Admirals, Generals, and
American Foreign Policy

1898 · 1914

RICHARD D. CHALLENER

Admirals, Generals, and American Foreign Policy

1898 · 1914

PRINCETON UNIVERSITY PRESS

Princeton, New Jersey · 1973

LCC 72-732

ISBN 0-691-06916-6

This book has been composed in Linotype Baskerville.

Printed in the United States of America
by Princeton University Press, Princeton, N.J.

For Martha

Contents

CHAPTER FOUR: Taft and Knox: The Military
    Dimensions of Dollar Diplomacy

CHAPTER FIVE: Wilson and Bryan: Moralism and
    Military Power

CHAPTER SIX: Conclusions   401

Acknowledgments

I AM deeply indebted to many institutions and individuals who have assisted me during the years that I have been engaged in the research and writing of this book. A grant from the Social Science Research Council provided several summers of research as well as support for a term of leave, while the Research Board of Princeton University provided funds for the typing of the finished manuscript.

I particularly want to thank the staffs of the Manuscript Division of the Library of Congress and the National Archives, especially those in the Foreign Relations Section, the Navy Department Section, the War Department Section, and the Office of Naval Records and Naval Library. Rear Admiral R. E. Eller, then Director of Naval History, kindly granted me access to the papers of the General Board, which were formerly located at the Naval Records Center in Arlington, Virginia, and the staff at that office was especially helpful. I am grateful, too, for the help that the librarians at the Ursinus College Library, Collegeville, Pennsylvania gave me with my research in the papers of Huntington Wilson.

Among the many individuals whose suggestions aided my research, I particularly want to thank Professors Walter Scholes of the University of Missouri, William Braisted of the University of Texas, and L. E. Ellis, now retired from Rutgers University. I am deeply indebted to numerous past and present colleagues at Princeton who have read all or portions of the manuscript and who furnished valuable criticisms: Joseph R. Strayer, Jerome Blum, Arthur Link, W. Frank Craven, and John Shy. I appreciate also the careful reading that Professor Ernest May gave to an earlier draft of the manuscript. Finally, at the Princeton University Press, Mrs. Eve Hanle provided needed encouragement, and Mr. Benjamin F. Houston edited the manuscript with a care and precision which went far beyond what any author has any reason to anticipate.

Princeton, N.J. RICHARD D. CHALLENER
April 1972

Abbreviations for Sources Frequently Cited

GB, Letters = Papers of the General Board of the United States Navy, Letters

GB, Proceedings = General Board of the United States Navy, Proceedings

GS = National Archives, Record Group 165, Department of the Army, Papers of the War Department General Staff

JB = National Archives, Record Group 225, Papers of the Joint Board of the United States Army and Navy

JB, Minutes = Joint Board, Communications and Minutes

Nav Rec AF 8 = National Archives, Record Group 45, Department of the Navy, Office of Naval Records and Naval History, Area File, Area 8 (Caribbean)

Nav Rec AF 10 = Office of Naval Records and Naval History, Area File, Area 10 (Far East)

Nav Rec Confid Comm AS = Office of Naval Records and Naval History, Confidential Communications, Asiatic Station, 1904-1906

Nav Rec Confid Ltrs = Office of Naval Records and Naval History, Confidential Letters

Nav Rec Subj File = Office of Naval Records and Naval History, Subject File, 1911-1926

SDCD = National Archives, Record Group 59, Department of State, Consular Dispatches

SDDF = Department of State, Decimal File, 1910-1927

SDMD = Department of State, Dispatches from the United States Minister to (country of origin)

SDML = Department of State, Miscellaneous Letters

SDNF = Department of State, Numerical File, 1906-1910

USNIP = United States Naval Institute Proceedings

Admirals, Generals, and
American Foreign Policy
1898 · 1914

ON the North China coast in the summer of 1900 units of the United States Navy were actively supporting the operations of an international military expedition then fighting its way toward the walled city of Peking. Within that city the American minister and his European colleagues were besieged by rebellious Boxer hordes, and it was still uncertain whether Minister E. H. Conger and his fellow diplomats could hold out until help arrived—uncertain, indeed, even if they remained alive. In Washington Secretary of State John Hay was frantically struggling to piece together a viable Far Eastern policy. Surprised by the magnitude of the Boxer uprising, he and President William McKinley, reluctantly and against their original intentions, had agreed to political and military collaboration with the European powers and had even gone to the extent of contributing several thousand American troops from the Philippines to the interallied military expedition. Hay was, however, trying to persuade the powers that they were merely conducting a "police operation" and not a war against China that would, he feared, inevitably produce the final partition of the Manchu Empire. To forestall that dreaded eventuality the Secretary of State had just put forth his "July circular" which asked all of the powers to respect the territorial and administrative integrity of China.[1]

On the last day of July, John Davis Long, the elderly bewhiskered Victorian who served as civilian head of the Navy, sat down at his desk to draft a special and urgent plea to the Department of State. The United States Navy, wrote its Secretary, was experiencing serious difficulties that required immediate assistance from the diplomats. To fulfill its Far Eastern mission the Navy must acquire a permanent naval station on the Chinese coast. Such a base, Long argued on behalf of the admirals—and, more specifically, at the behest of the Navy's newly-established General Board—was "a vital necessity" if the Navy was

---

[1] For "standard" accounts, see A. Whitney Griswold, *The Far Eastern Policy of the United States* (New York, 1938), 37-86, and Tyler Dennett, *John Hay: From Poetry to Politics* (New York, 1933).

both now and in the future to protect American citizens and American interests in Asia.[2]

The Secretary supported his request with an extended recitation of various problems then plaguing naval operations in North China. Of primary concern was the dearth of coal, the one, all-essential fuel without which a steam-driven navy was helpless. The Boxer crisis had erupted so rapidly that there had been no opportunity to accumulate an ample supply. Nor did the United States possess a ready source of coal anywhere in the Far East; in the Philippines the Navy had so far established only the most rudimentary of bases, and the supply of coal on hand was sufficient only for the needs of the continuing campaign against Aguinaldo. "To show the difficulty that is experienced in getting coal to our ships at Taku," Long confessed, "it is sufficient to state that it is shipped by our own colliers from Hampton Roads and from Cardiff, involving voyages of 12,000 to 14,000 miles."

In peace time the Navy could tolerate such logistic problems, but in the event of serious war in the Far East the shortage of coal might become a critical weakness. Moreover, Long continued, trouble in Asia was endemic. It was not only likely that there would be recurrent episodes like the Boxer uprising but also probable that these would recur with greater frequency. And, Long added, of all the nations "prominently interested in the maintenance of the affairs of Northern China," the United States was the only power which did not possess a naval depot on or near the coast of China—the British being established at Wei Hai Wei, the Russians at Port Arthur, the Germans at Kiaochow, and the Japanese but a relatively small distance from their own home ports.

The Secretary of the Navy asked for the Chusan Islands which lay just to the south of the mouth of the Yangtze River and were considered by American naval authorities to possess both economic and strategic value. The Chusans, admittedly, were situated on a part of the Chinese coast formerly claimed by Great Britain, but the Navy thought that the British claim might well have been abandoned. Of greater moment to Long and his associates was the question of diplomatic timing. The current uprising in China, they believed, offered a unique and opportune moment to press for the acquisition of these islands. The issue of annexation, however, was delicately and circuitously phrased: "It is possible that the islands desired can be obtained by our government as one of the results of the present circumstances in China, and it is suggested that negotiations for the acquisition be entered into at the proper time."

[2] National Archives, Record Group 59, Department of State, Miscellaneous Letters, John D. Long to John Hay, 31 July 1900. (Hereafter abbreviated as SDML.)

In this communication, the first of several of the general subject of Chinese bases, Secretary Long confined himself to the logistics of coal and the argument that the United States should possess a base because she was the only great power left out of the game. He might easily have chosen other arguments, for his operating difficulties in the summer of 1900 were real. The line of supplies and communication from the Philippines to North China was not only stretched beyond the limits of tolerance but rested upon an undeveloped naval facility at Manila. Indeed, it had already been necessary to secure Japanese permission to utilize the port facilities of Nagasaki as a point from which supplies bound for China could be transshipped.[3] To land both men and supplies in China the United States had been compelled to rely upon the facilities which Great Britain maintained at Tientsin.[4]

There was, of course, nothing unique in the desire of the United States Navy—or, for that matter, in the desire of any of the world's navies—to acquire overseas bases. It had long been evident that the transition from sail to steam had wedded navies more firmly to their bases than ever before in naval history. The effective operating radius of a warship was directly proportional to its consumption of coal and to the availability of coaling and repair stations. The history of European imperialism in the late nineteenth century is directly related to the efforts of European navalists to acquire, at strategic points throughout the world, a sufficient number of secure bases upon which to establish their naval power and make it effective.[5] The United States Navy had been no stranger to this same impulse. During and immediately following the Civil War it had sought naval stations in the Caribbean, and while its expansionist tendencies had been quiescent during the several decades of postwar naval decay, these had again acquired momentum in the 1890s as American naval power revived and an ever increasing number of Americans began to interest themselves in the prospects of a canal across the Isthmus of Panama.[6] Even in the nineties there had been in the Far East a few individuals in both the military and diplomatic services who had suggested that the acquisition of a Chinese port would serve the American national interest. The Chusan Islands, for example, had previously been mentioned in the

[3] SDML, Hay to Long, 12 and 18 July 1900.

[4] SDML, Hackett to Hay, 5 September 1900, enclosing a copy of a lengthy report prepared by Captain B. H. McCalla. Chapter Three contains a lengthier discussion of the navy's first attempt to secure a base in Far Eastern waters along with additional documentation.

[5] The definitive account remains Bernard Brodie, *Sea Power in the Machine Age* (Princeton, 1941), 93 and, especially, 105 ff.

[6] For convenient summaries see W. H. Calcott, *The Caribbean Policy of the United States, 1890-1920* (Baltimore, 1942), chs. 1 and 2, and Julius Pratt, *America's Colonial Experiment* (New York, 1950), 13-39.

final report of the Naval War Board established during the Spanish-American War to provide the McKinley administration with strategic guidance.[7]

But, in general, before 1900 these had not appeared to be issues of great urgency, nor had they been pursued with any great consistency. The Spanish-American War had been won before it was well started—if not as a consequence of American military prowess then certainly as a result of Spanish ineptitude and reluctance to fight. Once that "splendid little war" was over, most Americans, their ears still ringing with the oratory of the new Manifest Destiny, settled back to enjoy the beginnings of the imperial years and benefits of empire. There was a widespread belief that the acquisition of the Philippines—plus the addition of Hawaii and Guam and the establishment of a naval station at Manila—would be sufficient to maintain America's Far Eastern interests and unlock the doors to the Orient. An insular empire, stretching from Hawaii to the Philippines, would insure America's ability to tap the China market and become a Far Eastern power. Large territorial possessions in the European style would simply not be necessary. This, for example, was President McKinley's initial reaction, for his instructions to the Peace Commission had called only for the acquisition of Luzon and a naval station.[8] At the outset the Navy also seemed satisfied with such an insular empire. The Naval War Board, though it did mention the possibility of acquiring the Chusans, concluded that the creation of naval stations in Hawaii, in the Marianas (of which Guam is the principal island), and in Luzon "would largely meet the needs of the United States for naval stations, both for transit to China and for operations for war, if need be, in Eastern Asiatic waters."[9] In the Caribbean, moreover, the situation remained in a state of flux for some little time after the conclusion of the Spanish-American War: final agreements with Cuba were yet to be made, the route for the Isthmian canal had still to be determined, and Anglo-American differences over the Clayton-Bulwer Treaty of 1850 were as yet unresolved.

Unexpected and unwanted complications soon developed, especially in the Far East. There was the Philippine insurrection, most certainly not the reply which Americans had expected to William McKinley's well-publicized prayers for divine guidance on the Philippines. Then

[7] Papers of the General Board of the United States Navy, File 414-1, Report of the Naval War Board, 1898.

[8] Department of State, Paris Peace Commission, 1898, instructions sent to the Commission at Paris, 16 September 1898. See also H. Wayne Morgan, ed., *Making Peace with Spain: The Diary of Whitelaw Reid, September-December 1898* (Austin, Texas, 1965), 30-31.

[9] Report of the Naval War Board, 1898.

the Chinese situation grew ever more tangled until, as dramatically illustrated by the Boxer uprisings, the United States found itself being led into increasingly direct involvements in the cross-currents of Asian affairs. This involvement, moreover, took place against a background which to many seemed ominous—the prospect that China would be partitioned and that the presumably rich China trade, the economic magnet which had drawn Americans to the Orient, would shortly be divided up among the hungry European powers before the United States had sufficient opportunity to develop its own position.

Within the United States Navy not a few officers began to sense that the imperial years would be something less than glorious if they had to operate permanently under the restrictions and handicaps which prevailed at the time of their Boxer assignment. They began to think, in short, that they had settled for too little in 1898. More importantly, there emerged within the naval establishment in the spring of 1900 an organization which was specifically charged with the responsibility of providing the civilian Secretary with long-range advice and developing war plans and naval strategies. The War Board of 1898 had been a transitory phenomenon, an *ad hoc* creation intended to fulfill the urgent needs of a war for which there had been only the most meager advance preparations. And if the Spanish-American War had taught any military lessons, the one which it had underscored was the necessity to organize both of the American military services into more coherent, rational structures. Within the Navy one of the principal results of the ensuing reform movement was the establishment of the General Board. Its actual powers, to be sure, were severely restricted; its function was purely advisory; and it possessed no authority to command either the Secretary or the numerous, entrenched bureau chiefs to obey its wishes. But, for better or worse, the General Board did reflect naval thinking—at least reflected it insofar as ideas about naval strategy and naval policy were articulated by the high-ranking officers who comprised its membership: the chiefs of the Bureau of Navigation and the Bureau of Equipment, the President of the Naval War College, the chief of the Office of Naval Intelligence, and, above all, its president, the Admiral of the Navy and the victor of Manila Bay, George Dewey.[10]

The first meeting of the General Board took place in mid-April of 1900, less than two weeks after its formal establishment. The naval officers immediately agreed that their first task should be to draw up a list

10 The creation of the General Board is discussed at greater length in Chapter One. For the orders which established the General Board and officially outlined its purpose as well as its composition, see Papers of the General Board, Letters, I, Long to Admiral Dewey, 30 March 1900.

of desired naval stations in both the Caribbean and the Far East.[11] Indeed, the proposal for the Chusan Islands which Secretary Long put before John Hay at the end of July was largely the work of Captain Henry C. Taylor, one of the original members of the Board and a former president of the Naval War College at Newport. Even before informing Long about their desire for the Chusans, the naval officers had in fact decided that there were three acceptable sites on the Chinese coast. These sites were to be proposed to Secretary Long one at a time and in such fashion that, if any one should prove unacceptable, he would not realize that the General Board had already drawn up and prepared its request for an alternative site.[12]

Even though Secretary Long's eventual memorandum of July 1900 was phrased in circumspect language, it raised some very fundamental questions about national policy—above all, about the role of military power in achieving American political and diplomatic goals in the Far East. It seemed clear to the navalists that the aims of American foreign policy could be achieved only if the United States Navy was placed in a position where it could make its growing power effective upon the international scene. Certainly the Navy's request for a base in China raised questions about the extent to which the President and Secretary of State should pay heed to the presumed needs of the naval service, about the need, if any, for a military dimension to American foreign policy, and, ultimately, about the problem of reconciling force and diplomacy.

Few Americans living in 1900 would have openly stated the issues in these terms. The number of "realists"—to use terminology of the present—was severely limited. At the turn of the century American foreign policy was still publicly discussed and described in terms of broad, shining purposes, noble principles, and respect for long-established traditions. In more recent years George Kennan and others in the realist school of diplomatic historians have sharply, and properly, criticized the American record in that era for its excessive idealism, moralizing tendencies, and devotion to legal niceties.[13] In 1900, to be sure, there were special reasons for official caution in making public

[11] General Board, Proceedings, Minutes of the meeting of 17 April 1900. (Hereafter citations to the minutes of the General Board meetings will be given as GB, Proceedings.)

[12] GB, Proceedings, 29 June 1900.

[13] "I see the most serious fault of our past policy formulation to be in something that I might call the legalistic-moralistic approach to international problems. This approach runs like a red skein through our foreign policy of the last fifty years. . . ." George Kennan, *American Diplomacy, 1900-1950* (Chicago, 1951), 95. See also Robert Osgood, *Ideals and Self-Interest in America's Foreign Relations* (Chicago, 1953), and Kenneth W. Thompson, *Political Realism and the Crisis of World Politics* (Princeton, 1960).

statements about the needs of the military. William Jennings Bryan was about to launch the second of his several abortive campaigns for the presidency, and he planned to mount a crusade against the imperialism of William McKinley and the Republican administration. All the more reason, therefore, why John Hay and the President would solemnly depict their Far Eastern policies as motivated by a desire to protect and not despoil China, to assist the Chinese people rather than to line the pockets of American businessmen. It is not strange that in these circumstances there was no public discussion of the Navy's request for a base in China—indeed, almost two decades would pass before the official, published correspondence of the Department of State would contain even a single reference to the turn-of-the-century interest in the acquisition of a Far Eastern naval station on or near the Chinese mainland.[14]

The above is most certainly not the only possible interpretation of national policy in these years. By the mid-1960s many historians, most notably those of the "New Left," were contending that the expansionism of 1898—the acquisition of the Philippines, Hawaii, Guam, and Wake—was in reality a conscious effort to secure an "informal empire" that would guarantee American commercial access to the markets of Asia. It was, they contend, a systematic effort, deeply rooted in domestic social and economic conditions and deliberately designed to spread American capitalism without having to assume the burdens of territorial empire or the complexities of ruling vast colonial areas. "America's insular acquisitions of 1898," Thomas McCormick has maintained, ". . . were obtained . . . largely in an eclectic effort to construct a system of coaling, cable, and naval stations for an integrated trade route which could help realize America's overriding ambition in the Pacific —the penetration and ultimate domination of the fabled China market."[15] Furthermore, as Marilyn Blatt Young has summarized the argument, "The overall aim was . . . not an old-fashioned territorial empire, but a 'new empire,' whose rationale was commercial, whose style was 'anticolonial.' "[16] The Open Door policy thus becomes a form of anti-

[14] Department of State, *Foreign Relations of the United States, 1915* (Washington, 1924), 113-15.

[15] Thomas McCormick, *China Market: America's Quest for Informal Empire, 1893-1901* (Chicago, 1967), 107.

[16] Marilyn Blatt Young, "American Expansion, 1870-1900: The Far East," in Barton Bernstein, ed., *Towards a New Past: Dissenting Essays in American History* (New York, 1968), 177. The intellectual origins of the New Left interpretation are to be found in the writings of William A. Williams, whose *The Tragedy of American Diplomacy* (rev. edn., New York, 1964, p. 38) argues that "the Open Door policy became the strategy of American foreign policy for the next half-century. . . . [It] was in fact a brilliant strategic stroke which led to the gradual extension of American economic and political power throughout the world."

imperialist imperialism, a clever design to gain economic advantage in China without actually joining the ranks of the imperialist powers of Europe. From such a perspective the moralizing of a McKinley was largely verbiage intended to soothe the American public, while historians like George Kennan, so critical of turn-of-the-century moralism and legalism, have been taken in by the rhetoric and failed to comprehend the substance. Also from this perspective the quest for bases —whether McKinley's desire for a naval station at Manila or the larger views of the General Board—forms part of this larger national purpose: the conscious pursuit of a "new empire" in which American capitalism would reign supreme.

The pages which follow will be an examination of many of the various issues and events that have been differently interpreted by the "realists" and by the "New Left." Several observations must be made at the outset. First of all, whatever the relevance of the "realist" critique of American moralism and whatever the merit of the "New Left" interpretation of imperialism, the fact remains that the military dimensions of American foreign policy did begin to assume greater significance and importance after the Spanish-American War. The United States, both by design and by accident, had become involved in both the Caribbean and the Far East—and involved on a scale that would have seemed highly improbable before 1898. It was at last "emerging" as a world power. And, as a neophyte, the United States was finding it necessary to grapple seriously with issues that heretofore had been of secondary importance, to seek answers to questions that had not previously been raised. In these altered national circumstances the role of military men and military power in protecting and advancing America's position in the world was therefore an issue which necessarily assumed a new and different perspective.

The purpose of this study is to examine and measure the extent of change. To what extent did officers of the United States Army and Navy reflect upon issues of foreign policy? Did they develop opinions, offer recommendations, and, to any extent, participate in decision making? Conversely, did the civilian officials of government consult with or pay heed to the admirals and generals? How, and in what ways, did the President and the Department of State seek to make use of the military services in the formulation and execution of foreign policy? Was there any appreciable coordination of military and diplomatic policy? Does an examination of the civil-military relationship in the years from McKinley to Wilson lead to any generalizations which help in assessing the interpretations of either Kennan and the "realists" or William A. Williams and the "New Left"? And, ultimately, in the years from the Spanish-American War to the outbreak of World War

I, how effectively did the United States manage to reconcile force and diplomacy?

These and similar questions will be examined in greater detail in both their chronological and geographical context. This book, however, deliberately limits itself to a study of civil-military relations. That is, it analyzes the reciprocal relationship between the military services on the one hand and the President and the Department of State on the other. It asks, among other things, what the military reported to the civilians of the executive branch, whether they contributed to the policy-making process, and how the President and Secretary of State used them as the instruments of administration policies. It does not attempt to any appreciable extent to explore the Congressional dimension, nor does it try to examine in any great detail the many other groups or institutions in American society that may also have been influential in shaping a particular policy or set of foreign policy decisions in which the military services were involved. Thus, it cannot claim to be a full-fledged study of what is now termed "national security policy." But, except for the Caribbean, where the traditions of the Monroe Doctrine combined with a newly-intensified demand for an inter-oceanic canal, the United States did not have any policy which can properly be termed a "national security policy." The concept of a national security policy emerged in the United States only after World War II. It developed only after America had gone through two world wars and finally began to realize the importance of trying to coordinate the various strands of military, diplomatic, political, and economic policy into a coherent whole. Any attempt to organize a book about the pre-1914 period around a national security theme would therefore falsify the past by artificially imposing upon it a frame of reference that belongs to a much later period.

The issues and events examined in this book do not readily fall into tidy patterns about which the historian can construct either an evolving or a sequential narrative. For many reasons—ranging from the personalities of American leaders to the structure of institutions and the traditions of civil supremacy—the answers to the questions posed in the preceding paragraphs emerge only from an analysis of episodic materials and, in many instances, from an examination of information that is in the form of operational details rather than policy decisions at the grand level. This final caveat will become clearer after a consideration of the ideas and values of the leaders of the American military services and a description of the institutional framework within which they and their civilian superiors operated.

CHAPTER ONE

Ideas, Institutions, and Practices, 1898-1914

1. The "World View" of the Military Services

THE typical officer of the United States Navy was enthusiastic about the new American empire which had been acquired by the United States in 1898 in the Caribbean and the Far East. He was also convinced that his country was inevitably bound to play a role in world affairs commensurate to its size and wealth. To Captain Henry C. Taylor, the officer who formalized the General Board's request for the Chusan Islands, the United States was now fulfilling the dictates of destiny. "In 1898," Taylor wrote, "a duty which has haunted us for many years became plainly apparent." The Spanish-American War opened "tidal gates through which rushed upon us a flood of powers and duties which must be accepted and fulfilled—or we are not great. It is the test with which Fate tries our capacity for greatness."[1] A similar exhilaration with America's new role in the world existed in the lower echelons of the naval service. When Lieutenant John Hood concluded a technical article on the somewhat mundane subject of submarine cables, he felt compelled to express himself in the same imperial fashion: "We as a nation are following the inevitable law of evolution. We have left behind our swaddling clothes, and have entered the field of competition with the other great nations of the world. We are in the struggle for political supremacy and commercial pre-eminence whether we wish it or not and must advance always; for stopping means stagnation or decay."[2]

Such grandiose statements were but the naval expression of the current of Social Darwinism that had swept the United States in the 1890s and which is to be found throughout the writings of all those Americans—Theodore Roosevelt, Brooks Adams, Henry Cabot Lodge, Albert Beveridge—who had fought for the "large policy" in 1898. More specifically, however, naval officers viewed the world scene through the lens of Captain Alfred Thayer Mahan. By and large most officers at the turn of the century accepted without question the interpretation of world politics that had been proclaimed in the previous decade by

[1] H. C. Taylor, "The Fleet," *United States Naval Institute Proceedings* xxix, no. 4 (December 1903), 799 (hereafter abbreviated as *USNIP*).

[2] John Hood, "The Pacific Submarine Cable," *USNIP*, xxvi, no. 3 (September 1900), 487.

America's foremost exponent of seapower and its role in world history. There is indeed considerable justice in the half-facetious remark, attributed to a later Secretary of the Navy, that, to the average American naval officer, the United States Navy was the only True Church, Neptune was God, and Mahan was his Prophet.

To Mahan the only real world was the world of Social Darwinism in which the dominant, perpetual forces were rivalries and strife between nations. With the record of British history as his evidence, he had argued in countless books and articles that nations must expand if they are to achieve and retain greatness. There was a virtual moral obligation upon a great nation to extend both its foreign commerce and its territorial domain. Conflict, military as well as economic, was simply part of the inevitable pattern of events, a logical consequence of the laws of history. Trade itself created political rivalry. When a nation expanded its overseas commerce, it necessarily encountered rivals who wished to seize that trade for themselves, and the ensuing competition turned the rivals into enemies who, sooner or later, reached the stage of open conflict.

Long before the *Maine* had exploded in the harbor of Havana, Mahan had insisted that the United States must increase its trade with the Far East and had argued that construction of a canal across the Isthmus of Panama would provide the United States with clear-cut advantages in the growing struggle for access to the emerging markets of Asia. He had also warned that the opening of such a water route would pose new and severe problems for those who shaped national policy. The great states of Europe would attempt to block American commercial expansion either by establishing rival centers of power in the Caribbean or securing control over the trade routes to and from the Isthmus. The United States, as a counter move, must build its own naval stations in the Caribbean, acquire the Hawaiian Islands, and, above all, create a strong and powerful naval establishment. His prescription, resting on the basic assumption that expansion was a categorical national imperative, was a call to turn the Caribbean into an American lake, to begin the construction of an American overseas empire, and to create a naval establishment equal to that of any nation except Great Britain.[3]

It is therefore not difficult to explain why Mahan became the high priest of American navalists. He had provided a rationale for national expansion which, after all, turned upon the creation of a great Ameri-

[3] See William E. Livesey, *Mahan on Sea Power* (Norman, Oklahoma, 1947); W. D. Puleston, *The Life and Works of Captain Alfred Thayer Mahan* (New Haven, 1939); Margaret Sprout, "Mahan and the Gospel of Seapower," in E. M. Earle, ed., *Makers of Modern Strategy* (Princeton, 1943), 414-45.

can battle fleet. He had defined a purpose, a mission, for the New Navy. And he had interpreted the rise and fall of nations in terms of seapower—indeed, had exalted seapower as the key which unlocked world history.

Moreover, the attractiveness of Mahan's theories for the average naval officer was enhanced because in a very real sense they served to fill a gap in his own political education. The increasing professionalization of the Army and the Navy in the post-Civil War decades had, to be sure, affected the curricula at the two service academies and brought at least a modest increase in their liberal arts content.[4] But Annapolis had been slower to respond than West Point. The education of future naval officers continued to place great emphasis upon the technical and purely naval components and, as Admiral William S. Sims later complained, it was "cast in rigid form."[5] An evaluation of the Academy's program of studies at the turn of the century clearly indicated that the non-technical aspects of its curriculum were woefully inadequate by the contemporary standards of American civilian education. Indeed, even a decade after World War I a critical report of the Board of Visitors would call especial attention to the fact that the course of instruction at Annapolis "was devoid of any economics, of any substantial course in government, of any biology, geography, ethics, or social science, or of any of the literature of foreign languages."[6] The impact of Mahan's ideas upon men who were the products of this educational system is nowhere better revealed than in the memoirs of Bradley Fiske, an officer who entered the naval service in the 1870s and who, in the Taft era, assumed responsibility for the development of war plans. It was not until 1903, when he was briefly assigned to the Naval War College and happened to hear a lecture by its president, that he encountered the idea that war might be an instrument of national policy. As Fiske later confessed in his memoirs, until that time he had never had any clear idea "connected with war except that of fighting."[7] Having first encountered the philosophy of Mahan at this relatively late stage in his career, he immediately accepted—indeed, welcomed—it as something which not only explained the dynamics of world history but also served as a guide for the future.

Parenthetically, it should be added that, although Fiske himself was

[4] Samuel F. Huntington, *The Soldier and the State* (Cambridge, 1957), 237-39.

[5] Elting E. Morison, *Admiral Sims and the Modern American Navy* (Boston, 1952), 151 ff.

[6] Morison, *Sims*, 521.

[7] Bradley A. Fiske, *From Midshipman to Rear Admiral* (New York, 1919), 362; Warner R. Schilling, *Admirals and Foreign Policy, 1915-1919* (unpub. diss., Yale University, 1953), 5.

smitten by Mahan at the Naval War College, that institution was still not highly regarded by naval officers at the turn of the century and as yet did relatively little to increase their political education. Until well on into the first decade of the twentieth century its courses were given only in the summer and regarded by most officers as simply a pleasant interruption of the normal naval routines. Newport was still the most fashionable resort on the East Coast, and, as Yates Stirling later recalled, there were wives to be entertained and social functions to be attended.[8] Even Fiske was careful to specify that the experience at the Naval War College was considered by himself and his fellow officers to be "a vacation, and no one injured his health by too much hard work."[9]

In any event, the political ideas of the leaders of the United States Navy at the beginning of the twentieth century were virtual mirror images of the *Weltanschauung* of Alfred Thayer Mahan. Thus, Captain Asa Walker, one of the original members of the General Board would ask rhetorically, "With every nation in Europe suffering from a grievous attack of land famine, are not the acts of their legislatures, in increasing so enormously their navies, handwritings on the wall, needing no Daniel to interpret, foretelling that in the near future these nations will brave the woes dimly defined by the Monroe Doctrine, and wrestle for a slice of the rich lands of our hemisphere?"[10] Only two years after he had "discovered" Mahan at Newport, Bradley Fiske won the annual essay contest sponsored by the United States Naval Institute for an article which argued that Britain had achieved her present high estate only by waging a long series of successful wars on land and sea. "Every other great nation in history has done the same," he concluded. "Shall not we? . . . There is not a single reason to give, or to imagine, why the American people should not go through the same series of wars that all other nations have gone through."[11]

The official policy documents of the General Board clearly indicated that this group of officers, charged with the development of naval strategy, interpreted the world as did Mahan. The preamble to one of its early war plans revealed its conviction that the United States was caught up in a world of strife and inevitable competition between nations:

> History shows that trade rivalries brought about the successive humiliation of Holland, France, and Spain by Great Britain. The three great competitors for the world's trade are now the United States,

[8] Yates Stirling, *Sea Duty* (New York, 1939), 130-31.
[9] Fiske, *From Midshipman*, 363.
[10] Asa Walker, "Notes on Cuban Ports," *USNIP*, XXVI, no. 2 (June 1900), 339.
[11] Bradley Fiske, "American Naval Policy," *USNIP*, XXXI, no. 1 (March 1905), 10.

Great Britain, and Germany. Following the teachings of all history, two of these three must in the sequel be practically subordinated to the third. It may be expected that either Great Britain or Germany would profit so largely by the weakening of the other in a war with the United States that the power which stood aloof, suffering from no war exhaustion and husbanding her resources, would at the end of the war undoubtedly occupy the best position to control the trade of the world.[12]

When the General Board sought naval stations in the Caribbean, its argument was founded on the logic that once the United States began to build the Panama Canal, "aggression on the part of individual foreign powers could be assumed." Moreover, the danger to the United States would mount with the passage of time and become greatest when a completed canal increased commercial activity in the Caribbean. In support of this dire prediction the General Board pointed to the sequence of events which had taken place in the Middle East immediately following the completion of the Suez Canal. Each and every one of the European powers which profited from Suez and the consequent expansion of trade had either acquired new territory in the area or had materially strengthened existing strongholds. It followed, then, according to the General Board's logic, that the same cycle of aggression would be repeated in the Caribbean unless the United States took strong preventive measures.[13] As historical determinists, the naval staff could rest its case on the "law" that trade created rivalry and find it unnecessary to examine the range of possible political and economic differences between the Middle East and the Caribbean.

The General Board always was particularly suspicious of German intentions in the Caribbean. But German expansionism was interpreted as the consequence of impersonal forces which neither William II nor the German government could properly restrain. Various reports of the General Board insisted that the Germans themselves could not resist the pressures created by the growth of their population beyond the saturation point, by the need to expand domestic industries into foreign fields, and by the absolute economic requirements of guar-

[12] Papers of the General Board of the United States Navy, Op. 29, War Portfolio No. 1, Germany War Plan—Black Plan. When the original research for this book was done, the General Board papers were then located in the Naval Records Center, Arlington, Virginia; most have since been transferred to the National Archives. The citation is from a version of the Black Plan which bears no specific date but which was put together between 1911 and 1914. This version also includes a number of appendices bearing specific dates and containing additional information.

[13] Papers of the General Board of the United States Navy, Letters, II, Admiral George Dewey to Secretary William Moody, 7 October 1902. (Hereafter abbreviated as GB, Letters.) For a copy of this letter as transmitted to the State Department and contained in State's files, see SDML, Moody to John Hay, 21 November 1902.

anteed overseas markets. Thus, American naval strategists did not have to unearth specific examples of German activity in Latin America; it was sufficient to argue that German imperialism was propelled by great historical currents which made it inevitable that, when her domestic situation became intolerable, Germany would seek to resolve her internal crisis by a transatlantic adventure.[14] The same reasoning, indeed, even made it possible in 1919 for certain American officers to look beyond Germany after that country had been defeated in World War I. Using the familiar arguments about trade and conflict, the naval advisory group which accompanied Woodrow Wilson to Paris now built a new case that Great Britain was the rival to be feared. England, according to Wilson's naval staff, had always defeated her commercial rivals one by one. With Germany prostrate, Great Britain would most assuredly cast the United States in the role of the antagonist to be defeated.[15]

Within this broad framework of historical determinism there were naturally certain objectives of American foreign policy that the Navy believed it had a special obligation to uphold. Both the Monroe Doctrine and the Open Door in China occupied a special niche in naval thinking about foreign affairs. As Mahan himself once wrote, the United States had but two principal and permanent policies—the Monroe Doctrine and the Open Door—and all naval planning should originate with them.[16] Needless to say, the Doctrine, like the maiden in the oldtime motion picture serials, was always in danger of being violated by some rapacious foreigner. In the opinion of the General Board it was *the* barrier which prevented German expansion into Latin America.[17] Similarly, to Charles Sperry, the admiral who commanded the fleet during its famous cruise around the world, it seemed clear that it was only the protection afforded by the Doctrine which stopped the overcrowded and overdeveloped nations of Europe from embarking upon aggressive moves in the Western Hemisphere.[18]

Devotion to the principles of Monroe was a long-established tradition at the beginning of the century, but naval officers were not slow

14 General Board, version of Black Plan as previously cited.

15 National Archives, Record Group 45, Department of the Navy, Office of Naval Records and Naval History, Subject File, 1911-1926, Box 580, Memorandum 25 of the United States Naval Advisory Staff, Paris, 7 April 1919. (Hereafter abbreviated as Nav Rec Subj File.)

16 GB, File 404, Alfred Thayer Mahan to Secretary George von L. Meyer, 24 September 1910.

17 National Archives, Record Group 165, Department of the Army, Papers of the War Department General Staff, War College Division, File 6178/6, General W. W. Wotherspoon to the Chief of the General Staff, 14 December 1910. (General Staff papers will hereafter be abbreviated as GS.)

18 Papers of Admiral Charles Sperry, Manuscripts Division, Library of Congress, Sperry to his son, Charles Sperry, Jr., 6 November 1907.

to believe that the Open Door policy of John Hay also represented a binding commitment. The Navy, indeed, developed a Far Eastern consciousness more rapidly than the Army. As early as 1904 there were at least some high ranking naval officers who felt that the Open Door policy might be in future years more important to the United States than the Monroe Doctrine. In that year, when the Army and Navy began their first formal efforts to draft joint war plans, Admiral Taylor produced a long memorandum which argued that the growing American commitments in the Far East were "so important to our national life that we may expect in the future to find the sacredness of the Monroe Doctrine drop to second in the national mind, and our trade relations with Eastern Asia assume first place, and the primal cause of war."[19] A few years later, when the General Board developed its first plan for a possible conflict with Japan, its operating hypothesis was that "the first condition of possible war" was a conflict arising out of a Japanese challenge to the Open Door, specifically a Japanese attempt to extend their control over Manchuria.[20]

The Monroe Doctrine and the Open Door were not simply convenient fictions or myths to which naval officers paid lip service. They were genuine national commitments and possessed a living reality in their own right. Above all, they furnished a specific rationale for naval building programs. Since the Monroe Doctrine and the Open Door were *the* basic, established American policies, their defense was essential to the national interest and required the existence of a strong American battle fleet. In 1913, when the General Board was trying to persuade Secretary Josephus Daniels to endorse a firm, fixed naval building policy, the admirals put their case succinctly: "The General Board believes that an understanding of the navy's role as . . . an upholder of those doctrines and policies which have become a part and parcel of our national existence will fix a naval policy that will meet those demands."[21] Moreover, naval spokesmen argued, since the Doctrine had no official standing in international law and had never been formally recognized by any European country except Great Britain, there was all the more reason to construct a navy to protect it. "The Doctrine is just as strong," the General Board asserted, "as the armed and organized forces maintained to enforce it."[22] Or, as the admirals

19 National Archives, Record Group 225, Papers of the Joint Board of the United States Army and Navy, Subject File 325, Memorandum of Admiral H. C. Taylor, 10 June 1904. (Joint Board papers will hereafter be abbreviated as JB.)

20 GB, Op. 29, Folder 7, Strategic Plan of Campaign against Orange, 14 March 1911.

21 GB, File 446, Dewey to Secretary Josephus Daniels, 28 March 1913.

22 GB, version of Black Plan as cited.

argued in another context, the basic purpose of the battleship program was "to uphold the traditional policy of the Monroe Doctrine."[23] Mahan summarized the underlying assumptions of naval thought when he wrote in 1909 that, if the Germans should defy the Monroe Doctrine, "How do we propose to keep that national idol on its feet without a superior navy?"[24]

Another marked characteristic of the political thought of naval officers, a product of their general conservatism, dedication to discipline, and respect for hierarchical order in society, was the horror with which they regarded political disorder in other nations, most especially in those Latin American countries in which revolution appeared to be endemic. A commander who visited Honduras late in 1908 summed up his feelings in a scornful report:

> An insurgent leader appears before a town garrisoned by government troops. A notice is sent in from the jungle announcing an attack to be made at a certain time, demanding surrender. It is etiquette to surrender without delay. The officials march out carrying with them the receipts of the Customs House,—"the army" is apt to remain, as it is immaterial which side they serve. The insurgents come in, a new government is proclaimed, and what is more important, the Customs House is secured for the next "liberator" to appear.[25]

Even less flattering was the description of the revolutionary cycle in Haiti that was furnished by the commanding officer of the *Connecticut*: "The conspirator (called a 'candidate for President') gathers an armed force (by promises of political preferment, bribery, etc.), declares himself a candidate for President, and leads the Government forces against the Customs House, legislative chambers, or other points deemed to be the keys to the situation. . . . The Senators and deputies, through force of arms or bribery, confirm the claims of successful revolutionists."[26]

It was not merely junior officers serving on the Latin American station who looked with such pronounced disfavor upon that troubled area's political instability. In the early years of its existence the General Board drew up an elaborate plan for the seizure of Santo Do-

[23] GB, Letters, VII, Dewey to Meyer, 28 September 1910.

[24] Papers of Alfred Thayer Mahan, Manuscripts Division, Library of Congress, Mahan to Charles Stewart, 19 March 1909.

[25] Department of State, Numerical File, 1906-1910, Case 7357/428-34, William Metcalf to Elihu Root, 6 October 1908, enclosing report of Commander John M. Shipley of the *Des Moines*, 27 September 1908. (Hereafter citations from the Numerical File will be abbreviated as SDNF.)

[26] Nav Rec Subj File, WA-7 Haiti, Report of the Commanding Officer of the *Connecticut*, 7 August 1914.

mingo by the United States Navy in the event of war with a European power. This strategic document was preceded by a so-called "Information Section" that outlined the conditions of Dominican politics for the benefit of line officers who might be called upon to implement the planned operation:

> Until 1907 a revolution usually proceeded in the following order: a few leaders would borrow money and purchase arms and fit out a small force of 200 or 500 men in a country district, or purchase the allegiance of several of the important generals in the government service; an invasion of a seaport town or an uprising among the troops of the town would follow; the customs house would then be seized and these funds become at once the support of the faction. A fight usually took place in the suburbs or the streets of the town. Later scrip was issued and bought up at a discount by the merchants to facilitate customs house business. Those dues are always paid in United States gold. When Santo Domingo City passed into the hands of a revolutionary party it ceased to be a revolutionary party and became a government. The Congress elected the dictator as president and all revenues passed into the hands of the party in power, a minimum to be used for administration and the greatest part appropriated by the leaders in power. A new clique would then plot another uprising and the same sequence of events would follow. The leading men in power frequently leaving the country with their loot; though sometimes they would be assassinated or killed in a street fight.[27]

Typical of the naval attitude toward Latin politics was the judgment of Admiral Sperry that "the so-called revolutions are nothing more nor less than struggles between different crews of bandits for the possession of the customs houses—and the loot. . . . Conditions are the same except that the present despotisms are more cruel and bloodthirsty, if possible, than the old, since masquerading as governments by the people and for the people, they are not amenable to civilized opinion."[28] Admiral Charles Sigsbee, another member of the General Board and a onetime head of the Office of Naval Intelligence, believed that Latin American political incapacity was so pronounced that "it may even be asked if the Monroe Doctrine is not holding a large part of this hemisphere in check against Cosmic Tendencies."[29]

[27] GB, War Portfolio 1, Reference 5-D, Haiti-San Domingo Plan. The citation is from the revised version of the plan, dated July 1915. The original version of the plan was drafted in 1902, first seriously revised in 1905, and modified on numerous occasions thereafter.

[28] Sperry Papers, Sperry to Charles Sperry, Jr., 12 and 24 December 1904.

[29] Office of Naval Records and Naval History, Confidential Letters, Admiral

But what naval officers particularly emphasized was that the political turmoil and tangled finances of the Latin countries posed a constant threat to the United States. Charles Sperry was but one of many high ranking officers who categorically stated that the chronic bankruptcies and debt repudiations of the Latin American countries furnished "the simplest and readiest pretext" for the intervention of European countries into the Western Hemisphere.[30] Typical of the attitude which existed in the General Board was its observation in the "political" preamble of its Nicaraguan War Plan: "The unstable government of that country and the natural jealousy of the Latin American countries towards the United States and towards each other makes trouble a possibility at all times . . . and makes it necessary for this Government to stand by to intervene with a view to the protection of its own interests."[31]

In naval logic it therefore followed that the appropriate remedy for these conditions was the judicious application of American naval power. Admiral Taylor, dispatched to survey the Dominican and Haitian scene, advised his civilian superiors in 1903 that the only way to keep the two island republics in line was by permanently stationing American warships in the harbors of Santo Domingo: "It is fitting for us to substitute for the occasional visits of individual ships in times of outbreaks and petty wars, the practically continuous presence of a squadron of vessels. The people of those republics should again become accustomed to the presence in their waters of our naval forces which in times past they have accepted without opposition and with apparent satisfaction."[32] When the United States was embroiled in controversy with the Cipriano Castro regime in Venezuela, the naval observer, Captain Nathan Sargent, was equally explicit. The entire North Atlantic squadron should visit Venezuela, he advised, for "only such an argument . . . can be understood by the semi-enlightened and uncultivated members of the present administration which is headed by an untutored President. . . . Diplomatic representation and protests and even peremptory demands have no effect upon them, but they can appreciate the potential presence of a squadron of battleships, and such an appreciation would go far toward relieving the present tension."[33]

Charles Sigsbee to John Hay, 3 August 1904. (Hereafter citations from the Confidential letter file of the Naval Records materials will be abbreviated as Nav Rec Confid Ltrs.)

[30] Sperry Papers, Sperry to Charles Sperry, Jr., 6 September 1907.

[31] GB, War Portfolio 1, Reference 5-t, Nicaragua Plan, 22 June 1910.

[32] Papers of William H. Moody, Manuscripts Division, Library of Congress, Admiral Taylor to Moody, 30 December 1903.

[33] Nav Rec Subj File, VP-Protection of Individuals. Captain Nathan Sargent to Secretary Long, 20 January 1901.

Similar expressions of faith in the virtues of naval power came frequently from naval officers serving in the Far East. In 1905, to cite but one incident from many, the Standard Oil Company was having difficulty securing permission from Chinese officials to construct storage tanks at Chinkiang. There was, however, an unexpected visit to Chinkiang by a group of American naval vessels proceeding on a routine assignment. Overnight the local Chinese officials changed their minds, and to the visiting naval commander the lesson was obvious: "The unexpected appearance of our three vessels and the uncertainty as to their intentions were sufficient . . . and the representative of the Standard Oil Company is now free to improve his property and by so doing to enlarge the trade of this American corporation." As for the Chinese, he advised, "the *argumentum baculicum* is what they best appreciate, anything more considerate they look upon as weakness and correspondingly despise."[34]

The philosophy of "gunboat diplomacy" was clearly expressed in the policy statements of the General Board and in official naval regulations issued by the Department. When the Department of the Navy established its permanent Caribbean Squadron in the autumn of 1902, this new force was specifically assigned the policeman's mission: "It should be utilized to exert our influence towards maintaining order in those regions where disorder would imperil the lives and property of our citizens. This is a duty which naturally devolves upon this government because of its well defined policy towards those countries."[35] When the General Board sought funds to build a special class of light gunboats suitable for operations in Chinese rivers, it rested its case on the assumption that naval visits to the interior of China were essential "to maintain the political and commercial interests of the United States . . . in countries where disordered conditions impair the efficiency and justice of local administration." This mission was crucial in China "where the interests of civilization and trade demand constant watchfulness and care." Shallow-draft gunboats, however, were only a portion of the General Board's program, for the officers also believed that American battleships should pay frequent visits to Chinese ports. "This will supply that evidence of naval power which it is desirable to keep frequently within the actual view of the people of the East and which

[34] Office of Naval Records and Naval History, Area File, Area 10 (Far East), Commanding officer of the *Baltimore* to Secretary Charles Bonaparte, 17 December 1905. (Hereafter materials from the various Area files will be abbreviated as Nav Rec AF 10 or as Nav Rec AF 8, which is the main file for Caribbean materials.)

[35] GB, File 420-1, Moody to Commander-in-Chief, North Atlantic Squadron, 4 October 1902.

is a political asset the value of which should always be borne in mind."[36]

The Navy's world view, then, was strongly marked, if not dominated, by the more extreme tenets of Social Darwinism, especially as those doctrines had been interpreted by Alfred Thayer Mahan. The world in which the United States Navy sailed its ships was a competitive world in which there were many potential rivals and in which the possibility of conflict was ever present. It was a world in which seapower was dominant and in which the Navy—as America's traditional "first line of defense"—had a clear mission both to protect such "established" national policies as the Monroe Doctrine and the Open Door and to preserve law and order in those less fortunate parts of the globe where those conditions did not prevail. Naval power, all ranks firmly believed, provided the necessary means to exert that control and influence.

It was a rigid, frequently simplistic outlook. Since the actions of nations were governed by "the teachings of history," it was rarely necessary to examine anything except the laws of historical evolution as discovered by Mahan and the Social Darwinists. American policies were regarded as national constants; the Monroe Doctrine, for example, was in naval writings a fixed star by which the political course of the United States Navy could forever be charted. Policies and problems were reduced to their elementary, constituent elements with the nuances and the complexities generally eliminated. Thus the Doctrine was simply a permanent ban on European intervention in the Americas, and from naval writings one would gain no sense of the considerable transformation it underwent at the hands of Theodore Roosevelt. Similarly, the typical naval analysis of the revolutionary process in the Caribbean might be technically accurate, but its singleminded, unsympathetic concentration upon instability and corruption ignored the variables and rarely if ever showed an understanding of the underlying causes. Nor were questions raised about the possible limitations on the use of naval force for political ends. There were, as we shall see, exceptions among the officer corps, but in general there were few who had qualms about the virtues of "gunboat diplomacy."

The officers of the United States Army reflected the same competitive outlook upon the world—though obviously without the special concern with seapower and the rampant Mahanism that characterized naval thought. But at the turn of the century there were relatively few Army officers, as compared with their naval colleagues, who concerned themselves with the world scene. The Army was still on the periphery

---

[36] GB, Letters, VI, Dewey to Meyer, 30 December 1909.

of world politics. Its tradition was purely Continental, and its many difficulties in mounting the Cuban expedition in 1898 had furnished abundant evidence of that fact.[37] It had no "philosopher" like Mahan to give it a world mission and no instrument, like the New Navy, to exalt its role in history. Whereas officers of the Navy had been visiting Caribbean and Asian ports for decades, the officers of the Army had been concerned with the final campaigns against the Indians of the Great Plains and with the routines of garrison life in the many remote posts of the American West. By 1898, then, one would not expect the Army to have become involved in international affairs to the same extent as the naval establishment. The Continental tradition, moreover, died slowly after 1900, and the foreign policy horizons of the Army remained more closely tied to the Monroe Doctrine than to the Open Door. On the eve of America's involvement in World War I, for example, the only "plan" in the General Staff files (actually more a theoretical exercise than a genuine plan) for war with Germany anticipated American troops not on European soil but involved in the defense of Eastern cities against a German attack.[38] And Elihu Root's General Staff was long involved in the minutiae of administration rather than in the business of long-range planning.[39]

This is not to say that there were not Army officers who were exceptions—and important exceptions—to this general rule. For the mission of the Army did expand after the turn of the century. Army officers were drawn into Cuban affairs, involved in the construction and defense of the Panama Canal, handled the customs revenues of the Dominican Republic, and, above all, were concerned with the defense of the Philippine Islands. The Army did contain certain individuals like Leonard Wood who, for example, wrote extensively about matters of international politics and carried on an extensive correspondence with Theodore Roosevelt about Asian affairs. Those who, like Wood, became involved in the Philippines often turned their attention to the pattern of political events in Asia. After the Russo-Japanese war General Arthur MacArthur reported his own conclusions in the grandiose prose style which seems to be the hallmark of the MacArthur family: "How far reaching, and how permanent the effects of the recent war may be; and precisely what ultimate philosophical bearing it may have

[37] See Louis Morton, "Interservice Cooperation and Political-Military Collaboration," in Harry L. Coles, ed., *Total War and Cold War* (Columbus, 1961), 131-60, and Paul Y. Hammond, *Organizing the Common Defense* (Princeton, 1961), 61 ff.

[38] GS, Office of the Chief of Staff, File 9433, U.S. War Plans Against Germany. Among several documents in this file see, especially, F. L. Scott to M. M. Macomb, 24 February 1916.

[39] Otto L. Nelson, Jr., *National Security and the General Staff* (Washington, 1946), 73 ff.; Russell Weigley, *Towards an American Army* (New York, 1962), 174 ff.; and Hammond, *Common Defense*, 30.

upon the Problem of the Pacific, is not yet apparent, but for the time being Japan must be regarded as master of the ocean."[40] Similarly, at the newly-established Army War College in Washington there were a few officers like General Tasker Bliss whose outlook was global. As one of the Army representatives on the Joint Board when that inter-service group began its first tentative endeavors, Bliss could foresee a time in the not too distant future when Americans might "find ourselves fighting for our Monroe Doctrine on one side of the world and against somebody else's Monroe Doctrine on the other side of the world."[41]

Nevertheless, the involvement of the Army and its General Staff in foreign affairs was considerably less than that of the Navy. There was, for example, a brief period in 1911 when it appeared possible that the United States would intervene in China with military force as it had done at the time of the Boxer rebellion. But the Army staff quickly discovered that it was woefully deficient on information about the existing revolutionary situation in China. General Wotherspoon, the Assistant Chief of Staff, found it necessary to send a personal note to his opposite number in the Navy which began as follows: "I am called upon for a report as to the role of the Army in the protection of foreigners in China in view of the disturbed conditions there. My chief of staff wants to know what foreign troops etc. are there, also I would like ideas as to where in a general sense Americans have been concentrated and if in war they could take refuge in our ships etc."[42]

Once briefed on the Army's actual capabilities, Wotherspoon was then compelled to report that there was little that the United States Army could contribute. In comparison with the number of troops that other nations could send to China, he ruefully noted, the United States could furnish so few that her military commitment "would probably have little influence towards increasing the strength of our political representations at the capital of China."[43] The Army also resisted the temptation to expand its involvements. In 1912 Taft was so alarmed by the continuing revolution in Nicaragua that for a short time he contemplated the dispatch of the 10th Infantry Regiment to that Central American country. There was little enthusiasm in Army circles, and the civilian Secretary, Henry Stimson, at once objected. To Stimson it was far wiser to continue to rely upon the Marine Corps, even if this meant greater delay and expense. The appearance of Army troops in Nicaragua, he argued, might have international repercussions, where-

[40] SDML, Taft to Root, 26 January 1906, enclosing copy of report prepared by General Arthur MacArthur.

[41] JB, File 325, General Tasker Bliss to Dewey, 10 June 1904.

[42] GS, War College Division, File 6790 (War in China), especially 6790/13, Wotherspoon to Richard Wainwright, 9 November 1911.

[43] GS File 6790/15, Report by General Wotherspoon, 14 November 1911.

as the commitment of Marines would be in keeping with the historic functions of that force and less likely to cause misunderstandings.[44]

In the years after 1900 both services reached definite conclusions about the nations most likely to be friends and enemies of the United States. By the turn of the century the growing Anglo-American rapprochement had unquestionably reached such a stage that Great Britain had virtually ceased to be regarded as even a possible enemy. Indeed, according to the British naval attaché, the greatest change in American attitudes toward Great Britain since 1898 had occurred in the two American military services.[45] Mahan, writing to Roosevelt in 1906, summed up the new outlook: "British interests are not American interests, no. But taking the constitution of the British Empire and the trade interests of the British islands, the United States has certainty of a very high order that the British Empire will stand substantially on the same line of world policy as ourselves; that its strength will be our strength; and the weakening of it injury to ourselves."[46]

Mahan himself believed so strongly in the increasing identity of American and British naval interests that in 1906 he urged both Roosevelt and Root to abandon the historic American policy of insistence upon the immunity of private property at sea in time of war and, instead, to reconcile American maritime policy with British practices. He was insistent that, in the event of an Anglo-German war, American neutrality should not impede British seapower. Immunity of private property was, moreover, no longer in the national interest. "Great Britain and the British navy lie right across Germany's carrying trade with the whole world. Exempt it, and you remove the strongest hook in the jaws of Germany that the English speaking peoples have; a principal gage for peace."[47] Roosevelt and Root, in turn, submitted Mahan's proposals to the General Board for its advice. The naval strategists, themselves fearful that Britain was being tempted to adopt the traditional American thesis about immunity, returned the following unanimous verdict:

> The General Board is of the opinion that our interests are now so closely bound up with Great Britain that we should exert our diplomatic efforts to dissuade Great Britain from giving up the great advantage she now holds over Germany, due to her great navy and her

[44] Department of State, Decimal File 1910-1927 (hereafter abbreviated as SDDF), File 817.00/1907, Taft to Huntington Wilson, 28 August 1912. See also Papers of William Howard Taft, Manuscripts Division, Library of Congress, Presidential Series 3, Stimson to Taft, 29 August 1912.

[45] Arthur J. Marder, *The Anatomy of British Sea Power* (New York, 1940), 444.

[46] SDNF, Mahan to Theodore Roosevelt, 24 August 1906.

[47] *Ibid.*

excellent strategic position in regard to Germany's commerce. This great advantage would be lost to Great Britain if she should join with the United States in its previously mistaken policy of urging an international agreement to exempt private property from seizure in time of war.

British and American interests were parallel in the Western Hemisphere, the admirals continued, and the United States could certainly anticipate passive, if not active, British assistance in any war that might arise out of a European challenge to the Monroe Doctrine. Their report terminated on a note of hands-across-the-sea sentimentality: "The two great English-speaking nations seem destined to exert a great influence on the future progress of the world, the limitation of war, and the conduct of war when war is inevitable."[48]

There are innumerable references in like vein in Army and Navy records of the era. When Admiral Sperry took the White Fleet on its world cruise, he worked diligently for the cause of Anglo-American friendship in every British port of call. "I have quietly preached that doctrine from first to last," he wrote, "as the foundation to be cemented by 'ties of blood' . . . and that our community of interests being developed and apparent to all the world, it would be a natural alliance far stronger than any written treaty of alliance."[49] Army spokesmen echoed similar thoughts: Leonard Wood frequently noted that an understanding with Britain would provide the best solution for Far Eastern problems; Tasker Bliss informed the Joint Board in 1904 that the Army War College regarded war with Britain as the least probable of all possible conflicts; and the General Staff produced various studies that emphasized the improbability of war with Britain.[50]

These beliefs, to be sure, were not founded solely upon sentimentality or a presumed identity of interests. While Army leaders discounted the possibility of war with Britain, they were quick to point out that Canada was, after all, a hostage to British good behavior. As Tasker Bliss noted, Canada occupied such an exposed military position that it was always possible "to reimburse ourselves by more desirable property near home to replace that which we should have lost further away."[51] Similarly, both in the Army and the Navy there was at least a generalized recognition of the fact that Britain's increasing problems in Europe rendered it less and less likely that England could

[48] GB, File 438, Dewey to Secretary Bonaparte, 28 September 1906.

[49] Sperry Papers, Sperry to Mrs. Charles Sperry, 16 September 1908.

[50] Papers of General Leonard Wood, Manuscripts Division, Library of Congress, Wood to Theodore Roosevelt, 30 January 1908; JB, File 325, Bliss to Dewey, 10 June 1904; GS, Second Section, File 6200, 5a, various reports dealing with the fortification of Chesapeake Bay, November 1910.

[51] JB, File 325, Bliss to Dewey, 10 June 1904.

afford conflict with the United States. Nor were naval strategists always as sanguine as they had been in 1906 about the prospect of British assistance in a German-American clash. Later naval plans, for example, included the possibility that Britain might remain coldly neutral since, the British with their eyes ever peeled for the main economic chance, would realize the advantage of permitting their two strongest competitors to destroy one another.[52] Still, whatever the occasional doubts may have been, the fundamental attitude of the Navy was that of the young officer charged in 1910 with the responsibility of assessing the existing war plans of the General Board: "It is generally assumed that war with Great Britain is extremely improbable, and such a contingency is practically never thought of in our service."[53] It was a sentiment reciprocated in British circles, for, as Brassey's *Naval Annual* noted in 1903, "We do not mean to fight with America, nor she with us; and if war should break out between the two branches of the race, it will be in the nature of a civil war, and against civil wars it is impossible to prepare."[54]

With Germany it was far different. Admiral Dewey, throughout his long tenure as President of the General Board, never recovered from the acute case of Germanophobia he had acquired when Admiral Dietrichs sailed into Manila Bay in 1898. His feelings were shared fully by his colleagues on the General Board. In 1906, at the same time that these officers could write so glowingly about the rosy future of Anglo-American relations, they expressed the gravest of suspicions about Germany:

Germany wants to expand her colonial possessions. Especially it is thought that she is desirous of obtaining a foothold in the Western Hemisphere, and many things indicate that she has her eyes on localities in the West Indies, on the shores of the Caribbean, and in parts of South America. It is believed in many quarters that she is planning to test the Monroe Doctrine by annexation or establishment of a protectorate over a portion of South America, even going to the extent of war with the United States when her fleet is ready.[55]

Admiral Taylor, although willing to concede that most of the European powers had at least grudgingly accepted the Monroe Doctrine, warned that "Germany has been more sanguine than the others . . . and

[52] GB, version of Black Plan as previously cited.
[53] GB, File 425, Memorandum on the Preparation of General War Plans, 23 November 1909.
[54] *Brassey's Naval Annual, 1903* (Portsmouth, 1904), 110.
[55] GB, File 438, Dewey to Bonaparte, 28 September 1906.

showed by her actions in Haiti, and later in Venezuela in company with England, a desire to see how far she could go in testing the Monroe Doctrine."[56] Deep naval suspicion of Germany was a constant in the thinking of the General Board from 1898 to the outbreak of the European conflict in 1914. The completed "Black Plan" of 1914, on which the Board had been working for three years, stated unequivocally that "Black [Germany] will insist upon the occupation of Western Hemisphere territory under the Black flag, and Blue [United States] will then have to defend her policy by force, or acquiesce in the occupation."[57]

This plan, one of the two specific "color" plans drawn up by the General Board to meet the contingency of war between the United States and a designated foreign enemy, was the culmination of the General Board's strategic thinking about Germany. Based on the assumption of German aggression in the Caribbean, it presumed that the Imperial fleet would steam directly from its home ports to the Caribbean and attempt, as a first step, to secure a Caribbean base—perhaps the Venezuelan island of Margarita or in Haiti or the Dominican Republic—from which to conduct further operations in the Western Hemisphere. Naval planners did not anticipate direct operations against the United States; after 1905, indeed, the studies of the Naval War College presumed that at the most the German navy would make a feint at New England or possibly launch a raid to disrupt American preparations. Under the "Black Plan" the role of the United States fleet was to take the strategic defensive against these German moves; that is, to prepare itself to wage in the Caribbean the decisive naval battle that would thwart William II's imperialistic plans.[58]

Both services, however, were somewhat slower to discover the "natural enemy" in the Far East. The prevailing turn-of-the-century assumptions were that the interests of the United States, Great Britain, and Japan were similar, whereas Germany and Russia were considered the powers with whom American interests were most likely to clash. After the Boxer Rebellion had triggered a series of Russian moves in Manchuria, naval thinking for some years emphasized the Russian menace. Naval war planning in the first few years of the century was extremely casual, but it is still clear that the strategists of the General Board believed that the most likely Asian combination would

[56] JB, File 325, Admiral Taylor's memorandum of 10 June 1904.
[57] GB, version of Black Plan as cited.
[58] GB, War Portfolio 1, Atlantic Station: General Considerations and Data, 19 October 1910. See also Appendix B, Studies of the Naval War College, 1901-1915, which summarizes the evolution of the War College's thinking about the likelihood of a strike against the continental United States.

find the United States in partnership with the British and the Japanese in a war against Russia, Germany, and, possibly, France.[59] There were even in these years occasional, fleeting references to potential Japanese hostility; Army officers, for example, frequently reported suspicious Japanese activities in the Philippines.[60] But, by and large, until the aftermath of the Russo-Japanese war, the prevailing opinion in military circles was that Japan was a friend rather than an enemy; hence the most "pessimistic" forecast was that of Admiral Taylor when he wrote in 1904, ". . . nor do we need in the first instance to regard Japan as a probable enemy, though the result of the present war may cause us to change somewhat any plans based upon the certainty of an alliance of Japan with England and ourselves."[61]

The naval and military attitude toward Japan changed, and changed rapidly, in the next few years as Japanese-American tensions grew, especially at the time of the so-called "war scare" of 1907. In the eyes of the admirals and the generals Japan now clearly emerged as the most probable enemy of the United States in the Far East. The political dossier furnished by the General Board to its officers on the Asiatic Station made this explicit: "Of all the powers in the Far East, the United States will probably clash with none of them except Japan concerning interests in that region."[62] It was against Japan that the first of the famous "color" plans—the "Orange Plan"—was developed.

As early as the fall of 1906, and acting on specific instructions from President Roosevelt, the General Board began to draw up a tentative scheme to defend the Philippines and other American possessions in the Pacific from Japanese attack. Within a few years the General Board began formal preparation of a permanent, standing plan of operations. Completed in 1911 the "Orange Plan," despite later modifications and adaptions, remained *the* war plan of the United States Navy for conflict with Japan until the late 1930s, and its main provisions remained in force until superseded by the various "Rainbow" plans of the immediate pre-World War II era. Indeed, as early as 1909 the naval planners expressed satisfaction with their work; it was confidently noted that plans to deal with Japan were by far the most advanced and satisfactory, for the "question of Japan has already been

59 GB, Proceedings, 29 May 1902. See also GB, File 425, Sperry to Dewey, 18 January 1904 and War Portfolio 2, memorandum of 1 June 1904.

60 SDML, David J. Hill to Hay, 26 February 1901, a summary of some fifty documents that the War Department had furnished on the subject of Japanese activities in the Philippines.

61 JB, File 325, Taylor memorandum of 10 June 1904.

62 GB, War Portfolio 2, Asiatic Station: General Considerations and Data, February 1914.

given much thought by our officers, and the strategic situation seems reasonably clear."[63]

The "Orange Plan" assumed that, with the main American battle fleet permanently stationed in the Atlantic, the naval strength of the United States would, at the outset of any Far Eastern conflict, be far inferior to that of Japan. Hence the Asiatic fleet would be withdrawn from Far Eastern waters at the first suspicion of hostilities, while the Army garrison in the Philippines would withdraw to the fortress of Corregidor. For at least sixty days Japan would have a virtual free hand in the Pacific. But, within that interim, the full might of American naval power would be assembled in the Hawaiian Islands, and eventually the entire fleet would sail westward across the Pacific in a great offensive operation that would ultimately seek out and destroy Japanese naval power at its source—and, hopefully, rescue the beleaguered Army troops in the Philippines before they had been compelled to surrender.[64]

Both services contained at least some high-ranking officers who at certain times convinced themselves that war with Japan—and, it should be emphasized, a war disastrous to American interests—was imminent. On the occasion of the 1907 "crisis" several members of the General Board opposed Roosevelt's decision to send the main fleet into the Pacific since they were fearful that Japan would seize upon this as a provocative opportunity to initiate hostilities.[65] In the following years there were more than a few Army officers in the Phillipines who firmly believed, often on the slimmest of evidence, that Japan was about to launch a move against America's Far Eastern island possessions.[66] In 1913, on the occasion of another short but severe crisis in Japanese-American relations, Admiral Bradley Fiske, the Aide for Operations, stunned Woodrow Wilson and his cabinet with a memorandum which

[63] GB, Proceedings, 26 September 1906 and various items in the 425 file. The citation is from a memorandum of 23 November 1909 in the 425 file. See also War Portfolio 7, Naval War College Strategic Plan of Campaign against Orange, 14 March 1911.

[64] In addition to various documents in the War Portfolios just cited, see Louis Morton, "War Plan Orange: A Study in Military Strategy," *World Politics*, XI, no. 2 (January 1959), 221-50, and William Braisted, *The United States Navy in the Pacific, 1897-1909* (Austin, 1958). Braisted's principal conclusions are also contained in his two articles, "The Philippine Naval Base Problem, 1898-1909," *Mississippi Valley Historical Review*, XLI, no. 1 (June 1954), 21-40, and "The United States Navy's Dilemma in the Pacific, 1906-1909," *Pacific Historical Review*, XXVI, no. 3 (August 1957), 235-44.

[65] Sperry Papers, Sperry to Mrs. Sperry, 1 November 1908.

[66] This issue is discussed at greater length in Chapter Four. See also GS, War College Division, File 5288, which contains abundant material on the rumors that spread in 1911.

argued that "my studies of the race and its history leads me to the conviction that it is only a question of whether they themselves believe their preparations are sufficiently advanced to seize and hold the Philippines, Guam, and the Hawaiian Islands and inflict an enormous damage upon us before we can bring any adequate force in the Pacific that will decide whether they will go to war or not."[67] In official military thinking, then, there were sometimes echoes of the same fears and fantasies that appeared in the writings of Homer Lea, that eccentric but brilliant prophet of American doom, whose famous *Valor of Ignorance* had forecast not only an imminent war with Japan but also a conflict in which America would be defeated and invaded by her Oriental enemy.

Yet one must not exaggerate out of all proportion the extent of extremism in military circles about the imminence of war nor conclude that most officers lived in a perpetual state of apprehension about foreign threats. Comments about war and its prospects are, after all, part of the normal "shoptalk" of the professions of arms; often they are no more a sign of alarmism than a discussion of the statistical probabilities of death by cancer would be an indication of morbidity among a group of actuaries. And, especially in peacetime, pessimism about a nation's military prospects is one of the more prevalent attitudes of officers of any army or navy.[68] Military planners could also sometimes be aware of the objective factors which decreased the prospect of any conflict. The Army General Staff, for instance, once noted that a clear consequence of the Spanish-American War was the heightened respect which all European nations, save, of course, Germany, now showed for the Monroe Doctrine.[69] Planning documents occasionally reflected an awareness of the technological and logistical difficulties that militated against any European attack on America except in the most unusual circumstances. "Any European power, other than England," a naval memorandum pointed out in 1910, "must conduct operations against the continental portions of the United States by overseas expeditions pure and simple—expeditions so monumental that their transport and maintenance will be exceedingly difficult under the most favorable circumstances."[70] Thus, each year after 1900 the Navy planners discounted more and more the prospect that the German fleet might attack Eastern portions of the country and by 1913 had come to doubt even the possibility of a raid or a feint. Their general analyses rested

[67] Papers of Josephus Daniels, Manuscripts Division, Library of Congress, Admiral Bradley Fiske to Daniels, 14 May 1913.

[68] Huntington, *Soldier and the State*, ch. 3, 59-79.

[69] GS, War College Division, File 818, memorandum of 31 May 1904.

[70] GB, War Portfolio 1, Atlantic Station: General Considerations, 19 October 1910.

most frequently upon "possibilities" rather than "probabilities"—and not all their "possibilities," it should be observed, were entirely lacking in at least a degree of political sophistication. It was sometimes observed, for example, that the real danger of aggression in the Caribbean would occur if the United States became embroiled in a Far Eastern conflict, thereby tempting a European move for territorial acquisition in the West Indies. And the Navy's various plans for a campaign against Japan at least made mention of the many factors—ranging from Japan's financial problems after her conflict with Russia to her need for time to exploit her Manchurian gains—which might serve to deter an actual conflict.

Still, given the Navy's view of the world, war always did seem a possibility—and a possibility that demanded certain precautionary measures of naval policy. Thus the General Board unremittingly sought from its earliest days to commit the President and the Congress to a naval building program that would create a fleet of forty-eight battleships.[71] Equally important and an article of absolute faith to true believers in the gospel of Mahan, was the belief that the battle fleet must be kept together as a single unit and concentrated in the Atlantic. There were, to be sure, some very practical and political reasons for keeping the fleet in the Atlantic, reasons which had little or nothing to do with the best interests of naval strategy or policy. There was an almost total lack of adequate bases on the West coast of the United States; the Eastern states were anxious to keep the lucrative business of naval contracting firmly in their own familiar hands; and the principal Congressional committees which handled naval affairs were chaired by powerful Senators and Representatives who opposed changes that might deprive their home states of the naval business they had traditionally enjoyed.[72]

Even so, the General Board regularly affirmed that there were sound strategic reasons for keeping the fleet in the Atlantic. In reply to a specific request from the Secretary of the Navy in 1903 the General Board laid down the rule that "the proper military policy, taken as a general principle, for the distribution of the fleet, is the concentration of all the battleships in the Atlantic."[73] When fears of Japan began to rise and, in particular, when residents of California began to demand permanent naval protection, there were many discussions and debates about

[71] GB, File 446, Dewey to Daniels, 28 March 1913. This is the best summary of the General Board's position. It was published by Daniels in the Annual Report of the Secretary of the Navy for 1913, the first time that the Board's request had been given formal publication.

[72] Harold and Margaret Sprout, *The Rise of American Naval Power, 1776-1918* (Princeton, 1939), 277, 292-94.

[73] GB, Proceedings, 4 December 1903.

the wisdom of preserving the Atlantic concentration. But the General Board in 1907 reaffirmed its original stand: "At the present time, no European nation has a single battleship outside of European waters, which fact is considered a cogent reason that our entire battle fleet should be concentrated on the Atlantic Coast." Even if the enemy should be an Asian nation, the strategists continued, the best naval interests of the United States would be served by such a policy and by transferring the entire fleet, as a unit, to the Pacific at the time of emergency.[74]

This is not to say that the naval strategists were always either happy or content with this arrangement. Indeed, as will later be noted, there were significant waverings from the doctrine on the part of some. It was frequently argued that, if Congress would authorize a fleet of forty-eight battleships, then such a force could be divided into two units, one in the Atlantic and the other in the Pacific, and each would be of a size and composition that would enable it to operate independently of the other. But until Congress approved a navy based on the "two-ocean standard" (and also, until adequate facilities were built on the West coast) the General Board decreed that "The only possible arrangement is to concentrate our fighting forces in the Atlantic."[75] As Mahan advised Senator Perkins in 1911, division of the fleet prior to achieving the two-ocean standard would "be contrary to all sound military doctrine and practice. The people of the Pacific slope might *feel* themselves safer with half the battle fleet in their harbors, but *actually* they would be in greater peril, because they would have conditions favoring the destruction of our entire navy in detail."[76]

Another major precaution from the military point of view was to maintain a special watch on the Caribbean. The "strategy board" of 1898 had directed particular attention to the Caribbean as "one of the most interesting and vital regions of the world to the United States, considered from the viewpoint of commerce and of war . . . because our interests may be most seriously interrupted, by hostile navies, in time of war."[77] No sooner had the General Board been formally established in 1900 than it began to emphasize the same theme in report after report. Any war involving European powers would undoubtedly take place in the Caribbean, "for it is in South and Central American waters that the conflicts between the political and commercial policies

[74] GB, File 420-1, memorandum of 25 April 1907.

[75] In addition to the memorandum just cited, see also GB, Letters, v, Admiral Manney to Secretary Victor Metcalf, 15 August 1907, with attached comments by Admiral Dewey.

[76] Mahan Papers, Mahan to Senator George Perkins, 7 January 1911.

[77] GB, File 414-1, Report of the Naval War Board, 1898.

of our own and European nations seems to be most pronounced."[78] In 1904 the leading officers of the General Board and the General Staff began their first discussions about coordinating Army and Navy war plans, and, although the Navy was sorely tempted to a Far Eastern orientation, the eventual decision was that first priority should be given to a thorough study of the Caribbean as this was the most probable area of future hostilities.[79]

Many and varied arguments sustained this focus upon the Caribbean as the vital area of concern. All war planning assumed that the United States could not possibly be defeated by a European enemy unless that opponent had first secured a base of operations in the Western Hemisphere. It was also assumed that the only possible area in which such a base could be located was in the Caribbean. From this line of logic came the inevitable conclusion that the first strike by any European navy would be in that area and that the Caribbean would become the primary theater of operations. It was, of course, the technology of steam that underlay these assumptions. Admiral Sigsbee, when chief of the Office of Naval Intelligence, once carefully calculated the cruising radius of the German High Seas Fleet and proved to his own satisfaction that it could sail directly from its North Sea base to the Caribbean and reach the island of Santo Domingo without refueling. Though he did admit that to accomplish this considerable naval feat the Germans would have to cram their bunkers with coal as well as carry substantial amounts of it in special compartments constructed on open decks! But this study helped to persuade Sigsbee and others on the General Board that Santo Domingo, the limit of the German navy's cruising radius, would therefore be the special object of Germany's nefarious designs and the probable locale at which naval operations in a war with Germany would occur.[80]

The dominant reason for the Navy's desire to mount a permanent guard over the Caribbean was the Isthmian canal. For years the Navy had regarded construction of a canal across the Isthmus as *the* foremost naval need of the United States; the experiences of the war of 1898 had only confirmed that belief. Navalists were equally convinced that the primary role of the Navy in the Caribbean was to protect that canal, both during its construction and after its completion. Indeed, once the Panama route had been secured by Roosevelt's "big stick,"

[78] GB, Letters, I, Dewey to Long, 21 August 1901.

[79] Joint Board, Communications and Minutes, Dewey to Secretaries of Navy and War, 24 June 1904. (Hereafter citations from the minutes of meetings of the Joint Board will be abbreviated as JB, Minutes.)

[80] Nav Rec AF 8, Sigsbee to Morton, 22 April and 3 May 1905; also GB, Letters, I, Dewey to Long, 12 November 1901.

naval officers unanimously agreed that protection of the canal and the preservation of its neutrality had become a fixed national policy equivalent to the Monroe Doctrine and the Open Door.[81] Protection of the canal, in short, provided the Navy with a basic rationale for American intervention in the Caribbean as well as with another justification for enlargement of the fleet. In 1913, when the Navy was emphasizing its 48-battleship program, a substantial part of its case rested on the presumed need for additional naval strength to protect the canal.[82] In like vein, Admiral Dewey, making his annual request for the Navy's building program in 1910, summed up the attitude of the General Board when he argued for additional battleships on the grounds that to the traditional policies of the United States there had now been added a third: the preservation of the neutrality of the canal.[83]

In the years immediately following the Spanish-American War the Navy believed that there was one all-important requirement for an effective watch upon both the canal and the Caribbean: the acquisition by the United States of an extensive chain of naval bases and coaling stations throughout the "American Mediterranean." Indeed, the "strategy board" of 1898 had explicitly stated that it was now "obvious" that the United States would have to acquire bases outside American territory. In the Caribbean it had specified a need for bases not only in the immediate vicinity of the terminal points of the projected canal but also on the circumference or periphery of that sea.[84] The General Board, immediately upon its establishment in 1900, took up the same theme and emphasized that the protection of the Caribbean required bases both on the Isthmus and at the principal entrances and exits to that sea.[85] In the next few years there was probably no aspect of naval policy to which these officers devoted more of their time than the selection of appropriate sites for naval bases and coaling stations. In the summer of 1901, for example, the Board submitted two separate reports to the Secretary of the Navy about Caribbean sites; the following year it prepared two even more extensive recommendations, this time on a global basis. The same focus and emphasis pervaded all of its recommendations. America's need to control the Windward Passage was described as so pressing that "our right to establish ourselves at that point should be obtained at the earliest moment, irrespective of the

[81] GB, File 420, Dewey to William Griffin, 7 December 1912 is a typical statement.

[82] GB, File 446, Dewey to Daniels, 28 March 1913, a letter in which Dewey cites the preservation of the neutrality of the canal as a definite national policy.

[83] GB, Letters, VII, Dewey to Meyer, 28 September 1910.

[84] GB, File 414-1, Report of the Naval War Board, 1898.

[85] The details of this series of requests for Caribbean bases are discussed in Chapter Two.

future status of Cuba—whether it remain independent or be annexed by request." The reports stressed the strategic importance of Santo Domingo; insisted that the Cubans must be persuaded to cede the bases pledged in their own constitution; dealt with the possibility of acquiring such naval sites as Almirante Bay, Chiriqui Lagoon, Port Elena, and the Galapagos Islands; and, on one occasion, even hinted that the emerging interests of the United States might some day require a naval station at Bahia Hondo on the eastern tip of Brazil.[86]

This search for bases, as indicated in the introduction, was by no means confined to the Western Hemisphere. There was a similarly intense agitation for one or more Far Eastern bases to supplement the facilities to be created in the Philippines. The request for the Chusan Islands initiated in the summer of 1900 may have been triggered by the naval problems of the Boxer Rebellion, but it was simply part and parcel of a broader imperialistic thrust by the Navy to acquire a series of bases in all parts of the world in which the naval establishment was now both involved and interested.

But despite the intensity of the search, the Navy's enthusiasm for Caribbean and Far Eastern bases was relatively short-lived and produced few tangible results. One reason for the failure of naval hopes —a reason which will be elaborated in succeeding chapters—was political. In the Far East, for example, the Japanese showed not the slightest inclination to yield their lien upon portions of the Chinese coast coveted by the American navy, while the Department of State became increasingly cognizant of the conflict between naval desires and the concept of the Open Door. In Latin America, despite greater and sustained support from the State Department, Latin political leaders proved adroit in thwarting the wishes of the General Board. Ecuador, by placing a fantastic price tag upon the Galapagos, priced these islands out of the market; Peru always wanted to bargain port facilities at Chimbote for American diplomatic support in the perennial Tacna-Arica dispute; and on the Isthmus many a Central American foreign minister adopted the tactic of claiming that the cession of national territory was a matter of such acute political delicacy that such matters should be deferred until tomorrow—a mañana which somehow never dawned. Even the newly independent Cubans proved skillful in defending their national territory. Thus, the only tangible product of all the naval pleas for bases and stations in the Caribbean and Far East was Guantanamo Bay in Cuba. Moreover, only imperialistic forethought had produced Guantanamo. The United States, after all, had literally written the constitution of Cuba; had thoughtfully inserted in

[86] GB, Letters, II, Dewey to Moody, 30 September and 7 October 1902.

that document a clause which legally obligated the Cubans to furnish naval bases to the Navy; and had made acceptance of that constitution a condition of Cuban independence![87]

But with the passage of time members of the General Board began to lose some of their initial enthusiasm for foreign bases. Two individuals, Admirals Henry C. Taylor and Royal B. Bradford, had been responsible for much of the early drive that was initiated with the formation of the General Board in 1900. Bradford, chief of the Bureau of Equipment and an advocate of almost unlimited expansion, even encouraged the efforts of a group of private individuals—which included, incidentally, several bishops of the Methodist Church—to prove their solicitude for Liberia by obtaining an American naval station in that faintly independent African republic.[88] Taylor, on another occasion, endorsed a wholly unsuitable project for a coaling station in the Chinese harbor of Amoy. It was an implausible site, but, according to Taylor's catch-as-catch-can approach, since it was highly desirable to obtain a foothold somewhere in China, one might just as well begin with Amoy "as a step to some better place."[89]

The death of Taylor in 1904 relieved the General Board of his personal pressure for expansion and led at least one member of the Board to express the private thought that reason might now have a chance to prevail. Yet even before that time there had been second thoughts about the advisability of proliferating overseas naval stations. In the fall of 1902, at a time when he was actually endorsing one of the General Board's far-reaching proposals, Admiral Dewey expressed a growing concern. The United States, he suggested, might already have too many bases. Since all bases would have to be defended in time of war, their number might actually prove to be a weakness rather than a source of strength.[90] In the early months of 1903 the change in the outlook of the General Board became quite marked, and the tone of its communications became noticeably different. In reply to inquiries from the Department of State and other interested agencies about the desirability of certain naval sites, the General Board now began to express a new and cautious doctrine, namely: the idea that the concentration of naval strength in a particular area was more advantageous than the diffusion of American naval power at a number of separate, scattered locations. Soon thereafter the General Board was not only turning down specific opportunities to open negotiations for particular

[87] See especially David F. Healy, *The United States in Cuba, 1898-1902* (Madison, Wisc., 1963), 150-67.

[88] SDML, Long to Hay, 5 May 1899, with numerous enclosures.

[89] GB, Letters, II, Dewey to Taylor, 18 June 1903, particularly 9th endorsement.

[90] GB, Proceedings, 23 September 1902.

sites but also cutting back its formal list of desired bases and coaling stations.[91]

This change in the Navy's thinking about the desirability of overseas bases and the concentration of naval strength had its parallel in—and was undoubtedly influenced by—British naval thought. The dramatic and definitive redistribution of the British fleet, with its concentration in home waters and an attendant reduction in British overseas naval stations, did not officially take place until the regime of Lord Fisher as First Sea Lord in 1904. But there had been anticipations of these reforms under his predecessor, Lord Selborne. In 1903, at the very time that the General Board was beginning to change its own outlook, Selborne could write, with regard to overseas naval stations, that "the number of these bases and the money spent on them should be limited in the strictest manner to the absolute necessities of the Navy," and he actually initiated the first measures looking toward the concentration rather than the diffusion of British naval strength.[92]

The British naval moves were of course triggered by the growing might of the German navy. The change in heart of the General Board about the advisability of numerous foreign bases was the product of many and varied factors. One of the most influential was the obvious reluctance of the Congress to appropriate funds for the establishment and development of overseas naval sites. The Navy, it always should be emphasized, long prized and valued two locations above all others —Guantanamo Bay in Cuba and Subig Bay in the Philippines. These two naval bases were to be the keystones upon which the arches of American naval power would be erected in the Caribbean and Far East. All recommendations for additional sites, however, rested on the tacit assumption that these would only supplement Guantanamo and Subig and that the two locations in the Philippines and Cuba would be fully developed and fortified. But Congress was ever niggardly in its appropriations and unwilling to provide the Navy with the sums necessary to complete its plans for these two stations. In these circumstances, then, it seemed increasingly prudent to focus attention upon Subig and Guantanamo in the hope that at least the necessary funds for their development could somehow be secured. There was a consequent dampening of naval enthusiasm for additional foreign stations for which there was virtually no possibility of securing financial support from a recalcitrant legislature.[93]

---

91 *Ibid.*, minutes of 12 June 1903, 27 September 1904, and 20 December 1904. For a more detailed discussion of the issue, GB, Letters, II, Dewey to Moody, 24 March 1903.

92 Marder, *Anatomy*, 491-93. See also *Brassey's Naval Annual* for 1903, 110, and Colonel Roger Willock, *Bulwark of Empire* (Princeton, privately printed, 1962), 145.

93 Sprout, *Rise of American Naval Power*, 276-77.

At the beginning of the century the Navy had been convinced that the fleet could be refueled only at fixed land bases at which ample coal supplies could be stored. Much of the demand for overseas naval stations was created by the anticipated need for coal, especially in areas where naval operations appeared likely to occur. In 1898, at the time of the battle of Manila Bay, the Navy Department's search for coal for Dewey's fleet had been so intense that it had virtually overshadowed all other problems.[94] As previously noted, it was the logistics of coal that was emphasized in the General Board's first request for a base on the Chinese mainland in 1900. But by the middle of the decade the naval command began to believe that the fleet could be refueled at sea. The job of recoaling could be accomplished by specially built colliers that would accompany various naval units.[95] The emergence of the fleet collier obviously provided another reason why the acquisition of additional foreign naval stations began to appear of less significance to the General Board.

The voyage of the White Fleet around the world was equally influential. Whatever its political value may have been, that famous voyage had a great impact upon the outlook of the high command of the United States Navy. Beforehand naval theorists had assumed, in drawing up their hypothetical plans for war with Japan, that the fleet would have to put in at a Philippine naval base before it could possibly attempt any military action against an enemy. But so successful was the voyage across the Pacific that naval writers soon began to contend that the battle fleet could arrive in Far Eastern waters in a fully operational condition and would be ready to fight without a need to pause for repairs, refueling, or maintenance. The experience of the world cruise, in the judgment of the Joint Board, showed that the American fleet possessed a far greater cruising radius, coal endurance, and "power of self-maintenance" than any one had heretofore anticipated.[96] Similarly, the strategists revised downwards the amount of time—from 120 days to less than three months—that would be required to mount a naval operation in the Far East. The General Board, on the basis of the experiences of the White Fleet, therefore felt considerably less dependent upon the establishment of a major operational base in the Far East.

This does not of course exhaust the list of reasons why the Navy's views on the advisability of overseas bases began to be modified with the passage of time. There were certain specific decisons that affected

[94] Papers of Admiral George Dewey, Manuscripts Division, Library of Congress, Admiral R. B. Bradford to Dewey, 19 April 1902.

[95] GB, Letters, vi, Dewey to Meyer, 8 April 1909 and 23 February 1910.

[96] JB, Minutes, Dewey to Meyer, 8 November 1909.

base policy; for example, the General Board's interest in Almirante Bay and the Chiriqui Lagoon on the Isthmus of Panama came to a definite end in 1906 when two specially appointed boards concluded, after long study, that the defensive needs of the Panama Canal could be entirely fulfilled by a system of fortifications at its eastern and western termini.[97] The battle over the issue of Subig Bay also had an effect. The Navy, as will later be discussed in greater detail, was eventually compelled at the end of the Roosevelt administration to abandon its longstanding vision of a great naval bastion at Subig Bay and opted instead to locate its principal Pacific base at Pearl Harbor.[98] But in the course of this debate naval theorists began to draw distinctions between the tactical and strategic defense of American interests in the Philippines and the Far East. During the Taft era the argument began to be put forth that naval units in the Philippines, whether based at Subig or Manila, could provide only a tactical defense. The principal defense—the strategic defense—would rest with the main battle fleet, wherever it was concentrated, and could be accomplished "without a man or a gun at the spot." To those who accepted this line of reasoning, then, the issue of whether or not there was a major naval station at Subig Bay or elsewhere in the Far East seemed less crucial than heretofore. Or, to put the sentiments of the General Board more accurately, this line of argument as well as the presumed lessons of the voyage of the White Fleet made it possible for the admirals to swallow the bitter pill of their loss of Subig Bay and to concentrate their attention upon creating the center of Pacific naval power at Pearl Harbor.

There was, then, a relatively short period of time at the turn of the century when the Navy was intensely interested in proliferating overseas bases and coaling stations. This enthusiasm began to wane by about 1903, and for many and varied reasons: failure to win compliance from foreign governments, Congressional reluctance to appropriate funds, the presumed ability of the collier to meet supply needs, the Navy's eventual decision to give up on Subig Bay in favor of Pearl Harbor, and the capability of the battle fleet, as apparently demonstrated by its world cruise, to sustain itself far from its home bases. The net effect of these varied developments was not only to reduce the importance of additional bases but even, in the case of Subig Bay, to make this once-cherished location lose its centrality in naval thinking about the Pacific.

Yet, though enthusiasm waned, the General Board never entirely abandoned its interest in permanent foreign bases. Hopes for a Far Eastern naval station certainly lingered long after its acquisition was

[97] GB, Letters, IV, Dewey to Bonaparte, 12 April 1906.
[98] Braisted, *Navy in the Pacific*, ch. 5.

a political impossibility. The Board's revised list of desired coaling stations submitted in 1906 specifically drew attention to the elimination of its previous recommendations for a location in the northern waters of the Far East. Nevertheless, the report continued, its members still adhered to their original opinion that "such a location should be selected if future conditions be favorable."[99] The admirals were, above all, reluctant to knuckle under to the Army's insistence that Subig Bay was indefensible and long sought some way whereby at least a portion of their visions for that base could be realized. It is extremely unlikely that they were really convinced in mind or heart by the Army arguments; it is more likely that they were subdued and compelled to recognize, particularly after William Howard Taft, an advocate of the Army viewpoint, occupied the White House, that they would never be able to secure the necessary support for their proposed Philippine bastion.

Similarly there was a continuing if subdued interest in Caribbean sites, an interest which actually revived during the Taft era. Many of the practitioners of the rugged dollar diplomacy of those years were stimulated by the approaching completion of the Panama Canal to take a second look at the possible value of additional naval stations in the Caribbean. The opening of the canal, it was argued, would not only increase the volume of commercial activity in that region but also might tempt European nations even more than in previous years to secure a foothold. Alleged German interest in a series of commercial coaling stations in Haiti appeared to Admiral Dewey as an omen for the future. Europeans, he wrote, seemed to be more alert than Americans to the vast changes that would occur in the Caribbean when the canal was completed and in consequence were now trying to obtain appropriate sites from which to extend their influence in the future.[100] While the Navy had no interest in these specific Haitian commercial depots, it did begin to give at least qualified endorsement to several projects for the acquisition of bases, such as Chimbote in Peru and Ecuador's Galapagos Islands, which had lain dormant for nearly a decade. Naval spokesmen, to be sure, now de-emphasized the strategic value of such locations; their value was political and to be determined by the diplomatic advantage to be gained by preventing them from falling into the hands of a European nation. Such sites, so the naval reports argued, would now be of relatively little strategic value to the United States Navy but should be acquired if it was politically necessary to keep them out of the hands of Europe.[101]

[99] GB, Letters, IV, Dewey to Bonaparte, 12 April 1906.

[100] See, for example, SDNF, Case 838/802, Meyer to Knox, 21 June 1910, containing a lengthy statement by Dewey outlining the views of the General Board.

[101] This matter is discussed at some length in Chapter Four.

Another important dimension of the Navy's evolving attitude toward the complex subject of overseas bases was the development of the so-called "advanced base" concept. This, in brief, was the idea that the Navy in peacetime should develop a series of plans which would enable it, as the first move in any conflict, to seize an advanced, operational base in the area of probable hostilities. The ability to secure such a base at the very outset of war would, it was argued, obviate much of the necessity for acquiring and maintaining permanent American naval stations in the strategic locations of the Caribbean and Pacific.[102] "Advanced base" plans, as they evolved in the General Board and the various bureaus, called for the preparation and maintenance in time of peace of two fully equipped expeditionary forces, one at League Island in Philadelphia and the other at Cavite in the Philippines, with both ready for immediate action.[103] Advanced base planning received considerable attention, some of which was deliberately kept from Congressional attention. In 1906 a zealous officer in the Quartermaster section wanted the Navy's budget to include a special fund for the purchase of a three-month supply of rations for the advanced base stores at League Island. The request was denied, for his superiors feared that such an item in the naval budget would only serve to stir up Congressional suspicions and create fears on Capitol Hill that the Navy anticipated war in the near future. To avoid political repercussions it was deemed wiser to assemble stores and equipment as quietly as possible, utilizing, wherever possible, materials already on hand and available from regular naval sources.[104]

A number of relatively detailed "advanced base" plans were actually drawn up. There were several to be used as the opening move in an Asian conflict, including one which called for the immediate seizure of the Chinese port of Kiaochow. But by far the most structured of these plans was the one developed about 1904 for operations on the island of Santo Domingo—the Haiti-Santo Domingo plan, abbreviated in naval argot to the "Hi-Sd Plan." Based on the supposition that Germany would be the enemy and her Caribbean goal the two island republics, the "Hi-Sd Plan" outlined procedures for the immediate seizure of Samana Bay in the Dominican Republic and the Mole St. Nicholas in Haiti. Prompt establishment of American naval power in Hispaniola would forestall German plans since the United States fleet would be firmly based in the area of naval operations before the Impe-

---

[102] GB, File 408, a file devoted entirely to the advanced base concept.

[103] GB, File 408, Dewey to Morton, 3 February 1905. Also, for a summary of the history of the concept, see a memorandum dated 15 May 1913 and prepared for the Board by Commander W. H. Jackson. There is also a useful summary of early plans in Letters, IV, Dewey to Bonaparte, 3 August 1906.

[104] GB, Proceedings, 26 September 1906.

rial navy had reached the Caribbean. The Navy's plans were not only extremely detailed but also, through the instrumentality of the Joint Board, coordinated with those of the Army. It was one of the earliest examples of interservice cooperation. The completed plan, for example, provided that the naval landing forces would be relieved by Army units thirty days after the initial seizure, and specific Army units were designated for permanent occupation duty.[105]

The General Staff, when first consulted, did raise some objections. The "Hi-Sd Plan" called for the seizure of the two bases with or without the consent of the two Caribbean republics involved. Army planners had some qualms about aggressive action directed at two neutral countries and pointed out that, if the Dominicans or Haitians refused to accept American occupation, the United States might become involved in hostilities against them.[106] To meet this argument, naval planners simply pleaded their version of the national interest. In their view the need to establish an advanced base in the Caribbean before the arrival of the German fleet was so compelling that it overrode all other considerations, and the risk of Haitian or Dominican hostility therefore had to be accepted. But the prospect did not unduly alarm them. The people of the two island republics, so claimed the Navy's spokesmen, would certainly understand that the American action was also in their interest, for it would save them from the dangers of a permanent German occupation. Moreover, it was casually, if cynically, concluded, even if Haiti or Santo Domingo did resist, their armed opposition would be negligible, at the worst scattered guerilla operations that could be readily crushed, if not at the outset by the Marines then most certainly by the Army troops arriving a month later.[107]

In the latter years of the Taft administration the "advanced base" idea began to wane. In the Far East, for example, it became increasingly clear that American military strength was so limited that, in the opening stages of any conflict, all operations would have to be defensive and there would be no opportunity to seize an advanced base as a springboard for more ambitious endeavors. It was therefore recommended that the title of advanced base outfit be discontinued and the equipment on hand be redistributed to bolster general Pacific defenses.[108] But while the concept flourished, it offered—provided the

105 GB, War Portfolio 1, Reference 5-D, Haiti-Santo Domingo Plan and GS, War College Division, Report 818 (Memorandum of confidential file of problems, studies, and miscellaneous documents, 29 June 1907) and Second Section, File 7428 (Memorandum for the Chief of Staff, Intervention in Santo Domingo, 12 November 1912).
106 GB, File 425, General Adna Chaffee to Dewey, 1 March 1905.
107 GB, War Portfolio 1, Plan for the Seizure and Defense by the Navy of Samana Bay, Santo Domingo and Fort Liberty Bay, Haiti as advanced bases in time of war, September 1904.
108 GB, File 408, Dewey to Meyer, 26 February 1913.

moral issue is put aside—an ingenious solution to the naval problem posed by the fact that the United States would not possess its own permanent bases in the Caribbean and the Far East. The concept of early seizure of an "advanced base" was, in short, meant to be an alternative to the permanent possession of overseas naval stations, another way of achieving some of the strategic advantages which were supposed to follow from the ownership of bases in other countries.

Yet, as previously noted, neither the advanced base idea nor the change in the General Board's attitude after 1903 ever quite stilled the latent desire for actual ownership of permanent bases abroad. In 1913 the Navy readily participated in a scheme endorsed by that anti-imperialistic Secretary of State, William Jennings Bryan, to purchase the Mole St. Nicholas from Haiti.[109] In 1916 another liberal member of Wilson's cabinet, Josephus Daniels, the Secretary of the Navy, was advising the Department of State that, according to the General Board, a successful war against Germany in the Caribbean required American possession of Samana Bay.[110] Indeed, between the summer of 1914 and the American entry into World War I three years later, naval spokesmen, arguing the needs of national defense, manifested a strong and revived interest in various Caribbean and Central American sites, ranging from the Mole St. Nicholas and Samana Bay to the Danish West Indies and the Corn Islands of Nicaragua.[111]

2. THE EXTENT OF CIVIL-MILITARY AND INTERSERVICE COOPERATION

Before World War I there were no formal procedures or established institutions in the United States to promote or produce cooperation between the admirals and the generals, on the one hand, and the diplomats on the other. It was not until the very eve of a second world conflict, not until Franklin D. Roosevelt created the Standing Liaison Committee in 1938, that the first and still impermanent institutional arrangements for civil-military collaboration were created. The elaborately structured machinery that has existed in recent years, as exemplified by the National Security Council, was the result of the experiences of World War II when Americans finally agreed that it was necessary to institutionalize procedures for the coordination of diplomatic and military policy into coherent national policy. It is a commonplace of American history that the military services have all

[109] SDDF, File 811.34538, Bryan to John Osborne, 24 June 1913.
[110] SDDF, File 811.34539/1 and 2, Daniels to Lansing, 29 August and 22 December 1916.
[111] See scattered references in Arthur Link, *Wilson: The New Freedom* (Princeton, 1956), 332-38, and *The Struggle for Neutrality* (Princeton, 1960), 495-550.

too frequently been jealous rivals; the existence of interservice rivalry has been so well publicized that it is one of the clichés of American military history. Yet both before and after World War I more was accomplished in the United States to produce interservice cooperation than to bring about civil-military collaboration. As Louis Morton has justly observed, cooperation between the civil and the military in the United States has actually "lagged behind" interservice cooperation.[112]

The Spanish-American War, whose "horrors" were principally administrative and organizational, stimulated important reforms in the American armed forces. Elihu Root, appalled by the absence of any individual or group in the Army hierarchy that was centrally responsible for strategic or logistical planning, was the principal architect of change in the War Department. His reforms produced the Army War College, responsible for military studies and instruction, and, above all, the General Staff. The staff was to be the "brains" of the Army, the institution which would centralize strategic planning, maintain the proper degree of preparedness, and, in general, advise the Secretary of War on all important military matters. Root's reform was a major achievement in the professionalization of the United States Army, the point at which both responsibility and authority were placed in the hands of the professional officer corps. It created a military establishment much more centralized than in the past. It also produced an Army in which the lines of authority were more clearly delineated, for the General Staff possessed definite command functions. In the General Staff there existed an instrument authorized to speak in the name of the Army.[113]

The new organization admittedly did not live up to the original expectations. In the absence of a national consensus about military policy and a clear concept of national strategy, the General Staff became largely absorbed with its technical, organizational, and "managerial" functions. Moreover, as the bitter political fight involving the status of the Military Secretary, Fred C. Ainsworth, amply revealed, the General Staff faced an extended struggle simply to establish its authority within the military establishment. Thus, as more than one historian has

[112] Morton, "Interservice Cooperation." See also Ernest May, "The Development of Political-Military Consultation in the United States," *Political Science Quarterly*, LXX, no. 2 (June 1955), 161-80, and Fred M. Greene, "The Military View of American National Policy," *American Historical Review*, LXVI, no. 2 (January 1961), 354-77.
[113] In addition to the studies by Hammond and Nelson, there are excellent accounts of Root's work in Richard Leopold, *Elihu Root and the Conservative Tradition* (Boston, 1954), 38-46, and Philip Jessup, *Elihu Root* (2 vols., New York, 1938). See also Leonard D. White, *The Republican Era, 1869-1901: A Study in Administrative History* (New York, 1958), 134-53.

observed, the General Staff was still "growing to man's estate" at the time of America's active involvement in World War I.[114]

The comparable reform movement in the Navy did not result in the creation of a general staff system. What emerged in the spring of 1900 was the General Board, some of whose attributes have already been noted. The various bureau chiefs of the Navy retained their independence and did not, as in the Army system, report to and through the General Board. The members of the General Board held other equally important positions within the naval establishment and, in fact, seemed to have been appointed to it by virtue of their official assignments in the naval hierarchy. While the General Staff had been created by an act of Congress, the General Board was established only by a Navy Department order, lacked any degree of statutory independence, and was, in effect, the creature of the civilian Secretary. Its relations with other naval organizations—for example, the Naval War College and the Office of Naval Intelligence—were loose and informal, again in contrast to the Army system where the War College and the intelligence service were considered to be parts of a more structured scheme. Above all, the General Board advised and did not command.[115] Indeed, as one of Roosevelt's Secretaries of the Navy observed, the very title "General Board" was misleading, for instead of being a genuine policymaking group and the highest authority within the naval establishment, it actually resembled a "war board" which largely restricted itself to advising the Secretary on such matters as war plans and the composition and distribution of the fleet.[116] Yet however circumscribed its role, the General Board was the body which, as much by its composition as by its function, represented professional opinion in the naval service. And the seventeen-year tenure of Admiral Dewey, the Admiral of the Navy, as its presiding officer was a guarantee that its role would be far from negligible.

It sometimes seemed in 1898 as if the Army and Navy were merely skirmishing with the Spaniards and that the only real war was the conflict between the two American military services. Some institutional arrangement to coordinate their respective policies was a clear necessity. The eventual result was the creation, in the summer of 1903, of

[114] May, "Political-Military Consultation," 162, and Mabel E. Deutrich, *Struggle for Supremacy: The Career of General Fred Ainsworth* (Washington, 1962), 111 ff.

[115] Hammond, *Common Defense*, 50-71. For contemporary opinion, see H. C. Taylor, "Memorandum for a General Staff for the U.S. Navy," *USNIP*, xxvi, no. 3 (September 1900), 441-48, and Philip Alger, "Professional Notes," *USNIP*, xxix, no. 2 (June 1903), 493-95. There is valuable documentation on the origins of the General Board in G. W. Allen, ed., *The Papers of John Davis Long, 1897-1904* (Boston, 1939), especially 306, 311-12, 367-68, and 387.

[116] *Annual Report of the Secretary of the Navy, 1906* (Washington, 1906), 7.

the Joint Board. Composed of officers selected from the General Staff and the General Board, the Joint Board was given the mission "of conferring upon, discussing and reaching common conclusions regarding all matters calling for the cooperation of the two services."[117] But its powers were heavily restricted. It had no staff of its own; it could consider only those matters which the civilian service secretaries specifically put before it; and it could make only recommendations to the services and their secretaries. Moreover, the Joint Board was to consider only those items of military policy in which both services had an interest, and its range of activities was therefore considerably less than that of either the General Staff or the General Board. It was, indeed, primarily concerned with war plans and the possible acquisition of bases.[118] Thus over the years it dealt with such matters as the appropriate location for the Navy's desired base in the Philippines, the fortifications to be built for the Panama Canal, and the enlargement of the naval station at Guantanamo Bay in Cuba. But the Joint Board was not without importance. In 1903 it was involved in making plans to cope with possible Colombian retaliation for the *coup* in Panama, and the following year its debates succeeded in clarifying the war planning being pursued by the separate services. It agreed, as previously noted, upon a joint Army-Navy plan for seizure of Dominican and Haitian bases, and in 1907 it made specific recommendations to President Roosevelt on military dispositions in the Far East in the event of hostilities with Japan. Six years later it became involved in a sharp dispute with President Wilson when it made similar recommendations during another period of Japanese-American tension. Throughout the years of controversy with Mexico during the Taft and Wilson administrations the Joint Board was concerned with the coordination of many plans for possible military intervention.

But the Joint Board was severely damaged by the dispute between the Army and Navy that erupted after 1907 over the issue of Subig Bay. This bitter controversy, which has been the subject of several detailed studies, arose when the Army insisted that Subig Bay—the Navy's first and most highly prized location in the Philippines—was indefensible.[119] The admirals eventually yielded, but grudgingly, without conviction, and without grace. For years high ranking officers of the Army, especially the Chief of Staff, General Leonard Wood, remained stubbornly convinced that the Navy was trying to sabotage all

[117] JB, Minutes, 17 July 1903.

[118] See the studies of Hammond, Greene, Morton, and May that have been previously cited.

[119] Braisted, *Navy in the Pacific*, 216-23, for a general treatment as well as his article, "The Philippine Naval Base Problem" (cited above, n. 64).

agreements and covertly re-establish its former position at Subig.[120] More important, however, was the effect of this dispute upon President Roosevelt who was infuriated by it and moved to address a caustic letter to the services in which he roundly chastised them for their "one-sided consideration and vacillation." The Subig issue, the President thought, had been long settled; now he learned not only that the Joint Board planned to reopen the question but also that the Board was unable to reconcile the differences between the Army and Navy viewpoints. "By way of explanation," Roosevelt wrote, "I am further advised that it is not the policy of the navy to advise on anything but naval matters. I have had just such experience with army officers . . . but they justify their most trenchant critics when they act in such manner." Congress had for years been informed that there was agreement between the two services on Subig. But now, Roosevelt added in biting words, many Congressmen no longer believed either the General Staff or the General Board because of "the curious way" in which the Joint Board had mishandled the issue of Philippine defense. "It is quite evident," he concluded, "that there is some defect in method which ought to be removed."[121] When the Army General Staff requested a study by the Joint Board to determine whether or not the main battle fleet should be retained in the Pacific after the conclusion of the round-the-world cruise, Roosevelt, angered by this suggestion as much as by the issue of Subig Bay, tartly observed, "I should of course be glad to have the opinion of the Joint Board on this matter; but I cannot say that I will follow that opinion."[122]

The Subig Bay controversy, in short, undermined the position of the Joint Board and probably more than any other factor prevented it from evolving into a truly viable instrument of interservice cooperation. After Roosevelt left the White House, its role became less rather than greater. Taft paid it relatively little attention, and, in all the planning and discussions that preceded America's entry into World War I the role of the Joint Board was, to say the least, minimal. To be sure, Taft's general confidence in the preservation of peace and Wilson's aversion to military planning were important elements of this equation, but the bitter Army-Navy feuding over the Philippine naval sta-

[120] From 1909 on both the correspondence and the diary entries of Wood are filled with vitriolic references to the Navy's attitude on Subig Bay. See particularly the entries in his diary in May of 1913 at the time of the "crisis" in Japanese-American relations.

[121] GB, File 405, Roosevelt to Dewey, 11 February 1908. The letter is also printed in Elting E. Morison, *The Letters of Theodore Roosevelt* (Cambridge, 1952), VI, 937-39.

[122] JB, Minutes, Roosevelt's endorsement on a letter from General Bell to Taft, 7 February 1908.

tion had damaged the instrument as well as its potential for development.[123]

Interservice rivalries, the incomplete development of General Staff, General Board, and Joint Board, and the absence of any formal machinery for cooperation between the services and the civilian branches of government were formidable barriers to effective coordination of national policy. But there were other important reasons for the continuing lag. One most certainly was the importance of domestic politics in the appointment of the civilian secretaries who were responsible for the War and Navy Departments. When John D. Long was about to resign as Secretary of the Navy, Roosevelt's greatest concern was that his successor should be a Catholic and one who, in addition, came from "the Pacific slope."[124] Long himself represented the other side of this same political coin. "I am satisfied," he once wrote, "that it is not necessary that a Cabinet officer should be specifically familiar with the scope of his Department before assuming its duties. He is really the representative of his Department in the councils of the Administration, and does not so much represent the Department before the people as he represents the people in the Department."[125] Theodore Roosevelt, who was his own Secretary of the Navy as frequently as he was his own Secretary of State, seems to have considered just about everything except a potential Secretary of the Navy's familiarity with naval matters. The Civil Service reformer Charles J. Bonaparte was put in charge of the Navy because Roosevelt genuinely wanted him in the Cabinet and the only available vacancy was in the Navy Department. By the President's own admission the appointment was a "stopgap," and, as soon as the Attorney Generalship fell vacant, Bonaparte was shifted into that slot—where Roosevelt had wanted him in the first place.[126] Similarly, William Howard Taft was named Secretary of War in 1903 for reasons which had little to do with his knowledge of the Army and its problems. Taft's familiarity with the Philippines would admittedly be of great value in the administration of the military government of those islands, but the principal reason that Roosevelt wanted Taft in the Cabinet was to serve as his close, confidential "counselor and adviser in all the great questions that come up."[127]

Thus, in his seven years in the White House Roosevelt was served

[123] This point is amplified in Morton's "Interservice Cooperation."

[124] Roosevelt, *Letters*, III, 158, Roosevelt to Maria Longworth Storer, 4 October 1901.

[125] Quoted in Lawrence S. Mayo, ed., *America of Yesterday: The Diary of John D. Long* (Boston, 1923), 195.

[126] Joseph Bishop, *Charles J. Bonaparte, His Life and Public Service* (New York, 1922), 98-100, 112, 123, 128.

[127] Roosevelt, *Letters*, III, 426, Roosevelt to Taft, 14 February 1903.

by no less than six different Secretaries of the Navy. In consequence there was a discernible lack of administrative leadership in the department. As George von Lengerke Meyer observed when he took over the Navy for President Taft in 1909, none of Roosevelt's appointees had been able to gain command of his position or of the naval establishment during his brief tenure of office.[128] Nor is it surprising that, when Taft was Secretary of War, one of the highest ranking Army officers pointed out that it was actually Elihu Root, then the Secretary of State, who took the greatest interest in military matters of any of the members of Roosevelt's cabinet—"even more than the Secretary of War himself." As General Henry Corbin observed, "Mr. Taft undoubtedly has desires to be an excellent Secretary of War, but he is involved in so many projects that Army matters are left largely to the Department people."[129] Major General J. F. Bell, the first Chief of Staff to serve the full four-year term, once rather plaintively recorded his wish that "Mr. Taft would be able to take a little more part in the administration of the War Department."[130]

Officers of the Army and Navy increasingly realized, and sometimes complained, that they were not consulted or informed about the essentials of national policy. In 1908, as we have just noted, the Joint Board received Roosevelt's reluctant blessing to study the question of whether the fleet should return to its Atlantic base or be retained in the Pacific. After considerable study the Board, however, could reach only a vague and general conclusion: the region of concentration for the United States Navy should depend on the state of international relations. In the absence of international complications, the Board suggested, the fleet ought to be stationed in the area of America's greatest interests, but if there were war clouds on the horizon, then the naval concentration should be in the region of greatest danger. The members of the Board apparently recognized that this truism was singularly unhelpful, for they then went on to confess that they could not be more specific—for the simple reason that both the Army and Navy lacked accurate information about the actual state of American foreign relations. "What may be the facts determining the international relations only the Administration can know, and until this knowledge is communicated to the Joint Board, it cannot intelligently make recommendations as to the specific disposition of the fleet." Still, the Board did dare one tentative conclusion, but did so in a manner which clearly indicated the poverty of its information: "Although lacking such

128 M. A. DeWolfe Howe, *George von Lengerke Meyer, His Life and Public Services* (New York, 1919), 422-23.
129 Wood Papers, Corbin to Wood, 23 May 1906.
130 Quoted in Otto Nelson, *National Security*, 102.

knowledge of our international relations as would warrant the Board's making a definite recommendation as to the present disposition of the fleet, such information as the Board does possess, derived from the Information Divisions of the War and Navy Departments, renders it apprehensive of eventualities in the Pacific, and imposes upon it the duty of pointing out the danger of withdrawing the fleet from the region of threatening complications."[131]

More pointed was the complaint of General Bell, Chief of Staff. He had been compelled, he wrote, to base all of his plans for the second Cuban intervention in 1906 "on mere suspicion (created by newspaper articles) though I diligently sought to get information from the State Department." A year later he had a similar experience when he unsuccessfully sought to get information from the Department of State about the course of events that followed various racial incidents in San Francisco and created a Japanese-American "crisis."[132] Another member of the General Staff, General Wotherspoon, maintained that the War Department was "seriously handicapped" in making plans to cope with the Mexican revolution because the General Staff had no conception of the policies that the diplomats were pursuing towards Mexico. In all of these matters, as General Bell put the Army case, "they"—the civilian officials of the administration but "especially those in control of the State Department"—were

> so skeptical of any possibility of actual hostilities that they will not even take the trouble to keep the military and naval authorities informed of the progress of their negotiations. They consider such negotiations as extremely confidential, and if our Secretaries of War and Navy are well posted on them, they do not realize the importance of keeping their subordinate military hierarchy well informed also. . . . What in the Name of Heaven is a Commanding General in the Philippines to do, in order to be reasonably cautious and forehanded?[133]

Such complaints were not unjustified. In succeeding chapters of this book, specific aspects of the civil-military relationship will be examined at greater length, but it is accurate to state, in advance of the detailed evidence, that the Department of State was jealous of its legal and historic responsibility for the formulation and conduct of American foreign policy and unprepared to admit outsiders into its inner councils. In 1911 the General Staff, obviously surprised and unpre-

131 JB, Minutes, Dewey to Metcalf and Taft, 21 February 1908.
132 Wood Papers, Bell to Wood, 1 May 1911.
133 GS, War College Division, File 6320/8, Wotherspoon to Hill, 13 April 1911; Wood Papers, Bell to Wood, 1 May 1911.

pared, was informed that the Army might have to supply troops to guard the rail line from Peking to the sea. Lacking information about conditions in China, it asked the State Department for specific information about the number and location of foreign troops already in China and, in addition, sought permission for a staff officer to consult the files of the State Department. Back came a curt reply from Secretary Philander Knox which not only denied the request but also offered the gratuitous advice that the Army would be best advised to consult its own records.[134] Naval authorities received the same treatment when the Naval War College suggested the advisability of a joint Navy-State Department conference to consider issues likely to arise at the London Naval Conference of 1909. With more than usual asperity the Solicitor of the State Department wrote that, although the London Conference would indeed consider aspects of maritime law, "as the Department of State is charged with the administration of foreign affairs, and as this conference . . . falls within the jurisdiction of this Department, it would seem that the Department of State might well refuse to surrender its prerogatives."[135]

It was still sheer folly for an officer to make public statements about matters of foreign or national policy. Both services naturally received some of their sharpest reprimands during the administration of Woodrow Wilson when the President as well as his civilian secretaries were acutely tuned to the niceties of the historic separation of the military and the political in American life. When newspaper stories reported remarks by General William Gorgas about the then projected repeal of the Panama Canal tolls, Secretary Lindley Garrison, on specific instructions from Wilson, diligently searched Army regulations to discover if there were provisions that prevented public declarations by Army officers on "controverted political matters." Garrison reassured the President that, while there were no particular regulations, silence on such issues was part of the "common law" of the military establishment. As for himself, Garrison added, he had always "written a severe letter of condemnation to every officer who has given public expression of opinion upon any . . . political question. I have done this . . . upon the broad ground that officers of the Army should not take public part in political matters."[136] But the same attitude had prevailed in previous administrations. General Arthur MacArthur's public prediction of a future German-American conflict drew fire from Theodore Roosevelt, while the National Guard officer who reported it to him was told that he was unfit to hold a commission.[137] Similarly, President Taft rebuked the then Captain William Sims when that naval officer assured a London audience that, if England went to war, the United States would assist the British Empire "with every man, every dollar, every drop of blood." Taft at once wrote him that a naval officer must learn to "restrain himself within the limits of diplomatic intercourse" and, if asked to speak in a foreign country, "avoid invidious comparisons and limit his speech and expressions of friendship for the country whose guest he is, to language that will not indicate lack of friendship toward other countries."[138]

Of far greater significance than the attitude toward public statements was the fact that the principle of civilian control of both the formulation and execution of foreign policy was firmly established and maintained. "Civilian control," like "interservice rivalry," is another cliché; it is regarded as one of the "givens" of the American experience, a principle embedded in the Constitution. It is, however, a complex subject, for, as Samuel Huntington has pointed out, civilian control is actually complicated by the very Constitutional provisions that presumably guarantee it.[139] But whatever the problems and difficulties of establishing and maintaining it may have been, civilian leaders of the United States government in the early years of the twentieth century firmly believed that they exercised and should continue to exercise control in the field of foreign affairs. Officers of the Army and Navy were often censured, most notably during the administrations of Taft and Wilson, for both real and fancied attempts to make decisions that trespassed upon civilian authority in foreign policy. Secretary Philander Knox, for example, made a formal complaint to the Department of the Navy that Admiral William Kimball, the officer in charge of American forces in Nicaragua, was clearly exceeding his instructions by "exerting diplomatic pressure which had not been requested by this Department charged with the conduct of foreign relations."[140] Somewhat earlier, when a group of naval officers committed the unpardonable sin of making a courtesy call upon the Nicaraguan dictator, Zelaya, the entire Department of State was angered. Knox's haughty and humorless assistant, Huntington Wilson, laid down the law:

> This Department ventures the suggestion that when, in the future the Navy Department is good enough to comply with the request of this Department for the disposal of naval vessels as part of a political attitude, this Department might possibly frankly make known to

[137] Roosevelt, *Letters*, III, 676-77, Roosevelt to George H. Carter, 23 December 1903.
[138] Taft Papers, Letter press volumes, Taft to Meyer, 9 January 1910.
[139] Huntington, *Soldier and the State*, 177-79.
[140] SDNF, Case 6369/656A, Knox to Meyer, 14 January 1910.

the Navy Department this phase of the matter, in order that proper instructions may be given to commanding officers. . . . The necessity of this becomes quite apparent from a case like the present one, when the judgment of a legation expressed to the naval commander seems to have been more or less inadequate to its effect.[141]

Taft himself could also use the blunt phrase. Shortly after ordering a mobilization of American troops on the Mexican border in 1911, he learned that the Navy was still continuing to send small vessels into Mexican waters. His terse instructions to the Navy were "to keep the small fry" at home.[142]

The climax of this kind of "civilian supremacy" occurred during the Wilson administration when the political leadership was hypersensitive about possible military encroachments upon civilian responsibilities. The most famous incident, which will later be treated in greater detail, occurred in the spring of 1913 when Wilson, whose aversion to militarism was instinctive, became convinced that the Joint Board was trying to force his hand during a period of Japanese-American tension —above all, trying to reverse a decision made by the cabinet after full consideration of the facts. "It was a glorious thing," Navy Secretary Josephus Daniels joyously confided to his diary, "to see the President determined that . . . no officer of the Army or Navy should be permitted to make war plans . . . after they had been notified when such policy was contrary to the spirit of the Administration."[143] Other incidents, arising out of the Mexican intervention, revealed how quickly Wilson identified officers who seemed likely to disagree with his policies and insisted that they must adhere unswervingly to the dictates of the civilian policymakers.[144]

During the Roosevelt years, admittedly, the relationship was more complex, and on numerous occasions, naval officers in Latin America appeared to enjoy considerable freedom of action. Yet the principle of civilian control remained and was made particularly evident, even in the Caribbean area, once Elihu Root, a man with a strongly developed sense of legal proprieties, had succeeded John Hay as Secretary of State. In Santo Domingo, where the Navy had played a dominating role, the rough edges of policy were smoothed; it was made clear that authority lay in Washington and with the cabinet; and naval officers were reminded of the precise limits of their authority as well as of the

---

141 SDNF, Case 6369/107-08, Huntington Wilson to Meyer, 28 June 1909.

142 Papers of Philander Knox, Manuscripts Division, Library of Congress, Taft to Meyer, 14 March 1911. See also SDDF, File 812.00/922, Adee to Taft, 14 March 1911.

143 Daniels Papers, Diary, 17 May 1913.

144 Papers of Woodrow Wilson, Manuscripts Division, Library of Congress, Daniels to Wilson and Wilson to Daniels, both dated 11 August 1913.

rules which were to govern the landing of sailors or marines.[145] In 1907 the General Board, eager to expand the territorial limits of the Guantanamo naval base, suggested to Root that the second occupation of Cuba now provided an excellent opportunity to acquire the land without having to bicker with the usually recalcitrant Cubans. Root rejected the proposal. He wryly added that, by any set of standards, it would be improper for the United States government to put itself in the awkward legal position of negotiating with itself.[146]

It is quite possible to develop a considerable amount of sympathy for those Army or Navy officers who were called upon to act in what was called, sometimes euphemistically, "a political situation." Placed under strict civilian control, denied the right to express their opinions publicly, often given only the sketchiest of information, and normally excluded from the policymaking apparatus of the civilian government, they could readily find their situation embarrassing. But such an interpretation would be one-dimensional. There are other and equally important factors to be inserted in the equation of the American civil-military relationship: above all, the fact that the great majority of American naval and military officers continued to think primarily if not exclusively in terms of their own particular service, their own hierarchical values, their own customs and traditions. Their horizons were military horizons, and, in their own way, their view of the civil-military relationship was often as restricted and limited as that of their civilian counterparts.

This was true in matters of small as well as of major political import. It was a cardinal principle of the naval service that the officer in command of a vessel was solely and exclusively in charge of his ship and that he could not share or delegate any portion of the total responsibility. It was a principle that caused not a little friction with the Department of State. In 1907, to cite but one of several similar occurrences, the American consul at Chefoo complained with asperity about the great difficulty he had in obtaining an American warship whenever there was rioting in that Chinese port. He therefore asked that the American naval command in Shanghai be placed under standing instructions to send a vessel immediately to Chefoo upon the request of the American consul and without the necessity of referring such requests to higher naval headquarters. The Navy Department responded primly, that, while it would promise cooperation, it was contrary to established policy to bind a commanding officer to specific standing instructions. "Law and Navy regulations," the State Department was also informed, "make an officer responsible for any action he may take,

---

[145] SDML, Root to Bonaparte, 23 October 1905.
[146] SDNF, Case 4631/3-5, Root to Metcalf, 6 April 1907.

and he cannot be relieved of that responsibility by acting upon any instructions which he may choose to receive from any diplomatic or other official."[147]

Of even greater significance was the tendency of military men to limit themselves to the strictly military aspects of problems which, in actual fact, had political dimensions. Final decisions on issues of national policy, it was frequently said, were political decisions and as such could be made only by the political agencies of government. Moreover, relatively few officers really wanted to cross over the line that separated the military from the political. There was, in short, continuing respect for the traditional separation of powers and functions. What Army and Navy officers most frequently wanted was not participation in policy making but more accurate information about the decisions reached by the civilian government; they wanted to be told what the national policy was so that they, in turn, could chart their own military courses by it. "Bred in the tradition of civilian supremacy and separation of the political and the military," as Louis Morton has written, "the military asked only that they be given political guidance."[148]

An illustration of these tendencies was the turn-of-the-century discussion in the United States about the range and scope of the Monroe Doctrine. Prior to the celebrated Venezuelan debt episode, Theodore Roosevelt was himself raising the question and, at least in his private correspondence, indicating that he was not convinced that the United States should take the same attitude south of the Isthmus as it did in the Caribbean.[149] But when the General Board reported on the naval aspects of Caribbean defense, its approach was most circumspect. "Whether or not the principle of the Monroe Doctrine . . . covers all South America," Admiral Dewey wrote, "is not for the consideration of the General Board." The recommendations for Caribbean defense were therefore strictly military in character, almost exclusively confined to considerations of strategy and tactics. For, as Dewey continued, the Navy must limit itself to such recommendations and could only point out "the fact that the principles of strategy and the defects of our geographic position make it impracticable successfully to maintain naval control by armed forces beyond the Amazon."[150] Dewey and his colleagues, in short, were not tempted to cross into new terrain.

Even more striking was an interchange which occurred in 1912 when the Naval War College was asked to comment on recently completed plans for possible intervention in Mexico, a matter which, in

---

147 SDNF, Case 2283/3-4, Fowler to Department of State, 31 January 1907 and Newberry to Root, 12 March 1907.

148 Morton, "Interservice Cooperation," 137.

149 Roosevelt, *Letters*, III, 527, Roosevelt to Whitelaw Reid, 24 July 1903.

150 GB, Letters, I, Dewey to Long, 25 June 1901.

view of the then troubled Mexican-American relationship, was of major importance to both services. Admiral Frederick Rodgers, the President of the War College and one officer whose outlook went well beyond traditional limits, raised immediate objections. "It is evident," he commented, "that the plan is drawn up with a certain vagueness as to what is to be accomplished by going to war and how it is to be done." He was greatly distressed by the underlying assumption of the plan that the scope of any Mexican operation would be completely defined by the administration. This really meant, Rodgers argued, that "the General Board was thus relying upon the President to decide, without information, upon the very point which it is the duty of the General Board to advise him upon."[151]

Admiral Dewey remained unconvinced. In his rejoinder to Admiral Rodgers he contended that it was both sufficient and proper for the military services to wait until the eve of hostilities to obtain specific information about the government's policy. But, above all, it was the administration—the President and his Cabinet—which should determine and provide policy. "Policy," Dewey wrote with his usual firmness, "belongs to the cabinet, that is, to the supreme civil authority, and must be decided by that authority." The Admiral, furthermore, was disturbed by the implications of Rodgers' critique. The President of the War College seemed to be suggesting that war portfolios should be drawn up only through the joint efforts of the State, War, and Navy Departments. If so, Dewey wanted to register his strong disagreement. The contents of a naval war portfolio should be determined solely by naval officers. "Why include," Dewey asked, "in a naval portfolio many hundreds of pages of extraneous matter, whether a civil policy or army procedure, that can advance in no way the war operations of the naval commander-in-chief?" The object of war was victory; within that framework the naval officer should concentrate all of his attention upon the execution of the policies determined by his government:

> Military commanders should be historical students and should understand the policy of their country and the influences which it will have upon possible military operations. But they are themselves the prime instruments of war; and the purpose of war is to defeat the enemy. . . . A commander-in-chief should, therefore, rarely, if at all, be influenced by ulterior motives.[152]

All of these attitudes, both civilian and military, were present during the course of the extended debate of a proposal, first made during the Taft administration, to create a Council of National Defense. As ini-

[151] GB, File 425, Rodgers to Dewey, 12 March 1912.
[152] GB, File 425, Dewey to Rodgers, 19 June 1912.

tially proposed the Council would have included the Secretaries of State, Navy, and War; the chairmen of Senate and House military and naval committees; and the presidents of the two war colleges. Its proposed function was to coordinate national defense policy by bringing together representatives, both civil and military, of the executive departments and leaders of the national legislature. Moreover, there were certain enthusiasts within the ranks of the two services who even anticipated that the Council of National Defense would provide an opportunity for a genuine interchange of ideas and opinions between the civil and the military, especially between those responsible for America's military defense and those who conducted her foreign relations. General Wotherspoon, the Assistant Chief of the General Staff, prepared numerous and lengthy papers about "the need for coordinating military preparations and plans with the objects of the government in the development of national policies as to military strength."[153] Commander F. K. Hill of the Naval War College was far more explicit when he justified the proposed Council on the grounds that "no proper war plan can be made by military and naval officers without a thorough knowledge of the diplomatic conditions with all foreign countries as well as with the one against which the war is directed . . . and the diplomatic branch is the only one which can furnish correct knowledge of this."[154]

The very fact that such a Council could seriously be considered is in itself evidence that, with the expanding dimensions of American foreign and military policies, the first, faint crack was beginning to appear in the wall that traditionally separated the two. It was a first step toward the contemporary National Security Council and the involvement of the military in the mechanisms of policymaking. But it was only a first step, and a very halting one at that. The history of the proposed Council clearly indicates that, even if the need to coordinate the various strands of national policy was being felt, the traditonal, established attitudes remained very much in evidence and also that even the foremost advocates of the Council of National Defense had modest— one might say, even, parochial—interests in mind.[155]

From the outset, for example, the Department of State was not interested in participation. Secretary Knox on several occasions argued strongly against inclusion of his Department on the Council.[156] Within the Congress there were many outcries against the dangers of creating

153 GS, War College Division, File 6320-8, Wotherspoon to Hill, 13 April 1911, and File 6220, Wotherspoon to Wood, 30 August 1910.

154 GS, File 6320-8, Hill to Wotherspoon, 10 April 1911.

155 Hammond, *Common Defense*, 63-67.

156 GS, War College Division, File 6320-8, Wotherspoon to Commander W. S. Turpin, 6 April 1911.

a "super strategy board" so powerful and prestigious that it would escape civilian—and especially Congressional—control. Much was said about the threat of "Prussianizing" the American military structure by creating an institution in which the military could dominate the civilian—an argument put forth by, among others, Wilson's Secretary of the Navy, Josephus Daniels.[157] It is not surprising, therefore, that the representation of the State Department was eliminated from the proposal and that the bill to create the Council of National Defense languished for years on Capitol Hill. The Council of National Defense did not, in fact, appear until the rising tide of preparedness on the eve of America's entry into World War I provided the necessary momentum, and even then it was in a form far different from that originally anticipated.[158]

Moreover, the military advocates of the Council were principally interested in achieving certain immediate, and eminently practical ends. They hoped that the Council would reach agreement on long-term national policies so that they, in turn, could make their own long-range plans. That is to say, they were less interested in participation in and coordination of national policy than they were in securing Congressional support—and appropriations—for their own military and naval projects. This was more clearly the attitude of the Army than of the Navy. The Army, as Paul Hammond has emphasized, viewed the Council as a useful tool to combat the pork barrel politics of the Congressional military committees and thus "to protect it against the inconstancy and parochialism of politics."[159] Army leaders, for example, agreed with Knox that the participation of the Department of State was unnecessary. When Secretary of War Dickinson presented the Army's case for the Council it was on the very practical grounds that such a group would "determine a general policy of national defense and . . . recommend to the Congress and to the President . . . such measures relating to the National Defense as it shall deem necessary and expedient." General Leonard Wood, the Army Chief of Staff, was certainly one officer whose outlook, as previously indicated, was global and who took a genuine interest in international affairs. But Wood was pleased rather than saddened by the decision to eliminate the Department of State from the proposed Council and to substitute the chairmen of a half dozen major Congressional committees. Thus, Wood recorded in his diary the happy thought that this substitution

157 Daniels Papers, Diary, 26 January 1915. See also the commentary in E. David Cronon, *The Cabinet Diaries of Josephus Daniels, 1913-1921* (Lincoln, Neb., 1963), 93.

158 For a general discussion, see Robert E. Cuff, *The War Industries Board in World War I* (unpub. diss., Princeton University, 1966), ch. 1.

159 Hammond, *Common Defense*, 66.

opened the possibility "of getting six champions in Congress."[160] To Wood, as to others in the Army, a Council of National Defense would fulfill its major purpose if it could demonstrate the nation's military unpreparedness to Congress and help to fix a general, acceptable "National Defense policy" for which the legislators would be willing to provide long-term financial support.

The attitude of the Navy was more complex, for there were countervailing tendencies within that service. There were certainly those who, like Commander Hill and Admiral Rodgers, hoped to achieve a better coordination of military and diplomatic policy. And it was in large part for this reason that naval representatives argued strongly in behalf of the participation of the Department of State in the workings of the proposed Council. But Admiral Dewey, on the other hand, remained a traditionalist; in his view the Council of National Defense "deals with the political and financial aspects of war and includes military men only for the purpose of advising on the military capabilities of the country."[161] Moreover, like the Army, the Navy had certain tangible goals for which it sought Congressional support. Since 1903 the General Board had been firmly committed to the goal of a battle fleet of forty-eight capital ships. But it also knew that its goal would remain unrealized unless there was a firm national policy that called for a two-ocean navy. Thus the General Board, like the General Staff, saw the proposed Council as a means of creating a national military policy that would, in turn, support and carry forward its particular goals and circumvent the parochialism of the Congressional system.

Both services, it should be added, were becoming increasingly professionalized—and professionalization frequently reinforced both the traditional military distaste for involvement in "politics" and the separation of the worlds of the civilian and the military. It could, after all, be argued that an organization like the Council of National Defense might also increase civilian influence in military affairs, might lead to greater civilian intervention in those strictly military matters over which the professional officers were now exercising increased control. Thus, for every argument in behalf of a Council of National Defense to coordinate civil and military policy there could be another argument to the effect that the civilian world—ultimately, the world of politics—ought to be kept at a safe distance from the world of the military professional. As Paul Hammond has pointed out, there was in the Navy one strand of thought which led toward the creation of a Council of National Defense and another which led toward the creation of a Chief of Naval Operations who, as a trained and experienced

[160] Wood Papers, Diary, 10 November 1910.
[161] GB, File 425, Dewey to Rodgers, 19 June 1912.

professional officer, would be the effective governor of the naval establishment.[162]

3. Channels of Communication and Shared Assumptions

It is tempting to emphasize the negative aspects of the civil-military relationship in the United States as it related to foreign affairs: the lack of formal machinery to produce cooperation, the persistence of the principle of the separation of military and civil, the jealous attitude of the services towards the preservation of their own spheres of professional autonomy, and the equal reluctance of civilians to consider that army or navy officers might contribute to their work. But this is by no means the totality of the civil-military relationship; this is most assuredly not the complete history of the mutual relations of admirals, generals and diplomats in the evolution of American foreign policy in the decade and a half after 1898. It cannot be denied, of course, that much of that history does consist of instances of naval officers operating on the basis of insufficient political information and rampant Mahanism, just as it includes many examples of officers of the Department of State proceeding on their own policy courses without regard for the opinions of the military and considering the two services as silent servants whose mission was simply to execute the decisions of superior civilian wisdom. But, to repeat, such incidents are not the full story.

There were opportunities, after all, for communication—and often profitable communication—between the leaders of the military establishment and the civilian government. Much of this interchange was informal, sometimes conducted through irregular channels. The views of naval officers on duty in the Dominican Republic were simply passed on to Theodore Roosevelt by one of his Secretaries of the Navy when that individual felt they were of consequence. General Leonard Wood transmitted his concerns about Far Eastern political and military problems by the simple expedient of a lively exchange of personal letters with his erstwhile Cuban comrade-in-arms, Roosevelt. Admiral Sperry got his opinions about the improbability of war with Japan before the Cabinet by writing his old friend, Oscar Straus, then Secretary of Commerce and Labor. Insofar as there was any coordination of policy, it came about through the White House, that is, through the efforts of the President acting in his capacity as political leader of the government and as commander-in-chief of the armed forces. Much therefore depended upon the interest of the President himself. If the Chief Executive was an individual like Roosevelt, then there was a

[162] Hammond, *Common Defense*, 63-64.

clear opportunity for military officers to receive a hearing. For Roosevelt was himself always conscious of the factor of force and military power in international relations. As a former assistant Secretary of the Navy, he retained a personal interest in both its major and its mundane activities and possessed decided views on everything from the proper distribution of the fleet to the selection of individual Bureau chiefs. Thus General Bell, the same Army officer who was so critical of the Department of State, could write in praise of T.R. that "he gave me his complete confidence and would tell me anything he knew any time I sought information."[163] But with Chief Executives like Taft and Wilson the situation would be considerably different, for the former genuinely discounted the dangers of military involvements and the latter was innately suspicious of undue military influence.

But there were always at least a few civilian leaders who kept open lines of communications. Elihu Root, on becoming Secretary of State, would recall his own days in the War Department and make efforts to keep Army officers informed of his policies as well as pay attention to their reports. It was typical of Root that one of his first actions as Secretary of State was to drop a friendly note to Taft about the Dominican customs receivership. He had, he said, greatly enjoyed reading a report on Dominican finances which had originated in the War Department's Bureau of Insular Affairs and hoped that, in the future, such reports would be sent to him regularly as routine distribution.[164] There were, too, contacts between subordinate officials, especially after the semi-permanent geographic divisions began to appear in the Department of State. Knox's Division of Latin-American Affairs may well have considered the Navy as an agent of enforcement, but there were many discussions and conferences between officials of that division and officers of the Navy charged with military-diplomatic missions.

Of particular importance is the fact that the Navy did fulfill an often useful function in supplying information about events in countries and ports visited by vessels of the United States Navy. Whenever an American warship stopped at a foreign port, its commanding officer was required to send a detailed report to the Navy Department in Washington. In many, many instances—indeed, in virtually every instance when political issues were involved—these reports were routinely forwarded by the Navy to the Department of State for its information. The records of the Department of State further indicate that these naval reports were not merely acknowledged and filed; often they were

163 Wood Papers, Bell to Wood, 1 May 1911.
164 SDML, Root to Taft, 1 November 1905.

read with attention and respect; and often, too, they provided information which supplemented what was available to the State Department through its own resources.

That the Navy served as another set of eyes and ears for the Department of State is not really surprising. Communications were still primitive, not only in the Far East but especially in many of the lesser developed countries of Latin America. Radio was barely in its infancy, and the telegraph and telephone had not yet reached every section of every country; the Department of State therefore could not be in instantaneous communication with all of its representatives in foreign countries, especially with the consuls and vice-consuls in cities not of major importance. Thus naval vessels, cruising from port to port, could sometimes provide information more rapidly than it came through regular diplomatic channels. But of greater significance is the fact that the American foreign service was still politically dominated and the diplomatic representation of the United States in many foreign countries deficient in both quality and quantity. Particularly notorious was the state of the American consular service. Its appointees, chosen exclusively for political reasons, remained unsalaried until 1906 and received their remuneration in the form of fees charged for services presumably performed. Many, therefore, were solely interested in their own commercial ventures, possessed little if any knowledge of their official duties, and paid virtually no attention to the public business. It was also not until 1906 that the Department of State instituted even the semblance of an inspection system; thus, as the longtime head of the Consular Service himself confessed, the Department of State was often the last to know that a consul was not attending to his job.[165] The deficiencies of this situation were nowhere more obvious than in the lesser cities of Latin America where the financial rewards of the fee system were something less than spectacular and the calibre of American representation therefore especially poor.[166] Indeed, in some parts of the Caribbean the situation was so bad that the United States Navy went to considerable effort to prepare its own confidential list of reliable sources of information. Prominent on the General Board's list was a terse statement about the Dominican Republic: "Consular representatives of the United States—in general, not to be trusted."[167]

In such circumstances, then, the reports of naval officers from ports

[165] Katherine Crane, *Mr. Carr of State* (New York, 1959), 48-76.

[166] Dana G. Munro, *Intervention and Dollar Diplomacy in the Caribbean, 1900-1921* (Princeton, 1964), 20-23.

[167] Nav Rec Confid Ltrs, Darling to Commander-in-Chief, North Atlantic, 20 May 1903. The message continues, ". . . exception, possibly, our consular agent at Monte Christi, Mr. Petit, a native of Saint Thomas. Officers of the Navy report that the Consul General, Mr. Maxwell, at Santo Domingo City, is absolutely unreliable."

they visited carried a special importance in the flow of information that eventually reached Washington. This is not to say that the civilian officials of the State Department always so regarded these reports or considered them equal to those which came through normal diplomatic channels. Yet there were more than isolated occasions when that department used the services of the Navy to check upon the accuracy and authenticity of its own information. In Haiti, for example, in 1908 the American minister unexpectedly requested military assistance to guard against a threatened massacre of foreign residents. The State Department, before taking action, asked the Navy to send a qualified officer to Port-au-Prince to make his own investigation and, significantly, charged that officer to make an independent study without paying too much attention to the opinions of the various diplomats stationed in the Haitian capital.[168] In the Far East, on another occasion, it was through the report of a visiting naval commander that the Department of State first learned that the American consul at Canton had alienated Chinese opinion by mishandling indemnity proceedings that arose out of a massacre at Lienchow.[169] On more than one occasion, and especially in the Caribbean area, naval officers informed the Department of State that an American consul was dabbling in local revolutionary activities. During the Nicaraguan troubles of 1908-1909, Admiral Kimball, in charge of the special naval expeditionary force, proved to a skeptical State Department that the American consul at Managua was sending biased, distorted accounts of the Nicaraguan revolt because he was not only allied by marriage to members of the principal revolutionary faction but also actively working in their behalf.[170]

There was considerable consultation between military men and diplomats over the possible acquisition of overseas bases and naval stations. Such territorial acquisitions clearly involved the foreign relations of the United States and were issues which included many factors besides their purely military dimensions. What is notable, however, is the extent of civilian interest in the subject of bases. The Department of State was always scrupulous about consulting the appropriate military authorities whenever such a proposal was raised—whether it originated in military circles, in the diplomatic branch, or, as sometimes happened, with foreign governments. More importantly, the acquisition of overseas bases and naval stations commended itself to a wide variety of civilian opinion and, on many occasions, was actively encouraged by the Department of State. At the turn of the century

168 SDNF, Case 2126/170, Furniss to Root, 21 March 1908; /184-86, Metcalf to Root, 24 March 1908; /212-13, Metcalf to Root, 28 March 1908.

169 SDNF, Case 167/26-27, Newberry to Root, 24 September 1906.

170 SDNF, Case 6369/704-05, Meyer to Knox, 28 January 1910, enclosing one of Kimball's more vitriolic communications attacking Olivares.

there was strong and continuous support in the State Department, especially from John Hay, for the acquisition of Caribbean and Central American bases. At that time it was also standard practice for the Department of State, whenever the Navy had expressed interest in a particular Latin site, to instruct its own representatives in the country to investigate the possibilities. Moreover, even after 1903—that is to say, after the date when the Navy itself began to have second thoughts about the advisability of additional bases—many members of the American diplomatic service, especially in Latin countries, continued to manifest enthusiasm for the acquisition of bases and were constantly informing the State and Navy Departments that the present was an opportune moment for acquiring a particular site. To cite but one example it was the American minister in Peru who almost singlehandedly revived and sustained the project for the purchase of the port of Chimbote. Also, once the Latin American division of the State Department had been established, its strong suspicion of German intentions, nurtured during both the Taft and Wilson administrations, revived civilian interest in Caribbean bases—either in their acquisition by the United States or in measures to deny them to a European power.[171]

Virtually every one charged with responsibility for the direction of American foreign policy in Asia at one time or another endorsed the idea of an American base on or adjacent to the mainland of China. The interest of McKinley and Hay in a Chinese base was, to be sure, quite short-lived because of its obvious conflict with the principle of the Open Door. But the idea did not die. William Rockhill, the actual sponsor of the Open Door, seriously proposed a Korean site as an alternative, and various American ministers in Asia—Conger in China, O'Brien in Japan, Allen in Korea—urged the acquisition of a Far Eastern naval station. And, as in Latin America, there were enthusiastic subordinate officials in the diplomatic service. One of the most quixotic of all the Far Eastern projects originated in the fertile mind of the American consul at Amoy. Presumably eager to advance the interests of the Navy—and, one suspects, no less interested in his own pocketbook—he purchased in his own name a tract of land on one of the small islands in the harbor of Amoy and then generously offered to lease it to the United States Navy as a coaling station.[172]

Even more important, and as the many signs of interest in overseas bases indicate, those civilians who shaped American foreign policy in

171 These issues are discussed at greater length in Chapters Two and Four.
172 The Far Eastern base question is treated in greater detail in Chapter Three. On the specifics of the Amoy base project, SDML, Moody to Hay, 12 May 1902, with attached documents and GB, Letters, II, Dewey to Long, 25 November 1902. See also Seward Livermore, "American Naval Base Policy in the Pacific," *Pacific Historical Review*, XIII, no. 2 (June 1944), 113-35.

the first decade of the twentieth century shared and expressed many of the same ideas as those held by the generals and admirals. They sought many of the same objectives, were subject to many of the same fears. Thus, even in the absence of formal consultation and institutional procedures for civil-military cooperation, the result was a considerable amount of what might be described as "parallel thinking" on the part of the White House and the Department of State, on the one hand, and of the military services, on the other.

The writings of many scholars have, for example, conclusively shown that the economic motivation for American intervention in the Caribbean has been exaggerated and that the essential purpose of the Latin American policy of the United States—the "common thread" in the policies of the administrations from McKinley through Wilson—was to assure itself of political and military supremacy in an area that was considered vital to American interests. That is to say, control of the Caribbean was as important to the political leaders of the American government as it was to the General Board and the General Staff. Moreover, the same scholars have written extensively about the widespread Germanophobia which existed in civilian circles almost as strongly as it did in the ranks of the military. It is certainly true that some of the ideas prevalent in the General Board—for example, the concept of a German expansionist movement driven by irresistible internal forces or the belief that William II would or could send his entire fleet across the Atlantic—merely reveal the extent to which naval planners and strategists were dominated by an excessive Social Darwinism and isolated from the "real" political world. Nevertheless, civilians often echoed the same sentiments despite their greater familiarity with and direct involvement in international affairs. Thus, John Hay, according to his biographer, "believed that the German menace was substantial . . . [and] never lost the appearance of being very anti-German," while Roosevelt could state with complete conviction his belief that Germany intended "to make us put up or shut up on the Monroe Doctrine." Elihu Root, in later life, could defend his Cuban policy by remarking that no one could fully understand or appreciate the Platt amendment without knowing something about the character of William II.[173]

In the aftermath of the Spanish-American War, civilians as well as military were still uncertain about America's actual strength, prone to see foreign devils poised for Caribbean ventures, tempted to believe

[173] Tyler Dennett, *John Hay: From Poetry to Politics* (New York, 1934), 384; Jessup, *Root*, I, 314 and II, 310. For a general discussion see Munro, *Dollar Diplomacy*, ch. 1, as well as Dexter Perkins, *Hands Off: A History of the Monroe Doctrine* (Boston, 1941), ch. 6.

that Europeans must some day wish to challenge America in the Western Hemisphere. Having themselves tasted the heady wine of Social Darwinism, they too often viewed the world in terms of strife and struggle. William L. Langer, in his most recent analysis of European imperialism, has contended that much of the expansionism of the European great powers after 1870 was the result of fear of the unknown. The great states of Europe—emerging into a new industrial age, confronted by the rising forces of nationalism throughout the Continent, and disturbed by the emergence of a new, unstable state system out of the ruins of the post-Napoleonic concert—were led into imperialism less by the hope of commercial or political gain than by hypothetical fears of what might happen to them if they did not extend their colonial domain. Langer has coined the phrase "preclusive imperialism" to describe the post-1870 expansion of Europe, a movement which, in his interpretation, was motivated by the fears of the European nation states of the damages they might sustain if they did not enter the race for colonies in Africa and Asia.[174] Langer's interpretation seems particularly apt for the American experience. State Department, White House, and military services were especially concerned about hypothetical dangers in the Caribbean, about the damage that might occur to the American interest if the United States did not act, well in advance, of any possible European intervention. Any examination of the record of the Department of State's long concern with the sorry state of Dominican finances will clearly reveal this fear of future dangers, of ultimate and hypothetical evils, against which preventive action must be taken. If the Dominicans defaulted on their debts, then Europe might be tempted to move in and establish itself; if foreign creditors were not satisfied, then the gunboats of Germany—and even of Italy, of all nations!—were lurking just over the horizon to serve as bill collectors; or if the decisions of the Hague court about priorities were accepted as international law, then European military intervention in the Western Hemisphere would have legal sanction. The list of possible dangers was almost inexhaustible. The United States was never viewed as in clear and present danger, but the Republic might some day be threatened if it did not move promptly in the Caribbean to forestall hypothetical dangers that might become real if there was no such preventive action. This was a prevalent belief, expressed time and time again in the writings of Roosevelt, Hay, Root, and countless subordinates, and it was therefore not just military men who stressed the need to take positive measures to assure American dominance in the Caribbean. On the issue of political and military control in that region, then,

[174] William L. Langer, "Farewell to Empire," *Foreign Affairs*, XLI, no. 1 (October 1962), 115-30.

there was a common attitude—"parallel thinking"—in the White House and Department of State as in the War and Navy Departments.

Prominent also was the shared belief in the value of the show of force, the display—and possible employment—of military power to impress recalcitrant nations. In the era of imperialism, when the white man had as yet developed few qualms about his burden, this was standard international practice, as fully accepted by the United States as by the European powers. As John Hay explained when he authorized the visits of American gunboats to the inland river ports of China, "Even if this right were not explicitly granted to us by treaty, Rear Admiral Evans is unquestionably right in using it when like ships of other powers are constantly doing so."[175] And Hay, like the naval leaders, understood the persuasive power of the gunboat or other naval vessel as an instrument of American policy. "Some American gentlemen engaged in railway building and other large affairs in Ecuador," he once informed the Navy, "say that it would be a very great advantage to American interests generally in that Republic if a United States national vessel should occasionally, in passing by, stop at Guayaquil for a day or so. They say the effect on the public mind, and, incidentally, the effect on business interests would be advantageous."[176] Secretary Knox was equally definite about the show of naval force in Nicaraguan waters: "This Department regards the presence of these ships as important at this juncture for purely political reasons, quite apart from actual military considerations."[177] Indeed, the Taft administration, fully cognizant of the implications of the great disparity between the armed forces of the United States and the smaller Latin countries, relied heavily upon the calculated display of naval power as a method for accomplishing political objectives without resorting to direct intervention. In the words of Knox's chief assistant, Huntington Wilson, the best way to obtain political concessions from the Dominican Republic was to "synchronize the presentation of diplomatic notes with the arrival in Dominican waters of a first-class warship with landing forces."[178]

Yet it was still presumably an established tradition of American diplomacy that the United States did not intervene in the political affairs of other countries. Non-intervention, however, had never been an absolute doctrine, for throughout American history administrations had found "legitimate" exceptions, and the principle had in fact been weakened long before an activist like Roosevelt became President.

[175] SDML, Hay to Moody, 7 October 1903.
[176] SDML, Hay to Long, 25 February 1902.
[177] SDNF, Case 18432/20, Knox to Meyer, 17 March 1909.
[178] SDDF, File 839.00/659d, Huntington Wilson to Taft, 19 September 1912.

Nevertheless, the non-interventionist concept still retained sufficient popular standing for the administrations after 1898 to remain generally cautious about the actual practice of direct intervention, even in Latin America. They usually relied on the show of force, or sought such legal sanctions as the Platt amendment which would remove the stigma of illegality, or even maintained that an intervention, if actually carried out, was non-political in character, intended solely to protect American lives and property.

In any event, whatever the tradition, whatever the rationalizations, the political leadership explicitly recognized the *right* to intervene in foreign countries in order to protect American lives and property. In 1912 the Solicitor of the Department of State contended that such intervention (which he interpreted as non-political) was something which "the practice of nations has come to recognize" and also insisted that "such interposition by the one state as against the other is a matter of right, and, indeed, duty." Indeed, after surveying the American record, he candidly concluded that "no nation, it would seem, has with more frequency than has this Government used its military forces for the purpose of occupying temporarily parts of foreign countries in order to secure adequate safety and protection for its citizens and their property."[179] Others of course went much further. Roosevelt's "Big Stick"—epitomized by his actions in Panama and his famous orders to Admiral Bradford "to stop any revolution in Santo Domingo and keep that country in *statu quo* until the Senate has met"—was the symbol of an approach which was frankly interventionist. Roosevelt's outlook rested on the belief that great powers, like the United States, had a mission to preserve order in the unstable parts of the world. "More and more," he informed Congress, "the increasing interdependence and complexity of international political and economic relations render it incumbent upon all civilized and orderly powers to insist on the proper policing of the world."[180] William Howard Taft was, if anything, more explicit, when he explained to a Japanese audience that "we are living in an age when the intervention of a stronger nation in the affairs of a people unable to maintain a government of law and order to assist the latter to better government becomes a national duty and works for the progress of the world."[181]

The desire and willingness to utilize naval power either directly or

---

[179] Department of State, *Right to Protect Citizens in Foreign Countries by Landing Forces*, Memorandum of the Solicitor for the Department of State, 5 October 1912 (2nd rev. edn., Washington, 1929), 33. See also Dorothy Graber, *Crisis Diplomacy: A History of U.S. Intervention Policy* (Washington, 1959), especially 384 ff.

[180] As quoted in John Blum, *The Republican Roosevelt* (New York, 1954), 127.

[181] Ralph Minger, "Taft's Mission to Japan: A Study in Personal Diplomacy" *Pacific Historical Review*, xxx, no. 30 (August 1961), 289-90.

indirectly to accomplish political ends was widespread throughout the entire Department of State. Numerous indeed were the requests from ministers and consuls in foreign countries who believed that a firm display of naval force would produce salutary moral effects and counteract lamentable local tendencies to disorder. "Riots in Chefoo rarely, if ever, occur when warships are handy," advised the American consul in that Chinese city. "Do you know of a single instance when a United States warship was near at hand in time of trouble?"[182] Herbert Squiers, acting minister in Cuba, summarized the prevailing outlook when he requested a visit by American warships to Havana in the winter of 1904:

> It cannot be denied that such an exhibition of force and power impresses all people, and the display of a powerful fleet would undoubtedly counteract the impression left by our rivals . . . the German government never loses an opportunity to impress itself on every community, whether commercially or politically, and its policy in Cuba is no exception to this rule. . . . The Platt amendment is to many [Cubans] a menace, but when it takes the form of a powerful fleet, it is a substantial guarantee of their independence against their enemies, foreign and domestic.[183]

Thus, in an age when intervention was standard practice in the relationship between the great and the lesser powers, the use of the gunboat or, if necessary, the battleship as an instrument of diplomacy was not merely accepted but extolled by American civilian and military officials alike. This of course is not to say that the ideas of military and civilian were identical or that they shared the same system of values. Among the admirals and generals there were certainly many who thought almost exclusively in terms of coercive values, who valued force almost for its own sake, and who lived in a Darwinian thought world in which military power was the universal solvent for all political troubles.

Yet generalizations about either a "military" or a "civilian" mind are always dubious as are attempts to distinguish uniquely "military" or "civilian" attitude toward issues of American foreign policy. Indeed, the ranks of both the Army and the Navy included at all times officers who fit no military stereotype. Whatever the prevalence—even dominance—of the attitudes and ideas described earlier in this chapter, there were those who questioned, doubted, or even dissented. The same Commander Sargent who had excoriated the Venezuelans could

182 SDNF, Case 2283/3, Fowler to Department of State, 31 January 1907.
183 GB, File 420-1, Loomis to Moody, 6 February 1904, enclosing copy of Squiers' dispatch of 28 January.

also point out that the American minister in Caracas was like most American diplomatic officials in placing too much emphasis upon the presumed value of warships. "He overrates the importance of this fancied moral support," Sargent observed, and fails to understand that "the presence of the *Scorpion* is but an aggravation and is more hurtful than beneficial to his negotiations." On another occasion, when Sargent was sent to check the veracity of alarmist consular reports about unsettled political conditions on the Isthmus of Panama, he fired back an angry report in which he detailed the falsity of the news that Washington was then receiving. "I may mention," Sargent wrote, "that the only damage done the railway in the past year has been the cutting down of one telegraph pole. In the present unsettled and unpoliced condition of this country, this speaks fairly well for the character of the inhabitants and may be contrasted with the attempts at derailment, hold-ups of trains, robberies of express safes, stoppages of mail coaches and other perils of transportation in our own country."[184] Similarly, there were officers assigned to the Santo Domingo patrol who came to doubt the policies being pursued and the wisdom of the unchecked use of the American Navy to quell rebellion. Admiral Sperry flatly told Elihu Root that most of the American claims against the Dominican government were the result of collusion between foreign adventurers and corrupt local officials. Neither the government of the United States nor its navy, said Sperry, should attempt to enforce such tainted claims.[185] Later on a certain Captain A. F. Fechteler became convinced that the constant dispatch of warships to Dominican ports simply served to alienate public opinion. He advised his superiors in Washington that it would be a far wiser policy to announce publicly that the United States no longer intended to interfere in that country's affairs and then to leave the Dominicans alone to work out their own salvation.[186]

One of the most outspoken of all naval dissenters was Admiral Kimball, the officer in charge of the naval expeditionary force sent to Nicaraguan waters in the fall of 1909 and maintained there until the following spring. The occasion for his mission was the revolt which broke out late in 1909 against the Nicaraguan dictator, Zelaya, a man heartily detested by the American State Department and whose regime Knox had called "a blot on the history of Nicaragua." Official Washington was delighted at the revolt, openly supported the cause

184 Nav Rec AF 8, Sargeant to Long, 2 September 1901.

185 SDNF, Case 40/777, Minutes of the meeting of the American Delegation to the Second Hague Conference, 20 April 1907.

186 SDML, Bonaparte to Root, 22 May 1906, enclosing various communications from naval officers on the Dominican station.

of the revolutionary faction led by Estrada, and almost contemptuous-
ly rejected the claims of the faction led by Madriz, the man who had
actually succeeded Zelaya as head of the government and who had
enjoyed his support.

From one vantage point Kimball's work in Nicaragua appears as a
classic example of the absence of civil-military cooperation in foreign
affairs. Kimball clashed openly with the American consul at Managua
and disagreed sharply with State Department policy. Convinced that
the Estrada faction was acting in bad faith, Kimball tried unsuccessfully to persuade Knox and his advisers to recognize the regime of
Madriz. He charged that the followers of Estrada were stirring up
trouble in the hope of provoking an unnecessary American intervention. Behind Estrada, he argued, were American business interests
who not only supported the revolution for their own financial reasons
but who also controlled press coverage to such an extent that American newspapers received only distorted, biased accounts of the Nicaraguan situation. Indeed, the Admiral's sharpest attacks were
launched against the American community in Nicaragua, the group
which he held responsible for most of that nation's troubles. In the
spring of 1910, when he filed his final, lengthy report on his mission,
Kimball was, to say the least, outspoken:

> After forty years experience of and on American affairs, more or less
> tangled up in Latin American relations, I have come to the conclu-
> sion that much if not most of our government's troubles with Ameri-
> can claims against Latin American, and especially against Central
> American, governments arise from the fact that aid and protection
> is apt to be given to any American interest that is financially pow-
> erful enough to secure good council, no matter whether it be a legiti-
> mate interest or, as has so often been the case, a claim for spoils re-
> sulting from a fraudulent concession or monopoly worked through
> by the aid of corrupt and heavily bribed officials.

The typical American resident in Nicaragua, he continued,

> preserves and increases the natural arrogance and cock-suredness
> of his superiority to any living Latin thing . . . and freely exhibits
> these characteristics. . . . One of the chief requests to a naval officer
> by American residents as observed by me . . . has been for such ac-
> tion as would assert the superiority of the American employer's right
> to peon labor over the right of the country to the military service of
> the peon citizen.[187]

187 SDDF, 817.00/985, Meyer to Knox, 27 May 1910, enclosing copy of Admiral
Kimball's report of 25 May.

And he terminated his report with an eloquent request that the State Department, contrary to its practices, put its best and ablest representatives in Latin America rather than in Europe. Nowhere else in the world, Kimball noted, did an American representative serve as large an advisory role to a foreign government as he did in Central America where no government moved without consulting the minister or consul of the United States. What he asked for was the assignment of "such a United States representative in each community as would command its respect and could therefore control its action by proper advice based on knowledge, common sense, and standing with men of both nationalities."[188]

Another naval officer whose opinions were unorthodox was Admiral John B. Murdock who, as commander-in-chief of the Asiatic fleet, witnessed at first hand the Chinese revolution of 1911 that overthrew the Manchu dynasty. From the outset Murdock was sympathetic. The revolution represented a deeply rooted desire on the part of the Chinese to reform their outmoded institutions and "undoubtedly represents the will of the great majority of the Chinese people." It posed few threats to foreigners since it was directed against internal conditions. Murdock was impressed with the leadership of the revolutionary movement and, in his reports, caught some of the spirit that animated the group around Sun Yat-Sen:

> I am impressed with the sincerity and ability of the officials in charge of the revolutionary movement and with their confidence of eventually establishing an elective government for China, capable of controlling the country and developing peace and prosperity. They appreciate the difficulties they must overcome, but point to what they have already done in protecting foreign life and property through four months of disorder over an enormous territory as indicative of the ability of the people to rise to the demands imposed upon them by the common aspiration for a "new China."[189]

The true situation in China will never be understood until due allowance is made for the revolution in thought which has overrun the country. . . . It cannot be said to be fixed as yet and will undoubtedly be modified by contact with the conservatism of the north, but the

[188] SDDF, 817.00/985, the text of Kimball's report. See also the virtually complete file of Admiral Kimball's reports in Nav Rec Subj File, WA-7, Nicaragua, Correspondence of the Nicaraguan Expeditionary Force under Rear Admiral W. W. Kimball.

[189] SDDF, File 893.00/1181, Winthrop to Knox, 7 March 1912, enclosing Murdock report of 12 February.

past is gone forever, and a new China differing as yet in an unknown degree from the old has taken its place.[190]

The very size of the country and the magnitude of the revolution made disorder inevitable, but he cautioned his naval superiors in Washington against exaggerating its extent and maintained that the rioting was confined to a relatively small number of cities. The very perfection of the news-collecting media, Murdock suggested, was at fault; since the press acquired and provided almost immediate knowledge of scattered riots throughout China, it gave the false impression that disorder was universal. Moreover, the admiral emphasized that most of the journalistic reports, even those of the Associated Press, originated in Peking, which remained the center of the old, the dynastic, the traditional—and thereby were misleading. Implicitly he took the side of those who believed that the United States should extend early diplomatic recognition to the new regime then building in the coastal cities.[191]

Considerably different in tone were the reports from William J. Calhoun, the American minister in Peking, as well as the official attitude of the Department of State. Calhoun was by no means simply an advocate of the Manchu point of view; like Murdock, he had a grasp of the long-range forces at work in China. But his dispatches, up to the very moment of the Manchu abdication, suggested that the revolution could have been quelled if the great powers had been less neutral, more willing to lend support to the Imperial dynasty. He forwarded, with his obvious approval, those reports of his diplomatic colleagues in Peking which pressed for the dispatch of foreign troops to China to guard the rail link from Peking to the sea—a move suggested by many foreigners as necessary to prevent a repetition of the Boxer experiences but which also was indicative of the prevailing belief that the movement against the Manchus could be handled in the same traditional fashion. To Calhoun the disorders of 1911 and 1912 "were characterized by the awful barbarities which usually attend Chinese outbreaks once the normal restraint of law upon the population is removed." His dispatches frequently contained phrases such as "the flame of anarchy" and "anarchy and chaos . . . within limits of reasonable apprehension." Nor did the American minister judge the Manchu cause to be entirely lost: "It is not too much to say that the north is seething with unrest, and if the Manchus had a leader among them with a grain of courage, a *coup* can be

---

[190] SDDF, File 893.00/1224, Meyer to Knox, 29 March 1912, enclosing Murdock report of 26 February.

[191] SDDF, File 893.00/1269, Meyer to Knox, 17 April 1912, enclosing Murdock report of 18 March.

pulled off in the north more easily than the triumph of the republican movement was achieved."[192]

It is also clear that the Department of State heeded its own representative rather than Admiral Murdock—indeed, while the Admiral's reports did reach the Department, they seem merely to have been acknowledged and filed. Knox and his associates, moreover, were more perturbed by the uprisings than even the European embassies and foreign offices, were discussing the possibility of dispatching 2,500 American troops at a time when the other powers as yet had no plans to call for such an extensive force, and were unwilling to consider diplomatic recognition of the new regime being established in the coastal cities. Wedded to the financial tenets of "dollar diplomacy" and fearful that the 1911 revolution meant the end of their grandiose schemes for obtaining greater influence in China, Knox and his advisers were simply disinterested in the ideas of an observer like Admiral Murdock.[193]

This is not to claim that Murdock's interpretation of the events in China was either accurate or definitive. He, after all, was based in and around Nanking and the facts of geography dictated that he would be tempted to view the revolution through revolutionary eyes; his contacts were largely with those Chinese who were disenchanted with the traditional China of the Manchus. Calhoun, on the other hand, was in Peking, the heart of the old regime and a region still unaffected by the political ferment sweeping the coastal cities; again, his geographical location gave him a vantage point from which to assess the forces of drag and inertia in China and to understand the many obstacles to reform and change.[194]

Admiral Murdock and Admiral Kimball were two naval officers who do not fit a stereotype of the "military mind." Both had broader intellectual horizons than the assumptions of gunboat diplomacy, and both, if nothing else, saw certain dimensions which the Department of State either ignored or discounted. Moreover, the difference between a Murdock and a Calhoun was not simply a difference between a State Department and a Navy Department system of values; their differences were differences of experience, in temperament, even of perspective as conditioned by geography. Which, of course, leads back to the prior observation that, in the larger sense, sweeping generalizations about

[192] SDDF, File 893.00/1229, Calhoun to Knox, 8 March 1912, a typical report from the minister. See also his /1038 of 16 January.

[193] The reaction within the Department of State is further discussed in Chapter Four.

[194] Walter Scholes, "Philander Knox," in Norman Graebner, ed., *An Uncertain Tradition: American Secretaries of State in the Twentieth Century* (New York, 1961), 59-78. I am particularly indebted to Professor Scholes for the ideas contained in this paragraph.

the military mind in foreign affairs must always be qualified and tempered. The differences between what officers and civilians thought about various issues of American foreign policy cannot be reduced to a simple dichotomy; the factors of temperament, experience, and even of chance must enter the equation.

4. The Difference Between American and European Practice

The role of the military services in American foreign policy extended into many other matters beyond those so far touched upon in this incomplete survey. There were, for example, military representatives at the peace conference in Paris in 1898 which settled the Spanish-American war. Indeed, even before the delegation left Washington, McKinley had made it clear that he personally attached great importance to the views which Generals Merritt and Greene and Admiral Dewey would express about the advisability of retaining the Philippines and hoped that the delegates would pay attention to their recommendations. At Paris, moreover, one of the strongest presentations on behalf of keeping all of the Philippines was made by Commander (soon to be Admiral) Bradford; his testimony, according to one close observer, had a strong impact upon the delegation, even on its anti-expansionist members.[195] Similarly, Mahan was a member— and probably the most influential member—of the American delegation at the first Hague Peace Conference of 1899; the extent to which the head of the delegation, Henry White, deferred to the wishes of the advocate of sea power has been specifically noted by the most recent historian of that conference.[196] Officers of both services participated in the London Naval Conference of 1909, an international meeting which considered a wide range of maritime issues, especially the "rules" which should apply in time of war. At the conclusion of that conference the Department of State publicly announced that every major issue raised at the conference had been submitted to the General Board of the Navy for its advice and recommendations.[197] It was, as a matter of fact, general policy for the State Department to seek the opinions of the military services on those aspects of international law which touched the military interest; on such varied matters as the immunity of private property at sea, the neutralization of the Great

---

[195] H. Wayne Morgan, *Making Peace with Spain: The Diary of Whitelaw Reid, September-December, 1898* (Austin, 1965), 73-74, and Paolo Coletta, "McKinley, The Peace Negotiations, and the Acquisition of the Philippines," *Pacific Historical Review*, xxx, no. 4 (November 1961), 341-50.

[196] Calvin P. Davis, *The United States and the First Hague Peace Conference* (Ithaca, 1962), 74-75 and, especially, 175.

[197] SDNF, Case 12655/311, Memorandum of James Brown Scott, 15 March 1909.

Lakes, and the dropping of "projectiles" from balloons and what were then called lighter-than-air craft the General Board and the General Staff were at least invited to submit formal statements.[198] Succeeding chapters will consider some of the specific events of American foreign policy—the Dominican intervention, the "war scares" with Japan, the Mexican revolution—in which the military services were something more than merely the passive agents of civilian policy.

Yet one must be careful about claiming too much. Certainly the United States "lagged behind" the great powers of Europe in terms of the extent to which, for good or ill, military men had an influence upon foreign affairs. In a period of rising international tensions and competing alliance systems, national security was so crucial to European leaders that, especially in times of crisis, the opinions of general staffs were carefully weighed. In 1905, for example, the highly pessimistic military estimate of the French staff was one of the critical factors in the decision of the Paris government to seek a way out of the Moroccan imbroglio. In Germany and Austria-Hungary the military staffs had, indeed, achieved an influence which was to prove harmful to the interests of those states. The role of a Conrad in committing the Austrian Empire to war against Serbia and the restrictions which the famous war plan of Count Schlieffen placed upon Germany's freedom of diplomatic choice are two of the most familiar examples of the powers which some European militarists could exert.[199]

Great Britain, well before the outbreak of World War I, had come to realize the necessity for substantial coordination of military and civil policy. Her Committee on Imperial Defense was established in 1904 specifically "to obtain and collate for the Cabinet all the information and advice for shaping national policy in war."[200] But even before the creation of the C.I.D., British leaders paid considerable attention to the military dimensions of policy. When the negotiations for the second Hay-Pauncefote Treaty were just beginning, the Cabinet specifically requested that the Director of Military Intelligence submit a report on the effect that a revised treaty and a fortified canal, in American hands, would have upon Britain's naval position in the Caribbean. This and other Admiralty documents were distributed to and discussed by the Cabinet. Lord Lansdowne, in reaching his eventual deci-

---

[198] See GB, File 438 which deals with international law from the Navy's viewpoint. This is a very extensive file containing many examples of the cooperation between the Navy and the State Department on matters pertaining to international law on the high seas.

[199] Gordon A. Craig, *The Politics of the Prussian Army* (New York, 1956), 286-95. On Conrad, see Luigi Albertini, *The Origins of the War of 1914* (2 vols., London, 1952-55), II, 121-25, 172-75, and 453-65.

[200] Captain S. W. Roskill, *The Strategy of Sea Power* (London, 1962), 103-04.

sion, drew heavily upon their contents, especially in reaching his personal conclusion (which was, however, not that of the Admiralty) that Britain could permit a fortified canal since ultimate control of the Caribbean depended not upon concrete and guns on the Isthmus itself but upon the increasing naval power which the United States, with its growing fleet, could put into that sea. Similarly, in 1904, when Lord Fisher proposed his radical scheme for the redistribution of the British navy, the Cabinet had the benefit of a lengthy memorandum which explained in great detail why naval dispositions suitable for the age of sail had to be modified to meet the new technology of steam, the changes in the British alliance structure, and, above all, the rise of the German navy.[201]

By contrast with Great Britain—and specifically on these two issues —the United States fares poorly. Members of the General Board were not happy with the naval restrictions that the Clayton-Bulwer treaty had imposed, but there was no formal report by that group on the issue of fortification when the Hay-Pauncefote negotiations of 1900 and 1901 were under way. To be sure, in a letter to Theodore Roosevelt, John Hay did remark somewhat pettishly that "of course we have consulted the best naval opinion" and his report to the Senate did include a single memorandum from Admiral Dewey which seemed to indicate that the naval staff, like its British counterpart, believed that seapower and not fortifications on the Isthmus would provide the ultimate security for the canal.[202] But whatever the accuracy of Hay's contention may be (and this will be discussed later, in another context) the fact is that the Secretary of State made little of this document and that it was treated almost as an afterthought. Similarly, when the General Board drew up its plans for the distribution of the fleet, it did so in virtual isolation. As previously noted, the admirals consulted almost exclusively within their own circle and indicated their own lack of knowledge about the actual conditions of America's foreign relations.

But, in a broader sense, genuine coordination of civil and military policy did not become an issue of importance, in either Europe or America, until the world had experienced the shocks and disasters of total war. Both the Schlieffen plan and its French counterpart, Plan XVII, were drawn up by military experts in accordance with strict military logic, by military technicians concerned with the rapidity of mobilization, the capacity of railroads to concentrate troops, and the strategy of mass armies of conscripts. They were the work of military professionals—their supreme technical achievement—and not the re-

---

[201] J.A.S. Grenville, "Great Britain and the Isthmian Canal, 1898-1901," *American Historical Review*, LI, no. 1 (October 1955), 66-67; Marder, *Anatomy*, 48 ff.

[202] Dennett, *Hay*, 254 ff.

sults of a meaningful civil-military cooperation. In the summer of 1914, indeed, the very act of mobilization froze the possibility of diplomatic solutions to the crisis, effectively tied the hands of European diplomats. And once war had begun, virtually all Europeans assumed that politics and economics were adjourned, *sine die*, until the mass armies had produced a definitive military solution on the field of battle. It was a German field marshal who indicated that he did not wish to be bothered by mere economic concerns when he had a war to fight. In France it was not until the 1920s that there began to emerge the outline of a system of intergovernmental committees to coordinate the multiple dimensions of national defense. For France it required the experiences of total war and near defeat to produce the instruments for civil-military cooperation. In this sense, then, the "lagging behind" of the United States has to be considered in terms of a universal pre-1914 attitude toward war and the role of the military— in terms of the fact that it was not until the world had plunged into total war that it was realized, in Clemenceau's famous dictum, that war was too important to leave to the generals.[203]

[203] See the chapter by Hans Speier, "Ludendorff and the German Concept of War," in Earle, ed., *Modern Strategy*; R. D. Challener, *The French Theory of the Nation in Arms* (New York, 1955), 91 ff.

CHAPTER TWO

The Navy in the Caribbean in the Age
of McKinley and Roosevelt

1. THE SEARCH FOR BASES

AT the precise moment when the peace negotiations with Spain were opening in September of 1898, the Navy Department sent a set of confidential orders to Admiral William Sampson and Commodore Winfield Schley, the two ranking officers in Cuban waters. As a matter of highest priority they were directed to obtain all naval stations and all naval property left behind in Cuba by the departing Spaniards. Speed was essential. "It is possible," their orders read, "that the United States War Department may try to obtain custody of some of this property." If the Army was successful, then the Navy could obtain its bases and properties only by an act of Congress, and such action on Capitol Hill, as it was delicately phrased, "would create opposition from the other Department concerned."[1]

This incident, so typical of the deep interservice rivalries of 1898, revealed the speed and the enthusiasm with which the Navy was prepared to establish itself in the Caribbean just as soon as the Spaniards were driven from Cuba. It was also the opening episode in a new chapter in American policy in that region. In the immediate aftermath of the Spanish-American war the United States began to develop a consistent national policy for the Caribbean. That policy had two primary objectives: first, to build an American-owned and controlled canal across the Isthmus of Panama and, second, to transform the Caribbean into an American "lake" in which there would be neither European interference nor political instability in the countries of the Caribbean and Central America. To achieve the first objective the United States, with Theodore Roosevelt at the helm, sanctioned, if it did not actually sponsor, the Isthmian revolt of 1903 that produced Panamanian "independence" and, more important, the access rights for the long-sought canal. To secure the second goal the United States in 1904 proclaimed the "Roosevelt Corollary" to the Monroe Doctrine which sanctioned American intervention in the internal affairs of Latin countries which could not keep their finances in order and whose financial imprudence was thought to pose a danger of European intervention.

There were, of course, variations within the overall policy, and

[1] Nav Rec Confd Ltrs, Allen to Admirals Sampson and Schley, 22 September 1898.

American foreign policy progressed through a number of way stations along the path toward becoming the policeman of the Caribbean. For some time after 1898 the immediate concern was the problem of finding naval bases and, above all, determining the route for the interoceanic canal. The spectre of foreign intervention did not loom especially large until 1902 when the episode of the Venezuelan blockade produced fears of European interventions throughout the Caribbean to collect due bills from defaulting states. But it was not until two years later, when the Dominican Republic appeared to be involved in the same recurring cycle of international debt and repudiation, that the paranoid stage was reached and Washington responded with the Roosevelt corollary. Yet there were always certain limitations, certain hesitations. The burst of imperialism in 1898 was to a considerable extent a transitory consequence of wartime emotions. As those enthusiasms began to wane, it became clear within a few years that neither Congress nor the public would support further annexations of territory. Moreover, Roosevelt's imperious handling of the Panamanian revolt produced a certain degree of backlash which restricted his options when the Dominican troubles began the following year. Even if T.R. had been tempted by the prospect of direct intervention, he would have found it politically difficult if not impossible; as it was, the Customs Receivership which he put into operation in 1905 did not win the approval of a reluctant Congress until another two years had gone by. Similarly, the desire to prove to a skeptical world that Cuba was not simply an American ward made American policymakers at least initially hesitant to intervene for a second time in 1906. By 1905 the stage had been set for the arrival in the State Department of Elihu Root, a man who fully shared T.R.'s determination to maintain order and stability in the Caribbean but who preferred to use legal techniques rather than the "big stick."

How did the military services fit into this evolving Caribbean policy? This chapter examines several aspects of their involvement, beginning with the Navy's search for bases that started right after the Spanish-American war. It considers the Navy's role in the Venezuelan blockade, an episode which raises the controversial question of the extent to which Roosevelt used the fleet in the classic European manner as an instrument of policy to compel Germany to accept arbitration, and the part played by both military services in the "taking of Panama," an incident in which Roosevelt ostentatiously displayed the raw edges of American military power. It examines the Navy's role in Cuba, where it functioned under certain restrictions, as well as in Central America, where the restrictions were far less. A considerable portion of this chapter will focus on the Dominican Republic and its recurrent political upheavals, for the troubles of Santo Domingo were a matter of virtually continuous concern throughout all the Roosevelt years. Except for the Dominican materials, much of the content of this chapter is episodic, for it discusses, especially with respect to Central America, involvements that were sporadic, frequently disconnected, and incompletely documented. But taken together, all of these episodes—bases, Venezuela, Panama, Cuba, Central America, the Dominican Republic—were representative of the increasingly complex and expanded military dimenson of the Caribbean policy of the United States after 1900.

In the preceding chapter there was an extended discussion of the reasons which lay behind the Navy's interest in bases and coaling stations: the logic of Mahan, the pragmatic needs of a steam-driven navy, the strategic importance of the Caribbean, and the increasing demand for an Isthmian canal. Further elaboration of these "givens" of naval policy is unnecessary. What should be underscored, however, is the intensity of the Navy's initial enthusiasm for bases. That enthusiasm was revealed in many statements by naval officers but nowhere better than in a special report prepared in the spring of 1901 by Admiral Royal Bradford, a member of the General Board and Chief of the Bureau of Equipment. Indeed, the admiral himself thought that his report was of such importance that it should immediately be forwarded to the Department of State as an official expression of naval opinion. Admiral Bradford wanted the State Department to prepare special instructions for the American delegates to the forthcoming Pan-American Congress at Mexico City. The delegates should be made fully aware of the Navy's need for naval stations and bases on both the east and west coasts of the Isthmus and South America and, in addition, should be fully prepared to explain the Navy's case in detail to their Latin counterparts at the Congress. The best line of approach, Bradford suggested, would be for the American representatives to point out that the United States was committed by the Monroe Doctrine to preserve the independence of the Western Hemisphere from European aggression and therefore was entitled to the assistance of the Latin countries in the pursuit of that objective. But the Doctrine could not be preserved without a powerful American fleet, and that fleet, in turn, could not conduct successful operations at any great distance south of the territorial limits of the United States unless it had access to coaling stations and fortified bases.[2] The arguments of Bradford were, of course, scarcely new; what was unusual was his belief that an unsolicited report should be submitted to the State Department in an attempt to influence its judgment.

[2] SDML, Long to Hay, 27 July 1901, enclosing Bradford's memorandum of the 23rd to Long.

The initial vision of the Navy was far reaching. If all of its requests for bases and coaling stations had been successful, the United States would have become an imperial power beyond the wildest dreams of even the most ardent advocates of the "large policy" of 1898. It is, however, difficult to put together a precise or complete picture of the overall endeavor. In the first place, there were certain Caribbean sites in which the Navy's interest antedated 1898 and had actually originated in the era of the Civil War and its brief aftermath of expansion. On the other hand, the proposed acquisition of the Danish West Indies was handled so completely by the Department of State that the Navy's precise interest and influence in the project is by no means clear. Moreover, certain projects got started before the General Board was established, and, in consequence, one cannot be entirely certain of the extent to which they represented a genuine "naval" interest or were simply the special concerns of certain ardent expansionists within the naval establishment, such as Admirals Taylor and Bradford. Further complications arise from the long indecision in Washington about the actual location of the projected Isthmian canal and the long-drawn-out issue of whether or not the canal could be fortified. Finally, there was always a certain scrambling in the Navy's search for Latin bases, an opportunistic temptation to seek a particular piece of real estate, regardless of where it might fit into any overall scheme, simply because so many other proposals had been unsuccessful. Still, if any one document may be regarded as typical of the scope of the General Board's thinking at the height of its interest in Latin American acquisitions, it was the consolidated report prepared and submitted to the Secretary of the Navy during the summer and early fall of 1902.

Guantanamo Bay in Cuba, that report began, was the one location "indispensable to the efficiency of the naval force in the West Indies," and should be obtained "irrespective of the future status of Cuba." But the naval strategists placed equal emphasis upon the acquisition of bases on the Isthmus of Panama, since, in their judgment, the security of the projected canal could not be guaranteed merely by fortifying its termini. Colombia should therefore be asked to cede to the United States exclusive control of both Almirante Bay and Chiriqui Lagoon on the Caribbean side of the Isthmus regardless of whether the Nicaraguan or the Panamanian canal route was selected. On the Pacific side there should be a base in the Pearl Islands if the Panamanian route be chosen, at Port Elena in the event that the decision favored Nicaragua.[3]

[3] SDML, Darling to Hay, 1 November 1902, enclosing General Board No. 220, Dewey to Moody, 28 October 1902.

A second letter from the General Board accompanied this report. In the bureaucratic prose of that era it especially invited the attention of the Department of State "to that part of its report which involves the diplomatic relations of this government and asks that persistent efforts be made in this direction until the desired objects are accomplished." The cession of the Galapagos Islands, Ecuador's Pacific island group, to any foreign nation should be prevented since their strategic value was such that "they would become a menace to this country if any European power obtained a base at this point." Second, and more indicative of the broad sweep of naval thinking, was the flat assertion that "our future interests may demand that we have a base on the east coast of that continent [South America], preferably at Bahia, Brazil; and another on the west coast at Ferrol and Samanco bays (otherwise known as Chimbote)." Third, were the Danish West Indies, the island group which at that time the United States was still trying to purchase from Denmark. A treaty for their purchase had been negotiated, had cleared the Senate, but was still blocked in the Danish legislature. Hence the General Board did not directly mention these islands in its 1902 list of desired sites but instead asked for a base at Culebra, an adjacent small island off Puerto Rico and ceded with it to the United States in 1898.[4] But the omission of the Virgin Islands was merely tactical. Among themselves the admirals "understood" that their reference to Culebra should be interpreted as including the Danish islands as well. In executive session the General Board had agreed, before submitting their final list, that "Culebra included the Danish West Indies but that these should not be mentioned in the main report but stated in a confidential letter."[5]

During the years that the General Board actively pursued its expansionist policy, there were other reports, other targets, other priorities. The 1902 report, while truly representative of the broad scope of its Latin interests, also showed the first traces of the coming change of heart that would lead the admirals to conclude that concentration of naval strength was preferable to its diffusion and to focus their attention upon a few primary locations such as Guantanamo. The Galapagos, for example, had always previously been one of the "desired objects" for acquisition, but on the very eve of submitting their final report in 1902, the admirals revised their position to the simple recommendation that the acquisition of the Galapagos by a European power should be prevented. And language was softened; instead of saying,

4 SDML, Moody to Hay, 21 November 1902, enclosing General Board No. 284, Dewey to Moody, 7 October 1902.

5 GB, Proceedings, 23 September 1902.

as in earlier drafts, that the United States "will require" naval stations on the east and west coasts of South America, the completed report used the phrase "may require."[6]

A considerable portion of this search for Caribbean bases occurred during the time that John Hay was attempting to negotiate a new treaty with the British to replace the venerable Clayton-Bulwer treaty of 1850 and therefore revealed much of the Navy's attitude toward the two Hay-Pauncefote pacts. The Navy, needless to say, chafed under the restrictions imposed by the mid-nineteenth-century agreement with Britain. While Hay was still negotiating his first treaty with Pauncefote, the President of the Naval War College, Captain C. H. Stockton, published a long article which emphasized the negative effect that the Clayton-Bulwer treaty had upon the position of the United States and its navy in Central America and insisted that the United States must gain a clear right to build, protect, and fortify a canal entirely its own.[7] In 1900, when Admiral Bradford first proposed naval bases at Port Elena and Almirante Bay, he was clearly reacting against the first Hay-Pauncefote treaty, which assumed a neutralized canal and retained the non-fortification clauses of the older treaty. In his argument, for example, Bradford stressed the fact that, under the then pending treaty, the United States had assumed grave responsibilities for preserving the neutrality of the proposed canal but was severely handicapped by the continuing prohibition on fortifications at the termini of the canal.[8]

Yet there was no direct attack by the Navy on the non-fortification provisions of Hay's first treaty with Pauncefote, and the reason for this was not simply the traditional separation of the military from politics or the fact that the Navy was not fully consulted. Admiral Bradford, for example, seemed content with the proposal to establish fortified bases elsewhere on Colombian territory and, in fact, praised the first Hay-Pauncefote treaty for removing many of the strictures in the Clayton-Bulwer treaty. Dewey's response on the controversial issue of fortification was guarded. He had not, he informed Senator Morgan's committee, given the issue of fortification a great deal of time or thought and had generally believed that the defense of the canal would rest primarily with the Navy, not upon fortifications. Still, he was "not prepared to say that land defenses would be unnecessary."[9]

It seems, however, that the actual issue of fortifying the canal— which so angered Theodore Roosevelt and led to the failure of Hay's

[6] GB, Proceedings, 28 August, 23 and 26 September 1902.

[7] Charles Stockton, "The American Inter-Oceanic Canal: A Study of the Commercial, Naval, and Political Conditions," *USNIP*, xxvi, no. 4 (December 1899), 752-97.

[8] SDML, Long to Hay, 12 February 1900, enclosing copy of Bradford's report.

[9] Dewey Papers, Dewey to Morgan, 12 February 1900.

first treaty—was not a matter of all-consuming importance to the Navy. First, to the followers of Mahan, it was an axiom of strategy that national defense rested upon the battle fleet and not shore bases, on seapower and not fortifications. It was clear to them, as to the British admiralty, that control of the Caribbean—and ultimately of the canal —would depend upon the size and composition of the naval units that operated in it.[10] Second, it seemed possible to circumvent the non-fortification restrictions of the first Hay-Pauncefote treaty, if not the Clayton-Bulwer pact, by obtaining naval bases elsewhere in the area where the canal would be built. For while Article II of the ill-fated first treaty of John Hay stated that "no fortifications shall be erected commanding the canal or the waters adjacent," its provisions applied for a distance of only three maritime miles from either end. This clear-ly opened up the possibility of bases elsewhere in Colombia, Costa Rica, or even Nicaragua.[11]

More important, however, in naval thinking about the role of fortifi-cations in the defense of the canal was the geography of the Carib-bean. It is a body of water virtually landlocked and into which there are relatively few points of access for shipping. In consequence, as naval writers frequently observed, there were only a few positions "of commanding commercial and naval import"—the phrase used by the War Board of 1898.[12] Or, in the succinct words of Captain Stockton, "One cork is alone necessary for this bottle."[13] The "cork" which he and others had in mind was the Windward Passage between the eastern tip of Cuba and the Republic of Haiti on the western half of the island of Santo Domingo. The Windward Passage, they emphasized, provided the one route through which all naval traffic, commercial, or military, must pass to reach the Isthmus and any canal, whether Panamanian or Nicaraguan. Control of the Windward Passage was one of the absolute requirements for control of the Caribbean. As the General Board

10 See GB, File 414-1, Report of Naval War Board, 1898; P. C. Hains, "An Isth-mian Canal from a Military Point of View," *Annals of the American Academy of Political and Social Science*, XVII, no. 2 (May 1901); and, especially, "Inter-Ocean Canal" by Stockton, who wrote in 1899 that "the fact that the use of the Canal can be prevented by a naval predominance in the Caribbean has been called to your attention repeatedly" (p. 790). See also the discussion in Dennett, *Hay*, 248-60. For the British viewpoint, the best analyses are to be found in J.A.S. Grenville, "Great Britain and the Isthmian Canal, 1898-1901," *American Historical Review*, LI (Octo-ber 1955), 48-69, and Charles Campbell, Jr., *Anglo-American Understanding, 1898-1903* (Baltimore, 1957), 217, 238-39, and Appendix 4, 357 ff., a copy of the Admiralty Memorandum of 5 January 1901 which defined the British Navy's views on the value of fortification.

11 For the terms of the first Hay-Pauncefote treaty, see *Diplomatic History of the Panama Canal* (63rd Congress, 2nd Session, Senate Document 474, Washington, 1914), 289.

12 GB, File 414-1, Report of Naval War Board, 1898.

13 Stockton, "Interoceanic Canal," 767.

warned in 1901, "No solution of the problem of coaling and naval stations can be considered satisfactory which does not provide for military safety upon that route."[14] It was Guantanamo's geographic relation to the Windward Passage which made it so valuable to naval planners, while the sometimes almost paranoid fears which naval officers expressed about possible German intervention in Haiti or Santo Domingo were also directly related to Hispaniola's location astride the strategic passage. There were also, it should be added, other "corks" to the Caribbean, in particular the passages in the vicinity of Puerto Rico which gave strategic value to that island, the Dominican Republic, and the Virgin Islands. These passages—which, however, never received the same emphasis as the Windward Passage—could be controlled by naval bases at such possible sites as Samana Bay, Culebra, San Juan, or St. Thomas.

In any event, it is clear that naval strategists never expected to defend the canal simply by fortifications at its termini. They emphasized the role of seapower and counted on the acquisition of bases on the Isthmus. Above all, they believed that the key to control of the Caribbean—and therefore to the security of the canal—rested upon the acquisition of naval positions on the perimeter. These bases, controlling the principal passages into an essentially landlocked sea, would enable the United States Navy to put the cork into the Caribbean bottle. Positions on the perimeter, in short, were more important than fortifications at the termini of the proposed canal. "The general rule," Admiral Sperry noted, "is that you should seek to command a line of communications by being securely based on its flank rather than by holding only the terminus."[15]

It therefore seems that much of the barbed criticism aimed at John Hay for his first treaty with the British—above all, for accepting neutralization of an Isthmus canal that the United States could not fortify —was misdirected. His actions certainly indicated that he was aware of the dimensions of the naval strategic thought which has just been described. He was certainly working for the same goals as the Navy when he sought the purchase of the Danish West Indies, backed strongly the demands made on Cuba for the cession of naval bases, and authorized American diplomats on the Isthmus to open negotiations for the possible cession of naval stations in the vicinity of the proposed canal routes. He must have believed, as Tyler Dennett suggested many years ago, that he was building the American position in the Caribbean along the lines the Navy thought most important and

14 GB, Letters, I, Dewey to Long, 1 November 1901.
15 Sperry Papers, Sperry to Charles Sperry, Jr., 1 May 1905.

was actually increasing the security of the canal instead, as his friend Roosevelt charged, of threatening its safety.[16]

It should be emphasized that even though the Navy attached its highest priorities to bases on the perimeter of the Caribbean, it did regard Isthmian sites as of great value in protecting the canal. Above all, the General Board did not seek them simply as a device to circumvent the non-fortification provisions of the Clayton-Bulwer and first Hay-Pauncefote treaties. The admirals were just as interested after the second treaty had been negotiated and ratified, even after the British, in a supplementary note, had conceded the right to erect fortifications along the canal route. Heretofore the argument for additional bases had rested in part on the non-fortification clauses. Now the grounds were shifted. Naval strategists maintained that guns and concrete at the termini of the canal would provide insufficient protection. Efficient naval operations in the entire Central American area, it was explicitly argued, required more than just fortified bases at the two ends of the canal itself.[17]

In any event, the first naval approaches to the Department of State for coaling stations on the Isthmus were made towards the end of 1899. The two desired sites, both suggested by the 1898 War Board, were Almirante Bay on the Caribbean side and Port Elena on the Pacific. The impetus was a recent Congressional appropriation of the princely sum of $200,000 to be used by the Navy for the acquisition of naval depots on the Isthmus. Admiral Taylor's lengthy report—produced when the outcome of the first negotiations with the British was still uncertain—indicated the extent to which the Navy then wanted to escape from the restrictions of the Clayton-Bulwer treaty. What he wanted were major bases, capable of supporting fleet operations and carrying out extensive repair functions, and he further emphasized that the United States must possess full sovereign rights as well as rights to fortify whatever land might be leased or purchased.[18]

The Department of State immediately instructed the American minister in both Colombia and Costa Rica to open negotiations. What then transpired was a foretaste of difficulties to come. From the very beginning the Almirante proposal was in difficulties. Colombia's Minister of Foreign Affairs protested that the matter was "delicate," the timing, "inopportune." Soon he was maintaining that the cession of Colombian territory was an issue which "offers practically insurmountable diffi-

16 Dennett, *Hay*, 265-66.

17 SDML, Moody to Hay, 21 November 1902, enclosing Dewey to Moody of 7 October 1902.

18 SDML, Long to Hay, 12 December 1899, enclosing Bradford to Long of 6 December 1899.

culties." And, in truth, he was right, for Almirante Bay fell in disputed territory, in an area claimed by both Colombia and Costa Rica.[19] But the Colombians, who after all did have a considerable stake in the still unsettled question of the canal route, apparently did not want to appear entirely negative. They suggested politely that the tiny islets of New Providence and San Andreas—both, incidentally, several hundred miles out into the Caribbean and closer to Nicaragua than the Isthmus—might prove to be suitable. A somewhat less than enthusiastic Navy Department reluctantly agreed to send a vessel to investigate.[20]

The Costa Rican project started out more hopefully. Port Elena at least lay wholly within Costa Rican territory and was but twenty-five miles from the Nicaraguan town of Brito, assumed to be the Pacific terminal of the canal should the Nicaraguan route win approval. Naval officials were optimistic not only about obtaining the harbor but also about persuading Costa Rica to yield sovereign rights to the United States and sufficient land for adequate fortifications. Considerable effort was made to persuade the Department of State of the value of the harbor. The naval officer who examined it was asked to make a personal call on John Hay and to be prepared to answer any and all questions—especially about the need for sovereign rights, land for fortifications, and the inherent value of Port Elena to the Navy, even if the canal route should not be through Nicaragua.[21]

By midsummer of 1900 the American minister to Costa Rica was reporting that the President of that republic favored the proposal and that a definitive treaty, conceding all the Navy's wishes, was about to be drafted. The blow fell on the very day after the Navy had officially congratulated Hay and his assistants for their successful efforts. Abruptly, Minister Merry reported that the deal was off. President Iglesias, blandly maintaining that he personally was still in favor of the treaty, announced that his country's border dispute with Colombia put him in "a very difficult position," so difficult that he "could not at present make a move which would create animosity against him throughout Spanish America." But there was, he insisted, the prospect of mañana—if the Congress of the United States approved the Nicaraguan canal bill, then the situation would change, and he would be

[19] The opening of negotiations discussed in the correspondence just cited, but see also SDML, Long to Hay, 27 December 1899 and 26 March 1900, the latter of which emphasizes some of the difficulties involved.

[20] SDML, Hay to Long, 30 March 1900.

[21] Nav Rec Confid Ltrs, Allen to Commanding Officer of the *Philadelphia*, 3 April 1900; SDML, Long to Hay, 14 July 1900.

able to sign the lease with no delay or difficulty.[22] The Costa Ricans quite obviously were also playing the canal game!

The next moves were initiated by the Department of State and deserve mention simply as an indication of the support which John Hay was prepared to give to the Navy's proposals. On the basis of reports from Central America, the Secretary of State suggested to the Navy that the Colombian government had not in fact meant to close the door to all discussions of Almirante but simply wanted to get a specific cash offer from the United States. The Navy therefore was advised to name a figure that could be passed on to Minister Hart at Bogota—not, to be sure, a very precise figure since the negotiations were "in a very inchoate state." As Hay wrote, "I have revived the matter for your consideration in the supposition that the present condition . . . may afford a more favorable opportunity than existed at the time Mr. Hart's dispatches were written."[23] Similarly, when Hart was authorized to reopen the issue, his instructions from the State Department included a strong statement, which had actually originated in the Navy Department, about the need for fortifications at Almirante. Hart was to tell the Colombians that, while other countries might object to the fortification of the canal, "it is likely that the people of this country will not consent to build a canal unless controlled by this government at all times."[24] John Hay, in other words, was working for a fortified base in Colombia at the very same time that he was agreeing in the first Hay-Pauncefote Treaty to an unfortified canal—further evidence that his general policy must be assessed not simply in terms of the treaty with the British but in its totality.

But there were no results. The Navy frequently inquired hopefully about possible progress in the negotiations; just as frequently the Department of State responded in the negative.[25] Soon the Navy began to get restive. It was the continuing lack of success in this matter that led Admiral Bradford, in the summer of 1901, to make his suggestion that American delegates to the Pan-American congress should be asked to work in the Navy's behalf. Then, too, the Navy sought, and won approval for the idea that the Isthmian Canal Commission, headed by Admiral Walker, should be involved in its endeavor. At the Navy's request, Hay instructed Walker that he should consider the possibility of acquiring sites for naval bases in reaching his decision

22 SDML, Long to Hay, 3 November 1900 and Hay to Long, 15 November 1900, the latter enclosing a copy of Minister Merry's dispatch of 4 November.

23 SDML, Hay to Long, 1 August 1900.

24 SDML, Long to Hay, 3 November 1900, with endorsement by Alvey Adee on instructions to be sent to Hart.

25 SDML, Long to Hay, 5 March 1901.

about the proper route for the proposed canal.[26] Naval authorities even held talks with a promoter who claimed to hold rights in the Chiriqui region of Colombia (a lagoon near Almirante Bay) and was obviously eager to peddle them to the Navy. This time it was the Department of State which applied the necessary amount of cold water. It informed the eager admirals that "In view of the somewhat stale and decidedly doubtful nature of the titles offered, their purchase would . . . involve simply the purchase of a lawsuit." Moreover, they were reminded, even if these private titles were valid, the Navy could not obtain the necessary territorial sovereignty without direct negotiations with the government of Bogota.[27]

Further pursuit of the details of these two futile endeavors would be highly unrewarding. The pattern established in the 1900-01 negotiations with Costa Rica and Colombia remained unchanged. There were admittedly several brief flurries over Port Elena, occasions when Minister Merry felt that President Iglesias was about to change his mind and grant a two-hundred-year lease.[28] And the Navy, hoping to help its cause, ultimately proved willing to yield on its demand for full sovereign rights, conceding that it would be sufficient to obtain merely extraterritorial rights of control and administration within a lease.[29] However, Colombia, with the canal route remaining unsettled, never showed any signs of willingness to lease Almirante; the approved tactic was to inform Washington that any cession of national territory would require a special session of the Colombian legislature and the "government might be undone by granting such a concession."[30] But there always appeared to be a slight opening in the Colombian door. Their foreign minister kept suggesting, as he had previously done, that the two Caribbean islets would be suitable and hinting that his government would greatly prefer to consider the entire question of bases "when a declaration for the Panama Canal has been made by the United States."[31]

These Colombian statements—made of course at a time when the final decision on the canal route had yet to be reached—indicate the complex relationship between canal, naval bases, and emerging Latin nationalism. On the one hand, there was the United States, eager to settle the canal question, anxious to secure naval stations for its protection, and prepared to consider the availability of such bases in its final

[26] SDML, Hay to Long and Walker, 24 April 1901.
[27] SDML, Hill to Long, 18 May 1901.
[28] SDML, Hackett to Hay, 5 August 1901.
[29] SDML, Adee to Long, 4 September 1901, but see also Long to Hay, 14 February 1902.
[30] SDML, Hay to Long, 10 December 1901.
[31] SDML, Hay to Long, 9 December 1901.

choice of a route. On the other hand, there were several Latin states whose politicians had to consider the political risk of ceding national territory to the "Colossus of the North" but who were also sufficiently lured by the canal enterprise to hint that a favorable American decision about the route would affect their attitude on the cession of naval bases. Early in 1902, for example, the Costa Ricans openly tipped their hand. To the displeasure of both the Navy and the Department of State they suggested that the proposed lease for Port Elena ought to be combined with a project to secure a right of way through Costa Rica for the interoceanic canal. It was indicated that both proposals would be facilitated if combined into one.[32]

But none of these suggestions ever resulted in a base for the Navy. After passage of the Spooner Act and the final decision in favor of the Panama route, the Navy shifted its attention to the Pearl Islands, lying in the Gulf of Panama and close to the proposed site of the Pacific terminus. But the Navy had no more success with this project than with those that had preceded it.[33] The admirals, however, kept trying, and their interest in bases in Central America definitely persisted well after the General Board decision of 1903 to concentrate rather than diffuse naval strength. Indeed, the Navy's reaction to the revolt of November 1903 that created the Republic of Panama was instantaneous; the admirals saw tangible advantages in an independent Panama no less quickly than the political leaders and diplomats. Within a week of the famous *coup* on the Isthmus, the General Board had supplied John Hay with a special report that called attention to the naval importance of Almirante Bay, Chiriqui Lagoon, and the Pearl Islands, all three of which now lay within the territory of the week-old republic. "Considering the recent political changes on the Isthmus," the General Board delicately suggested, "this seems an opportune moment to bring the subject once more to your attention and to request you consider it in any new negotiations that may be undertaken."[34]

But it was not an opportune moment. The Roosevelt administration had recognized the independence of Panama with a haste that bordered on the indecent, but it was also anxious to prove to a skeptical world that the Panamanian revolt had been genuine and the new state not a puppet of Washington. Hence there were no negotiations. Nor did the Navy get State Department support in 1904 when it argued that three articles in the new American treaty with Panama authorized the United States to purchase land and establish such naval stations

[32] SDML, Hay to Long, 11 January 1902, enclosing copy of Minister Merry's dispatch of 6 December 1901. Also, Long to Hay, 17 January 1902.

[33] SDML, Hay to Long, 18 January 1902.

[34] SDML, Moody to Hay, 10 November 1903, enclosing General Board report of the same date.

and fortifications as might seem necessary for the defense of the canal.[35] Whether these clauses in the Panama treaty might eventually have borne fruit and produced naval stations outside the limits of the Canal Zone was a matter never put to a final test. In 1906 there were new studies within the military establishment of the defense needs of the proposed canal. A special National Coast Defense Board concluded—and its verdict was sustained by the Joint Board of the two services—that it would be sufficient to fortify the termini of the canal itself and to include the necessary coaling stations within these fortifications.[36] This decision, reversing the postulates of the preceding years, finally brought an end to the Navy's unrewarded search for bases on or near the Isthmus and Central America. The General Board's revised list of desired bases in 1906 specifically eliminated Chiriqui Lagoon, Almirante Bay, and the Pearl Islands. Since all of the requirements for the defense of the canal could be met by fortifications at the termini, "outside depots may be dispensed with."[37]

Guantanamo Bay, astride the Windward Passage at the southeastern tip of Cuba, was, however, the prize which the Navy most avidly sought. The first formal meeting of the General Board took place on April 17, 1900. In the course of that meeting the officers present voted unanimously to inform their civilian superiors that, of all possible sites for a naval base in the West Indies, their first choice was Guantanamo.[38]

This unanimity, however, was deceptive, for both before and after this recommendation there was considerable debate in naval circles about the appropriate sites to be selected in Cuba. Two years earlier the War Board of 1898 had been unable to choose between the respective merits of Santiago and Guantanamo; even after its decision of April 1900 the General Board had second thoughts, and it was not until a year and a half later that a 3-2 vote reconfirmed the earlier recommendation that Guantanamo was the most important location in Cuba.[39] Adding complexity was the fact that General Leonard Wood, the military governor of Cuba, preferred Santiago and, as was his custom, expressed considerable dissatisfaction with the Navy's choice.[40]

Moreover, with the passage of time the Navy's appetite for Cuban bases actually increased. Towards the end of 1900 it asked the Department of State to obtain both Guantanamo and Cienfuegos in any set-

[35] GB, Letters, III, Dewey to Morton, 29 September 1904.
[36] JB, Minutes, Dewey to Bonaparte and Taft, 2 April 1906.
[37] GB, Letters, IV, Dewey to Bonaparte, 12 April 1906.
[38] GB, Proceedings, 17 April 1900.
[39] GB, Proceedings, 26 November 1901 and Letters, III, Dewey to Bonaparte, 1 February 1901, a summary of naval opinion about Guantanamo.
[40] Wood Papers, Wood to Julian Cendoya, 29 August 1904.

tlement with Cuba. A year later, and after the passage of the Platt amendment, it had expanded the list of desired sites to four, having added Havana and Nipe Bay to the two previously mentioned. The General Board was at pains to insist that, while Guantanamo was the single most important location, naval needs in Cuba could not be satisfied by less than four bases. Naval spokesmen launched a special effort to obtain a base in the harbor of Havana, the capital of the new republic. On behalf of his admirals, Secretary Long addressed a personal plea to President Roosevelt to enlist his support in convincing the reluctant Cubans that the United States could better protect them from foreign enemies if it had a naval station at Havana. "The Platt amendment makes provision for stations at such points as shall be agreed with you," Long wrote, "and the very fact that in all past time the neighborhood of Havana has been recognized as the proper place for a naval station would probably weigh very much with you in regarding it as the proper place for the future."[41] The argument for Havana, incidentally, was primarily political. Whereas Guantanamo was the most strategic location in the West Indies in view of its location on the Windward Passage, Havana, as the center of government, was regarded as the most likely location for an enemy attack—and also, though this was not mentioned in writing, the most likely location for an American intervention in Cuba should that ever prove necessary.

Naval officers could never complain of a lack of general civilian support for their Cuban goals. President, Secretary of State, and Congress all insisted upon naval stations. The Platt amendment made it a precondition of the American evacuation of Cuba and the establishment of a free Cuban government that the Cubans "sell or lease to the United States lands necessary for coaling or naval stations at certain specified points to be agreed with the President of the United States."[42] Roosevelt was adamant. In the spring of 1902, when the Cubans apparently wanted to place some limits upon the cession of bases and the rights to be accorded the United States, Roosevelt inquired of Hay if there was anything more that he personally could do. As he put it in another letter, "Whatever is done about reciprocity, the naval stations are to be ceded and in the near future. . . . The question itself is not a matter open to discussion by the Cubans. It is already contained in their constitution, and no discussion concerning it will be enter-

---

[41] Nav Rec Confid Ltrs, Long to Roosevelt, 13 December 1901. On the "political" aspects of the Navy's interest in Havana, see GB, Letters, I, Dewey to Long, 1 November 1901. For the 1900 requests, SDML, Long to Hay, 21 December 1900, enclosing the General Board report of 7 December.

[42] For the complete text of the Cuban-American Treaty of 1903, see, among others, A. S. Link and William Leary, eds., *The Diplomacy of World Power* (London, 1970), 70-72.

tained."[43] In 1903, faced with further Cuban delays, T.R. began looking about for his Big Stick. Would it be possible, he wondered "to let
the Cuban people know as delicately as possible that those coaling stations must be ours, and that they are laying themselves up for grave
trouble in the future if they do not immediately put them in our possession." Rumors that the Cuban congress might adjourn without final
action led Roosevelt to ask his Secretary of War, "What do you think
of this: Would it not be a good plan to put our troops thus peaceably
on the lands we intend to take as coaling stations?"[44] As with Roosevelt
so with Hay. Never did the Secretary of State retreat from the position
that the obligation to cede coaling stations was "a substantial part of
their constitution" and therefore not negotiable.[45]

The Navy's difficulties, then, were with the Cubans who, having
been compelled to accept the Platt amendment and incorporate it in
their constitution, tried thereafter to salvage whatever they possibly
could from the situation. They were dead set against yielding a base
at Havana, strongly opposed the cession of four bases to the United
States, and objected to the inclusion of the so-called Fort Toro area
within the proposed boundaries of Guantanamo. At other times they
tried to combine the issue of the coaling stations with American recognition of the long disputed Cuban claim to the Isle of Pines, arguing
that the United States should definitively relinquish that island before
they turned any bases over to the United States.[46] By the spring of
1903 those Americans who were dealing with the Cubans had lost most
of their patience; the American minister in Havana, Herbert Squiers,
was writing to Hay that the Cubans "are twisting and squirming in
every possible direction to escape their obligations, even such as they
have already agreed to."[47]

But Roosevelt and his Department of State, though insistent about
the cession of bases, were willing to take some account of Cuban sensibilities. President Palma was told as early as the spring of 1902 that the
American government appreciated the Cuban objection to an American naval base in Havana and recognized that it would not be fair for
the United States to insist upon maintaining its own armed forces in

[43] Roosevelt, *Letters*, III, 367, Roosevelt to Hay, 23 October 1902. See also p. 85,
Roosevelt to Root, 1 June 1901, as well as the summary in Jessup, *Root*, I, ch. 15.
[44] Papers of Elihu Root, Manuscripts Division, Library of Congress, Roosevelt to
Root, 15 March 1903.
[45] Papers of John Hay, Manuscripts Division, Library of Congress, Hay to Squiers,
24 October 1902.
[46] R. H. Fitzgibbon, *Cuba and the United States, 1900-1935* (Menasha, Wisc.,
1935), 94-112, a good summary. See also David Healy, *The United States in Cuba,
1898-1902* (Madison, 1963), 143-44.
[47] Fitzgibbons, *Cuba*, 105.

the immediate vicinity of their capital city.[48] John Hay, rightly suspecting that a number of influential Americans wished to keep the Isle of Pines under the American flag, privately admitted to Squiers that he did not blame the Cubans for "being suspicious of our Senate and feeling that it wants both coaling stations and the Isle of Pines."[49] While he would not put the bases and the Isle of Pines in the same package, he did sign a separate treaty with Cuba—a treaty that the U. S. Senate, in fact, would not ratify—which relinquished the Isle of Pines and did so "in consideration of the concessions of coaling and naval stations."[50] Still, President and Secretary of State always maintained firm pressure on Palma's government. In late 1902, for example, the Cuban government formally protested the continuing presence of American artillerymen in the forts of Havana. To soothe ruffled Cuban feelings the Army was prepared to withdraw this small force, but the War Department suggested—and Roosevelt put its suggestion in the form of a message to Palma—that the best solution for the problem would be for the Cuban government to settle the question of bases and then simply let the United States reassign the artillerymen to these new locations.[51]

Naval leaders, needless to say, were not entirely pleased with the administration's willingness to make some concessions to the Cuban point of view. Admiral Taylor later told his version of a meeting—attended by President Palma, Secretaries Hay and Moody, and himself —at which the Cuban chief executive informed the Americans that his country would never agree to include Fort Toro within the boundaries of the Guantanamo reservation. To Taylor's great displeasure, Hay sided with the Cubans and accepted a boundary line far closer to Cuban wishes than to those of the General Board.[52] Moreover, the administration was willing to settle for the cession of two bases and even informed the Cubans of this at a time when the Navy was still firmly insisting that four were absolutely essential. Hence the treaty that was finally signed in the summer of 1903 provided for but two sites, Guantanamo and Bahia Hondo, the latter meant to serve as a substitute for Havana but one which would still provide the Navy with a station on the northern coast of Cuba.[53]

The Navy, however, soon decided that Bahia Hondo had little if any

48 Hay Papers, Hay to Squiers, 24 October 1902; Roosevelt, *Letters*, III, 369-70, Roosevelt to Palma, 27 October 1902.

49 Hay Papers, Hay to Squiers, 19 May 1903.

50 Fitzgibbon, *Cuba*, 99.

51 SDML, Root to Roosevelt, 25 October 1902.

52 GB, File 406, undated memorandum (probably March 1902) prepared by Captain Swift. Also, in the same file, personal letter from Admiral J. E. Pillsbury to Dewey, 27 September 1906.

53 Fitzgibbon, *Cuba*, 99.

potential as a naval station, while almost as quickly it began to express dissatisfaction with the size of the Guantanamo reservation. By April of 1905 the General Board was urging the Department of State to re-open negotiations with the Cuban government for an enlargement of that base. Guantanamo, the admirals contended, could not be de-fended from attack unless artillery could be mounted outside the exist-ing boundaries. Therefore, in the pious words of the General Board, it should "be impressed upon the Cuban authorities that it is impera-tive for the assurance of their own political integrity that Guantanamo be *securely* held by the United States."[54] It was thus but a short step to the next formal suggestion that the United States exchange its un-wanted lease at Bahia Hondo for an enlargement of the naval station at Guantanamo. Since the Cubans had always been sensitive about the Bahia Hondo lease because of its proximity to Havana, the first though highly tentative overtures began as early as 1905.[55]

The second occupation of Cuba in 1906 whetted the Navy's hopes for success in its quest for enlargement of Guantanamo. In September of that year American warships and a special delegation, headed by Secretary of War Taft, were dispatched to Cuba to cope with a rebel-lion against the Palma regime. In the circumstances Admiral J. E. Pills-bury, commander-in-chief of the Atlantic fleet, unburdened himself to Dewey:

> It looks very much now if the United States would again have pos-session of the island, although this may be temporary. I have always believed, as did many others, that when we had possession of the island before, we should have taken the amount of land necesssary for the defense of the naval station, no matter what the Cubans might say afterwards. If we gain temporary possession once more, wouldn't this be a good time for the General Board to do something about enlargement?[56]

The General Board did think it appropriate, and, after some dis-agreement, eventually secured the endorsement of the Joint Board for the proposed exchange and enlargement. Thus in April of 1907 there was a formal request to the Department of State to open negotiations. The American military establishment relied heavily upon the fact that the Cubans would be under duress, though the Joint Board tried to be circumspect in alluding to the advantages it anticipated from the American occupation of Cuba. "The alteration in our relations with

[54] GB, Proceedings, 26 April 1905.
[55] GB, File 406, confidential memorandum of Lt. Commander Charles Rogers, 2 May 1906.
[56] GB, File 406, Pillsbury to Dewey, 27 September 1906.

Cuba," it suggested, "may make the government of that island now more willing than ever to accede to a request for extension."[57]

Elihu Root, however, quickly dashed the Navy's hopes. The failure of the Cuban "experiment" in 1906 had been a genuine embarrassment to the Roosevelt administration. In point of fact, the second occupation had been assumed with the greatest reluctance. Root himself was increasingly conscious of growing anti-Americanism in the Latin countries. He therefore sent back the polite but firm reply which has previously been alluded to:

> It would afford me pleasure to give your request the usual formal direction, were it not for the anomalous position in which such a request would place this Government if addressed to an administration which, while representing the Republic of Cuba, is in substance and fact carried on by the United States through its own agencies. It does not strike me as suitable that this Government should negotiate with itself to enlarge or modify the conditions of an engagement which, under a treaty, it has entered into with the independent government of Cuba for the use of the naval station at Guantanamo.[58]

And that was that, the line to which Root adhered throughout his tenure as Secretary of State. The following year the Joint Board made another attempt, again to no avail, to interest the Department of State, using the argument that the Cuban predilection for civil war always posed the possibility of American intervention and made the Guantanamo base of the greatest importance. Moreover, the admirals now at last confessed the real issue that lay behind their desire for the extension: the lack of water at Guantanamo, not the alleged strategic or political value of additional land. The Navy, despite tireless efforts, had been unable to find a source of fresh water on the Guantanamo reservation—and this, more than any other consideration, had spurred its many requests for extension.[59] But it was not until the second occupation had ended and until the Taft administration had come into office that the State Department was finally willing to act. Eventually, as will later be noted, the Taft administration plunged into another seemingly endless round of negotiations with the Cubans who, in their turn, again demonstrated an uncanny ability to thwart the naval purpose. Indeed, the one constant in the entire Cuban base equation was the skill with which Cuban authorities, even under the Platt amend-

57 GB, Letters, IV, Dewey to Metcalf, 30 January 1907, and File 406, Meyer to Knox, 13 July 1909. See also JB, Minutes, 22 March 1907.

58 SDNF, Case 4631/3-5, Root to Metcalf, 6 April 1907.

59 GB, File 406, Meyer to Knox, 13 July 1909; JB, Minutes, Dewey to Taft, 29 January 1908; SDNF, Case 4631/11-12, Meyer to Knox, 13 July 1909.

ment, were able to keep the Navy from attaining its goals. One conclusion is abundantly evident: had it not been for the American insistence that the Platt amendment serve as the precondition for Cuban independence, there never would have been even a single American naval station anywhere on the island of Cuba.

While the Navy's desire for Cuban bases was steadfast, its interest in and influence upon the unsuccessful American attempt to purchase the Danish West Indies, (or Virgin Islands) was less clear. Admiral Bradford, admittedly, was personally very much involved, but naval records indicate that in the Danish matter the Navy followed rather than initiated the action. Moreover, by the turn of the century, the attempted purchase already had a long and complex history. An earlier treaty for the purchase of the islands had failed in the Senate in 1870; the Republican platform of 1896 had called for their annexation; and at the time of the Spanish-American war the advocates of expansionism had manifested a clear interest in them. But the Navy itself was often equivocal about their value. The Naval War Board of 1898, for example, had pointed to the general strategic importance of the area around the Dominican Republic, Puerto Rico, and the Danish West Indies, but it had focused its primary attention upon the Windward Passage. Moreover, in selecting possible sites for naval bases in the northeastern Caribbean, Mahan and his associates had opted for Samana Bay in the Dominican Republic rather than St. Thomas in the Virgin Islands. Their reasoning was primarily financial, for they assumed that the United States would have to purchase all of the Danish islands to get St. Thomas, whereas they thought that Samana Bay could be acquired by itself. Nor were the naval advisers of 1898 strongly committed to their recommendation. At the end of their report they appended a paragraph which noted that they had "just heard" of another promising site for a coaling station in the northeastern Caribbean—the island of Culebra, only 55 miles from Puerto Rico and 23 from St. Thomas.[60] It is true that in the fall of 1898 Admiral Bradford sent a special memorandum to John Hay emphasizing the importance of purchasing the Virgin Islands from Denmark, but the main thrust of his argument was that they should be obtained in order to keep them from falling into the hands of Germany. Even Bradford confessed that, with other sites for naval stations now available in the area, the islands actually had less strategic value to the Navy than before the Spanish-American War.[61]

After 1898, as we have seen, the Navy generally regarded the Wind-

[60] GB, File 414-1, Report of Naval War Board, 1898.
[61] Charles Tansill, *The Purchase of the Danish West Indies* (Baltimore, 1932), 224, 390-92.

ward Passage as of greater strategic importance than the passages to the east of the Dominican Republic. It did not, however, neglect the northeastern Caribbean. The admirals could on occasion argue that Puerto Rico was "isolated" and could not adequately be defended if the only American naval station was located at Guantanamo and the fleet organized for the defense of the Windward Passage. Indeed, during the several years when the General Board was enthusiastic about the proliferation of bases, Dewey could be quite expansive about general needs in the northeastern Caribbean, that is, in the area of the Virgin Islands. "In view of the Isthmian canal and the German settlements in South America," he wrote in 1901, "every additional acquisition by the United States in the West Indies is of value. The further east the acquisition, the greater the value as against aggression from European bases; the further south the acquisition, the greater the value for aggressive action on our part against localities in South America."[62] Stated in less provocative terms, Dewey's argument was that the northeastern Caribbean had a special value in protecting American interests in northern South America, that is, from the Orinoco to the Amazon.

Nevertheless, the Navy was not deeply involved in the informal and formal efforts to purchase the Danish islands which got underway in 1899 and which lasted until the fall of 1902 when the treaty of purchase was finally rejected by the Danish legislature. At Hay's request, to be sure, Admiral Bradford met with and encouraged the Danish adventurer, Captain Lee Christmas, when that colorful promoter sought to initiate an American offer in 1899. On the other hand, the ensuing negotiations were entirely in the hands of Hay and his advisers, especially Henry White, while the Department of State, in contrast to the way it handled negotiations for Cuban or Isthmian bases, communicated very little with the Navy and showed minimum interest in requesting the opinions of the General Board.[63] In point of fact, if the Navy had been asked, it might well have been embarrassed, for American naval authorities were poorly informed about the various harbors in the Virgin group. There was information in the naval archives about St. Thomas, but as late as the fall of 1901 Dewey had to confess that "St. John, in the Danish group, offers, as far as we know, a most excellent harbor; but our knowledge of it is limited, as it has been little visited by our officers."[64] To remedy this deficiency the Navy sought and gained permission to send one of its vessels to the Danish islands to

[62] GB, Letters, I, Dewey to Long, 12 November 1901.

[63] Tansill, *Danish West Indies*, 240, and Allan Nevins, *Henry White* (New York, 1930), 203-16.

[64] SDML, Long to Hay, copy of General Board No. 187, Dewey to Long, 12 November 1901.

examine various harbors and anchorages. The Danish government, however, became suspicious and began to ask questions about the purpose of the naval visit. As a consequence Hay finally counselled the General Board that it would be wise to postpone its examination "until the negotiations upon which we are now engaged with Denmark shall be decided one way or the other."[65]

Moreover, while the Navy sought a strong position in the northeastern Caribbean, the difficulty was that there always seemed to be several possible locations. During the time of the negotiations with Denmark there was still talk about the possibility of acquiring Samana Bay, the Dominican harbor long considered a great naval value. More important, there were the Puerto Rican sites—San Juan and the island of Culebra—which had the distinct advantage of already being American territory. Indeed, in the summer of 1901, while negotiations with Denmark were still proceeding, the General Board decided that it would go ahead and select its preferred site for a northeastern Caribbean base without waiting for the eventual settlement of the Danish question. Its choice fell on Culebra, with San Juan to serve as a supply and reserve collier base.[66]

There was only one formal report submitted by the General Board on the subject of the Danish West Indies. This document, moreover, did not reach the Department of State until mid-November of 1901, scarcely two months before the final treaty was signed and almost two years after the formal negotiations had begun. Even this document showed the ambivalence of the General Board's formal position on the Danish islands. While it endorsed their acquisition, it dwelt principally with the general strategic importance of the northeastern Caribbean, the naval value of Haiti and Santo Domingo, and the danger to the United States if Germany managed to acquire the Danish islands. It placed so much emphasis upon the German threat that it appeared as if the General Board was less interested in the islands for the sake of the United States Navy than as a means of denying them to the empire of William II. The strongest statement about their value to the United States Navy was simply the assertion that "in addition to such points as Puerto Rico (and Culebra) . . . both St. Thomas and St. John would be valuable possessions, while their occupation by a foreign power would be a decided menace to us."[67]

In summary, then, the driving force behind the attempted purchase of the Danish West Indies was not located in the General Board. The

[65] SDML, Hay to Long, 1 and 26 April 1901.

[66] GB, Proceedings, 26 June 1901, and Letters, I, Dewey to Long, 25 June and 21 August 1901.

[67] SDML, copy of Dewey to Long, 12 November 1901, as cited.

Navy was certainly interested in establishing a position in the northeastern Caribbean, but other sites seemed available, and, when the Navy did express its formal opinion, it emphasized the importance of denying the Danish group to Germany. This is not to say that the General Board would not have gratefully accepted their purchase. Early in 1902, when the formal treaty was finally signed, several members of the Board wrote confidently about their "probable acquisition" and began to lay plans for naval surveys of the forthcoming American possession.[68] And the Danish islands appeared, as we have seen, in the list of bases submitted by the General Board in the fall of 1902. When the treaty failed to pass the Danish legislature, the Navy was convinced that German machinations were to blame—a sentiment shared, it must be added, by many Americans including the President and the Secretary of State. The General Board had absolutely no doubts. It was Germany, wrote Admiral Sperry, which "pulled the strings" and led the Danes to reject the treaty.[69] The General Board, indeed, had been almost hypnotized by the alleged German threat from the very beginning. Its one report to the Department of State in 1901 was studded with blunt references to "German interests." It was in the more sophisticated offices of the Department of State some one altered the document by substituting "European" for "German."[70]

Two other sites in which the Navy was interested—Chimbote in Peru and the Galapagos Islands, the possession of Ecuador—were seriously pursued for only a relatively brief time during the short period of intense interest in the proliferation of overseas bases. Neither project culminated in success; both had dimensions of comic opera. Yet both also indicate other significant aspects of the Navy's post-1898 quest for bases: the way in which interested representatives of the Department of State were sometimes more zealous than the admirals as well as the fact that certain Latin countries were tempted to use the lure of naval stations as a way of involving the United States in their problems—or, at the minimum, of easing a strain on their national finances. American imperialism, after all, was not entirely a one-way street. In not a few countries there were special interest groups, revolutionary factions, and even governments which imagined that their own advantage would be served by American involvement or intervention.

Of all the nations on the west coast of either Central or South America, only Peru managed to qualify in the eyes of the United States

[68] GB, Letters, I, Crowninshield to Long, 27 February 1902, and Nav Rec AF 8, Bradford to Long, 25 January 1902.

[69] Sperry Papers, Sperry to Charles Sperry, Jr., 29 November 1904. For Hay's opinion, see Hay Papers, Hay to Roosevelt, 15 April 1903.

[70] SDML, copy of Dewey to Long, 12 November 1901, as cited.

Navy as a "friend." Naval planners, when considering such states as Colombia, Ecuador, Chile, and Peru, invariably singled out the latter as the only reliable country. The reason for Peruvian "friendship" was simple: Peru wished to enlist the support of the United States in the three-cornered Tacna-Arica dispute, a permanent, never-ending territorial quarrel between Peru, Ecuador, and Chile. Over the years the United States had, in point of fact, tended to sympathize with the Peruvians, especially against the Chilean claims. It is therefore not surprising that the government in Lima was tempted to make offers to the United States, especially at such moments when the Tacna-Arica controversy seemed to be in a new stage of crisis.[71]

There had been correspondence in the 1890s between the State Department and its Peruvian legation about the possible acquisition of Chimbote. In 1902 Theodore Roosevelt asked the General Board for a memorandum on its naval value, while, as previously noted, the Board had included Ferrol and Samanco bays (that is, Chimbote) on its 1902 list of sites that might be desirable in the future and which, in the Board's assessment, might "readily be obtained" from a friendly Peru.[72] The Peruvians were certainly friendly, but the price was hardly right. Their offer in 1902 of a 99-year lease on Chimbote was notable for the number and variety of attached strings: an American guarantee of Peruvian territorial integrity, American mediation of the Tacna-Arica dispute, an American "gift" to Peru of ten million dollars if the disputed territories were awarded to Chile, the construction of fortifications at Callao, the gift of several third-class warships, and reductions by the United States on the duties levied against several Peruvian products that entered the American market.

However, by the time that this Peruvian "offer" actually reached the Navy in 1903, the General Board was emerging into its new period of caution about the advisability of adding new holdings. It simply sat on the issue for some time, then finally produced a guarded document as ingenious as it was circumspect. A coaling station at Chimbote, Dewey advised, might have considerable strategic advantages if, in the future, the United States developed "certain political attitudes" towards the republics of South America. But, he quickly added, the General Board refrained as a matter of policy from offering its own opinions about international relations and fully understood that any decision about Chimbote would be a political decision made by the civilian administration. Thus, his report continued, "the General Board just wishes to

---

[71] Seward Livermore, "American Strategic Diplomacy in the South Pacific," *Pacific Historical Review*, XII, no. 1 (March 1943), 42-49. Also, GB, Letters, III, Dewey endorsement on report of 24 March 1903.

[72] SDML, Moody to Hay, 21 November 1902, enclosing General Board report of 7 October 1902. See also GB, Proceedings, 28 August 1902.

indicate which is the best port in case the government wishes to act." After this typical disclaimer of interest in political affairs, Dewey happily switched to purely military considerations. Since the new line of the General Board was the concentration rather than the diffusion of naval energy, the recommendation was that the purchase should be deferred until a later date.[73]

Whenever attempts were made to revive the issue in the next few years, the General Board adhered to the "standard" reply about the concentration of naval strength. It spurned overtures that originated with the American consul at Callao, showed no interest in the inevitable offer that came from a group of American promoters who claimed to hold rights to coal fields in the area of Chimbote, and failed to respond favorably to reports from Admiral Henry Glass, the commander of the Pacific fleet, when he found that the American consul at Callao and "prominent" Peruvians were anxious to lease the bay to the Navy.[74] The Navy, indeed, became so provoked by these offers that the General Board finally voted unanimously against accepting Chimbote even if the Peruvian government offered it unconditionally to the United States—an unlikely prospect, in any event! To make absolutely certain, Admiral Glass was sent specific orders. He might examine the facilities of Chimbote, but he must realize that his examination was solely for the purpose of preparing a plan of defense to be used if Chimbote should become an advanced base in time of war in the Pacific and was not meant to be a prelude to any proposal for a lease or concession.[75]

Chimbote did not again become an item for discussion until the very end of the Roosevelt years. Once more the Peruvians took the initiative. Combs, the American minister, reported to Root a conversation with the Peruvian Foreign Minister: "After discussing the port of Chimbote . . . and offering it to our government for the use of its fleet at any time, he brought up what was evidently the purpose for which he had invited me"—naturally, a request for American help in the latest round of the Tacna-Arica fight. The State Department was sceptical, and Alvey Adee's marginal notation was tart: "Peru offers us Chimbote for our naval vessels. *Timeo Danaos.*"[76] The issue was left

[73] On the Peruvian "offer," see SDML, Hay to Moody, 28 January 1903, enclosing dispatch from the legation in Peru dated 21 December 1902. In the same file see also, Hay to Moody, 12 February 1903. In the naval archives the best summary of negotiations is GB, Letters, VI, Dewey to Meyer, 8 April 1909. On the Navy's reaction in 1903, see GB, Letters, II, Dewey to Moody, 24 March 1903 and SDML, Darling to Hay, 8 April 1903.

[74] GB, Letters, III, Taylor to Glass, 19 April 1904.

[75] GB, Proceedings, 19 December 1904, and Letters, III, Dewey to Glass, 9 December 1904.

[76] SDNF, Case 944/57, Combs to Root, 12 February 1909.

pending for the incoming Taft administration, but, regretably, the men who assisted Philander Knox failed to share Adee's fears of Greeks and Peruvians. Chimbote, consequently, again became an issue.

One reason why naval interest in Chimbote never became very strong was that, in the eyes of the strategists, Peruvian harbors were less valuable than the Galapagos Islands belonging to Ecuador. These Pacific islands, located on the Equator and presumed to command the Pacific approaches to any canal route, were a major focus of the Navy's attention for a number of years. In the comedy of errors that marked the various negotiations to acquire the Galapagos, two features were constant: the intention of Ecuador to conduct a virtual raid on the United States Treasury, and the passion with which representatives of the Department of State sought, always in vain, to advance their version of the Navy's interest.

As with Chimbote, there had been stirrings of American interest in the Galapagos before the Spanish-American War, but the principal attempts to acquire a naval base began early in 1899. Archibald Sampson, the American minister in Quito suggested their purchase, while Admiral Royal B. Bradford at the Bureau of Equipment was naturally the naval officer most enthusiastic about the proposal. By mid-April of 1899, John Hay had authorized Sampson to make discreet inquiries about the possibility of leasing a naval station.[77] What emerged from a seemingly endless exchange of reports and cables was the great discrepancy between the value assigned to the Galapagos, on the one hand, by the United States Navy and, on the other, by the Ecuadorian government of President Alfaro. Bradford, anticipating purchase "at a moderate cost," suggested one million dollars as a fair price for the entire group or, if that were unacceptable, a lease on Chatham Island at $5,000 per year. President Alfaro appraised his real estate considerably higher. Twenty million dollars was the price tag which he placed on Chatham Island by itself. Early in the proceedings the Ecuadorians for the first, but far from the last, time began to hint, with remarkable lack of subtlety, that other nations lusted after the Galapagos and were prepared to pay the handsome sums that the niggardly government in Washington rejected. The French were reported as offering 300 million francs—then the equivalent of 60 million dollars—for the entire group, while England, Germany, and several private com-

[77] GB, File 414-1, an undated memorandum (probably late 1902 or early 1903) summarizes all the correspondence between the State and Navy Departments on the Galapagos between 1899 and 1902. See also SDML, Long to Hay, 14 April 1899, enclosing a Bradford memorandum on the subject. In addition to Livermore's account in "American Strategic Diplomacy," see J. Fred Rippy and E. Parks, "The Galapagos Islands: A Neglected Phase of American Strategic Diplomacy," *Journal of Hispanic History*, IX, no. 1 (March 1940), 37-45.

panies were said to be seriously interested in all or part of the Galapagos.[78]

Minister Sampson excelled in reporting the fearsome details of any and all rumors to Washington. It was typical of his approach to inform the Department of State that the Ecuadorians believed that the danger of European seizure of the Galapagos was intensifying and that, in these circumstances, he needed additional instructions on the procedures he should follow to negotiate their purchase. His eagerness to close a deal was more than obvious. Congress, too, added some pressure, for in December 1899 a resolution was passed requesting information from the administration about the reported danger that Ecuador would sell the Galapagos to a foreign power and about the steps that were being taken to prevent such a dire eventuality.[79]

The record of the ensuing negotiations is a record of confusion. At times it appeared certain that the United States could acquire a lease without any difficulty if it would accept the Ecuadorian price tag. But at other times the President of Ecuador, like political leaders on the Isthmus, contended that it was "beyond his power" to sell national territory and that all would depend on the reaction of the Ecuadorian congress. The game of the Galapagos continued through 1901, with the State Department—each time at the Navy's request—patiently instructing Sampson to pursue each and every new lead. By the end of the year, however, civilian patience was beginning to wear very thin. When the Navy submitted yet another request for a further effort, Adee scribbled a note suggesting that Sampson might be instructed to tell the government of Ecuador that it was doubtful if any European power would care to purchase the Galapagos "in view of the well-understood feeling in the United States that such a proceeding would not be favorably regarded by our Government and people."[80] It was a clear forecast of the policy eventually adopted by both State Department and Navy after all efforts had failed: namely, that while the United States was not going to purchase the islands, no European power would be permitted to acquire them either.

The Navy retained its interest, as already indicated, up until the very moment of submitting its consolidated list of desired bases in the fall of 1902. With their location on the Pacific route to the canal area, the Galapagos were of particular significance during that period when the provisions of the Clayton-Bulwer treaty were still in force and

78 There are numerous documents in SDML, especially Long to Hay, 11 July 1899, 13 July 1900, and 2 December 1901. See also Department of State, Diplomatic Dispatches, from the American Minister in Ecuador, Sampson to Hay, No. 194, 31 March 1900.

79 SDML, copy of Senate Resolution of 6 December 1899.

80 SDML, marginal comments of Alvey Adee on Long to Hay, 2 December 1901.

when the first Hay-Pauncefote treaty was under consideration, for they lay outside the geographical area in which there could be any treaty restrictions on the United States or its navy. There were periods of considerable optimism in the Navy about the prospects for success, especially when, according to the naval interpretation of Ecuadorian politics, the liberal and reportedly pro-American party won control of the republic's government.[81] Naval spokesmen, of course, complained about the improbable value placed on the islands by the government in Quito; even an enthusiast like Bradford termed the asking price "not only ridiculous but exorbitant." Still the Navy dispatched inquiry after inquiry to the Department of State inquiring about "progress" and sometimes offering gratuitous advice of its own—such as the suggestion that the diplomats ought to remind Quito that American possession of the Galapagos would better enable the United States to help Ecuador in preserving the Monroe Doctrine.[82] A certain edginess even crept into the naval correspondence when repeated inquiries produced no favorable results. On one occasion, when the Department of State had again asked the Navy to state its opinion of the value of the Galapagos, the reply was almost brusque. In previous correspondence, the Bureau of Equipment said, it had fully set forth its views on the desirability of the islands, the proper location for bases, and the price that might properly be paid. "The notes of the Bureau have been very full. The Bureau has in no manner changed its opinions on this subject; as a matter of fact, each step in the progress of construction of a trans-Isthmian canal accentuates its importance."[83]

In the summer of 1902 the Navy's attitude began to change. Even Bradford had become increasingly aware of the difficulty, if not impossibility, of reaching an agreeable price; the selection of the Panama route led the Navy to pay attention to the strategic potential of the Pearl Islands, far closer to the actual Pacific terminus of the canal; while the whole issue of the desirable number of foreign naval stations was about to be raised. In any event, once the General Board reached its decision to strike the Galapagos from its list, the admirals stayed with that decision. Future inquiries brought from the Navy an almost standard reply: the Navy no longer wanted to acquire the Galapagos but believed American interests would be distinctly menaced if they fell into the hands of a European power. In 1904 Sampson tried to scare up the bogey of transfer to Chile. But the General Board, when consulted by the State Department, was not impressed. Chile was not

[81] SDML, Long to Hay, 26 March 1900.

[82] For signs of the Navy's irritation as well as its tendency to offer gratuitous advice, see SDML, Long to Hay, 13 July 1900, and Bradford to Long, 30 November 1901.

[83] SDML, Long to Hay, enclosing report of Admiral Bradford, 7 February 1902.

a naval power and could scarcely hope to command the Pacific. Chilean acquisition of the Galapagos was therefore "a matter of indifference." To which the State Department understandably concurred.[84]

Archibald Sampson was by this time the only onetime enthusiast for the islands whose ardor had not been dampened. Long after it was obvious that the game had been lost he kept batting up new proposals. In April of 1903 John Hay was moved finally to try his hand at discouraging him. It was undesirable, Hay wrote, to initiate any new efforts, for "Every time the matter has been breached, the exigencies of the government of Ecuador shows to be beyond anything we could reasonably entertain. I am unable to give you any instructions at present, except to transmit to this Department any offer or suggestion which may be made you directly by the Ecuadorian government." Given this slightest of openings Sampson naturally was ready by the end of the year with still another proposal, this time a lease for the islands to be obtained through the instrumentality of an American loan to Ecuador.[85]

Something in the Ecuadorian air—possibly the altitude of Quito itself—affected those who represented the Department of State in that country. William R. Fox, Sampson's eventual successor as minister, became similarly enamored of the Galapagos. By 1906 he was busy reporting that only a revolution in Ecuador had prevented a French loan to that country which would have been secured by a lien on the Galapagos.[86] By the following February, Fox was advancing the schemes of a certain C. E. Brooks who wished to serve as go-between in a new scheme. Alvey Adee alerted Root with a covering note:

> Minister Sampson tried hard to induce us to negotiate for the Galapagos and snarled himself up somewhat, but—on the repeated advice of the Navy—we told him that we did not wish the islands and warned him not to encourage any proposals for their sale to us. The Galapagos question has cropped up from time to time ever since I came into the Department. We have answered again and again that we don't want them ourselves and will not let Ecuador sell them to any non-American power. But—Ecuador needs twenty million dollars.[87]

[84] On the Navy's eventual loss of interest, see Nav Rec Confid Ltrs, Taylor to Moody, 8 September 1902; GB, Letters, II, Dewey endorsement on memorandum of 30 December 1903. On the Chilean "scare," SDML, Moody to Hay, 14 January 1904.

[85] Hay Papers, Hay to Sampson, 15 April 1903; SDML, Adee to Moody, 16 December 1903, enclosing Sampson dispatch of 31 October 1903.

[86] SDNF, Case 1305, Fox to Root, 9 September 1906.

[87] SDNF, Case 1305/1, Adee memorandum for Root, attached to Fox dispatch of 1 February 1907.

On this occasion Root didn't bother to ask the Navy's opinion but did check with Paris to discover if by chance the rumors of French interest had substance. Pichon, the French Foreign Minister, issued the expected denials and added that, having once lived in the West Indies, he personally wished that he could sell all of France's West Indian possessions to the United States. (To which Adee, incidentally, noted that Pichon had the power to carry out his wish—"if we have any desire to buy more volcanoes."[88])

By 1908 Fox had found a German threat, "substantiated" by dozens of clippings from the Ecuadorian press, and even conjured up a Japanese menace. One of his clippings described a scheme whereby Ecuador would sell the Galapagos to Chile, after which the Chileans would, in turn, lease or sell them to Japan. "Men, perhaps countries, with foresight," Fox advised the Secretary of State, "are looking forward to the completion of the Isthmian Canal, and to a vantage ground to be gained by a foothold in these islands." He evoked no response. Elihu Root forwarded his latest information to the Navy, but the admirals took no action, and the materials simply ended up in a file in the Office of Naval Intelligence. The State Department returned the now standard reply: the Navy was disinterested in the Galapagos but the United States would permit no foreign nation to acquire them.[89] And there the matter rested until the stalwarts of the Taft State Department resurrected it for one last chance on the boards.

In its search for Latin American bases, then, the Navy received strong support from the Department of State—indeed, almost too much support from some of the Department's representatives. The number of occasions on which Hay authorized negotiations for naval stations indicated that he consciously assisted in the process of turning the Caribbean into an American lake, and was well aware of what the Navy claimed it needed to assure the defense of that sea and the projected canal. If this endeavor produced only Guantanamo, it was not through any deficiency in the structure of civil-military relations or differences between the civilian and the naval goals. The reasons were in Latin America—in the growing distrust of the Latin countries for American purposes, in their increasing reluctance to cede national territory, and, paradoxically, in the misguided efforts of some Latin regimes to use the lure of naval bases to involve the United States in their affairs.

[88] SDNF, Case 1305/4, Henry White to Root, 28 June 1907, with marginal comments by Adee.

[89] SDNF, Case 1305/10, Fox to Root, 20 April 1908; Nav Rec Subj File, WA-7, 08/294 Register, Office of Naval Intelligence reports on Ecuador, 1891-1918.

2. VENEZUELA AND THE GERMANS

In the colorful Caribbean career of Theodore Roosevelt no episode has been more controversial or subjected to such widely variant interpretations as the Anglo-German intervention in Venezuela in 1902-03. This European blockade produced a widespread belief in the United States that the Monroe Doctrine was under attack and was clearly a primary reason for Roosevelt's enunciation, two years later, of the famous "Roosevelt Corollary." During World War I Roosevelt publicly described the episode in terms of an "ultimatum" which he had served upon the recalcitrant government of William II and which compelled the Germans to arbitrate their dispute with the Venezuelans. For many years skeptical historians searched the records for evidence of such an ultimatum but concluded that Roosevelt's wartime version of the incident was yet another example of his propensity for myth-making. More recently, however, the detailed analyses of Seward Livermore and Howard Beale have indicated that there was more substance than shadow to Roosevelt's recollections. They contend, in brief, that the President may well have called the German attention to the presence of the American fleet in the Caribbean and used it as an instrument of policy to convey a warning to Germany that arbitration was preferable to intervention.[90]

But naval records, as Livermore noted, do not entirely resolve the controversy. They are partial and fragmentary; some bits of evidence, as with many documents, can be fitted into any of several possible interpretations; and the historian is therefore still tempted to claim either too little or too much.[91] Still, at the very least, the attitudes and opinions of a number of naval personnel who had first-hand involvement in the Venezuelan affair form a significant aspect of the entire episode.

The Navy quite clearly was among the first to raise the spectre of German intentions in Venezuela. Nearly two years before the debt episode reached its climax, the naval policymakers worked themselves into a considerable frenzy over alleged German interests in the tiny

[90] The standard interpretations are Dexter Perkins, *History of the Monroe Doctrine*, 214-23, and Henry Pringle, *Theodore Roosevelt* (New York, 1931), 198-203. The newer and more convincing arguments are to be found in Howard K. Beale, *Theodore Roosevelt and America's Rise to World Power* (Baltimore, 1956), 395 ff., and Seward Livermore's pioneering article, "Theodore Roosevelt, the American Navy, and the Venezuelan Crisis of 1902-03," *American Historical Review*, LII, no. 3 (April 1946), 452-71.

[91] Beale, for example, makes much of the decision to turn Culebra into a naval base. But he never points out that this decision was based not on the Venezuelan decision but primarily on the difficulties the Navy was then encountering in securing bases in Cuba. See Beale, *Roosevelt and America's Rise*, 416.

island of Margarita, which lies just off the coast of eastern Venezuela and is less than two hundred miles from British Trinidad. In March 1901 Commander Nathan Sargent of the *Scorpion*, a more or less permanent observer in these waters, filed a lengthy report which, as he put it, ought to be of interest to both the Navy and State Departments. Sargent claimed that Germany meant to acquire Margarita as a foothold on the northern coast of South America, a site which could also be used as a supply and coaling depot for the Imperial navy. His evidence was the recent visit of a German naval craft, the *Vineta*, to Margarita where it had spent three months in the summer of 1900 taking soundings and making surveys of many harbors. It was most unlikely, suggested Commander Sargent, that this was simply "unselfish hydrographic work for the benefit of mariners in general." Venezuela, moreover, had many debts to Germany and might, he thought, accept a compromise settlement by which her indebtedness would be cancelled in return for a 99-year lease on Margarita.[92] Sargent, incidentally, had already discussed his concerns with Herbert Loomis, the minister at Caracas, as well as with J. A. Orsini, the American consular agent at Carupano, a small Venezuelan port near Margarita. Orsini informed him that it was "common knowledge" among German merchants on Margarita that the Imperial government was about to lease the island and that it was no secret to them that the visit of the *Vineta* had been a preliminary step in this process.[93]

The General Board immediately forwarded Sargent's report to the State Department, even before making its own examination of his findings. It further requested that, when diplomatic relations permitted, Venezuela should be asked to let the United States make its own survey of Margarita and its environs. John Hay, in turn, launched his own inquiries in Berlin, soon receiving from the American chargé, John B. Jackson, a German denial of any interest in Margarita.[94] The Department appears to have been satisfied, though Senator Henry Cabot Lodge, that firm defender of the principles of Monroe, was not. Having himself discussed the matter at some length with Sargent, Lodge remained convinced that so much smoke definitely suggested the presence of a German-fed fire. The Senator therefore suggested both a warning to Venezuela not to sanction any German lease of Margarita and a decision to station both a powerful American cruiser and a gun-

[92] Nav Rec Subj File, WE-10, Venezuela-Margarita Island, ONI Register 460, 1901, No. 01-460 N-11-a. This file contains Sargent to Long, 15 March 1901, as well as a later Sargent report of the 26th.

[93] ONI Register 460, as cited. Orsini to Sargent, 20 March 1901.

[94] GB, Proceedings, 23 April 1901; Letters, 1, Dewey to Long, 24 April 1901; and SDML, Hay to Long, 10 April and 13 May 1901, the latter including a long dispatch from the American legation in Berlin dated 24 April 1901.

boat at La Guaira, the port of Caracas. "There is no place in the world at this moment," Lodge wrote, "where it is so important that we should have a warship as at La Guaira. . . . The mere presence of one of our ships there would, I think, be sufficient to prevent trouble."[95]

Lodge later claimed that it had been difficult to persuade Secretary Long to send such a vessel. But the Navy was fully prepared to continue its watch over the region. A second vessel was sent to check the accuracy of Commander Sargent's reports. This additional investigation—conducted, incidentally, in such secrecy that only two officers aboard the ship knew the purpose of its mission—satisfied the naval command in Washington that Sargent had been correct.[96] Thereafter, the General Board focused considerable attention on Margarita, especially in the drafting of its war plans for the Caribbean. Margarita ultimately came to occupy, along with Santo Domingo, a special place in naval war plans as one of the most likely targets of any aggressive German move in the Western Hemisphere. Indeed, by the time that the "Black Plan" was formalized in the Taft era, Margarita had emerged as the most logical site for the German fleet to seize as an advanced base for wartime operations in the Caribbean. To American naval strategists it seemed clear that the German navy must be aware of Margarita's great geographic advantages, that is, its location at a point that the German fleet could reach without having to pass close to American positions in the Caribbean. Moreover, the American naval officers contended, the fact that the Germans had so carefully surveyed the island and had demonstrated so much interest in it around 1900 seemed proof of their strategic awareness.[97]

But, no matter how great the naval suspicion of German intentions in Margarita, the Navy's attitude toward the whole Venezuela question was just as heavily influenced by its intensive dislike for the Venezuelan dictator, Cipriano Castro, who had a long record for "persecuting" American interests. This also was a shared attitude. The President and Department of State were equally hostile to Castro. To Roosevelt he was, simply, "the villainous monkey."[98] In any event, in the months prior to the Anglo-German blockade of 1902 the attention of both American diplomatic and military personnel in Venezuela had been directed largely against the alleged misdeeds of Castro and his regime.

[95] *Papers of John Davis Long*, Lodge to Long, 1 June 1901, 365-66.

[96] GB, File 409, Hackett to Commanding Officer of *Mayflower*, 17 May 1901, and in ONI Register 460, Commander Adams to Long, 12 June 1901, a dispatch which confirms the observations of Sargent.

[97] See the role assigned to Margarita in the various versions of the Black Plan, as cited in Chapter One.

[98] For evidence of Roosevelt's continuing antagonism toward Castro, see Hay Papers, Roosevelt to Hay, 30 August 1904.

Throughout 1900, for example, Herbert Loomis supplied the Department of State with extensive reports about Castro's wrongdoing and emphasized the point that his actions were responsible for the revolutionary disturbances in the country. As far as Loomis was concerned, it was only the presence of foreign warships in Venezuelan waters that preserved even the semblance of internal order. He therefore strongly urged Hay to order American naval vessels to make frequent, informal, and unpublicized visits to La Guaira, a policy which Hay, in turn, endorsed in April 1900 and soon asked the Navy to implement.[99] Commander Sargent was the naval officer most frequently involved, at the request of the Department of State, in investigating the various incidents that occurred in Venezuela. The normal tone of his reports about alleged Venezuelan interference with American business concerns was anti-Castro. According to Sargent, the Castro regime, knowing it was unpopular with its own people, interfered with American business since the dictator and his followers realized that they should lose no time "in filling their own pockets while they still have the opportunity." Sargent noted that visits by Italian and German warships were frequent, but, instead of dwelling upon the dangers of foreign intervention, he drew the conclusion that these European naval visitations usually had the beneficial effect of compelling Venezuelan authorities to enforce rules and regulations long ignored. He observed quite bluntly that diplomacy had virtually no effect on "the semi-enlightened and uncultivated members of the present administration . . . but they can appreciate the potential presence of a squadron of battleships."[100] Sargent, as previously indicated, gradually became less bellicose and came to the conclusion that the American minister counted too heavily upon the influence of naval power, but he always believed that units of the Navy should be kept in the general vicinity— for example, in Trinidad—so that they could reach La Guaira in less than twenty-four hours.[101]

The summer of 1902 produced new revolutionary disturbances in Venezuela. At the request of diplomatic officials, the Navy investigated many incidents arising from their latest insurrection against Castro. Its particular assignment was to determine if a naval blockade, imposed by the Castro forces against certain revolutionary-held towns, was effective or simply a "paper" blockade. Before long, however, both American diplomatic and naval personnel concluded that the revolt against Castro was far less significant than it had initially appeared,

[99] Nav Rec AF 8, Loomis to Hay, 22 March 1900.
[100] Nav Rec Subj File, VP-Protection of Individuals, Sargent to Long, 20 January 1901.
[101] Nav Rec AF 8, Sargent to Long, 10 March 1901.

with the result that the two American naval vessels then in Venezuelan waters were withdrawn.[102] In August the American Minister cabled the State Department that the commander of a German war vessel at Puerto Caballo had warned Castro forces not to bombard that rebel-held city without giving notification in advance and had further informed the Venezuelans that he would land his own sailors to protect German lives and property if Puerto Caballo was attacked. Although the State Department replied that the German commander should be told that, if German sailors were landed, the United States would do likewise, it emphasized the importance of informing the Venezuelan government that there must be no bombardment of Puerto Caballo without prior notification. The primary concern, then, was still with the actions of the Venezuelans.[103] This, too, remained the attitude in naval circles. When the Orinoco Steamship Company asked for American naval help in reclaiming two of its ships which had fallen into the hands of the revolutionaries, the State Department reluctantly concluded that international law would not sanction the dispatch of American gunboats into the interior waterways of Venezuela. Admiral Taylor, who had been consulted by the State Department, fully accepted its authority to rule on the precepts of international law but added his own opinion of the Venezuelans: "International law presumes that nations influenced by it are of the family of modern civilized nations and that the edicts of international law cannot be followed by savage nations." It was Taylor's own opinion that the Venezuelans had committed sufficient misdeeds to justify sending American gunboats up the Orinoco to convey vessels of the steamship company and to protest strenuously any seizures.[104]

Throughout the autumn of 1902 the emphasis in naval correspondence remained upon the events of the continuing revolution against Castro. There were frequent reports that the "decisive battle" was about to be fought. If and when that happened, the Navy wished to have its own vessels at hand to protect against eventualities.[105] But, above all, when the Anglo-German blockade did occur in early December, it failed to produce any unfavorable comments from those American naval officers then in the Venezuelan area. Their reports to the Navy Department about the forthcoming blockade were factual and laconic, with merely additional suggestions that the presence of American warships might be advisable. Commander S. W. Diehl of the

[102] SDML, Adee to Long, 9 August 1901.
[103] Nav Rec AF 8, Bowen to Hay, 14 July 1902; Hill to Long, 1 August 1902; and Adee to Cowles, 21 August 1902. See also SDML, Hill to Long, 1 August 1902.
[104] Nav Rec AF 8, memorandum of H. C. Taylor, 22 September 1902.
[105] Papers of William Moody, Manuscripts Division, Library of Congress, Taylor to Moody, 14 October 1902.

Marietta, who had himself made many previous tours of observation in the Caribbean, was the principal naval officer who witnessed and reported the European blockade and intervention. Diehl most certainly was not disturbed by the presence of German and British warships. Indeed, he noted with some satisfaction that once the Anglo-German action had actually begun, Venezuela had quieted down remarkably. He thought that the *Marietta* ought not to be too visible, since her occasional use as a medium of communication between the British and German ships and their shore positions "makes the Venezuelans suspect our official neutrality and makes our disinterestedness suspect." Diehl continually stressed that American interests in Venezuela were safe, that communications remained open, and that both the American Minister and consul agreed with him that the immediate presence of the *Marietta* was unnecessary.[106] The Minister, Herbert Bowen, was himself so pleased with Diehl that he sent a special note to John Hay to praise the naval officer for his assistance, sound advice, and ability to get along with the Venezuelans as well as with the members of the blockading squadrons.[107] As for Diehl, he too stressed his good relations with the British and German officers, while virtually all his hostile comments were directed at the Castro regime. After the crisis had eased (and only two days after Bowen had left Caracas to serve as an arbitrator) Diehl reported that Castro immediately resumed his familiar practice of putting a squeeze on foreign merchants to get the revenues his regime so desperately needed. "Surely," he noted sardonically, "a country gets the government it deserves."[108]

Those who patrolled the Venezuelan beat, having long disapproved of the Castro regime, viewed its difficulties with equanimity, if not outright satisfaction. Only at the higher echelons did there appear even the slightest of hints—and this in connection with the maneuvers of the full American fleet in the Caribbean at the very moment when the Anglo-German blockade was occurring—that the United States Navy was anything more than a passive bystander. But the fact that the Navy had some fifty ships on maneuvers in the Caribbean at the precise moment of the blockade was by no means the result of Venezuela's international difficulties. It was a naval effort that had been decided long before December of 1902 and for which there had been months of planning. Heretofore the Navy had never held peacetime maneuvers as a unit; it was, as Admiral Taylor frequently complained, simply a navy of single ships and would never be genuinely strong until it had

---

[106] Nav Rec AF 8, Diehl to Moody, 30 November and 14 December 1902.

[107] Nav Rec AF 8, Bowen to Hay, 23 January 1903, a dispatch forwarded by State to the Navy.

[108] Nav Rec AF 8, Diehl to Taylor, 24 January 1903.

learned "to think in squadrons." Theodore Roosevelt, the first President to believe in the importance of large-scale peacetime maneuvers, had authorized the Caribbean naval mobilization in the late spring of 1902 and had stressed the fact that these operations, the first in the American experience, would be of the utmost professional importance.[109]

The American fleet, commanded naturally by Admiral Dewey, was thus on maneuvers off Culebra when the European intervention began. On the 14th of December Admiral Taylor, who accompanied the fleet, did check with the Navy Department in Washington to reconfirm previously made plans to divide up the fleet for the Christmas holidays and send some of the vessels to Trinidad—"just across the road from Venezuela," as Taylor put it. It was evident that he and Dewey were uncertain about the delicacy of the Venezuelan situation and wanted guidance from Washington. The reply which came from the Navy Department was that Dewey must keep a vessel constantly at San Juan in Puerto Rico so that uninterrupted communications could be maintained with the fleet.[110] A very liberal interpretation of this brief exchange, occurring when Roosevelt was in communication with the German representatives in Washington and clearly trying to get them to abandon the blockade, certainly permits the speculation that the American fleet was being used as a political makeweight. Admiral Taylor suspected as much. "So far, it seems to us down here," he wrote Secretary William Moody in mid-December, "that our country is rapidly becoming the big policeman on the corner watching the smaller folks to see that they do not get too noisy at their sports. It is a singular accident that all these things should come about just as we achieve this very powerful concentration in this corner of the 'American Mediterranean.' "[111] Similarly Captain William Cowles, then acting director of ONI and, since he was Roosevelt's brother-in-law, close to the President, could write that the presence of the fleet in Caribbean waters was "probably a convenience to the Administration in discussing the Venezuelan situation." And Dewey, in January 1903, made an entry in his journal which noted the "effect on foreign powers" of the maneuvers, especially since they took place at the same time as the European demonstration against Venezuela.[112]

Yet all of these comments were guarded as well as ambiguous. At

---

[109] Roosevelt, *Letters*, III, 275 and 283, Roosevelt to Dewey, 16 June 1902, and to Thomas C. Platt, 28 June 1903.

[110] Nav Rec Messages Sent in Cipher, 1 June 1898 to 1 September 1906, Moody to Dewey, 15 December 1902. See also Moody Papers, Taylor to Moody, 14 December 1902.

[111] Moody Papers, Taylor to Moody, 14 December 1902.

[112] Beale, *Roosevelt and America's Rise*, 417.

the most they reflect a conscious sense of the Navy as a watchful presence, alert to the possibility that things might get out of hand. Moreover, even Cowles added the comment that, while the Navy's presence may have been a political convenience, this had not been anticipated or expected by any one in the administration—had been, in other words, a fortuitous advantage.[113] Nor do the available written records of the Navy indicate that there was any naval pressure upon Roosevelt to take any particular stand about Venezuela or any formal expression of fear about a threat to the sanctity of the Monroe Doctrine. Naval records, in short, simply support the conclusion that whatever the President may have done about the blockade of Venezuela, his action was, as with so many of his diplomatic efforts, personal and individual, something he did on his own initiative and responsibility. The fleet, after all, was in the Caribbean in accordance with a longstanding plan for peacetime maneuvers and professional improvement. Whatever opportunistic use was made of its presence, whatever the "ultimatum" that was sent, the initiative was with Roosevelt, not the Navy.

It is also clear that, as soon as the Anglo-German intervention had ended, Cipriano Castro once again reoccupied the center of the stage as the Latin "dictator" most distrusted by the Roosevelt administration. By the summer of 1904 the President had reached the conclusion that Castro was "riding for a fall" and that, in such circumstances, "if he has to have a fall, we had better give it to him." The plan which most appealed to Roosevelt was the seizure of the Venezuelan customs houses and their operation either by Belgian agents or other representatives selected by the Hague court. It was an idea which, again, originated in the White House and which was primarily Roosevelt's.[114] There was, however, ample naval cooperation with this particular scheme. By October of 1904 the General Board, at Roosevelt's prompting, had worked out a tentative plan for naval seizure of the Venezuelan customs houses against anticipated Venezuelan resistance. Moreover, those naval officers who developed the plan professed to be alarmed by evidence of German influence in Venezuela. They called special attention to various reports, originating in the consular service and passed on to the Navy, which claimed that the Castro regime intended to purchase its naval ordnance from the German armaments firm of Schneider-Creusot. By March 1905, when Roosevelt was in fact perilously close to intervention, his naval advisers informed him that their overall Venezuela Plan, on which they had been working for three years, was now "in as complete a state as practicable" and that

[113] Ibid., 417.
[114] Hay Papers, Roosevelt to Hay, 9 September 1904.

the cruiser division, supported by 600 Marines, could sail on a moment's notice.[115]

Eventually Roosevelt abandoned his scheme, one to which he had been especially attracted, and there was no intervention. But the American attitude toward Castro remained one of thinly disguised hostility. Even Elihu Root, a man whose patience with Latin nations surpassed that of any other American statesman of the period, chastised Venezuela for her "great ingenuity in destroying every American interest in her country" and confessed that he had had to hold himself in "with both hands to keep from acting under the influence of irritation."[116] It was not until the last months of the Roosevelt administration that Venezuelan-American relations began to turn the corner. Castro had finally been ousted and his successor, President Gomez, indicating a desire to settle all outstanding claims, suggested that he would welcome the visit of an American warship at La Guaira. Thus, at the request of the Department of State, the small gunboat Dolphin, commanded by Lt. Commander Thomas Washington, was assigned the mission. It received a rousing welcome at the Venezuelan port, while Commander Washington, who filed extensive reports of his visit, suggested that, with the exile of Castro, there should be no further Venezuelan-American difficulties. The Department of State was especially pleased with Washington's diplomacy, gave his visit credit for paving the way for the later work of Minister William Buchanan, and even sent a special letter of commendation to the Navy Department. Assistant Secretary Robert Bacon observed that he had read the naval officer's reports "with a feeling of genuine pleasure. Our navy can generally be counted on to do the right thing, and I take off my hat to them.... Good for Washington. His name did not do him any harm." It was a successful example of another role frequently played by the naval officer, that of the ambassador of good will—this time, to be sure, with an assist from a man who happily bore the name of the first commander-in-chief of the Army.[117]

3. THE NAVY IN NABOTH'S VINEYARD

It was in the Dominican Republic and on the Isthmus of Panama, however, that military officials played their largest role in the execution of American foreign policy during the Roosevelt years. Indeed, in

115 Nav Rec Confid Ltrs, Darling to Loeb (Roosevelt's secretary), 28 March 1905. Also GB, Proceedings, 20 December 1904.

116 Root Papers, Root to Albert Shaw, 22 May 1908.

117 SDNF, Case 4832/67, Root to Buchanan, 21 December 1908, and /67, Washington to Newberry, 13 January 1909; and /71, Bacon to Adee, 16 January 1909.

the affairs of Hispaniola naval officers long enjoyed not only a very free hand but also an opportunity to participate in the actual making of policy.

The history of Dominican-American relations, especially of America's long interest in Samana Bay, predates the Civil War and includes numerous colorful, exotic, and morally dubious projects. Ulysses Grant, after all, once even authorized his personal secretary to negotiate a treaty for the purchase of the island republic.[118] But Grant's involvement was rivaled by the later effort of the General Board when, early in 1903, it sponsored a Dominican mission carried out by two junior naval officers. In February of that year Lieutenants Crosley and Smith, armed with passports describing them as journalists on a current events assignment, arrived in the Dominican Republic to carry out a task for which they had been carefully selected by Admiral Taylor of the Bureau of Navigation.

Lieutenants Crosley and Smith had a fruitful visit. Within a few weeks they claimed that "there remains no section of the country and water surrounding Fort Liberty Bay about which we have not complete data for military use." Then, casting aside their protective cover as junketing journalists, they made contact with the revolutionary faction headed by the Dominican general Horacio Vasquez. To their great pleasure they were told that Vasquez and his followers ardently hoped for American intervention in the affairs of the revolution-torn Republic—and would pay a price for assistance. General Vasquez "openly proposed to me," Crosley recorded, "that if I, as an American naval officer, would take a proposition looking toward peace without further bloodshed to the authorities in Santo Domingo City, when he returned to the Presidency, he, Vasquez, would grant the United States a concession in Samana Bay for a coaling station." Lieutenant Smith, meanwhile, busied himself collecting evidence to show that Germany was financing the Vasquez faction and was anxious for his success. "I assume that the Germans would not so assist," Smith wrote in the ominous tone reserved for discussion of the German "threat," "unless they were to receive something in return; the fact that Vasquez offered to promise me a concession in Samana Bay for services rendered shows that he had such offers in mind."[119]

The General Board was thoroughly impressed by the report of the two junior officers and at once drafted its own special memorandum to be transmitted to the Department of State. Santo Domingo, the

---

[118] See the colorful account in Allan Nevins, *Hamilton Fish* (New York, 1935), 252-78. A more balanced interpretation is David Donald, *Charles Sumner and the Rights of Man* (New York, 1970), especially 436-44 and 468-80.

[119] Nav Rec AF 8, Lt. W. S. Crosley to Admiral Taylor, 6 May 1903.

strategists argued, would be the most logical target of a European aggressor intending to make war on the United States; conversely, the plans of such an aggressor could most readily be thwarted if the United States itself possessed Samana Bay and Fort Liberty Bay. Dewey's group reasoned that, since the Dominican people were friendly, the present moment was opportune for the Department of State to take action that would ultimately bring the island republic under the control of the United States. The General Board was even convinced that, if the right man were sent to represent America in the Dominican Republic, it would be easy "to develop a request for some sort of occupation by the United States, and this would virtually secure to us control of this most important strategic point in the Caribbean." The timing, too, was urgent. Dominican finances were chaotic, with the consequent danger that European creditors might close in on the Dominican Republic as they had previously closed in upon Venezuela. It was naturally the German pressure that seemed most ominous: "It is certain that Germany has recently taken steps to acquire concessions in Santo Domingo; she failed because the President [Vasquez] failed. Another time the one with whom she deals may be more successful."[120]

There was, to be sure, nothing novel or truly distinctive in these reports, with their emphasis upon the presumed German threat and the familiar argument about Caribbean strategy and the Dominican Republic's location athwart major passages into that sea. Nor was naval interest, as we have noted, a new phenomenon; one of the first and clearest signs of the Navy's revival in the '80s and '90s had been its renewed interest in the acquisition of Samana Bay in the Dominican Republic and the Mole St. Nicholas in Haiti. Just prior to the outbreak of war in 1898, Admiral A. S. Crowninshield, at the specific request of the Navy Department, had visited Santo Domingo and discussed with President Ulises Heureux a scheme whereby Samana Bay would be ceded to the United States in return for the admission of certain Dominican exports into the United States on a duty-free basis. Mahan's War Board, though tentative in its conclusions, had also fixed upon Samana Bay as a possible site for naval acquisition.[121]

The early concern was largely strategic. While, as we have seen, Guantanamo was the prize Caribbean site and the Windward Passage given first priority, the island of Santo Domingo always occupied an important place in the Navy's strategic planning. Indeed, in their vari-

120 Nav Rec AF 8, copy of General Board memorandum of 8 May 1903.

121 Nav Rec Confid Ltrs, Crowninshield to Long, 28 February 1899. See also W. H. Calcott, *The Caribbean Policy of the United States, 1890-1920* (Baltimore, 1942), 113, and Selden Rodman, *Quisqueya: A History of the Dominican Republic* (Seattle, 1964), 116.

ous memoranda the members of the General Board were always much more "positive" in their assertions about its value than in their statements about the naval merits of the Danish West Indies or Puerto Rico. In fact, the Board's memorandum on the Virgin Islands, which we have previously noticed, put more stress on the value of Santo Domingo than upon the Danish possessions. The General Board had no sooner been established in 1900 than it focused upon the island: "In the development of war plans for a possible campaign in which the West Indies will be the scene of hostilities, the Board believes that Haiti or Santo Domingo is of great importance and must be defended if the overall campaign is to be successful." Its seizure by a hostile power "might easily cause what would otherwise be a short campaign to grow into a long and intensive war." Samana Bay, the best harbor on the island, "is undoubtedly a great bait for aggression" and "constitutes a standing menace to . . . the United States."[122]

Thus the Navy always maintained a very special watch over the island and its two republics. It was specifically mentioned in the standing orders given the Caribbean Division, with the commander of that naval force charged "to keep himself informed as to conditions existing in the island . . . and frequently to visit these republics."[123] Lieutenants Crosley and Smith were by no means the only naval officers who engaged in undercover activities. Admiral Taylor once carefully explained to his chief, Secretary Moody, that while the training ship *Buffalo* was ostensibly carrying out a routine training mission in Dominican waters,

> one of her officers is doing the work of the General Board, making secret examinations of the surrounding land and water. This has been going on for three years; that is, ever since the General Board was instituted. It is much needed, for when the day comes, we must not be as ignorant . . . as we were of Cuba.[124]

The ultimate proof of the Navy's strategic concern was the fact that its most specific and detailed "advanced base" plan was drawn for the single purpose of seizing that island at the outbreak of any war with a European power. Though with the passage of time other targets in the Caribbean—Margarita, Cartagena, Puerto Rico, and even Cuba—came to receive at least equal emphasis in strategic planning, the island of Santo Domingo was never far from the watchful eye of the General Board. On the eve of America's entry into World War I, for

[122] GB, Letters, I, Dewey to Long, 23 April 1901.

[123] GB, File 420-1, Moody to Commander-in-Chief, North Atlantic Station, 18 October 1902.

[124] Moody Papers, Taylor to Moody, 22 December 1902.

example, the Board was still insisting that the proper protection of Caribbean interests demanded possession of Samana Bay.

The United States could undoubtedly have secured Samana Bay in 1898 as a base to use against Cervera's fleet. President Heureux, whose treasury was chronically empty, was neither the first nor the last Dominican leader to think of offering it to America in return for assistance. From the American consul in the Dominican capital there came dispatch after dispatch indicating that Heureux would not object to seizure of the bay by the United States on some convenient pretext, such as the satisfaction of an unpaid claim. "Let your government come and take it," he is reported to have said.[125] But neither the State nor Navy Departments liked the proposal, at least in the terms in which it was put. "This Department," Secretary Long wrote, when his opinion was asked, "does not care to acquire a coaling station in Samana Bay by a process of seizure."[126] The State Department, both then and for some time afterwards, showed no desire to get involved in the tumultuous politics of the Dominican Republic. In contrast to its response when bases in Cuba, on the Isthmus, or even in the Galapagos were at issue, it simply acknowledged and filed naval communications about Samana Bay. After all, during the years immediately following the Spanish war when the Navy was most intensely interested in the acquisition of bases, there always seemed to be a reasonable prospect of purchasing the Danish islands. Nor, in point of fact, did the General Board itself actively pursue Samana Bay before 1903 as an object of Board policy. Individual members might wish for its acquisition, but the Board itself never included Samana Bay on any of its various, consolidated lists of desired naval stations. When the Board asked early in 1901 that Hay be specifically informed about the importance of the island, its request was simply that the Department of State should undertake diplomatic measures intended to prevent any portion of the island from being ceded to a European country.[127]

Indeed, in the years immediately following the Spanish-American War there were relatively few interchanges between the admirals and the diplomats on the subject of "Naboth's Vineyard." There were of course the usual naval visitations sponsored by the Department of State to gain information and show the flag. Hay, for example, once specifically asked a naval vessel to stop at a particular Dominican port and communicate with the agents of the American Dye Wood Com-

---

[125] SDML, Day to Long, 8 May 1898. Also Department of State, Consular Dispatches, Dispatches from the Consul at Santo Domingo, Grimke to Day, 10 April 1898. (Hereafter citations from various consuls will be abbreviated as SDCD.)

[126] SDML, Long to Day, 12 May 1898.

[127] SDML, Hay to Long, 18 January 1901, acknowledging receipt of a General Board report of 13 December 1900.

pany because "the gentlemen who are engaged in business there think it would have a favorable effect upon their interests."[128] However, by 1903 civilians and military alike were becoming profoundly alarmed by Dominican developments—by the inauguration of a new revolutionary cycle in that land of revolution, the bankruptcy of the Dominican government, the increasing pressures exerted by foreign creditors, and the fear that Europeans, encouraged by a recent decision of the Hague tribunal, would be tempted to use their gunboats as bill collectors, as in Venezuela.

Naval spokesmen were increasingly worried by the twin spectre of Dominican political disorder and financial insolvency. The General Board's memorandum that resulted from the Crosley-Smith mission was clearly an outgrowth of that fear. "The feeble and chaotic conditions of the government in that island," as Dewey put it, "make it easy for any country to obtain concessions without great expense."[129] By the summer of 1903 the General Board was sufficiently alarmed to take what for it was an unusual intervention in political affairs; it sent a confidential memorandum to Secretary Hay which stressed that naval officers familiar with the Dominican Republic believed that the ultimate financial crisis could be expected at any hour:

> The information indicates that the country is bankrupt, and the only means it now has of obtaining money is by borrowing from merchants at high interest and by allowing the merchants to bring their goods in free of the duties. Consequently the whole country is running behind more and more, and it is predicted that very soon the government will not be able to raise any money at all with which to pay its foreign debts.[130]

By year's end Admiral Taylor, convinced that the two republics on the island were "governments and nations only in name," was attempting to persuade the Secretary of the Navy that "it seems highly expedient . . . to indicate by a peaceful show of force the interest which the United States feels in the island." He argued, further, that "the time has arrived when it is fitting for us to substitute for the occasional visits of individual ships in time of outbreaks and petty wars, the practically continuous presence of a squadron of vessels in that vicinity."[131]

As the turmoil spread in the Republic, naval officers were unanimous in their almost open contempt for the Dominican political scene. Admiral Charles Sigsbee, who commanded the Caribbean squadron,

[128] Nav Rec AF 8, Hay to Long, 1 July 1902.
[129] GB, Letters, I, Dewey to Moody, 6 May 1903.
[130] Nav Rec Confid Ltrs, Moody to Hay, 22 July 1903.
[131] Moody Papers, Taylor to Moody, 30 December 1903.

and who in 1905 would be deeply involved in the establishment of the Customs Receivership, suggested that the only way to deal with such a country was by denying it sovereign rights. When his bile was running free, Sigsbee even contended that the Dominicans could never awaken to reality until some foreign power seized their customs houses and they had experienced a taste of foreign occupation. He found a racial explanation for their political backwardness:

> The Spaniard has intense and aggressive pride; the Negro is highly imitative and lacks a sense of proportion. Conjoin these qualifications and we have the Hispano-Negro, with his lofty declarations and his poor performance.[132]

Junior officers familiar with the Republic fully concurred. What can be done with a country like Santo Domingo, complained Commander William Southerland, where the population "look upon revolution as they do upon any other fiesta?"[133]

Even officers familiar with Dominican problems and politics showed the same tendencies. When Sumner Welles the architect of Franklin Roosevelt's "Good Neighbor" policy, wrote his massive, definitive study of *Naboth's Vineyard*, he specifically singled out Commander A. C. Dillingham as one officer who "thoroughly understood" that republic.[134] Dillingham, indeed, was considered so well acquainted with the Dominican situation that on two separate occasions, at the request of the President and of the Department of State, he was charged with major responsibilities for the handling of American relations with Santo Domingo, and in addition he was one of the two Americans most responsible for working out the eventual customs receivership. But in his correspondence with the Navy Department, Dillingham also could write in a vein which suggested that the only good Dominican was one who obeyed American orders. In 1904 he told the Department:

> Of course, we appreciate the rights of neutrals as guaranteed by international law, but in the promises the principles of international law can hardly be applied; international law can be applied only as it suits the convenience of the United States.[135]

Discovering that the Morales regime was little improved over the government it had succeeded, he wrote scornfully to Admiral Sigsbee:

---

[132] Nav Rec Confid Ltrs, Sigsbee to Hay, 3 August 1904.

[133] Nav Rec AF 8, Southerland to Bonaparte, 21 April 1906.

[134] Sumner Welles, *Naboth's Vineyard* (2 vols., New York, 1928), II, 624-25.

[135] SDML, Dillingham to Commander-in-Chief North Atlantic Squadron, 11 February 1904, forwarded by Navy Department to State.

They simply set down and make what they can of the customs houses, and make very little effort to drive their enemy out of the country. . . . As long as there is an [American] man-o-war in the locality, these officials will stir themselves, but when the man-o-war leaves, they do as little as possible.[136]

Deprecatory comments about the Dominican political scene were by no means confined to naval circles. In February 1904 Theodore Roosevelt expressed himself in his usual, forceful manner:

Santo Domingo is drifting into chaos, for after a hundred years of freedom, it shows itself utterly incompetent for government work . . . sooner or later it seems to me inevitable that the United States should assume an attitude of protection and regulation in regard to these little states in the neighborhood of the Caribbean.[137]

Believing the republic on the verge of dissolution, he told President Eliot of Harvard, "If I acted purely in accord with the spirit of altruistic humanitarian duty, I would grant the prayers of the best people in the island and take partial possession of it tomorrow." However, the Dominican financial and political crisis came to a head immediately following the Panama venture, and Roosevelt, if nothing else, realized that it might be impolitic to get involved in still another direct Latin intervention. Hence his correspondence was also filled with comments such as his frequently quoted statement that "I have as much desire to annex Santo Domingo as a gorged boa constrictor might have to swallow a porcupine wrong-end-to." Thus, in the winter and spring of 1903-04 he still hoped, if at all possible, to avoid direct intervention, desired no annexation or political control, but increasingly thought that some further American involvement was both inevitable and unavoidable.[138]

Meanwhile, the Navy clearly expected a major assignment. On January 4th, 1904 Admiral Wise was ordered to take his squadron to Guantanamo—"secret and confidential for the protection of American interests, especially in Haiti-Santo Domingo."[139] (Wise's squadron, incidentally, was the training squadron. The Navy had nothing else then available, for, as Admiral Taylor had to confess, "the truth is that . . . everything else was on the keen jump at other points such as the Isthmus of Panama."[140]) The Army General Staff, equally convinced that

[136] SDML, Dillingham dispatch of 11 February 1904 as cited.
[137] Roosevelt, *Letters*, IV, 724, Roosevelt to Theodore Roosevelt, Jr., 10 February 1904.
[138] Roosevelt, *Letters*, IV, 734 and 740-41, Roosevelt to Joseph Bishop, 23 February 1904, and to Charles Eliot, 4 April 1904.
[139] GB, File 420-1, Darling to Wise, 5 January 1904.
[140] Moody Papers, Taylor to Moody, 29 February 1904.

a major intervention was pending, initiated special efforts to acquire additional information about routes to the interior of the republic and about the actual condition of the Dominican railways.[141]

Soon the Navy did draw a political involvement. Roosevelt complained that he was unable to gain a clear picture of what was happening in Santo Domingo. Its government, desperate for financial help, was offering to trade Samana Bay for American assistance, while W. F. Powell, who served in the dual capacity of American minister to both Santo Domingo and Haiti, was not providing the sort of information which Roosevelt desired. T. R. requested that Admiral Dewey "with the assistance of Mr. Loomis, and Admiral Taylor and Commander Sargent . . . go to Santo Domingo, investigate conditions, and give me a full, impartial searching account of the situation as it now presents itself to the eyes."[142] The naval domination of the committee, with only Assistant Secretary Loomis representing the Department of State, was striking. Soon thereafter the reports on the Dominican Republic submitted by Commander Dillingham commended that officer to the Department of State. He was called to Washington for special talks with Loomis, and the latter, in turn, specifically asked the Navy to designate him as Senior Officer in Dominican waters and assign several ships to his command.[143]

The roulette wheel of Dominican politics had by this time spun Carlo Morales into the presidency, and the United States wished to stabilize his regime against the continuing insurrection led by the followers of Juan Jimenez. Morales had proclaimed a blockade of the ports controlled by Jimenez. Thus, the first issues confronted by the Navy in providing support for Morales dealt with the blockade and the prevention of shipments of armaments for the insurrection through that blockade. If the United States wished to put an end to the revolutionary cycle in the Dominican Republic, Admiral Frederick Wise soon contended, it must stop the importation of arms and "permit the Morales government to stop the sending of ammunition to the Jimenez faction."[144] A particular sore point with the Navy was the alleged activity of a New York company, the Clyde Steamship Company, in allowing its vessels to carry munitions to any faction in Santo Domingo which had sufficient cash to pay for the consignment. Admiral A. S. Barker, Commander-in-Chief of the North Atlantic fleet, entered a vehement protest: "It would seem from what . . . I learn that certain

[141] Papers of General Tasker H. Bliss, Manuscripts Division, Library of Congress, Bliss to Chief, 2nd Division, General Staff, 14 January 1904.

[142] Roosevelt, *Letters*, IV, 734, Roosevelt to Dewey, 20 February 1904.

[143] Moody Papers, Taylor to Moody, 29 February 1904; SDML, Hay to Moody, 26 March 1904 and Darling to Hay, 28 March 1904.

[144] Nav Rec AF 8, Wise to Moody, 12 February 1904.

Americans are responsible in great measure for this unfortunate state of affairs in San Domingo as they bring arms and ammunition to the different parties."[145]

But the Navy's initial attempts to cope with blockade and arms shipments produced an awkward situation. Both Minister Powell and the Morales government complained that the Navy's practices in the harbor of Santo Domingo City were hampering legitimate neutral commerce and actually aiding the government's enemies. Hay, while taking note of the complaints, virtually washed his hands of the problem. He noted that, since the harbor was on the firing line between government and insurgent forces, the Department of State was scarcely in a position to judge the best procedures to employ, and therefore he decided that these "must be left to the discretion of the naval commander," acting under the Navy Department's own instructions.[146] In February 1904, when a launch from the *Newark* was convoying a Clyde steamer in Santo Domingo harbor, it was fired upon by the insurgents. The American commander, in retaliation, landed 300 sailors and established them in positions from which they could shell the rebel camp. The followers of Jimenez immediately fled. This incident, though trivial, indicated the degree of local initiative enjoyed by naval officers in Dominican waters. It was also specifically commended by the Department of State.[147]

The problem of dealing with the Clyde Company turned out to be slippery. The Department of State had to accept the fact that, in international law, there were no grounds for stopping Clyde steamers and that the company had every right to carry on legitimate commerce. John Hay took the position that the basic problem was one of false consignments—that is, barrels which carried the label, for example, of pork products but which contained arms hidden in the bottom. Clyde officials, in turn, protested their inability to stop these practices. Navy Secretary Moody was far from satisfied. In his judgment the Clyde Company was using the guise of lawful commerce to carry on a lively, indiscriminate arms trade with all corners—"arms are concealed and entered as codfish, and distributed fairly to each faction, the government *de facto* paying all the bills." The United States, he argued, ought to withdraw all protection from Clyde vessels and notify the company of this decision. But Hay demurred. He was willing to caution the Clyde Company once more but insisted that naval commanders must

145 Nav Rec AF 8, Barker to Moody, 15 February 1904.

146 Nav Rec AF 8, Hay to Moody, 3 March 1904.

147 Nav Rec AF 8, Powell to Hay, 24 February 1904, copy furnished to Navy Department by State.

still retain sufficient discretion to protect all legitimate neutral commerce but deny help to vessels engaged in illegitimate trade.[148]

The influence of Commander Dillingham rose rapidly after his appointment as Senior Officer. In one of his early reports he suggested that there was much confusion in the handling of Dominican affairs because no one naval officer had been designated to exercise overall command. In consequence, he believed, too many different officers were trying to carry out their own individual ideas. Moreover, he felt that there could never be a consistent American policy as long as the Navy followed its standard practice of dispatching individual ships on "spasmodic" visits to trouble spots when needed and then moving them somewhere else as soon as the trouble ceased. Under such procedures, Dillingham pointed out, naval policy was episodic, for the officers involved in Dominican affairs never had a genuine opportunity to learn more than the bare facts of a situation. He therefore recommended the establishment of a permanent naval force in Dominican waters under the command of a single officer. John Hay, when informed of the commander's opinion, particularly commended it to the Navy Department for serious consideration.[149]

In April 1904 Dillingham—along with Morales and Powell—was apparently convinced of the reality of an Italian threat to seize the Dominican customs on behalf of unpaid Italian claimants. In a confused cable to Washington, Dillingham notified his superiors that he might have to take preventive action to forestall the Italians and assume possession of the customs houses in the name of the United States. Ordered not to take such a step, Dillingham later defended himself by maintaining that he never would have moved without specific authorization from the Navy Department. Furthermore, in the very unlikely event that the Navy did not provide such instructions, he never would have proceeded with his plan unless the Italians had actually started to use force and were in the act of taking the Dominican customs. Dillingham went on to argue that he had never really expected the Italians to seize the customs, for he doubted if any European government would interfere in a matter which was clearly the business of the United States. But the typical lingering doubt of the naval officer could not be entirely eliminated: ". . . with the information I had from our chargé d'affaires, with the late decision of the Hague Tribunal, and

---

[148] On the operations of the Clyde Steamship Co., see Nav Rec Subj File, VP-Protection of Individuals, a file which includes many dispatches concerning the company's involvement in Dominican affairs in the early months of 1904. Also, AF 8, Moody to Hay, 7 March 1904 and Hay to Moody, 9 March 1904.

[149] Nav Rec AF 8, Dillingham to Moody, 3 and 4 April 1904, and Hay to Moody, 24 April 1904.

remembering the actions of the German government at Port-au-Prince not long ago, I could see many possibilities!"[150]

However complicated and unconvincing his explanation may now seem, it apparently satisfied naval authorities. Soon thereafter Dillingham was actively engaged in negotiations with both the Morales and Jimenez forces in an effort to secure a truce in the Dominican civil war. The naval commander, for example, suggested to Morales that his own talks with Jimenez had led him to believe that an end to hostilities could be arranged, on terms favorable to the government, if Morales would adopt a moderate approach.[151] Shortly thereafter a peace commission was established, and Dillingham personally attended its meetings in the hope that his personal influence could keep the talks from breaking down. When a truce was finally arranged, observers generally gave the credit to Dillingham. "In my opinion," Admiral Sigsbee reported to the Navy Department, "the organization of this peace conference was due largely, if not wholly, to the good offices exercised on each side by Commander Dillingham, who seems to have the confidence of both sides in this revolution."[152]

While the commander may have been harsh in his judgments of the quality of Dominican political life, Dillingham was by no means lacking in appreciation of the complex issues involved. He was relatively confident that, with judicious American help, the *status quo* could be maintained and Morales maintained in office until the American Congress met in the late fall of 1904 and presumably dealt definitively with the Dominican question. He realized that it was the presence of his warships which had made his diplomatic efforts successful. In glowing terms he wrote that their presence gave the Dominicans a sense of confidence in the future. Yet he was also sufficiently realistic to understand that the Navy's involvement in Dominican affairs might lead the people of that country to assume that the United States would give them so much material assistance that they would be content to let the United States solve their problems for them.[153] Dillingham also realized early in his mission that the constant presence of American warships removed the temptation for other nations to interfere: "The most important effect of the actions that we have taken in the affairs of Santo Domingo in the past few months is in showing to foreign powers that the United States considers it its own affair to look after this

150 Nav Rec Messages Sent in Cipher, Moody to Dillingham, 18 April 1904; AF 8, Dillingham to Moody, 22 April 1904.

151 Nav Rec AF 8, Dillingham to Moody, 16 May 1904.

152 Nav Rec AF 8, Sigsbee to Moody, 8 June 1904.

153 Nav Rec AF 8, Dillingham to Moody, 16 May 1904.

Republic, and so long as we continue this policy, there is no danger from any other power in Santo Domingo."[154] Dillingham, in short, was no alarmist about the European "threat" and valued the presence of American warships primarily as a visible evidence of American interests in Santo Domingo. His position, he noted, would be far different if the naval vessels of other countries were still visiting the island, but such visits had ceased with their recognition of the primacy of the American interest.[155]

Whether Dillingham was as successful at peacemaking as he thought, is, of course, an issue open to some question. Still, the presence of so many warships in Dominican harbors, the undisguised assistance given to the Morales regime, and the absence of visits by the naval vessels of other countries could only have had a powerful effect upon the rebels—and also upon the followers of Morales—in convincing them of the merits of peace. After the truce, moreover, naval observers began to manifest at least a guarded optimism about the future of the Republic. As Admiral Sigsbee reported, no one could begin to predict how long Morales could retain his power, but the revolution against him had been the first revolt in Dominican history that had failed—which, if nothing else, gave Morales a certain unique prestige. Even a more skeptical naval observer, Admiral Sperry, found some consolation in the apparent willingness of the various Dominican factions to accept American guidance even if for no stronger reason, as he put it, than the fact that "the ruin is so great that the loot is trifling."[156]

The interposition of the United States in 1904 had of course done nothing more fundamental than to provide support for the Morales regime. It had as yet not dealt with the basic financial problems of the Republic, above all, with the many defaulted foreign debts which were the root cause of Santo Domingo's difficulties with the United States as with Europe. The solution most frequently put forth was that the United States should take over the administration of the Dominican customs houses and ultimately impose a fiscal administration which would guarantee the Republic's ability to repay her international obligations.

The history of these various arrangements—the two protocols between the United States and the Dominican Republic, the Senate's objections to and rejection of the first protocol, the so-called *modus vi-*

154 Nav Rec AF 8, Dillingham to Moody, 5 June 1904.

155 Nav Rec AF 8, Dillingham report of 16 May 1904.

156 Sperry Papers, Sperry to Charles Sperry, Jr., 24 December 1904; Nav Rec AF 8, Sigsbee to Moody, 8 June 1904.

vendi of 1905, and the revised and finally accepted treaty of 1907—has been told by many authors and in considerable detail.[157] What needs to be pointed out, however, is the considerable role that the United States Navy had in this sequence of events. Naval officers, to be sure, were not the first to suggest supervision of the customs. It had long been obvious that in the Dominican Republic, as elsewhere in Latin America, the customs houses were the principal source of governmental revenues as well as the "security" against which foreign debts were pledged and that any solution to the Republic's finances must inevitably involve the customs houses. Moreover, the Dominican "crisis" had been triggered late in the fall of 1903 by a Belgian suggestion that the creditors of the Republic should unite to seize the customs houses to prevent yet another pending default. And the customs issue was still very much alive after Morales came to power. In his desperate search for American assistance, Morales had himself suggested a wide variety of schemes, including some form of American involvement with the Dominican customs—though, clearly, Morales would have preferred other "solutions," such as American loans or the leasing of Samana Bay to the United States.[158] (Parenthetically, it might be noted that while Morales, Minister Powell, and some naval officers, such as Captain Wise, suggested the leasing of Samana Bay, the General Board still made no formal request. It was only in the report submitted by Admiral Dewey and his investigating group that the acquisition of this base was actually proposed.)[159]

But naval officers had been early advocates of schemes for American control and/or possession of the Dominican customs. One of the earliest recommendations from Commander Dillingham, made early in 1904 and before he had been named Senior Officer, was that the only way to end the revolutionary cycle in the Republic was through American possession of its customs houses. According to his analysis, the Dominican merchant class had a vested interest in revolution; it lent money at exorbitant rates of interest to financially pressed governments and, in return, received inflated paper money with which to pay off its own customs obligations. The net effect of this system and the many conditions attached to the loans was to reduce the amount of revenue available to the government as well as to stimulate further

---

[157] The latest and most complete account is Munro, *Dollar Diplomacy*, 87 ff., but see also J. Fred Rippy, "The Institution of the Customs Receivership in the Dominican Republic," *Hispanic American Historical Review*, XVII, no. 4 (November 1937), 419-57.

[158] Munro, *Dollar Diplomacy*, 90.

[159] For additional examples of the opinions of naval officers, see Welles, *Naboth's Vineyard*, II, 426-27.

political disorder.[160] Likewise, the report submitted in mid-March of 1904 by Admiral Dewey's investigating group called for an American intervention in which possession of the customs houses was one of the principal recommendations.[161]

But Roosevelt, as we have noted, was reluctant to assume such responsibilities. He did not approve the acquisition of Samana Bay, and it was not in fact until the very end of 1904 that American representatives in the Dominican Republic were officially authorized to open negotiations for a customs receivership. Again the naval establishment had a significant role. Commander Dillingham was appointed by Roosevelt as one of the special commissioners to conduct the negotiations with Morales. He and the new American minister, Thomas Dawson, then worked out the complicated arrangements whereby the Dominican customs were Americanized and the receivership, after several false starts, initiated.[162]

The projected transfer of the customs to American control was, however, a source of some friction between the administration and its naval representatives in the Republic. Most of the Dominican "experts" predicted that the transfer would produce political disorder. The insurrection against Morales was still proceeding, and, while that regime clearly welcomed the coming American involvement, it was equally obvious that many Dominicans did not. Indeed, even while the final terms of the protocol were still being negotiated, Commander Dillingham had notified Washington of the need for additional warships in the principal Dominican ports and had suggested to Secretary Hay that Admiral Sigsbee's squadron should arrive at the Dominican capital on the day before the terms of the convention were publicly announced.[163] Sigsbee, who had now assumed control of the naval force, feared that the transfer could not be made peacefully and that he would have to employ coercive measures. While confident that bloodshed could be averted, Sigsbee believed that the transfer could not be affected "independent of naval power." He promised to offer naval protection to the Morales regime during the actual transfer of authority and, in addition, to assist that government by landing its officials at various ports so that they could explain the terms of the receivership to local residents.[164] The Roosevelt administration, however, found the tenor of Sigsbee's reports disturbing. He was soon notified not to take possession of any customs houses and to use every possible

160 Nav Rec AF 8, Dillingham to Moody, 6 January 1904.
161 Rippy, "Initiation of the Customs Receivership," 442.
162 Munro, *Dollar Diplomacy*, 99-101.
163 SDML, Dillingham to Morton, 10 January 1905.
164 Nav Rec AF 8, Sigsbee to Morton, 23 January 1905.

effort to avert hostilities between the Dominican factions. He was specially cautioned, above all, not to intervene between the factions except in case of an absolute necessity to protect American lives and property.[165]

Sigsbee was unhappy with these instructions and claimed not to understand the limits of his authority. He continued to believe—and cited Minister Dawson as well as President Morales in support of his views—that article seven of the pending convention "justified, even required, the United States to take prompt military action, if necessary, to transfer the customs houses" and to land its naval forces in support of the Morales government.[166] But by this time it was already becoming evident that the United States Senate would not support such an interpretation of the protocol and was objecting to the clauses which obligated the United States to guarantee the territorial integrity of the Dominican Republic and bound America to support the Morales regime. Thus, with the protocol stalled in the Senate, Admiral Sigsbee never received a green light to proceed with his recommendations, while he, in turn, began to lapse back into sardonic comments about the Republic, its political and financial problems, and its treatment by the United States. By mid-April of 1905, for example, Sigsbee was suggesting that the United States ought to abandon its traditional respect for the right of revolution and simply deny to the Dominicans the right to stage revolts against the regime in power. The Republic, as he saw it, was simply a country "where revolution is nothing more than a scramble for office, largely at the expense of foreign nations." The admiral conceded that it might be a dangerous precedent for the United States to interfere with the sovereignty of a weak nation, but, on the other hand, the insurrections in Santo Domingo were costing the United States Navy upwards of two million dollars per year—"an amount of money about equal to the whole annual revenue of San Domingo."[167]

The United States Senate, as is well known, did balk at the protocol negotiated by Dawson and Dillingham. It was the well-publicized arrival of an Italian warship at Santo Domingo on March 15, 1905 that finally led the Roosevelt administration to proceed with the establishment of the customs receivership but to create it under the terms of a special *modus vivendi* proposed by the Morales government as an alternative to the protocol. But the historical decisiveness of the Italian visit is, at best, conjectural. It seems clear that Roosevelt had made up

[165] SDML, Morton to Sigsbee, 28 January 1905, a copy of orders sent by the Navy and forwarded to State for its information.

[166] Nav Rec AF 8, Sigsbee to Morton, 18 February 1905.

[167] Nav Rec Subj File, VN-Naval Policy, Sigsbee to Morton, 3 April 1905. See also AF 8, Sigsbee to Morton, 9 and 23 February 1905.

his mind to act well before the Italian vessel hove into sight and that one of his standard tactical devices was to try to frighten dissenting Senators about the foreign danger to the Dominican Republic.[168] But in the Dominican Republic, on the other hand, it is equally clear that both Morales and Dawson were frightened by the possibility of an Italian intervention.[169] Sigsbee, however, left a mixed record. On the day that the Italian ship arrived, he cabled Washington of his strong suspicion that the Italians would seize the customs houses if the United States Senate did not accept the protocol. But he also assured the naval authorities that he would consider himself governed by his standing instructions not to intervene. Also, once the *modus vivendi* was in force, he immediately advised Colonel George Colton to take immediate possession of the customs house in the Dominican capital "otherwise the Italians may take it" and also to secure the customs at Samana Bay to remove "a great bait to European aggression."[170] Yet in his detailed report to the Navy Department, Sigsbee explained that what he had really feared was an insurrection in Santo Domingo City and that he had therefore advised Colton to act at once to prevent such an occurrence from happening. Moreover, his emphasis on Samana Bay was but a conditioned Navy reflex. He had no evidence of any Italian move in that area but simply believed that its strategic location was such that any foreign power intervening in the Dominican Republic would seize it in preference to all other locations.[171] It would therefore seem that the fortuituous arrival of the Italian warship provided the pretext rather than the reason for the *modus vivendi*. Even to the admiral in command, its appearance was not an immediate peril but rather an omen of what might happen some day if the Senate did not approve the receivership.

The United States showed no inclination to relax its military watch over the Republic once the *modus vivendi* went into operation. In the summer of 1905 when the Navy wished to withdraw some of its vessels for routine summer cruises, the word quickly came back that "It is the wish of the President that an adequate force be kept in Santo Domingan waters."[172] The Customs Receivership was put in the hands

---

168 Some historians have argued also that T.R. inflated the Japanese-American "crisis" of 1906-07 for its effect on Congress which was failing to respond to his naval building programs. See Mowry, *Era of Roosevelt*, 189. For evidence that Roosevelt was seeking to impress the Senate with Santo Domingo's problems, see his correspondence in late 1904 and early 1905 in vol. IV of his *Letters*.

169 Munro, *Dollar Diplomacy*, 101-06.

170 Nav Rec AF 8, dispatches from Sigsbee to Morton dated 4, 21, and 22 April 1905.

171 Nav Rec AF 8, Sigsbee to Morton, 3 May 1905.

172 Nav Rec AF 8, Darling to Commander-in-Chief, 3rd Squadron, North Atlantic Fleet, 24 June 1905.

of the Bureau of Insular Affairs of the War Department, and Roosevelt bluntly replied to a note from Secretary Taft, "As for Santo Domingo, of course you are right. American citizens in the customs house are there to stay until we ourselves take them out, and no revolutionists will be permitted to interfere with them."[173]

But the involvement of the Army in the administration of the customs houses began to produce changes in the American attitude toward Dominican problems. Colonel George R. Colton, the Army's man in the Dominican Republic, viewed affairs differently from Admiral Sigsbee. Early in his administration of the customs he sent a long dispatch to Secretary Taft, beginning with the statement that his report

> was sent in a spirit . . . of that which I believe to be my duty to the Secretary of War personally and the President of the United States. It would not have been written for consideration by the subordinates of another Department which I cannot but feel have been, through lack of careful consideration, in a measure possibly responsible for some of the existing conditions here, especially with relation to certain complications and the resulting attitude of the Dominican people toward the United States.

What worried Colton was simply that "the claims of the San Domingo Improvement Company and its operation in the past is the source of public scandal involving the credit of the United States Government." To Colton it was clear that the Dominican people regarded the awards given to that company as unjust, something which only the superior force of the United States had compelled them to accept. Colton quickly convinced himself that many of the operations of the San Domingo Improvement Company had been morally dubious and had produced a demoralizing effect upon the conduct of government in the Republic. American support of the claims of the Improvement Company had been ill-advised. "I do not believe," Colton concluded, "that the protecting power of the United States should be perverted by allowing another dollar to be exacted from the people of this country in that behalf until the whole matter has been honestly and fearlessly investigated."[174]

Colton was soon complaining about the practices pursued by the United States Navy in boarding vessels in Dominican waters. He did not wish to abandon the search of commercial vessels for illegal arms and ammunition; what he wanted was due process, particularly due process according to Dominican and not American law and practice. But when he complained to the Department of State, he was informed

---

[173] Roosevelt, *Letters*, IV, 1159, Roosevelt to Taft, 8 April 1905.
[174] SDML, Colton to Taft, 19 June 1905.

that the discontinuation of naval boarding would simply increase the chances of revolution by permitting arms to reach the anti-Morales forces.[175] Precisely the opposite was true, Colton replied, for if the impression became widespread "that we are going to carry things with a high hand here, regardless of the law, it will endanger the Treaty in the end." He ended one report to Taft with a refreshing note rarely evident in naval accounts: "As regards revolutions and rumors of revolution, it will be understood that in a country such as this such things are an ordinary topic of conversation, but as a rule mean nothing."[176]

Colton's reports went from Taft to President Roosevelt and gradually began to make the Administration aware of its one-dimensional view of the Dominican debts. Roosevelt turned one of Colton's reports over to Dr. Jacob Hollander, the financial expert who had been appointed to supervise and adjust the Dominican debt, with a note which said that, if the colonel's statements were true, then the United States would have "to take sharp measures" to dissociate itself from the debts of the Improvement Company and, in addition, support the Dominican government in its refusal to pay anything but the legally valid claims of the company.[177]

But no one, least of all Roosevelt, was prepared to sanction any policy which might jeopardize the American grip on the customs houses under the *modus vivendi*. Late summer of 1905 brought repeated rumors from the naval watch that further disorders were imminent. Colton himself accepted these reports as valid and, indeed, asked Washington for additional warships.[178] But the real "culprits" on this occasion were Admiral Royal E. Bradford, Sigsbee's successor on the Dominican police beat, and his chief, Charles Bonaparte, one of Roosevelt's many Secretaries of the Navy and a man who clearly was only serving time in that post until another cabinet appointment became available. Bradford was an alarmist about the danger of revolution, while Bonaparte faithfully furnished Roosevelt with copies of his pessimistic cables and reports. Indeed, Bonaparte fully shared the views of his naval command. "It is the general opinion of this Department," he informed Roosevelt, "evidently shared by Admiral Bradford, that we shall have trouble in Santo Domingo, probably in the Monte Christi area."[179] He was communicating Bradford's reports to the President, he added, so that the Navy could have its orders in advance of the ex-

175 SDML, Colton to Taft, 25 June 1905.
176 SDML, Colton to Taft, 21 June 1906.
177 Roosevelt, *Letters*, IV, 1259, Roosevelt to Jacob Hollander, 3 July 1905.
178 SDML, Major General Bates to Root, reporting the view of Colton in his dispatch of 28 August 1905.
179 Papers of Charles J. Bonaparte, Manuscripts Division, Library of Congress, Bonaparte to Roosevelt, 4 September 1905.

pected uprising. It was, of course, these communications from Bonaparte that prompted Roosevelt's famous order so often cited as the very epitome of his "big stick" in action:

> As for the Santo Domingo matter, tell Bradford to stop any revolution. I intend to keep the island in *statu quo* until the Senate has had time to act on the treaty, and I shall treat any revolutionary movement as an effort to upset the *modus vivendi*.[180]

Bonaparte's compliance, needless to say, was complete and immediate. "Of course this is strictly confidential," he informed his own assistant, "but requires prompt action on the part of the Department. President's message should at once be cabled to Bradford and Bureau of Navigation should be instructed to provide reinforcements even if this interferes with other contemplated arrangements."[181]

But both the President and the Secretary of the Navy began to run ahead of Bradford. The Admiral, though pleased with his new orders, no longer thought the danger immediate and had decided that the critical period in the Republic's revolutionary history would not come until later in the year. Moreover—and it is, unfortunately, typical of the often fantastic fluctuations in "informed" opinion about Dominican affairs—the junior officers in Bradford's command soon began to report conditions of political tranquillity while Colonel Colton, in the eyes of these same naval officers, now appeared to be the alarmist about possible insurrection.[182] But, in any event, Bradford had instructions which virtually gave him *carte blanche* to intervene on American terms throughout the Republic. He could board any and all commercial vessels; his squadron was to protect all the customs houses whether the officials in them were American or Dominican; and the Morales government had to obtain Bradford's permission if it wished to land supplies of arms or make any landings of any sort outside the immediate vicinity of the capital. The admiral was specifically told that he had authorization to intervene to put down all disorders of an insurrectionary character; while it was desirable to avoid any resort to force, "yet should it become necessary there should be no hesitation in so doing." Roosevelt, incidentally, saw and approved these orders.[183]

---

[180] SDML, Darling to Bradford, 10 September 1905. Also contained in Bonaparte Papers, Bonaparte to Darling, 6 September 1905. See also Bonaparte to Roosevelt, 4 September 1905.

[181] Bonaparte Papers, Bonaparte to Darling, 6 September 1905.

[182] SDML, Darling to Root, 13 September 1905, and Bradford to Bonaparte, 10 September 1905.

[183] Bonaparte Papers, Bonaparte to Roosevelt, 27 September 1905; SDML, Bonaparte to Root, 28 September 1905.

The arrival of Elihu Root in the Department of State in the fall of 1905 began to smooth the rough edges of the Roosevelt-Bonaparte approach. As elsewhere in the Caribbean, Root did not so much change the main lines of policy as he tightened the ground rules and strengthened the legal underpinnings. Under Hay, for example, the State Department had paid little attention to many aspects of the administration of the Customs Receivership. In July 1905 a young naval officer had written to the Department for advice, noting that he had just been assigned by the Navy for special duty at Monte Christi under the Department of State. He received a laconic reply that, since the Customs Receivership was under the direction of Colonel Colton, the State Department had little authority in a matter which actually came under the jurisdiction of the War Department.[184] With Root, however, it was different. As previously noted, he asked Taft to furnish him regularly with copies of Colton's monthly reports. And when Minister Dawson cabled that "an American customs official" named Morris had been wounded in a raid by smugglers on a customs house, Root seized the opportunity to make a special point:

> In describing Mr. Morris as an American customs official, Mr. Dawson, of course, means that Morris is an American who is an official in the Dominican customs service. The whole system of revenue collection in Santo Domingo at the present time exists under Dominican authority solely, and the officers engaged in administering it are executing the laws of the Dominican Republic under the authority of the Dominican Government, and are in no sense American officers or acting under American authority. It seems important to see that this distinction is understood by all officials and representatives of our government.[185]

It is doubtful if Dawson had been aware of this distinction; the "of course" in Root's message was gratuitous. But the point had been made, and the Secretary of State underlined it. The Navy was told it might send a ship to investigate the incident but that when it visited a trouble spot its purpose was solely to protect American lives and property—and then only in the event that the local Dominican authorities could not furnish adequate protection.[186] Root, moreover, never thought that the United States should continue to operate the customs houses under the *modus vivendi* if the Senate finally refused its advice and consent to the treaty:

184 SDML, Adee to Bonaparte, 14 July 1905.
185 SDML, Root to Bonaparte, 25 October 1905.
186 SDML, Root to Bonaparte, 9 November 1905, setting forth the conditions that governed intervention.

The result will be sooner or later an uprising against the Dominican Government to which the customs officers supposed to represent the United States, though not legally doing so, would have to yield, to the greater injury of our prestige and credit, or which would be suppressed by a use of force on the part of our Government difficult to justify on constitutional grounds.[187]

Root had no desire to end the attempt to bring order to the Republic or to abandon all controls. He welcomed a Dominican request to assign an American Army officer to train a rural police force. This, the Secretary told Taft, was a good idea since it "would contribute to the influences in Santo Domingo tending to preserve tranquillity and to make easier the operation of the pending treaty if ratified by the Senate."[188] He refined the standing orders for Admiral Bradford. American forces could be landed but only upon receipt of a notice from the Dominican authorities that they were themselves unable to preserve order. Yet the Republic was by no means a free agent in its affairs. The flat prohibition on the importation of armaments remained; naval vessels continued to enforce it by boarding and searching commercial shipping; and the Morales government still had to secure American permission to receive arms for its own forces.[189] Root, moreover, recognized the right of the Navy to continue to recommend about Dominican affairs. In the fall of 1905, when there were again signs of a political storm in the Republic, the Secretary of State furnished Bonaparte with copies of the cables he had just received, noted that his department believed that the American role should be one of neutrality between the contending factions, but concluded that "if you see any occasion for any change of instructions to our Minister in Santo Domingo, or think any change of attitude on the part of our Government desirable, I beg that you will advise me."[190]

The long-deferred revolution against Morales finally took place in the winter of 1905-06. Soon he became just one more ex-president of the Dominican Republic. Root's policy was non-intervention, which proved viable since there was in fact no movement in the Republic against either the receivership or American interests. Colonel Colton, moreover, was quick to praise the Navy and its current commanding officer, Commander William Southerland. "Present naval policy and wise action Southerland," he cabled to Taft, "prevented serious com-

[187] SDML, Root to Taft, 16 November 1905.
[188] SDML, Root to Taft, 1 November 1905.
[189] SDML, Root to Bonaparte, 9 November 1905; Bonaparte Papers, Bonaparte to Root, 2 January 1906.
[190] SDML, Root to Bonaparte, 30 December 1905.

plications." What Colton meant by "wise action" was later explained in some detail:

> The naval policy of non-interference in the political situation has prevented the possibility of embarrassing complications, and the wise course of Commander W. H. Southerland in extending his good offices in the direction of peace, has gained for us the good will of all parties, and dispelled any doubts that may have been entertained as to the correctness of American intentions toward the Republic.[191]

As Dominican politics began to simmer down during 1906, the Navy began to exhibit a new "correctness" in its Dominican behavior. Late in March Commander Southerland reported that the entrance to the harbor at Santo Domingo City was beginning to silt over and that larger vessels could no longer enter. But he had few regrets. The Dominican Congress was about to discuss the terms of the revised treaty with the United States; thus Southerland believed it was not good policy to keep naval vessels in the harbor at that critical time.[192] Soon afterwards, noting that the United States was not very popular with the Dominicans, he suggested that naval vessels should be sent by the United States only when the necessity was absolutely clear and then only if it was made clear to the Dominicans that the United States had no intention of interfering between the rival political groups.[193]

By this time, too, a number of junior officers had come to sense some of the difficulties inherent in the employment of American naval power to achieve political ends in the island republic. Their reports began to mention some of the injustices that had been committed as well as to strike a note of skepticism that would have appeared heresy in the "heroic" days of Sigsbee and Dillingham. Commander A. F. Fechteler suggested, for example, that the Dominicans could protect their own customs houses if they wanted to and that Americans were in no danger during an uprising if they would simply "mind their own business and keep out of the line of fire." Rumors of yet another possible Italian intervention struck Fechteler as ludicrous; in retrospect he even interpreted the "threat" of March 1905 as a farce. According to the Commander, the Italian agent in Santo Domingo, a man named Bancalari, was currently threatening a naval visitation and had frightened the Dominican government, which, in turn, had communicated its fears to the American Minister, Dawson. But it was simply a colossal bluff, a

191 SDML, Taft to Root, 1 February 1906, forwarding several reports from Colonel Colton.

192 SDML, Bonaparte to Root, 24 March 1906, forwarding copy of a Southerland dispatch.

193 SDML, Southerland to Bonaparte, 5 April 1906.

bluff which Bancalari thought he could carry off, since a year previously he had succeeded in "bulldozing" both Dawson and Morales with his empty threats of Italian intervention. Fechteler's assessment of Dawson was harsh:

> Foreign intervention (with ensuing complications) seems to be a nightmare with our minister, and foreign creditors will naturally take advantage of that. However, should foreign men-of-war come with the idea of interfering, it could only have the very excellent result of clearing up the situation. It is surely humiliating to have to make pleas and concessions and all that sort of thing in order to keep them away.[194]

Commander William Braunersreuther, whose small vessel was a part of Southerland's naval force, was even more heretical in his views. The customs receivership, he believed, only served to drive money out of the country, decreased the volume of currency in circulation, and created economic hardship for small businesses in the Republic. Rumors were circulating that the owners of one plantation intended to sell their lands to the Navy for a coaling station. Their effect, Braunersreuther maintained, was to convince many Dominicans, even some who had once been convinced of American honesty, that the aim of the United States was simply to acquire territory. Among the illiterate Dominican masses hatred of Americans was so intense, he charged, that parents "are quieting their children with the threat 'There comes an American. Keep quiet or he will kill you.'" Braunersreuther compared the attitude of the Dominicans with that of the citizens of Alsace-Lorraine when the Germans attempted their forced Germanization of the two conquered provinces, and the French-speaking population, in return, tried to inculcate their children with their own personal hatred of the German conqueror.[195]

There is no direct evidence that such naval reports had any specific influence upon the civilian government of the United States—though all were in fact transmitted to the Department of State by the Navy. But their general effect must certainly have been to reinforce the increasing tendencies under Root to assume a more correct relationship. Yet it must also be emphasized that among the military policymakers there was no tendency to question the inherent value of the receivership or the assumption that Dominican peace was best maintained by the discreet use of naval power. Colonel Colton, for example, reported

---

[194] SDML, Bonaparte to Root, 22 May 1906, enclosing copy of Fechteler report; also Newberry to Root, 24 July 1906.

[195] SDML, Newberry to Root, 4 May 1906, enclosing copy of Braunersreuther's dispatch of 22 April 1906.

after the forced resignation of Morales that "It has become a settled conviction among Dominicans that revolutions against the general government cannot succeed as long as the revenue collecting machinery is removed from the possibility of capture and used as a basis for hostile operations."[196] Even during the tumult that had preceded the fall of Morales, Colton continued, there had been general public acceptance of the principle of American control of the customs houses and thus there had been no necessity to use force to protect them: "Thus it will be seen that the Customs Receivership has been accepted not only as an inviolable condition but as an independent moral force, making for the peace of the country, and the reconciliation of the hitherto warring factions."[197] Commander Southerland, though far more modest in his claims, generally agreed with these conclusions. While he admitted that American control of the Dominican customs did not prevent all revolutionary activity, he maintained that it assured the Dominican government, without effort or expense, a guaranteed income. Similarly, while he never felt that naval power was the ultimate check on Dominican revolutionary tendencies, he always viewed the Navy's role as that of a valuable deterrent:

> The Navy Department will understand that the presence of warships does not prevent revolution, although it is clear to me that they have a deterrent effect. They assure the safety of the customs houses though, to be sure, an American landing of troops during an insurrection would undoubtedly lead to serious clashes with the local population.[198]

Thus, while American policy toward the Dominican Republic increasingly flowed into regular channels, the general objective remained unchanged as did the means employed to attain it. This was again made obvious in the summer of 1906 when there was yet another political tempest in the country. This time Secretary Bonaparte informed Roosevelt that the naval command believed that Southerland had sufficient forces on hand unless the President wished to return to the policies pursued in the preceding year when Admiral Bradford had been given so much latitude. That is to say, the naval policymakers now believed that their strength was sufficient to carry out a policy that was limited to the protection of American life and property and the prevention of interference with the *modus vivendi*.[199] A month

196 SDML, Taft to Root, 1 February 1906, enclosing Colton report; also relevant is Taft to Root of 6 January 1906.

197 SDML, Taft to Root, 1 February 1906, as cited.

198 SDML, Southerland to Bonaparte, 5 April 1906, a copy of Southerland dispatch forwarded to State.

199 Bonaparte Papers, Bonaparte to Roosevelt, 21 June 1906.

later another letter from Bonaparte showed how little the general objective had changed. He reported that he and Root had together decided not to relieve one warship stationed at Santo Domingo City by another but instead to assign both to the Dominican capital,

> so as to satisfy the native statesmen that the failure of Congress to ratify the treaty would not lead the Government to abandon its interest in the island. This conviction has unquestionably been impressed on the intelligent minds of these eminent, though dusky, personages by this time. . . .[200]

To elaborate further upon the Dominican story during the era of Roosevelt and Root is unnecessary since, in fact, it soon ceased to be a story. By mid-summer of 1906 Minister Dawson was informing Root that he and Southerland were cooperating famously and that his own preference for diplomatic solutions was properly counterbalanced by the naval officer's concern for military precautions.[201] By the end of the same year Colonel Colton was observing that quite a few American naval vessels were being maintained in Dominican harbors with nothing to do, their crews bored and restless, and the good effect of their presence having long since vanished. The Customs Receivership was, he judged, a great success:

> It has forced the Dominican leaders to choose some other means of securing a living than by inciting revolution against the existing government . . . there is evidence of a general breaking up of their former plan of life, and if they are convinced that no other alternative remains, they will no doubt eventually become good citizens.[202]

Above all, he claimed that through the operations of the receivership, the Republic had "been raised from chaos commercially and the point of dissolution politically to a position of comparative order and efficiency as a nation."

The Dominican Treaty finally managed to win Senatorial approval in 1907 and was also endorsed, though not without the exertion of considerable diplomatic pressure, by the Dominican legislature. In the summer of 1907 the United States withdrew from active intervention in the Republic's affairs. The role of the Navy thereafter began to fade. Americans lost their remaining fears of foreign intervention. The chargé d'affaires, Fenton McCreery, cheerfully sent Root an account of

[200] Bonaparte Papers, 7 August 1906.
[201] SDML, Dawson to Root, 24 July 1906.
[202] SDNF, Case 620/4-8 and /12-17, Colton to Taft, 13 November 1906 and 8 February 1907.

several interviews he had held with the Dominican Minister of Foreign Affairs. That official had expressed his fear that an Italian naval vessel, currently visiting the Jamestown Exhibition, would eventually head for Santo Domingo on a debt-collecting jaunt. Commented McCreery: "These are for your wastebasket. Serious though the situation might become in the future, it has its ludicrous aspect at present. I sent this to prove that I am trying to have a little fun out of San Domingo, if possible."[203]

Once the Treaty had been passed, it became even clearer that the Department of State was effectively in command of the receivership. The new regulations, drafted in the War Department's Bureau of Insular Affairs by General Edwards, tightened the arrangements previously in force under the *modus vivendi*, increased American control of the customs, and eliminated certain practices which had persisted when, under the *modus vivendi*, the receivership had operated under Dominican law. But it was a State Department control. The Bureau of Insular Affairs, which exercised immediate supervision, was subject to directions from the President through the Secretary of State. William E. Pulliam, the new Receiver General, clearly understood. When he departed on his assignment in November of 1907, he wrote Root, "I believe I understand and appreciate the attitude of the State Department on the Dominican Receivership and shall exert every consistent effort to bring about the desired result." It was also symbolical of the change that all drafts on the funds controlled by the Receivership now went through the Department of State before being executed by the Bureau of Insular Affairs.[204]

For the remainder of the Roosevelt administration the trouble spot on the island of Santo Domingo was not the Dominican Republic but its neighbor, Haiti. Revolution had long been predicted for that republic, but Haiti had somehow managed to remain quiet until January of 1908. At that time insurrection broke out against the regime of its aged, dictatorial ruler, Alexis Nord. The headquarters of the movement was in the St. Marc area, and one of Nord's first reactions was to announce a blockade of St. Marc as well as his firm intention to shell the disaffected area. Commander G. R. Marvell, of the *Eagle*, promptly sailed to St. Marc where he not only protested against the proposed bombardment but also succeeded in preventing it. He also reported, to the discomfiture of the Department of State, that the leader of the insurrection was using the American consulate at St. Marc as his headquarters. The Haitian government, meanwhile, complained that Com-

203 SDNF, Case 1199/194-95, McCreery to Root, 27 June 1907.
204 SDNF, Case 1199/293-94, Pulliam to Bacon, 27 November 1907.

mander Marvell's conduct was serving only to aid the cause of the revolutionaries.[205]

But, as the various reports began to get back to Washington, the Department of State sided with the naval commander. When other sources seemed to confirm the involvement of the American consul, Root simply dismissed him from the service and closed his consulate.[206] (It later turned out, it should be added, that the consul himself was not guilty, but Root decided not to reopen either his case or the consulate.[207]) Marvell's own detailed report of his actions at St. Marc clearly indicated that he had kept in communication with Minister Henry Furniss at Port-au-Prince, had worked with the minister in framing his protest against the bombardment, and had, in fact, gone to St. Marc at the specific request of American diplomatic representatives in Haiti. With this evidence at hand, Alvey Adee agreed that Marvell's actions had not only been proper but merited a special commendation; moreover, the Assistant Secretary added, Nord's determination to shell St. Marc was "brutal in the extreme and deserved a severe protest."[208]

There ensued a brief controversy with Nord about whether or not the defeated rebels should be granted asylum in American consulates. While this issue remained unsettled, a completely unexpected cable arrived from Furniss. In it the Minister maintained that he and the European diplomatic officials in Port-au-Prince believed that a warship should be permanently stationed at the Haitian capital, with the United States, France, Britain, and Germany taking turns in furnishing the naval watch. But since Furniss provided no details with his request, he was sharply questioned: "Report by cable what possible need there seems to be for permanent station warship at Haiti. . . . You have not reported either that lives or property of foreigners ever in danger."[209] Furniss finally answered that President Nord had told both the British and French ministers that there was grave danger of a general massacre of foreign residents if the revolt grew in intensity. He added that while he personally could neither confirm nor deny the danger, he did know that Nord was a man prone to paroxysms of rage and capable of ordering the rashest of actions. American naval officers, he indicated, had convinced him of the need for the permanent assignment

---

[205] SDNF, Case 2126, especially documents /43 through /53 which chronicle the progress of the uprising. For a general account, see L. L. Montague, *Haiti and the United States, 1714-1938* (Durham, 1940), 188-96.

[206] SDNF, Case 2126/53, Root to Furniss, 22 January 1908.

[207] SDNF, Case 2126/61-100, various documents and dispatches in February 1908.

[208] SDNF, Case 2126/61-62, Adee memorandum attached to Marvell's report of 18 January 1908.

[209] SDNF, Case 2126/170-71, Furniss to Root and Bacon to Furniss, 21 and 23 March 1908.

of a warship with a large landing force aboard at the Haitian capital.[210]

The State Department, as we previously noted, remained skeptical and decided to make an independent check before authorizing any action. Captain Potts of the *Des Moines* was therefore asked to investigate and specifically charged by the Department of State not to make his mission known to the American diplomatic representatives in Haiti nor to base his findings "too much" upon the opinions of the European diplomats at Port-au-Prince.[211] His reports, however, only confirmed the estimate formed by Furniss and were much appreciated by the State Department. "This is interesting!" wrote Robert Bacon on the margin of Potts' report, "Potts said opinions formed by consultation with many persons, feels rumor of attack on foreign subjects . . . has foundation in fact." Alvey Adee added, "I think it may now be safe to confirm these Haiti telegrams with a bunch of warships at Port-au-Prince." Thus, with a strong assist from the Navy, the Department of State reached its conclusion:

> More than two years' continuous smoke suggests *some* fire dangerously near the historical explosive called Haiti. The only hope of better things is Nord's death of old age, and a comparatively pacific revolution with the installation of a decently civilized successor. Nord's tyranny, however, may precipitate a revolutionary movement at any time, and, if it comes, the story of Touissant L'Ouverture and Soulonque may be repeated. Moral, keep ships there![212]

So a naval watch was established over Haiti. It was a purely American watch, since Root politely discouraged British suggestions that it might be shared among the interested powers.[213] There was, however, no direct intervention, and the Republic of Haiti was spared the kind of controls imposed upon its neighbor. Throughout the remainder of the Roosevelt years, the situation remained generally unchanged—despite the fact that revolutionary outbreaks grew in intensity and, on one occasion in late 1908, the diplomatic corps in Port-au-Prince seriously considered the possibility of joint landings. Elihu Root, who was

---

[210] SDNF, Case 2126/180, Furniss to Root, 25 March 1908.

[211] SDNF, Case 2126/184-85, Metcalf to Root, 26 March 1908, a copy of the orders which Metcalf prepared for Potts and cleared with Root before they were sent. For the text of the orders, see Nav Rec Messages Sent in Cipher, Metcalf to Potts, 26 March 1908.

[212] SDNF, Case 2126/212-13, Bacon memorandum of 30 March 1908 attached to copy of Potts' report on the Haitian situation; /185 1/2, Adee memorandum of 1 April attached to another Potts cable; and /218, Adee to Bacon, 20 March 1908.

[213] SDNF, Case 2126/267, Sir Esme Howard to Root, 27 March 1908 and attached documents.

making American policy, wanted no joint operations with European nations and wished to avoid any intervention except in an emergency when American life and property were clearly endangered.[214] When Albert Shaw suggested to him that he should "add a black pearl to your crown of glory" by effecting a Dominican or Panamanian solution to Haiti's problems, the Secretary declined the honor. Such a solution might be advantageous, but it was unfeasible:

> The Haitians are suspicious of us. They are densely ignorant and really believe that we want to gobble up their country, and we have to be very careful about volunteering any interference in their affairs lest we be met with an outcry of protest. . . . Of course they have good reason for doubting the advantage of too close an association between the United States and a black man's government.[215]

At least one naval observer was skeptical. Commander Shipley, after surveying the Haitian scene, observed, "It is deplorable but true that they cannot govern themselves. Affairs may go on in the future as they have in the past—but no better. The one question is how long the civilized nations of the world will permit such conditions to exist."[216] But the United States, as it turned out, was willing to "permit such conditions" until the era of Woodrow Wilson when the Navy was finally used as the instrument of a policy of outright intervention.

4. Intervention on the Isthmus

On the Isthmus of Panama the Navy enjoyed an unprecedented opportunity to execute American foreign policy in the opening years of the twentieth century. This is not to imply that the Navy "made" Isthmian policy but simply to emphasize that, given the new American sensitivity about the Isthmus, it was called on many times to carry out coercive measures which originated in a Department of State that often relied upon naval vessels as instruments of political policy. Moreover, the circumstances in Central America were such that naval officers frequently received considerable latitude and discretion in the interpretation and implementation of these orders.

In the spring of 1900, for example, there were many reports from American consular agents on the Isthmus of imminent political disorders and appeals for the dispatch of naval craft to stand watch. The *Machias*, under Commander Logan, was sent with orders to remain in

[214] SDNF, Case 2126/349, Root to Furniss, 4 December 1908.
[215] Root Papers, Albert Shaw to Root, 11 December 1908, and Root to Shaw, 16 December 1908.
[216] Nav Rec AF 8, Shipley to Newberry, 19 December 1908.

the vicinity of the Isthmus and make certain that transit across the Isthmus remained free and open, as prescribed by the Treaty of 1846 with New Granada.[217] There then followed various incidents which were typical not only of the way that the State and Navy Departments tried to meet the problem of Panamanian political disorders but also of the way in which the two departments often ended up wrestling with one another. The Navy, which soon wanted the *Machias* for other and non-political duties, began to express reluctance at the prospect of keeping a vessel permanently on the *qui vive* at Panama—especially after Commander Logan began to indicate that the men with whom he discussed Panamanian affairs felt there was little cause for anxiety. It was the Department of State which wanted the *Machias* to remain and which only grudgingly agreed to release it as the Navy's requests mounted.[218] The strongest advocate of the presence of the *Machias* was the American consul, Cobbs, whose expressions of alarm were frequent and loud. In the judgment of Commander Logan, however, the consul was a victim of "undue anxiety" and the danger of interference with the freedom of transit was slight.[219] The naval officer, to be sure, was narrowly and strictly interpreting his orders, but his lack of concern points up the fact that it was often the civilian and not the military representatives of the United States who exerted the pressure to keep naval vessels on political duty.

This particular incident ended in confusion. In July of 1900 revolutionary oubreaks, so frequently predicted, finally occurred. The *Machias* had long since departed, and the Consul's plea for the immediate dispatch of a warship elicited a reply from the Navy that none could be present for at least a week. When the Department of State protested that it had assumed that a ship was to be stationed permanently at the Isthmus, the Navy simply responded with the argument that it had previously notified the diplomats of the departure of the *Machias*. Here was a typical example of the imperfect coordination of policy which resulted when two separate and theoretically equal agencies of the executive branch, each with its own separate interests to maintain, worked through the form of written requests and formal correspondence.[220]

Since rioting was an annual occurrence on the Isthmus, the summer of 1901 also brought many reports of possible interruptions to transit. On this occasion, however, when the Department of State requested

217 Nav Rec AF 8, Consul Gudger to Hill, 7 April 1900; Consul Cobbs to Hay, 16 April 1900; and Long to Hay, 24 May 1900, forwarding various reports from Commander Logan.

218 Nav Rec AF 8, Long to Hay, 24 May 1900, and Hay to Long, 29 May 1900.

219 Nav Rec AF 8, Logan to Long, 12 June 1900.

220 Nav Rec AF 8, Cobbs to Hill, 16 July 1900, and numerous attached documents.

the assignment of a naval vessel to the Isthmus, Alvey Adee furnished an extended commentary on the 1846 Treaty for the guidance of naval officers. The obligation to keep the transit across the Isthmus free and open was not, Adee emphasized, a primary obligation of the United States but rather an international guaranty of the obligation of Colombia to preserve that transit. Therefore, in the event of interruptions, the first step was to call upon the Colombian authorities to fulfill *their* obligations. But then, Adee continued, if Colombia was unable to do so, the United States might "exercise" its own guaranty of the treaty "in any proper way sufficient to prevent interruption or embarrassment of transit." By such means, the Department of State contended, the United States would thereby help Colombia in the performance of her own duties. But naval commanders were also cautioned to avoid actions which might suggest that American intervention to protect the neutrality of the railroad was in behalf of a revolutionary faction or even of the Colombian government—that is to say, since the neutrality of the railroad was an international guaranty, the United States had no obligation to recognize the belligerent rights of *any* Colombians who might threaten the freedom of transit, whether governmental or revolutionary forces.[221]

This was helpful but still somewhat obscure, for it left much to the judgment of the naval commanders who had to assess the circumstances and interpret their general orders. The Department of State often found it difficult to be more specific. In 1901, for example, when the president of the Panama Railroad Company asked for military protection for his property, the State Department, in sending very general instructions, had to fall back on the statement that further action would have to depend upon additional information about the ability of the Colombian government to meet its obligations.[222] A year later, in answer to similar and specific Navy requests for policy guidance, the answer came back that the Department of State would have to rely heavily upon the judgment and discretion of the naval commander on the spot.[223]

But by the time of the 1901 disturbance the Navy had already girded itself, with considerable enthusiasm, for further requests for operations at the Isthmus. Both the General Board and the Naval War College began to work up detailed plans for landings and had undertaken an intensive, confidential search for information about landing sites, trails to the interior, and strategic locations along the line of the

[221] Nav Rec AF 8, Adee to Long, 6 August 1901.

[222] Nav Rec AF 8, Adee to Long, 8 August 1901.

[223] Nav Rec Confid Ltrs, Moody to Commanding Officer of the *Cincinnati*, 20 September 1902.

Panama railroad—all described as places "such as we would be compelled to occupy in case of disturbances there."[224] Convinced that the political situation on the Isthmus was disturbing, the Board decided to distribute its tentative plan of operations to all naval officers in the vicinity for their guidance. Captain Perry of the *Iowa* was sent a copy of the plans with instructions to make an immediate check on every trail and landing place both to confirm the accuracy of the plans and to assure his own complete familiarity with the area.[225]

The Navy got no immediate opportunity to put its plans into operation. Once again the officers sent to the area reported that the danger of revolution had been grossly exaggerated. Captain Sargent, whose dissenting opinions have previously been noted, suggested sarcastically that "of the American interests in danger, the most conspicuous is that of this ship's company which, after a long siege of the tropics and but a few weeks change of climate, has by force of circumstances been sent here in the wet and most unhealthy season of the year."[226] Perry of the *Iowa* reported with a similar touch of sarcasm that "but for the accounts in the New York papers, still arriving, no one here present would suspect that there was any impending trouble."[227] Sargent, incidentally, was severely reprimanded for the tone of his negative report. Acting Secretary of the Navy Frank Hackett deleted the last sentence of his dispatch before sending it to the Department of State since, in his masterful understatement, "it would seem to question the action of the State Department in making a request for naval aid."[228]

There was, however, "trouble" before the end of the year. Between the closing months of 1901 and the Panamanian uprising of November 1903 the United States did in fact land its forces on several occasions to protect the transit and enforce its interpretation of the Treaty of 1846. After the landing in November 1901, Colombian military authorities were told that, to quell an uprising, they could not shell the city of Colon without giving the residents at least four days in which to flee. Faced with the prospect of an extended delay, the government forces abandoned their scheme and simply departed from the vicinity of Colon.[229] In the following May American naval officers, summoned by the consul and representatives of the United Fruit Company, successfully "persuaded" a revolutionary faction not to attack government

224 GB, Letters, I, Lt. Commander Underwood to Pacific Mail Steamship Co., 6 September 1901, and Dewey to Sigsbee, 9 September 1901.
225 Nav Rec Confid Ltrs, Long to Perry, 10 and 16 September 1901.
226 Nav Rec AF 8, Sargent to Long, 8 September 1901.
227 Nav Rec AF 8, Perry to Long, 23 September 1901.
228 Nav Rec AF 8, Hackett to Sargent, 11 September 1901.
229 Nav Rec AF 8, Lt. Commander Henry McCrea to Long, 26 November 1901.

forces.[230] The most significant interventions, however, took place in the fall of 1902 when rumors of revolution became numerous. Secretary Moody, reporting the situation to Roosevelt, was persuaded that the revolutionists meant to attack both the line of the railroad and the city of Panama. Since the United States was then negotiating with Colombia for the purchase of the property of the New Panama Company, Moody believed that this American intention combined with the provisions of the 1846 Treaty to give the United States "a prospective interest in that property" and the right to prevent any destruction of the railroad properties. He therefore wanted a strong naval force at both Colon and Panama City with orders that these forces be prepared to occupy strategic points along the length of the railroad.[231] By September there were in fact four companies of marines and three warships actively involved in maintaining the transit across the Isthmus. The Navy's tactics were varied. It prohibited Colombian government troops from placing obstructions along the rail line to hamper the movement of revolutionary forces, provided American armed guards for the trains on the railroad, and permitted government troops to travel on the trains only if unarmed. The naval officers on the spot were convinced that their mission had been vital; to Commander McLean of the *Cincinnati* it was only the presence of the naval vessels which had prevented the disruption of rail communications and free transit across the Isthmus.[232]

Coincidentally it was in October 1902 that the Navy established its Caribbean squadron, a permanent unit of the fleet with a mission, more political than military, to preserve law and order throughout the Caribbean area. With the Navy being called upon to provide ships for so many and different "trouble spots" throughout the entire area, the Department believed it necessary to organize and institutionalize its procedures for serving as the enforcement agency of the Department of State. While the immediate situation at the Isthmus was but one of many factors that led to the creation of the Caribbean division, its standing orders called special attention to the Navy's responsibilities in the area where the canal would be built: "It should fulfill our treaty obligations with all those countries and particularly with Colombia."[233] There was also, in the autumn of 1902, a new urgency and a new note

[230] Nav Rec AF 8, McCrea to Moody, 16 May 1902.

[231] Nav Rec Confid Ltrs, Moody to Roosevelt, 12 September 1902, and Moody to Commanding Officer of the *Cincinnati*, 20 September 1902.

[232] Nav Rec AF 8, McLean to Moody, 16 and 23 September 1902, and Commander W. B. Diehl to Moody, 17 November 1902. See also Moody Papers, Taylor to Moody, 13 November 1902.

[233] GB, File 420-1, Moody to Commander-in-Chief, North Atlantic Station, 4 October 1902.

of stridency in the orders which went out to the Isthmian commanders from the Navy Department. Secretary Moody flatly wrote, "The Department believes it wise to have United States forces at hand to insure our rights as set forth in the treaty and to protect the interests of the United States in the event of military leaders of either party being unable to control their forces."[234] Similarly, the commander of the *Cincinnati* received explicit instructions that "Any transport of troops which might contravene these provisions of the treaty should not be sanctioned by you, nor should use of road be permitted that might convert the line of transit into theatre of hostilities." The rights of the Colombian government received, at best, backhanded recognition: "transportation of [Colombian] government troops not in violation of the treaty and which will not endanger transit or provoke hostilities may not be objectionable."[235]

Clearly then, in the months after the passage of the Spooner Act and while the Hay-Harran Convention was still pending, the United States was moving more forcefully on the Isthmus. In contrast to its earlier interpretation of the 1846 Treaty, it was setting itself up as the arbiter of that treaty and, in the name of the treaty, using its navy to regulate the activities of Colombian government forces as well as of insurrectionists. It was not a very large step from this to the situation in the fall of 1903 when, with Colombian unwillingness to ratify the Hay-Harran Convention, the United States openly interpreted the treaty of 1846 against the government at Bogota and welcomed the revolt that created an independent Panamanian state.

The Navy did, to be sure, occasionally insert a few modifiers which showed at least minimal awareness of Latin feelings. The orders establishing the Caribbean division ended on a hortatory note, instructing all officers

to advance these interests by the cultivation of friendly relations with the people of those countries. Whenever possible a more cordial feeling should be developed by greater intercourse with the natives and their officials, by being familiar with their language and habits, and by the avoidance of any assumption of superiority. This latter attitude is considered by the Department to be of utmost importance.[236]

The commanding officer of the *Wisconsin* was also told in the fall of 1902 that he should remember that Colombian-American relations

234 Nav Rec Confid Ltrs, Moody to Roosevelt, 12 September 1902.

235 Nav Rec Confid Ltrs, Moody to Commanding Officer of the *Cincinnati*, 20 September 1902.

236 GB, File 20-1, orders of 4 October 1902, as cited.

were strained and negotiations for a canal treaty stalemated "on account of a feeling of irritation on part of Colombian representatives."[237] Irritation there certainly was, even though John Hay eventually did decide to have the Navy loosen some of the restrictions initially placed on Colombia's use of the railroad and to limit American "interdiction" to grave threats of disorder.[238] Certainly, too, the various incidents on the Isthmus in the fall of 1902, which distressed Harran in Washington as well as other Colombians, were a main factor in the increasing unwillingness of Colombia to agree to the canal treaty so eagerly sought by the United States.

In the biggest intervention of all—Roosevelt's well-publicized "taking" of Panama, with or without the consent of the cabinet, the Congress and the public—the Navy served simply as the executive agent for a Presidential policy. In the formal Navy records, the confidential correspondence as well as the copies of cables sent in cipher, there are no direct references to Panamanian affairs until November 2, 1903—at which date of course the cables literally began to buzz with activity. Commander John Hubbard, of the *Nashville*, the vessel on the spot at Colon when the insurrection occurred was privy to no secrets abouts its imminence. Three weeks before, indeed, he had reported to Washington that while three-quarters of the local population would welcome a canal on almost any terms and would follow a competent leader in that direction, "such a leader is now lacking, and it isn't believed that in the near future these people will take any initiative steps."[239] On orders from the Navy Department Hubbard had then left for Guantanamo, spent some time in Jamaica, and did not return to the Isthmus until the evening of November 2nd. All was quiet, and, despite much talk of revolution, no Panamanian actions had taken place. On the morning of the 3rd a Colombian gunboat carrying 400 to 500 troops arrived, but Hubbard, still lacking specific orders, decided he could not prevent the Colombians from landing their forces.[240] This is scarcely the record of a man with foreknowledge.

There is, however, little need to retell the familiar story of the hour-by-hour progress of the Panamanian revolt on November 3rd, for it has been subjected to detailed analysis by many historians. But, again, the formal records of the Army and Navy fail to indicate that the two services were deeply involved in the chain of events that led

[237] Nav Rec Messages Sent in Cipher, Darling to Casey, 29 October 1902.

[238] Miles P. du Val, *Cadiz to Cathay* (Stanford, 1940), 183-85, a brief account of the entire episode.

[239] Nav Rec, Letters and Endorsements from the Commanding Officer of the U.S.S. *Nashville*, 28 May 1903 to 5 January 1904, Hubbard to Moody, 17 October 1903.

[240] Nav Rec, Letters from the *Nashville*, as cited, Hubbard to Moody, 8 November 1903.

to the *coup*. To be sure, some months beforehand, at the suggestion of the Chief of the Army General Staff, Roosevelt did interview two captains who had recently been working in behalf of Army intelligence on the Isthmus. But these two officers, instead of providing their President with new information about political conditions at Panama, found themselves amazed at the detailed knowledge already possessed by Roosevelt. According to one account, the two captains thereupon abandoned their own private thoughts of resigning from the Army and leading the Isthmian revolt themselves.[241] In mid-October the Navy Department dispatched a considerable series of cables which alerted various naval units to possible operations on the Isthmus in early November. These messages, however, contained neither political information nor policy guidance; they were purely operational in character. Even Roosevelt's sharpest critics have admitted that these cables did not of themselves imply formal intervention and were not licenses to act.[242] It is also clear from the historical record that the plotters in Panama got their hints about what to expect not from naval sources but from Hay and Roosevelt.

It was only on the evening of November 2nd, the night before the *coup*, that the orders began to stream out from the Navy Department. Their character was such as to indicate that in this venture the Navy was the transmission belt for Presidential action rather than an active maker of policy. One of the most striking features of these last-minute cables, indeed, is the lack of co-ordination which was revealed. The cable to Hubbard on the evening of the 2nd, for example, directed him to prevent any hostile force from landing at Colon, especially Colombian troops, and to occupy the line of the railroad. But the orders were delayed, and Hubbard did not receive them until after he had permitted the Colombians to land. His reply on the 3rd, which must certainly have caused consternation in Washington, was the accurate statement that so far there were no signs of an uprising though one might occur before the day was over.[243] There was also similar confusion over Hubbard's responsibility for sending a force to Panama City, on the other side of the Isthmus, to prevent a Colombian bombardment. Commander Hubbard, claiming that reports of the shelling were exaggerated, argued that his commitments in Colon prevented compliance. Eventually, of course, the Navy's role *was* decisive. The later arrival of warships on both sides of the Isthmus—above all, the arrival of the *Dixie* with explicit orders to prevent Colombian retaliation—

241 Du Val, *Cadiz to Cathay*, 303-05.

242 The standard accounts of the Panama affair are Pringle, *Roosevelt*, ch. 6, and Dwight Miner, *The Fight for the Panama Route* (New York, 1940), ch. 10.

243 Miner, *Fight for Panama*, 360-63.

effectively persuaded the Colombian forces that it was hopeless to try to undo the revolt.[244] Still the cryptic nature of many of these orders and the need for secrecy must have baffled as much as enlightened naval officers on the Isthmus. Their contribution was to follow orders and, as it turned out, to furnish reports to Washington which helped the Administration to determine what was actually happening and supplemented the information which came from consular sources.

Both Army and Navy were more deeply involved in the policymaking process after the *coup* when they sought to commit the Administration to a number of military recommendations designed to protect the new Panamanian state from Colombia. The considerable concentration of naval strength on the Isthmus immediately following the uprising naturally deterred the Colombians, but the question soon arose as to whether the government at Bogota would long tolerate the new Republic. American naval authorities at first thought the Colombian danger was minimal; Admirals Henry Glass and Joseph Coghlan, two senior officers who had been rushed to Panama, were convinced that a limited amount of naval patrolling would be sufficient to protect the new American ward.[245] But the Army soon began to sound the alarm bell and, almost out of the blue, forecast a Colombian land invasion.[246] At first, the Army's warnings merely annoyed naval authorities in Washington and fanned the familiar flames of interservice rivalry. Admiral Taylor bluntly cabled the marine commandant on the Isthmus

> Let the Department know through proper channels of your daily operations. . . . Please also remember that the Army, which has only a couple of officers down there, is furnishing the President every day with pages of cipher cable, most of which, though dealing with small matters, is of considerable interest. Let your scouting be thorough and extending a long distance and give us daily accounts of it.[247]

In any event by early December both the Navy and War Departments had become definitely worried. Admiral Glass was authorized to place marines near the frontier of the new Panamanian state, told to seek all possible evidence about Colombian intentions, and badgered with inquiries about the ability of his forces to withstand a Colombian attack. On the 10th orders were even prepared in Washington —though not actually sent—for Glass to position his sailors and ma-

---

[244] Nav Rec Confid Ltrs, Moody to Hay, 5 November 1903, enclosing various dispatches from the *Nashville*, and forwarded to State as soon as received. For summary, see du Val, *Cadiz to Cathay*, 335.

[245] Du Val, *Cadiz to Cathay*, 362.

[246] Nav Rec Messages Sent in Cipher, Moody to Glass, 3 December 1903.

[247] Nav Rec Confid Ltrs, Taylor to Elliott, 4 January 1904.

rines so as "to prevent forcibly hostile entrance by land to State of Panama." While Washington did draw back from the full implications of such action, there was another week at least during which Glass received orders which stressed that his positions must be strong enough to resist attack and, if attacked, should be held.[248] On the 18th and 19th of December, however, there was a definite change in official thinking in Washington. Thereafter, for example, Glass was told that he was to draw in his outposts if they became liable to attack, that his positions were for observation and not resistance, and that the Administration had decided to restrict active military operations in Panama to the defense of the rail line across the Isthmus. He was specifically instructed to disregard any previous orders which might appear to be in conflict with these latest expressions of national policy.[249]

These early December alarms had set various military groups into motion in an effort to inaugurate a vastly expanded American military role in the defense of Panama. The prime mover was the Army General Staff which for some time continued to fear the probability of a Colombian land attack.[250] The Staff, in turn, was influenced by its own observer on the Isthmus, Captain Cloman, a former military attaché in Panama who was now operating under an assumed name and in the guise of a lumberman. Cloman liberally furnished the War Department with lengthy reports that focused on the strategic importance of the Yavisa, an area near the southern neck of the Isthmus, stressed that Colombia could mount a force of 15,000 soldiers, and wrote off any Panamanian help as negligible.[251] General S. B. Young, the Chief of Staff, prepared a summary of Cloman's reports for his chief, the Secretary of War. Elihu Root, in turn, supplied Roosevelt with copies and directed the Joint Board to consider the entire issue at a special meeting two days before Christmas.[252]

The members of the Joint Board strongly supported the recommendations put before it by the General Staff. Admiral Dewey, as senior officer, reported back to the two service secretaries that, if the United States became involved in a war for the defense of Panama, American forces must occupy not only the entire line of the railroad

[248] Nav Rec Confid Ltrs, Moody to Roosevelt, 14 December 1903, and Messages Sent in Cipher, Moody to Glass, 3 and 11 December 1903. The file includes a copy of a proposed message of 10 December which was vetoed by Roosevelt and not sent. See also du Val, *Cadiz to Cathay*, 362-65.

[249] Nav Rec Messages Sent in Cipher, Moody to Glass, 18 December 1903.

[250] GS, File 818, 29 June 1907, Memorandum of Problems and Studies of the Army War College. This memorandum contains a copy of a Root to Roosevelt letter of 23 December 1903 that spells out the fears of the Chief of Staff, General S. B. Young.

[251] JB, File 326-1, 21 December 1903, a report prepared for Root by General S. B. Young and based on Cloman's findings.

[252] GS, File 326-1, Loeb to Moody, 23 December 1903.

but also the "strategic area" of the Yavisa. He himself was a strong advocate of preventive measures, action to forestall Colombia in advance:

> The Board is also of the opinion that it would tend materially to continue the maintenance of peace if the Yavisa region could now be occupied by a strong force. It appears to the Board that neglect to prevent possible enemies from obtaining possession of the large quantity of supplies and establishing a strong foothold in Yavisa is almost a deliberate invitation to them to take a step which would be certain to bring on hostilities—a step which they might otherwise hesitate to take.[253]

When both service secretaries sent this recommendation to Roosevelt, the President had before him the Joint Board's opinion that the United States should undertake a not inconsiderable military venture in the name of prevention.

But if the Joint Board had ever had a chance, its recommendations came too late. For several days the compasses in both the White House and the Department of State had been veering toward caution. The danger of political repercussions was beginning to suggest caution. The orders sent Admiral Glass on the 18th and 19th were an indication of this, as was Roosevelt's own message to Secretary Moody two days before the Joint Board meeting: "Would it not be well to issue instructions down at and around Panama that under no circumstances must they fire unless fired upon? If there should be a brush with Colombia, I want to be dead sure that Colombia fires first."[254] John Hay, too, was urging Moody to make certain that a scheduled visit of American warships to Cartagena should "under no circumstances take on the aspect of threatening war."[255]

President Roosevelt eventually turned down the recommendations of the Joint Board, but he did not do so lightly. "The military reasons for taking possession of Yavisa are strong," he informed Admiral Walker, "yet it seems to me that they may be outbourne by the political reasons, so as to make it inadvisable to take it just now."[256] In his formal "overruling" (the word is T.R.'s) of the Joint Board, Roosevelt extended this line of reasoning. The military reasons for desiring the Yavisa were good, while the Joint Board was entirely correct in presenting its views to him and, from a military point of view, pressing for their acceptance. "But it seems to me," Roosevelt wrote in summary, "that the political reasons against seeming to court a clash with Colombia out-

[253] JB, File 325 (War Plans), Dewey to Moody and Root, 23 December 1903.
[254] Roosevelt, *Letters*, III, 674, Roosevelt to Moody, 21 December 1903.
[255] Moody Papers, Hay to Moody, 23 December 1903.
[256] Roosevelt, *Letters*, III, 677, Roosevelt to Walker, 23 December 1903.

weigh the military disadvantages of allowing them to seize unop-
pressed a valuable base of operations against us."[257]

There were further alarms about Colombia's intentions for at least
another six weeks. Yet the naval representatives on the Isthmus had
never been as fully persuaded of the Colombian threat as their
superiors on the Washington boards. Even at the height of the December "scare" Admiral Glass, with the naval officer's faith in the virtues
of seapower, had remained confident that his sailors and marines could
indefinitely contain any Colombian advance. "Land movements," he
had advised, "are almost impossible, and we could perfectly control
the main waterways."[258] (Though this confidence, to be sure, may have
reflected a desire to preserve the Navy's prerogatives and to keep the
Army out as much as it represented an unbiased estimate of Colombian strength.) But even Glass had a few moments of doubt in January
1904, while the official planners in the General Board, convinced that
Colombia would never accept the loss of her Panamanian province,
continued to perfect their plans for possible military action.[259] But Colombia did nothing, nor did Washington abandon its eventual decision
to pursue a cautious approach. Ultimately, the United States reverted
to its original interpretation of the 1846 Treaty; that is, it would protect the neutrality of the railroad and the proposed canal route but it
would go no further. It would not defend Panama's borders. When
there were reports of a possible Colombian move in the Chiriqui Lagoon, Admiral Coghlan got specific orders that he was not to interfere
with a Colombian landing anywhere in Panama except within the strategic limits of the canal zone.[260] Roosevelt, once overzealous, returned
to the "correct" approach, and, while he recognized the right of his
military advisers to present their military recommendations, he overruled them on the solid ground of the ultimate superiority of political
to purely military considerations.

There was but one last touch of deviousness. When Congress began
to make its customary investigatory noises, Roosevelt sought to assemble documentation to defend his Panama policy. His personal secretary wrote Secretary Moody at the Navy Department:

The President would like to be advised if the papers and documents
which have been submitted by you from time to time to the President really have any bearing upon the separation of Panama from
Colombia. It does not seem to the President that the purely military

257 Roosevelt, *Letters*, III, 677-78, Roosevelt to Leslie Shaw, 24 December 1903.
258 Nav Rec AF 8, Glass to Moody, 21 December 1903.
259 Nav Rec AF 8, Coghlan to Moody, 26 January 1904, and Confid Ltrs, Taylor
to Elliott, 4 January 1904.
260 Du Val, *Cadiz to Cathay*, 376-77.

dispatches of our forces come under that head. For instance, observations by Army and Navy officers as to the probabilities of success of invasion along different routes, or as to the possibilities of resistance by the Panama troops, or as to the quality of the Colombian troops, or as to our own plans in the event of military complications, are none of them called for by the resolutions and would none of them be proper to give out. Simply send over to the President copies of all documents called for under the wording of the [Senate] resolution. Also please send the President a private memorandum as to the dates when we began to have correspondence relating to such matters as those given above, which the President does not regard as being called for by the resolution.[261]

Once the Republic of Panama had been established, the United States became its patron, proper and generally correct, though always prepared, with its military forces in the Canal Zone, to maintain order throughout the new republic. As Minister Barrett noted in 1904, "the masses of people are schooled and experienced in all kinds of uprisings, agitations, and popular excitements, and great harm might be done on some occasion if there were not a force, like a company of marines, convenient at Ancon, the effect of whose moral presence, even if they did not participate in preserving order, would maintain quiet or protect property."[262] Indeed, the decision of Panama not to maintain a standing army—a decision presumably made in the interest of internal political tranquillity—owed much to the influence of the United States which suggested that the marines in the Canal Zone could be used by the Government of Panama to preserve order.[263]

A new attitude toward Panamanian affairs became evident once Elihu Root succeeded Hay as Secretary of State in 1905. Root, as we have previously noted, insisted that strict obedience be paid to legal norms and hoped to regain some of the Latin American friendship that had been lost by the high-handedness of Roosevelt and Hay. The new Secretary, it must be emphasized, was thoroughly convinced that the United States had both the right and the duty to protect its interest in the Caribbean and on the Isthmus—and to do so by force, if absolutely necessary. But he was equally positive that there must be no hint of illegality or irregularity in American actions. "The Latin American people," he once observed, "are perfectly willing to sit at the feet of Gamiel if Gamiel won't kick or bat them on the head."[264]

[261] Moody Papers, Loeb to Moody, 30 January 1904.

[262] W. D. McCain, *The United States and the Republic of Panama* (Durham, 1937), 59-60, quoting Barrett's dispatch of 13 December 1904.

[263] McCain, *U.S. and Panama*, 48-55.

[264] Root Papers, Root to Albert Shaw, 3 January 1908.

The new demeanor of Gamiel became evident at the time of the national elections in Panama in 1906. There was widespread apprehension that the fledgling state would be unable to withstand the political tensions of an electoral campaign and that, at the very minimum, military forces of the United States would have to intervene to protect life and property. Moreover, the Panamanian government made it clear that it would welcome American intervention, naturally on its behalf. Indeed, it was obviously seeking active American support for its cause.[265] The commanding officer of the *Colombia*, the vessel then assigned to Panamanian duty, suggested that it might be advisable to prepare careful plans so that, at a moment's notice on election day, special trains could rush marine detachments into Colon and Panama City.[266]

Elihu Root, however, had anticipated such demands and had already undertaken an effort to define the terms under which the American military might intervene. As early as December of 1905 he tried to make it clear that the United States intended to exercise an impartial attitude during the Panamanian election campaign. The 1903 treaty with Panama, he argued, gave the United States no rights to interfere in the domestic politics of that country and authorized intervention only if internal disorder appeared to threaten the construction and, ultimately, the operation of the Panama Canal.[267] In February 1906, in one of the longest memoranda that he composed while Secretary of State, Root tried to spell out the precise details of American authority on the Isthmus. His memorandum informed the War Department that the clauses of the 1903 Treaty "did not contemplate relieving the Government of Panama from all responsibility for the maintenance of public peace and constitutional order, nor do they place the onus for such maintenance, in the first instance, upon the United States." The Panamanian government should not rely upon the power of the United States "to protect them from the results of indifference and indiscretion on their part."

Root then turned to the question of American responsibility if the turmoils of a political campaign should create a situation—"which God may forbid"—that the Colombian authorities could not control. Armed bands, he noted, might try to prevent an election or overthrow a government. If so, then American representatives in Panama would have several important questions to answer: Did such acts threaten the Republic itself? Were the insurrectionaries so well armed that Pana-

---

[265] McCain, *U.S. and Panama*, 63 ff. and, especially, 70.

[266] Nav Rec AF 8, Commander J. M. Bowyer to Governor Charles Magoon, 19 June 1906.

[267] SDML, Memorandum of the Second Assistant Secretary, with attachments, 1 December 1905.

manian authorities could not cope with them? Above all, was there any threat to the construction of the canal? Such questions, Root continued, were essentially military questions and, in the main, would have to be answered by American military authorities in Panama. It was therefore the responsibility of the War Department to draw up, in advance, instructions sufficient to cover such emergencies and to make them available to all Army officers in the area. Properly informed of the nature and scope of their authority, these officers "could act promptly and efficiently but without exceeding their jurisdiction."[268]

Root, in short, was both trying to regularize procedures and to draw a clear line between interference in Panamanian politics and intervention in emergencies that might threaten the canal. The core of his policy remained the protection of the canal. "The construction of the Isthmian Canal," he firmly stated, "is . . . a national endeavor of the United States, and measures which interfere with that work and are calculated to obstruct, hinder, or delay its accomplishments, are interferences with the rights and privileges of the United States and must be dealt with accordingly."[269]

Secretary of War Taft did in fact draft the instructions that Root requested. While emphasizing that the State Department did not intend to restrict American powers in the event of an emergency, Taft also underscored the point that there must be no military intervention unless the emergency was grave and beyond the powers of Panama to handle.[270] Thus, in June 1906, when the commander of the *Colombia* wanted to have the troop trains ready and loaded with marines, Governor Charles Magoon of the Canal Zone supplied the naval officer with copies of all the correspondence between himself, Root, and Taft on the subject of intervention.[271] Commander Bowyer was thus well informed of the guidelines set by the War and State Departments. The trains, it must be added, were in fact readied, for fears of insurrection rose as the Panamanian elections neared, but there was, happily, no need for the marines since the voting was conducted smoothly and without disorder. On the day following, all American authorities in Panama—Governor Magoon of the Canal Zone, Commander Bowyer, and the American minister—unanimously recommended that the *Colombia* be released and the marine complement returned to American soil.[272] For the naval officers, moreover, there were official compli-

[268] SDML, Root to Taft, 3 February 1906.
[269] *Ibid.*
[270] Nav Rec AF 8, Taft to Magoon, 26 April 1906.
[271] SDML, Bowyer to Bonaparte, and Root to Bonaparte, 3 July 1906.
[272] SDML, Magoon to Root, 2 July 1906.

ments from the Department of State because "they have left nothing undone to strengthen the influences of the civil authorities in their efforts to preserve peace and public order . . . without in any way embarrassing these civil authorities or the Government of Panama by a display of force."[273] The threat of American intervention had certainly been present throughout the Panamanian election, but the manner of handling American power had been regularized and was far different than in the period before Root.

5. CUBAN AND CENTRAL AMERICAN AFFAIRS

But if political affairs on the Isthmus proceeded smoothly in 1906, they broke down completely in Cuba at precisely the same time. The Cuban crisis in the early fall of that year was an acute embarrassment to Washington; the "Pearl of the Antilles," once given independence, was meant to be a Caribbean showpiece, a government which would demonstrate to a skeptical world that Cuba could conduct her own affairs and was not simply a puppet dancing on the American string. The troubles, moreover, were entirely unexpected. Root, as a matter of fact, had only recently put on paper his conviction that the Cubans had conducted themselves "admirably" and had been far more successful at self-government than anyone in Washington would have dared to hope at the time of their independence.[274] Adding to the difficulties was the fact that the insurrection against President Estrada Palma in 1906 occurred at a moment when Root was in Latin America on his well-publicized good-will tour, the American minister to Cuba was in Europe, Roosevelt was at Oyster Bay, and Secretary of the Navy Bonaparte, as was his custom, was absent from his desk more than he was present.

In these circumstances, then, the first intimation of serious trouble appears to have come in the form of a cable from Frank Steinhart, the Consul General in Havana, which informed Roosevelt that the Cuban president wanted the immediate dispatch of two American warships since he could no longer preserve order in his country. Palma promised that within a few days he would get the Cuban Congress to make an official request for "forcible intervention."[275] Theodore Roosevelt at once took firm hold of the policy reins. Through numerous actions

273 SDML, Bacon to Bonaparte, 23 July 1906.
274 Root Papers, Root to Charles Eliot, 18 June 1906.
275 SDNF, Case 244/113, Steinhart to Roosevelt, 13 September 1906. For a general account of the episode, R. H. Minger, "William H. Taft and the U.S. Intervention in Cuba in 1906," *Hispanic American Historical Review*, XLI, no. 1 (February 1961), 75-89.

the President made it clear that he, and he alone, intended to define the scope of the American response. Notable from the outset of the crisis was the extent of his control over the employment of American military force and his measured use of the instruments of coercion. Thus Bonaparte was authorized to send two naval vessels as promptly as possible but strictly and only "to protect American interests." Steinhart was told that Roosevelt was relutant to intervene and also that he was not prepared to do so until the Cubans had exhausted every possible countermeasure.[276]

But as the insurrection grew, Roosevelt adopted a dual policy. On the one hand he directed the Navy to prepare for the worst, to speed up its preparations to send additional ships, and to make ready as many marines as possible. "We should have a large force of marines in Havana," he wired from Oyster Bay, "at the earliest possible moment on any ships able to carry them."[277] But at the same time he refused, at least for the moment, to authorize any naval landings that could be interpreted as intervention in Cuban political affairs. Thus, on the same day that he authorized the naval build-up, Roosevelt made certain that cables went to naval officers in Cuban waters instructing them "to take no part in the troubles in Cuba other than to protect American interests." Even these actions could occur only in cases of necessity and after clearance had been received from the American chargé d'affaires in Havana, Jacob Sleeper.[278] The President also tried to keep his larger preparations secret. When it was decided that the naval force should include three battleships, Roosevelt decreed that the announcement of their sailing orders should be handled "so as to give misleading information" and to suggest a long-anticipated shakedown cruise.[279]

Inevitably there was confusion at the Cuban end of the chain of command. On September 13, Commander Colwell of the *Denver*, one of the first vessels to reach the scene, visited President Palma in company with Steinhart. He quickly concluded that the insurrection was far more serious than even Palma realized. Colwell was convinced that the rebel forces had sufficient strength to seize Havana, following which there would be an uprising of "low negro and lawless elements." Sleeper, told by Cuban officials that they could no longer guarantee American lives or property, wanted a force of American sailors ashore. The two therefore decided on their own authority to land a

---

[276] SDNF, Case 244/114, Bacon to Steinhart, 10 September 1906.
[277] SDNF, Case 244/118, Roosevelt to Bacon, 12 September 1906.
[278] SDNF, Case 244/106 1/2, Bonaparte to naval commanders in Cuban waters, 13 September 1906.
[279] Nav Rec Messages Sent in Cipher, Bonaparte to Commanding Officer of the *Louisiana*, 14 September 1906.

battalion of marines from the *Denver*, later claiming that their action had the approval of President Palma.[280]

Later the same day the chargé had second thoughts, especially after he had received the State Department's warning, dated the 12th, which specified the restrictions which were to apply to any intervention. Sleeper then asked Colwell to withdraw his marines, but his request was refused by the naval officer. It was not until the 14th, by which time Sleeper had reconfirmed the "no landings" instructions with Washington, that the naval forces were returned to their ship.[281] Commander Colwell remained unrepentant. He defended his conduct on the grounds that he had never received any orders beyond those which had initially sent him to Cuba and that, in the absence of specific instructions, he had no accurate understanding of the administration's policy. Then, moving to the offensive, he maintained: "I do know that the immediate effect of my landing on the evening of the 13th was to prevent the occupation of Havana that evening by rebels, with probably much disorder and probable bloodshed. The effect of my landing was an immediate armistice."[282]

Effective the landing may have been, but the wrath of Roosevelt was soon felt in Havana. "You had no business to direct the landing of those troops without specific authority from here," he cabled Sleeper. "They are not to be employed in keeping general order without our authority. . . . Remember that unless you are directed otherwise from here the forces are to be used only to protect American life and property."[283] The President still clearly hoped to avoid a general intervention and, at the very least, regarded the action taken by Sleeper and Colwell as premature.

But the crisis worsened. When Roosevelt finally became convinced that Cuba "had fallen into the insurrectionary habit," he dispatched his battleships and an expeditionary force. Secretary of War Taft was made responsible for this force and charged with the responsibility of trying to negotiate a settlement between the warring Cuban political parties. It was also made clear that the military were to be under firm civilian control. Strict limits were set upon their sphere of operations. The Navy, for example, was directed to supply the Department of State with a copy of every set of orders issued by naval authorities that pertained to Cuban affairs—and for some time virtually buried the Department of State with copies of naval correspondence on nearly

[280] Nav Rec AF 8, Colwell to Bonaparte, 4 October 1906.

[281] SDNF, Case 244/106-121, various documents from Sleeper and Colwell relating to the initial landing.

[282] Nav Rec AF 8, Colwell report of 4 October 1906, as cited.

[283] SDNF, Case 244/121, Roosevelt to Sleeper, 13 September 1906.

every conceivable subject.[284] When Army units were sent to Cuba, their marching orders were strict:

> The President of the United States deems it of utmost importance that American forces should not be engaged in any conflict with Cubans, but that disorders by Cubans should be suppressed by Cubans . . . troops, therefore, are not to take part in any active way in the suppression of disorder except in an extreme emergency in which [it is] absolutely necessary for them to protect life and property.[285]

Great care was exercised in the choice of an Army officer to command the troops sent to Cuba. When General Frederick Funston was suggested for the post, Taft at once vetoed his appointment on the grounds that the situation demanded a commander who could work easily with civilians and who had "more pliancy and diplomacy" than Funston.[286]

Yet this second intervention in Cuba was more than just an illustration of the principle of civilian control. At the Washington level there was also a considerable amount of civil-military cooperation and consultation. When Roosevelt directed that the Navy must keep the State Department informed of all its actions, Navy Secretary Bonaparte could reply that his department had already been in close touch with Root's assistants and that from the beginning practically all of the Navy's orders to its Cuban vessels had been at the suggestion of the State Department.[287] Bonaparte himself believed so strongly in the need for coordination that he suggested that the naval commander in Cuba should be clearly placed under the control of the Secretary of War, Taft.[288] Moreover, the military did have an opportunity to influence certain specific aspects of the intervention. Roosevelt's initial suggestion, for example, had been to prepare and dispatch a force of marines. But Admiral Converse persuaded the Acting Secretary of State, Robert Bacon, that if three battleships were assigned to the Cuban mission, it would be possible to get 2,000 sailors to Havana in less than five days and to do so in far greater secrecy than if the marines were used. Bacon, in turn, convinced the President of the merits of this suggestion. Thus it was on the admiral's recommendation that the decision was taken to employ the force of battleships.[289]

[284] Nav Rec Confid Ltrs, Newberry to Root, 25 September 1906.

[285] GS, File 132, Report of Major General James F. Bell, Chief of Staff, on his assignment in Cuba, no date but marked as received on 29 January 1907.

[286] Root Papers, Taft to Roosevelt, 3 October 1906.

[287] Bonaparte Papers, telegram, Bonaparte to Roosevelt, 18 September 1906.

[288] Bonaparte Papers, 18 September 1906, a detailed letter sent in support of telegram cited above.

[289] Nav Rec AF 8, Bacon to Roosevelt and Roosevelt to Bacon, 13 September 1906.

Taft's mission to Cuba, as is well known, failed to solve the political crisis and led shortly to the second American occupation of that island, an intervention about which the Administration had been and remained reluctant. But in Central America, where revolution appeared endemic, the same niceties of behavior were not always observed, even in the era of Elihu Root. America's paramount interest in the canal made her exceptionally sensitive to the preservation of law and order in adjacent countries. Root, to be sure, always hoped to find other than military means to cope with Central American unrest. The various Central American peace pacts which he sponsored as well as the Central American Court of Justice were juridical efforts in that direction, endeavors which, at best, were only sporadically successful. But, successful or not, the State Department never thought it prudent to adopt a hands-off attitude. As a result naval officers on duty in Central American waters long continued to play a significant role in the affairs of that region. And there were always those who wished them to do more. Frederick Palmer, a journalist who accompanied the fleet on its tour round the world, was so appalled by what he had seen in Central American ports of call that he took it upon himself to write a lengthy letter to Theodore Roosevelt. The gist of his communication was that no regions of the world were worse governed than Guatemala and Nicaragua and that the only solution for their chronic condition was "to give our ministers resident the power of advice and suggestions and have our cruisers call more frequently." Roosevelt was sufficiently impressed by Palmer's observations to forward his letter to the State Department. But on its margin Alvey Adee, conscious of the dilemma that was posed, scratched a plaintive note, "How could we do this without actually acquiring all these little countries?"[290]

The record of the Navy's involvement with the small states of Central America is voluminous. It is also composed of numerous incidents long-forgotten and trivial in the extreme, many of which suggest low comedy rather than high international drama, confusion rather than coordinated policy. A few of these episodes should, however, be cited to indicate the flavor as well as the objectives of the naval role in Central America.

Typical of the many minor incidents in which the Navy was involved was one which occurred in the spring of 1906 when a revolt appeared imminent in Guatemala and a vessel loaded with arms for the insurrectionists slipped out of San Francisco harbor. Since the ship carried an American flag, the State Department could and did order the Navy to seize the ship before its arrival in Guatemala. But the Navy was late

---

[290] SDNF, Case 6775/607-08, Frederick Palmer to Roosevelt, with marginal comments by Adee on the copy that T.R. sent to Root.

in getting to the scene. Its only accomplishment was to report that the American consul at the port where the ship had arrived was an agent for the insurrection. The revolt shortly collapsed, leaving the Navy with the tricky question of what action to take about the still uncaptured vessel that had supplied the abortive uprising. A hurried conference between Navy and State Departments led to the decision that there were no legitimate grounds for seizure, and the orders for capture of the vessel were abruptly rescinded.[291]

The desire to use the Navy to keep the peace was, however, always a constant. In 1907, when Root was hopeful that the Central American Peace Conference, then about to be held in Washington, would produce peace-keeping machinery, a certain Commander Glennon began reporting his fears of a pending conflict. He suggested that the United States might best prevent such a war by sending a note to each government "in the name of humanity" stating that it would regard the initiation of conflict as an unfriendly act and would feel justified in seizing the ports and customs houses of any aggressor. Glennon was immediately reminded of the forthcoming Washington conference and advised that pacific conditions should not be interrupted prior to that gathering.[292] Yet Root, whatever his hopes for juridical solutions, also made certain that the Navy continued to keep a sufficient number of American naval vessels on the Central American coast to guard American interests. Toward the end of the year—in fact, just three days after the end of the Washington conference—the commanding officer of one naval vessel reported from Honduras that the situation was so quiet in La Union that "even the street barriers . . . are down." He asked that his and other ships be withdrawn, but the State Department was unconvinced. Acting Secretary Bacon at once advised the Navy that removal of the ships would be unwise and asked the Navy to keep at least one vessel on each Central American coast until such time as the relations between the Central American states had been stabilized as a consequence of the agreements reached at the Washington conference.[293]

It was, above all, the policies of Zelaya, the Nicaraguan dictator, which caused the greatest concern in Washington about the prospects for Central American peace. The final breaking point in Nicaraguan-American relations did not occur until the administration of President Taft, but long before that time Zelaya had angered a long and impos-

[291] Nav Rec AF 8, Newberry to Bonaparte, 8 June 1906, and Converse to Commanding Officer of *Marblehead*, 16 June 1906; Messages Sent in Cipher, Newberry to *Marblehead*, 15 June 1906.

[292] SDNF, Case 6775/103-04, Glennon to Metcalf, 23 August 1907.

[293] SDNF, Case 6775/265-66, Bacon to Metcalf, 2 December 1907.

ing series of American consuls, ministers, naval officers, and officials of the Department of State. Many would have welcomed the opportunity to deal severely with him. It was, for example, fear of a Zelaya-sponsored war which had provoked Commander Glennon's recommendation to seize the customs houses of an aggressor. W. L. Merry, the American minister to Nicaragua and Guatemala, believed that no improvement in Nicaraguan political or economic conditions was possible as long as Zelaya ruled. He was convinced that Nicaragua's ultimate objective was a union of Central American states under its dictatorial control.[294] His successor, John C. Coolidge, worked himself into a rage over conditions in Nicaragua and, literally, resigned his diplomatic post in protest. "The government of Nicaragua is utterly false," he wrote, adding that friendly pressure was to no avail since "there is no real friendship, and the only pressure known to this government is force." Concluding his dispatch—"which," Adee wrote on its margin "seems to have been written in the incubation stage of Mr. Coolidge's fit"—the American minister offered a series of reasons why it was inconsistent with the dignity of the United States to continue diplomatic relations with Zelaya.[295] After Coolidge's departure, America was represented by a chargé d'affaires, J. H. Gregory, Jr., whose opinion of Zelaya was, if anything, lower than that of his predecessor. Gregory's acid reports stirred Adee to observe, hopefully, "that if the resignation habit becomes chronic in Nicaragua, it might be a good post to which to send men we are tired of."[296]

In any event, the problem of coping with Central American disorder, especially disorder sponsored by Zelaya, constantly troubled the Department of State. In 1907 there were reports of pending war between Nicaragua and Honduras. But, as so often was the case, the reports were obscure and contradictory. In March, on the advice of Dean Wood, the consul at La Ceiba, the Department of State asked the Navy to send a ship to that Honduran port. In reply the Navy cited a cable of its own, received the same day from the commanding officer of the *Marietta*, then also at La Ceiba, which categorically denied the existence of any danger to American interests.[297] Several days later, to underscore its point, the Navy Department forwarded another dispatch from the *Marietta* which described Consul Wood as so uncouth and undignified "as to be totally unfit for his position" and as com-

294 SDNF, Case 6775, various dispatches from Minister Merry in January and February of 1908.
295 SDNF, Case 6369/42, Coolidge to Root, 19 November 1908, with Adee postscript.
296 SDNF, Case 6369/70, Gregory to Root, 30 December 1908.
297 Nav Rec AF 8, Newberry to Root, 21 March 1907.

manding no respect from either Honduran officials or American residents. (When the message was eventually acknowledged some weeks later, the State Department simply noted laconically that "the Department has accepted Wood's resignation."[298])

When reports of trouble continued to mount the Navy dispatched the *Chicago* and the *Princeton* to Amapala which, according to current rumor, was about to be shelled by Nicaraguan forces. Blunt orders were issued to "prevent such bombardment by use of such forces as may be necessary." The justification for such orders was that the rumored bombardment would be "in violation of the customs of modern warfare among civilized nations."[299] There must, however, have been further talks with the Department of State, for these orders were soon rather drastically rewritten. The two naval commanders were now told that a Nicaraguan bombardment of Amapala could only be permitted if due notice were given in advance to the residents and if noncombattants were given full opportunity to evacuate the town. "After that," the new orders read, "you will not take steps to prevent capture of Amapala by bombardment or otherwise."[300] The State Department, grappling with the problem of legitimacy, had decided that the United States could justify no greater intervention than a demand that civilians be given an opportunity to evacuate Amapala.

Meanwhile a comparable threat of bombardment appeared to be developing on the east coast at La Ceiba. Maintaining that the city would burn to the ground if shelled, the commander of the *Marietta* decided that the only way to prevent the destruction of American interests at La Ceiba was to order the Nicaraguans not to make any such attack.[301] In a number of reports Lt. Commander Fullam attempted to convince Washington that he had acted within the discretion permitted by his orders. He rested his case on the argument that Central American warfare was simply a conflict between political factions—in this case, between two men, Bonila of Honduras and Zelaya of Nicaragua—and involved no patriotic or nationalistic interests. Neither country, claimed Fullam, could properly claim belligerent rights, and if the United States conceded to either the right to bombard cities, it would in fact be surrendering all of its own rights to protect its citizens and their property. "To admit the sovereign rights of any so-called government," Fullam decreed, "and to officials on this coast today . . .

[298] Nav Rec AF 8, Commanding Officer of *Marietta* to Newberry, 24 March 1907, and Denby to Metcalf, 13 April 1907.

[299] Nav Rec Messages Sent in Cipher, Newberry to *Princeton* and other vessels, 1 April 1907.

[300] Nav Rec Messages Sent in Cipher, Newberry to *Princeton* and other vessels, 8 April 1907.

[301] Nav Rec AF 8, Lt. Commander W. F. Fullam to Metcalf, 1 April 1907.

would be to invite anarchy and to surrender all protection for foreign interests."[302]

But this phase of the chronic Nicaraguan-Honduran problem blew over almost as quickly as it had developed. No incidents actually took place. Thus, the Department of State, while tempted to argue with Commander Fullam and his assumptions, generally kept its opinions to itself. It was well over a month before Root sent a letter to the Navy which contained a mild rebuke to Fullam for issuing such orders on his own responsibility—and even that rebuke was not for his objective but for the manner in which he had delivered it. It was the opinion of the State Department that the naval officer could have prevented the shelling of La Ceiba by reaching an oral understanding with the authorities in that port.[303] Then, as the correspondence began to mount, Fullam continued to defend himself with the counter argument that high surf had prevented him from landing, that he had provided the American vice-consul at La Ceiba with a copy of his proclamation, and that, above all, the only orders which he had previously received were "to exercise discretion protecting American interests."[304] Ultimately the Department of State yielded and accepted Fullam's pleas. The episode ended when Acting Secretary Bacon wrote the Navy that he had high confidence in Fullam's discretion, believed that he had handled himself well in a trying situation, and had not meant his earlier correspondence to be regarded as a censure of his actions.[305]

Throughout the remaining months of 1907 there were other instances when, at the behest of the State Department, naval vessels were sent to Central American waters on political missions. In August, for example, the Navy was asked to report on the probabilities of conflict between Nicaragua and, now, Guatemala.[306] It was not, however, until late in the year that another major flurry took place. This episode involved the forceful policies of the new commander of the *Marietta*, Commander W. J. Maxwell, and the antics of an American adventurer with the improbable name of Lee Christmas. Both Maxwell and Mexican diplomatic sources reported that Christmas was recruiting American residents in Guatemala for a filibustering expedition against Honduras. Naval vessels were at once directed to be on the lookout for the alleged expedition, but the "threat" rather rapidly vanished when the President of Guatemala gave varied assurances that he would not permit any filibustering expedition to base itself on Guatemalan soil.

302 Nav Rec AF 8, Fullam to Metcalf, 17 April 1907.
303 Nav Rec AF 8, Metcalf to Fullam, 22 April 1907, enclosing copy of a letter from the Acting Secretary of State.
304 Nav Rec AF 8, Fullam to Metcalf, 8 May 1907.
305 Nav Rec AF 8, Bacon to Metcalf, 21 May 1907.
306 SDNF, Case 7357/7, Adee to Metcalf, 21 August 1907.

In the interim, however, Commander Maxwell had notified Washington of his intent to sink any vessel carrying arms for such an expedition or, indeed, any suspicious ship that might attempt to escape search. In addition his reports carried dark allusions to British interests presumably in back of the filibustering movement.[307]

This naval initiative was a bit too much for the Department of State. "Commander Maxwell," observed Adee, "seems to be rather cocky and to have his own ideas of international duty." But the Department of State took no action since Maxwell had not carried out any of his threats and the affair of Lee Christmas quickly evaporated.[308] But within another few weeks Commander Maxwell went well beyond the limits which even a charitable officialdom could tolerate. Without warning he requested the assignment of two destroyers and a full battalion of marines at the Honduran port of Puerto Cortes, stated that he would seize the customs houses if there was any uprising in Honduras, and indicated he would not recognize any new regime unless ordered to do so by his superiors in Washington.[309]

As Adee noted, this was the sort of request which made officials in the Department of State "very nervous." James Brown Scott, the Solicitor, was asked to advise if there were any precedents in international law for the actions contemplated by Commander Maxwell. Assured that there were none, Root then informed the Navy that Maxwell had exceeded his authority by proposing an action which "appears to be a matter for the exercise of the political discretion of this government."[310] The Navy Department, meanwhile, was itself becoming disenchanted with Maxwell. One of his communications made a cryptic request for naval authorities in the United States "to investigate operations of tropical fruit company, 42 Broadway, New York City, also Pennsylvania State Senator Sisson."[311] When asked to explain his actions at Puerto Cortes, Maxwell produced replies which the Navy in Washington found unconvincing. He denied any actual intent to seize customs houses, admitted that he had sent his request for assistance "before I realized that the mere presence of the *Marietta* was enough to stop all further action" and attempted to fall back on the familiar complaint that his standing orders were insufficient. The Navy therefore decided to solve the problem of its quixotic commander by

---

[307] SDNF, Case 7357/44-46, Maxwell to Metcalf, 26 December 1907, with copies furnished to the Department of State.

[308] SDNF, Case 7357/44-46, Bacon to Adee, 16 January 1908.

[309] SDNF, Case 7357/53-54, Maxwell to Metcalf, 17 January 1908.

[310] SDNF, Case 7357/53-54, Root to Metcalf, 27 January 1908.

[311] Nav Rec AF 8, Maxwell to Metcalf, 16 January 1908, and Metcalf to Maxwell, 30 January 1908.

abruptly changing his orders and sending the *Marietta* to the more stable surroundings of Tampa, Florida.[312]

The Department of State tried but could turn up nothing more convincing than the usual crop of rumors to substantiate the reports sent by Maxwell. But the diplomats, even if without evidence, remained unwilling to withdraw all vessels from Central American coasts. After the departure of the *Marietta* the only naval craft, except for a collier, left on the east coast of Honduras was the *Dubuque*. When the Navy also asked to remove it, the State Department was reluctant. Robert Bacon, fearful of an eventual though unspecified outbreak, observed, "I am rather loath to let vessels go until the conventions [of the Central American Peace Conference] are ratified by Guatemala."[313] Similarly, American diplomatic representatives in Central America wanted a naval watch to be preserved at all times. Minister Merry commended his department for keeping vessels near the Nicaraguan shore: "In my opinion they cannot be better employed . . . 'eternal vigilance is the price' of understanding the situation in Central America and nothing political can be taken for granted." His successor, Gregory, consistently argued that the constant presence of American warships had a salutary effect upon Zelaya and his schemes for Central American domination.[314]

August of 1908 brought further trouble to Honduras. This time, though, the "culprit" was not a zealous naval officer but the American consul at Puerto Cortes. Consul Brickwood, without providing any advance warning, abruptly got in touch with the President of Honduras and told him that he should ask the United States government to send a warship to Puerto Cortes. The State Department, properly regarding this as a clear overstepping of consular functions, demanded an immediate explanation. While conceding that his message had been poorly phrased, Brickwood claimed that he was merely responding to a request which had actually originated with the government of Honduras. Root was unimpressed and cautioned Brickwood to work with and through the American minister and not to deal directly with the Honduran government.[315] Soon the consul was in further difficulty for exaggerating local dangers. He reported in detail on a riot in Puerto

---

[312] Nav Rec AF 8 contains a sheaf of communications between Maxwell and his superiors in the Navy Department in Washington for the months of January and February of 1908. His report to Metcalf on 17 February is particularly relevant. See also Messages Sent in Cipher, Metcalf to Maxwell, 17 January 1908.

[313] SDNF, Case 7357/91-93, Bacon to Adee, 26 February 1908.

[314] SDNF, Case 7357/104, Merry to Root, 29 February 1908.

[315] SDNF, Case 7357/202-03, Bacon to Dodge, 4 August 1908. Brickwood's reply, dated 5 September, is filed with /519, Metcalf to Root, 17 November 1908.

Cortes, described the participants as "men liable to commit murder without the slightest provocation," and predicted serious outbreaks in the imminent future.[316] The Department of State this time sought an independent analysis of the situation in that port, and Commander Craven of the *Dubuque* drew the assignment. Craven characterized the same riot "as little more than a drunken row among the sailors at the barracks" and as "devoid of any political significance." It was his report that the State Department accepted as correct. "You see," Adee wrote in the margin, "that Commander Craven does not share Mr. Brickwood's hysterical apprehensions."[317]

Throughout the remainder of the Roosevelt administration the naval watch in Central America remained. Even Commander Maxwell got back into good standing with the State Department for a report which showed that charges brought against an American consul were false.[318] But it was Commander John H. Shipley who most clearly impressed the officials of the Department of State. In late October 1908 he sent the Navy a report, soon forwarded to Root's department, which commented at length on political, social, and economic conditions in Honduras. Much of what he wrote was standard fare—the contrast between the poverty of the masses and the wealth of a few great families, the observation that revolutions were merely "farces"—but Shipley went on to emphasize that in a country like Honduras the customs houses provided the key to political control. He suggested that the United States ought to assume control of the Honduran customs and that, if this were done, there would be no further uprisings since there would be nothing tangible for an insurrection to acquire. Honduras, Shipley added, was so close to the United States that it had a mission "to extend a helping hand. Could not the proposition of temporarily taking over the Customs, in case of danger of any port falling into the hands of the insurrectionists, come from the Honduran government itself?"[319]

His report struck a responsive note in the Department of State. Adee commented that it was well conceived, well expressed, and based on considerable knowledge of the way in which the United States was then proceeding in the Dominican Republic. Though the proposition as phrased was impractical, the Assistant Secretary continued, the

---

[316] SDNF, Case 7357/567, Brickwood to Department of State, 12 December 1908.

[317] SDNF, Case 7357/569-70, Newberry to Root, 22 December 1908, forwarding copy of Craven report of 12 December.

[318] SDNF, Case 7357/281-82, Adee to Root, 7 August 1908, commenting on one of Maxwell's reports.

[319] SDNF, Case 7357/428-34, Metcalf to Root, 6 October 1908, forwarding copy of Shipley's report of 27 September on conditions in Honduras.

basic idea was a good one. Bacon concurred, adding that he had already considered a similar solution of the Honduran problem with Dr. Jacob Hollander, the expert on the Dominican customs. It seemed to Bacon that a remedy along the lines suggested by Commander Shipley was the only practical one that could be foreseen for bankrupt countries like Honduras.[320]

To generalize about these Central American episodes that have just been described is difficult. They were, after all, largely minor—an abortive attempt to seize a vessel suspected of carrying arms for an insurrection, threats issued but never carried out to prevent a coastal bombardment, a mission to check the accuracy of a consul's reports. They deserve at best only a small footnote in the broader sweep of the Latin American policy of the United States. But, taken together, they were manifestations of an increased desire to police those areas adjacent to the canal where no Secretary of State or President believed that civil discord could long be tolerated or doubted that the display of naval force was a valid way of securing this objective. It should also be clear from these scattered incidents that the Navy's role as a supplementary and valuable source of information for the Department of State was substantial.

These incidents also indicate, as evidenced by the examples of Commanders Fullam and Maxwell, the continuing problem of coordinating policy when two separate departments, each with its own values and procedures, had to work together through a system of formal requests and written correspondence. The extent of this difficulty was well illustrated when Commander John Hood, assigned to the Latin American division, asked the Navy Department for additional information. Well aware of the problem encountered by his predecessors in interpreting their standing orders, Hood asked that all officers assigned to Caribbean duty be given better information about the Latin American policy of the United States government.[321] But to this request Secretary Truman Newberry could only respond, first, that ships were assigned to protect American interests in countries where revolution was frequent; and, second, that "it is impracticable for the Department to lay down any general policy to be pursued at the different ports . . . except the general one that the interests of Americans must be protected."[322] Newberry contended that Naval Regulations provided an adequate answer for most situations, while special cases, which fell outside Regulations, would always have to be referred back to Washington. Given

[320] SDNF, Case 7357/428-34, Adee to Bacon, memorandum of 7 October 1908.
[321] Nav Rec AF 8, Hood to Metcalf, 16 November 1908.
[322] Nav Rec AF 8, Newberry to Hood, 1 December 1908.

this as the prevailing attitude, it is a wonder that there were not more rather than less instances of naval officers in conflict with civilian policy.

Any attempt to generalize about the role of the military services in these disparate, episodic Caribbean and Central American ventures runs the risk of merely stating the obvious. The Navy quite clearly was being used as an instrument of national policy; the mission assigned the Caribbean squadron to maintain order and stability simply underscores that obvious dimension of gunboat diplomacy. It is equally clear that both civilian leaders and military officers shared the same objective of building and guaranteeing American hegemony in the Caribbean. Indeed, at the very moment when John Hay was being publicly criticized for neglecting American security in his first treaty with Lord Pauncefote, the Secretary of State was actually trying to secure the Navy's objectives by obtaining other and seemingly more available sites for naval stations.

Both the formulation and the execution of American policy lacked any real coherence. The Navy's search for bases, to cite but one illustration, was marked by a hit-or-miss approach on the part of naval authorities. It was complicated by the fact that, at the time when the search was most intense, the Cuban question was still unsettled and the definitive route for the canal as yet undetermined; it was undercut by the unwillingness of Congress to appropriate funds to purchase or maintain bases; and it was further obscured by the ambivalent attitude of naval officers whose expression of ideas was always inhibited by the tradition that military men offered no advice on political questions. Thus, while the General Board might recommend the acquisition of, say, Chimbote, naval officers would also insist that their recommendation hinged upon the development of the administration's political policy, a matter about which they professed, at least outwardly, to have no opinions of their own. The inevitable result was a series of cryptic remarks about the advisability of securing Chimbote which left about as much unsaid as was actually stated. Policy coherence was equally inhibited by the archaic manner in which two separate and distinct entities within the executive branch—the State Department and the Navy—functioned as watertight compartments, each living according to its own customs and procedures, and dealing with each other at arm's length through the mechanism of formal correspondence. It was difficult to achieve coherence when, as has just been noted, a naval officer seeking guidelines on the administration's policy in Latin America could only be told that it was "impracticable" for the Navy to set down any general rules except that "the interests of Americans must be protected."

Similar problems emerge on the civilian side of the equation. So much of what happened in Latin America in this period depended almost entirely on the decisions, if not the whims, of Theodore Roosevelt, especially in the period before Elihu Root became Secretary of State. While T.R. may well have used the presence of the fleet in Caribbean waters to strengthen his hand in the Venezuelan episode of 1902, he also played his cards so close to his vest that he obscured the fact that both civilian and military leaders were actually expressing more anger at Castro of Venezuela than at William II of Germany. In Panama he simply used the Navy as the blunt instrument of his intensely personal policy; in the Dominican Republic he allotted to certain naval officers a not inconsiderable role in shaping the course of events; and in Cuba he kept the Navy under tight leash to prevent the escalation of an intervention he had never desired. There were reasons why each episode was handled differently, but the role of the Navy in these events can more readily be interpreted as a chapter in the biography of Theodore Roosevelt than as part of an evolving, coherent pattern of civil-military relations.

Throughout the entire period, however, one constant was the administration's concern with the problem of intervention—how, under whose auspices, under what circumstances could the United States interpose its coercive power, especially its naval power, to achieve its political goals. And, in particular, how was such intervention to be justified? The Roosevelt corollary was deliberately designed to provide a rationale sanctified by the name and the tradition of Monroe. In Panama, Cuba, and, eventually, the Dominican Republic, the United States secured treaties which provided a legal authority and justification for intervention. But elsewhere, especially in Central America and in incidents where no European threat could plausibly be adduced, the issue remained. Should America interpose its military power to prevent a filibuster, to stop rebels from shelling a Central American port, to seize a customs house to quell an insurrection? While, in the last analysis, the canons of international law and the shibboleths of the older non-interventionist tradition were usually honored more in the breach than in the observance, they still had to be considered. Moreover, after the criticism engendered by the Panamanian episode, even Roosevelt was less inclined to reach first for his big stick. This is certainly one of the prime reasons why Elihu Root labored so long to promote Central American peace through juridical means—via peace pacts, a Central American court, and the neutralization of Honduras.

Root sought the same goal of political stability but hoped to secure it by law rather than by direct intervention through the instrumentality of the United States Navy. But neither Roosevelt nor Root were successful in their endeavors, and, as Chapter Four will demonstrate, Taft and Knox also wrestled with this same issue of intervention—with the question not only of the legitimacy of coercive methods but also of the proper employment of military force in the support of national policies.

In one sense, of course, Roosevelt and the Navy were eminently successful in reconciling force and diplomacy. On those many occasions when they chose either direct or indirect intervention, the small and underdeveloped nations of Latin America had no choice but to accept American demands. The overwhelming discrepancy between the power of the United States Navy and the armed force of any Latin country virtually guaranteed an American "success." Roosevelt, Hay, and Root were fully aware of American predominance; they knew full well that in many instances a mere "show of force" would be sufficient. In fact, they counted upon it. In the terminology of the present, they relied on the "overkill" potential of the Navy to act as a deterrent that would either prevent a revolution or channel its course. Commander Southerland summed up the assumptions of the era well when he wrote, "While the presence of warships does not prevent a revolution, it is clear to me that they have a deterrent effect." Outwardly, then, there was American "success" in reconciling force and diplomacy. The Caribbean was turned into an American preserve, no European interventions occurred after Venezuela, and in country after country the presence of American warships helped enforce and maintain stability and order. But neither civilian nor military considered the long-term consequences of such success—the eventual growth of an intense, often bitterly anti-American nationalism that fed upon the antagonisms generated in this era of using force, direct as well as indirect, to achieve American political ends.

CHAPTER THREE

Asia and the American Military, 1898-1909

1. THE SEARCH FOR BASES

MAJOR Morris Foote, who commanded the 9th Infantry during the China Relief Expedition, was growing increasingly worried about the American future in China. "It seems to me," he informed his superiors early in 1901, "that the United States will be very much left out if we do not take our concession now when we can. It is Minister Conger's business, but if we want any 'open door' in Tientsin, we better hustle around and get that little piece of river front at once, or otherwise our merchants will have to play second fiddle."[1] Major General Adna Chaffee, Foote's commander and the officer in command of all American army units involved in the suppression of the Boxers, agreed. It was clear to Chaffee that there was going to be continued disorder in China and that the United States Army must therefore possess a guaranteed position for the "undisputed footing for its troops and stores."[2] The general soon initiated an extended correspondence with E. H. Conger, the American minister in Peking, in which he attempted to persuade that diplomat of the necessity for an American concession at Tientsin. To his colleagues in the army, Chaffee expressed even stronger opinions. The United States, he wrote, would have to maintain troops in China "for a long time, which cannot be more definitely expressed than by the term Years." Tientsin, Chaffee argued, should be the army's base since it commanded the military route to Peking, the capital of China and seat of the Manchu government.[3]

It is appropriate to open this chapter with another section on the military pressures for bases—this time, for a base in Chinese waters. As in Latin America, the quest for new naval bases and coaling stations was one of the first manifestations of the expanded role of the military in American foreign policy at the beginning of the new century. In Asia it took the form of strong recommendations that the United States establish a military presence on or adjacent to the mainland of China and thereby extend the range of American imperialism some thousands of miles beyond the original limits of the so-

[1] SDML, Foote to General Adna Chaffee, 17 February 1901.

[2] SDML, Chaffee to E. L. Conger, 21 February 1901.

[3] Papers of General H. C. Corbin, Manuscripts Division, Library of Congress, Chaffee to Corbin, 26 January 1901.

called "insular empire" that stretched from Hawaii to the Philippines. In the Far East, as in Latin America, the Army and the Navy were also involved in the major issues of foreign policy that arose during the administrations of McKinley and Roosevelt: in the Boxer Rebellion, in the continuing problem of intervention in Chinese affairs, and, particularly, in the definition and interpretation of the Open Door policy. In the first half of the decade the military services would also be concerned with the growing Russian-American rivalry over Manchuria, while in the years after 1905 they would become deeply involved with the implications of the rise of Japanese military power that flowed from Japan's striking victory over Russia in 1904-05. It is around these themes that this chapter will be organized.

Civilian policy in Asia is more complex than in Latin America and far more difficult to summarize. Indeed, the Open Door—both shorthand for and symbol of all Far Eastern policy—has enjoyed almost as many different interpretations as there have been historians who have written about it. To the older generation of Samuel F. Bemis and A. Whitney Griswold, the Open Door policy was part and parcel of the "great aberration" of 1898 that produced Asian involvements contrary to the national interest.[4] At another extreme, Akira Iriye, one of the most recent scholars in the field, has described the Open Door as a "myth" and maintained that, even at the moment it was first proclaimed, it was no more than "a negative response to the public demand for a positive and vigorous assertion of American rights and interests in China."[5] The Kennan critique suggests that the Open Door is the very epitome of the "legalistic-moralistic" strain in American foreign policy, while the very different assumptions of the "New Left" lead to the conclusion that the Open Door was merely the handmaiden of American capitalism, a shrewd scheme to produce the American economic conquest of China without the formal trappings of empire.

Even with this welter of possible interpretations, several points seem clear. Among all the policymakers, civilian as well as military, there were great expectations in 1898, followed by equally great fears that the Boxer Rebellion presaged the division of China among the great powers and the disappearance of the presumably vast China market. Moreover, once Washington had proclaimed the Open Door policy, several options were presented to American diplomacy. The United States could, at least in theory, try to maintain the policy by creating a military presence in China and by engaging in the same game of

---

[4] Samuel F. Bemis, *A Diplomatic History of the United States* (4th edn., New York, 1955), 463-502, and A. Whitney Griswold, *The Far Eastern Policy of the United States* (New York, 1938), 36-87.

[5] Akira Iriye, *Across the Pacific* (New York, 1967), 81.

power politics that was played by the Europeans. The United States could also hope to preserve the Open Door through international cooperation. Or, as a third option, America could rely in the main upon some other great power—presumably Great Britain or Japan—to keep other nations from slamming the Chinese door in American faces. The available evidence suggests that in the confused period which stretched from 1898 through and even well beyond the formal settlement of the Boxer question, all three of these alternatives had their proponents within the American government and that the United States was at one time or another tempted by each of them. The military power politics option, which will be considered in greater detail in succeeding pages, was clearly present in the minds of more than just a handful of American civil and military leaders; moreover, the concept of providing the military in Asia with at least a minimum of leverage was never totally abandoned. Yet it is also clear that by the time Theodore Roosevelt became president in 1901, the United States had decided that it could never attempt to maintain its Far Eastern policy by force of arms. When Russia effectively moved to close off Manchuria to other nations, T.R.'s correspondence fairly bristled with hostile references to Czarist mendacity. But though his noise was loud, he fully understood that there was simply no body of opinion in the United States to sustain a policy of pushing American differences with Russia to any ultimate conclusions. Implicitly if not explicitly Roosevelt came to rely upon the Japanese to guard the Open Door and, by challenging the Russians in Korea and Manchuria, to work in the American interest.

The Russo-Japanese war ended that phase of America's Far Eastern policy. Roosevelt thereafter sought, amid growing signs of latent Japanese suspicion, first, to allay that suspicion and, second, to sponsor some kind of an Asian balance of power in which Russia and Japan would mutually deter each other from controlling the Far East. Roosevelt's often-quoted phrase that the Philippines were the "Achilles heel" of America's position in the Far East is rightly interpreted as proof that he had become fully aware of the limits of American power in Asia and the vulnerability of the American position. Yet at the end of his years in the White House, T.R. was by no means prepared to abandon all pretense that the United States was a Pacific power. His decision to dispatch the entire fleet of battleships into the Pacific and thence on around the world was typical Roosevelt. It was, on the one hand, a conciliatory move intended to demonstrate that there was absolutely no imminent threat of war with Japan, while, on the other, it was designed to point out to Tokyo that the latent military power of the United States could, if necessary, be deployed in the Pacific.

This capsule summary of American policy in Asia suggests several preliminary and paradoxical observations about the role of the military services. First, the "heroic phase" of military involvement—the period when the admirals and the generals played the greatest role—came at the very outset. Their search for bases coincided with and was part of the process of formulating and defining the concept of the Open Door. Also, the two services enjoyed their greatest freedom and largest opportunity to influence policy at the time of the Boxer uprising. But then, as other contingencies arose, the military actually had less success in securing bases in Asia than they had in Latin America. And, except at the beginning, the military services enjoyed less operational freedom throughout the decade than they possessed in Latin America. They and their civilian superiors were, after all, dealing with the great powers. Even a minor involvement in Chinese affairs might well produce not merely a Chinese reaction but a response from the European nations that had interests in China. The Army and Navy enjoyed no situation comparable to that in Latin America where the Europeans kept out and where the heaviest competition would be, at the most, a Dominican gunboat or the protest of a rebel junta.

Also, for the Navy as well as for the civilian leaders of government, the period of greatest expectations was at the very beginning of the century. Thereafter the admirals and the generals, like Theodore Roosevelt, became increasingly aware of the limitations of their power. When, as we shall later see, the Army successfully vetoed the Navy plans to base American naval power in the Philippines, the Navy was compelled to agree that Pearl Harbor in Hawaii—many thousands of miles from the Asian mainland—would have to serve as the focal point for American naval strength in the Pacific. But, and again like Roosevelt, the Navy was never prepared to abandon all of its earlier assumptions. By the end of the decade the Navy, encouraged by the presumed "lessons" of the round-the-world-cruise of the fleet, was preparing itself to reassert more than a few of its earlier assumptions about its ability to function in the Eastern Pacific.

The Army's strong interest in a concession at Tientsin was a clear example of the thrust for Chinese bases which arose in military circles as a direct consequence of the experiences of the Boxer Rebellion. In the Introduction to this book we have described the logistical problems encountered by the fleet operating in North China waters in the summer of 1900 and how this led the Navy to engage in extended correspondence with the Department of State about the possibility of acquiring the Chusan Islands. The Navy's interest was both intense and sustained. When no answer was forthcoming to its first request, the

Navy pressed for a reply. By October of 1900 the General Board was pleading military necessity: "The plans of a naval campaign in Asiatic waters in case of a war in which the United States may become involved make it imperatively necessary that we have the right to use a naval port on the coast of China."[6]

Even at the risk of repetition it must be emphasized that this general desire for Asian bases was by no means a new concern of the Navy. In the 1890s, when the break-up of the Celestial Empire first appeared as a possibility, a number of naval officers, with some support from diplomatic circles, had advocated the acquisition of naval stations in China. Yet the effort had been, at best, sporadic; there had been no formal requests that engaged the attention of the McKinley administration or its Department of State. And it is a matter of record that military logic rather than any well-formulated political strategy had led the United States into the Philippines in 1898.[7] Mahan's Strategy Board, convened to provide plans for the planless Navy, had in that same year recommended the acquisition of naval stations in the Philippines and Guam and had also tentatively pointed to the Chusans. But it had been cautious in its approach, pointing out that the first two sites might be sufficient for naval needs and also noting that naval stations could be liabilities as well as assets. A prudent nation, Mahan had warned, did not multiply their number "beyond the strictly necessary."[8] Even more indicative of the continuation of naval caution prior to the Boxer affair was an article that appeared in the December 1899 issue of the U. S. Naval Institute *Proceedings* over the authoritative signature of Captain Charles Stockton, then president of the War College at Newport and a few months later to be one of the original members of the General Board. Stockton argued that, if the United States wished to develop a sphere of influence, it must obtain a naval station either in Korea or North China equal in importance to any facilities developed on Luzon. But Captain Stockton also highlighted the problems such a base would entail. A base in the waters of North China would not for years serve any significant American commercial interest; it would have to be fortified against potential enemies; and its defense might well require an American capacity to secure command of the seas in East Asia. Since these were major stumbling blocks, Stockton warned, "the acquisition of such territory should not be entered into lightly, and all the contingencies likely to follow should be carefully

---

6 SDML, Long to Hay, 29 October 1900, a verbatim copy of a General Board report. The original can be located in GB, Letters, 1, Dewey to Long, 10 October 1900.

7 See the discussion in Braisted, *Navy in the Pacific*, 3-20, as well as the impressionistic account in Louis Halle, *Dream and Reality* (New York, 1958), 176-88.

8 GB, File 414-1, Report of the Naval War Board, 1898.

examined." The president of the Naval War College personally thought that the Far Eastern game was worth the candle, but he conceded that, if the government opted against such a course, he would also be satisfied with a naval station on Luzon for "then the Philippines will serve our naval needs."[9]

Hence, it was the events of the summer of 1900 that were decisive in stirring a sustained naval effort. The initial arguments of the General Board, as we have seen, emphasized strategy and logistics—the vast distances from Manila to Taku and the shortage of coal in the western Pacific. But Army and Navy officers were also prepared to take advantage of China's troubles and believed that the Boxer uprising had created a political opportunity for action. Most assumed as a matter of course that there would be more disorders in China. The Manchu empire, if not destined for immediate collapse, would certainly have to yield further, more extensive concessions to the great powers. "To be candid," Chaffee wrote the War Department, "it is probably as good a way as any, for eventually it will come. China is doomed to disruption, to be divided up, so why not now?"[10] Quite a few naval officers suggested that, once the Boxer movement was suppressed, the eventual reckoning with the Chinese authorities would provide an ideal opportunity to obtain the desired base. As early as June of 1900 Admiral Louis Kempff, who commanded the naval forces off Taku, informed the Navy Department that he would favor keeping a port in northern China "if final arrangements should make such a step appear appropriate to the authorities in Washington."[11] By October the General Board was putting its case obviously if clumsily; it asked the Secretary of the Navy "to consider the propriety of presenting now to the State Department the question of whether, in the settlement of the China situation, it would not be possible and desirable to get the State Department to request a port for this government."[12]

The details of the Navy's continuing quest for Far Eastern bases have been chronicled in several articles by Seward Livermore as well as in the lengthier narrative of William Braisted.[13] It is therefore unnecessary for this study to duplicate their excellent and pioneering work. But, in brief, what happened was simply that the General Board continued to manifest its interest in a China base. When its several requests in 1900 brought no fruits, the Board sought in the following year to reopen the issue, this time advocating a secondary choice,

9 Charles Stockton, "The American Inter-Oceanic Canal," 777.

10 Corbin Papers, Chaffee to Corbin, 10 April 1901.

11 SDML, Long to Hay, 28 July 1900, enclosing Kempff report of 22 June 1900.

12 GB, Proceedings, 9 October 1900.

13 Braisted, *The United States Navy in the Pacific, 1897-1909*, and Livermore, "U.S. Naval Base Policy in the Pacific" (cited in Chapter One, n. 172).

Samsa Bay. As Captain Crowninshield then noted, "The [General] Board fully agrees that it is most important not to defer the acquisition of some valuable harbor through diplomatic processes, and it is hoped that the Board's suggestions to the State Department may be of some avail later."[14] In the summer of 1902 the civilian heads of the Navy Department asked the Board to reexamine its needs for foreign naval stations; the firm reply of the naval strategists was that "For the more complete protection of our interests in the Far East, the vicinity of the Chusan Islands in China is looked upon by the Board as of first importance as a base."[15] Indeed, to the members of the Board it was incumbent upon their Secretary to "initiate persistent efforts . . . in this direction until the desired objects are accomplished."

By late 1902, to be sure, the first doubts about the wisdom of the policy of seeking additional bases were beginning to appear even within the membership of the General Board itself. A minority of its members were beginning to feel that the United States could over extend its commitments and that the need to protect scattered bases would be a liability in time of war. But at least for the moment, and since such ardent expansionists as Admirals Bradford and Taylor remained on the General Board, there was no change in the Board's advocacy of a China base. Its proponents, indeed, long argued that such a naval station would be of particular utility in time of war. Individual officers who visited the Far East, either on special assignment or routine tours of duty, also continued to plead for the acquisition of a naval station.[16] The Chusans, it should be added, always remained the favorite site, for, as Admiral Dewey pointed out, the most likely theater of naval operations was in the area of northern China and "all our studies . . . indicate that the Chusan group is best."[17] Moreover, even after the Bradford-Taylor era had passed, the General Board continued to manifest its interest. In a special report of 1906 the Board called attention to the fact that it was now eliminating the Chusans from its list of desired overseas bases. But, it quickly added, it was "still adhering to its original opinion that such a location should be selected if future conditions be favorable."[18]

Many were the reasons why the admirals were unable to realize their Far Eastern dreams. First and foremost was the fact that in the

14 GB, Letters, I, Crowninshield to Long, 18 October 1901.
15 GB, Letters, II, Dewey to Long, 30 September 1902.
16 GB, Proceedings, 23 September 1902. For the views of individual officers, see SDML, Hackett to Long, 5 September 1900 (communicating the opinions of Captain B. H. McCalla); Sperry Papers, Sperry to Admiral Bradford, 29 November 1902 (Sperry's opinion); and GB, Proceedings, 7 May 1903 (opinions of Admiral Charles Stockton).
17 GB, Letters, II, Dewey to Moody, 18 June 1903.
18 GB, Letters, IV, Dewey to Bonaparte, 12 April 1906.

second set of Open Door notes, issued in the summer of 1900, the Mc-Kinley administration had, for better or worse, committed itself to respect for the territorial and administrative integrity of China. The Open Door was often—though, significantly, not always—cited by diplomatic officials as a reason why the State Department could take no action. When, for example, General Chaffee pressed Conger about the Tientsin concession, the American minister pointedly reminded him that "the emphatically declared policy of the United States is that it would not make the present military movements in China a pretext for securing possession of Chinese territory."[19] In 1901, when the Navy Department asked for a "progress report" from the diplomats, William Rockhill, the State Department's reigning China expert and, indeed, the real author of the Open Door notes, believed that the only reply that could be given to the General Board was that it was "inexpedient" to negotiate with the Chinese for a base. "This is a very delicate and difficult matter," he advised John Hay. "Everything considered, I think that it will be a pretty difficult question to settle without giving a rather serious blow to the policy which we have been very consistently following in China."[20]

But it was not simply the scruples of the Open Door which blocked the Navy. Washington had to consider the attitude of the other great powers. "Once the subject is broached," Rockhill observed, "all the other Powers who have not got naval stations on the coast of China and who are anxious to secure them, will commence again pressing their claims with renewed energy." Nor, for that matter, were the other Far Eastern powers anxious to welcome the United States into their heretofore exclusive club. The Navy had unfortunately gotten interested in sites which were located either within the spheres of influence of other nations or which were subject to various treaty provisions that presumably prevented China from yielding them to other nations. When, for example, John Hay asked Conger to look into the possibilities of Samsa Bay, he was reminded by his minister in Peking that existing treaties between China and Japan would make it necessary to consult the Japanese. "Japan claims a sort of mortgage right to the province of Fo Kien," he pointed out, "and it is understood China has agreed that if any part of the province is to be alienated, it shall be to Japan."[21] Discreet inquiries in Tokyo soon produced expressions of

[19] SDML, Conger to Chaffee, 25 February 1901, forwarded by the Minister to Hay on 1 May 1901.

[20] SDML, Rockhill to Hay, 6 December 1901, attached to Long's 2 December 1901 request for a "progress report."

[21] Department of State, Dispatches from the U.S. Minister to China, No. 455, Conger to Hay, 20 November 1900. (Hereafter citations from the various collections

regret couched in all the niceties of diplomatic language. The Japanese Foreign Minister said no, but "because of the very friendly relations of the two countries, it was with regret that circumstances were such as, in the opinion of his Government, made it necessary to decline to give a favorable response which otherwise would be given with pleasure."[22] Oriental regret or not, his statement marked the effective end of the Samsa episode. Similarly with the Chusan Islands. These, in essence, fell under a British veto. When England had returned the islands to China in the 1880s, she had received a Chinese promise that they would never be ceded to another power. The Navy had counted upon the burgeoning sentiments of Anglo-American friendship to conquer this hurdle, but it remained an obstacle that kept their goal from being fulfilled.[23]

Yet it is all too easy to exaggerate the difficulties with foreign powers or the conflict between the principle of the Open Door and the desire for bases. It is also too easy to express shocked indignation, as did George Kennan in his *American Diplomacy, 1900-1960*, that American statesmen would so desert principle as to advocate, even temporarily, the acquisition of a naval base in China.[24] There were always quite a few American diplomats and officials who gave serious thought to the question of a Far Eastern naval station. Some of the more enthusiastic proponents, to be sure, were to be found in the second echelon of American officialdom in the Far East. John Fowler, who served for years as the consul at Chefoo was informing the Department of State before the end of 1898 that the United States must have a place in China from which to bring its military power into play. As he bluntly advised his superior, "If we intend to protect our interests in North China by our own guns and by our own coal, we must have a base in North China." He chided the Navy for being slow to recognize its own needs and claimed that while he had been advocating a China depot for more than a year, he had found the Navy Department unable to grasp its importance. Fowler was even convinced that if the United States and its navy had been more alert on the issue of a base then "perhaps the political question in North China would not have assumed so acute a phase."[25]

Higher officials in China were also advocates of a naval station.

of ministerial dispatches will be abbreviated as SDMD with the country of origin indicated.)

22 SDMD, Japan, No. 524, Buck to Hay, 11 December 1900.

23 GB, Letters, II, Dewey to Long, 7 October 1902; SDML, Rockhill to Hay, 6 December 1901, as cited.

24 Kennan, *American Diplomacy*, 34-35.

25 SDCD, Chefoo, China, Fowler to Moore, 27 October 1898.

E. H. Conger, the diplomat whose famous message from Peking during the Boxer siege gave the world the first hint that the legations were holding out, was an early proponent. Conger, no friend of the China that was or had been, long advised the Department of State that the best, if not only, remedy for the plight of the Manchu government was to have the western powers develop her latent, still untapped resources. But to accomplish this mission, he insisted, the westerners would have to surmount both the latent opposition of the Chinese people and the inability of the Manchu dynasty to cope with the problem of preserving law and order. "As a consequence," wrote Conger late in 1898, "the interests of the foreigners must be safeguarded by foreign armed forces scattered throughout the Empire wherever large investments are made." Summarizing his views, he wrote:

> It is true that the integrity of China can easily be preserved by an alliance of a few of the great powers. But to what end? If simply to preserve the old China without possibility of material development or trade progress, then it is not worthwhile. But if real progress is to be made, mines opened, railways constructed, orientalism must eventually give way to occidentalism. In my judgment this is bound to occur. It may and it may not be soon, but the sooner it comes the better . . . In any event, we should see to it that as many doors are left open as possible, and we ought to be ready, either by negotiation or by actual possession, to own and control at least one good port from which we can potently assert our rights and effectively wield our influence.[26]

It is true that Conger did hesitate when Hay suggested in the fall of 1900 that he should look into the matter of Samsa Bay. But his hesitation was tactical and based on his belief that it was not an opportune moment to act, since the United States was negotiating the Boxer settlement with the Manchu authorities and the last of the disturbances had not yet been suppressed. While he advocated caution, he also told Hay that "to me a naval station for us somewhere on this coast seems very important, and I have heretofore recommended it." Less than a week later, after reminding the Secretary of State that a request for Samsa would conflict with the Open Door commitment, Conger broached another solution. "If Samsa is impossible, would not Chusan with the consent of England answer the purpose?"[27] His reaction was similar when the Army pressed for a concession at Tientsin. He made clear to General Chaffee his doubts about acting while negotiations with the Chinese government were still in progress, but he also pri-

[26] SDMD, China, No. 82, Conger to Hay, 3 November 1898.
[27] SDMD, China, Nos. 455 and 459, Conger to Hay, 20 and 23 November 1900.

vately encouraged the American consul in Tientsin to protest the attempts of other powers to secure sections of the river front and permitted him to notify foreign officials in Tientsin that the United States was interested in a tract.[28] Moreover, a year later, Conger returned to the subject of an American base without benefit of outside prompting. One of his dispatches of September 1901 reminded the Secretary of State of his long interest in the acquisition of a naval base and went on to suggest that, since the Boxer settlement had finally been reached, "the present time would appear to be opportune for making such a demand upon the Chinese government."[29]

Chinese ports, like those in Latin America, contained a number of zealous subordinate American officials who tried to engineer schemes that would benefit both the Navy and their own pocketbooks. One such project revolved around the possible accession of a coaling point in Amoy harbor—a location in the Formosa strait that was on an offshore island even closer to the Chinese mainland than either of those two recently famous islands, Quemoy and Matsu. The scheme for an Amoy station originated in the fertile brain of Dr. Carl Johnson, the vice-consul at Amoy, who had purchased some property on the island when its owners defaulted on their taxes. When Captain (later Admiral) Charles Sperry visited Amoy in 1902, Johnson first proposed to sell or lease his property to the Navy. The scheme, as outlined by Johnson, was entrancing if legally dubious. Amoy, he claimed, was neutralized, outside the Japanese sphere of influence, and perhaps about to be turned into an international settlement where foreigners would live under the kind of rule that existed in Shanghai. The vice-consul would sell outright for fifteen thousand dollars or, if the Navy preferred, would build a "go down" and jetty to be leased for twenty-five years at an annual rental of $2,500. Johnson argued persuasively for the rental:

If the Navy Department were to begin the erection of a building for a coaling station it would be reported by the foreign consuls to their respective governments and might possibly lead to a protest from some one of them. If the storehouses were built by a private party and leased to the government afterwards, it would be much less likely to attract attention. After it had been used this way for a few years, the title could be quietly transferred to the Government without exciting comment.[30]

[28] On Conger's reaction to the Tientsin proposals, see SDMD, China, No. 489, 31 December 1900, and No. 551 of 27 February 1901.

[29] SDMD, China, No. 738, Conger to Hay, 13 September 1901.

[30] Sperry Papers, Sperry to Bradford, 7 February 1902, and, especially, SDML, Moody to Hay, 12 May 1902. The latter file contains a vast amount of Johnson's

At the time Johnson made his proposal, the Navy had already been unsuccessfully pursuing its Far Eastern will-o'-the-wisp for several years. This perhaps accounts for the great amount of attention which this scheme attracted and the number of naval officers who bit hard on the Amoy bait. Sperry thought it was feasible, while Admiral Bradford, the General Board's foremost enthusiast for bases, persuaded the Secretary of the Navy to have the State Department make inquiries about the possibility of such a transfer.[31] Eventually Conger replied that the Chinese would not object and that, since no territorial rights would be ceded, there would be no grounds for a Japanese protest.[32] The General Board first endorsed the scheme but then early in 1903, when its members were beginning to question the entire subject of overseas bases, reversed itself. A majority of the Board ultimately took the position that Amoy was unsuitable; it could not be fortified and would therefore be of no value in time of war; and, above all, it was too far south of the vital area of North China and too close to the Philippines to be of real assistance in any foreseeable naval operations.[33] But this was not a unanimous judgment. The commander-in-chief of the Asiatic squadron continued to think that the Navy should acquire Amoy since, in his opinion, the United States ought to have a hand in the disposition of territory in that portion of China. The irrepressible Bradford argued that, since it was desirable for the United States to get a foothold on the coast of China, the Navy might as well begin with Amoy. Poor as that location was, it could at least serve as "a step to some better place."[34] But the Amoy project, supported by logic no better than this, was officially dead. Several years later, when an American businessman tried to interest the Navy in a warehouse on Amoy, the General Board rejected his proposal by simply referring back to and reproducing the arguments put forth in its decision of 1903.[35]

It was not just consuls or ministers in China who saw some merit in the Navy's early-twentieth-century eagerness for a station in China. In the summer of 1900, when excitement over the Boxer uprising was at a maximum, even William McKinley showed interest. According to John Bassett Moore, the Assistant Secretary of State, the President seemed to "favor seizing a port as the European powers have done."

correspondence concerning Amoy, including the specifics of the proposal discussed in the text.

[31] SDML, Moody to Hay, 12 May 1902, which includes a long report prepared by Admiral Bradford.

[32] SDMD, China, No. 1096, Conger to Hay, 22 September 1902.

[33] GB, Proceedings, 23 September 1902.

[34] GB, Letters, II, Dewey to Bureau of Equipment, 9th endorsement by Bradford, 18 June 1903.

[35] GB, Letters, IV, Dewey to Bonaparte, 5th endorsement, 11 July 1906.

And Hay's interest was not merely a momentary aberration. The Navy's first formal request to him was submitted in the summer of 1900; it was three months later, when he presumably had had sufficient time to consider it, that he initiated his request to Conger to investigate the possibility of securing Samsa Bay. As a matter of fact the State Department did not, at least initially, rule out the possibility of securing a concession as part of the Boxer settlement. David Hill, acting Secretary during one of Hay's frequent absences, replied to one of the Navy's many requests for a progress report with the statement that "the question of renewed or enlarged 'concessions' to the United States in treaty ports may very properly form part of the eventual negotiations with China for the settlement of all pending questions."[36]

Thus there was interest in official Washington. But, as we have noted, the possibility of international complications and, above all, the commitment to the Open Door concept were powerful deterrents. It was soon realized that the United States would be greatly embarrassed if, at a time when it was arguing that the powers should not use the Boxer uprising as an excuse to partition China, the American government served its own demands on China. Still, Hay did not flatly reject the Navy's various proposals; there was a note of sympathy for the Navy's requests, even a hint that at some indefinite future date the issue might be reopened. For example, when he reported to the Navy in the fall of 1901, the Secretary of State wrote, "I beg to say that the negotiations for the purpose referred to are extremely difficult at this moment, and, in my judgment, it would be expedient to postpone for a while the consideration of the subject."[37]

The attitude of William Rockhill, the one-man Far Eastern division of Hay's department, perhaps best indicated the dilemma of those who wished to assist the Navy but who were fully aware of the difficulties raised by its proposals. He penned notes which argued that the attempt to secure a base in China would be a blow to established policy. Also, when he was asked his opinion about the Amoy project, Rockhill pinned a newspaper clipping to his reply—a clipping which emphasized the current unwillingness of the Chinese government to make further territorial concessions. But he immediately offered an alternative. Why not, Rockhill suggested, attempt to secure a site in Korea? He had just heard from Horace Allen, the American minister in Seoul, about several magnificent harbors in Korea which could probably be obtained by the United States for naval use. Korea, Rockhill added, had the political advantage of being outside the area in which the usual restrictions on American policy applied. "I feel certain that if a

---

[36] SDML, David J. Hill to Long, 11 December 1900.
[37] SDML, Hay to Long, 9 December 1901.

naval station on the coast of southern Korea were acceptable to the Navy Department," he advised Hay, "there is no man in the world who could manage to secure it, with the necessary privileges, as well as Allen. Looking over the question from a purely political view, I should say that it would be an excellent thing if we had a coaling station in Korea."[38]

Hay concurred with his Far Eastern expert and forwarded Rockhill's suggestion to the Navy Department with a covering note of his own which pointed out that a Korean base could probably be acquired more readily than one in China.[39] Horace Allen, needless to say, was enthusiastic. A man who yielded to no one in his distaste for the Korean government, Allen was willing to sanction almost any tactic that would produce a naval station for his government. After a visit to Korea by Admiral Rodgers had acquainted him with the Navy's intense desire for a Far Eastern base, Allen endorsed Rodgers' choice of Sylvia Bay in strong language. Noting that the Koreans would probably refuse to sell or lease the bay, he continued:

> If the place is seriously desired there is the precedent of England's taking Port Hamilton nearby, and of her maintaining more or less of a claim to it even though she gave it back to China. . . . If it should by any chance become necessary to bring pressure to bear upon these people in the settlement of a claim, the occupation by our naval forces of this harbor would promptly bring them to terms. At the same time such action would, as matters go in this part of the world, give to the United States an interest in this particular part of Korea that would prevent Sylvia Bay from going to any one else, and when Korea has finally brought upon itself the crash that seems inevitable, this harbor would probably fall to us. It is also possible that, once having occupied the port, a lease might be negotiated on amicable terms.[40]

But, as with Amoy, it was the General Board which ultimately spurned the Korean suggestion. The strategists decided that its location was too far removed from the probable center of naval action in China—too far to the north, as Amoy had been too far to the south. Moreover, they reasoned that if Japan was an ally of the United States, they would have access to Japanese ports, and a Korean site would be of little additional value. Conversely, if Japan was an American enemy,

[38] SDML, Rockhill to Hay, 4 June 1902, and Hay to Moody, 9 July 1902, enclosing a Rockhill memorandum of 3 July.

[39] SDML, Hay to Moody, 9 July 1902.

[40] SDMD, Korea, No. 534, Allen to Hay, 21 November 1902. For an interpretation of Allen's attitude toward the Koreans and their government, see Fred Harrington, *God, Mammon, and the Japanese* (Madison, 1944), 183 ff.

any base in Korea would be indefensible, an immediate casualty to Japanese naval action. The General Board, therefore, could see no advantage in the acquisition of Sylvia Bay or, for that matter, any Korean site.[41] Clearly, then, though both the military and the diplomats were interested in a Far Eastern station, they were working at cross purposes. Rockhill and Hay saw an opportunity to satisfy the Navy without doing violence to their China policy; the General Board, which tested projects according to strict naval and strategic logic, was simply not interested.

As we have seen, the General Board's enthusiasm for bases waned after 1903. In the Far East, with the failure to secure any of its desired sites, the naval strategists also turned to the advanced base alternative —that is, the seizure, at the outset of hostilities, of a base from which to conduct future operations. The General Board began to develop plans, admittedly somewhat rudimentary, to capture certain Far Eastern locations and to accumulate a so-called "advanced base outfit" in the Philippines.[42] Admiral A. S. Crowninshield made clear the connection between the advanced base concept and the failure to secure regular bases when he wrote a fellow officer that the General Board had been trying to obtain permanent stations in the Far East,

> and suggestions looking to this end have been made to the State Department . . . but without effect, the State Department having declined to enter upon this matter, at least for the present. We are therefore thrown back upon the necessity of seizing an advanced base when war actually is imminent.[43]

Then, too, the unwillingness of Congress to appropriate funds led the Navy to concentrate its efforts upon a single location, Subig Bay in the Philippines—a decision about the Far East which paralleled its decision to focus upon Guantanamo in the Caribbean. Also, especially after the successful voyage of the White Fleet, naval writers began to emphasize the argument that fleet colliers could fulfill many of the functions heretofore assigned to land bases. Thus the General Board's standard reply to inquiries about Far Eastern bases was that of Admiral Dewey in 1908: "The practice of coaling from colliers will doubtless become the rule in the future as has generally been the case in the past, the colliers accompanying the fleet and obtaining their coal from Olongapo and Cavite."[44]

41 GB, Proceedings, 12 June 1903, and Letters, II, Dewey to Moody, 18 June 1903.
42 GB, File 408, which is entirely devoted to the advanced base concept. As previously noted, the most useful paper is Commander Jackson's May 1913 report entitled "A History of the Advanced Base."
43 GB, Letters, I, Crowninshield to Rodgers, 18 October 1901.
44 GB, Letters, V, Dewey to Metcalf, 8 October 1908.

It was thereafter only in civilian circles that the idea of a base in China was kept alive. The ink was scarcely dry on the Root-Takahira agreement, which eased various tensions between the United States and Japan, when the American ambassador in Tokyo reopened the issue. Ambassador Thomas J. O'Brien, acting entirely on his own initiative, wrote Elihu Root that he assumed it would be in the American interest to have one, possibly two, coaling stations on the Chinese coast: "I suggest that the present may be a good occasion to secure these rights; also that at this time Japan might consent to a Chinese cession in the northerly part of Fukien, in case a harbor in that province should be preferred by us."[45] O'Brien had apparently been reading old files in the Embassy and had noted the Japanese refusal, almost a decade earlier, to permit the Chinese to cede territory in the Formosa area. His inquiry produced not a flicker of interest in the Navy. Referred to the General Board, it was simply acknowledged and filed.[46] Shortly afterward, when the Consul General at Hong Kong transmitted an offer, apparently originating with a religious order, to lease land on Amoy, the Navy was also not interested. The newly formed Far Eastern Division of the State Department nevertheless was worried that the admirals might be tempted. In transmitting the appropriate papers to the Navy Department, it added a special note which observed that, if the land were to be used for naval purposes, special permission would have to be secured from the Chinese government. But, the Far Eastern Division added, "China will never consent to this transaction except under compulsion. This is especially true now when China is seized with the fever of 'rights recovery' and is so strenuously demanding the annulment of almost all her concessions previously granted to foreigners." The State Department, however, need not have worried. Back came the now standard naval response: the United States Navy could rely on colliers to supply the needs of its Far Eastern units.[47] Most assuredly the search for a base in China had completely ended.

The Open Door policy of the United States has sometimes been regarded as an idealistic commitment to the territorial and administrative integrity of China, with the United States acting as the friend and patron of China in contrast to European powers who sought further concessions and spheres of influence. The search for a naval station in Chinese waters, if viewed from this perspective, can only seem an aberration, an abandonment of principle. But the long-standing mili-

[45] SDNF, Case 478, O'Brien to Root, 4 November 1908.

[46] GB, Proceedings, 28 November 1908.

[47] SDNF, Case 14928/3-5, Wilder to Root, 25 June 1908, with attached memoranda prepared by Solicitor James Brown Scott and the Far Eastern Division.

tary and civilian interest in the various projects for such a base also suggests that there was another, contemporary interpretation of the Open Door, a concept held by not a few military and diplomatic officials concerned with Asian affairs: namely, the acquisition of a naval base somewhere in the Far East from which the United States would be able to make effective use of its naval power, might be able to intervene, with force if necessary, in the event of a future Boxer-type uprising or the political collapse of the Manchu regime.

This concept, to be sure, never became dominant, but it was present in quite a few diplomatic and military minds. To the naval strategists the issue was clear and simple: the collapse of China was almost certain, future disorders were inevitable, and the theater of operations would be in North China. Since the Philippines were too far distant, every consideration, whether of simple logistics or the implementation of contingency plans, led directly to the necessity for a naval station. For, as Captain Bowman McCalla observed, without a base the United States could not land its forces, protect American lives and property, or defend the national interest unless some other country, such as Great Britain, would graciously permit the United States to use its facilities and concessions in China.[48] A similar appreciation of the role of naval power was present in certain civilian minds. If, as we have seen, the proposals for a base on Chinese soil posed a conflict with the principle of the Open Door, then the suggestion could be made, as by Rockhill, that the Navy look elsewhere where the political strictures would not apply. Indeed, Rockhill's sponsorship of the Korean proposal confirms other evidence that the sponsor of the Open Door notes was by no means unprepared to include the element of coercion in his China policy. His biographer, Paul Varg, has pointed out that Rockhill believed that the Chinese would have to reform their antiquated governmental structure to survive in the twentieth century but also felt that such reforms would have to be imposed on a recalcitrant China by the west. In such circumstances, then, it was proper for the United States to be in a position where, if necessary, pressure —perhaps military pressure—could be brought to bear.[49]

Moreover, whatever the moral dilemmas produced by the principles of the Open Door, the Department of State never had any reservations about the right of the United States to use force to protect American interests in China. As we have previously noted, John Hay readily endorsed the Navy's plans to send gunboats into the interior waterways of China on the grounds that the practices of other nations as well as existing treaties made this a matter of right. In the fall of 1900, when

[48] SDML, Hackett to Hay, 5 September 1900, enclosing comments of McCalla.
[49] Paul Varg, *Open Door Diplomat* (Urbana, Ill., 1952), 30.

the Navy was making its first requests for a naval station, David Hill, Acting Secretary of State in the temporary absence of Hay, made the American position clear. The State Department, he so informed the Navy, upheld the right of naval landings at any point on the Chinese coast whether or not the location was a treaty port or foreign concession legally open to foreigners. Such action could not be interpreted as "hostile" when the government of the United States deemed it necessary to protect the lives of its citizens or their interests. Hill was quite emphatic in maintaining that "the question of whether any power should land troops is a question for each power to determine for itself." Whatever statements may have previously been given to the Chinese, he added, none had been "designed to forego the right which this Government had always held, and which on occasion it has exercised in China and in other countries, to land forces and adopt all necessary measures to protect the life and property of our citizens, whenever menaced by lawless acts which the general or local authority is unwilling or impotent to prevent."[50]

As in Latin America, some of the strongest voices raised in approval of naval visits and coercive measures came from American consuls in China. When Ragsdale, the consul in Tientsin, got word in the fall of 1900 that McKinley planned an early removal of the American troops employed in the Boxer uprising, he objected strongly. The United States, he insisted, must "maintain sufficient forces here to secure the position of American interests missionary and mercantile until the final settlement of the present troubles shall be made."[51] Fowler, the consul at Chefoo, constantly complained about the inaccessibility of American warships, extolled their value in times of trouble, and insisted upon the need to show the flag at regular intervals.[52] Indeed, any survey of consular reports from China would show that these individuals were, if anything, more anxious than their naval colleagues to have American naval power regularly displayed in their vicinity. For, as one American diplomat phrased the prevailing sentiment in the consular service in the Far East, "A consul who has not the support of his military will have little influence in the present government there, which is essentially military."[53]

That American consuls were so enamored with the trappings of military power is not surprising. They were, after all, primarily representatives of the business community, and at the turn of the century

[50] SDML, Hill to Long, 11 December 1900. A good example of Hay's beliefs on this subject is SDML, Hay to Moody, 7 October 1903.

[51] Nav Rec AF 10 (Far East), Ragsdale to Department of State, 4 October 1900.

[52] Nav Rec AF 10, Fowler to Department of State, 4 January 1901.

[53] SDMD, China, No. 615, Squiers to Hay, 21 August 1900.

American businessmen, like their counterparts in Europe, regarded it as a proper function of even laissez-faire government to protect their foreign properties from native interference and unrest. Those with interests in the Far East were especially insistent. At the height of the Boxer disturbances, John Foord, the President of the American Asiatic Association, openly informed John Hay that "for any effective participation in the settlement of China's future, it is absolutely necessary that the naval and military representation of the United States at important points in the Empire should bear some appreciable relationship to the size of the commercial and other interests possessed by Americans there."[54] In like vein, A. W. Bash, speaking for the American-China Development Company, a group of financiers promoting the Hankow railway project, doubted the wisdom of removing American troops and relying upon diplomatic techniques. "We would lose our interests," Bash wrote the Secretary, "if we withdrew in such fashion . . . and I hope that the military energy will be continued and that, at the proper time, one of our new battleships will be dispatched to the scene."[55]

To write more on this point is virtually unnecessary, for the outlook of businessman, consul, and naval officer in the Far East was similar. Their desire to show the flag and, if necessary, employ coercive measures, is one of the "givens" of the age of imperialism. To be sure, those who thought they understood the Oriental mind always added that demonstrations of military power had an especial impact upon the Chinese and were therefore all the more important. "I think it right, proper, and advisable," Rear Admiral Evans wrote, "that our Ministers and other diplomatic officials and any special commissioners sent on important missions should when practicable be conveyed in a war vessel, for in the eyes of the Eastern peoples, this adds prestige and importance to their mission."[56] Alfred Thayer Mahan was even more direct:

As regards the Chinese, I have found out something in my experience with my children. When they have done wrong, if you insist on their doing something, they sometimes can't *will* to do it. Consequently, after some disastrous failures, I adopted this plan which always worked. I required no amends at the moment, no promise for the future. I just gave them a good whaling and let them go. The same thing rarely occurred again.[57]

[54] SDML, Foord to Hay, 21 August 1900.
[55] SDML, Bash to Adee, 14 August 1900.
[56] Nav Rec AF 10, Evans to Moody, 18 November 1902.
[57] Mahan Papers, Mahan to Rear Admiral Rouverie Clark of the British Admiralty, 19 December 1900.

The Navy soon constructed a special fleet of gunboats to patrol Chinese waters. All of the various strands of the General Board's thinking about Asia and the proper role of naval power were reflected in the orders which established this force. Its role was to show the flag and— a telling phrase—"to protect Americans and foreign residents and interests in China and other semi-civilized countries." Another vital function was "to maintain the political and commercial interests of the United States, more particularly in countries where disordered conditions impair the efficiency and justice of local administration." The interior river ports of China required special attention since they were in an area "where the interests of civilization and trade demand constant watchfulness and care." For, the General Board added: "This will supply the evidence of naval power which it is desirable to keep frequently within the actual view of the people of the East and which is a political asset the value of which should always be borne in mind."[58]

The history of the United States Navy in the Far East after 1900 is filled with episodes in which naval officers acted upon these assumptions and stereotypes. But it is unnecessary to chronicle them in their entirety, from the more serious to the trivial. There would be little merit in an extended narrative which simply described the typical venture of the U.S.S. "X" as it moved to Chinese port "Y" to protect missionary or commercial group "Z." Rather, in the pages that follow attention will be focused upon several major events—the Boxer Rebellion, the tensions with Russia over Manchuria, several contemplated interventions in China, the growth of Japanese-American rivalry, and the world cruise of the White Fleet—in which the military were involved in the mainstream of American foreign policy and something more than the silent agents of civilian policy.

2. The Boxer Rebellion and Military Intervention in China

Paradoxically, the Navy, and to some extent the Army, enjoyed their greatest independence at the very beginning of the twentieth century when the Boxer Rebellion involved the United States for the first, but not the last, time in an international police operation. That the American military had a considerable role in the Boxer affair was to a large extent a matter of chance. In the first place, in the summer of 1900, the Philippine insurrection was still in progress, and the United States therefore had far more military strength on hand in the Pacific than it

[58] GB, Letters, v, Dewey to Metcalf, 25 April 1907, and vi, Dewey to Meyer, 30 December 1909.

was to have available for years to come. Thus, when the siege of the legations began, Washington could contribute a significant increment of power to the international military venture that was mounted. Second, the fact that the official representatives of the United States in China were besieged in Peking and, in fact, cut off from communication with the outside world meant that considerable autonomy had to be delegated to the responsible military officers in China. Finally, the sheer factor of distance between Washington and North China made it impossible for McKinley and Hay to direct every detail of policy.

Initially the Navy was more than a little reluctant to become involved in the Chinese disturbances. Admiral George C. Remey, then the commander of the Pacific fleet, was not looking for new fields to conquer. When Admiral Louis Kempff was first sent to Taku, Remey warned him that the most important function of the Navy in the Pacific "lies entirely within Philippine waters. True, the United States does have interests north of Hong Kong, but in their extent they are comparatively of a minor character." Basking in the comforting thought of a growing Anglo-American friendship, Remey was prepared to let Britannia rule the Asian waves and bear the principal burden:

> For many years there has been a well-understood international agreement that, in cases of local disturbance and danger, the naval vessels of different nationalities present would cooperate and those of any nation would look out for the interests of all foreign nations. In view of the very cordial relations now existing between Great Britain and the United States, this agreement may be more than ever relied upon.[59]

It should be added also that neither Remey nor Kempff were especially prescient in diagnosing the potential seriousness of the growing disturbances in China. In early June, when the full force of the storm was about to break, Kempff was still advising the Navy Department that the disorders were the consequence of a lack of rainfall and incipient famine. A report which, incidentally, described the Boxers as members "of what we might designate an 'Athletic Association'" indicated his lack of concern: "Should a sufficient rainfall come soon it will be safe to predict that disturbances of any serious nature will not take place."[60]

The American legation in Peking had been warning about possible trouble since the fall of 1899 and continued to do so on into the spring of 1900. Indeed, at one point in April of 1900, Conger asked for the presence of a warship for at least a short period of time and

---

[59] Nav Rec AF 10, Remey to Kempff, 4 June 1900.
[60] Nav Rec AF 10, Kempff to Long, 3 June 1900.

pointed out that serious trouble might be imminent if the Imperial authorities remained passive.[61] But it is doubtful if any diplomat in Peking, including Conger, fully appreciated the extent of the crisis until it erupted in early June. Certainly neither Hay nor Rockhill at their desks in Washington were seriously engaged. In March, Conger, acting in concert with the other diplomats at the Chinese capital, had suggested that, if the Manchu government continued to take no action, all the powers with interests in China should join in a naval demonstration off the coast. The suggestion was received without enthusiasm. Hay counseled that a joint naval demonstration would not be appropriate "in view of the attitude of this Government toward the political situation of the European powers in China."[62] The Department of State sent copies of Conger's cables to the Navy with an indication that one or two vessels might be sent to protect the rights of American citizens, including the interests of missionaries whose position "through long acquiescence (has) become a vested right."[63] But, prior to the actual outbreak in late May and early June, this was the limit of warning and response. Also, the Navy had been further informed that its ships, if used, would operate solely for the purpose of "independently protecting" American interests.

Thus the June uprising, though not unexpected, produced improvised, occasionally frantic policymaking at all levels. Once Kempff arrived at Taku, Conger asked him to act in concert with the European and Japanese naval commanders in the event that Peking was placed under siege. Kempff accepted the charge. But when his superior, Remey, first learned of the admiral's early actions, he anxiously cabled the Navy Department of his growing fear that Kempff "cooperates with foreign powers to an extent incompatible with American interests."[64] General Arthur MacArthur, commanding in the Philippines, was at first opposed to the release of any troops from his command for duty in China on the grounds that the more important military operations in the Philippines would be seriously weakened. To add to the confusion, the naval command off Taku was long uncertain about the extent of its authority to act in conjunction with other naval forces whether the issue was that of joining the bombardment of the forts at Taku or participating in the joint relief expedition.[65] In Washington,

[61] Nav Rec AF 10, Conger to Admiral J. C. Watson, 5 April 1900, and Conger to Kempff, 18 and 25 May 1900.

[62] Nav Rec AF 10, Hay to Long, 10 March 1900, forwarding copy of Conger's request.

[63] Nav Rec AF 10, Hay to Long, 15 March 1900.

[64] SDML, Long to Hay, 6 June 1900, forwarding copy of Remey's cable to Long.

[65] SDML, Long to Hay, 8, 11, and 18 June 1900, various dispatches from Kempff to Long. Also Nav Rec AF 10, Remey to Kempff, 4 June 1900.

of course, larger issues were immediately posed: above all, to what extent should the United States act in military and political concert with those European powers whose China policies it had so frequently deplored?

Eventually the military commanders got their orders. These instructions clearly reflected the many conflicting forces that affected the Administration's policy. They showed a realization that distance and poor communications made it necessary to grant considerable latitude to the military authorities as well as a counterbalancing desire to maintain overall civilian control. They indicated the intent to protect Americans and American interests in China but also a desire not to stray so far into co-operation with Europeans that violence would be done to established tradition. Kempff, for example, was instructed by the Navy "to protect American national interests as well as the interests of individual Americans." The very next sentence, however, was a plea for prudent behavior: "Whatever you do, let the Navy Department know plan of concerting powers in regard punitive or other expeditions and keep us informed of forces you will need in order that Government may properly discharge the obligations that its very large interests put on it."[66] General Chaffee's orders were the work of Elihu Root, the newly-appointed Secretary of War and, in the absence of Hay from Washington, McKinley's principal adviser. Chaffee was told to cooperate fully with Kempff and, if possible, to communicate with Conger— "in general observe his wishes and answer to his demands in regard to his protection and that of the interests which he represents." But the commanding general was also informed that he might "freely" confer with the representatives of other powers and

> wherever it shall appear to you that the American interests which you are to protect will be best served by that course, you will act with the forces under your command concurrently with the forces of other powers. You will, however, avoid entering into any joint action or undertaking with other powers tending to commit or limit this Government as to its future course of conduct, and you will avoid taking any action having any object except the protection of American interests herein charged upon you.[67]

It is small wonder that, three weeks later, Root attempted to be more specific in the charge laid upon Chaffee. He was then told that the American government wished to maintain friendly relations with all

[66] SDML, Hackett to Remey and Kempff, 18 June 1900, copies of orders sent by the Navy to its Far Eastern commanders.

[67] SDML, Corbin to Chaffee, 30 June 1900, a copy of orders sent by Root to Chaffee and furnished to the State Department on 9 July 1900.

Chinese not involved in the "outrages" as well as to cooperate with the efforts of Li Hung Chang, the Viceroy of the province of Chili, to end the rebellion. Chaffee could still consult freely with other national commanders and was "at liberty to agree with them from time to time as to a common official direction of the various forces in their combined operations." Still, as Root's orders finally admitted, "Much must be left to your wise discretion and that of the Admiral."[68]

There was no cause for Washington to worry excessively about the "wise discretion" of its commanders. Chaffee, Kempff, and Remey possessed a strong sense of suspicion about the wily European and retained much of the traditional American attitude toward involvement with Europeans. General Chaffee, for example, soon developed an intense skepticism about the intentions of Germany. Once Count Waldersee had belatedly arrived on the Chinese scene with his grandiose Teutonic projects, the American general strongly resisted his plans to extend the range of allied military operations. Since the German had not gotten to China until the siege of Peking had been lifted, Chaffee suspected that he merely sought some spectacular military engagement to win glory for German arms.[69] Towards the end of his tour of duty Chaffee so strongly objected to one of Waldersee's schemes that he received a special commendation from the Vice President-elect, Theodore Roosevelt.[70] Nor were Kempff and Remey prepared to embark upon what they interpreted as glory hunts. One proposal for an allied naval venture in the early fall of 1900 produced the scornful comment from Remey that "I can scarcely attribute such extensive preparations for so insignificant an objective to any other reason than a desire for either personal or national aggrandizement on the part of the Allies." Remey confessed that he had been briefly tempted to cooperate because of the obvious need to retain Allied unity before the Chinese but added almost plaintively, "I hope the Department will understand how very hard it is to withstand the pressure of the seven principal powers in an affair of this kind. It would be so much easier to act in concert with the others and have all their undivided opinion to justify me."[71] Admiral Kempff, in turn, was most suspicious of the Russians, whose policies he thought were perfectly "in keeping with that persistent and consistent glacier-like movement . . . of that country in the acquisition of lands which lie adjoining."[72] He consistently ex-

---

[68] SDML, Corbin to Chaffee, 19 July 1900.

[69] Root Papers, Chaffee to Root, 5 October 1900.

[70] Corbin Papers, Chaffee to Corbin, 16 March 1901; SDML, Root to Hay, 18 February 1901, enclosing copy of 15 February 1901 message from Chaffee; Roosevelt *Letters*, III, 14, Roosevelt to Chaffee, 16 March 1901.

[71] Nav Rec AF 10, Remey to Long, 2 October 1900.

[72] SDML, Kempff to Long, 27 June 1900.

pressed the view that the objectives of all the nations then involved in China were "more than just the protection of life and property, and I do not consider it proper for the lives of our military men to be offered up in order to aid them in their hidden schemes."[73]

Indeed, Kempff's initial reluctance to cooperate in naval ventures actually produced some criticism of his alleged refusal to act while great issues still hung in the balance. In mid-June a conference of the Allied admirals decided to shell and then seize the forts of Taku, that is, the fortifications in the outer harbor at Tientsin. When Kempff did not participate in the operation, there was some newspaper criticism as well as adverse comment in the Department of State. But Kempff, who naturally defended his conduct in several lengthy dispatches, was not apologetic and did not base his case upon the uncertainty of his orders. He had not acted, he reported, because he believed it was against American policy to become entangled with other powers; moreover, he was convinced that the shelling of the forts would stir Chinese anger to such a pitch the lives of Americans in other parts of China would be endangered. Since the military forces of the Chinese government had made no hostile moves against the United States, Kempff doubted if he had authority to commit an act of war against a country with which the United States was at peace.[74] While much of his attitude reflected American traditionalism, Kempff may well have been wiser than he thought. For the seizure of the Taku forts did not turn out, as anticipated, to be the magnificent show of allied strength that would "bring the Chinese to their senses" but, as much historical evidence now shows, simply stirred the Boxers to new outbreaks and led directly to the siege of Peking.[75] A junior ensign reported at the time: "I know that the general impression at Tientsin before the taking of the forts was that a show of force was all that was necessary to make the Chinese come to terms immediately; and the feeling after the capture of the forts was that of regret for having precipitated the whole affair by this action."[76] Washington, too, came to appreciate Kempff's caution, for it fitted into its evolving policy of trying to demonstrate that the United States was neither at war with the Chinese government nor binding its own policies too closely to those of the Europeans.

National policy was of course always determined by the civilian administration. The Army and Navy, for example, were not consulted

[73] SDML, Kempff to Long, 1 July 1900.

[74] SDML, Long to Hay, 28 July 1900, enclosing Kempff report of 22 June. See also Long to Hay, 21 July 1900, forwarding a copy of Kempff's report of 17 June.

[75] Victor Purcell, *The Boxer Uprising: A Background Study* (Cambridge, 1963), 245 ff.

[76] Nav Rec AF 10, Ensign Pettingill to Senior Squadron Commander, Asiatic Station, 15 January 1901.

about the wisdom of cooperating at arm's length, about using the services of Li Hung Chang, or about the second set of Open Door notes released by Hay in late July. Moreover, once the legations had been rescued, the Boxer movement brought under control, and communications restored, the administration tightened some of the reins which had been loosely drawn during the period of more trying circumstances. For example, when it appeared that Admiral Remey might cooperate with the Allies in seizing several Chinese forts for use as winter headquarters, he was immediately ordered to take no such action without further instructions.[77] Nonetheless, between June and the fall of 1900, there were a number of decisions which, while of secondary magnitude, clearly showed that military advice influenced the general evolution of administration policy. In mid-July the Allied conference of admirals off Taku recommended that each of the governments involved in China's affairs issue orders which would forbid further trade in armaments with the Chinese. This proposal, to be sure, came to Washington as a formal recommendation from the French and German governments, but it also carried a strong endorsement by the American naval command in China.[78] Root was skeptical about its effectiveness and doubted the power of the President to interfere with the arms trade, but he nevertheless approved. Soon Remey had orders "to use every exertion to prevent importation into Chinese ports of arms which may reach enemy hands."[79]

Naval officers had, quite properly, a distinct influence upon the force levels to which the McKinley administration agreed. Kempff and Remey, as we have noted, were specifically given responsibility for recommending the number of troops that ought to be committed. The former officer responded with some early recommendations that were far beyond the military capabilities of the United States, but his messages on this subject did much to create the sense of urgency which developed in Washington in late June and early July. Kempff maintained that the United States, if it was to have a proportionate representation in the relief expedition, should contribute 10,000 men; he asked specifically for four infantry regiments, 500 cavalry, and a battery of field artillery.[80] His estimate of urgent military needs was a major factor in McKinley's decision to send troops from the Philippines and to

[77] Nav Rec AF 10, Long to Hay, 1 October 1900, and Remey to Long, 2 October 1900; SDML, Long to Hay, 1 October 1900.

[78] SDML, Long to Hay, 17 and 19 July 1900.

[79] SDML, Hay to Long, 18 July 1900. All of these documents cited from State Department files are also to be found in the Area 10 file of Naval Records.

[80] SDML, Kempff to Long, 24 June 1900, forwarded on the same date to the State Department. See also two additional reports from Kempff attached to Hackett to Hay, 7 July and 21 August 1900.

contemplate the assignment of an additional two or three Philippine regiments on a standby basis.[81]

Conversely, once Peking had been taken, the decision to carry out a prompt reduction in the American military commitment, a matter on which McKinley felt strongly, also involved the military leaders in China. McKinley, running for re-election against the anti-imperialist Bryan, wanted to get Chaffee and his soldiers out of Peking at the earliest possible moment.[82] Within ten days after the city had been freed, Chaffee was notified that there might be an early decision to withdraw his forces, while the general, in his replies, indicated that he could, within a matter of weeks, get along with a substantially reduced force.[83] But McKinley wanted to move even more rapidly and began to make dramatic, if not radical suggestions. By September he had gone beyond the simple desire to move Chaffee and his troops out of Peking; he was also suggesting that Conger and the legation should be removed to Tientsin, that all negotiations with Chinese authorities should be conducted from that city, and that all of Chaffee's troops should be returned to the Philippines as soon as possible.[84] There was, needless to say, a great flurry over this proposal, which went further than either military or diplomatic authorities desired. McKinley was eventually persuaded to accept a gradual, phased reduction in Chaffee's command. This compromise, however, came about only after simultaneous telegrams arrived from Conger and Chaffee which were phoned to the President and "changed the whole course of affairs."[85]

One would naturally expect the Army and Navy to advise on force levels. These were matters, almost entirely military, on which it was precisely their function to counsel their commander-in-chief. But the Army and Navy in China also provided the administration with a wealth of non-military information during the duration of the crisis. Since sources of information were scanty and the legation cut off from all communications for nearly three months, the military became a second set of eyes and ears for the administration. Both service secretaries, Root and Long, went to considerable pains to make certain that all relevant Army and Navy dispatches got to the Department of State. (Though, conversely, the State Department routinely sent to the services only those messages which pertained to military matters.) It is also

[81] Root Papers, McKinley to Root, 3 July 1900.

[82] Dennett, *Hay*, 314-15, and Margaret Leech, *In the Days of McKinley* (New York, 1959), 525-26.

[83] SDML, Corbin to Chaffee, 25 August 1900, and Chaffee to Corbin, 4 and 19 September 1900.

[84] Root Papers, copies of McKinley to Hay, 9 and 14 September 1900.

[85] Hay Papers, Adee to Hay, 14 September 1900, reporting impact of the two telegrams on the President.

clear that these dispatches were read and utilized. In mid-July, for example, Admiral Crowninshield commended Remey for the frequency and quality of his reports which he said had been of value not only to the Navy Department, "but also in many cases to State, War, and the President."[86] Later on, when Theodore Roosevelt wanted to score the conduct of both European troops and American missionaries during the Boxer episode, he cited the many reports of American Army officers as his evidence.[87]

There were several instances when information collected by the military proved of immediate value to civilian policymakers. From the beginning of the Boxer disturbances, Hay and McKinley had searched for a responsible Chinese official with whom to deal and had, with great misgivings, come to favor Li Hung Chang, the Viceroy of Chili. While he was eventually named by the Imperial government as the official Chinese plenipotentiary, many of the powers were reluctant to deal with him, in large part because of his reputed sympathies for and connections with Russian imperialist ventures.[88] Since the end of May, American naval officers at Canton had kept in touch with Li; at one point they thought they had buttoned up an arrangement whereby he would be brought to Tientsin aboard an American warship; when that fell through, the Navy blamed the British and reported that it was British action that prevented Li Hung Chang from reaching North China.[89]

In mid-August the Russian chargé in Washington protested that the Allied admirals had agreed among themselves that, even if Li should reach North China, they would not permit him to make contact with the Manchu authorities. The Russians politely suggested that the United States government might wish to instruct Admirals Kempff and Remey to dissociate themselves from that decision.[90] Remey, naturally, was immediately asked to explain. To the great pleasure of the Department of State, Remey replied that there had been no formal decision by the admirals to ban Li although there had been an informal discussion of the possibility of doing so. Moreover, he had strongly dissented from the opinions of his fellow admirals, supported the cause of Li Hung Chang, and made certain that his dissent was made a matter of record. "He was the first and most reliable man to look to for a settlement," Remey commented, "and I have acted on this idea, believing it to be in accordance with the policy and views of the United States

[86] Nav Rec AF 10, Crowninshield to Remey, 26 July 1900.
[87] Roosevelt, Letters, III, 752, Roosevelt to Mahan, 18 March 1901.
[88] Dennett, Hay, 310-11.
[89] SDML, Long to Hay, 25 July 1900, enclosing Kempff to Long, 29 June 1900.
[90] SDML, Adee to Long, 17 August 1900.

Government."[91] Once armed with Remey's report, Hay informed the Russians that his own investigation showed that the Allied admirals had reached no final decision about Li and that, even in their informal discussions, the American admiral had dissented from the prevailing sentiments.[92] Since Hay at that time was trying to win support for Li Hung Chang and also to appease the Russians, Remey's actions had presented him with a useful diplomatic opportunity. It was indeed not long before Remey got a special cable which commended him for his dissent.[93]

Another episode, relatively unimportant in itself, cast a faint light on the American future in Asia. In late August of 1900 the American consul general in Shanghai reported an "alarming situation" at Amoy created by the landing of some 300 Japanese troops on that island.[94] Amoy, the site of the terminus of the proposed Hankow railway which the American-China Development Company was promoting, was already of some interest to Washington; the administration had already been asked on several occasions by the promoters of the rail venture to support their claims against reportedly increasing Japanese inroads in the province of Fo Kien.[95] But Amoy was also an area about which, as Alvey Adee noted, the administration had little current information and would have to reply upon the reports that came from the Navy. Hay consulted with the President and soon orders were issued to the *Marietta* to make an immediate investigation:

> Proceed to Amoy and report circumstances of Japanese landing. Does it amount to occupation? We allow to other powers, and on occasion would ourselves exercise, discretionary right to land and protect national citizens and interests against Chinese, or when imperilled beyond power of control or provincial authority to protect. Does either condition exist at Amoy?[96]

Meanwhile, the Japanese were going to considerable lengths to explain to the United States that the "propinquity" of Amoy to Japanese-

[91] SDML, Remey to Bureau of Navigation, 21 August 1900, transmitted to State Department on the same date. Additional information is in a longer Remey to Long communication, 24 August 1900, but which was not given to the State Department for another month. Nav Rec AF 10 contains virtually the same documentation as the Miscellaneous Letter file of the State Department. It is therefore cited only when the appropriate naval document did not appear in the State Department materials.

[92] SDML, Adee to Long, 24 August 1900.

[93] Nav Rec AF 10, Long to Remey, 26 August 1900.

[94] SDML, Adee to Long, 26 August 1900.

[95] SDML, A. W. Bash to Adee, 14 August 1900.

[96] SDML, Adee to Long, 24 August 1900.

held Formosa created special problems. Amoy, they claimed, had been the point of origin for most of China's "evil designs" against Formosa. Their landing had been made necessary, the Japanese alleged, by various anti-foreign riots at Amoy and the burning of a Japanese temple.[97]

The American vice-consul at Amoy, Dr. Johnson, was the same man who, within a year, was to tempt the Navy with a lease for a coaling station at Amoy and who was already trying to impress naval officers with its strategic importance. It is hardly surprising that he found the Japanese landing unwarranted. In any event, Johnson was questioned by the naval investigating group when it arrived at Amoy, and reported that the alleged burning of a Japanese temple was a transparent fraud. What had burned, according to the vice-consul, was a room in a private house, then rented by a Japanese priest. "It was clear from the beginning to the end," he informed the officers of the *Marietta,* "that the burning of the rented room, which was not attended by any disturbance whatever, had no influence—excepting an excuse—on the conduct of the Japanese. They seemed to have set out to occupy the port and were bent on doing it."[98]

The naval officers, when they filed their own report, sustained the vice-consul's verdict. Commander C. G. Bowman informed the Navy Department—which passed his findings on to State—that the circumstances at Amoy had not warranted Japanese intervention, that Chinese authorities were successfully maintaining order, and that the preservation of foreign interests depended upon an early Japanese withdrawal.[99] The outcome of the Amoy affair, however, was anticlimactic. Assistant Secretary of State David Hill had a quiet talk with the Japanese minister in Washington, expressing his hope that the Japanese would soon withdraw and the American desire that no nation would upset the delicate Chinese balance by taking unilateral action. More to the point was the action of the British who, at China's request, landed a few of their own troops at Amoy and thereby neutralized the Japanese position. A few days later the Japanese left.[100] At most the incident was a faint foreshadowing of Japanese-American differences still on the far horizon. But it had given the Navy an opportunity to provide the Department of State with information on which to base its own actions.

[97] Department of State, Communications from the Japanese Legation in Washington, Minister Takahira to Hay, 29 August 1900.

[98] Nav Rec AF 10, Johnson to Commander Green of the *Marietta*, no date but clearly in the latter part of August 1900.

[99] SDML, Hackett to Hay, 5 September 1900, forwarding copy of Commander Bowman's report.

[100] Department of State, Communications from the Japanese Legation, Memorandum of conversation between Hill and Takahira, 4 September 1900, and Hackett to Hay, 5 September, as cited.

Once the Boxer disturbances were quelled, the military receded into the background, while the diplomats, emerging from their enforced inactivity, resumed their dominant role. The McKinley administration dispatched its ranking Asian expert, William Rockhill, to conduct the negotiations to settle the Boxer affair. Chaffee's troops, gradually but drastically reduced in the fall of 1900, were cut to a mere legation guard in the following spring. It was increasingly obvious that the United States government was reluctant to become directly involved in Chinese affairs and, above all, had no intention of trying to preserve the Open Door by the wholesale employment of the techniques of power diplomacy.

Yet military power was by no means entirely eliminated from the Chinese equation. American diplomats wished to preserve at least the rudiments of a power position. Both Conger and Rockhill, to be sure, had had their fill of purely military solutions by the fall of 1900. They complained bitterly about the manner in which European officers, especially the Germans, hampered the work of diplomacy with their military schemes; they were angered by the intention of the Europeans to retain their military forces intact until the Manchu government had agreed to pay an indemnity; and they protested strongly against a plan to construct a "veritable fortress" in the heart of Peking as protection against another burst of violence.[101] Conger prophesied that there was no real safety in military defenses and that everything depended upon the spirit and willingness of the Imperial government, when restored to full power, to implement the demands placed by treaty upon it.[102] But neither diplomat wanted American military power reduced to a nullity. By March of 1901 even Rockhill was "strenuously" protesting Washington's decision to remove all of Chaffee's troops except a small legation guard, for he and Conger insisted that, for years to come, a strong force must be kept at the legation. At one time, indeed, Conger suggested that a force of 1,000 American soldiers should be permanently maintained at Peking. It was a recommendation, he informed Hay, which he regretted, but if the United States was "to retain any prestige with foreign powers or with China, we must assume our share of the burden."[103] Eventually Washington determined to keep no more than a tiny military complement as a Legation Guard—one company of the 16th Infantry, less than 200 soldiers. But though a token force, it was to be a symbol of America's continuing interest in the preservation of its stake in China. For, as Conger summarized the issue:

[101] Hay Papers, Rockhill to Hay, 19 February and 18 April 1901; SDMD, China, No. 542, Conger to Hay, 21 February 1901.

[102] SDMD, China, No. 536, Conger to Hay, 16 February 1901.

[103] SDMD, China, No. 488 and No. 519, 29 December 1900 and 31 January 1901. See also Dennett, *Hay*, 322.

While it is understood that we will not take territorial indemnity nor participate in the division of the empire and consequently are placed at a considerable disadvantage in the negotiations, yet we ought to do our full share in compelling a settlement that will avoid dissolution. The presence of even a small body of U. S. troops will be a potential in that direction and would give us at least a shadow of a claim for recognition of some sort if the Empire does go to pieces.[104]

In a certain sense, after the excitement of the Boxer period and the collapse of the great schemes for naval bases, the history of the Army and the Navy in China was anticlimactic. China herself, always assumed to be on the verge of a fatal illness, obstinately refused to die; the expected partition of the Manchu empire, for many and varied reasons often little understood by American observers, never took place. The Navy continued to investigate minor alarms, visit ports and inland rivers, and return reports to Washington which were dutifully passed on to the Department of State to be read, acknowledged—and filed. The calibre of naval reporting varied markedly, for not all of the senior officers assigned to the Asiatic station cared greatly about Far Eastern politics. Rear Admiral Frederick Rodgers, who succeeded Remey, generally confined himself to routine operational reports. Admiral Evans was more concerned with international affairs, but his dispatches often dealt with problems no more serious than his extended efforts to collect the names and locations of various American missions in China which might need protection in future disorders.[105] The work of protection, moreover, became so routine and was so firmly in the hands of the Navy that, when trouble threatened in the Yangtze valley in 1908, Rockhill, now serving as minister to China, could simply write that "it is assumed . . . that under the existing arrangements of the Navy Department, the proper commanding officer is in a position to insure the prompt dispatch of a vessel to any port whenever the protection of American missionary . . . interests might make such a step advisable."[106]

But the naval officers were still firm in their conviction that these routine operations were important in furthering American interests. Gunboats, they thought, made it possible for American missionaries to perform their labors in the vineyard of the Lord. After Admiral

[104] On the final decisions regarding the size of the Legation guard, see SDML, Root to Hay, 7 March and 21 May 1901. The quotation is from Conger's 519, 31 January 1901, as cited.

[105] Nav Rec AF 10, Evans to Moody, 2 June 1903 is a representative example of his reporting; Rogers' routine and non-political dispatches are scattered in the AF 10 file in the fall of 1902.

[106] SDNF, Case 1518, Rockhill to Root, 23 November 1908.

Charles Train, commander of the Asiatic fleet, had visited China's inland waters, he concluded, "My trip up the river convinces me that the presence of gunboats is essential to the safety of the many missionaries living along its banks." Outbreaks were always possible; the only restraint "is the actual visible presence of force."[107] Naval reports also continued to show much interest in the development of American trading and financial enterprises and the ways whereby the naval presence presumably fostered their growth and safety. When Admiral Evans visited the upper reaches of the Yangtze in 1902, much of his final report was a laudatory account of the efforts of the American-China Development Company to promote the Hankow railway and the ultimate value of this project for American prestige in the Orient.[108] Junior officers continued to pride themselves on their minor interventions with local officials to persuade them to abandon some practice that restricted American trade.

It was typical of most officers assigned to duty in China that they always tended to see dangers lurking over the horizon and to maximize the prospects for a renewal of disorder. When Admiral Evans summarized his findings early in 1903, he emphasized the likelihood of outbreaks along the line of the Canton-Hankow railway, wrote of his readiness to use a force of 500 marines then in the Philippines, and concluded on the pessimistic note that the general situation in China "calls for deep and careful consideration of those in authority in regard to the protection of American interests in China."[109] A few years later, Commander Nathan Sargent of the *Baltimore* wrote a long report which chronicled the return of Shanghai to its customary tranquillity. Sargent nonetheless ended with a gloomy forecast that "the storm which apparently is brewing may not break at all, but all old residents appear to be a unit in their conviction that it is coming, and it would seem that we cannot afford to ignore this consensus of opinion."[110] Commander Smith of the *Chattanooga* visited the Yangtze in 1907 and could see neither signs of unrest nor indications of Chinese antipathy toward Americans. But he too ended his report with the comment, "Every one I talked to qualified his remarks by saying that no one can tell when there will be an uprising and that there is unrest beneath the surface."[111]

The ideas contained in these reports about China were of course but a reflection of the general outlook—the gospel of expansion derived from Mahan—which we have previously discussed. Obviously naval

[107] SDML, Train to Bonaparte, 11 November 1906.
[108] Nav Rec AF 10, Evans to Moody, 6 October 1902.
[109] Nav Rec AF 10, Evans to Moody, 2 May 1903.
[110] Nav Rec AF 10, Sargent to Commander-in-Chief Asiatic Fleet, 4 January 1906.
[111] Nav Rec AF 10, Smith to Commander-in-Chief Asiatic Fleet, 20 May 1907.

officers long interpreted their role as that of preserving Anglo-Saxon ideas of law and order in a semi-civilized country. As in Latin America they also tended to send back to Washington opinions which they had picked up from their conversations with members of the American community in China—consuls, businessmen, and, especially in China, missionaries. Given their frequent changes of station and assignment, the many pressures of the naval service, and their general lack of an informed background on Chinese affairs, few naval observers had the opportunity to develop independent conclusions. The opinions cited in the previous several paragraphs bear witness to the derivative nature of many of their judgments.

It was certainly possible for naval officers to encounter American missionaries who desired, even insisted upon naval protection. Not a few missionaries, frightened by the Boxer Rebellion and such incidents as the "Lienchow massacre," were as apprehensive about the future as any Mahan-oriented naval officer. The American commander of the *Wilmington*, investigating aspects of the Lienchow affair, conferred with Dr. Wisner, the American head of a missionary college at that location. To Wisner a stray bullet fired at one of his buildings had appeared a clear threat not merely to his own life but to the entire mission. On this occasion, however, the naval observer was skeptical. Though prepared to send marines if the situation appeared urgent, he found no threatening signs and commented that, while "every foreign mission runs a certain risk of mob violence . . . apparently Dr. Wisner's nerves are more highly strung than is suitable for mission work in China, and a remote danger seems to him immediate and threatening."[112] A few years later Rockhill encountered an angry Episcopalian bishop at Hankow who complained bitterly about his inability to secure American gunboats to protect his mission school. The bishop sharply told Rockhill that

> It might be well to remind the Naval Department of the situation here in China, which is one of constant instability, and perhaps suggest that American residents would appreciate the presence of American ships so that they would not be so wholly dependent upon the courtesy of our British cousins, however unfailing and constant we are glad to acknowledge that courtesy to be.[113]

But it is also true that, in the light of the Boxer experience, at least a few of the missionaries were slowly beginning to question their long-accepted reliance upon gunboats and their insistence that the Chinese

[112] SDNF, Case 167/26-27, Newberry to Root, 24 September 1906, forwarding copy of report from the *Wilmington*.
[113] SDNF, Case 1518/230-31, Rockhill to Root, 4 December 1908.

must be compelled to live up to the specific letter of the law in every extra-territorial treaty. The decade after 1900 was, however, very much a transitional decade, during which the missionary view of China was exceedingly slow to change. According to the most recent historian of the American missionary effort in China, those who popularized the movement in America continued to paint a rather bleak picture of the Chinese as backward heathens whose characteristics were guile and deceit.[114] Nor does one find in either Navy records or missionary papers any strong expression of doubt about the value of the gunboat in sustaining the cause of Christ. It was not until the decade of the 1920s, when Chinese nationalism had become an accomplished and often hostile fact, that the missionaries came to realize that the United States Navy was an obstacle rather than an asset in the fulfillment of their work. It is therefore not surprising that in the earlier years the touring naval officer often reflected in his reports an exaggerated picture of the same bleak view of the Chinese character that prevailed in missionary circles.

We have already discussed the extent to which American consuls in China believed in showing the flag and impressing the Chinese with naval power. All that needs to be added is to point out that these same individuals, in their frequent contacts with visiting naval officers, further spread the image of China as a nation in which disorder was always imminent. This was, for example, especially true of Henry Fowler, for years the consul at the important Chinese port of Chefoo. He was angry in 1901 because he could not obtain naval protection since, as he put it, "the trouble season" in Chefoo was about to begin.[115] A year later Fowler was organizing a militia among the American residents of that city since he was convinced that the next outburst in China would occur not in Peking but in the treaty ports.[116] In 1906, at the height of the boycott movement, Chefoo remained quiet, one of the few peaceful areas in all China, but to Fowler the tranquillity was deceptive. Actually, he wrote, "the situation is worse than it was in 1899. All China is in a ferment, a spark is only needed to create the greatest and most sanguinary outbreak the world has ever seen." The following winter, when his naval protection was removed, Fowler was outraged, again drew comparisons with the situation on the eve of the Boxer uprising, demanded the return of the naval watch, and observed that riots rarely occurred when warships were handy.[117] When Rear Admiral J. H. Dayton unexpectedly inherited command of the Asiatic

114 Paul Varg, *Missionaries, Chinese, and Diplomats* (Princeton, 1958), 105-22.
115 Nav Rec AF 10, Fowler to Hay, 4 January 1901.
116 SDCD, Chefoo, China, Fowler to Department of State, 18 January 1902.
117 Nav Rec AF 10, Fowler to Department of State, 18 December 1905 and 3 February 1906; SDNF, Case 2283/1-3, Fowler to Root, 31 January 1907.

fleet, one of his first acts was to seek out Fowler at Chefoo. Confessing that he had lost touch with Chinese affairs, Dayton asked the American consul to provide him with the necessary political background and estimate the probability of future danger.[118] Thus, it was inevitable that the reports filed by naval officers who served in the Far East would reflect the views of men like Fowler and other like-minded members of the American community, such as the consul at Newchang who insisted that Chinese merchants "are nervous about the stability of trade that is not supported by the show of gun boats." Quite typical was the demand of a junior officer that the Navy should provide more naval visits to the upper Yangtze—especially since he prefaced his report with the observation that "All the Americans were quite pointed in their complaints at the infrequency of the visits of American gunboats."[119]

But, whatever the prevailing tendencies and attitudes, there were always a few exceptions, naval officers who discounted rumors they heard or who questioned the need to respond to a request for naval assistance. Even Admiral Evans, after his Yangtze tour in 1902, felt confident enough in his own judgment to turn down the consul at Canton when he asked for a gunboat. Having just visited the region and talked with foreign as well as American residents, he believed that there was no genuine prospect of an uprising.[120] A few even had sufficient independence of judgment to question basic assumptions. After observing the boycott movement in Canton in 1905, Commander Tillman maintained that there would be no violence "unless it is brought about by some foolish or unwarranted action by some American or European." He was sufficiently heretical to dare the suggestion that American businessmen in Canton, who were losing money from the boycott, would prefer to have some of their properties destroyed in rioting rather than have the boycott continue—"for violence would undoubtedly mean an indemnity and a stronger action by the American government than merely diplomatic protests."[121] Similarly, Commander Sargent, an officer whose views, especially in Latin America, were well regarded in the State Department, testified that the Chinese boycott probably owed as much to the immigration policies of the United States government as it did to local circumstances in China.[122] Reactions such as these were, to be sure, relatively rare, but always in sufficient number

118 Nav Rec AF 10, Dayton to Fowler, 8 September 1906.

119 SDCD, China, Newchang, Henry J. Miller to Hill, 21 September 1901, and SDNF, Case 1813/7, Newberry to Root, 2 July 1907, copy of report by Lt. H. P. Perrill.

120 Nav Rec AF 10, Evans to Moody, 2nd endorsement, 24 December 1902.

121 Nav Rec AF 10, Tillman to Commander-in-Chief Asiatic Fleet, 25 October 1905.

122 Nav Rec AF 10, Sargent to Commander-in-Chief Asiatic Fleet, 4 January 1906.

to make it unwise to proclaim sweeping generalizations about the rigidity or bellicosity of naval thought.

During the years from the Boxer Rebellion until 1906, the Navy did maintain a small force of battleships in the Far East. Though, as we have seen, these ships had no opportunity to intervene in China on the grand scale, the General Board was convinced that these units, by no means equal to the naval strength of potential rivals, were an essential component of national policy. In 1905 Admirals Train and Stirling recommended that the battleships be brought back to American waters and their place taken by a force of armored cruisers. They called attention to various technical problems that had arisen, especially the continuing lack of adequate repair facilities in the Philippines, but the General Board pointed to the larger political interests of the United States and the Far Eastern war then raging between Russia and Japan. "The political conditions existing in the East now," the Board replied, "together with the war in progress, are such that the Department deems it inadvisable to deprive the fleet of a battleship."[123] A year later Admiral Train wished to assign several destroyers to the reserve. Again the General Board demurred, focusing its attention on the general political situation in China and the presumed need to have vessels in readiness for possible action.[124] The General Board, in short, continued to believe that the Navy had a broad, general political mission to preserve order in China. Thus, too, when the Board sought authorization to maintain an advanced base unit and a force of 1,000 marines in the Philippines, one of its principal arguing points was the troubled political condition of China.[125]

But, in actuality, there was only one time when there was any real prospect of a major intervention in China, one that might conceivably have rivalled the scale of operations in 1900. That was in late 1905 and early 1906 when an anti-foreign boycott seriously troubled Chinese-American relations, and, when for some time, Roosevelt seriously considered a military response. The President had initially tried diplomacy, indeed had tried to adjust American immigration policies to meet some of the Chinese grievances that were the underlying cause of the boycott. But, as anti-American demonstrations increased, T.R. began to lose patience. Dissatisfied with Chinese explanations, he informed Root that the time had come when "I think we shall have to speak pretty sharply to the Chinese government."[126]

Thus, it was the President who came to take the strongest of stands,

123 Nav Rec AF 10, Stirling to Morton, 28 February 1905, and Morton to Train, 19 April 1905.
124 Nav Rec AF 10, Newberry to Train, 22 May 1906.
125 GB, Letters, II, Dewey to Moody, 15 June 1903.
126 SDML, Roosevelt to Root, 16 November 1905.

and who began to believe that the Chinese would have to be confronted with American strength. Even as he was writing to Root about the need for "speaking sharply," he was beginning to reach for his big stick.[127] Secretary of the Navy Bonaparte was directed to meet with Root and Admiral Converse to consider plans for military action. The first decision was to increase markedly the number of American vessels assigned to Far Eastern duty. The conferees agreed, however, that in view of the naval strength already in Chinese waters, "it does not seem practicable to do much more than what has been ordered with a view to producing a suitable moral effect."[128] But Roosevelt found this insufficient. Within less than a month he had directed both services to draw up plans for a military demonstration. There was naturally a period of intense activity for the General Staff and the General Board, with both eventually agreeing that the appropriate location for such an operation would be in the vicinity of Canton. Before long their joint plan called for the landing of no less than 5,000 troops (Roosevelt himself once suggested 15,000, plus reinforcements, as necessary) at Canton.[129] Roosevelt's comrade-in-arms from Cuba, General Leonard Wood, was deeply involved in this planning and wrote the President enthusiastically of his arrangements to dispatch 5,000 soldiers from the Philippine Division—men who, according to Wood, would be young and vigorous, embarked in a state of combat readiness, and well briefed about the geography of the Canton area.[130]

The policymaking role of the services in this venture was minimal. To be sure, the volume of correspondence about conditions in China showed a marked increase, for both Army and Navy supplied the Department of State—and sometimes the President directly—with a great number of reports from officers in the Far East. Some of these no doubt added to the feeling that China was on the brink of another abyss. It was Admiral Train's opinion, for example, that "the only restraint was the visible presence of forces."[131] Taft, absent from Washington on his well-publicized visit to the Orient, sent Roosevelt an extensive report, prepared by an Army officer in Manila, which described a general weakening of Chinese national strength and the growth of anti-foreign sentiments from Peking to Canton.[132] Such re-

---

[127] For a general discussion of Roosevelt's attitude toward the boycott, see Beale, *Roosevelt and America's Rise*, 238-52.

[128] Bonaparte Papers, Bonaparte to Roosevelt, 15 November 1905.

[129] GB, Proceedings, 27 December 1905; GS, File 820, memorandum prepared by General J. G. Bates, the Chief of Staff, "Memorandum of an Emergency Force to be taken from the Philippines Division for Service in China," 6 February 1906.

[130] Wood Papers, Wood to Roosevelt, 25 February 1906, and to Taft, 11 April 1906.

[131] SDML, Train to Bonaparte, 11 November 1905.

[132] SDML, Taft to Root, 6 January 1906.

ports, from all indications, were read and digested in the Department of State; Root, in fact, specifically thanked the Navy for its many helpful dispatches on the nature and extent of the boycott.[133] Roosevelt was also in frequent correspondence with Leonard Wood, exchanging private letters in which the two veterans rather jauntily discussed the feasibility of conducting operations in China with 5,000 soldiers instead of the 10,000 that Wood actually wanted. "It would be an act of utter folly," Roosevelt noted, "to under-estimate our foe, who would beyond all comparison be more formidable than they showed themselves to be in 1900."[134]

But none of the military records show any involvement in fundamental policy issues. The Army and Navy advised on the number of ships and troops that might be used, engaged in the technical aspects of joint war planning. There was also discussion with the President about the one issue that greatly troubled the Army Chief of Staff: namely, whether it was wise to weaken the Philippine garrison by taking all the troops for the proposed China operation from those islands.[135] But neither the documents of the Army or the Navy reveal any discussion of the fundamental wisdom—or lack of wisdom—of the proposed Canton operation or its possible political consequences. From start to finish, it was the President's show, a proposal which originated in the White House with a man who felt that the Chinese might have to be taught an American military lesson.

Nothing, fortunately, ever came of the proposal to put 5,000 soldiers ashore at Canton. The ultimate military result was only the preparation of yet another set of plans that eventually gathered dust in the military archives. And, as with many of Roosevelt's schemes, there is always some uncertainty about the President's commitment to it. He certainly seemed serious about action in the early weeks of 1906, but he may have expected that the threat of using force would be sufficient to achieve his purpose.[136] By April he had just as certainly cooled off and was now writing Wood, "I do not believe there will be any expedition to China, but I wanted to be sure that if it was needed we would not be unprepared."[137] The reasons why there was no American intervention were many and complicated; they ranged from the fact that the Manchu government was doing more to control the boycott than Roosevelt ever admitted to the patient efforts of Rockhill in educating Americans, including the President, to a better understanding of the

---

[133] Nav Rec AF 10, Root to Bonaparte, 3 February 1906.

[134] Wood Papers, Roosevelt to Wood, 2 April 1906.

[135] GS, File 820, Bates to Taft, 6 February 1906.

[136] Beale, *Roosevelt and America's Rise*, 244-45.

[137] Wood Papers, Roosevelt to Wood, 2 April 1906.

causes of Chinese unrest.[138] But, above all, there was the sheer unpredictability of events in China, where the anticipated disorders never got sufficiently out of hand to give Roosevelt his chance. As Secretary Bonaparte observed, in evident perplexity, when transmitting a bundle of naval reports to Elihu Root, "The reports from China are as contradictory as ever, and the riots expected for the New Year didn't occur."[139] In any event, with the dampening of the boycott movement, the China scene became quiet, and it was not until the era of Taft and Knox, when the more organized forces of Chinese nationalism stirred revolution against the Manchu government, that the United States again seriously contemplated the armed enforcement of American interests in China.

3. THE RUSSIANS AND MANCHURIA

The military services were concerned after 1900 not only with the future of China but also with the changing pattern of internationl relations throughout the Far East. In the aftermath of the Boxer Rebellion both the Navy and the Department of State showed a consistent interest in and apprehension about Russian moves in Asia, especially in Manchuria. Secretary of State Hay long assumed that the Russians would utilize the plight of China to further their traditional plans for expansion in Asia, either by doing favors for the Manchu court or, more simply, by moving their forces directly into Manchura.[140] When the Czarist government in 1900 did assume military control of Manchuria, Russia quickly emerged, in the opinion of official Washington, as the prime enemy of the Open Door and the nation most likely to thwart American political and economic purposes in Asia. Even as late as the outbreak of the Russo-Japanese War in 1904 Theodore Roosevelt could think in terms of a dauntless Japan fighting the American war for preservation of the Open Door against the onslaught of the Slav. Indeed, for some years after 1900, when many Americans basked in the sunlight of an assumed Anglo-American entente and regarded Japan as a probable Far Eastern partner, it is not fantasy to write of a Russian-American rivalry in Asia.[141]

That rivalry, as noted, centered on Manchuria and took form as

---

[138] Varg, *Open Door Diplomat*, 59-70.

[139] Nav Rec AF 10, Bonaparte to Root, 22 March 1906.

[140] Root Papers, Hay to Root, 6 September 1900.

[141] The best monograph is still E. H. Zabriskie, *Russian-American Rivalry in the Far East, 1895-1914* (Philadelphia, 1946), 45-64, but see also W. A. Williams, *American-Russian Relations, 1781-1947* (New York, 1952), 37-42, and, on Russian policy, see Donald Treadgold, "Russia in the Far East," in Ivo Lederer, ed., *Russian Foreign Policy: Essays in Historical Perspective* (New Haven, 1962), 531-76.

early as the summer of 1900 when the Czarist government gained possession of the port of Newchwang and control of the rail line from that city to Peking. John Hay made several attempts to secure Russian promises to protect the Open Door in Manchuria but was not sanguine about the prospects. "Of course," he wrote in September of that year, "she will not be bound by any pledges that she finds it convenient to break. But we must try to make it inconvenient."[142]

The opportunity "to make it inconvenient" began to develop within the year. American diplomats in Asia, who fully shared Hay's apprehensions about the Russian presence in Manchuria, pressed for action; Herbert Squiers, the chargé in Peking, asked that naval vessels make occasional calls at Newchwang. And, parenthetically, he coupled his request with mild but pointed comments about the observable tendency of the Navy to focus its attention on the larger and more attractive Chinese ports.[143] Henry Miller, the consul at Newchwang, was more direct. Noting that American trade through Newchwang was of increasing importance, he wanted this fact transmitted to the naval command in Asia and given "proper recognition" by the Navy in the form of frequent naval visitations.[144] Since the Russians always had a gunboat of their own at Newchwang, Miller advocated an agreement between the United States, Japan, and Great Britain that one of these three nations would always have a war vessel on hand at the Manchurian port. He counted heavily upon the presence of naval power as the only way to preserve an Open Door and argued that his proposal "would make it quietly known to the public that none of our rights in Manchuria had been surrendered. . . . If we want to maintain an open door, we should be guarding the present situation more carefully."[145]

The Department of State immediately endorsed Miller's recommendation. The Navy was asked to detail a ship for a "friendly visit" to Newchwang and, in addition, was told that "a report by its commander on the observable nature and purposes of the Russian occupation would be expedient." That the State Department attached considerable importance to this naval mission was indicated by the fact that the then rarely used classification of "confidential" was placed on all of this correspondence, while Henry Miller, the consul who had first suggested the visit, was simply told that a naval vessel was enroute to Newchwang and given no hint of the broader purposes.[146]

The Newchwang assignment fell to Captain (later Admiral) Charles Sperry, commander of the *New Orleans* and one of the most politically

142 Root Papers, Hay to Root, 6 September 1900.
143 SDMD, China, No. 680, Squiers to Hay, 29 July 1901.
144 Henry B. Miller to Squiers, no date, enclosed with No. 680, as cited.
145 SDCD, China, Newchwang, Miller to Hill, 21 September 1901.
146 SDML, Adee to Long, 11 and 13 September 1901.

conscious officers in the naval service. On this particular occasion in 1901, he and Miller immediately conferred and, not surprisingly, reached almost identical conclusions. Sperry's report of his visit to Newchwang closely paralleled the dispatch sent by the consul soon afterwards. Both men were concerned about measures that might be necessary to protect American interests in Newchwang if and when the Russians retired, as they had long been promising to do. Sperry and Miller suspected a Russian stratagem, not a genuine evacuation. They were convinced that the Russians would merely withdraw to the city's outskirts, leaving the port to the mercy of bandits and various marauders. The foreign residents, left without protection, would thus be compelled to ask the Russians to return, thereby providing them with a built-in justification to make their occupation permanent. To circumvent this presumed scheme, both Americans asked that an American gunboat be stationed at Newchwang throughout the entire winter of 1901-02.[147]

But when the Department of State first requested naval cooperation, the Navy hesitated, alleging its pressing need for warships in the Philippines and citing the harsh climate at Newchwang as excuses.[148] Admiral Remey, still commanding in the Far East, was also skeptical; he doubted if the Russians ever intended to withdraw from Newchwang and suggested that, even if they did, it would be simpler and wiser to advise the few Americans at Newchwang to remove themselves to some point of safety.[149] But Minister Conger added the weight of his influence to the request for a naval watch at Newchwang. The Navy, faced with mounting pressure, finally yielded.[150] The *Vicksburg*, a vessel inappropriately named for this semi-arctic duty, barely made it into Newchwang before the harbor was frozen solid for the long Manchurian winter. But, however inauspiciously, the naval watch on Newchwang had begun. Captain Sperry was delighted, for he correctly believed that it was his report on conditions at Newchwang which had influenced the decision. "I was not called upon to make a political policy recommendation," he wrote a friend, "and I did not do so, but I do think that my sketch of the situation was significant." In this observation he was correct, for, while others had previously endorsed the assignment of a vessel to Newchwang, it was Sperry's report which in fact had first spurred the State Department to its decision.[151]

---

[147] Nav Rec AF 10, Sperry to Junior Squadron Commander, U.S. Naval Force on the Asiatic Station, 21 September 1901.

[148] SDML, Long to Hay, 23 October 1901.

[149] Nav Rec AF 10, Remey to Long, 8 and 12 October 1901.

[150] Nav Rec AF 10, Conger to Hay, 28 September 1901; SDML, Long to Hay, 2 and 19 November 1901.

[151] Sperry Papers, Sperry to Crowninshield, 20 December 1901.

Thereafter naval observers filed numerous reports on the New-chwang situation. It is almost superfluous to say that these breathed a strong, hostile note about Russian purposes. Sperry was convinced (in-correctly, it must be added) that it was only the timely arrival of the *Vicksburg* that thwarted the devious Russian plan to evacuate and re-turn, "picking up the abandoned rights of others in the process." Deep and abiding was his distrust of Russia. "The partition of China can hardly be said to be going on," he commented cynically, "as that might imply that some other nationality than Russia was getting a chance, which is not the case."[152] Even Admiral Remey agreed to the assign-ment of one of his vessels to Newchwang. Though he never believed that the presence of the *Vicksburg* was essential to protect American lives and property, he ultimately accepted the political logic that it "exerts considerable restraint on Russian aggression in Manchuria."[153]

But even in ice-bound Newchwang the Navy was not freed from civilian control in Washington nor permitted to let its anti-Russian sentiments reach extremes. Late in the winter of 1901-02 there was a riot between sailors from the *Vicksburg* and Russian police.[154] To the suspicious Sperry it was not just a typical brawl between sailors and shore patrol but an incident that the Russians had exploited for the specific purpose of causing friction.[155] The Navy took a serious view. Secretary Long piously informed John Hay that the trouble had not originated with the American sailors but was a consequence of "the unwarranted aggression of the Russians." Long, whose report simply reflected the views of those officers directly involved in the affair, ar-gued that the Navy had been proceeding on the assumption that New-chwang was a regular treaty port in which all foreigners enjoyed equal status. It was therefore "unbearable then to have, in a treaty port, American sailors arrested by Russians, particularly if the consular courts still have jurisdiction."[156]

The Navy got not sympathy but a stinging rebuke. Hay, in his re-sponse, observed that while foreign rights in Newchwang had not been usurped, the situation was "a delicate one calling for the utmost for-bearance and consideration on all sides to avoid friction":

> It cannot be supposed that the machinery of a temporary adminis-tration . . . can be as complete and as fully provided with a system of institutes as will render the maintenance of order as easy as would be the case were the same officials dealing with questions in

152 Sperry Papers, Sperry to Admiral Watson, 3 November and 16 December 1901.
153 Nav Rec AF 10, Remey to Long, 31 December 1901.
154 Nav Rec AF 10, Long to Hay, 10 March 1902.
155 Sperry Papers, Sperry to Watson, 27 April 1902.
156 Nav Rec AF 10, Long to Hay, 10 March 1902.

their own country. It is the opinion of the Department that all the parties, in the interest of order at Niu Chwang should so far as possible unite to that end without too strict an insistence upon technical prerogatives.[157]

The Navy, in short, should be more understanding. Hay thought it ought to work out special regulations governing shore leaves and, as a model for the Navy to emulate, suggested the State Department's instructions to Consul Miller. He had been told to use "utmost circumspection and forbearance" in working with the Russians, and that the State Department did not expect that "he will stand upon his exact consular prerogatives . . . but will freely and frankly lend his aid . . . waiving import technicalities where the circumstances seem to require it, deeming that the maintenance of good relations and order are the main consideration, always provided that individual rights are not sacrificed."[158]

Two weeks later the Navy was reprimanded in even sharper terms. Captain E. B. Barry of the *Vicksburg* demanded an apology from the Russian civil administration at Newchwang, while Consul Miller, disregarding his own instructions, acted as the intermediary in delivering the Navy officer's demand. This time the Department of State firmly asserted its prerogatives:

> The Department of State regrets that, in spite of all the efforts that have been made to maintain a *modus vivendi* at Niu Chwang, Captain Barry saw fit to demand an apology from the Russian civil administrator for what appears to have been an error of judgment as to the culpability of certain American seamen, and especially that he made this demand in the manner that he did: namely, through the U. S. Consul, in what the Department of State cannot but regard as intemperate in tone. It is to be said also, however, that the Consul was at fault in transmitting Captain Barry's letter without instructions from the Department of State authorizing him to do so.[159]

The Navy got the message. There were no further troubles at Newchwang. The naval watch, however, lasted on into succeeding winters, though it was not always continuous, and the tone of the reports that came back to Washington was uniformly anti-Russian.

Naval officers like Captain Sperry believed that war between Russia and Japan was inevitable. When it came they were, like their Presi-

---

[157] SDML, Hay to Long, 31 March 1902.

[158] SDML, Hay to Long, 2 April 1902, enclosing a note from the Russian Foreign Office concerning the naval allegations.

[159] SDML, Hill to Long, 11 April 1902.

dent, unashamedly pro-Japanese.[160] But on numerous occasions they were given to understand that they must observe "strict neutrality." Indeed, at the outset of the conflict, Roosevelt asked the State Department to make it clear that, if fighting occurred between Russian and Japanese vessels in neutral Chinese ports, the Navy would in no way interfere "without positive instructions from the Navy Department."[161]

The United States Navy, in consequence, had opportunity to do little more than observe the fighting, but even this was subject to severe restrictions. Admiral Evans wanted to station a battleship at Nagasaki to follow the progress of the war from the Japanese homeland. The suggestion was promptly vetoed. Evans was also told that the presence of large numbers of American vessels near the actual theater of war would be undesirable.[162] The issue of protecting Americans in Newchwang inevitably arose, but the administration, whatever its pro-Japanese sympathies, wished to preserve a strictly neutral role and decided to withdraw the cruiser then at that port to avoid "unnecessarily embarrassing situations."[163] When the British government decided to send its Asiatic fleet into North China waters, the American commander in the Far East requested permission to proceed north as far as Shanghai and Chefoo. Back came the reply, "for reasons diplomatic U. S. fleet cannot be permitted to the north of Shanghai."[164] About the only special mission that the Navy received was an assignment in the spring of 1905 to find out what had happened to the Russian fleet in the disastrous battle at Tsu-Shima, the naval engagement that ended the last faint Russian hopes of victory. But this request, which came directly from Theodore Roosevelt, reflected no political interest but simply the insatiable curiosity of a former Assistant Secretary of the Navy who was forever fascinated by naval detail. "President very desirous that you obtain from Russian officers in Manila the most minute accounts," the cable to Admiral Train read, "and all the information they can give regarding the recent battle and effects of Japanese gun fire, torpedo boats and tactics and whether they believe mines and subs were used. What do they attribute the Japanese victory to? Give full reports."[165]

---

[160] Sperry Papers, Sperry to Charles Sperry, Jr., 23 January 1904. On Roosevelt's pro-Japanese opinions, see Blum, *Republican Roosevelt*, 131, 134-37.

[161] Nav Rec, Confidential Communications, Asiatic Station (1904-1906), Moody to Evans, 6 February 1904. See also in the same file, Morton to Stirling, 28 August 1904. (Hereafter citations from the Confidential Communications file will be abbreviated as Nav Rec Confid Comm AS.)

[162] Nav Rec Confid Comm AS, Moody to Evans, 9 February 1904.

[163] Nav Rec Confid Comm AS, Moody to Evans, 12 March 1904.

[164] Nav Rec Confid Comm AS, Cooper to Moody, 8 May 1904, and Darling to Stirling, 8 July 1904.

[165] Nav Rec Confid Comm AS, Converse to Train, 6 June 1905.

Naval officers were emphatically warned off politics. At the outset of the Russo-Japanese war one of the first dispatches from St. Petersburg relayed a Russian protest about the attitude of the American naval commander in the Manchurian harbor of Chemulpo. Czarist officials charged that the Americans had been the only foreigners at Chemulpo who did not protest the Japanese attack against their vessels. And that they were also the only foreign naval personnel who did not receive the Russian sailors aboard their ships after the attack. This, reported Ambassador Robert McCormick, "has created bitter feeling here. Official denial or explanation would have excellent effect as the incident as reported taken here to confirm statements in British newspapers, read by Emperor himself, that the United States government is very hostile to Russia."[166] It was immediately made clear to the Navy that its officers should in the future avoid giving such signs of their sentiments. The details of what had happened at Chemulpo were reported incorrectly; nevertheless, the incident accurately reflected the basic anti-Russian sentiments of the American armed services. By March of 1904 Roosevelt was sufficiently concerned to send a special note to Secretary Taft when he read newspaper statements that attributed anti-Russian statements to General Chaffee:

> The Lieutenant General should, as a matter of course, be more than careful about saying anything tending to cause international bad feeling, and above all at a time when we are having difficulty in preventing the feelings of one or the other of the combatants from being hurt. . . . Our Army and Navy officers must not comment about foreign powers in a way that will cause trouble.[167]

By the fall of 1904 the Secretary of State also felt it necessary to direct a special memorandum to both the Army and Navy about the attitude of their officers. In Hay's rather circumspect language,

> In recent personal conversation with the Russian Ambassador, he has adverted to the attitude of the military, naval and civil officers of the United States in China with reference to the present contest between Russia and Japan. While indisposed to make specific statements in individual cases, allusion is made to instances of personal and official action on the part of officers which, when coming to the attention of the Russian representatives, cause an impression of unfriendliness.[168]

---

[166] SDML, Adee to Moody, 25 February 1904, enclosing copy of McCormick's dispatch from St. Petersburg.

[167] Roosevelt, *Letters*, IV, 744, Roosevelt to Taft, 7 March 1904.

[168] SDML, Hay to Morton and Taft, 1 December 1904.

The remainder of Hay's message, needless to say, discussed the need for circumspection and conduct becoming a neutral.

4. WAR PLANS IN THE PACIFIC AND THE RISE OF JAPANESE POWER

Although the Russo-Japanese war provided no major role for the Navy, it proved to be something of a watershed in military planning. Until the "lessons" of that conflict were learned, the war plans of both services had been not only somewhat casual but, to the later historian, appear to have been designed to meet contingencies whose probability was, to say the least, remote. It will be recalled from our earlier discussion that, when the Army and Navy first engaged in efforts at joint planning, the Navy had tended to envisage the Pacific as the more likely theater of operations and the Open Door as perhaps some day rivalling the Monroe Doctrine in significance.[169] While joint planning thereafter proceeded on the assumption that the Caribbean should receive priority, the Pacific-mindedness of the Navy, in which expansionism was far from dead, was always noticeable. In thinking about a Pacific conflict, the naval planners assumed for some years that Japan would be a friend and that England, also, could be relied upon. The anti-Russian sentiments of the General Board made its strategists further assume that the goal of Czarist policy was the control of all Manchuria. All of which, therefore, led to some hazy assumptions about a tri-cornered conflict in which the United States, Japan, and Great Britain might wage war against Russia, France, and possibly Germany.[170] When for example, Admiral Remey was asked to testify before the General Board on Asian strategy, he began his presentation by noting that Britain and Japan might theoretically be regarded as the nations most to be feared since they could do the greatest damage to American interests in the Far East. But, he continued, "in the present state of affairs, they are more likely to be aligned with us than against us . . . [and] the Japanese like Americans best of all foreigners."[171] Typical also was Admiral Sperry's enthusiastic reception of the renewal of the Anglo-Japanese alliance in 1905 as

> the best guarantee of peace both in Europe and in the East . . . that can be devised. . . . With England holding the route to the East with her fleet, Japan ready to put a million of men anywhere under the

[169] See pages 17-18.

[170] See various documents cited in Chapter One, especially GB, Letters, I, Hackett to Rodgers, 16 February 1901, and JB, File 325, Admiral Taylor's memorandum read at the 4 June 1904 meeting of the Board.

[171] GB, Proceedings, 29 May 1902.

shadow of the fleet . . . the Pacific becomes a closed sea with ourselves one of the inside partners.[172]

The plans that were made were of the General Board's own devising, most certainly not the result of any dialogue with the Department of State or other civilian policymakers. Staff studies, occasional briefings from officers with Far Eastern experience, and reports of the Office of Naval Intelligence furnished the raw material. The most frequent hypothesis—a conflict with a coalition of enemies composed of Russia, Germany, and France—rested upon generalized and surface observations. Russia was a potential enemy in consequence of her Manchurian policy, while Germany appeared a Far Eastern rival after her actions in Samoa, her apparent interest in the Philippines in 1898, and her role during the Boxer Rebellion. France entered the picture simply because since the 1890s she had been the ally of Czarist Russia. The complexities of the European system and, above all, the rivalries between the powers that would have made such a combination virtually impossible were mysteries to the admirals and never considered in their planning. So too were the considerable changes which the European alliance system was actually undergoing in the early years of the twentieth century.

Yet if the Navy's ideas about Far Eastern wars and coalitions were superficial and general, they were actually not far out of line with the main thrust of civilian policy. The leading members of the Roosevelt administration, the President in particular, were similarly pro-Japanese and anti-Russian. So annoyed was Roosevelt by Russian policy that on one occasion in 1903 he wrote Hay that he hadn't "the slightest objection to the Russians knowing that I feel thoroughly aroused and irritated at their conduct in Manchuria; that I don't intend to give way and that I am year by year growing more confident that this country would back me in going to an extreme in this matter."[173] Similarly he expressed great pleasure at Japan's initial victories in her conflict with Russia, writing one of his sons that "strictly between ourselves—for you must not breathe it to anybody—I was thoroughly pleased with the Japanese victory, for Japan is playing our game."[174] The basic difference between his point of view and that of the Navy's was in degree and not in kind. Roosevelt once chanced to read some of the lengthy letters on Far Eastern affairs that came from the pen of Captain Sperry and found himself in general agreement with the naval officer's point of view about Russia's Far Eastern objectives. But at the same time T.R. believed that Sperry was far too pessimistic about the future

[172] Sperry Papers, Sperry to Charles Sperry, Jr., 9 October 1905.
[173] Roosevelt, *Letters*, III, 520, Roosevelt to Hay, 18 July 1903.
[174] *Ibid.*, IV, 734, Roosevelt to Theodore Roosevelt, Jr., 10 February 1904.

and, unlike the naval officer, doubted the inevitability of Russia's Man-churian policy. Russia, he cautioned, was still an underdeveloped pow-er; while the future might perhaps belong to her, "it is the future, and not the present."[175] Roosevelt, in other words, had a more sophisti-cated understanding of the elements of national power and, unlike the typical Navy officer, was not prey to generalized fears about the in-evitability of Russian expansion.

Roosevelt and Hay also shared ideas similar to those of the Navy about the growing friendliness of Great Britain. A whole series of quo-tations can be readily assembled to match such an expression as the following from Roosevelt: "We are closer in feeling to her than to any other nation . . . and probably her interests and ours will run on rather parallel lines in the future."[176] Indeed, as several of his critics have cor-rectly pointed out, Roosevelt's Far Eastern policy sometimes suffered because, contrary to expectations, British and American interests in the Far East were not parallel and expected British support therefore did not materialize.[177] Moreover, the Department of State in these same years also fell victim to the same sort of blindness that showed itself in the strategic thinking of the Navy—the failure to realize that what happened in Asia was frequently determined by the balance of power in Europe and the changing pattern of alliances and rivalries on the Continent. American statesmen, themselves not involved in Eu-ropean affairs, were tempted to construct Far Eastern policies which were irrelevant because they failed to take sufficient account of the all-important European dimension to Asia's affairs. It is therefore some-thing less than just to criticize the Navy for constructing an unsophis-ticated model of world politics when civilian policymakers often made the same kind of error. Perhaps it should simply be pointed out that all American policymaking, whether civilian or military, labored under the still dominant tradition of non-involvement in European affairs and thereby took place in at least a partial vacuum.

In any event, within a few years after its conclusion, the Russo-Jap-anese war had exercised a decisive influence upon military thinking about Far Eastern politics and strategy. First, with the defeat of Rus-sia, no more was heard in the Navy of a Russian threat. Instead, Japan began to emerge as the nation with whom conflict seemed most likely. Second, a great and bitter debate, related to the growth of Japanese military power, erupted between the Army and Navy over the proper location for the American naval station which presumably would be

---

175 *Ibid.*, III, 112-13, Roosevelt to George Becker, 8 July 1901.

176 *Ibid.*, III, 97, Roosevelt to Henry Cabot Lodge, 19 June 1901.

177 The argument is forcefully made, though considerably overstated, in Griswold, *Far Eastern Policy*, 87-132.

the bastion of American strength in Asia. The Navy remained insistent that it must be at Subig Bay in the Philippines, while the Army vehemently argued that Subig, with its geographic similarities to ill-fated Port Arthur, could never be defended against a determined Japanese thrust and that the services must therefore look elsewhere. Third, there was an increasing debate over the proper location of the American fleet, above all, over the question of whether or not any portion of it should be permanently stationed in the Pacific.

These three issues also had important implications for American foreign policy. What was involved, after all, was the defensibility of the Philippines—whether they were the "Achilles heel" of the United States—and, ultimately, the viability of America's position in the Far East. Nevertheless, the debates and discussions over Japanese power, and especially those over Subig Bay and the location of the fleet, were largely conducted within and confined to military circles. Certainly, too, the arguments over Subig and the concentration of the fleet were decided by military people, primarily on the basis of military logic, without reference to the Department of State or considerations of American foreign policy. Yet the ultimate decision—especially the abandonment of Subig Bay for Pearl Harbor—cast a long shadow in American diplomatic history. In the 1930s, when Japan finally embarked on her long-deferred program of expansion, the United States Navy was based in a location many thousands of miles from China and the Asian mainland as a consequence of military decisions made a generation previously.

Japan, it should be noted, did not emerge as a potential enemy solely as a consequence of her Far Eastern victories in 1904-05. There had been occasional suggestions before that date of the possibility of Japanese-American difficulties. Thus, while Admiral Remey was staunchly pro-Japanese and believed that it would be safe to rely on her as friend and potential ally, he could also tell the General Board in 1901 that "it is clear that she covets the Philippines." He observed that if the Asian political picture changed and if the Russian threat to Japanese interests should vanish, then "no sentiments of friendship" would deter Japan's quest for the Philippines.[178] But suggestions of this sort were extremely rare in the Navy before the Russo-Japanese war. It was in the Army, where the Philippine commitment was deep, that suspicions of Japan rose earlier and in sharper form. In January 1901, for example, Army intelligence turned up a mass of papers which appeared to implicate a Japanese consular official in the continuing Philippine insurrection. The lower echelons of the Military Information Division,

[178] GB, Proceedings, 29 May 1902, and Nav Rec AF 10, Remey to Long, 7 October 1901.

convinced that the consul had operated with the connivance of the government in Tokyo, believed, in the words of one Army captain, that "The Japs now feel they can dare to intrigue in the Philippines and see in them a field of exploitation." Of especial concern was the doctrine clearly enunciated in the captured papers, the concept of "Asia for the People of Asia, a doctrine, an ideal perhaps, a desire to obtain the attainment of oriental ideals by occidental methods, a doctrine big with danger for the continued supremacy of the Anglo-Saxon race in the Far East."[179] The Philippine commander, General Arthur MacArthur, was also concerned and forwarded the documents to Washington with a covering note in the portentous prose that was his custom:

> The conclusion arising from a perusal of these papers is almost irresistible that Japanese interference is one of the elements of sustaining the insurrection in these islands. What force is to be attributed to it is not yet apparent but it is believed that the hostile attitude of the Japanese and possibly the Japanese Government itself demands the closest consideration by our government in Washington.[180]

MacArthur demanded "drastic action," specifically the removal from the Philippines of the Japanese officials implicated in the papers. A year later MacArthur's successor, General Chaffee, was equally convinced of Japanese intrigue. Papers found on a Japanese military observer gave him "positive proof" that some Japanese and some insurrectionists were attempting to form an offensive and defensive alliance.[181] Shortly afterwards, when Leonard Wood acceded to the Philippine command, he, too, began to speculate about a Japanese threat to the islands, and in his many letters to Theodore Roosevelt he tried to convey the thought that "Japan is now superior to us in the Pacific Ocean, and can take the islands whenever she wants them."[182]

But prior to the Russo-Japanese war none of these incidents had produced any measurable impact on civilian policy centers in Washington. In 1901-02 the Navy, in the course of routine Pacific voyages, turned up evidence of some Japanese interest in Wake and Midway islands. On each a few Japanese birdhunters had been found, a discovery which led naval officials to suggest that the presence of these ci-

179 SDML, Hill to Hay, 26 February 1901, a substantial file of reports sent by the Army to the State Department. The quotation is from a report by Captain John Taylor, Division of Military Information, 4 January 1901.

180 SDML, Hill to Hay, as just cited; the quotation is from a letter, Arthur MacArthur to the Adjutant General, 10 January 1901.

181 SDML, Root to Hay, 8 April 1902, enclosing a dispatch, Chaffee to Corbin, 10 January 1902.

182 Wood Papers, Wood to Roosevelt, 13 December 1905.

vilians could perhaps later be parlayed by the Japanese government into claims for ownership of Midway and Wake.[183] The Department of State did, to be sure, follow up these reports since both islands were to form links in the projected trans-Pacific cable. Hay therefore informed Tokyo that no settlements, temporary or otherwise, could be considered by the United States as providing a basis for later Japanese claims to sovereignty over the islands. When the Japanese promptly and emphatically denied any such intent, the State Department was entirely satisfied. Indeed, some of its officials were more disturbed by the continuing insistence of the Navy that all the Japanese on the islands should be removed. Alvey Adee, convinced that the Japanese disclaimer was sufficient, thought it highly inappropriate that the Navy should insist upon the deportation of "these poor devils."[184] Eventually, given further Japanese denials of official interest in the islands, the Navy abandoned its demand, and the case of the birdhunters disappeared. While Hay may well have thought that the Japanese did have some latent interest in acquiring Wake, his final note on the subject indicated the attitude that generally prevailed in the State Department at that time: "Consarn islands anyhow. We've got too many to keep the run of."[185]

The attitude was similar when the State Department examined the various Army documents that alleged Japanese involvement in the Philippine insurrection. David Hill, the Assistant Secretary, scrutinized them carefully but was not persuaded of their significance. He reported that they had "at first a very portentous appearance." But closer examination, he continued, showed that most of the presumably hard information was rumor or gossip. Hill also pointed out that the Army documents showed quite clearly that, in early 1899, when the Japanese had become fully aware of America's desire to keep the Philippines, the government in Tokyo had actually abandoned some of its tentative plans to help the Philippine insurrectionists. All that Hill would admit was that the Japanese consul and military attaché in Manila had been engaged in "unfriendly intercourse with the enemy" and should therefore be recalled.[186] Nor did Leonard Wood initially succeed in persuading Roosevelt that there was a potential though remote

[183] SDML, Adee to Long, 16, 18, 21, and 27 August 1902 (all pertaining to Wake); Long to Hay, 26 October 1900, enclosing an early naval report on the presence of Japanese settlers. Also, Hay to Long, 9 November 1900, 10 January, 16 March, and 8 April 1901, and Long to Hay, 12 March and 5 April 1901 (all pertaining to Midway).

[184] Hay Papers, Adee marginal comments on Hay to Long, 18 August 1902.

[185] Hay Papers, Hay to Adee, 15 August 1902. For a brief discussion of the place of Midway, Wake, and Guam in naval thinking, see Earl S. Pomeroy, *Pacific Outpost: American Strategy in Guam and Micronesia* (Palo Alto, 1951), 30-34.

[186] SDML, Hill to Hay, 26 February 1901.

danger to the islands. "I do not for a moment agree, however, that Japan has any immediate intention of moving against us in the Philippines" was the Presidential reply to one of Wood's early letters. Roosevelt buttressed his opinion with a detailed analysis of Japan's involvements in Korea and Manchuria, the delicacy of her relationship with Britain, and the other international complications which restricted Japan's freedom of action. "No man can prophesy about the future, but I see not the slightest chance of Japan attacking us in the Philippines for another decade or two, or until the conditions of international politics change."[187]

In the immediate aftermath of the Russo-Japanese war there was still some ambivalence in the American military attitude toward Japan. Early in 1906 Admiral Dewey could blurt out that the next American war would probably be with Germany or Japan. But Lieutenant Frank Marble, then the naval attaché in Tokyo, found Dewey's remarks not only indiscreet but astonishing.[188] Indicative of this continuing ambivalence was a long report on conditions in the Pacific filed by General MacArthur at the end of an extensive Asian trip. In it MacArthur made it clear from the outset that the principal fact to be kept in mind by Americans was that Japan now "must be regarded as master of the ocean." The general could dwell also upon the community of interests that still bound Japan to the United States, yet balance this against the possibility that domestic politics in Japan might force the government into a conflict with the United States that none of its leaders wanted. MacArthur thought that the improbability of war between the countries was such that it removed "the question of the Philippines, as far as violence is concerned, from the domain of immediate apprehension," but he also added the qualification that "the possibility of such violence must always be considered in discussing experiences and policies touching American Pacific interests."[189]

The Russo-Japanese war did not cause Japanese-American rivalry but rather created the conditions in which rivalry might develop. It destroyed Russia's position in Asia and provided dramatic evidence of Japan's growing military power. But of greater importance was popular dissatisfaction in Japan with the terms of the Treaty of Portsmouth that had emerged under the aegis of Theodore Roosevelt and for whose presumed shortcomings many Japanese blamed the American President. Japanese-American relations were soon exacerbated by the immigration policies of the United States and, above all, by a series of

187 Wood Papers, Roosevelt to Wood, 22 January 1906.

188 Sperry Papers, Marble to Sperry, 13 May 1906.

189 SDML, Taft to Root, 26 January 1906, enclosing copy of General MacArthur's report.

discriminatory measures undertaken in several Western states, the most notable of which was the decision of the San Francisco school board to require children of Oriental parentage to attend special, segregated schools. The rapid growth of these potentially serious irritants, the journalistic furor generated by certain elements of the "yellow press," and the occasional diplomatic alarms that were sounded even led some historians to write of a Japanese-American "crisis" in 1906 and 1907.

The extent of the crisis was considerably exaggerated, and it has been put in proper perspective by recent and detailed studies of Roosevelt and his policies.[190] It is certainly unnecessary in this book to examine the minutiae of Japanese-American relations in these few years. But within the broad framework of civil-military relations there is much to discuss.

First, if not foremost, is the fact that both the Army and the Navy developed a genuine concern about the rise of Japanese power and its implications for the United States. The General Board, as we have briefly noted in the preceding chapter, began seriously in the autumn of 1906 to draft strategic plans for a possible war with Japan. This was the first phase of the "Orange Plan," the first plan in American military history that was drafted in peacetime for the conduct of a specific war against a designated enemy. It was initiated, so the planners said, "in view of the possibility of strained relations with Japan." As early as September 1906 an outline had been prepared "of the preliminary steps, necessary preparations, probable movements, and general policy on the part of the Navy in case war with Orange should seem imminent in the near future."[191] By June 1907, perhaps the moment of greatest worry during the entire "crisis," both service boards were deeply involved in planning for various contingencies. At a special meeting of the General Board the principal paper put before the naval officers was specific in its discussion of the probabilities of war and studded with value judgments about the tenor of Japanese policy. The report, read by Captain Sargent, not only summed up the work so far accomplished by the naval planners but also revealed the emotional bias that had already developed in naval circles:

Making all due allowance for exaggeration in current reports, it cannot be doubted that the present attitude of the Japanese agitators is

190 The "classic" monograph, Thomas A. Bailey, *Roosevelt and the Japanese-American Crises* (Stanford, 1934) should be supplemented by Raymond Esthus, *Theodore Roosevelt and Japan* (Seattle, 1967) and Charles Neu, *An Uncertain Friendship: Theodore Roosevelt and Japan, 1906-1909* (Cambridge, 1967).

191 GB, Proceedings, 26 September 1906.

such as to render possible international complications which may result in war.

Having observed that even a peace-loving nation like the United States could, as in 1898, be roused to war fever, Sargent asked rhetorically:

If such was the case with us, how much more may it now be with a bellicose people whose heads are already turned by successful war waged against an implacable enemy, and whose feelings are being worked upon by adroit politicians with subtle arguments of race antipathy and alleged details of persecution of compatriots?[192]

Indeed, by the time that President Roosevelt was ready to dispatch the fleet on its world cruise, the state of mind of some members of the General Board bordered on panic. These naval officers were convinced that somewhere, somehow, the Japanese would find a provocation to strike the American fleet during its voyage. As Admiral Sperry later recalled, these "war fiends" and "war hawks" simply "could not believe the fleet would go home . . . and I said in exasperation one day that such talk made me question their intelligence." In a calmer mood Sperry added, "Even such wise men as Wainwright and some of the staff were stubbornly confident that a row was imminent."[193] The Army General Staff similarly possessed those who were alarmed to the point of irrationality. A memorandum prepared in 1908 in the office of the Chief of Staff argued that the peacetime garrison of the Hawaiian Islands must be immediately reinforced and made capable of quelling any and all uprisings against American authority. Reinforcement, the planners contended, was urgent since the Hawaiian islands contained 15,000 Japanese males, all capable of bearing arms and many with previous military experience, and only 3,000 Americans—"a grave menace to the safety of the islands."[194]

There was a growing awareness of the strategic problems of the Pacific and the difficulty that the United States would face in defending its interests in any conflict. The flaws in America's Far Eastern military position were, unfortunately, becoming all too readily apparent. Above all, it was the situation at Subig Bay in the Philippines (sometimes spelled Subic and also known in military circles as Olongapo) around which a growing controversy began to rage.

Early in the century Subig had been chosen as the site at which the Navy would construct its principal naval station and which would be-

192 GB, Proceedings, 14 June 1907, report read by Captain Sargent.

193 Sperry Papers, Sperry to Mrs. Sperry, 1 November 1908 and to Charles Sperry, Jr., 6 January 1909.

194 GS, File 3195, Major General Bell to Robert Shaw Oliver, 3 August 1908.

come the keystone of America's Far Eastern defenses. A specially appointed board had selected it in 1901 after making a not inconsiderable investigation of possible alternative sites in the Philippines and, incidentally, after failing to get the government in Madrid to turn over to the United States Navy certain long standing Spanish plans for the naval development of Subig.[195] Since that date it had been an article of faith with the General Board, especially with Admiral Dewey, that Subig was the one and only suitable location in the Philippines. Of the many naval documents endorsing Subig, a General Board report of 1907 was typical. This statement began with a flat assertion that "without a fortified base in the Philippines, the Asiatic Fleet cannot keep open the lines of communication for supplies from the United States or between the Army posts within the Philippines, without which supplies the United States could not hold command of the islands." This was followed by the sweeping assertion that "Subig Bay occupies the same position in relation to the control of the Philippines (as does Guantanamo to the Caribbean) and its protection by fixed defenses is of the gravest importance, not only that the fleet may protect Manila, but that it may have facilities for docking, repairing, and provisioning in those distant waters."[196] The involvement of Admiral Dewey in this enterprise was both total and personal; whenever the Subig Bay site was criticized, he drew upon his own experiences and prestige to defend it. A private letter from Dewey to the Secretary of the Navy in 1903 typified the Admiral's intense feelings:

> I can state from my own experience that upon leaving Mirs Bay in April, 1898, I fully expected the Spanish fleet at Subig as from my strategical study of the situation that is where they should have been. Had they been in Subig Bay and had that bay been more properly defended, my victory at Manila would have been much more difficult an one.[197]

In 1903 and 1904 the Navy's commitment became absolute. Once the General Board had abandoned its quest for bases throughout the Caribbean and the Far East, the natural corollary of this decision was to focus the Navy's efforts upon two sites, Guantanamo and Subig. The General Board explicitly stated in April 1904 that "It is the policy of the General Board to concentrate upon Guantanamo and Olongapo and to discourage expenses elsewhere until these two are equipped as

[195] GB, Letters, I, Dewey to Long, 26 September 1901, and File 405, Dewey to Metcalf, 18 February 1908, a summary of the General Board's recommendations on Subig over the years. On the failure to get Spanish plans, File 405, Hay to Long, 16 September 1901.

[196] GB, Letters, v, Dewey to Metcalf, 4 March 1907.

[197] GB, File 405, Dewey to Moody, 16 June 1903.

naval bases and adequately defended." Suggestions that other sites, such as Cavite in the harbor of Manila, should also be developed met firm resistance. "Every dollar available for such purposes ought rather to be spent at Olongapo."[198]

Though the Navy had placed all of its eggs in the Subig basket, little was done to bring its dream of a great Philippine naval bastion even close to reality. In 1903 the Joint Board noted that, despite American possession of the Philippines for five years, "not a gun has been mounted nor an earthwork raised to protect any of the harbors."[199] A year or two later, when Admirals P. H. Cooper and Yates Stirling wanted to remove some of the naval forces in the Far East, they rested much of their case upon what they called the "utter defenselessness" of the area.[200] In 1907, at a special White House conference with Roosevelt, the naval command made a point of bringing the lack of adequate defenses in the Philippines to the personal attention of the President and warned that "the consequences of neglect or decay may be nothing less than national disaster."[201] Moreover, as we have noted, prevailing strategic doctrine called for the maintenance of the American fleet in the Atlantic. Consequently, there were never more than two or three battleships in the Pacific, and, in point of fact, the last of these were taken from the Asiatic fleet after the Russo-Japanese war. The Asiatic fleet, in short, ultimately consisted of a cruiser squadron and some gunboats.

Thus, when the naval planners began to work on the Orange Plan, their starting point was the continuing inadequacy of the base at Subig Bay and the obvious inferiority of available naval power in the Pacific. The initial American posture must obviously be defensive:

> Owing to the preponderance of naval and military power possessed by Japan in the Pacific Ocean, the United States would be compelled, whilst preparing for the offensive by the assembly of its fleet in the Atlantic, to take a defensive attitude in the Pacific, and maintain that attitude until reinforcements could be sent from the Atlantic to the Pacific.[202]

The plans drawn up in 1906 and 1907 called for the concentration of all of the defensive efforts of both the Army and the Navy at Subig. Two considerations dictated this decision: the fact that neither service had sufficient strength in the Philippines to defend more than one lo-

---

[198] GB, Letters, ii, Dewey to Moody, 30 March 1904.

[199] JB, Minutes, Dewey to Moody, 19 December 1903.

[200] Nav Rec AF 10, Cooper to Moody, 8 May 1904, and GB, File 420-1, Stirling to Morton, 10 August 1904.

[201] GB, Proceedings, 26 March 1907.

[202] JB, Minutes, Meeting of 18 June 1907.

cation and the existence at Subig Bay of a floating drydock, the one facility essential for the repair of battle damage and the only drydock available to the Navy anywhere in the Pacific.[203] However, the Navy also planned to withdraw most of the Asiatic fleet, except two monitors and five torpedo boats, from Far Eastern waters and remove these vessels to some safe assembly point where, out of reach of the Japanese Navy, they could await the arrival of the Atlantic fleet and prepare for an eventual offensive back across the Pacific. Naval planners, in short, were starkly realistic about American losses and Japanese potential in the opening phases of any conflict. It was assumed, for example, that no reinforcements could reach the Philippines in less than ninety days. Japan would consequently enjoy three months of virtually uncontested supremacy in Asian waters, during which time the Philippines would be "at the mercy" of the Japanese attacker. Planning documents suggested that the Hawaiian Islands might be lost, that there might also be Japanese attacks upon the Canal Zone in Panama, and—in moments of panic—that the Japanese might even dare an attack on the West Coast of the United States.[204]

The strategists hoped, however, that the combined forces at Subig Bay could hold out and the United States maintain at least a foothold in the Philippines until the great relief effort was launched with the Atlantic fleet. In the opinion of the Navy's planners, the successful defense of Subig Bay would be "the only thing that could save us from overwhelming reverses in the early stages of war."[205] In the spring of 1907, therefore, the General Board asked that all of the "advanced base materials" in the Philippines—that is, the supplies and equipment long maintained at Manila for use by marine and naval forces in offensive moves such as the seizure of a base on the Chinese mainland—be transferred to Subig and used to bolster its inadequate defenses.[206] As the General Board summarized the situation and its strategy in the spring of 1907: the military policy of the United States, in the event of war with Japan, would be to transfer the Atlantic fleet to the Pacific, via Suez, a voyage that would require three months, during which time all Pacific defenses would be:

> concentrated at Subic Bay, at which point all available Army forces would also be rallied, and the attempt would be made to hold this bay with the floating drydock as a base to be occupied by the Atlan-

[203] GB, Letters, v, Dewey to Metcalf, 17 June 1907.
[204] GB, Proceedings, 14 June 1907, Sargent memorandum, and Letters, v, Dewey to Metcalf, 4 March 1907.
[205] GB, Letters, v, Dewey to Metcalf, 4 March 1907.
[206] GB, Letters, v, Dewey to Metcalf, 17 June 1907.

tic fleet on its arrival; there would, however, be a strong probability that Subic and the Philippines would fall, leaving the United States thereafter with no point of support for its fleet, and giving to Japan the prestige of a decided initial success.[207]

Ironically the gravest threat to the Navy's strategy was not the navy of Imperial Japan but the Army of the United States. The more the Army studied the presumed "lessons" of the Russo-Japanese war the less it liked Subig Bay. Actually, the Army's disenchantment with Olongapo had started well before that date when General Leonard Wood, newly appointed as the Philippine commander, began to oppose the site. But the early critics of Subig were unable to command any substantial audience until the General Staff had examined in detail the implications of Japan's striking victories in the Far East.

Leonard Wood was as bitterly opposed to Subig as Dewey was in favor of it. To the former Rough Rider it became a personal San Juan hill to be assaulted no matter what the cost. In mounting his campaign against Subig, Wood tried to enlist the support of his Army colleagues in the Philippines, the General Staff in Washington, and his onetime comrade-in-arms, Theodore Roosevelt. To Wood it was axiomatic that Manila, not Subig, was the key to the Philippines. He stridently proclaimed that he who "holds Manila, will, in the eyes of the world, hold the Philippines, whatever happens elsewhere."[208] His preference for Manila, to be sure, had strong overtones of the age-old Army-Navy rivalry. A fortified Subig, Wood once pointed out to the General Staff, would be garrisoned by the Marine Corps, and, should that happen, "the increase will be used as an excuse for cutting down the [enlisted] strength of the Army" and also "might serve as an entering wedge to carry the transfer of the defense of our insular possessions entirely to the Navy and its adjunct Marine Corps."[209] But the essence of his argument was always that, since Manila was the capital and most important city in the Philippines, it was the point around which the defense structure should be built. Moreover, since Wood was, if nothing else, a realist about Congressional willingness to appropriate money for the military services, he doubted if there would ever be sufficient funds to maintain a strong Army garrison or an adequate naval force in the Philippines. He thus envisioned a situation in which a beaten Navy would seek refuge in a Subig Bay that the Army could not properly defend, a military disaster leading to the eventual loss of both naval base and Philippine capital. In his solution all available forces, both Army and Navy, should be used to bolster the defenses of Manila in

[207] GB, Proceedings, 14 June 1907.
[208] Wood Papers, Wood to General W. H. Carter, 9 May 1904.
[209] Wood Papers, Wood to General Tasker Bliss, 25 October 1904.

the hope of establishing "one place in the Philippines where we can keep our flags up and maintain ourselves."[210]

Leonard Wood even found one naval officer, Rear Admiral William Folger, then commander of the Navy's forces in the Islands, who not only agreed with him but who even had the temerity to try to "educate" Dewey and the General Board about the shortcomings of Subig Bay. Folger, indeed, called it a "rat trap."[211] Then, in June 1904, Wood began through his personal correspondence with Roosevelt to try to influence the President. Roosevelt was at least sufficiently stirred to send a copy of Wood's letter to Admiral Dewey and to accompany it with strict instructions that the Admiral of the Navy was to give him a personal letter in reply.[212] The expected happened. The General Board convened, once again endorsed Subig Bay, and declared that Wood's strategic vision was myopic: he who controls Subig Bay, the General Board decreed, controls the city of Manila and therefore the Philippines.[213] Admiral Dewey, in reply to the President's request, argued that even the Spaniards had reached the inevitable conclusion that Subig Bay was the only logical site for a naval base. Moreover, since this was 1904 and Japan still appeared to be a friend, Dewey's answer glowed with optimism about the prospects for a successful defense of the Philippines and took sharp issue with Wood's pessimistic conclusions about the weakness of America's Far Eastern position.[214]

Theodore Roosevelt sided with his naval chiefs. As yet he did not see the islands as the "Achilles heel" of America. No sooner had he received Dewey's report than he sat down and fired off a reply to Leonard Wood, a terse document that was intended by Roosevelt to end the controversy for once and for all:

I send you Admiral Dewey's report on behalf of the General Board. . . . I agree with this report. The question as to choosing between Subig Bay and Manila has been gone over with great care, and while I did not of course take part in the discussions among the military and naval officers, which finally induced them with practical unanimity to decide upon Subig Bay, I entirely agree with the decision to which they came. If we are ever reduced in the Philippines to a condition when the fleet is of use only in assisting the Army to repel an

[210] Wood Papers, Wood to Bliss, 1 June 1904.

[211] Wood Papers, copy of Folger to Moody, 1 June 1904, and Folger to Wood, 14 and 20 September 1904.

[212] Wood Papers, Wood to Roosevelt, 1 June 1904. A copy of this letter is also in GB, File 404-1, Loeb to Dewey, transmitting Wood's letter to the General Board on behalf of the President.

[213] GB, Proceedings, 1 September 1904.

[214] GB, Letters, III, Dewey to Roosevelt, 4 August 1904.

attack upon Manila, I think that the end of our possession of the Philippines is in sight.[215]

Roosevelt was almost as fully committed to Subig as the Navy and believed that its fortification was essential to the success of his entire Far Eastern policy. The President never doubted that his Asian policies would be bankrupt if the United States did not develop a fortified base from which to exercise its military power. About the same time that Wood was assaulting Subig Bay, one of Roosevelt's critics in the House of Representatives, Congressman Elijah Burton, attacked the administration's naval policies, proposed a program of naval disarmament, and contended that no foreign power posed any threat to the Philippines. Roosevelt's response was sharp and fully revealed his unquestioning belief in the reciprocal relationship of military power and diplomacy:

> The one unforgiveable crime is to put one's self in a position in which strength and courage are needed, and then to show lack of strength and courage. . . . To be rich, aggressive and yet helpless in war, is to invite destruction. . . . Mr. Williams, for instance, is against the fortification of Subig Bay. He affects to regard the fortification of Subig Bay as a menace to the independence of the Philippines; with which it has nothing in the world to do. . . . Mr. Williams's attitude about Subig is monstrous in view of what we have seen happen before our eyes to the Russians at Port Arthur because of their unpreparedness. If we are to have a naval station in the Philippines; if we are to have a fleet in Asiatic waters, or to expect the slightest influence in Eastern Asia where our people hope to find a market, then it is of the highest importance that we have a naval station at Subig Bay. If we are not to have that station, and are not to have a navy, then we should be manly enough to say that we intend to abandon the Philippines at once; not to try to keep a naval station there; and not to try to exercise that influence in foreign affairs which comes only to the just man armed who wishes to keep the peace. China is now the sport and plaything of stronger powers because she has constantly acted on her belief in despising and making little of military strength afloat or ashore, and is therefore powerless to keep order or repel aggression from without. . . . The little powers of Europe are powerless to accomplish any great good in foreign affairs because they lack the element of force behind their good wishes.[216]

Subig Bay, then, was the key position from which Roosevelt's America, "the just man armed," could exert its influence. It was small won-

[215] Wood Papers, Roosevelt to Wood, 5 August 1904.
[216] Roosevelt, *Letters*, IV, 735-37, Roosevelt to Burton, 23 February 1904.

der that he took the debate so seriously, responded so sharply to Leonard Wood, and later on, when the Army began to score effective points against Subig, reacted intensely and emotionally.

The sailors had won the Subig battle of 1904. Wood, of course, was still unconvinced, while Admiral Folger, to his surprise, was not removed from his post. He surmised what had happened when his broadside hit the General Board:

> Admiral Higginson met Admiral Taylor who said, "Write Folger, for God's sake to keep his hands off Olongapo." Then the fat was in the fire, and I got letters saying "Oh, you've gone and done it" etc. and letters came telling of a sort of stupor and disinclination to talk on the part of the General Board. . . . You realize that the death of Taylor removed the blind unreasoning element, and permitted the rest of the world to do a little thinking—and hence the delay in my execution which at one time seemed imminent.[217]

But gradually the Army General Staff began to grow more critical of Subig. By the autumn of 1907 Colonel Hugh Scott, a true convert, was gleefully reporting to Wood on the growing number of staff officers in Washington who had been won to the anti-Subig cause.[218] Wood himself seized upon the occasion of William Howard Taft's visit to the Philippines in 1907 to press upon the Secretary of War all of his arguments about the folly of Olongapo—a move of no little importance to the Army since the controversy over Subig lasted on into the next administration and Taft in time became an advocate of the Army point of view.[219] Nevertheless, as late as the spring of 1907, when Roosevelt conferred with his military and naval advisers about the defensibility of the Philippines, the General Staff, though obviously without enthusiasm, could still assure Roosevelt that the Army could "protect Subig Bay against any probable force of an enemy for 120 days."[220] However, in the fall of 1907 the General Staff, still being prodded by Wood, began to bring up its heavy guns and won Roosevelt's grudging approval for a re-examination of the entire issue of Subig Bay. What had once been a closed issue became a major controversy.[221]

The report produced by the Staff in January 1908 was a bombshell

[217] Wood Papers, Folger to Wood, 14 September 1904; for Wood's reaction, see his letter to Roosevelt, 21 October 1904.

[218] Wood Papers, Scott to Wood, 21 December 1907.

[219] Wood Papers, Diary, 24 September 1907.

[220] In addition to the various General Board memoranda and letters previously cited, an excellent summary of the issues in the dispute is a report to be found in the Taft Papers, Series 2, Meyer to Dickinson, 22 March 1911.

[221] JB, Minutes, 6 November 1907, and the following items in the Wood Papers: Wood to Taft and Roosevelt, 1 November 1907; Taft to Wood, 4 November 1907; and Wood to Agwar, 18 November and 23 December 1907.

which blew the admirals from the quarter deck. Major General J. Franklin Bell, as Chief of Staff, put the Army firmly on record with the flat assertion that

> no matter how much further study may be put upon the subject it will be found that no land fortifications of any kind whatsoever can be erected covering the bay which will enable the Army to hold it against a serious land attack with any such land forces as Congress is at all liable to authorize the permanent maintenance of in the Philippine Islands.[222]

The Staff maintained that it was only applying the "lessons of the Manchurian War." It made much of the unfortunate resemblance between Subig Bay and the Russian naval base at Port Arthur which had fallen an easy victim to Japanese attack. Moreover, the Army added, the effect of Japanese heavy ordnance at Port Arthur had been so crushing that military men not only questioned the defensibility of Subig but even had grave doubts about such presumably impregnable bastions as the French fortifications on the German border and the fortress of Gibraltar.[223] Leonard Wood, never to be stilled, was now writing, almost with relish, that the Japanese could throw five times as many soldiers against Subig as the Army could possibly find to man its defenses. Olongapo, he predicted, "will prove a veritable death trap for our navy and the force left there to defend it, if the control of the sea is sufficiently lost to permit the landing of troops on the coast of Luzon."[224]

This time the Navy yielded. The Joint Board, called into session, accepted the logic of the Army's argument. After observing that both military and political conditions had changed in the Far East, it decreed that Subig should be abandoned in favor of a concentration of defenses at and around Manila:

> Subig had all the necessary requisites while Japan was a friend but not when Japan passed to a possible enemy . . . and when it was known that she had the means to destroy the naval base, the aspects of the whole case were changed entirely, and it was the duty of military authorities to change.[225]

The reaction in the White House was immediate. Soon after the Joint Board had doomed Subig Bay, Theodore Roosevelt lashed out at his military advisers. He was also angry with them for what

---

[222] JB, Minutes, meeting of 29 January 1908.
[223] JB, Minutes, Dewey to Taft, 5 March 1908.
[224] Wood Papers, Wood to General J. P. Storey, 24 July 1907.
[225] JB, Minutes, Dewey to Taft, 5 March 1908.

he termed their "academic" handling of the problem of adequate defenses for the Hawaiian Islands and irritated at their refusal to advise on any dimension of a problem except its purely military aspects. But his most scathing comments were reserved for the Joint Board for its "vacillation" and "one-sided" consideration of the Philippine defenses. Time and time again, Roosevelt fumed, he had been assured that Subig was the one and only acceptable site, that it could be made impregnable, and that the decision in its favor was final. On the basis of their advice, he further complained, he had informed the Congress of these plans. But now he was suddenly told that all his information had been incorrect. Roosevelt ominously concluded that the "curious way" in which the Joint Board had dealt with the Philippine matter had not only irritated Congress but had also made it unwilling to believe the Army or Navy on any major issue.[226]

Much of Roosevelt's criticism was ill-tempered if not unwarranted. He, after all, had authorized the services to re-examine the issue of Subig, he had long corresponded with Leonard Wood about the proposed site, and his own closest adviser, Taft, had for some time been convinced by the Army's arguments.[227] But, in a broader context, the incident revealed the existing lacunae in civil-military relationships even when the President was a man who was attuned to military questions and took an interest in their technical details. The apparatus of military policymaking was so constructed that the President was on the periphery, while the members of the Cabinet—save, of course, for the two service secretaries—were far removed from the issues at hand. Moreover, the military boards had in fact operated in a vacuum. Dewey, to be sure, could attempt to mollify Roosevelt by arguing that the change in service attitudes towards Subig was simply the inevitable consequence of a fundamental change in Japanese-American relations. Nonetheless to many Americans the entire affair would appear as yet another, and particularly egregious, example of an interservice rivalry that had culminated in the unexpected reversal of a policy to which the nation had been committed.

There would be further arguments over the question of a Pacific naval base that would last well into the time of the Taft administration. The Navy would attempt to reopen the case of Subig; the Army would complain that the Navy was cheating on the decision of 1908; and there would be controversy over the question of whether or not Manila Bay—with its fortress on Corregidor—could be an acceptable substitute. Nevertheless, the decision reached early in 1908 was funda-

---

[226] GB, File 425, Roosevelt to Metcalf, 11 February 1908.
[227] For Taft's attitude, see GB, File 405, Taft to Metcalf, 21 January 1908.

mental. Further development of Olongapo was cancelled. It was agreed that, in the event of an Asian war, the floating drydock at Subig would immediately be taken into Manila bay to find refuge behind the guns of Corregidor.[228] Soon thereafter the Navy decided to establish its principal Pacific station at Pearl Harbor in the Hawaiian Islands and that site became the locus of America's naval strength in the Pacific.[229]

5. THE WAR SCARE OF 1906-07 AND THE WORLD CRUISE OF THE FLEET

The ultimate importance of the various developments and issues we have just discussed—the rise of Japanese military power, the increasing fear of Japanese intentions, the continued study of the "lessons" of the Russo-Japanese conflict, and the re-evaluation of Philippine defenses—lay in their relation to national policy, above all, to American foreign policy. The historian, admittedly, can produce few neat and tidy documents which "prove" a pattern of military influence upon either the Secretary of State or the President. Yet much can logically be inferred which indicates that, even without formal acknowledgment, there was considerable civilian awareness of the broad problems of Asian policy that were being raised by military men.

Roosevelt, Taft, and Root were, first of all, recipients of a wide variety of military information, ranging from the formal reports of the service boards to the private correspondence of such a politically conscious general as Leonard Wood. Moreover, Leonard Wood did not confine his own advice to military detail but commented extensively on international affairs. He always made a considerable point of telling Taft that belief in the imminence of a Japanese-American war was widespread among the Philippine population and that "the idea of trouble with Japan could not have been so widely disseminated without pretty systematic work" by the Japanese themselves.[230] To the Secretary of State, Wood wrote at great length about

the Japanese agitation in these Islands, which is persistent and widespread: when one lands in the remote islands, one of the first questions asked is "Has the war between the United States and Japan commenced?" The Japanese have made these people believe that

[228] JB, Minutes, Dewey to Metcalf, 5 March 1908.

[229] For summaries of the issues and the decisions reached, see Taft Papers, Meyer to Dickinson, 22 March 1911, as cited, and GB, Letters, VI, Dewey to Metcalf, 27 May 1908, and File 404, Dewey to Meyer, 26 January 1911.

[230] Wood Papers, Wood to Taft, 13 April 1907.

they are their friends and will guarantee them independence in case we should be forced out. . . . I don't know that we should expect anything else from Japan; her policy, of course, is "Asia for the Asiatics," as soon as she is able to do so, what might be described as a Monroe Doctrine embodying this principle.[231]

He informed Roosevelt that while, in his opinion, it might be "rubbish" to think that the Japanese would attack the American fleet during its world cruise, at the same time "it is not altogether an impossible proposition." Moreover, while Wood clearly recognized that Japan's economic and financial situation seemed to preclude the possibility of war, he pointed out that the very same logic could be turned to support the proposition that these conditions "may even make war necessary."[232] Leonard Wood, in short, wanted the leaders of the Roosevelt administration to believe that the "crisis" in Japanese-American relations was not something that had been entirely manufactured in the newspapers but had a basis in what he considered reality.

The historian must then ask about the extent to which such opinions were shared by the civilian administration in Washington. From time to time aspects of the Navy's estimate of the situation did appear in official correspondence. For example, in the fall of 1906 Roosevelt sent his Secretary of Commerce, Victor Metcalf, to California in an effort to persuade the Californians to soften their discriminatory policies towards Japanese residents of that state. Prior to Metcalf's departure for the West Coast, Elihu Root furnished him with a long memorandum, a memorandum which included such statements as the following:

Japan is ready for war, with probably the most effective equipment and personnel now existing in the world. We are not ready for war and we could not be ready to meet Japan on anything like equal terms for a long period; the loss of the Philippines, Hawaii, and probably the Pacific coast, with the complete destruction of our commerce on the Pacific, would occur before we were ready for a real fight. . . . While we would ultimately drive them out of our own country, there is little or no prospect of our ever being able to inflict any effective reprisals upon Japan, and the loss suffered by us would probably be permanent and irrevocable. . . .

If they see that the tendency of events is going to lead to war, they will not hesitate an instant to bring it on at the most favorable time for them; and that will be, first, before we can have made adequate preparations and, second, before the Panama Canal is finished so

231 Wood Papers, Wood to Root, 25 January 1908.
232 Wood Papers, Wood to Roosevelt, 30 January 1908.

that we can get the bulk of our Navy into the Pacific in time to save our Asiatic squadron.[233]

This memorandum, to be sure, is about the only "panicky" letter to be found in the files of the Department of State. Its existence does not mean that either Root or the President believed war to be imminent. It was probably written in an alarmist vein to impress upon Metcalf, and the Californians whom he would visit, the importance of moderation in handling the Japanese question.[234] But the memorandum does indicate that the Secretary of State was well aware of many of the fears that existed in the minds of American military men in the fall of 1906; much of what he wrote reflected and paralleled the gloomy predictions to be found in the early versions of the Orange Plan as it began to take shape at that time. The letter might also be interpreted as an indication that the administration feared what might conceivably happen if tensions with Japan were permitted to grow and get completely out of control. Similarly, by the summer of 1907—and even before the Joint Board had reversed itself on Subig Bay—Roosevelt was beginning to write in his private correspondence of the Philippines as the "Achilles heel" of America.[235] Such statements not only marked a striking change in the President's attitude but also were a clear indication that the pessimistic estimates of men like Leonard Wood had finally impressed themselves upon Theodore Roosevelt.

It must always be emphasized that Roosevelt and Root did not regard war as an immediate possibility at the time of the "crisis" in Japanese-American relations. Although there may actually have been one or two fleeting moments of doubt—perhaps briefly in the summer of 1907—such moments were rare. Most assuredly the President did not succumb to the irrational fears that afflicted certain minds on the General Board. He was, above all, angered with the Californians and believed that much of the friction with Japan arose from actions taken by his fellow Americans—actions which he, as President, could not morally defend and sought to have changed. When he analyzed Japan's situation, Roosevelt properly and accurately concluded that, from the Japanese point of view, conflict with the United States made no sense. Japan, according to his realistic estimate of that nation's best interests, faced a difficult financial condition, needed time to recover from the effects of her war with Russia, and, above all, wanted an opportunity to develop her new stake in Korea and North China. Yet Roosevelt also could write, and at length, of potential long-

[233] SDNF, Case 1797/13, Root to Bonaparte, 27 October 1906.
[234] Bailey, *Roosevelt and the Japanese-American Crises*, 25.
[235] Roosevelt, *Letters*, v, 761-62, Roosevelt to Taft, 21 August 1907.

range discords and differences; he could envisage, at some date in the distant future, a war with Japan. But—and this was the crucial estimate—it would occur long after he had left the mansion on Pennsylvania Avenue.[236]

Yet the "crisis" of 1907 cannot simply be written off as no crisis at all or as a fantasy of the imagination. It is noteworthy how frequently the word "war" appeared in the vocabulary of American policymakers, both civilian and military, in these years. The possibility of conflict, however remote, was never removed from their consciousness. At a cabinet meeting early in 1908 Elihu Root expanded at some length on the various reasons why Japan was in financial straits because of excessive expenditures for armaments. Theodore Roosevelt cut into Root's discourse with acid comments about Americans who were unworried about Japan, "certain 'sublimated sweetbreads' who closed their eyes to any chance of trouble with Japan."[237] William Howard Taft, easy-going and optimistic, was both before and after the period of tension the cabinet official most likely to discount the prospects for conflict. Yet in 1907, when he was in Japan and involved in the discussions that led to the Taft-Katsura agreement, he felt it necessary to cable Washington, "Am satisfied that the Japanese government is most anxious to avoid war; that they are in no financial condition . . . [to risk it.]"[238] Thus even to a man like Taft the likelihood of armed conflict had at least to be taken into consideration and was not so irrelevant a factor that it was unnecessary even to mention it.

Moreover, in the spring and summer of 1907 there was closer consultation between American military leaders and the civilian administration than at any time since the outbreak of the Spanish-American conflict. In March 1907 members of the General Board attended a conference at the White House, an occasion which the naval officers seized to press the President for reinforcements for the Philippines and to emphasize the deficiencies in the defenses at Subig Bay.[239] In mid-June Roosevelt specifically inquired about the plans being prepared by the General Staff, the General Board, and the Joint Board to be put into

[236] Roosevelt, *Letters*, v, 717-18, and 728-29, Roosevelt to Root, 13 July and 26 July 1907. For a first-hand account, see M. A. DeWolfe Howe, ed., *George von Lengerke Meyer* (New York, 1919), 363, 365-66, 370-71, 383-85.

[237] Howe, *Meyer*, 383.

[238] Knox papers, copy of Taft to Roosevelt cable of 18 October 1907. As Ralph Minger has noted, "in all of this a note had been injected—the possibility of war was certainly prevalent for it hung uneasily over all the conversations. An evidence is that everyone with whom Taft spoke, Japanese or American, touched upon the subject of war if only to deny its possibility." Minger, "Taft's Mission to Japan: A Study in Personal Diplomacy," *Pacific Historical Review*, xxx, no. 3 (August 1961), 288.

[239] GB, Proceedings, 26 March 1907.

force in the event of trouble with the Japanese. The President's inquiry spawned innumerable meetings of the various service boards and led to a full-scale meeting of the Joint Board which, in turn, sent its conclusions directly to the President.[240] The culmination of this activity was a conference in late June at Roosevelt's Long Island home on Oyster Bay at which the representatives of the two services discussed their recommendations with Roosevelt.[241]

The discussions at Oyster Bay produced not only talk but limited recommendations for action: transfer of coal supplies from Cavite to Subig, a similar transfer of the "advanced base" materials from Manila to strengthen the defenses of Olongapo, and the shipment of mines to that harbor—all of which were described as preliminary measures that would actually be implemented in the event that trouble appeared to be imminent. There was also an agreement between the President and his military and naval advisers to concentrate all of the defenses at Subig (this, of course, was just before the Army began to mount its final offensive against Subig), to send the American battle fleet to the Pacific, and "when their preservation demands action" to withdraw the few armored cruisers then in Philippine waters to a point of safety where they could ultimately rendezvous with the main Atlantic fleet. Roosevelt had, in short, endorsed in principle the main features of the Orange Plan: the concentration of the Philippine defenses at one location, the removal of naval vessels that might be overwhelmed in the initial engagements, and the dispatch of the main battle fleet to the Pacific.[242]

There was of course no commitment to action; these were measures to be implemented only if war seemed imminent. When General F. C. Ainsworth, the Adjutant General, transmitted the War Department's instructions to Leonard Wood, he added a special note: "The President states definitely that he has no apprehension of war nor does he expect that there will be any, but desires that the material for the defense of Subig should be at hand and plans for its defense matured."[243] Furthermore, the fact that Wood's instructions, dated the 6th of July 1907, did not reach the Philippines until early September would certainly indicate that the War Department was not moved by any special sense of urgency. Wood, to be sure, was permitted to carry out a few of the recommendations—for example, to transfer material from Manila to Subig—but he was also cautioned that he was to act "as

240 JB, Minutes, meeting of 18 June 1907. See also GB, Proceedings, 15 and 17 June 1907, and Wood Papers, F. C. Ainsworth to Wood, 6 July 1907, a summary of the discussions in Washington military circles.

241 Howe, *Meyer*, 362.

242 Paragraph based on documents cited in footnote 240.

243 Wood Papers, Ainsworth to Wood, 6 July 1907.

quietly as possible and without ostentation, so as to avoid it being inferred either at home or abroad that preparations are being made for war."[244]

Thus, at a time of rising tensions with Japan, Roosevelt had kept in close touch with his service boards and had endorsed their strategic planning. While he did not expect conflict and hoped to adjust American policies, especially the policies of the Californians, to meet some of Japan's grievances, he was not so certain of the success of conciliation that he neglected the military dimension of the problem. Moreover, it is difficult to believe that his choice of such measures of accommodation as the Taft-Katsura agreement and the so-called "Gentleman's Agreement" did not also reflect Presidential awareness of the military weakness of America's Far Eastern position. In this sense, certainly, American foreign policy showed an awareness of the difficulties that any conflict with Japan would produce.

There was always a dualism in Roosevelt's approach—a combination of the elements of force and diplomacy—which came especially to the fore in his decision to send the fleet, first, into the Pacific and, then, on around the world. The announcement that the main fleet was to set forth on such a mission was virtually guaranteed to quiet any talk of a Japanese-American conflict; no one, after all, could imagine such a globe-circling jaunt if there was any danger of war, however remote, in the months ahead.[245] There was also the conscious desire to promote "good will" through visits to Asian ports. But, by the same token, the "showing of the flag" by such a powerful force of battleships would be tangible evidence of the growing naval strength of the United States and a warning, however disguised, that the United States could eventually put a formidable fleet into the further reaches of the Pacific. Evidence of both purposes are to be found in the President's writings—ranging from his statement that the sending of the fleet helped to quell rumors of war to his later boasts that he had dispatched it after detecting a certain faint "air of truculence" in Japanese communications.[246] Also, as a practical consideration, the former Assistant Secretary of the Navy envisioned the cruise as a great laboratory experiment that would provide invaluable performance data which might be of great assistance to the Navy if it ever did have to fight far from American shores.

As we have previously noted, it was the long-established policy of the United States to keep its main battlefleet concentrated in the At-

---

[244] For Wood's reaction to these orders, see Wood Papers, Wood to Roosevelt, 13 December 1907.
[245] Bailey, *Roosevelt and the Japanese-American Crises*, 220-24.
[246] Howe, *Meyer*, 365-66.

lantic. This, the General Board had ruled in 1903, was "the proper military policy, taken as a general principle." To the strategist, adhering to Mahan's theory that the sole objective of naval operations was to secure command of the seas, it was logical to insist that "Concentration is the true principle, and no departure from this rule should be seriously considered."[247] Practical considerations, of course, were also involved in the decision to favor the Atlantic. The admirals firmly believed that the actual size of the fleet was insufficient to permit a division into Atlantic and Pacific components and that such a division could not even be considered until a "two-ocean" standard had been achieved. Moreover, Congressional reluctance to build the number of capital ships desired by the General Board made the achievement of such a standard seem so far distant as to be virtually inconceivable. The lack of docking and maintenance facilities in the Pacific was another important factor; here again the unwillingness of certain important Senators and Congressmen to permit the western states to share in the pot of gold of naval expenditures worked to preserve the naval monopoly of the Eastern and Gulf states, and thus to keep the battle fleet in the Atlantic.

This is not to say that there had not been debates about the merits of the established policy or that the viewpoint of the admirals had always been unanimous. At the outbreak of the Russo-Japanese War the commander-in-chief of the Asiatic fleet, Yates Stirling, had suggested that the United States ought to keep a naval force in Asian waters that would be "large enough to cope with the fighting force of any possible enemy near or liable to arrive before our reinforcements should come."[248] The General Board had even hinted that strategic doctrine should be squared with political considerations. In 1903, anticipating the imminence of the war between Russia and Japan, it had suggested the advisability of stationing no less than three battleships in the Pacific.[249] In 1905 there was another, more extended discussion of these issues in the General Board, the outcome of which was a cautious statement that "the question about the distribution of battleships compels a recognition of the limitations which political situations place upon strategic dispositions." The members of the Board, in keeping with strict naval theory, agreed that the dispersal of the fleet beyond effective supporting distances would weaken its military effectiveness; but they also suggested that "the influence which a small group of heavy ships exerts upon political complications, when near the scene

[247] GB, Proceedings, 4 December 1903, and Letters, v, Dewey to Metcalf, 25 April 1907.
[248] GB, File 420-1, Stirling to Morton, 10 August 1904.
[249] GB, Proceedings, 4 December 1903.

of trouble, is frequently apparent."[250] The General Board, in short, was tempted by the thought that a few battleships, capable of making a demonstration in the Pacific, would actually have greater effect on the Asian scene than the existence of a unified fleet thousands of miles away in the Atlantic.

Such statements, phrased in general if not oblique language, represented the outer limits of the General Board's thought about the relation between politics and the disposition of the fleet. Others, to be sure, felt more strongly. The occasion of the Board's discussions in 1903 prompted Admiral Taylor to write Mahan for his judgment on the distribution of the fleet. Mahan, faithful as always to the principle of concentration, stressed the importance of a unified fleet but, to the surprise of Taylor and the General Board, argued that it ought to be located in the Pacific. His was a political, not a strategic judgment. No European power, Mahan asserted, seriously contemplated any attempt to weaken the American position in the Caribbean, for none could hope to "make a permanent assertion against us on this side of the Atlantic. Great Britain has abandoned the idea; who better than she could maintain it?" But the Far East was fluid; against the Far Eastern interests of the European powers, the United States could "take the offensive, always the best attitude." Therefore, Mahan counseled:

> to remove our fleet—the battlefleet—from the Pacific would be a declaration of policy and a confession of weakness. It would mean a reversion to a policy narrowly American, and essentially defensive, which is militarily vicious. . . . The American question, the Monroe principle, though not formally accepted, is as nearly established as is given to international questions to be. The Pacific and Eastern is not in that case, and is the great coming question.[251]

However much the General Board might be attracted to the Pacific, it could not be persuaded by Mahan's vision of the American destiny in Asia. His letter, indeed, was not read to the naval strategists until a year had passed, while the only outcome of the discussion was a decision to make no recommendation—which meant, of course, reaffirmation of the standing policy of concentration in the Atlantic.[252] No less striking was the Board's renewal of its faith in the same policy in the spring of 1907 when not a few of its members actually feared conflict with the Japanese. Concentration in the Atlantic should be the permanent policy since

[250] GB, Proceedings, 24 January 1905.
[251] GB, File 420-1, Mahan to Taylor, 7 December 1903.
[252] GB, Proceedings, 24 January 1905.

Every European power now recognizes that the occupation of a distant colony by the enemy can have no effect upon the ultimate result of war. The battle fleet will alone give command of the sea and insure communications between home and colony, and any war, other than one exclusively between continental European nations, will be won by the fleet obtaining command of the sea.

Even more important was the fact, according to the admirals, that

At the present moment no European nation has a single battleship outside of European waters, which fact is considered a cogent reason that our entire battle fleet should be concentrated on the Atlantic Coast. If war should result from any infraction of the Monroe Doctrine, it would be necessary for the aggressive European power to sustain its contention in American waters south of the U. S., therefore, the best strategic position of our battle fleet units would be on the Atlantic coast.[253]

The Board recognized that many, both within and without the naval establishment, advocated keeping at least a portion of the fleet in the Pacific. But such a policy, it countered, might well produce a disaster comparable to that which had befallen the Russian navy in its war with Japan. If there should be war with a European power, a divided American fleet could be defeated in detail by its enemy. Moreover, a concentrated fleet based in the Atlantic was always preferable, even in the event of war with Japan:

Of course, in this case, Japan only being under consideration, it would be better to have the battle fleet in the Philippines, and with our base at Olongapo assured, we would be ready for any emergency with that country; but as we must also be prepared for possible trouble with European nations in the defense of the Monroe Doctrine, it would be unwise for us to put all our battle fleet in the Pacific waters. We have not nor shall we have in the near future, a sufficient number of battleships to hold both places at the same time against the attacks of a European and a Japanese force, or either of them.[254]

A divided fleet was possible only when the number of battleships had reached thirty or possibly after the completion of the canal made rapid transit from one ocean to the other a possibility.

Thus, the Atlantic commitment was retained as the appropriate permanent, peacetime policy. Strategically committed to the goal of

253 GB, Letters, v, Dewey to Metcalf, 25 April 1907.
254 GB, Letters, v, Dewey to Metcalf, 25 April 1907.

winning command of the seas with a unified fleet, the naval theorists feared that, however dangerous the situation in Asia might be, a Pacific concentration might tempt a European reaction in the Caribbean. It was, it might be added, a decision which in several ways resembled the British solution recently carried out by Lord Fisher—a withdrawal of outlying naval forces for concentration upon the command of the Atlantic and a similar belief that there was the greatest of perils in the wide dispersion and fragmentation of naval power.[255]

All of these considerations were much on the minds of naval experts in the late spring of 1907 when the decision was made to send the fleet on its world cruise. That decision, however, was related not merely to the continuing discussion about the disposition of the fleet but also, and more immediately, to the strategic portions of the Orange Plan. Naval records on this point are admittedly something less than satisfactory, but the inference seems clear.

When the General Board, in response to Roosevelt's inquiries, began to hasten its planning in June of 1907, one of its sub-committees, headed by Captain Sargent, recommended strengthening American naval forces in the Pacific. The United States should send to the Pacific coast "a force of battleships of such size as would enable this country, in case of war with an Asiatic power, to protect that coast and the Hawaiian Islands from raiding attacks." Sargent's committee based its recommendation on the postulates of the Orange Plan as well as on previous discussions about the possible merits of stationing battleships in the Pacific. It pointed out that naval units in the Philippines would, according to plan, be withdrawn at the outset of hostilities and that basic American strategy called for the rendezvous of all units of the fleet in the Hawaiian Islands. It might be advisable, the report went on, to protect that strategy by the prior establishment of a battleship squadron in the Pacific. While conceding that it was breaking with established practice, the sub-committee argued that the overall naval strength of the United States—with twenty-two battleships and ten armored cruisers either in service or virtually completed—now made it possible to re-examine the familiar postulates about naval concentration. Indeed, suggested the sub-committee, "the broad principle of concentration may have become subject to some degree of modification . . . and the concentration of the whole at a distance of 11,000 miles from a threatened point may not be a logical application of strategic principles."[256]

The assembled board, however, did not accept the full recommen-

[255] Arthur J. Marder, *From the Dreadnought to Scapa Flow* (London, 1961), 40 ff., 106-07.

[256] GB, Proceedings, 15 June 1907, Sargent report.

dations of its sub-committee. What emerged from its discussion was
a compromise. There would be no division of the fleet; the principle
of concentration was inviolable. But the full Board did recommend
that "at as early a date as practicable, not less than 16 battleships be
assembled in the Pacific." To preserve secrecy it was further agreed
not to put this recommendation in writing but to transmit it verbally
to the Secretary of the Navy.[257] On June 18th the recommendation to
send sixteen battleships to the Pacific was put before the Joint Board
which was meeting to determine a unified Army-Navy approach to
the Japanese problem. What the Joint Board then approved was a
resolution which called for the full battle fleet of the United States to
be "assembled and despatched for the Orient as soon as practicable."[258] The resolution was by no means a "war move" and was not
to be immediately undertaken; rather it was a move to be implemented
only at the point in time when war appeared to be imminent. But it was
in keeping with the basic strategy of the Orange Plan; that is, it was a
precautionary move to concentrate the Atlantic fleet and move it into
the Pacific in line with a strategy which called for the assembly of all
American naval strength in the Hawaiian Islands and an eventual
trans-Pacific offensive against Japan.

It was this latter recommendation that was put before Theodore
Roosevelt ten days afterwards at Oyster Bay. What emerged from the
discussion was far less provocative—a decision to transfer the main
battle fleet to the Pacific ocean in the fall of 1907, probably in October.[259] It would appear as if the refinements were the work of the President who took the proposed transfer of the fleet from one ocean to the
other and turned it into his multi-purpose world cruise. There is unfortunately no record of any full naval discussion of the entire global
proposal. But what apparently happened was this: a project to transfer
the fleet from the Atlantic to the Pacific, originating in naval circles
as a precautionary move to be undertaken in the light of the strategy
of the Orange Plan, was transformed by the President into a plan for
a global cruise with many and varied implications, of which the purely
miliary were to become of lesser consequence.

The famous voyage was entirely peaceful, and, despite many rumors
of Japanese plots against the fleet, no incidents occurred. But the debate over the disposition of the fleet continued. By the summer of 1907
the General Board was involved in further controversy with Roosevelt
over this familiar issue. Shortly after the transfer to the Pacific had
been approved, the General Board sent the President a letter which

257 GB, Proceedings, 17 June 1907.
258 JB, Minutes, meeting of 18 June 1907.
259 See summary of discussions in Wood Papers, Ainsworth to Wood, 6 July 1907.

caused Roosevelt to believe that his top ranking admirals were about to abandon the principle of concentration. Their letter seemed to suggest that the General Board wanted to divide the fleet—retaining six battleships in the Atlantic while sending the remainder to the Pacific— and believed that the overseas interests of the United States had now developed to such a point that separate fleets were necessary in both Atlantic and Pacific.[260] Dewey, in rebuttal, contended that Roosevelt had misunderstood the Board's position; it had, he claimed, simply been trying to underscore the inadequacies of the existing fleet while pointing to the objectives that future building programs should achieve. That is, the General Board believed that, with the obvious growth of America's interests in the Far East, all future naval construction programs should focus on the creation of a genuine two-ocean navy. But these, Dewey insisted, were considerations for the future. For the present, and with the fleet that actually existed, the General Board had no intention of departing from the established principle of concentration of naval strength in one, undivided fleet. The Board, Dewey continued, agreed that the force to be transferred to the Pacific in October should consist of the full complement of battleships then in service.[261] With Dewey's letter, the incident blew over, but it was a harbinger of pending difficulties with Roosevelt— and of the Navy's problem in discussing such an issue with a President whose own devotion to the principle of naval concentration was, if anything, even stronger than that of the admirals.

At this point the Army began to play the role of devil's advocate. The General Staff, once it began to worry about the state of Philippine defenses, not only directed its fire against Subig Bay but also tried to influence the permanent disposition of the battle fleet. In January 1908, concurrently with his campaign against Subig, General Bell raised the question of how long the fleet should remain in the Pacific. With a pessimism that would have done credit to Leonard Wood, Bell sketched out his forebodings of a war with Japan. Without a powerful American fleet in the Pacific, Bell maintained, the defense of both the Philippines and Hawaii would be "a difficult if not impossible task," while enemy raids might even extend to the west coast of the United States. After adding a few gloomy touches about the lack of supplies, the potential hostility of Japanese residents of Hawaii, and the inadequate size of Army garrisons in the Pacific possessions, Bell concluded that "a policy should be adopted which will maintain a battle fleet in the Pacific

---

[260] GB, Letters, v, Metcalf to Dewey, 8 August 1907, and General Board's second endorsement, 2 August 1907, on a letter from Admiral Manney.

[261] GB, Letters, v, Dewey to Metcalf, 15 August 1907.

Ocean until conditions so change as to permit of its removal without danger to our insular and Pacific Coast possessions."[262]

The Joint Board, early in 1908, devoted two full sessions to the issues raised by the General Staff. The outcome was a curious compromise, a document which revealed a certain petulance with civilian authority for failing to keep the military informed about political conditions but which also showed the traditional military reluctance to speak out on issues which involved both politics and strategy. The Joint Board reaffirmed its commitment to the principle of concentration; the fleet, it decreed, should remain as a single unit until such time as Congress provided sufficient funds for a two-ocean navy—for a fleet in each ocean that would be capable of safeguarding American interests without assistance from the other. But where should the existing fleet be located? That, said the Joint Board in language that was neither loud nor clear, would depend upon the general state of international relations. In time of complications, the fleet should be stationed in the area of greatest danger; in time of peace, in that of greatest national interest. Even this highly generalized recommendation was rendered an innocuous truism by the qualification that immediately followed: "What may be the facts determining the international relations only the Administration can know, and until this knowledge is communicated to the Joint Board, it cannot intelligently make recommendations as to the specific disposition of the fleet." Yet the admirals and generals did dare a tentative conclusion, a suggestion presented almost wistfully:

Although lacking such knowledge of our international relations as would warrant the Board's making a definite recommendation as to the present disposition of the fleet, such information as the Board does possess, derived from the Information Divisions of the War and Navy Departments, renders it apprehensive of eventualities in the Pacific, and imposes upon it the duty of pointing out the danger of withdrawing the fleet from the region of threatening complications.[263]

It was perhaps wise of the Joint Board to be circumspect. Roosevelt held strong views about the concentration of the fleet and, as we have seen, had suspected that his admirals were being tempted to abandon that principle. Thus, the Joint Board's apparent wavering angered him as much, if not more, than its recommendation over Subig Bay. Con-

---

[262] JB, Minutes, Bell to Taft, 7 February 1908.
[263] JB, Minutes, meeting of 19 February 1908, and Dewey to Taft and Metcalf, 21 February 1908.

vinced that he knew as much about the proper disposition of the fleet as the Joint Board, his rejection of its advice was blunt and to the point: "I should of course be glad to have the opinion of the Joint Board on this matter, but I cannot say that I will follow that opinion; for I feel that the battle fleet should not be divided between the two oceans; and I doubt if, at present, we can permanently care for it in the Pacific."[264] A year later, when there was a Congressional recommendation in favor of dividing the fleet, the President again reacted with his customary vigor. In cabinet discussions, as one member later recalled, Roosevelt was "most emphatic" in his opposition. Also, as between the two oceans, Roosevelt vastly preferred the Atlantic—and for reasons which showed that his political sophistication was superior to that of his Army and Navy advisers. The legislature of Nevada and California had just passed new discriminatory laws aimed at Japanese residents of those states, and Roosevelt told the cabinet he was therefore glad that the American fleet was not then in the Pacific. Had the battle fleet been stationed in the Pacific, he said, the United States could "never explain to Japan that the actions of the two state legislatures had not been with the approval of the Federal Government."[265]

Thus, by Presidential decision the fleet remained on its traditional, established station, though the issue would long remain under discussion and continue to be debated during the administration of his successor.

Roosevelt, as we have seen, did not expect that the "crisis" with Japan would lead to conflict. Nonetheless, when the White Fleet was ready to sail on its world cruise, the President did not disregard the many rumors of fantastic Japanese plots against it. From Paris Ambassador Henry White cabled a report, which had originated in the office of his naval attaché, that a scheme was afoot to blow up units of the fleet when it arrived in the harbor of Rio de Janiero. There were other and similar reports, ranging from the confidential notes of William II about secret agreements between Mexico and Japan to stories about a Japanese plot to torpedo or mine American vessels once they had reached Asian waters.[266] All proved to be sheer fantasy. Nevertheless, the Treasury Department was instructed to make thorough investigations, a special warning was sent to Admiral Evans before the White Fleet arrived at Rio, and his vessels actually got a precautionary escort

264 Roosevelt's endorsement on Manney letter cited in footnote 260.

265 Howe, *Meyer*, 416, 419-20.

266 SDNF, Case 10799, especially /1-7, which includes White to Root, 23 December 1907, and Dudley (the Minister in Brazil) to Root, 7 January 1908. See also NF, Case 1797/348, Charlemagne Tower (the Minister in Germany) to Root, 10 July 1907, which relays the Kaiser's warnings.

into that harbor.[267] In Roosevelt's judgment "it was extremely improbable that any attempt will be made, yet anything of that sort would be so disastrous that we should take every precaution."[268] The warnings and investigations showed not only that the President was maintaining a tight control over the fleet but also was determined that nothing should interfere with the fulfillment of its role as an instrument of policy.

For Roosevelt was clearly using the battle fleet as a political instrument. Nothing illustrated his purpose more clearly than the careful way in which the decision was reached to permit it to stop at Japanese ports. The administration made absolutely certain that the Japanese government would welcome such a visit. Once satisfied on that point, it then made doubly certain that no action by the fleet or its personnel should appear provocative.

In the summer of 1907, when American newspapers first announced that the fleet would sail into the Pacific, there were immediate fears of an unfavorable Japanese reaction. From Tokyo the American ambassador pointed out that, while the official reaction of the Japanese government had been calm, the appearance of the American fleet in the Pacific might "have an unfavorable effect upon the mind of the average Japanese."[269] The care with which the Roosevelt administration treated these warnings was indicated when some months later General James H. Wilson sent a long letter to Secretary of State Root. Wilson's report, to be sure, was secondhand, based on his correspondence with an old friend then serving in the Japanese diplomatic service. According to Wilson, "though the Japanese do not want dominion over the Pacific, they will stand firm in making the Inland Sea a *mare clausum*, [and] . . . any visit of our fleet to that Sea or to any port of Japan, even under all assurances that can be given that theirs is a peaceful and complimentary visit, will result in rioting and serious disturbances."[270] Elihu Root at once replied that Wilson's information checked with reports he had received from other sources and added, "I shall see that the part that relates to the possibility of our fleet visiting Japan comes to the attention of the President."[271] The American government sought carefully and in advance to get assurances from Japanese authorities that a visit to their country would be welcome. A final decision was,

[267] SDNF, Case 10799/15-25, Dudley to Root, 3 January 1908, and /48-50, Dudley to Root, 25 January 1908. See also Nav Rec Confid Ltrs, Metcalf to Commander-in-Chief, Pacific Fleet, 4 March 1908.

[268] Howe, *Meyer*, 384-85.

[269] SDNF, Case 1797/298-300, Luke Wright to Root, 10 July 1907.

[270] SDNF, Case 8258/77, Wilson to Root, 7 January 1908.

[271] SDNF, Case 8258/77, Root to Wilson, 8 January 1908.

moreover, delayed until every conceivable interested party had been consulted. Even after the basic decision had been reached, there was a momentary pause in the late spring of 1908 when Ambassador Thomas J. O'Brien, apprehensive of an unfavorable reaction by the Japanese public, suggested that it might not be wise to send the entire battle fleet into Tokyo harbor. O'Brien thought it might be prudent to limit the visit to only one or two squadrons, thus minimizing the full display of naval might.[272] Again Washington checked with Tokyo. Roosevelt reaffirmed the original decision to send the full complement of sixteen battleships into Tokyo only after the Japanese government had officially informed him that there would be great disappointment in Japan if the entire American fleet did not appear.[273]

Even greater care was taken in the selection of the officer who would command the fleet when it moved into the Pacific. Captain Robley Evans (universally known as "Fighting Bob") had commanded the sixteen battleships on the cruise around Cape Horn but had fallen ill while proceeding up the west coast of South America. He was replaced by Admiral Charles Sperry. In selecting Sperry, Roosevelt singled out a former member of the General Board who, as we have seen, had not been caught up in the anti-Japanese fever that had existed in high naval circles and who, moreover, had always taken especial pains to make certain that his views on international politics came to the attention of his civilian superiors. Early in 1907, for example, Sperry had produced a long memorandum in which he had argued that, while the Anglo-Japanese alliance assured Japanese control of the Eastern Pacific, the best interests of the United States would be served if Japan, Britain, and the United States remained in accord. Minimizing present differences between Japan and America (which he called "incidental"), Sperry maintained that Japan's conquest of Korea had relieved the pressures of population that had motivated her expansionist policies and that the Japanese, for many reasons, could not risk a break with the United States. "Apart from any sentiment of traditional friendships," Sperry wrote, "it seems impossible that any responsible Japanese statesman should contemplate a rupture with this country, for which there is no adequate motive, and which would entail great expense."[274]

The recipient of this memorandum was Oscar Straus, Secretary of Commerce in the Roosevelt cabinet and—certainly from Sperry's point

[272] SDNF, Case 8258/355, O'Brien to Root, 16 April 1908.
[273] SDNF, Case 8258/356, Root to O'Brien, 21 May 1908.
[274] Sperry Papers, Sperry to Oscar Straus, 4 February 1907. On the transfer of command from Evans to Sperry, see Damon Cummings, *Admiral Wainwright and the U.S. Fleet* (Washington, 1962), 180 ff.

of view—a useful transmission belt for his opinions. Straus not only read Sperry's letter to the assembled cabinet but also supplied a copy to Taft before the Secretary of War left on his own visit to the Far East.[275] Admiral Sperry was quite conscious of what he was attempting to do; indeed, he later speculated about the possibility that his letters might actually have influenced the development of American policies towards Japan in 1907.[276] While this would seem to be a reflection of the Admiral's ego, it is clear that when Roosevelt selected Sperry to replace Admiral Evans a year later he did so in the full knowledge that he was selecting an officer who shared many of his own views, was not affected by the anti-Japanese virus, and was well suited to implement his own policies.

Once Roosevelt had appointed Sperry, he treated him to careful and personal instructions. His assignment to take the fleet into Japanese ports, Roosevelt wrote, was far more difficult than the task which Evans had accomplished in sailing around the tip of South America. "I need not tell you," the President warned, "that you should exercise the most careful watch while you are in Oriental waters." While Sperry's most important task was to prevent any attack upon American ships by some "fanatic," the diplomatic mission was of almost equal importance. He must, instructed the President, "prevent there being any kind of action by any of our men that would give an excuse for the feeling that we had been in any way guilty of misconduct. Aside from the loss of a ship I had far rather we were insulted than that we insult anybody under these peculiar conditions."[277] Parenthetically, it should be added, once the fleet had arrived in Japan, Roosevelt continued to conduct some of his personal diplomacy with the Japanese through Sperry. In particular, he sent the admiral a personal message to be delivered to the Emperor—and about which he gave no advance information to the American ambassador in Tokyo. When Sperry later related this incident to Elihu Root, the Secretary of State was not surprised. Long familiar with Roosevelt's tendency to bypass orthodox channels, Root merely grumbled, "It should have come through the State Department."[278]

Admiral Sperry proved to be an adroit diplomat. Before giving Roosevelt's message to the Emperor, he got in touch with Ambassador O'Brien and provided him with a copy to be transmitted to the Japanese well in advance of the scheduled audience. The Emperor, Sperry explained, "does not like surprises."[279] Also on his own initiative,

275 Sperry Papers, Straus to Sperry, 11 February 1907.
276 Sperry Papers, Sperry to Mrs. Sperry, 12 July 1908.
277 Sperry Papers, Roosevelt to Sperry, 21 March 1908.
278 Sperry Papers, Sperry to Mrs. Charles Sperry, 6 April 1909.
279 Sperry Papers, Sperry to Charles Sperry, Jr., 30 October 1908.

Sperry corresponded and cooperated with a legendary figure in the Japanese foreign office, Mr. Denison, an elderly American who had been an adviser to the Japanese for more than four decades.[280] The details of the fleet's visit to Tokyo were arranged through the auspices of Denison. Sperry was always alert to the possibility of trouble. Later he wondered if all the anxiety about the visit had been warranted, for, as he noted, every aspect of his stay in Tokyo had proceeded smoothly and had been marked by a genuine and enthusiastic Japanese welcome. But at the time of the visit he felt that he "had been walking on eggs" and wrote, in some surprise, that "it has finally dawned on me that there was an almost distressing nervous tension in the Japanese government circles which broke happily."[281] Summarizing his visit, the admiral wrote:

> I was not prepared to find such nervous tension existing in governmental circles as undoubtedly did, but the reaction after my first talk at the Grand Hotel was almost hysterical. Everybody had a scare, and if I had blundered with that fleet back of me, it would have been bad business.[282]

The voyage around the world proved to be an adroit combination of the olive branch and the sword. In Washington it was realized that it could benefit American foreign relations in general and not merely with Japan. The Australian government, for example, literally besieged Washington with requests for a visit by the American fleet to Melbourne. Elihu Root agreed that it would be "good business" and would help to cement relations that, at some future date, might be invaluable. "The time will surely come," he told Roosevelt, "although probably after our day, when it will be important for the United States to have all ports friendly and all causes of sympathy alive in the Pacific."[283] Once again Sperry was the right man for the task. For, as he later observed, he used the occasion, whenever he visited British harbors, to spread the gospel of Anglo-American friendship and the mutuality of British and American interests.[284] Like Root and Roosevelt, he felt that Anglo-American friendship was a vital key to America's future position in the Orient.

But if the voyage promised to promote Anglo-American friendship it also promised to complicate relations with China. American diplomats in China, especially William Rockhill and Edwin Denby, unleashed a veritable flood of messages warning of the danger of sending

---

[280] Sperry Papers, Sperry to Mrs. Charles Sperry, 23 October 1908.
[281] Sperry Papers, Sperry to Charles Sperry, Jr., 30 October 1908.
[282] Sperry Papers, Sperry to Charles Sperry, Jr., 6 January 1909.
[283] SDNF, Case 8258/143-45, Root to Roosevelt, 21 February 1908.
[284] Sperry Papers, Sperry to Mrs. Charles Sperry, 9 September 1908.

the entire American fleet into any Chinese harbor. They feared that the Chinese would misinterpret the purpose of the visit. The Chinese, they pointed out, were in the midst of a campaign to try to regain the extra territorial rights they had been compelled to yield to the western powers, and many regarded the United States as a champion, or at least a potential champion, of their cause. To Rockhill it seemed more than possible that the Chinese would regard a visit by the battle fleet as a portent that the United States was ready to become "an active participant in upholding all Chinese pretensions."[285] Denby, the consul general at Shanghai, feared that Chinese agitators in that city would interpret an American naval visit as an American endorsement of their campaign against Japan and might even regard the presence of the battleships as a signal "that the time has come to act overtly against Japan and that a powerful friend may be there to help." The visit, at the worst, might strike a spark that would set the Chinese tinderbox aflame; it might, at the least, simply produce Chinese resentment at the United States for her failure to assist the cause of China. Thus, the advice of these two old China hands was that the Department of State should consider the impact of the proposed visit in terms of its effect not only on Chinese political affairs but also upon Sino-Japanese relations. "The advisability of sending a great American fleet to Chinese waters," suggested Denby, "depends on the answer to this question: 'Does the American government wish to arouse China's public sentiment against Japan?' "[286] Rockhill was equally blunt: "I am definitely of the opinion that if the American government has not definitely decided to intervene now by force in the affairs of the East, the visit of the American forces to Chinese waters should be circumspectly arranged."[287]

Since the Roosevelt administration had no desire to incite trouble, it accepted this advice and decided to limit the number of ships that would visit Chinese ports. The decision was made in the Department of State and the Navy simply notified of the action taken. It was agreed to send only eight battleships to Amoy and none at all to Hong Kong. A gratified Rockhill soon sent back his expressions of great pleasure at this discreet use of naval power.[288]

The world voyage of the "White Fleet" thus had clear diplomatic and political significance. But it had perhaps its greatest impact upon the Navy. The voyage proceeded far more smoothly and efficiently than

285 SDNF, Case 8258/355, Rockhill to Root, 19 April 1908.

286 SDNF, Case 8258/386, Denby to Root, 18 April 1908.

287 SDNF, Case 8258/400, Rockhill to Root, 21 April 1908.

288 SDNF, Case 8258/401, Root to Wilder, 5 June 1908, and, especially, /414, Rockhill to Root, 4 May 1908 and /425, O'Brien to Root, 19 June 1908.

any one had even dared to hope. The Navy Department had anticipated that it might require 120 days for the fleet to steam across the Pacific; the time actually required was only 90. There had been considerable fear that the coaling of the fleet would pose great difficulties, but coaling the vessels from accompanying colliers proved no great obstacle. (Though it should be mentioned that the Navy actually possessed so few colliers that it was compelled to charter them from foreign governments.) Naval experts had also been fearful that the battleships, upon arrival in Far Eastern waters, would be in need of extensive repairs and would therefore have to spend time at such a site as Subig Bay before being able to undertake further operations. This also appeared to be a mistaken assumption.[289]

These favorable results had an almost immediate effect upon strategic planning. Naval planners began to revise downwards the amount of time necessary under the Orange Plan to bring relief to the beleaguered Philippines—and, obviously, to revise upwards their hopes for its defensibility. The success of fleet colliers reinforced the belief that overseas naval stations were not as essential as had once been believed. Also, since the fleet had presumably arrived in Far Eastern waters in a state of combat readiness, the General Board was to become more optimistic about its chances of engaging in immediate operations even if the Navy did not possess a great bastion at Subig Bay.[290] Thus the way was open for the Navy—especially since by the time Roosevelt left office it had twenty-five battleships in being and six more under construction—to raise again with the incoming President, William Howard Taft, the issues of the Subig Bay and the disposition of the fleet.

Most of the conclusions for this chapter should at least have been implicit in the preceding pages. When the military sought bases on or near the Chinese coast, they were, in effect, challenging the assumptions of 1898 that an "insular empire" reaching from Hawaii to the Philippines would suffice for the American purpose in the Far East. Both the logistical and operational difficulties that arose during the Boxer Rebellion and the widespread belief that disorders would continue in China led to a quite systematic attempt by the Navy to establish American naval power on the mainland of Asia. True, it would still have been an "informal" and at least technically an "insular" empire, comprising ports of entry, coaling stations, naval bases and not vast

[289] See Annual Report of the Secretary of the Navy, 1908 (Washington, 1908), 297 ff.

[290] GB, Letters, v, Dewey to Newberry, 24 February 1909, a subject discussed again in Chapter Four.

land areas to rule or administer. But the geographic and, more important, the political and military implications of informality would have been extended for some thousands of miles. Actually, the periphery of such an insular empire would have been located at the very center of the imperialist rivalries and great power clashes of the Far East. But for the many reasons that have already been cited, the Navy achieved none of its goals. However, it should be re-emphasized that this "military option" commanded considerable attention, was not confined solely to members of the General Board, and was in the backs of many minds on numerous occasions. It simply will not do, as Akira Iriye contends, to interpret the Open Door notes as merely a negative response by John Hay to the military and their "hardline" commercial allies who wanted a vigorous and aggressive China policy. The various issues posed by the "military option" were discussed over too long a time and attracted too many proponents for such a conclusion to be valid. A Rockhill, for example, might veto the concept of a base in China, but he was quick to suggest a Korean alternative. Moreover, the military did not really launch their serious campaign for a naval base until after, not before, the notes had been sent, while the critical approaches to foreign nations with interests in the Far East also came at a later date.

Events in the middle of the decade, above all, the rise of Japanese military power, undercut the Navy's original assumptions. These changed conditions were taken into account in the drafting of the Orange Plan as well as in the interservice struggle that resulted in the Navy's decision to abandon Subig Bay for Pearl Harbor. The evidence suggests that in varying ways much of what the services were thinking about the Far East did get through to civilian authorities in Washington, particularly to the President. Roosevelt obviously had other sources of information, and his Far Eastern decisions were based on a multitude of considerations—for example, the reluctance of Congress to authorize the number of battleships that Roosevelt wanted and his own belief that the California legislature was in large part responsible for the troubles with Japan. But it is impossible to imagine that his decision to conciliate Japan was not also the product of his own familiarity with naval thinking, his correspondence with officers such as Leonard Wood, or his own direct participation in such conferences with military leaders as the Oyster Bay meeting of June 1907.

Both services learned much from their first decade of continuous involvement in the Far East. The great expectations of 1898 vanished amid the complexities and problems of the years that followed. Both the Army and the Navy learned, along with Roosevelt, that the Philippines were not the stepping stone to Asia but rather the "Achilles heel" that the President termed them. Still, at the close of the decade, the Navy was by no means prepared either to abandon the concept of the Open Door or simply to retreat all the way back to Pearl Harbor. While the Orange Plan might postulate initial American disasters, it also anticipated a triumphant American return across the Pacific to the sources of Japanese power. It was a forecast that did not become a reality for more than a generation but which was fulfilled in 1945 at the end of a conflict fought along lines that the authors of the original Orange Plan would easily have recognized. Though, it should be added, the road back from Pearl Harbor—with its bloody stopovers at Tarawa, Iwo Jima, and Okinawa—was more costly and more arduous than any naval strategist in the first decade of the century could ever have anticipated.

CHAPTER FOUR

Taft and Knox: The Military Dimensions
of Dollar Diplomacy

1. THE NEW ADMINISTRATION

In March 1909, when President William Howard Taft and Secretary of State Philander Knox took office, one of their very first acts was to establish a naval watch in the Caribbean to prevent ex-President Cipriano Castro from regaining control of Venezuela. In February 1913, when the two men were on the verge of leaving office, one of their last acts was to send units of the fleet up and down the Central American coast in an effort to convince citizens of those countries that the inauguration of Woodrow Wilson would not mean an open door for revolutions in Latin America. Throughout all four years the President and his Secretary of State were consistent in their employment of the military services as instruments of administration policy. Moreover, military men were never permitted to forget that, in the eyes of the administration, their function was to serve as the obedient servants of the Department of State and the White House. When a junior officer commanding the *Marietta*, then in Honduran waters, complained that the Bluefields Company, an American-owned enterprise active in Central America, was trying to involve the United States Navy in its own nefarious business operations, Alvey Adee firmly and unequivocally laid down the administration's line:

> The banana question is merely one of rivalry between American interests. First one side and then the other makes it worthwhile for the local authorities to side with it, with a see-saw result which is wearisome. Our naval officers can't influence the result one way or the other. The *Marietta* is not in Honduran waters, however, on banana police duty, but to exert a moral influence towards political tranquillity at this juncture when we are after bigger game than bananas.[1]

The inauguration of Taft and the appointment of Knox produced no substantial changes in the established patterns of civil-military relations, or, for that matter, in the basic objectives of American foreign policy. Most aspects of their highly publicized, frequently criticized "dollar diplomacy" had in fact been anticipated by Roosevelt, Hay,

[1] SDNF, Case 19475/55-56, Commander Hill to Meyer, 2 June 1909, and Adee interoffice memorandum, 29 July 1909.

and Root. Most of the issues which arose and in which the military were involved—in Cuba, in Nicaragua, in the Dominican Republic, and even in the Far East—were basically similar to those which their predecessors had faced, and thus this chapter will examine a set of problems not unlike those which have been previously explored. In Mexico, however, administration and military services confronted a social revolution far different from the insurrections, coups, and uprisings which had previously been the staple fare of Latin American policy.

But with Taft and Knox there were important changes of emphasis. Intervention in Latin America was far more aggressive, far more harsh than under Root's regime of legality. In the Far East there was a determined, abrasive effort to pump American capital into China and thereby to achieve greater American political leverage on the Chinese government. Taft himself was not nearly the activist in foreign policy that Roosevelt had been, and he shared none of Roosevelt's sense that America was involved in the European much less the world balance of power. Whereas the first Moroccan crisis of 1905 had triggered an impressive display of Rooseveltian activism, the second, and far more serious, crisis of 1911 caused scarcely a tremor in the White House. Similarly, and to the frequent despair of his military advisers, the easygoing Taft discounted fears of the potential danger posed by Japan as simply the natural reaction of military alarmists. Since Taft and Knox shared many beliefs in common, it is often difficult to separate the role of the President from that of the Secretary. Still, it does seem clear that Knox was far more in control of the apparatus of American foreign policy than Root or Hay had been.[2] As Huntington Wilson, Knox's principal assistant, later recalled: "Philander Knox, in his quiet, matter-of-course way, was still more the complete autocrat in his domain. Like a *cordon bleu chef* who allows no one to interfere in his kitchen, he had it tacitly understood that, outside of Congress, no official from the President down was to say or do anything that touched upon foreign relations without his approval in advance."[3]

Historians have labelled this the era of "dollar diplomacy." The phrase is shorthand for what was a sustained effort to secure both economic gain and political influence in the Far East and the Caribbean through the systematic investment of American capital. Knox was personally committed to the cause. Once, when seeking an appropriation from Congress, he instructed his assistants to draft a memorandum

[2] Henry Pringle, *The Life and Times of William Howard Taft* (2 vols., New York, 1939), ii, 678-715 deals with his foreign policy. On Knox, see Walter Scholes, "Philander Knox," in Graebner, *Uncertain Tradition*, 59-78.

[3] F. W. Huntington Wilson, *Memoirs of an Ex-Diplomat* (Boston, 1945), 199.

that "would be especially emphatic on the China and Latin American points." According to the Secretary's reasoning, "China and Latin America are recognized by the world as the regions of richest potentiality for foreign commerce, and it happens that China and the rest of the Far East, and Latin America, are geographically, by tradition, and by common consent, two fields pre-eminently adapted for American enterprise."[4] Taft was no less adamant. When Theodore Roosevelt grew alarmed and warned that intensified American efforts in Manchuria might incur the wrath of Japan, Taft blandly dismissed his one-time mentor's advice and stated bluntly, "We are not [going] to abandon our rights to equal opportunities under the Open Door Principle."[5] Assistant Secretary Huntington Wilson also scorned the Roosevelt warning, referring to it as "his absurd theory that in return for Japan's amiable acquiescence in our exercise of our undeniable right to regulate immigration, we should abandon the political and commercial position which we hold as of right in Manchuria."[6] Huntington Wilson's own abrupt resignation from the State Department in 1913 was triggered by Woodrow Wilson's decision that America would not participate in the financing of loans to China, a decision which struck to the very heart of Huntington Wilson's firm belief that "dollar diplomacy" was vital to American interests.[7]

Yet "dollar diplomacy" has been examined by many historians, and there seems little reason to analyze it further and even less need to raise the old and familiar question of whether the administration's policies were primarily designed to foster the political interests of the United States or, more simply, largely intended to make greater profits for the business and financial community. To be sure, certain aspects of the administration's policies, such as the desire to sell battleships to Argentina and thereby benefit the Bethlehem Steel Corporation, did draw the Navy into the financial toils of the administration. But for the purposes of this study it is more relevant to examine how the Army and Navy fitted into those issues that, as Adee said, were "bigger game than bananas."

More than a few military leaders complained about the treatment that they received in the "kitchen" presided over by that *cordon bleu chef*, Philander Knox. They maintained that their views were neither as carefully weighed nor as frequently sought as in the years when the former Rough Rider had been President. Commander Hill of the Naval War College, aware that Knox and the State Department had

4 Papers of F. W. Huntington Wilson, Ursinus College Library, Collegeville, Pa., Knox to Wilson, undated but filed in 1909 folder.

5 Taft Papers, Letterpress volumes, Taft to Roosevelt, 17 January 1911.

6 Huntington Wilson Papers, Wilson to Knox, 23 December 1910.

7 Huntington Wilson Papers, H. Wilson to Woodrow Wilson, 19 March 1913.

no enthusiasm for the proposed Council of National Defense, commented sharply:

> If the State Department is not represented then the Department will do as it has done in the past—establish policies without regard to the military preparedness of the country to carry through these policies. . . . The State Department is allowed to go ahead and make these policies without regard to the military branches, and, if trouble ensues, then the onus falls on the military branches and the State Department steps out.[8]

To which General Wotherspoon replied, "It is useless to discuss the unwillingness of the State Department to do what we would like, and hard to believe that had we a Hay, a Blaine, or a Root to deal with we might not have had a different answer to our suggestions."[9]

In one sense, however, there was probably more rather than less discussion between military officials and the Department of State than in the past. The departmental reorganization carried out by Knox, which led to the creation of the now familiar geographic divisions, undoubtedly increased consultation between officials at the second echelon when the Department of State wished military support for a particular diplomatic decison. When, for example, a crisis arose in Nicaragua, it was now quite simple for the proper official in the Latin American Division to get in touch with the appropriate naval officer with whom to discuss the details of what the Navy was expected to do.

Knox's department, however, was especially insistent upon its prerogatives, upon obtaining military obedience to its wishes, and upon maintaining the shibboleths of civilian supremacy. There were frequent and sometimes peevish complaints, more so than in the days of Hay and Root, about military initiatives in the areas reserved to the Department of State. In November 1910 Assistant Secretary Hugh Gibson compiled for Knox's benefit a long list of occasions when naval officers were judged guilty of having disseminated information about foreign affairs and, by so doing, of having brought "serious harm" to the national interest.[10] When naval officers in Nicaragua appeared to be exceeding their instructions, another official wrote bluntly that

> the diplomacy of naval officers in Central America has become harmful to the carrying out of the State Department's policy in these countries. I would suggest that the Navy Department be requested to instruct its officers in this matter and to the end that an intelli-

[8] GS, War College Division, File 6320-8, Hill to General Wotherspoon, 10 April 1911.

[9] GS, File 6320-8, Wotherspoon to Hill, 13 April 1911.

[10] Huntington Wilson Papers, Gibson to Knox, 12 November 1910.

gent cooperation, at least in Central America, be agreed on between the two branches of the service.[11]

Huntington Wilson's anger when three naval officers committed the error of paying a formal call upon the Nicaraguan dicator, Zelaya, has been previously noted. During a later Nicaraguan intervention, when certain Navy officers contended that the uprising could not be handled properly without the assistance of the Army, the same Wilson promptly informed Knox that "This . . . seems to suggest comment on matters of policy involved beyond the question of policy." Within a few days, he had persuaded Taft to send the Navy Department a strong letter which spelled out the State Department's demand that the Navy understand the requirements of civilian policy.[12]

Friction was not confined to major issues of policy such as the proper handling of Central American insurrections. One of the most peevish exchanges concerned the actions of a Navy captain sent to Constantinople at the time of the Young Turk revolution. Leishman, the American minister, had requested the presence of several warships to provide protection for American citizens in the event that disorder spread out of control. Soon, however, Leishman began to charge that Captain Marshall, the officer placed in charge of the naval force, had neglected his responsibilities and conducted himself in a manner liable to cause great embarrassment to the United States.[13] In Washington the two departments concerned began to exchange communications on such subjects as whether Captain Marshall had acted with excessive independence, had failed to consult with the legation in Constantinople, and had visited various Turkish ports without informing anyone of his plans. The State Department raised the grave charge that Marshall had threatened Turkish officials with reprisals, an action which, at a time of national unrest in Turkey, might have had serious repercussions.[14]

The extensive correspondence between the State and Navy departments indicated, at least in this instance, that the diplomats were correct and that naval independence had bordered upon irresponsibility. But it also revealed once again the familiar problem, which plagued the Taft administration as it had bothered preceding administrations, of coordinating the efforts of two independent, executive departments,

[11] SDNF, Case 19475/59, John J. Gregory, Jr. to Adee, 6 July 1909.

[12] SDDF, File 817.00/1940a, H. Wilson to Taft, 4 September 1912; also /2003B, H. Wilson to Taft, 23 September 1912, draft of telegram Wilson prepared for Taft's signature.

[13] SDNF, Case 10044/289, Leishman to Knox, 9 June 1910.

[14] SDNF, Case 10044/348-49, Leishman to Knox, 27 July 1910, to which is attached a lengthy memorandum by the Chief Clerk, Wilbur Carr, summarizing the Department's objections to Marshall's procedures.

each with its own procedures and established ways. The Navy Department defended Captain Marshall with its standard argument that, although Naval Regulations did specify that naval commanders should pay attention to the advice of civilian officials, these basic regulations also stipulated that "a commanding officer is solely and entirely responsible to the Navy Department for all official acts in the administration of his command."[15] The State Department countered by pointing out that Captain Marshall had, during his three months in Turkish waters, sent only three messages to the American legation and that two of the three had been sent during the first week of his visit. As Adee wryly observed, the meager information furnished to Leishman must, at the least, have left the Minister in some doubts as to Captain Marshall's intentions.[16]

This incident was trivial except for the fact that it did stimulate the Department of State to greater efforts to guarantee naval compliance with civilian wishes. What the State Department wanted was clear. On this occasion, as at other times when the two departments were at odds, the diplomats cited the actions of a certain Captain Shipley as the example to emulate. In the eyes of the Department of State Shipley was indeed the perfect model of the modern, and politically correct, naval officer. Before visiting the Latin port of San Pedro, he had checked with local American consular officials and worked out with them the appropriate date for his visit. Fearing that the municipal officers of San Pedro would try to lodge certain protests with him rather than send their complaints through diplomatic channels, Shipley had informed these men on arrival that he would not accept their representations and would immediately forward any and all notes to the American minister.[17] By citing these and other examples of Shipley's deference to civilian authority, it was obvious what the Department of State wished to establish as the norm of naval conduct. The Navy was in the somewhat paradoxical situation of playing a larger role than in the past and of even having a better opportunity to consult with subordinate officials in the State Department but at the same time of operating under greater restrictions.

2. FAR EASTERN ISSUES, 1909-1913

Taft and Knox expended a vast amount of their diplomatic energy upon the Far East, especially China. And, as has just been noted, their

15 SDNF, Case 10044/351-56, Winthrop to Knox, 16 August 1909.

16 SDNF, Case 10044/351-56, Adee to Meyer, 28 August 1909.

17 SDNF, Case 10044/351-56, Adee to Meyer, citing the Shipley report of 29 April 1909 as the "model" for the sailors to emulate. The full text of this highly admired dispatch is in Case 7357/629-30, Meyer to Knox, 1 May 1909.

primary objective was to attain greater political influence and economic gain by and through the investment of American capital in that country. But, in contrast to Latin America, the military component of dollar diplomacy in Asia was relatively small. The bulk of the correspondence not only in the Taft and Knox papers but also in the files of the Department of State deals with political, diplomatic, and financial affairs—with such matters as the possibilities of securing a particular financial concession, estimates of the attitudes of other Asian powers toward American economic interests in China, or the political gains which might be anticipated from economic success. Much of the correspondence is promotional in character and devoted to the task of trying to convince a reluctant Wall Street community that it should support American diplomacy with its dollars and overcoming the skepticism of numerous bankers who felt "that while it was all right to be making history, their business was to make money."[18]

There are many reasons why the military dimensions of American policy in Asia were less than in Latin America. Taft and Knox could readily persuade small Latin states with the logic of the gunboat, and they had no outside competitors. In China they faced a complex international situation. Knox, despite his eagerness to expand the American role in China, was well aware of the limits beyond which policy could not go. Thus, when Taft was once invited to speak on the subject of Far Eastern policy, his Secretary of State cautioned him that "in the case of China, you are hardly in a position to guarantee the realization of any roseate hopes that might be indulged in on such an occasion." The President, Knox pointed out, "could not pledge the United States to a pro-China policy in opposition to the aims and acts of other powers."[19]

Moreover, between 1909 and 1913 there were no "incidents" to mar Japanese-American relations. Nothing happened to threaten the series of agreements that had been worked out in the closing years of the Roosevelt administration. Taft, who could draw on his own experience in the Philippines, his visits to the Far East, and his personal talks with Japanese leaders, had absolutely no fear of a possible war with Japan. Indeed, as we have previously noted, not a few military leaders were tempted to make adverse comments about the ease with which the President and his entire administration seemed to discount any and all chances of conflict with the Japanese.

In the Army, especially among officers who served in the Philip-

[18] Knox Papers, Division of Far Eastern Affairs, Memorandum of conversation with Morgan and Co., 14 July 1910. For illustrations of the promotional nature of dollar diplomacy, see H. Wilson Papers, H. Wilson to Knox, 1 September 1910, and, a particularly fine example, H. Wilson to Julius Kahn, 6 July 1911.

[19] Knox Papers, Knox to Taft, 20 August 1910.

pines, doubts about Japanese intentions continued to be expressed. The correspondence of such officers as Generals Wood and Bell always reflected an undercurrent of belief that, as Wood put it, "trouble with Japan must occur sooner or later."[20] From time to time more extreme views came out into the open. In the early fall of 1909, for example, General Duvall, then commanding in the Philippines, supplied Washington with full details about the operations of Japanese spies in the islands. In addition, he dispatched a series of cables to the Adjutant General which suggested that Japan was preparing to strike a blow in the imminent future. Taft himself examined the correspondence but quickly concluded that he did not "think there is anything to be done, and I don't regard the matter as of any particular significance."[21] Duvall, it should be added, was too much of an alarmist for his fellow officers, and the General Staff questioned him sharply about the basis for his reports. Soon after he had raised his alarm, General J. G. Harbord of the Philippine Constabulary filed a report critical of the work of Army Intelligence in the Philippines and of the fears of Duvall. "I find on arrival here," wrote Harbord, "that General Duvall has been completely obsessed with the idea that there is going to be a Jap invasion" and that "he talks with such indiscretion that business has been somewhat affected by the tone of his alarm."[22]

Again in 1911 a group of Army officers in the Philippines became excited about rumors that the Japanese were about to purchase a million tons of rice in Saigon and Bangkok. They constructed a "rice curve" which was intended to prove that such purchases were a harbinger of trouble and claimed that similar studies of Japanese activity in the rice market in 1903 had provided advance information about Japan's intention to make war on Russia. The General Staff was skeptical, but Leonard Wood did pass these reports on to the Department of State for further evaluation—with the added comment that, if the estimates were correct, then there was "fair ground" for the inference that Japan contemplated war.[23] The State Department promptly exploded the rumors. Its consuls in the two Indochinese cities reported that Japanese purchases of rice had increased only from 27,000 to 80,000 tons and suggested that purely economic factors, such as a pending famine in China, accounted for the larger purchases.[24]

There was actually only one incident in Japanese-American relations

[20] Wood Papers, Bell to Wood, 11 May 1911, and, for the Wood quotation, Diary, entry of 10 November 1910.

[21] GS, File 4359, numerous reports from September 1909 through March 1910. For Taft's reaction, see, in this file, Taft to Dickinson, 11 October 1909.

[22] Wood Papers, J. C. Harbord to Wood, 16 April 1910.

[23] GS, File 5288, Army War College Report, a file which contains virtually all the correspondence on the 1911 "scare." But see also Wood Papers, Wood to Knox, 20 March 1911.

[24] GS, File 5288, Knox to Wood, 29 March 1911.

which had even slight military overtones. This was the well-publicized Magdalena Bay episode of 1911-12 which involved the effort of a group of American promoters to sell a vast area of land in lower California to a Japanese syndicate that planned to develop and colonize the region with Japanese laborers. It led ultimately to a Senate resolution, sponsored by Senator Henry Cabot Lodge, which declared, without specific reference to the Monroe Doctrine, that the United States viewed with "great concern" such transfers of private property.[25]

The Navy's formal involvement, as we shall see, was marginal. The individual who tirelessly fanned the flames of controversy and who stirred the Senate was Lodge. It was the senator from Massachusetts who made speeches denouncing the project and who furnished Taft with letter after letter in which he submitted his "evidence" of nefarious Japanese intentions. Lodge envisioned a military threat. "Magdalena Bay is valueless commercially," he informed Taft early in 1912, "the only value that Magdalena Bay can possibly have is a military and strategic value, which would be very great indeed, and that is probably the reason for Mr. Blackman [the principal promoter] finding his only possible purchaser among the Japanese."[26] It should be added that Knox most emphatically did not appreciate the zeal of Senator Lodge. After he and Taft left office, Knox commented bitterly in a letter to his former chief about the work of "Lodge, that liar." He promised Taft that "the time is certain to come when I will even up with that gentleman for his repeated falsehoods about the conditions of foreign affairs since 1909." For, as Knox put it,

> Two things happened during your administration that really hurt us with foreign governments. One was the false and insulting position of Congress toward Russia, which had Lodge's approval, and the other was the row which he kicked up about the Japanese trying to get Magdalena Bay, which not only hurt their feelings but the Resolution the Senate passed to save his face, after the State Department had shown him up as a mare's nester, was resented by the Latin Americans who justly felt that it put a crimp in their sovereign right to make such commercial dealings with other powers as they saw fit.[27]

The United States Navy, to be sure, had once been interested in Magdalena Bay, having formerly secured permission from Mexico to keep a coaling vessel in its waters and to use the region for target prac-

---

[25] For a general account, see Perkins, *Hands Off*, 271-74.

[26] Taft Papers, Presidential Series 2 (Letterpress volumes), Taft to H. Wilson, 5 April 1912, a summary of the Lodge memos.

[27] Knox Papers, Knox to Taft, 28 April 1914. Taft himself commented that Lodge "started in on Magdalena Bay, having been fooled by a lawyer who was hunting a defunct client." Pringle, *Taft*, II, 714.

tice. But early in 1911 Mexican authorities notified Washington that the permission had expired and that Mexico did not wish to renew it for another three-year term. The Navy, however, did not seek renewal. It simply informed the State Department that the Navy had not taken advantage of its permission to use Magdalena Bay for some years. According to the naval experts various technical developments in gunnery practices and in the refueling of warships now made it unnecessary to make use of the bay.[28]

This occurred some months before rumors of a Japanese interest in Magdalena Bay got into West Coast newspapers and before Lodge had started to express his concerns. Once the issue had arisen, however, it was handled almost exclusively at the level of White House and Department of State—by correspondence between the promoters on the one hand and Taft and Knox on the other, by formal and informal communications with the Japanese Foreign Office. While the State Department discounted the rumors that members of the Japanese government had any direct interest in the proposed purchase, it was just as strongly opposed as Lodge to the sale of land in Lower California that might lead to the establishment of any Japanese community. It made its hostility to the project abundantly clear to the American promoters; it also got the Japanese government to "volunteer" statements denying any official interest or involvement in the project.[29]

The United States Navy played only a bit part in the episode. Its opinion, as far as can be determined, was not solicited, nor did its views, if any, become a matter of record. The Army and Navy attachés in Tokyo did assist Ambassador Charles P. Bryan in an effort to determine if there was any substance to the stories that, despite official denials, members of the Imperial government were involved. But neither they nor the ambassador could turn up any information, while Ambassador Bryan suggested that the American promoters were simply trying to inflate the value of their holdings in Magdalena Bay by circulating rumors that the Japanese government was interested in the scheme.[30] That Bryan's suspicion was at least a possibility is suggested by an incident which occurred in the fall of 1911 when the promoters adopted a tactic which surely smells of blackmail. Their spokesman, after loudly professing his patriotic devotion, "confessed" that the owners of the land really wanted to sell their Mexican holdings to Americans rather than Japanese. But, he averred, they were being pressured

28 SDDF, File 811.34512/58, Meyer to Knox, 14 January 1911.

29 SDDF, File 894.2012/10, Knox to Allen (the promoter of project), 14 August 1911; /13 Taft to Knox, 5 August 1911; /44, Memorandum of State Department conversations with Japanese minister, 5 April 1912; and /36B, H. Wilson to Taft, 12 April 1912.

30 SDDF, File 894.2012/39, Bryan to Knox, 4 April 1912.

by the Japanese syndicate to sell at the earliest possible date and needed to know if there was any chance that their land could be sold to Americans. Furthermore, the spokesman added, J. P. Morgan had indicated a willingness to advance a million dollars to help the cause of an American purchase, but Morgan needed further encouragement. The Secretary of the Navy had promised to write Morgan a letter indicating the Navy's interest in Magdalena Bay. What he now sought, said the spokesman, was a similar letter to Morgan from the Department of State. This gambit, needless to say, failed. The State Department, after professing that this was an issue of naval strategy which the diplomats were not competent to judge, then took the offensive; it pointed to all the political and international difficulties that would arise if the Secretary of the Navy actually wrote such a letter and why it would be inadvisable. The point was made—and no more was heard on that score.[31]

Though the Navy was not fully engaged in the Magdalena Bay episode it did continue to debate and discuss the familiar issues of where to concentrate the fleet and what to do about the ill-fated Philippine naval station. These were matters which lasted on into the Taft era. But since both have already been treated in considerable detail and since they did not bear as directly upon foreign affairs in the Taft years as they had during the Roosevelt administration, they can be discussed in more abbreviated fashion.

As we have previously noted, a Navy Department order of February 1908 had cancelled future development of Subig Bay and had pointed to Manila Bay as the only area in the Philippines that the Army could make secure.[32] The General Board, however, was unwilling to accept this as the final, irrevocable decision. Refreshed, it returned to the fray in the spring of 1909 and tried to secure a reversal of the order. Even when the Board submitted plans and estimates for a naval station at Cavite on Manila Bay, it still contended that "this in no way changes its opinion that Olongapo is the desirable location for this base and station."[33]

In building its case in 1909 for a return to Subig, the General Board put forth a host of reasons and rationalizations. The navalists hit hard upon the argument that the cost of building any naval station at Manila would be prohibitive. Then, they maintained that, in the last analysis, the Army could guarantee only the safety of Corregidor and not the entire Manila area. If this were true, they argued, why prefer

---

[31] SDDF, File 894.2012/18, Latin American Affairs memorandum of conversation between Wilbur Doyle and Allen, 4 October 1911.

[32] See pages 240-41.

[33] GB, Proceedings, 21 June 1909.

Manila to Subig since neither could be rendered genuinely secure? "It is not a question between Olongapo and Cavite," their argument ran, "since the Army is not willing to guarantee the land defenses of either. It is a question of having a Naval Station with docking facilities at Olongapo or having none at all."[34]

But the General Board relied most heavily upon the presumed "lessons" of the world cruise, the prospect that the United States would soon be able to maintain a separate fleet at Pearl Harbor, and the operating advantages which would accrue when the Panama Canal was opened. From these it drew several arguments: notably, that the time necessary to send adequate naval reinforcements to the Philippines could and would be drastically shortened and that, in such circumstances, the prospect of a devastating Japanese attack would be lessened. The admirals drew a sharp distinction between the "tactical" and "strategic" defense of the Philippines; the former depended entirely upon the actual forces available at a given location, while the latter "may be effective without the presence of a gun or a man at the threatened point." The thrust of this argument was that if the United States had a strong battle fleet anywhere in the Pacific—whether based in the Philippines, at Pearl Harbor, or even on the Pacific coast of the United States—its "strategic defense" against the invasion of the Philippines would probably be sufficient to obviate the danger of such an attempt. The sum of this equation was, of course, that Subig Bay was still the preferable site, all the more so since, according to the admirals, they no longer needed as "extensive" a facility as they had once desired. In point of fact all the General Board now wanted was permission to build a relatively small docking and repair station at Olongapo. And, as a concession to the Army, it was willing to concede that, at the first sign of international danger, the floating drydock at Subig should be towed into safer waters behind the guns of Corregidor.[35]

But the Navy was now dealing with William Howard Taft, the one-time Secretary of War who had previously been converted by Wood and the General Staff to the anti-Subig cause. Hence the President's first reaction to the Navy's request to reopen the issue was to tell his Secretary of the Navy, "I have read the report of the General Board on Olongapo, but it does not convince me that you ought not to make an arrangement now for the establishment of a naval station at Cavite. I think that is what ought to be done."[36] General Wood, ever on the alert, sought out the President to reaffirm his and the Army's opposi-

---

[34] GB, Letters, VI, Dewey to Meyer, 27 May 1909.

[35] GB, File 405, Taft to Meyer, 7 June 1909, with second endorsement by Dewey, 21 June 1909.

[36] GB, File 405, Taft to Meyer, 7 June 1909.

tion. "The other day I was called to Washington to dine with the President, and discuss the question of Subig Bay and Manila," he confided to a friend, "and I think that the navy yard and naval base will land on the beach in front of Manila."[37]

Nevertheless Taft did direct one more Joint Board study. With it another round in the familiar debate opened. W. Cameron Forbes, governor of the Philippines, was consulted and made clear his preference for a naval base at Corregidor. Thus, in short order Taft, like Roosevelt before him, found himself confronted with conflicting advice. Also, like T.R., he was anxious to reach a final settlement of the troublesome issue. When Forbes raised the Corregidor question, Taft wrote almost plaintively that the recommendation was of sufficient importance to examine seriously the problem of whether or not there was sufficient space for a naval station at Corregidor. "I should think it doubtful," he wrote. "We must hurry up this decision and must have a statement authoritative as to the cost and wisdom of the various proposed sites. I am not stiff in the matter of having the thing at Manila, but you might talk the matter over with Wood and see what he thinks of the new suggestion."[38]

Final agreement, wondrous to state, was reached by the Joint Board in November 1909. Moreover, the Navy got what it had been seeking: permission to develop Olongapo on a restricted basis as a docking and repair station, with the understanding that the floating drydock would be removed to Manila if war threatened. The Army, as its part of the bargain, was specifically relieved of any responsibility for the defense of Subig.[39] Leonard Wood, needless to say, was displeased. In an attempt to mollify him, General Bell tried to explain what happened in the Joint Board: "The Army members were not altogether satisfied, for the reason that they were a unit in preferring that the naval station be established on the island of Corregidor. But the result of the deliberations of the Joint Board represents the most advantageous compromise that could possibly be arrived at as a unanimous verdict."[40]

Although the Army staff was not satisfied, the compromise of November 1909 proved to be definitive. This is not to say, however, that the voices of the Army dissenters were thereafter stilled. Time and time again Wood growled about the naval logic based upon the so-called "lessons" of the world cruise. "In view of the experience gained

[37] Wood Papers, Wood to Major J. K. Thompson, 24 July 1909.

[38] Taft Papers, Taft to Meyer, 16 September 1909, enclosing correspondence with Forbes. Also, JB, File 305, Taft to Meyer, 16 September 1909, a copy of the same letter.

[39] JB, Minutes, 5 November 1909, and File 305, Meyer to Dewey, 15 November 1909. GB, Letters, VI, Dewey to Meyer, 24 November 1909.

[40] Wood Papers, Bell to Wood, 16 December 1909.

on the recent trip around the world," he sniffed, "they think they will not want a naval base but can keep their ships in repair while in the fleet. No one but a fool would be deceived. The trip around the world was made under ideal conditions; it was nothing more than a leisurely yachting trip."[41] Once he became Chief of Staff, Wood remained the angry watchdog, always barking at the Navy for spending excessive sums on Olongapo and, according to him, trying surreptitiously to build it up as a major naval station. Typical was a protest of Wood in 1912 that the General Board was maintaining its "shifty attitude" about Subig and violating its agreement to spend no more than $300,000 annually on the site.[42] What particularly angered Wood and the General Staff was the decision of the Navy to close down the facilities which it had previously maintained at Cavite and transfer these to Olongapo. Hence in 1911 the Army General Staff again prepared for action and persuaded Secretary Dickinson to take its case to the President. In 1911 it was the Army that was now asking that the issue be re-examined, that the case for Manila and Corregidor be re-opened, and, above all, that the Navy be ordered to cease and desist further development of Subig.[43] Once again the two service secretaries presented their briefs to Taft. But this time Taft sided decisively with naval opinion, accepting the Navy's counter argument that the General Board was doing no more than "building at Olongapo a small docking and repair station which is too small to encourage an enemy to any great effort and which will be abandoned at the outbreak of war." Taft refused to put the issue once more before the Joint Board:

> I do not think it is at all the same question which was presented as to whether a great naval station should be established at Olongapo or established at Pearl Harbor; nor is it the same question as to whether the real defense of the Islands should be made at Corregidor Island near Manila or at Olongapo. It is only the question of the establishment of a naval repair station which could be abandoned in time of war, if necessary. . . .[44]

The Army lost this battle and with it, the war. Wood and his allies might argue that Secretary Dickinson had presented their case imperfectly; they could even find some members of the General Board who agreed with them (but who would do nothing since Admiral Dewey

[41] Wood Papers, Wood to General Arthur Murray, 9 November 1909.

[42] Wood Papers, Diary, 12 February 1912.

[43] Taft Papers, Presidential Series 2, Meyer to Taft, 1 April 1911, enclosing Dickinson to Meyer, 27 March 1911.

[44] Taft Papers, Taft to Dickinson, 3 April 1911.

remained the adamant defender of Subig); but they could not get their arguments before the Joint Board. The only consolation, if any, which remained to the General Staff was to be able to point to the discomfiture of naval authorities in times of tension with Japan—for example, in May 1913—and claim that the problem of Philippine defense would be far less difficult if the Navy had accepted its advice.[45] The Army of course did not change its mind. In the archives there is a note of 1914 from General Wotherspoon to Admiral Knapp about the problem of defending the Philippines; it reads, not very surprisingly, "we want to ask what you think about bringing up this question again. I am with General Wood very seriously impressed with the gravity of the situation out there, and something more than this continual exchange of correspondence . . . should be done." Either, suggested Wotherspoon, the present "upbuilding" of Olongapo should cease or, if continued, should be "under proper authority as the result of agreement between the two services."[46]

There was also continuing discussion about the creation of a fleet of battleships in the Pacific. Even before the Taft administration came into office, the General Board, as we have seen, had been moving in that direction. Its advice in the spring of 1908 had been that the Atlantic concentration should be maintained until Congress had authorized a navy large enough to support separate battleship fleets in each ocean.[47] But clearly it thought that that day was now coming. And by February of 1909, only a few weeks before Taft took office, the General Board decided that the long awaited time had finally arrived. The number of battleships completed, or virtually completed, now stood at thirty-one, whereas the "magic number" that would permit division of the fleet into separate units had always been calculated at thirty.[48]

In making these recommendations the General Board called attention, as before, to the defense of Subig Bay. But it was with a different twist. In previous years naval strategists had asked for an impregnable naval base in the Philippines because the main fleet would be concentrated far away in the Atlantic. But, as we have just seen, at the time Taft came to the Presidency the General Board was reopening its campaign for Olongapo, claiming that the Navy needed only a limited docking and repair station at Subig and that its defense would be best secured by "strategic" rather than "tactical" measures. Thus an important argument in behalf of the naval campaign for Subig was that the

---

[45] Wood Papers, Diary, 15 May 1913.
[46] GS, File 2041, Wotherspoon to Knapp, 24 April 1914.
[47] See page 258.
[48] GB, Proceedings, 20 February 1909.

naval station could be properly defended if a Pacific fleet was established. As the General Board put it, "a Pacific battle fleet would [provide] strategic protection . . . to the naval station at Olongapo." In fact, the strategists claimed, an American fleet at any point in the Pacific would deter the Japanese since "a fleet anywhere in the Pacific would render such an attempt too dangerous to be considered."[49]

Nevertheless the Navy did not achieve its goal of a Pacific battle fleet. Whenever the time for making decisions arrived, it was always concluded that the Atlantic concentration had to be continued. The number of battleships in being might permit a separate Pacific fleet. But the continuing lack of naval facilities in the Pacific still posed genuine operating and maintenance problems; equally important, higher costs in the Pacific made the establishment of a fleet of battleships in that ocean appear economically impossible. Late in 1910 the General Board again re-examined the whole question of concentration and, despite its earlier recommendation, reaffirmed the standing policy of locating the battle fleet in the Atlantic.[50] Its own studies showed, for example, that a Pacific fleet of seventeen battleships and eight armored cruisers would raise naval costs by nearly four million dollars a year. Coal cost three dollars a ton in the Atlantic but had to be figured at eight dollars per ton in the Pacific—with the estimate running to as much as eleven dollars if it had to be transported in American-owned vessels.[51]

Moreover, when the time for decision arrived, the General Board, despite the pull to the Pacific, continued to see valid reasons for maintaining the entire American fleet in the Atlantic. Its decision of 1910 had both a political and military underpinning and was in harmony with its outlook earlier in the century. The admirals admitted that there was no nation with which war was probable, but they regarded Germany and Japan as the two countries "which approximate this state most closely." Then, they continued, while "it is impossible to say that either is the more probable antagonist, . . . it is sure that Germany would be the more formidable." The strength and power of the German fleet was such that, in the event of war with that country, the United States would have to be prepared to act with the utmost speed and, if at all possible, secure the initial advantage. "But in case of war with Japan," the General Board went on, "while it would probably be impossible to prevent Japan from seizing Luzon, and Guam, and perhaps raiding Pearl Harbor, Japan could not retain Luzon or Guam for

---

[49] GB, Letters, v, Dewey to Newberry, 24 February 1909.
[50] GB, Letters, vii, Dewey to Meyer, 10 November 1910.
[51] Nav Rec Confid Ltrs, Dewey to Meyer, 17 November 1910.

the reason that we could, eventually, send a fleet to the Japanese coast that would overwhelm the Japanese fleet, isolate Japan from the world, and bring her to terms."[52] Thus the Atlantic retained the priority it had enjoyed since the turn of the century. And the statement itself, it might be added, was a remarkable foreshadowing of the "Europe-first" strategy that the American military services would endorse a generation later on the eve of World War II.

Between 1909 and 1913 the "China policy" of the Taft administration revolved around political and, especially, financial concerns. The prospect of a serious military involvement arose only once in the fall and winter of 1911-1912 when the Manchu dynasty was toppled by revolution. This is not to say, however, that the Taft administration did not maintain the same kind of naval watch in Chinese waters that its predecessors had formalized or that it was not fully prepared to use the Navy to guard American lives and property in China. Typical as well as prompt was the reply of Huntington Wilson in September 1911 when the State Department was warned that American missionary interests were threatened by rioting: "You will of course request our Admiral to send gunboats where they will afford the greatest security to Americans."[53]

American diplomats in China were, as in previous years, always conscious of the potential for what they euphemistically called "trouble." A typical report from the American legation at Peking in the spring of 1910 began with the observation that there were no signs of immediate danger or of any growth in anti-foreign sentiments; but it closed with the standard, generalized warning, "China is undoubtedly passing through a serious domestic crisis and the situation contains many elements of danger. It is easily seen how an anti-dynastic movement or trouble of purely domestic origin may be deflected into an anti-foreign crusade."[54] There were moments also when American diplomats in China took the threat seriously. Later on in the spring of 1910 Minister William J. Calhoun became convinced that disorders threatened in many Chinese cities and that there were signs pointing to an outbreak as serious as that of the Boxer uprising. He suggested to Washington that the warships of all the nations with interests in China ought to be distributed at different ports on the Chinese coast so that they could "provide a far greater range of protection than would be obtainable by the concentration of forces. . . ." Then, when Admiral Hubbard, the American naval commander in the Far East, refused to participate in

---

[52] GB, Letters, VII, Dewey to Meyer, 10 November 1910.
[53] SDDF, File 893.00/541, H. Wilson to Calhoun, 7 September 1911.
[54] SDDF, File 893.00/369, Frank F. Fletcher to Knox, 5 March 1910.

such a scheme, Calhoun strongly complained to the Department of State.[55] His complaint about naval independence produced no results, but the administration was moved by his report. In short order the Navy was instructed to send the *Buffalo* to Manila so that there would be available in the Far East a vessel capable of transporting upwards of 900 soldiers and marines to the Chinese danger scene. The matter was thought of sufficient importance that Taft himself made the necessary arrangements with the War Department, while the Navy Department was placed under the strictest of orders to preserve complete secrecy about the purpose of the *Buffalo*'s visit to the Philippines.[56]

The Taft administration, in short, remained on the *qui vive* and acted as previous administrations had acted. But the flurry in the spring and early summer of 1910 was short-lived, and, in general, the State Department did not operate on the assumption that China was on the abyss of revolution. In the summer of 1910, Rear Admiral Hubbard sent the Navy Department a long report in which he, like Calhoun a few months previously, outlined his growing fears of revolution in the not distant future. As Hubbard saw the situation in China, it would be "conservative, I think, to say that all the elements needed to produce such an occurrence are now existing, excepting only organization and a leader." What the admiral sought was a guideline for his conduct if and when the expected revolution should occur. Would the United States, he asked, follow its "traditional policy of non-interference," or "would it be expected that we would join with other foreign powers in some form of interference which is commonly accepted out here these powers would probably exercise?" Hubbard wanted a license to act. While he recognized that American interests in China were still small, he was personally convinced that the United States government had no intention of abandoning China to the other powers. "That being so," he concluded, "it would seem that we should be getting into readiness to assert, if necessary, whatever claims we may think our due."[57] The Navy Department bucked his message to the Department of State, adding that the admiral was considered to be "a careful and competent observer, and the Navy Department places great confidence in his judgment."[58] Although this was but a few months after the American legation in Peking had expressed similar fears, Assistant Secretary Huntington Wilson chose to minimize the admiral's findings. The Department of State, he replied, did not antici-

[55] SDDF, File 893.00/411, Calhoun to Knox, 4 June 1910, enclosing copies of his correspondence with Hubbard.

[56] Nav Rec Confid Ltrs, Meyer to Commander-in-Chief Asiatic Fleet, 9 July 1910.

[57] Nav Rec Confid Ltrs, Hubbard to Meyer, 26 July 1910.

[58] Nav Rec Confid Ltrs, Winthrop to Knox, 2 September 1910. A complete file of this correspondence is also in SDDF, File 893.00 beginning with /430.

pate any serious uprisings in China in the near future. Revolutionary elements did exist, but they had been present for at least two decades; moreover, Wilson added, the jealousies among the various revolutionaries and their chronic inability to cooperate with one another had made it relatively easy to suppress outbreaks. "We have no information to make us believe," Wilson concluded, "that this condition has changed."[59]

But within a year conditions did change. From the very beginning of the revolution against the Manchu dynasty the Department of State was seriously concerned. In mid-October 1911, when the movement was then but a few weeks old, Philander Knox was already informing Taft that the "rebellion in China is most serious since the Taiping revolution." Although he conceded that foreign interests had been respected and that the regime might possibly survive, the Secretary of State concluded that "as this is anti-dynastic in origin, it is anyone's guess how long it will remain suppressed."[60] The extent of his alarm was indicated by a note which he sent Taft before the month was out:

I am informed by Admiral Wainwright that the Pacific Fleet of 5 armored cruisers has planned a cruise to Hawaii for next month and the Admiral inquired whether it is desired that they be prepared to proceed to China, if necessary. It is my opinion that, although the present situation looks by no means desperate, no one can tell what the future developments may be and that we may be considered remiss in our duty if we did not at least prepare to render our nationals in China every assistance in our power in case of need and that, therefore, the squadron should by all means so arrange their preparations that they might proceed to China later if ever the situation seems to call for it.[61]

Though the President was offered several days to consider this proposition, Knox had his answer within twenty-four hours. Taft immediately informed his Secretary of State that he approved his suggestion and had instructed Navy Secretary Meyer to make his plans accordingly.[62]

The events which followed have previously been discussed in other sections of this book. We have observed, for example, that Admiral Murdock was more inclined than Minister Calhoun to show sympathy for and understanding of the Chinese revolutionary movement led by Sun-Yat-Sen. We have also considered some of the administrative dif-

59 SDDF, File 893.00/432, H. Wilson to Meyer, 15 September 1910.
60 SDDF, File 893.00/565A, Knox to Taft, 13 October 1911.
61 SDDF, File 893.00/610A, Knox to Taft, 27 October 1911.
62 SDDF, File 893.00/611, Taft to Knox, 28 October 1911.

ficulties that the Army confronted when it was asked to prepare plans for possible operations in China.[63] What remains to be discussed, then, is the readiness of the Taft administration to become involved militarily in the Chinese revolution.

In October 1911 the State Department was, in fact, more concerned about Chinese affairs than the European foreign offices. In mid-October the Far Eastern Division advised Knox that the United States should concentrate naval strength in Chinese waters "meanwhile making confidential inquiries of our War Department as to what land forces would be available in case of necessity." In addition, it recommended that American citizens in China should be advised to "concentrate in such open ports as are accessible to foreign men of war." Knox's Far Eastern advisers, however, cautioned that the United States should be careful not to assume the initiative and should attempt to pursue a cooperative policy with the other powers, especially Great Britain.[64] But when Knox, pursuing the recommendations of this memorandum, made inquiries in Europe and Japan, he found that none of the foreign offices—including even the Japanese—as yet shared his concern. The British doubted if the danger warranted the expense and inconvenience of concentrating foreign residents in the Chinese ports, while the Japanese were still dubious about the prospect of intervening, even if asked to do so by Britain.[65] Nor did any of the foreign offices believe, as Knox had asked, that further measures might be necessary. Knox soon retreated. When "sensational" reports of a possible American intervention began to appear in the press, the Secretary denied them. He then went on to say that he had merely exchanged views with the other powers and had received reassuring notes which indicated that no further action in China seemed necessary at this moment.[66]

By November, however, all observers of the Chinese scene had decided that, from their point of view, the situation was becoming critical. Knox was no longer in advance of European opinion. Nor was it a case of considering intervention simply to protect foreign lives and property. The Japanese, for example, had begun to talk about an intervention on the scale of that of 1900 to protect the railroad from Peking to the sea, and the British soon inquired if the United States would be willing to participate in a joint effort to keep the railroad open. Amer-

[63] See page 25.

[64] Knox Papers, Correspondence, II, Memorandum of Far Eastern Affairs Division, 14 October 1911.

[65] SDDF, File 893.00/638, Knox to American embassies in Tokyo, Paris, London, and Rome, 14 October 1911.

[66] Knox Papers, Correspondence, II, Knox to Taft, 17 October 1911. See also John G. Reid, *The Manchu Abdication and the Powers, 1908-1912* (Berkeley, 1935), 242 ff.

ican diplomatic personnel in Peking strongly endorsed this request.[67] So did Knox. His reply to the British inquiry was instantaneous: "This government will take part with others in protecting under the protocol of 1901 the railway to the sea provided such action becomes necessary. What forces will probably be needed and when? Soldiers may be preferable to marines except for special emergencies."[68]

It was at this point that the Army General Staff was brought into the picture and asked to prepare a report on its capabilities for operations in China. There were some Army officers who advocated an extensive intervention. Captain John Fair of the 4th Cavalry sent several urgent letters to the Army War College in which he argued for the immediate dispatch of five regiments from the Philippines plus the preparation in the United States of a relief expedition of at least division strength.[69] But the General Staff was much less sanguine. It concluded that the United States Army could do relatively little to influence the overall situation in China. The Philippine garrison comprised only 15,000 men, and according to the Staff, no more than 5,000 to 7,000 could be dispatched to China. The total number of available troops could be expanded to 25,000 to 30,000 men if soldiers in the United States were used. But such an effort, the Staff went on, would severely tax the resources of the miniscule United States Army and, in addition, would take months to complete—by which time the situation in China surely would have changed greatly. For these reasons the General Staff showed no enthusiasm for assuming a broad, general role in China as part of a larger international force guarding the interior railways. It therefore suggested that if the administration decided to employ the Army, it ought to limit its involvement to the protection of a particular treaty port, Shanghai being preferred.[70]

The recommendation of the General Staff was based on the underlying assumption that the Chinese revolution would spread, that disorganization and confusion would be nationwide, and that the intervention of the powers would be massive. Army planners, for example, assumed that it would take 100,000 foreign troops to guard the Peking railway and "assure a hearing to foreign governments in connection with international affairs." They also assumed large-scale military intervention by the Japanese and the Russians, acting at the behest of other powers. Thus when the possible American contribution of troops

[67] SDDF, File 893.00/638, /644, and /648, Williams (Peking) to Knox, and Schuyler (Tokyo) to Knox, 7-10 November 1911.

[68] SDDF, File 893.00/648, Knox to Williams, 10 November 1911.

[69] GS, War College Division, File 6790/22 (War in China), Capt. J. S. Fair to President, War College, November 1911.

[70] GS, File 6790/15, Report of General Wotherspoon, 14 November 1911, copy furnished to State.

was measured against this formidable array, it appeared both negligible and incapable of affecting the political outcome. The Army Staff therefore was driven by its own logic to suggest that the United States should restrict its military endeavor to the occupation of a single city and to hope that such a limited operation would put the United States in a stronger position "to have her demands considered" at the time of ultimate settlement.

The General Staff's estimate was given to the Department of State and eventually sent to Taft for his examination. There is no direct evidence of its effect upon policymaking. The issue of how many troops to furnish for possible operations in China was complex. It was affected not merely by Staff estimates but by many and varied developments, ranging from the progress of the Chinese revolution to the varying policies of the European powers with interests in China. It seems certain that Knox never envisioned an intervention on the scale suggested by the Army planners. Also the Secretary of State wished to pursue policies in China in cooperation with the other powers, had no desire to have the United States assume the initiative, and on occasion even showed some awareness of the need for "safeguarding . . . Chinese sensibilities."[71]

Nevertheless, Knox was always prepared to act and to pledge American military support. When he was informed in late November of the evolving plans in Peking to protect the railway, he immediately advised Minister Calhoun that the United States was prepared to send a full regiment of troops, plus supporting forces, to a total of 2,500 men.[72] But again he was out in front of opinion in Peking. The European representatives in the Chinese capital were still drafting their plans and, at least for the moment, were asking their respective governments to do no more than bring their legation guards up to the maximum strength authorized by the protocols of 1901. Thus, Calhoun informed Knox that the preliminary plan to guard the railway called for no more than 500 American soldiers. In these circumstances, he did not recommend the dispatch of as sizable a force as the Secretary had suggested.[73] Knox, however, was not to be entirely denied. To make his point and underscore American readiness to participate he instructed Calhoun to inform his diplomatic colleagues that the United States stood ready, "on short notice when and as the need actually arises," to furnish from 500 to 2,500 troops to uphold its obligations under the Boxer protocol.[74]

[71] SDDF, File 893.00/679, Knox to Calhoun, 23 November 1911.
[72] SDDF, File 893.00/701, Knox to Calhoun, 28 November 1911.
[73] SDDF, File 893.00/699, Calhoun to Knox, 27 November 1911.
[74] SDDF, File 893.00/701, Knox to Calhoun, 28 November 1911.

There was considerable discussion in the next few weeks about the number of troops that should be sent, but there is no need to examine the details of the various diplomatic interchanges. Ultimately the figure of 500 was established; then, in early January 1912, when the European and American representatives in Peking decided that the time to send the troops had finally arrived, this was the actual number of soldiers that the United States furnished for the proposed railway guard.[75] Yet Knox was always anxious to indicate his willingness to provide more. Even when he issued instructions for the dispatch of the 500 soldiers, the Secretary of State asked Calhoun to make certain that the Chinese government knew that the United States had been prepared to send a larger force but had decided against such action only after it had been informed that the situation on the Peking railway was less acute than had been feared.[76] Similarly, he told the War Department that he wished only to send a battalion but was prepared to dispatch a regiment.[77] (On the other hand, when responding to Senate inquiries about the reason for assigning troops to China, Knox concentrated upon the legal power of the President to use troops to protect American lives and property in foreign countries and failed to mention the larger contingents he had been prepared to use.[78])

There was a truce between the Chinese government and revolutionaries in December 1911; early in 1912 the Emperor abdicated, and the Chinese Republic was proclaimed under the leadership of Yuan Shih-k'ai. This did not, of course, put an end to rioting and disorders; nonetheless this rapid sequence of events meant that there was never an opportunity—or excuse—for a foreign intervention on the scale of the Boxer enterprise. Thus, too, the dispatch of the 500 American soldiers was anticlimactic and of no great consequence. Indeed, the entire episode revealed only the extent to which the American Secretary of State was prepared to consider the employment of troops—not merely for the traditional protection of American lives and property but to participate in an international scheme to keep open the railway from Peking to the sea.

With the passage of time after the accession of Yuan, the American concerns about possible intervention gradually lessened. There was, to be sure, another flare-up in March 1912 when the Navy thought it might have to land sailors.[79] There were also innumerable reports from naval officers in China that found their way into the files of the Department of State; and, as we have seen, those from Admiral Murdock

[75] SDDF, File 893.00/907, Stimson to Knox, 10 January 1912.
[76] SDDF, File 893.00/903, Knox to Calhoun, 9 January 1912.
[77] GS, File 6790/34, Knox to Wood, 18 January 1912.
[78] SDDF, File 893.00/989, Knox to Senator W. J. Stone, 30 January 1912.
[79] SDDF, File 893.00/1229, Calhoun to Knox, 29 March 1912.

often showed considerable sympathy for the aims of the Republic as well as a reluctance to put his sailors ashore.[80] But to quote these reports would be merely to add further illustrations of the long naval watch maintained over the affairs of China and of the role, which Admiral Murdock well fulfilled, of the Navy in furnishing an additional set of eyes and ears for the Department of State. In any event, by the end of 1912 and with the departure of the politically minded Murdock, naval reports had again become routine and were sent by a commander whose primary interest was in operational matters.

3. Central America: Nicaragua and Honduras, "Bigger Game than Bananas"

Though the diplomats often complained of naval behavior, they counted heavily upon the presence of the Navy in Caribbean waters as an instrument of policy. Dollar diplomacy, as practiced by Taft, Knox, and Huntington Wilson, had a strong military dimension and placed heavy reliance upon the "moral value"—and ultimate authority—of naval power, whether discreetly or overtly displayed. One of the most common phrases in Knox's correspondence with the Navy was the request "for the disposal of naval vessels as part of a political attitude." This policy, to re-emphasize a previous observation, was by no means original with the Taft administration; what was different was the frank, open emphasis upon its centrality.

What the State Department would have welcomed, and in fact was hopefully seeking, was a clear, legal right to intervene in the affairs of such countries as Nicaragua and Honduras. The "Root solutions"—inter-American peace pacts, the Central American Court of Justice—had not proved especially effective. Political unrest was still endemic. Many of the State Department's policy papers in the Knox era complained about the lack of a Platt amendment for Central America—that is to say, the absence of any treaty or convention which provided the United States with the legal justification that it had for intervention in Cuba, or, for that matter, in Panama. There were many complaints about the difficulty to finding acceptable grounds for American intervention. As Philander Knox himself wrote Taft early in 1909, all that the Department of State had been able to accomplish up to this moment

> had amounted to little more than the friendly assertions of a duty. There should be some conventional right to intervene in Central American affairs promptly, without waiting for outbreaks and with

[80] SDDF, File 893.00/1203 and /1224, Murdock to Meyer, 18 and 26 February 1912.

a view to averting rather than quelling disturbances. The United States and Mexico jointly or the United States alone should be in a position to apply an effective remedy at any time.[81]

Taft, writing to Knox about a conversation he had had on the same subject with the Mexican ambassador, was less diplomatic in his phraseology; he had told the Mexican diplomat that his administration would "not be content until we have secured some formal right to compel the peace between those Central American Governments and used the expression 'to have the right to knock their heads together until they should maintain peace between them.' "[82]

To find a legal means to knock Central American heads together was not easy. Neither the United States nor Mexico had actually signed the Treaty of Washington, the basic pact drawn up under Root's sponsorship. Various attempts to interest the Mexican government in co-sponsoring a new treaty which would, among other goals, guarantee the neutralization of Honduras proved abortive, since Mexico neither wished such a close partnership with the United States nor shared the same concern for the fate of Honduras.[83] Indeed, the one venture in Mexican-American cooperation in the spring of 1909 created only discord. During a period when war between Nicaragua and El Salvador appeared imminent, the Mexican government was persuaded to assign one of its gunboats to Central American duty and to instruct its commander to cooperate with American naval units. But, to the displeasure of the Department of State, Mexico almost immediately protested that the American naval commander had ordered her gunboat to take actions which might have involved the use of force and had given these orders at a time when vessels of the United States were lying idle. To the Mexicans this was "an effort to crowd Mexico into a hostile action against Nicaragua from which it would be difficult to back out."[84] An investigation, needless to say, was launched. Eventually the Department of State was satisfied that there had been a misunderstanding and that the American naval command had issued no such instructions. But the Mexicans were not convinced—and Mexican-American cooperation came to a quick and early end.[85]

81 Knox Papers, Knox to Taft, 28 September 1909.
82 Taft Papers, Letterpress volumes, Taft to Knox, 22 December 1909.
83 SDNF, Case 18920, Knox to de la Barra, 26 March 1909.
84 SDNF, Case 18920/3, Thompson to Knox, 15 April 1909. On the origins of the proposed venture in Mexican-American cooperation, see Knox Papers, Translation of conference with de la Barra, 14 March 1909.
85 SDDF, Case 18920/3, Knox to Mexican Embassy, 17 April 1909. Also Case 18432/126-27, Meyer to Knox, 8 May 1909, enclosing a copy of the report from Captain Moore of the *Colorado*. For the orders under which American naval units operated, see Nav Rec Messages Sent in Cipher, Winthrop to Moore, 21 April 1909.

Throughout 1909 officials of the State Department, as well as their legal advisers, continued to wrestle with the legalities of intervention but had great difficulty in finding acceptable grounds upon which to base their intended actions. Late in the spring of that year there was fear of yet another Zelaya-sponsored filibuster, this one directed against El Salvador. The *Colorado* was first given an uncomplicated order "to stop any expedition crossing the Gulf of Fonseca." But supplementary instructions, issued two weeks later, only clouded the issue. The commander was now allowed only "to use force if necessary but to avoid the use of force as far as practicable, particularly within the three-mile limit." A further cautionary note was added: "Should armed conflict become inevitable use every effort to compel opponents to take initiative."[86] It had not been easy to agree upon these orders. State Department officials had wished to base intervention on the argument that the United States had a moral right—indeed, a moral duty—to take action to guarantee observance of the Washington conventions. James Brown Scott, the Solicitor of the Department of State, was formally consulted but rendered a strongly dissenting opinion. Intervention by the *Colorado*, he pointed out, would be in violation of international law unless a request to act came from the government of Nicaragua, "a fundamental principle of international law being the recognition of the sovereignty and independence of each individual nation." The United States, Scott noted, was simply a third party to the dispute between Salvador and Nicaragua. It, therefore, had no legal case for intervention. At the most it had a moral right to call the attention of both countries to their international obligations and to insist that they fulfill them.[87]

For some time the Department of State toyed with the idea of preparing a memorandum to the Navy based upon Scott's advice. Finally, however, it was decided to send the supplementary orders just cited to the *Colorado*. For a second time Scott was consulted, this time for help in drafting a memorandum which would justify the possible use of force and legitimize the authorization given the *Colorado*.[88] The Solicitor was still troubled. He attempted a draft memorandum but found it "difficult as no recognized principle of international law exists on which to base actions outlined in telegrams, as such action rests upon a question of government policy rather than a legal right." An indication of his hesitation was the fact that he included a wide variety of possible reasons that might be cited: Salvador's request for assist-

[86] Nav Rec Messages Sent in Cipher, Winthrop to Moore, 24 April and 6 May 1909.
[87] SDNF, Case 18432/92, Scott to H. Wilson, 23 April 1909, and /91, Memorandum for the Solicitor, 19 April 1909.
[88] SDNF, Case 6369/189, H. Wilson to Scott, 26 April 1909.

ance, possible threats to American property at La Union, humanitarian considerations, the fact that a Central American war would be "an international nuisance detrimental to the interests of the United States," and even the contention that the United States, by intervening, would represent "the common conscience of humanity."[89] Four days later Scott suggested in another note that it might be well to cite the Monroe Doctrine as another justification for action, since the Doctrine had imposed "correlative duties upon the United States to see that the Central American states conduct themselves properly." To be sure, Scott admitted, this argument lost much of its force unless there was some danger of European intervention. However, since Salvador had recently had some difficulties with Italy, there was at least a chance to buttress the State Department's case—that is, if any one took this as a threat to the Doctrine.[90]

In the fall of 1909 there was another and similar exchange with the legal authorities. The United States was then contemplating seizure of the Nicaraguan port of Corinto as reprisal for the execution by Zelaya of two Americans captured while serving in the rebel army. Once again the Solicitor's office expressed grave reservations. The Assistant Solicitor insisted that the Department must generalize its case against Zelaya for offenses against human decency, otherwise the seizure of Corinto would appear no different to the world than the German seizure of the Chinese port of Kiaochow.[91] James Brown Scott once more pointed out that there was no legal right upon which the contemplated action could be based. He insisted that the American case would have to rest on grounds of policy—the policy of maintaining peace in Central America.[92] Though both men agreed with that policy, they had underscored the legal problems inherent in the Knox policies and the general difficulty of finding an acceptable legal justification for intervention.

Adding to the complexity of intervention in Central America was the familiar problem of communicating the wishes of the Department of State to its naval representatives. Captain Austin Knight, one of the officers involved in the fiasco with the Mexican gunboat, prefaced his defense with pointed remarks about the absence of specific instructions and the extent to which he had been kept in the political dark:

> I have received no word from the Department beyond the original order to proceed here and protect American interests and remain

[89] SDNF, Case 6369/189, Scott to H. Wilson, 27 April 1909.

[90] SDNF, Case 6369/189, Scott to Adee, 1 May 1909.

[91] SDNF, Case 6369/342, Memorandum of the Assistant Solicitor, 29 November 1909.

[92] SDNF, Case 6369/343 and /345, Memoranda by Solicitor Scott, undated but in response to /342.

on the coast until further orders. And I have no information from the chargé d'affaires beyond the dispatches already quoted, none of which give any clue to the cause of the strained relations to which they refer.[93]

Indeed, by midsummer of 1909 the civilian hierarchy of the Navy Department had come to feel slighted and so informed the State Department. Acting Secretary Beekman Winthrop told Knox that compliance with the policies of his department was difficult since the Navy had "received no explicit and definite expression of the views of the State Department concerning the attitude that should be observed by naval officers in Nicaraguan waters as part of a political attitude of the State Department towards the officials of that country." In the absence of such guidance, Winthrop added, the Navy could only act in accordance with the principles of international custom and the regulations of the United States Navy.[94]

Taft and Knox had inherited the problem of Zelaya and Nicaragua from their predecessors. All of the difficulties just mentioned—the problem of communication between civil and naval authorities, the inability to find legal justifications for intervention, the desire of the Department of State to assure complete naval obedience—were always present in the development of American policies towards Nicaragua after 1909. Therefore, a closer analysis of Nicaraguan-American relations during the four years of the Taft administration will indicate the general pattern of civil-military relations in that period.

Certainly Knox and his associates detested Zelaya even more fervently than those Americans who, during the Roosevelt years, had written their own vitriolic reports in the "incubation stages" of their fits of anger. Former Minister Gregory, brought back to Washington and put in charge of a newly-established training program for foreign service candidates, informed neophytes that "the sixteen years of his [Zelaya's] Presidency over Nicaragua have left no public records except the devastation of his unfortunate country." The sole method for dealing with him was by threatening severe reprisals if he stepped out of line; Zelaya and his regime, Gregory fondly recalled, "were frightened of Roosevelt. They knew he had been a soldier in Cuba and probably was a very strong man and might get on his horse some day and ride down there."[95] Huntington Wilson, the Assistant Secretary who specialized in Latin affairs, was particularly proud of the role of the United States in finally bringing down the Zelaya regime; he had been,

[93] SDNF, Case 18432/50-52, Capt. Austin M. Knight to Meyer, 16 March 1909.
[94] SDNF, Case 6369/154, Winthrop to Knox, 16 August 1909.
[95] SDNF, Case 6369/184, copy of talk given to new members of the Department by Gregory, 17 June 1909.

Wilson later recalled, "guilty of murder and rape, as well as robbing his countrymen by graft to the extent of making himself a multi-millionaire."[96] President Taft himself rejoiced before a Pittsburgh audience that his administration had refused "to tolerate and deal with such medieval despots as . . . Zelaya" and had "accomplished the elimination of Zelaya and Zelayism."[97]

From the ranks of the Navy there emerged equally intemperate prose. Commander William S. Benson, after a period of service on the Nicaraguan coast, described Zelaya as an absolute dictator who maintained himself in power by completely unscrupulous methods. He was so unpopular among his own people, Benson reported, that a revolution

> would be accepted with delight by a very large majority of the people, even by employees of the present government, they having already secured enough booty while in office to make them comfortable the rest of their lives under a stable government.[98]

Benson, along with his fellow officers, was thoroughly convinced that the only way to keep Zelaya in check was by keeping naval vessels in the vicinity. The General Board felt likewise and prepared a general plan for operations in Nicaragua, which began with the following political preface:

> The unstable government of that country and the natural jealousy of the Latin American countries towards the United States and towards each other make trouble a possibility at all times, and the large American interests in that locality and the position of the United States as the leading power in the Western Hemisphere make it necessary for this government to stand by to intervene with a view to the protection of its own interests and in the interest of humanity and fair play.[99]

At the very outset of their administration Taft and Knox embarked upon a policy of using the Navy to check Zelaya and keep Nicaraguan-sponsored revolts from spilling over into other Central American countries. One of the first orders given to the Navy in March 1909 informed the admirals that the State Department believed it would "be politically expedient to keep for the present two naval vessels in Nicaraguan

---

[96] Huntington Wilson Papers, Memorandum submitted to S. B. Bertron summarizing the accomplishments of the administration, January 1913.

[97] Huntington Wilson Papers, draft prepared for Taft speech in spring of 1910.

[98] SDNF, Case 6369/128-30, Benson to Meyer, 21 June 1909.

[99] GB, War Portfolio 1, Nicaragua, Reference 5-t, Nicaragua Plan, as approved by the General Board on 22 June 1910.

waters."[100] The reasons, Knox made clear, were political rather than military. During the next few months there were numerous, and often conflicting, reports about the imminence of a Nicaraguan venture in Central America. Nothing, however, happened—though all observers were convinced that it was the presence of American vessels which had proved "sufficient to prevent Nicaragua from making any hostile movement in the Pacific." When even the rumors of Nicaraguan activity began to die down, the American chargé in Salvador indicated that "it is generally believed that thanks to the energetic and prompt action of the United States, President Zelaya is now powerless to disturb the peace of Central America."[101]

It was also hinted in the Department of State that perhaps the time was becoming ripe for carrying out measures against Zelaya. "Mr. Root said a year ago," Adee noted, "that this state of things in Central America would logically and necessarily end by the intervention of the United States and Mexico, ostensibly to protect the neutrality of Honduras, but practically to clip Zelaya's wings."[102] But there was in fact no American action until, in November 1909, the long delayed, long-anticipated revolution against Zelaya broke out. Zelaya ultimately resigned in favor of one of his lieutenants, José Madriz, and fled the country in December. The United States maintained a technical neutrality but made no secret whatsoever of its sympathy for the revolutionary forces, led by one Juan Estrada. As Huntington Wilson later recorded, the State Department frankly favored "the party opposed to Zelaya and opposed any faction that would return to his uncivilized methods."[103] The execution of two Americans, Cannon and Groce, who were serving in the Estrada army when captured by government troops, provided the excuse for a final rupture of diplomatic relations with Zelaya and, as we have already noted, led to discussion of the possibility of seizing Corinto as reprisal. But the State Department was confident that, in the long run, the Estrada forces would triumph over both Zelaya and his successor, Madriz; it decided, at least for the moment, against forcible intervention.[104]

The Navy immediately drew an important role. At the outset of the insurrection a vessel was dispatched to Corinto because "the United

[100] SDNF, Case 18432/9, Knox to Meyer, 10 March 1909.

[101] SDNF, Case 18432/82, Frazier to Knox, 18 March 1909. Among the many documents in this file that relate to the situation in April and May of 1909, see, in particular, /112, Meyer to Knox, 29 April 1909 and /153, 14 May 1909, also from Meyer to Knox and transmitting a report from the commanding officer of the *Colorado*.

[102] SDNF, Case 18432/12, Adee memorandum of 11 March 1909.

[103] Wilson, *Memoirs*, 209.

[104] SDNF, Case 6369/355, a long memorandum by Huntington Wilson dated 26 November 1909.

States government wishes to make it apparent that it is watching carefully the progress of events."[105] Then, on the very day that diplomatic relations were broken, Rear Admiral William W. Kimball was appointed to head a special Nicaraguan Expeditionary Force, which included a force of some 1,000 marines, 700 from the Philadelphia Navy Yard and the remainder from the garrison in the Canal Zone. Kimball sailed on the 5th of December and was expected at Corinto by the middle of the month. His initial orders were far from explicit, for he was only instructed to be prepared to carry out assigned operations in the area of Nicaragua for a period of perhaps two months.[106] While the admiral was enroute to Corinto, the State Department wrestled with the question of definitive instructions. There was talk in Washington, even on the part of the President, about the "regrettable duty" of direct action against Zelaya. But Kimball was finally given instructions not to land any of his marines without specific authorization from Washington (although he was allowed to embark his force on two small islands in the Gulf of Corinto that belonged to Salvador). The Navy, taking no chances, instructed Kimball to prepare and submit plans for landings on both coasts of Nicaragua, for the maintenance of important coastal areas, and for an advance into the interior.[107]

Zelaya, however, resigned in favor of Madriz and fled Nicaragua. Kimball, after studying his orders, decided that the United States did not want Zelaya in its custody and therefore took no steps to impede his departure. This was essentially the admiral's own decision, but no one in the State Department raised any objections.[108] Soon, however, Admiral Kimball was at odds with the Washington policymakers and offering his own decided opinions about the proper course of action to follow in troubled Nicaragua. He began to send various reports, originating in his own naval command, which blamed much of the trouble in the country on the American-owned Bluefields Steamship

[105] Nav Rec Messages Sent in Cipher, Meyer to Commanding Officer of the *Vicksburg*, 18 November 1909.

[106] Nav Rec Confid Ltrs, Meyer to Kimball, 1 December 1909, and Knox Papers, Wainwright to Knox, 7 December 1909.

[107] Nav Rec Messages Sent in Cipher, Meyer to Kimball, 11 and 27 December 1909; Confid Ltrs, Meyer to Kimball, 15 December 1909; Taft Papers, Letterpress, Taft to Knox, 22 December 1909; Knox Papers, memorandum of discussion with Special Representative of Mexico, 15 December 1909.

[108] Both State and Navy archives contain an abundance of material on the Nicaraguan Expeditionary Force. See SDDF, File 817.00 (Nicaragua), which is complete but confusing since it contains many documents that were originally part of the 6369 "case" file used in the numerical filing system. For the Navy's role, there is a full documentary record in Nav Rec Subj File, WA-7, Nicaragua, Correspondence of the Nicaraguan Expeditionary Force. The most useful single document in both collections is Admiral Kimball's final report, dated 25 May 1910. On the flight of Zelaya, see WA-7, Correspondence, Kimball to Meyer, 23 December 1909.

Company, a concern which, according to Kimball's junior officers, enjoyed monopolistic privileges granted by Zelaya and supported him in all of his endeavors.[109] Then, towards the end of December, Kimball had an extended interview with Madriz, the new leader of the "government" forces, and was favorably impressed with his many and varied promises, which ranged from a pledge to hold free elections to an offer to find a recreational area for Kimball's sailors and marines.[110]

This burgeoning interest in Madriz soon brought Kimball into sharp conflict with the State Department, for both Knox and his Latin American Division firmly believed that "Estrada represents majority aspirations and the best elements of Nicaragua."[111] Its "official" neutrality was biased in favor of Estrada and founded on the growing assumption that the revolutionary forces were gaining control of the country, with the end of the Zelayists in sight. Soon, too, there was a sharp interchange between Kimball and the State Department. Estrada's representatives in Washington charged that the admiral was intervening in Nicaraguan affairs on behalf of Madriz by putting pressure upon Estrada to negotiate with Madriz and even claiming that Estrada's future relations with the United States depended upon his willingness to initiate peace negotiations.

Philander Knox, insisting that the State Department was strictly neutral and opposed to action on behalf of either faction, was openly critical of Kimball's conduct. "In these circumstances," he noted, "the Department of State has seen, with a certain amount of surprise, the above indication that Rear Admiral Kimball has felt justified in exerting diplomatic pressure which has not been requested by this department charged with the conduct of American foreign relations." He found Kimball guilty of "exceeding the object of his presence in Nicaraguan waters" and made pointed comments to the effect that the State Department had always assumed that the admiral would always "precisely reflect" its point of view. Knox did, however, soften the blow with a final comment that the Department of State found Kimball's dispatches both interesting and valuable.[112]

The Navy quickly got the hint. Kimball was immediately ordered to follow a policy of the strictest neutrality and, above all, to refrain from bringing diplomatic pressure to bear on either Nicaraguan faction. The admiral, needless to say, denied any intervention although some months later, in his final report, he readily conceded that he had un-

[109] Nav Rec Subj File, WA-7, Nicaragua Correspondence, Kimball to Meyer, 12 and 23 December 1909.
[110] Nav Rec Subj File, WA-7, Nicaragua Correspondence, Kimball to Meyer, 31 December 1909.
[111] Knox Papers, Memorandum of 15 December 1909, as cited.
[112] SDNF, Case 6369/656A, Knox to Meyer, 14 January 1910.

successfully tried to arrange an armistice between the factions. That effort, he contended, had failed solely because of what he termed the "bad faith" of the Estrada faction.[113]

Even sharper differences soon emerged between Admiral Kimball and the American consular agent, José de Olivares, who had remained at his post in Managua. Olivares steadily fed the State Department a diet of ecstatic reports about the progress of the insurrectionary forces under Estrada and Chamorro, insisted that Madriz would always fail to inspire public confidence, and maintained that all right-thinking Nicaraguans sided with the Estrada revolution.[114] Kimball disagreed completely. By mid-January 1910, in a series of dispatches, which without question were read in the State Department, he characterized the recent reports of Olivares as "totally false."[115] In Kimball's opinion, Madriz was sincere in proposing reform, while those who followed Estrada and Chamorro did so in the expectation that the insurrectionists would permit them to retain their ill-gotten gains and monopolies. He believed that most newspaper accounts appearing in American dailies

> appear to be colored by the politically active American interests in this country, the farming of the revenues, and the working of the monopolies authorized by Zelaya. . . . If Estrada wins and establishes a dictatorship, these interests will be maintained by him. . . . All interested American citizens and all true Zelayists are naturally strongly in favor of Estrada because he was once a Zelaya protégé and held the beef monopoly from him. . . . These people, plus one faction of the conservative party, may be able to raise enough money to corrupt the military chiefs for bringing about the downfall of Madriz, but I do not think this is probable.[116]

Kimball soon turned to arguments *ad hominem*. "Attention is called to the fact," he reported, "that the U. S. Consul at Managua [Olivares] is connected by marriage with an influential conservative family and that, therefore, he has great facilities for learning the conservative point of view." The Estrada faction, Kimball next charged, was desperate to obtain American intervention and contemplated staging an incident that would require a landing by the United States Marines. "The pro-American interventionist branch of the conservative party,

---

113 Kimball's report of 25 May 1910 is now located in the 817.00 file but was originally classified as /985 of Case 6369.

114 SDNF, Case 6369/683, Olivares to Department of State, 21 January 1910. See also his /742 and /744 of 8 and 10 February 1910.

115 SDNF, Case 6369/659, Winthrop to Knox, 15 January 1910, enclosing two recent reports from Kimball.

116 SDNF, Case 6369/985, Kimball report of 25 May 1910.

to which the American consul at Managua belongs . . . as is evidenced by his reports to the State Department, is quite capable of making the plot . . . but is lacking in the necessary courage." In another report Kimball maintained that Olivares was openly promising his assistance to those who would take up arms in behalf of Estrada.[117]

The Department of State was sorely tempted to reply with equal asperity to these intemperate reports. After reading Kimball's account of the plot to stage an incident, the chief of the Latin American Division scribbled a note to Huntington Wilson, "I think you will want to read this report of Kimball. It indicates that the Mexican Consul General at Managua is busy furnishing the admiral with some information. . . . I regret very much that Admiral Kimball should be so against the policy of neutrality between the two factions."[118] Wilson, in turn, informed the Secretary of the Navy that "the remarks of the Rear Admiral hardly seem to indicate that frame of mind which is conducive to the cordial cooperation which, to attain good results, is so necessary between the two branches of the government."[119] And the Navy was further asked to explain why other naval officers on Nicaragua's east coast also appeared to be intervening in behalf of Madriz.

But Kimball was not entirely discounted or discredited. The American chargé d'affaires in Panama accompanied Kimball's expedition and was fulsome in his praise for the admiral's intelligent and disinterested labors.[120] Moreover, with the passage of time, civilian officials in Washington began to suspect that, even if Kimball was not correct in his Nicaraguan estimates, Olivares was equally prejudiced and biased. In February of 1910, for example, Olivares began to fire off daily cables which charged that the Madriz faction threatened American lives and property and that he would soon have to request the landing of Kimball's marines. He also maintained that the situation in and around the town of Matagalpa was so serious that it was his duty to request that Admiral Kimball send a field hospital corps under suitable military escort to the region.[121] Kimball angrily denied the existence of such dangers. He first informed Olivares that he "had no apprehension of danger to Americans at Matagalpa if my advice is followed and proper neutrality maintained." He then sent off his own dispatches to Washington which argued that the reports of Olivares were "constructed to give false views as to the true political and military condi-

[117] SDNF, Case 6369/704, Kimball to Meyer, 28 January 1910 and /744, Kimball to Meyer, 10 February 1910.

[118] SDNF, Case 6369/762, Doyle to H. Wilson, 17 February 1910.

[119] SDNF, Case 6369/762, H. Wilson to Meyer, 19 February 1910.

[120] SDNF, Case 6369/686, Weitzel to Knox, 6 January 1910.

[121] SDNF, Case 6369/777, Olivares to Knox, 10 February 1910.

tions in the country."[122] When these conflicting reports were brought to the attention of Philander Knox, his wrath now fell not on the admiral but on the consul:

> Independently of the despatches of Admiral Kimball, who takes a more moderate and often dissenting view from your own, the Department has the impression that your reports are inclined to be exaggerated, due perhaps to excessive enthusiasm on your part. You are to reconsider your request to the admiral. Department considers it ill advised and will not authorize any such action unless fully persuaded of its necessity. . . . If you really believe ground for serious apprehension for safety of Americans, you may at your discretion visit personally that place and report by telegraph. If in your calm and deliberate judgment it is your duty to do this you will call upon the local *de facto* authorities for such guard. . . . Hereafter you need not cable daily unless you have important information and you will make every effort to be wise and conservative in your judgments.[123]

The aggrieved consul naturally defended his conduct at some length, the gist of his argument being that, since he was located in the Nicaraguan capital, he could see "the situation as it actually exists," while the admiral, from his station off Corinto, was isolated from the mainstream of Nicaraguan affairs.[124]

Estrada and Chamorro failed to capture Managua, and even Olivares admitted that the revolution was losing some of its impetus. Kimball, still unsuccessful in his varied ventures at peacemaking, suggested to Washington that, if given a free hand, he could

> take charge of the government at any time and straighten things up a bit preparatory to the coming of their regularly appointed administrative officers, with no show of force and just a few squadron officers to lend a hand. Though in theory Nicaraguans hate Americans, they actually have a child-like faith in our kindness, helpfulness, and innate fairness.[125]

His suggestion found no takers. What happened was simply that, with the waning of the revolution, Kimball's force was gradually depleted

[122] SDNF, Case 6369/745, Meyer to Knox, 10 February 1910, a copy of Kimball dispatch of 9 February. See also Nav Rec Subj File, Nicaraguan Correspondence, Kimball to Meyer, 1 February 1910.

[123] SDNF, Case 6369/744, Knox to Olivares, 11 February 1910.

[124] SDNF, Case 6369/751, Olivares to Knox, 12 February 1910.

[125] Nav Rec Subj File, WA-7, Nicaraguan Correspondence, Kimball to Meyer, 16 February 1910.

by the Navy Department, and in mid-March 1910 his marines were returned to Panama. Convinced that the revolutionary force was spent, the admiral urged recognition of the Madriz regime as the legal government.[126] But this was another of Kimball's recommendations that found no favor in the Department of State. When the British made a similar request at the same time, Knox informed London that he would be most gratified if Great Britain withheld recognition; he considered Madriz to be anti-American and excessively pro-Mexican, wanted more explicit promises from his regime, and, above all, regarded it as simply a continuation of the Zelayist party. As one official wrote in explanation of the American refusal to recognize Madriz, "Much as we would regret the wars and confusions that might ensue, it is clear that things must be worse in Central America before they are better."[127]

Meanwhile, the center of controversy shifted to Nicaragua's east coast where the Madriz forces, having surrounded Bluefields, threatened to shell it if the Estrada troops did not surrender the customs houses within twenty-four hours. Commander William W. Gilmer, the American officer on the spot, promptly informed both sides that they must not engage in any hostilities within the town, carry out any bombardments, or maintain any units larger than 100 men within Bluefields.[128] Gilmer's orders produced a not inconsiderable flurry. Madriz protested bitterly that, since Bluefields was now the main seat of the insurrection, the actions of Captain Gilmer were preventing him from destroying his enemy—at the minimum, he suggested, the United States ought to make Estrada get out of Bluefields so the two opposing sides could have their battle.[129] (Gilmer reported the bitterness of the Madriz forces, for "the Americans have checkmated them at every turn." His own departure, he added, would surely lead to the capture and destruction of Bluefields by Madriz.[130]) The Department of State and the Navy both made elaborate searches of their records to find precedents for Gilmer's action. The latter, at least, had difficulty; Admiral Wainwright ruefully reported to the State Department that there were no written records which either sustained or established such a precedent, though he personally remembered incidents in Santo Domingo when naval officers had warned revolutionary leaders not to

126 SDNF, Case 6369/843, Kimball to Meyer, 24 March 1910.

127 SDDF, File 817.00/907, draft of State Department memorandum on Nicaraguan policy, Dawson to H. Wilson, 18 April 1910 (after this date all documents in Case 6369 bear the 817.00 number).

128 SDDF, File 817.00/942, Moffatt to Knox, 17 May 1910.

129 SDDF, File 817.00/969, Luis F. Corea to Knox, 23 May 1910.

130 SDDF, File 817.00/943 and 957, Gilmer to Meyer, 18 and 19 May 1910.

open hostilities in an area where American lives might be endangered.[131] The Department of State, in turn, produced several lengthy defenses of Gilmer. These touched upon literally dozens of arguments but tried to minimize the extent of the American intervention (mostly "admonitions," Knox maintained) and contended that the "United States took only the customary step of prohibiting bombardment or fighting by either faction within the unfortified and ungarrisoned commercial city of Bluefields."[132] It was thought wise to send copies of this defense to all American legations in Latin America to try to counteract the Madriz charges.

The furor over Bluefields soon passed, if for no other reason than the obvious fact that neither faction in Nicaragua was sufficiently powerful to challenge the United States Navy, however disguised its interposition might be. Admiral Kimball, at least, got in the last word. His final report, which reached the Department of State late in the spring of 1910, was a pungent, opinionated document. His principal point was to charge that the continuation of the civil war in Nicaragua was a direct consequence of the bad faith of the Estrada faction and its unwillingness to make peace. As noted in the first chapter, he scored the American residents of Nicaragua for their shortsightedness and arrogance. Five months in Nicaragua had made him despair of getting accurate information and "disbelieving any and all information offered, official or otherwise." Angrily he asked the rhetorical question, "I have never been able to understand how the comparatively small commercial interests backing the revolution could control practically the whole American press and give such generally false views, even when the official reports of the American consuls, so partisan that they were never reliable, supported those views."[133]

His report went unheeded. The Department of State merely acknowledged its receipt and filed it without comment. Diplomatic recognition was refused. The Department of State continued to growl at Madriz and to send occasional warships to Nicaragua to impress him. Then, late in the summer of 1910, the Estrada-Chamorro forces unexpectedly emerged victorious and took control of the government. There was, needless to say, great joy in Washington. Once the new regime had come into power, the involvement of the Navy in Nicaraguan affairs again became minimal. Indeed, the reports which came from naval officers who stopped at Corinto were largely devoted to com-

---

[131] SDDF, File 817.00/1488, Wainwright to Charles Williams, Solicitor's Office, 31 May 1910.

[132] SDDF, File 817.00/186-87, J. Reuben Clark to Knox, 20 June 1910.

[133] SDNF, Case 6369/985, Kimball report of 25 May 1910.

ments upon the rare phenomenon of political tranquillity in that region.[134] It was to be another two years before the United States was again involved in a direct military intervention.

In the interim, and especially after the accession of the pro-American president, Adolfo Diaz, in 1911, Secretary Knox busily pursued various projects, notably the Knox-Castrillo convention, that were intended to stabilize Nicaraguan finances and provide the United States with a clear right of intervention. But the Knox-Castrillo convention encountered strong opposition, was long delayed in the Senate and finally rejected. During the period of Senate debate, the *Vicksburg* was in Nicaraguan waters, and its commander asked the chargé d'affaires at Managua, Franklin Gunther, if it would be advisable for his ship to remain at Corinto. Gunther replied that, although the convention had been approved by the Nicaraguan legislature, the present moment was critical in Nicaraguan affairs. Therefore, he advised,

> the mere presence of at least one American war vessel at Corinto has a strong moral effect and is of great assistance to the Government in its efforts to preserve complete tranquillity. Should some small, hysterical popular uprising suddenly grow to alarming proportions, the effect might be deplorable upon the resolutions of our Senate when it comes to consider in its next session the Knox-Castrillo convention.[135]

The State Department, in short, wanted several warships on the Nicaraguan coast so that when the Convention came before the Senate those gentlemen would have before them the image of a peaceful, orderly Nicaragua.

The sudden revolt in Nicaragua of August 1912 caught both Washington and Managua by surprise. President Diaz and his supporters, demoralized by the uprising, immediately sought and obtained from the Navy a landing force of over a hundred officers and men to protect threatened American property.[136] Early reports from both the naval command and the American minister, George T. Weitzel, were relatively optimistic about the chances of preserving order. Within another week, however, this mood vanished. Weitzel began to call for additional military assistance, especially for the presence of a landing force at Corinto. He identified the insurrection, led by Luis Mena, with the onetime followers of Zelaya and therefore as dangerous to the best interests of Nicaragua and the United States. His ominous con-

[134] SDDF, File 817.00/1470, Dawson to Knox, 17 November 1910, and Cooper to Meyer, 25 and 27 November 1910.

[135] Nav Rec, Area File 1911-1927, Central Pacific, Gunther to Commanding Officer of the *Yorktown*, 15 October 1911.

[136] SDDF, File 817.00/1825, Winthrop to Knox, 6 August 1912.

clusion was that "the Government of the United States will have to consider handling a very difficult and serious problem which may require a large force in Nicaragua, primarily to protect the lives and property of Americans and other foreigners and secondarily to reestablish some semblance of order."[137]

The naval command, however, responded far more slowly to the presumed dangers of the Mena-led revolt. Commander Terhune of the *Annapolis* felt that he could control matters within his area. "I have powerful influence here," he cabled the Secretary of the Navy. "*Annapolis* is very popular with government which would welcome forcible intervention on the part of the American government."[138] When Weitzel urged that all of his marines be sent to Managua, Terhune reserved his decision on the grounds that he could make no such move unless he received a written statement from the Nicaraguan government that it was unable to protect American lives and property.[139] However, as the revolt grew in intensity, Terhune did agree to sending the marines to the Nicaraguan capital, but he still would not endorse Weitzel's requests for even greater forces. "The American minister," he reported, "is very anxious for an American army of occupation of 2,000. Such a force may be necessary to suppress rebellion with force. I cannot recommend so many lives to be risked in dispute with which American Government is not interested vitally."[140]

Soon thereafter Major Smedley D. Butler and 350 marines were sent to Managua. But Weitzel, supported now by Butler, still felt that this was insufficient. As the revolution continued to grow and the Diaz troops began to suffer major defeats, he urgently demanded the assignment of a large military contingent to Nicaragua.[141] The Department of State, well aware of the differences between Terhune and Weitzel, sided with the latter and formally requested the Navy to supply additional sailors and marines. Soon there was a real flurry of activity in Washington; the upshot of many meetings between State and Navy officials was an agreement by the Navy to send sizable forces. The battleship *California* was ordered to Panama, at which point it was to take on board some 750 marines for possible service in Nicaragua.[142]

Within the State Department, however, there was considerable sen-

[137] SDDF, File 817.00/1841, Weitzel to Knox, 11 August 1912.

[138] SDDF, File 817.00/1848, Cone to Knox, 12 August 1912, forwarding Terhune cables of 10 and 11 August 1912.

[139] SDDF, File 817.00/1857, Meyer to Knox, 13 August 1912, forwarding Terhune cable of the 12th.

[140] SDDF, File 817.00/1864, Meyer to Knox, 15 August, forwarding Terhune cable.

[141] SDDF, File 817.00/1883, Weitzel to Knox, 21 August 1912.

[142] SDDF, File 817.00/1885, Doyle to Adee, a Latin American Affairs Division memorandum, 21 August 1912, and /1892A, H. Wilson to Weitzel.

timent that even these reinforcements would be inadequate. Huntington Wilson, who was running the Department during the summer absence of Knox, began to consider adding 1,200 infantry from the Army garrison in Panama. He discussed the Nicaraguan situation with President Taft, demanded sufficient troops to protect the Legation at Managua and preserve communications with the coast, and compared the situation to the Boxer uprising of 1900.[143] He maintained his pressure on Taft, for he was convinced that the administration's entire Nicaraguan policy was on the verge of total collapse. In late August Wilson wired Taft, who had gone to Massachusetts, that the "Zelaya liberals" (his term for the followers of Mena) hated the United States and that Army troops should be dispatched at once.[144] Taft was momentarily convinced and immediately notified the War Department that the 10th Infantry should be alerted to sail for Nicaragua within forty-eight hours, prepared to cope with a situation "analogous to the Boxer trouble in China."[145]

But in deciding to throw the 10th Infantry into the breach, no one had counted on the negative reaction of Taft's newly-appointed Secretary of War, Henry L. Stimson. He immediately responded that, in his judgment, the State Department had failed to consider the vastly different political implications of using the Army rather than the marines, especially the impact on world opinion. Stimson also observed that Nicaragua was further removed from and less vital to the United States than Mexico and that the Nicaraguan outbreak seemed less grave than the current revolution in Mexico—a clever reference to Taft's then well-known reluctance to permit any American intervention in Mexico despite a mounting number of border incidents.[146]

Stimson's logic had its effect. Taft decided to hold up his orders. Instead, he asked the Navy to give him precise figures on the number of marines that could be made available.[147] Then the picture changed abruptly. The naval command in Nicaragua had remained confident, even in the face of Weitzel's mounting pleas for additional force, that the Navy could control the situation. Apparently an optimistic report from the *Denver* reached Taft just when the President was having second thoughts about the employment of the Army and persuaded him

[143] SDDF, File 817.00/1919A, H. Wilson to Taft, 27 August 1912.
[144] SDDF, File 817.00/1919B, H. Wilson to Taft, 29 August 1912.
[145] SDDF, File 817.00/1904, Forster (Taft's Secretary) to H. Wilson, transmitting copy of Taft's telegram to his Secretary of War, Henry L. Stimson.
[146] Taft Papers, Presidential Series 3, Stimson to Taft, 29 August 1912. The incident is not mentioned in Henry Stimson and McGeorge Bundy, *On Active Service* (New York, 1947), but in 1931, as Secretary of State, Stimson refused to permit the use of American troops in later Nicaraguan troubles (181-82).
[147] SDDF, File 817.00/1907, Forster to H. Wilson, 28 August 1912; Taft Papers, Letterpress, Taft to Forster, 28 August 1912.

to revoke his orders for the 10th Infantry. In any event, as he explained the circumstances to Stimson:

I am very glad we were able to revoke the order. I made it on the recommendation of Wilson of the State Department because I feared very much a situation in which 4 or 500 of our marines might be surrounded by a lawless band of cutthroats and overwhelmed with numbers, and murdered in cold blood. I was determined to avoid the possibility of such a contingency, and it was not until I got word from the Commander of the *Denver* that this danger was not imminent that I was able to do what was very satisfactory to both you and to me, that is, to keep the army out of these disturbances in Central America.[148]

Once additional ships and sailors had been assigned to Nicaraguan duty, the Navy's confidence naturally increased even more. Admiral Southerland, who assumed the overall command, positively assured Washington that with the promised increment of 750 marines, "I can control the situation."[149] Weitzel, however, still argued for Army troops "on grounds of kindness and mercy to the Nicaraguans," while in the Department of State, Huntington Wilson remained skeptical.[150] When Southerland cabled that he needed no further reinforcements and that he only intended to use his marines to guard the rail line from Managua to the sea, Wilson called an immediate conference with naval authorities in Washington to express his doubts. With Knox still absent from Washington, he continued to press Taft for greater action and, in the process, proved himself more militaristic than the military. Complaining about the Navy's actions to the President, Wilson claimed that if Southerland did no more than drive the rebels off the rail line, the insurgents would still be free to avenge themselves upon Americans and other foreigners elsewhere in Nicaragua. He made it clear to Taft that he and his colleagues in the Department of State would not be content until all of the Mena forces "are sufficiently cowed to become impassive." Unless the rebels were eliminated, he argued, American prestige would suffer throughout all of Latin America, with a consequent increase in trouble in Mexico, Cuba, and Panama. If America proved reluctant to act in Nicaragua, then, according to Wilson, the authority of American words would be lessened everywhere: "We think if the United States did its duty promptly in Nicaragua, it would strengthen our hand and lighten the task not only in Nicaragua but in

---

148 Taft Papers, Letterpress, Taft to Stimson, 2 September 1912.

149 SDDF, File 817.00/1933, Twining to Knox, 31 August 1912, enclosing a copy of Southerland's dispatch of the 29th.

150 SDDF, File 817.00/1937, Weitzel to Knox, 4 September 1912.

all Central America and even have some moral effect in Mexico." Thus there should be extensive military preparations, "even if they should prove to have been out of proportion to the necessities."[151]

Taft could not be moved. Wilson had to accept a naval policy which seemed to him far less than the Nicaraguan situation demanded. Although the marines soon opened the rail line to Managua, they infuriated Wilson and his associates by announcing that they would permit neither the government forces of Diaz nor the revolutionaries of Mena to transport troops or munitions upon it.[152] Even more infuriating was Admiral Southerland's subsequent report that, by controlling the railroad, he had reduced the insurrection "to the status of an ordinary Central American revolution" and created a situation which "will compel both parties soon to open negotiations, at which time the American minister, with the moral support of our presence, will be able to induce compliance with the wishes of our government."[153]

Huntington Wilson, of course, wanted the railroad to be denied only to the revolutionaries and open to the government forces. It was only the rebels who should be punished since Mena's revolt lacked "even the pretense of contending for a principle," was in "the category of anarchy rather than ordinary revolution," and was "the most inexcusable in the annals of Central America."[154] Once again the Assistant Secretary sought Presidential backing. He drafted a letter for the President's signature, a letter which, if Taft approved, would be sent as an official communication from the White House to the Navy Department. The draft which Wilson prepared left no doubts about Wilson's belief that the Navy was excessively neutral in its conduct and had failed to mount a forthright campaign. It began with the flat assertion that Mena's rebels were simply bandits and that the United States had hoped to produce a speedy end to the uprising so that "the moral effect upon the whole revolution-ridden region of Central America and the Caribbean should be greatest." But, the draft continued, Admiral Southerland "may not have grasped fully the purpose and scope of the policy of this government." His intention "to observe a strict neutrality and not allow the Government forces to use the railroad . . . [was] inconsistent with our recognition of the legal Government." Southerland was also criticized for being mild in his attitude toward the "revolutionary disturbers" and holding discussions with them. Finally, in the draft which Wilson wanted Taft to sign, there was mention of the pos-

151 SDDF, File 817.00/1940a, H. Wilson to Taft, 4 September 1912.
152 SDDF, File 817.00/1957, Downs to Knox, 9 September 1912.
153 SDDF, File 817.00/1959, Admiral Southerland to Meyer, 9 September 1912.
154 SDDF, 817.00/1940b, H. Wilson to Weitzel, 4 September 1912.

sibility that Army troops might yet have to be employed and operations conducted well beyond the line of the Managua railway.[155]

Huntington Wilson also wrote directly to Admiral Converse, the acting Secretary of the Navy, though in a more restrained, diplomatic fashion than was his custom. Modestly he began, "I hope you will pardon me for feeling some anxiety . . . and for again raising the question of whether or not it would be practicable to have it understood that in all policy matters the Admiral will seek completest accord with the minister and be guided by the judgment of the Legation, referring any points of disagreement to the Government here before taking any action inconsistent with the views of the minister." His reference was to another specific complaint from Weitzel that Admiral Southerland claimed that his orders would not permit him to force the revolutionaries out of a position known as the Barranca. Wilson made it clear that the State Department wanted the Navy to insist that Southerland obey the minister's wishes.[156]

On this occasion Huntington Wilson got much of what he wanted from President Taft. The Chief Executive agreed that the rail line was to be kept open for use by the troops of the Nicaraguan government and denied to the rebels, a policy deliberately intended to strengthen the hand of the Diaz government. Southerland received new orders, tougher and more explicit in their tenor.[157] But there was irony in the situation, irony which Admiral Southerland did not overlook. Just three hours before his new, Wilson-inspired orders arrived, the Admiral had accepted the surrender of Mena and 700 of his followers. Mena was reported to be a very sick man and his troops virtually at the point of starvation. Southerland lost no time in pointing out to Washington that all of this had been accomplished, as he had predicted, within the framework of his original orders and before the new instructions reached him.[158]

Only one rebel force still remained operative in Nicaragua, a small band led by one of Mena's followers, Zelodon. By this time Southerland was in fact better tuned to the wishes of the Department of State and prepared to employ more forcible methods. He announced that, if Zelodon's troops threatened any government positions, he would substitute his own sailors and marines for the soldiers of Diaz. South-

[155] SDDF, File 817.00/2003B, H. Wilson to Taft, 23 September 1912.

[156] SDDF, File 817.00/2005, H. Wilson to Converse, 25 September 1912.

[157] SDDF, File 817.00/2014, Doyle to H. Wilson, 23 September 1912, informing him of his discussion with the President and of the orders given by Taft. See also /2010, H. Wilson to Weitzel, 24 September 1912.

[158] SDDF, File 817.00/2018, Weitzel to Knox, 25 September 1912, forwarding Southerland's report on the conclusion of operations against Mena.

erland also indicated that he was prepared to occupy positions other than those on the railway itself.[159] When Zelodon refused to surrender, Southerland, counting little upon any assistance from Diaz' troops, decided that he would force the issue. "From all my experience," he noted, "I have every reason to believe that the Government forces will remain inactive and simply follow on our heels to reap the fruits of our work." He decided, on his own authority, to order Zelodon to surrender and, if he refused, to attack with his own marines.[160] Events followed on schedule. When Zelodon spurned the order, Southerland smashed the rebel position in an attack that resulted in the death of the rebel leader as well as in several fatalities among the marines. This action effectively ended the rebellion, even to the satisfaction of Weitzel.[161] Admiral Southerland at last got a telegram of congratulations from the Department of State. But the naval officer, like Kimball before him, got the last word. The final sentence of his summary report read:

> In justice to the officers and men of my command I desire to invite the attention of the Navy Department to the fact that under the Department's orders of 29 August and prior to receipt of 24 September orders, a force of marines and bluejackets had penetrated to the heart of this country, through towns, re-laying rail tracks, repairing bridges . . . [and] opened the rail line from Corinto to Granada and has taken the chief instigator of the present trouble—and this without losing a single American life by a hostile shot. . . . The revised orders came at a time when, as a result of previous operations, our force of marines and bluejackets were in positions from which they could best carry out such orders.[162]

In Nicaraguan affairs the Department of State had pushed its views and tried to enforce its policies on the Navy Department more strenuously than on any other occasion between the Spanish-American War and the First World War. The dogged persistence of Huntington Wilson succeeded in getting Admiral Southerland to pursue a far harder line than the naval officer felt necessary. But the Nicaraguan example also fully revealed the inherent, fundamental problem of policy coordination in the absence of any formal machinery. The State Department, to make its policy effective, had to go to the unusual length of

[159] SDDF, File 817.00/2022 and /2044, Southerland to Meyer, 27 and 29 September 1912.

[160] SDDF, File 817.00/2045, Southerland to Meyer, 3 October 1912.

[161] SDDF, File 817.00/2050-51, Southerland to Meyer, 3 October 1912 and Weitzel to Knox, 4 October 1912.

[162] SDDF, File 817.00/2119, Meyer to Knox, 23 October 1912, forwarding a copy of Southerland's long report of 27 September 1912.

appealing directly to the President and securing his personal intervention with the Navy.

After the collapse of the Mena revolution, American naval forces were gradually withdrawn from Nicaragua, though a legation guard remained on into the 1920s. The Navy's suggested force of 50 men was raised to 100 at the request of Minister Weitzel who feared that the smaller number would simply permit the Nicaraguans to "get the idea that the United States is giving tacit consent to a renewal of revolution."[163] All parties, however, agreed on the advisability of the legation guard; even Southerland described Nicaragua as a "semi-savage country—more so than any of the other Central American states—and will remain so until its revolutionary activities have ended."[164] But, at the end of 1912, all was apparently quiet on the Nicaraguan front. As one marine commander thankfully wrote towards the latter part of December, "Today ends a week of religious festivities, during which there were no disturbances."[165]

Honduras, geographically next to Nicaragua, caused Taft and Knox almost as much trouble as Nicaragua. Her political weakness made her a constant temptation to more aggressive neighbors, while her chronic bankruptcy always raised the spectre of foreign intervention. A major Honduran crime in the eyes of the Department of State was the fact that the regime of President Miguel Davila was considered pro-Zelaya and to have gained power only through the assistance of the detested Nicaraguan leader. As Huntington Wilson wrote with his characteristic bluntness, "Honduras has politically, financially, and economically about as bad a record for stability as could be found on the face of the earth."[166] Philip Brown, who served as minister in the Taft era, set down a succinct bill of charges: a weak government with a president of dubious honesty; a demoralized treasury which operated without a budget and no fixed income. "Occasionally a mule train with money from the coast arrives, but no one knows exactly what becomes of it."[167]

The United States Navy consequently played a role in preserving law and order in Honduras comparable to its part in Nicaragua. Naval officers regarded the presence of American warships in Honduran waters as a prerequisite for political tranquillity. The commander of the *Tacoma* once noted that the people of Honduras interpreted the

[163] SDDF, File 817.00/2174, Weitzel to Knox, 14 December 1912.

[164] SDDF, File 817.00/2164, Southerland to Meyer, 14 November 1912.

[165] SDDF, File 817.00/2184, Andrews to Knox, 26 December 1912, forwarding report of a Marine Corps officer, Charles Long, dated 8 December.

[166] Huntington Wilson Papers, H. Wilson to William Hoster, 24 June 1911.

[167] SDNF, Case 7537/41, Brown to Knox, 16 April 1909.

presence of American vessels as tangible evidence of American support for the government of Davila. If the ships should be removed, he
warned, the entire governmental structure "might fall like a house of
cards."[168] But therein lay the difficulty. The Department of State was
not anxious to appear as the abiding prop of the Davila regime nor did
it appreciate the way in which the government of Honduras pointed
to the occasional visits of American naval craft as proof that Washington was prepared to assist it against its various enemies, domestic and
foreign. The general policy, therefore, was to keep vessels away from
the coast of Honduras except in times of emergency and, if possible,
to place the Davila regime in the position of having to request American assistance rather than having it constantly on hand.[169] There was
also a further problem, previously mentioned, which rose to the fore
during Zelaya's reported filibustering activities early in 1909: namely,
the absence of any clear legal right for American intervention in the
affairs of Honduras, a consequence of the fact that the treaty which
presumably guaranteed her neutrality had not been signed by the
United States.

To the Department of State the neutralization and stabilization of
Honduras would provide the foundation for the Central American stability it so avidly sought. Knox firmly believed that a radical change in
the position of Honduras would, above all, help to clip the wings of
Zelaya and Nicaragua, since it was the weakness of Honduras which
tempted the Nicaraguans to violate the peace of Central America.
Eventually he produced familiar proposals for Honduras: a new
treaty, to be signed by the United States and Mexico, which would
guarantee the neutrality of Honduras, provide grounds for American
intervention, and include various provisions for American financial
advisers and supervision of the customs. The Knox-Davila convention,
though winning the approval of the government of Honduras, never
did manage to gain the support of the United States Senate.[170] Yet in
placing the proposal before the Senators, the Taft Administration not
only made clear its desire to build an orderly Honduras but also produced its classic rationalization of "dollar diplomacy." As Knox told
the Senate:

> I think ratification of the Convention is particularly important to us
> because the question really at issue is can or can not this government

[168] SDNF, Case 18432/57-58, Hood to Meyer, 22 March 1909.

[169] SDNF, Case 7357/664 and /665, Brown to Knox, 12 August 1909.

[170] Among the numerous sources for this plan, one of the best is to be found in
the Knox papers, Memorandum of the Secretary's conversation with the Special
Ambassador of Mexico, 15 March 1909. For a clear secondary account, see Munro,
Dollar Diplomacy, 164-65.

have a beneficial and constructive policy in the neighborhood of the Caribbean, the Panama Canal, and the Central American Republics . . . it [is] increasingly impossible for the United States to sit by and see this whole region racked with turbulence and insurrection. . . . More than this, the question seems to be, is it better that our duty be done now with dollars or perhaps later with bullets?[171]

One of the strong arguing points used by the administration in behalf of the Convention was that its ratification would presumably make it less necessary to land sailors and marines than heretofore. It was the absence of such a convention, so the argument ran, which made it necessary for marines, at that very moment, to be protecting the rail terminal at Puerto Cortes, to have been sent recently to Ceiba, and a few months earlier to have been assigned to Amapala "prepared to use force if necessary to protect Americans and their interests from the violence of the Commandante."[172] Presumably, then, if the Convention passed and stabilization followed, such interventions would be unnecessary. Others felt, however, that the Navy ought to have a permanent role. From 1907 through 1910 Minister Brown argued steadily that the United States ought to obtain a naval base in the Gulf of Fonseca as a way of guaranteeing the achievement of its political objectives in Central America.[173] It was, however, not a proposal which then commended itself to the Navy. The General Board just as consistently replied that such a base would have no strategic value. But, as it often did, the Board was careful to point out that it was confining itself to the military dimensions of the situation and not expressing any opinion about the possible political value of a base.[174]

It is unnecessary to chronicle the many occasions during which there was naval activity in and around the waters of Honduras. These ranged from the anti-filibustering moves, earlier described, which were aimed at Zelaya to the frequent occasions when the Department of State authorized a naval landing to protect American lives and property in a time of disorder. The best example of the difficulties which the Department of State and the Navy encountered in intervening without a legal mandate occurred late in 1910 and early in 1911 when revolution against the Davila regime finally took place.

This was one revolt which did not surprise Washington. Reports of a possible uprising had persuaded Knox to send the *Tacoma* to Puerto

171 Taft Papers, Presidential Series 2, Knox to Taft, 23 January 1911.

172 Taft Papers, H. Wilson to Taft, 26 February 1911, a memorandum prepared to help the President in "selling" the treaty.

173 SDNF, Case 7055/1, Brown to Root, 28 May 1907, and /2, Brown to Knox, 20 January 1910.

174 SDNF, Case 7055, attachments to dispatches just cited, Newberry to Root, 2 July 1907 and Meyer to Knox, 23 February 1910.

Cortes on an "observation mission" well before the fighting broke out.[175] Moreover, the Department of State had come into possession of information which indicated that the expedition against Davila was being prepared in New Orleans and that the insurgents planned to use a small vessel, the *Hornet*, then in that Louisiana port. It was also well known that the ranks of the insurgents included an American Negro adventurer, known as Lee Christmas, who had a long record of involvement in various Central American imbroglios. The Department of Justice, acting on Knox's request, searched the *Hornet* while it was still at New Orleans but could find no ammunition aboard nor anything that could serve as a legal pretext to keep the vessel from sailing.[176] Once in the Caribbean, however, the *Hornet* quickly acquired a cargo of arms, ammunition, and revolutionaries. In early January it landed the revolutionary leaders on the coast of Honduras, where the insurrection was formally launched and a provisional government under Manuel Bonilla, established. While all of this had been happening, the State and Navy Departments had been endlessly discussing the question of whether or not the suspected vessel could be seized, but no appropriate legal justification could be unearthed. To complicate matters further, the *Hornet*, which was flying an American flag on arrival in Honduras, was promptly sold for the munificent sum of one dollar to a citizen of Honduras and thus formally entered the service of the revolutionary leader, Bonilla, under the Honduran flag.[177]

The wheels spun furiously in Washington. The crucial question was the policy to be adopted toward the revolution—whether to support the Davila government against Bonilla, to remain entirely neutral, or follow some third approach. Naturally there was much discussion about the possibility of taking the sting out of the *Hornet* by simply authorizing the United States Navy to seize the vessel. The Latin American Division favored the direct approach of forbidding either side to shell any Honduran town.[178]

The Navy was instructed to keep a close watch on the *Hornet* while an investigation was launched to determine whether or not she had violated American neutrality laws—and hence would be subject to seizure. But the captain of the insurgent vessel informed an American officer that, unless the United States employed force against him, he intended to use the *Hornet* to further the cause of the Bonilla movement. The American naval officer thereupon simply put forty of his

175 SDDF, File 815.00/897-98, Dodge to Adee, 6 December 1910.
176 SDDF, File 815.00/926, Fowle to Knox, 20 December 1910, and /934, Doyle to Dodge, 21 December 1910.
177 SDDF, File 815.00/974, Commander Davis to Meyer, 10 January 1911.
178 SDDF, File 815.00/975, Weitzel to H. Wilson, 11 January 1911.

men aboard the *Hornet*—and was congratulated by the State Department for his prompt action.[179] Naval officers carried out the further wishes of the Department of State by informing both sides in the civil conflict that certain cities, notably the capital, Puerto Cortes, were out of bounds for any military operations.[180]

There were howls of Honduran protest. The Davila regime, which sought American assistance, bitterly objected to the ban on fighting at Puerto Cortes. Davila complained plaintively, and correctly, that his troops would fight only if they could enjoy the protection furnished by the defenses of the capital; if forced to fight in open country, they would desert—and the victory would be won by Bonilla. As a minimal concession he asked that the Navy let him keep his troops in Puerto Cortes and use its defenses in any fighting that might develop.[181] The Department of State, well aware of the effect that its prohibition would have, estimated that Bonilla would eventually triumph but did not wish to become involved as an active supporter of either group. It therefore decided that the best possible solution would be to maintain the prohibition on fighting, invite both sides to declare an armistice, and offer the deck of an American warship as "neutral ground" upon which, it hoped, representatives of the two contending groups could select a third person to head the government of Honduras until national elections could be held.[182]

To Davila there went a flowery telegram from President Taft which expressed a sincere desire to help Honduras and thanked him for his interest in avoiding further bloodshed.[183] To the United States Navy there went orders which flatly stated that the United States could not permit a continuation of the fighting, especially in the capital, where "You will at once notify both parties that no fighting will be permitted within the town of Puerto Cortes."[184] It was an effective gambit which denied to each side the opportunity to get at its opponent. Both Davila and Bonilla soon agreed to an armistice (though not without many persuasive efforts by the American naval command to assuage sorely wounded Latin *amour propre*), and a special commissioner, sent from Washington, served as an intermediary in the selection of a new gov-

[179] SDDF, File 815.00/997, Cooper to Meyer, 17 January 1911; /1015, Cooper to Meyer, 23 January 1911; and /1020, Knox to Meyer, 24 January 1911.

[180] SDDF, File 815.00/1040, Memorandum of Second Assistant Secretary, 30 January 1911, and /1053, Knox to Meyer, same date.

[181] SDDF, File 815.00/1081, McCreery to Knox, 6 February 1911, and /1084, McCreery to Knox, 7 February 1911.

[182] SDDF, File 815.00/1053, Knox to Meyer, 31 January 1911.

[183] SDDF, File 815.00/1041, Taft to Davila, 31 January 1911.

[184] SDDF, File 815.00/1053, Knox to Meyer, 31 January 1911; /1075, Davis to Meyer, 2 February 1911; and /1075, McCreery to Knox, 4 February 1911.

ernment.[185] Clearly it was a solution which rested upon American naval might. The American warships in the harbor of Puerto Cortes so dwarfed the contending armies that no other choice but obedience was open to them. Moreover, since Puerto Cortes was the capital city and thus the key political position, the prohibition on fighting for its control had effectively compelled both factions to negotiate. Yet the United States could screen its actions by arguing that it was defending the lives and property of innocent foreigners and protecting a defenseless city from attack. It could even cite the Hague Convention—which forbade the bombardment of defenseless towns—as a moral precedent. It was an ingenious, cosmetic way to handle the "problem" of revolution without actually landing the marines, and to deal with a small Central American state in which the United States might lack a conventional right of direct intervention but could rely on the deterrent power of the Navy.

It was also one Central American incident in which Navy and State Department worked in harmony. Naval officers supplied much of the actual information on which the State Department built its policy—and, in the process, also provided convincing evidence that one American consular agent was actively involved in promoting the Bonilla revolution.[186] Captain Cooper of the *Marietta*, the senior officer at the time, ultimately received much praise from the civilian commissioner who supervised the peace negotiations. His action in seizing the *Hornet* had convinced both sides of the impartiality of the United States, while "his insight into the military, geographic, and strategic circumstances . . . made it possible for me to hope to induce the warring factions to accept an agreement."[187]

There remained the problem of the *Hornet* which still lay at anchor in Puerto Cortes in the hands of the United States Navy. The investigation conducted by the Department of Justice dragged on slowly, but eventually the lawyers in Washington decided that the *Hornet* had violated American neutrality laws and should be brought back to New Orleans where a Federal Court would hold further hearings on the charges.[188] The Department of State was now embarrassed. Bonilla,

[185] SDDF, File 815.00/1284, Thomas Dawson, Special Commissioner, to Knox, 30 April 1911, a report on his work as intermediary. On the Navy's role, see /1124, a long State Department memorandum of 18 February 1911.

[186] SDDF, File 815.00/1021, Latin American Affairs memorandum, 27 January 1911.

[187] SDDF, File 815.00/1284, Dawson report of 30 April 1911.

[188] SDDF, File 815.00 contains numerous reports on the *Hornet* as well as extensive correspondence bearing on the interdepartmental debate between the State and Justice Departments over appropriate procedures. They are to be found scattered in the file from late February through mid-April 1911. For a typical view of the naval establishment, see /1220, Meyer to Knox, 31 March 1911.

after all, had by now become the head of one of the major factions in Honduras, enjoyed the support of quite a few American residents of that country, and was himself irate at the indictment drawn by the Department of Justice. To the annoyance of Attorney General Wickersham, the Department of State requested a *nolle prosse*. Wickersham rather testily asked Knox to specify the international reasons which justified abandonment of the case and indicated that, in his opinion, it should not be dropped.[189] Knox, in turn, had to secure Presidential support and get Taft to direct that the indictment against Bonilla and the *Hornet* be dropped. But at least Knox and his associates had sufficient grace to admit that their action was based not on law but on policy. They conceded that it was intended only to avoid the embarrassment that would follow any attempt to prosecute a man who had just become an important official in another country. On the margin of the last State Department document in the file, Alvey Adee scribbled a fitting epitaph for the case:

> Treason is ne'er successful;
> What's the reason?
> When it succeeds,
> It is no longer treason.[190]

4. Miscellaneous Tasks: From Selling Warships to Policing Liberian Tribes

Nicaragua and Honduras furnished virtually continuous fields for naval employment during the Taft-Knox era, but the Navy also fulfilled a wide range of miscellaneous assignments behind which there were political purposes. Many were trivial but at least showed the extent to which the Navy was put to the service of the Department of State.

One of the very first missions it received in March 1909 was to conduct a search for the whereabouts of ex-President Cipriano Castro of Venezuela, one of the villains of the Roosevelt period, who was, according to rumor, about to sneak back into the Western Hemisphere and attempt to regain his lost power. Castro's possible return—described as "an eventuality which would be disastrous not only to America but to all other foreign interests in that Republic"—was considered sufficiently serious to prompt a cabinet-level discussion, out of which there came orders to the Navy to send vessels to observe Cas-

189 SDDF, File 815.00/1245, Wickersham to Knox, 11 April 1911.
190 SDDF, File 815.00/1316, Clark to H. Wilson, with attached comments by Adee, 7 April 1911.

tro's movements and report all possible information.[191] The Department of State could not, of course, order Castro's seizure, much as it would have liked to. Thus, the Navy's assignment, if Castro landed at Trinidad and then set sail for Venezuelan coast, was simply to shadow his movements, thereby providing all interested parties with information and preventing him from achieving any surprises.[192]

The actual outcome was anticlimactic. For several weeks a number of American naval vessels scurried about the Caribbean on the lookout for the ex-dictator of Venezuela. But Castro was also cordially disliked by Britain, France, and the Netherlands; their governments agreed to deny him entry into any of their Caribbean possessions, while France was prepared to deport him to Europe if he showed up at Martinique.[193] Faced with these not inconsiderable barriers, Castro gave up and returned to Europe on his own—whereupon the naval watch, which had earned the special thanks of the Department of State, was abandoned.[194] It was an incident scarcely worth a footnote in the Navy's history but a portent of the promptness with which the Taft administration moved at the first faint indication of possible political trouble in the area adjacent to the canal.

In the Castro affair the Navy was no more than the executive arm of civilian policy, but on other occasions it was brought closer to the mainstream of "dollar diplomacy." The Navy was sometimes deeply involved in the extensive efforts of Philander Knox and the Department of State to persuade the Argentine government, then involved in a South Atlantic naval building race with Brazil and Chile, to order three battleships from American shipbuilders rather than from European or Japanese competitors.[195] To gain this Argentine contract, presumably worth twenty-three million dollars, was a major objective of the administration. It was also an endeavor, according to Taft, "brought about directly by the untiring efforts of the Department of State." Indeed, as the President once bragged in a speech before an audience of Pittsburgh businessmen, it was a classic example of the way in which American diplomacy could be "a matter of practical interest" to the business community.[196]

The effort of the diplomats had indeed been untiring. Their campaign was directed not only at the Argentines but also at the Navy De-

[191] Huntington Wilson Papers, H. Wilson to Meyer, 29 March 1909; Nav Rec AF 8, H. Wilson to Meyer, 29 March 1909. See also Howe, *Meyer*, 429.

[192] Nav Rec Messages Sent in Cipher, Meyer to *Maine*, 30 March 1909.

[193] SDNF, Case 3136/153A, H. Wilson to Meyer, 9 April 1909.

[194] SDNF, Case 3136/163, Knox to Meyer, 14 April 1909.

[195] Seward Livermore, "Battleship Diplomacy in South America," *Journal of Modern History*, XVI, no. 1 (March 1944), 31-48.

[196] Huntington Wilson Papers, draft of speech prepared for Taft by the State Department, probably spring of 1910.

partment to persuade the admirals to share design secrets with the South Americans. Actually, the possibility of gaining the Argentine contract had arisen late in 1908 and the first inquiries were initiated by Elihu Root, but it was the incoming Taft administration which took up the matter in earnest as one of its first moves in the spring of 1909. Huntington Wilson informed the Argentine minister that American shipbuilders were "exceedingly anxious to secure a share of the orders for warships" and pointedly reminded him that Americans had already purchased a considerable share of the Argentine government loan that would finance its building program.[197]

The nub of the issue, however, was the willingness of the Navy to cooperate. Argentina soon made it clear that her officials would have to gain access to certain United States naval publications before they could decide which nation would win the desired contract.[198] The Department of State, in requesting the Navy's cooperation, stressed the desirability of gaining for American shipbuilders as large a share of the Argentine naval contract as possible.[199] Similarly, the Bethlehem Steel Company, itself angling for a portion of the order, asked the Navy's permission to use government designs for underwater torpedo discharge tubes and fire control mechanisms. Both then and later Bethlehem officials accompanied their requests with pointed remarks about the competitive disadvantages faced by American shipbuilders when they tried to outbid Europeans firms that enjoyed strong governmental support.[200]

There was, at first, some reluctance on the part of the Navy. It regarded certain matters as confidential and not for release to any foreign government. But the General Board eventually opted for maximum cooperation.[201] It was always encouraged in this direction by the Department of State which rarely missed an opportunity to impress upon the Navy the importance of foreign orders for domestic firms. A decisive influence was the endorsement of the Bureau of Ordnance which happily discovered that the interests of the United States, of the naval establishment, and of the private shipbuilders were identical, especially when it came to building ships and providing war material "for . . . those countries affected by the Monroe Doctrine."

197 SDNF, Case 1070/42, Memorandum of Secretary's conversation with the Argentine minister, 7 March 1909.
198 SDNF, Case 1070/45-46, Argentine Legation to State Department, 12 April 1909.
199 SDNF, Case 1070/42A and /45-46, Knox to Meyer, 12 April 1909.
200 SDNF, Case 1070/55-59, Meyer to Knox, 5 June 1909, which includes Bethlehem Steel correspondence with the Navy. See also Nav Rec AF 10, Knox to Meyer, 8 December 1909.
201 Nav Rec Confid Ltrs, unsigned memorandum of 11 March 1909, spelling out the Department's policy of cooperation.

Such orders, the Bureau agreed, would both add to American prosperity and increase the resources that would be available to the Western Hemisphere in time of war.[202] Hence the General Board was ultimately willing to permit the use of confidential designs and devices provided only that measures were taken to preserve their confidential nature.[203]

Naval officials never delved deeper than the justification via prosperity and Monroe. They never sought to learn the purpose behind the Argentine building program nor the effect that a naval race between Argentina, Brazil, and Chile might have upon South American politics. Their eventual cooperation with the State Department was complete. In June 1909 various Argentine newspapers alleged that American armor plate was inferior to that of the British and that the United States government was about to launch its own investigation of the defects. Knox at once asked the Navy "to make a statement denying this as concisely and completely as possible." The admirals were happy to comply, with the result that Huntington Wilson was soon able to assure the Argentine government that the United States Navy considered American steel to be as good if not actually better than any manufactured in Europe.[204] But, in fairness to the naval officers, it should be added that the State Department also showed no concern for the political dimensions of the South American naval race and demonstrated, especially when it also authorized a similar campaign to elicit orders from Chile, that its primary interest was the profit of American business. In any event, it is not surprising that in the fall of 1909 Knox could receive a glowing letter from President Charles Schwab of the United States Steel Company in which that industrialist praised the Secretary for his efforts on behalf of American industry and added that, if the Argentine contracts were awarded to the United States, "it will be a great achievement for you as well as for America."[205]

The Navy had a hand not only in Central American politics, the search for Castro, and Argentine battleships but even in the tangled affairs of the nominally independent West African republic of Liberia. Founded as a home for ex-American slaves and the occasional recipient

[202] SDNF, Case 1070/55-59, Meyer to Knox, 5 June 1909, to which is attached endorsement of Bureau of Ordnance, 14 May 1909. Another copy of this correspondence is in Nav Rec Confid Ltrs, 14 May 1909.

[203] SDNF, Case 1070/55-59, Meyer to Knox, 5 June 1909.

[204] SDNF, Case 1070/61-62, H. Wilson to Meyer, 11 June 1909, and several attached telegrams intended to provide the Argentines with the reassuring words of the naval establishment.

[205] SDNF, Case 1070/76, Schwab to Knox, 4 September 1909. The Livermore article, "Battleship Diplomacy," also stresses that the State Department's motive was to make profits for American steel firms.

of past favors from the United States, Liberia had long been a "cause" for certain Americans, especially those involved in mission work.[206] There was a small but vocal group, prominent among whom was a Bishop Hartzell of the Methodist-Episcopal Church, which wanted the United States to play a far more active role as guardian and benefactor of the African republic. Its favorite gambit, proposed with more or less consistency from the turn of the century to the Taft era, was the proposal that the United States should acquire a naval station in the Negro republic. The proponents of this scheme surmised that, as the owner of a naval base, the United States would then exert a greater influence over Liberian affairs. But, naturally, when trying to sell their proposal to the Navy, they emphasized the advantages which would presumably accrue to the Navy and to general American commercial interests.[207] In the early years of the century, these friends of Liberia had some hopes of success, for they enlisted the interest of Admiral Royal B. Bradford, that enthusiast for overseas bases who, in those days, seemed ready to acquire foreign bases by the job lot. The Navy did send a special mission to Liberia to investigate its harbors and coastal waters. The Liberian government, pathetically anxious to secure American assistance, proved embarrassingly eager to cede almost any bit of coastal territory that the Navy could use.[208]

But the venture died quickly. John D. Long, described by one missionary as a man "who failed to have a vision of our necessities," doused the proposal with liberal quantities of particularly cold water. The Navy's own investigation showed that Monrovia was the only feasible site for a base but that even its harbor was sadly deficient in meeting minimal naval requirements for a coaling station.[209]

Liberia long continued to have both internal and external problems equal if not superior to those of any Caribbean republic. When the Liberian government sent a mission of its own to the United States to request help, Congress, after some delay and opposition, agreed in March 1909 to send a special commission to investigate and make recommendations. The range of problems to be studied included tribal disorders, finances, and continuing border disputes then causing diffi-

206 One of the few studies of Liberian-American relations is Raymond Bixler, *The Foreign Policy of the United States in Liberia* (New York, 1957); pages 20-36 deal with the issues raised in this study.

207 For a brief summary of various proposals developed in the Navy between 1899 and 1902, see GB, File 414-1, a staff memorandum used in the preparation of the Board's comprehensive report on coaling stations in October 1902. See also SDML, Long to Hay, 5 May 1899, enclosing letters of Bishop Hartzell and Admiral Bradford, and Hay to Long, 9 May 1899.

208 SDML, Hay to Long, 8 January 1900, conveying the Liberian offer.

209 GB, File 414-1, staff memorandum cited in note 207.

culties between Liberia and neighboring British and French possessions.[210] The Liberian Commission, which included several Negroes as
well as missionaries and government officials, spent some months in
Liberia and eventually submitted its report to Knox in the fall of 1909.
Although Knox's instructions to the Commission had made absolutely
no mention of the long dormant project for an American naval base,
the final report included it among its many recommendations.[211] It
was, however, one suggestion that found absolutely no favor in Washington. Though, as time was to show, the Taft administration was willing to share in the financial reorganization of Liberia and assume some
responsibilities as a member of an international financial protectorate,
neither the Navy nor the Department of State had any interest in the
kind of permanent involvement that a naval base would have
created.[212]

The question remained, however, of the extent of assistance to be
rendered the Liberians. To Huntington Wilson, whose political judgments rarely exhibited the quality of mercy, Liberia was a country
saddled with an inexperienced government that had gotten into unfortunate disputes with its neighbors and made far less political or economic progress than adjacent, European-controlled colonies.[213] The
recommendations of the special commission were still pending when,
in the late winter of 1910, the American minister in Monrovia began
to sound the alarm with a series of urgent dispatches that chronicled
increasing native disorders and growing friction with Britain and
France. The State Department, still waiting the final decision on long-
term assistance, decided to send a cruiser "to contribute, as far as it
can, by the moral effect of the ship's presence, and by cruising on the
coast, to tranquilizing the present uprisings and difficulties."[214]

Captain W. B. Fletcher, who drew the assignment as commanding
officer of the *Birmingham*, was no tranquilizer. He quickly developed
a strong aversion to the Liberian government and concluded that its
dominating purpose was to involve the United States in its own domestic difficulties. The Department of State, in turn, soon decided that
Captain Fletcher, despite careful briefings before his departure,
"failed to understand the meaning of 'moral support' to the Liberian
government."[215]

[210] SDNF, Case 12083/190C, Knox's instructions to the Liberian Commission, 13
April 1909.
[211] SDNF, Case 12083, Report of Liberian Commission, 11 October 1909.
[212] Bixler, *U.S. in Liberia*, 24.
[213] Huntington Wilson Papers, Wilson to Rev. J. H. Eccleston, 14 December 1909.
[214] SDNF, Case 882/314, Knox to Meyer, 25 February 1910.
[215] SDNF, Case 882/338, interoffice memorandum, H.A.F. to H. Wilson, July 1910,
commenting on Fletcher reports of late April.

Typical was a cable which Fletcher sent in late April: "Trouble at Cape Palmas caused by mismanagement and incompetence of authorities here who have tried to commit me to use force and who have rejected an offer suggesting method for peaceful settlement."[216] The irascible Fletcher filed many reports in like vein. He expressed surprise at the patience of the European governments in tolerating Liberian malpractices, charged the Liberian government with cowardice in dealing with native rebellions, and flatly asserted that "a strong white man's rule should exist here." The Liberians, he wrote, were unable to govern their own country, while "their civilization is a veneer of frock coats and tall hats, with a faculty for writing high sounding phrases. They have no mind and no depth." He found the native tribes justified in their hatred of the government. Fletcher claimed that the government in Monrovia had stage-managed the recent visit by the American commission. It was "very skillfully handled and permitted to see and hear only such matters as was intended they should." Above all, Fletcher was loud in his complaints that it was ridiculous to send a naval vessel to Liberia every time there was feud between the government and some tribe.[217]

Fletcher's judgments were, at least in part, sustained by the American minister, Ernest Lyons, who also had a dim view of the sense of responsibility possessed by Liberia's leaders and of their inability to cope with problems whose resolution required only a minimum of energy. It also soon became apparent that the Liberian government had been led to expect far too much of the United States and that the guilty parties were the chargé, Ellis, and an American adventurer, Frank Flowers, who used his vague connections with the legation to claim that he spoke (and promised) on behalf of the United States government.[218] But, even with these extenuating circumstances, the State Department was intensely dissatisfied with Captain Fletcher. Its bill of particulars against the naval officer charged that, instead of lending moral support to the Liberian government, he had favored arbitration between the government and the rebellious tribes and had been prepared to deal with the rebels as equals. Furthermore, he had used harsh language and showed a complete inability to establish good personal relations with Liberian authorities—a charge which, if anything, was an understatement. As for his comments about the shortcomings of the Commission, the State Department replied that they were "absurd, and inasmuch as the Captain is not aware of the full report of the Commission, he is incompetent to pass upon the thoroughness of its in-

216 SDNF, Case 882/342, Fletcher to Meyer, 28 April 1910.
217 SDNF, Case 882/353 and /364, Fletcher to Meyer, 14 and 17 April 1910.
218 SDNF, Case 882/773, Lyons to Knox, 11 May 1910.

vestigations."[219] The Navy reassigned Fletcher, who was soon succeeded in Liberia by Captain Luby of the *Des Moines.* Thereafter the Department of State noted, with pleasure, that civil-military relations over Liberia now proceeded with far less friction.[220]

But Captain Luby had no more use for the Liberians than Fletcher; his comments about their conduct were equally harsh. After observing a wide assortment of indiscretions by government troops—which ranged from indiscriminate firing on anything that moved to the theft of cattle—he sent a personal note to the head of the Liberian government:

> Such an occurrence renders your organization unworthy of the name of "government." If you cannot control the rabble that you brought here from Monrovia and called a military force, how can you expect to inspire any confidence in the native tribes who have recently surrendered, surely expecting that some regularity and decent order would accompany whatever penalties the Government felt justified in inflicting? Personally I am disgusted and did my official obligations permit, the *Des Moines'* anchor would not rest an hour longer on the bottom.

The outspoken captain concluded, "Such a travesty on government, I warn you, will not be allowed to exist much longer in the twentieth century, or I am mistaken." The Liberians answered that Captain Luby had written his dispatch while in an excited state of mind. Not so, shot back the naval officer, for the letter was "one of the most deliberate acts of my life. I was indignant, righteously and justly indignant, as would be any civilized man upon getting reliable information as to such an incident."[221]

In his more temperate moments Captain Luby reported that there was actually little foreign interference in Liberia, while most of the disturbances, which had previously concerned the legation, were of comic opera dimension. He did, however, end the native insurrection. Unlike Fletcher, he informed the rebels that he was directed by the government of the United States to support the government of Liberia and had no authority to mediate between the contending parties. Soon the insurrection ended, and, with Luby's assistance, an amnesty was arranged. Philander Knox was pleased by this example of a naval officer who followed the Department's suggestions; his firm stand with the

[219] SDNF, Case 882/388, interoffice memorandum, H.A.F. to Wilson, as cited.

[220] SDNF, Case 882/377, Knox to Meyer, 24 June 1910.

[221] SDNF, Case 882/385, Lyons to Knox, 30 May 1910, enclosing copies of Captain Luby's correspondence with Liberian officials.

natives had, in the Secretary's opinion, influenced their prompt decision to surrender.[222]

The surrender of the native rebels put an end to the "heroic" days of naval involvement in Liberia. To be sure, when the Navy Department made its usual suggestion that the *Des Moines* could now be removed elsewhere, the State Department countered with the request that the presence of an American warship at Monrovia would be valuable until such time as the last of the tribal disorders had been wholly settled and the nation's finances reorganized.[223] Eventually the United States, while unwilling to assume sole responsibility for Liberia, did float a loan and set up a receivership in company with several European states.[224] While these negotiations dragged on, Captain Luby grew more disenchanted with each passing month. He furnished Washington with extensive reports about the shortcomings of the Liberian government, began to feel, as had Fletcher, that some foreign power must assume direction of the country, and complained that American influence was only serving to keep an unworthy regime in power. "The Liberian government," he wrote despairingly, "in my opinion, must rest on its record and is answerable for its merits, which are few, and its demerits, which cry to Heaven." The State Department merely nodded; indeed it frequently commended Luby for his discretion, tact, and valuable reports.[225] For Luby might be as outspoken as Fletcher but, in the eyes of the State Department, at least he obeyed instructions.

5. A FAMILIAR THEME: CARIBBEAN BASES AND ISTHMIAN DEFENSES

Naval involvements in the affairs of Liberia or in promotional efforts to sell battleships to Argentina were new and exotic aspects of civil-military relations in the Taft era. But the Navy also pursued various matters which had long been on the agenda. It continued to concern itself with the defenses of the Panama Canal, with bases in the Caribbean, and, as always, in the never ending problems of the island of Santo Domingo.

By the time that Taft and Knox came into office, work on the Pan-

222 SDNF, Case 882/377, Knox to Meyer, 24 June 1910, and /386, Meyer to Knox, 1 July 1910.

223 SDNF, Case 882/409, Winthrop to Knox, 7 September 1910, and attached documents.

224 Bixler, *U.S. in Liberia*, 36.

225 SDNF, Case 882/400, Winthrop to Knox, 15 August 1910, forwarding copy of Luby's report of 24 July 1910.

ama Canal had progressed to such a point that its completion, while not immediately in sight, was no longer simply a far distant prospect. In consequence, both civil and military policymakers gave increased attention to the effects that the opening of the canal to commercial traffic would have upon politics and military affairs in the Caribbean. One clear result was a revival of interest in the subject of naval bases to protect the approaches to the canal. Another was that the Taft administration had to make the final decision about fortifications for the canal itself.

As we have seen, the issue of canal fortifications had been much debated some years earlier. The Joint Board had ruled in 1906 that the proper defense of the canal should be a system of fortifications at each terminus.[226] But no action had been forthcoming to implement this recommendation during the remaining years of Roosevelt's term in office. Both military services now believed firmly that fortification was essential. General Tasker Bliss summed up the Army's point of view in a letter to General Goethals: "The world expects us to fortify; part of it wants us to fortify, the rest of it is either indifferent or sees no plausible pretext on which to base an objection."[227] General Wotherspoon, at that time head of the Army War College, was similarly moved to an extended discussion not only of fortifications but also of the strategy of the Caribbean and the role of force in international relations. He felt that the United States must be the "sole judge" of the measures it took to protect the canal and that the exercise of American responsibilities in the area of the canal would assuredly involve the use of force. "For any one to claim," he observed "that force will not be required is to ignore the experience of the past. Just to uphold the treaty of 1846, the United States has had to use armed force at least ten times in the previous 55 years." What especially angered Wotherspoon was the contention that the canal could best be protected not by fortifications but by international agreements that would guarantee its neutrality. Such agreements, he argued, would involve the United States, "in those entangling alliances which it has been the highest effort of our nation to avoid." He then attacked

> those dreamers and sentimentalists (generally, by the way, not of military age and thus not liable to military service) who long for the great era of peace when there will be no wars or rumors of war and when the pruning hook shall take the place of the sword, [who] ignore these teachings and apparently refuse to go deeply into the

[226] JB, Minutes, 2 April 1906, Dewey to Bonaparte and Taft.
[227] Bliss Papers, Bliss to Goethals, 16 December 1909.

question of the effectiveness of neutrality agreements as exemplified in history.[228]

The Navy's planners felt as strongly about fortifications. In 1909, when asked to make an official statement on the subject, the General Board merely produced a document which was little more than a paraphrase of its earlier pronouncements. The line of argument, not surprisingly, was that fortifications were essential to preserve the neutrality of the canal and maintain the various international obligations assumed by the United States under the Hay-Pauncefote treaty.[229]

Civilian opinion echoed that of the military leaders. Knox and Wilson drew up a memorandum on fortifications which made the sweeping statement that "the whole world has unobjectingly observed the execution of the act of 1902 which provided for the construction of the canal and direction to the President to make such provision for its defense as may be necessary for its protection." Equally uncompromising was their conclusion that "the right to defend and protect is an indisputable incident to exclusive ownership."[230] Taft was no less explicit. To one critic of fortifications, he wrote, "I do not think it safe, with a property worth 400 millions of dollars, to leave it where any irresponsible nation, of which there are too many, could suddenly descend upon it with a fleet and greatly disable or injure it." On another occasion the President adopted the line that "We built the Canal partly for military reasons, and we certainly would be very foolish if we gave our enemy the same opportunity to attack us, that we have expended 500 millions to have to protect us."[231]

There was no thought, however, of erecting an Isthmian equivalent of Gibraltar or Singapore. Theodore Roosevelt, for example, had contended that the principal value of fortifications would be to provide protection against the rash act of some Latin dictator who might decide to embarrass the United States by a sudden strike at the canal. Hence the argument for fortifications was most frequently put in terms of their value in preserving the general security of the Caribbean rather than in furnishing a great bastion against a European attack. Taft thought in like vein. His principal argument on behalf of the canal fortifications was, "Suppose we had a man like Castro at the head of

[228] GS, War College Division, File 6178/6, Wotherspoon to Wood, 14 December 1910.

[229] GB, Letters, v, 2nd endorsement on Dewey to Wright, 24 February 1909.

[230] Huntington Wilson Papers, undated memorandum in folder "Knox Correspondence."

[231] Taft Papers, Letterpress, Taft to H. S. Drinker, 25 November 1910, and to David Starr Jordan, 23 February 1911.

a Central American or South American country and he were to get one or two warships and violate his obligations."[232] Thus, if there was any argument with military leaders over the proposed fortifications, that debate was over their size, extent, and, of course, cost. Taft always presumed that the principal cost would be the original outlay for construction and that a few battalions of coast artillery would be a sufficient garrison. He therefore resisted military attempts to expand the fortifications beyond what appeared reasonable to his civilian eyes. When the Army, for example, asked for an additional appropriation of four or five million dollars to build barracks for four or five infantry regiments, the President demurred. "If they are needed," he countered, "we can have them there promptly when war is declared and can house them without investing five million dollars in an expensive post." Taft had his way—to the obvious displeasure of his Chief of Staff, Leonard Wood, who complained that the President simply "does not seem to appreciate that thirty minutes possession of the locks by an enemy determined to do harm to them would put them out of use for a year or more."[233]

The issue of additional naval stations and bases in the Caribbean was more complex. Several long dormant proposals—Chimbote, the Galapagos, the Pearl Islands—were revived. The impetus for several of these came from the Department of State or from its representatives in Latin America rather than from the Navy. The General Board was still of the opinion that additional bases in the Caribbean were, from a strictly naval point of view, of dubious value, and, if and when the naval planners endorsed a possible acquisition, their acceptance was usually qualified and lacking in enthusiasm. One cannot go to the extent of saying that the civilians in Knox's Department of State were always more interested in bases than the military, but there were at least several projects in which such tendencies were present.

In 1910, for example, various private individuals with interests in the Cocos Islands, a group some five hundred miles west of the Isthmus and belonging to Costa Rica, tried to interest the military in acquiring them as an adjunct to the canal's defenses. Since at least one influential senator was concerned, the State Department thought it wise to get the official opinions of the two military services. Neither showed any interest whatsoever and denied that the Cocos had any value in the defense of the canal.[234] On the same date the services turned down a similar in-

---

[232] Taft Papers, Letterpress, Taft to James Gordon Bennett, 19 December 1910.

[233] Taft Papers, Letterpress, Taft to Dickinson, 28 December 1910; Wood Papers, Diary, 29 December 1910, comments on learning that Taft had disapproved the Army estimates for 1911 that requested funds to establish garrison posts in the Canal Zone.

[234] SDNF, Case 16698/1, March to Knox, 1 June 1909, and attached documents.

quiry about the merits of the Pearl Islands. But on this occasion the Latin American Division of the State Department was not satisfied and asked the General Board to make a thorough reexamination of the possibility of utilizing one or more of the islands in the defense system of the canal. The Navy gave the request short shrift. Its curt reply was to the effect that the Navy already possessed accurate charts of the islands, had examined them in detail on many previous occasions, and therefore believed that it would serve no useful purpose to make yet another investigation.[235] The Army War College expressed the prevailing opinion of both services when in 1912 it rejected the idea of acquiring outlying islands near the Isthmus to strengthen the canal's defenses. The permanent defenses being constructed in the Canal Zone would be sufficient. If the fleet was present, then these fortifications would more than meet any possible requirements; but even if the fleet was far distant, it would be better to concentrate all of the defense effort at fortified sites on the Isthmus than to scatter various defensive positions in and around the area. According to this analysis, which accorded with the studies of the General Board, there were "no detached positions near the Canal Zone, other than those now being fortified, the defense of which would add more to the security of the Canal than would employment of equal forces and resources within the Canal Zone."[236]

The possibility of acquiring Chimbote in Peru was again raised in the spring of 1909 when, according to the American minister, the Peruvian Foreign Minister freely offered it to the United States for the use of its fleet. The Navy gave a highly qualified endorsement. First, the General Board summarized all of the previous negotiations, stressing the many concessions and compensations which the Peruvians had formerly demanded and emphasizing that acceptance of the current offer should only be on the basis that Chimbote was freely offered with no strings of any sort attached. Second, and equally important, it specified the many reasons why, from a strictly naval point of view, the United States no longer needed a coaling station in that area and could take care of the needs of the fleet by the use of colliers.[237] For various reasons the Department of State took no action, but Adee noted that the approaching completion of the Panama Canal, in his judgment, made the acquisition of a coaling station more important than it had previ-

[235] GS, File 4520, Bell to Dickinson, 1 October 1909; SDNF, Case 16698/12, Doyle to Wilson, 13 November 1909, H. Wilson to Meyer, 2 December 1909, and Meyer to Knox, 30 December 1909.

[236] GS, War College Division, File 6178 is a complete record on the Pearl Islands question. See, especially, 6178/23, Meyer to Dickinson, which enclosed a report of the Strategic Committee of the Naval War College, dated 21 November 1911.

[237] GB, Proceedings, 8 April 1909, and Letters, VI, Dewey to Meyer, 8 April 1909.

ously appeared.[238] In the fall of 1911 Minister H. Clay Howard again revived the proposal. This time the American minister was interested in tying the Chimbote proposition to various schemes designed to get the Peruvians to order submarines for their navy from the United States, while the Peruvian government, in turn, still hoped through the cession to get American support in its long-standing dispute with Ecuador.[239] The Navy first took the attitude that such a station remained, as the admirals had always maintained, of no particular naval value and that it might be unwise to acquire Chimbote while other and more important positions remained undeveloped. But then the naval planners reversed themselves. They notified the State Department that their negative reaction had been based solely upon naval considerations but that they were prepared to change their minds if there were overriding political considerations. Ultimately the General Board recommended accepting Chimbote on the grounds that such a naval station would provide a foothold for intervention on the west coast of South America and help to protect the one and only country in that area which, according to the admirals, had a consistent record of friendship with the United States.[240]

Much the same reaction was exhibited when the Galapagos issue again came to life. The General Board once more argued in the summer of 1909 that the practice of coaling the fleet from colliers made the Galapagos unnecessary. But it could also envisage possible political advantages in acquiring them simply to take them off the international market. In 1910, however, the General Board paid more attention to the approaching completion of the Canal and conceded that, while the United States still did not need the islands, their acquisition made more sense with each passing year. Its endorsement was nevertheless backhanded:

> But, it must also be remembered that while the acquisition of the islands does not seem at present necessary except as a means of preventing the acquiring of influence in that region by a foreign power, yet nevertheless all the indications of the future point to an increase in the strategic value of the islands and that there seems no possibility of any decrease in that value. There can be no doubt as to the increase in the value of all land near the Panama Canal, both stra-

[238] SDNF, Case 18991/1-4, Adee memoranda of 14 April and 26 October 1909, attached to the Navy's original response, Meyer to Knox, 9 April 1909.

[239] SDDF, File 811.34523/4, Howard to Knox, 7 August 1911.

[240] SDDF, File 811.34523/8, Winthrop to Knox, 16 August 1911, and /11, Meyer to Knox, 11 November 1911. Also /12 and /14, two State Department memoranda, 22 November and 11 December 1911 which summarize thinking in the Latin American Division and the views of the naval officers they consulted.

tegically and commercially, so that, even as a financial measure, the acquirement of the islands would be remunerative and wise.[241]

In 1911 the Navy finally stated its willingness to purchase the islands and, on this occasion, clearly looked ahead to the strategic considerations which would apply when the canal was finished. But throughout these interchanges, it was the Department of State which generally seemed to be more interested and to be querying the Navy, even in the face of negative responses, about the merits of the Galapagos. The chief of the Latin American Division, for example, expressed considerable fear in 1910 that rumors of European interest in the Galapagos suggested "a carefully thought out effort on the part of certain European governments to secure control of the trade routes to the canal," while Huntington Wilson several times kept the issue alive by referring to alleged projects, sponsored by European governments, to obtain the islands.[242]

Moreover, the State Department was clearly behind the proposal, made early in 1913, to secure a base in the Gulf of Fonseca from Nicaragua. Its goal was to find a means of supporting the Diaz government, for the base proposal was but part of a larger treaty, involving rights for an American canal in Nicaragua, that would have provided immediate financial aid to that bankrupt nation. It does not even appear that the General Board or any one in the Navy was consulted at that time, for the measure was rushed hurriedly to the Senate on the eve of the administration's departure from office.[243] In Nicaraguan affairs, to be sure, this was not unusual. As far back as 1907 officials of the State Department, as well as their representatives in Central America, had considered the possibility of a base in the Gulf of Fonseca in terms of the political advantages that might accrue. "I think," Assistant Secretary Bacon had written, "that the matter of getting coaling stations in the Pacific is more important than the Navy admits." The Navy, when approached, had always given the same response about its lack of strategic value and only occasionally hinted that there might be political reasons that conceivably ought to be taken into account. Its recommendations, however, were always firmly against the acquisition of any site in the Gulf.[244]

The question of Caribbean bases also involved the Republic of Haiti

[241] GB, Letters, VI, Dewey to Meyer, 30 June 1910, and VII, Dewey to Meyer, 1 October 1910.

[242] SDDF, File 822.014/177, Latin American Affairs memorandum, 26 September 1910, and /176a, H. Wilson to Dickinson, 19 April 1911.

[243] Link, *The New Freedom*, 331-33.

[244] SDNF, Case 7055/1, Brown to Root, 28 May 1907, Newberry to Root, 2 July 1907, and Bacon to Adee, 10 July 1907; /2, Brown to Knox, 20 January 1910, and Meyer to Knox, 21 June 1910.

whose strategic location, as we have several times observed, made the Navy exceptionally interested in its affairs. During the Taft administration the particular issue which arose was whether or not the United States would permit the Haitians to grant naval concessions to Europeans. In June 1910 the Department of State was informed that the government of Haiti was about to grant monopolies of its coastwise shipping to a French commercial group and possibly also to a certain Hans Rankl, who was reputed to be an agent for the German Hamburg-America line. Those granted monopolies would also, according to the reports, be permitted to establish their own coaling stations at various points along the Haitian coast.[245] The government of President Antoine Simon was at once warned that the United States would not look with favor upon such concessions. Minister Henry Furniss added that the number of coaling stations seemed to be excessive, far more than would be necessary for the conduct of any purely commercial ventures. Indeed, their number was so great that they could be of value to a European power only if some military purpose was involved.[246]

The General Board, provided with the relevant diplomatic documents, soon produced a lengthy report of its own. The admirals, needless to say, opposed the rumored concessions. As defenders of American commerce, they saw these grants as harmful to American shipping interests. The imminent completion of the Panama canal, the naval board argued, would greatly increase Caribbean trade, "and, if there is going to be trade increase, all practicable steps should be taken to see that U. S. citizens are not debarred from it." The naval strategists, like Minister Furniss, were also convinced that the number of coaling stations involved could only mean that they were intended to serve a military purpose in time of war. Indeed, the admirals professed to see an emergent pattern in recent European activities in the Caribbean. This new European interest in Haiti, taken in conjunction with indications of French and German interest in the Galapagos, could only indicate

> that the German and French merchants, at least, if not their military officials as well, are thoroughly awake to the advisability of hemming in the approaches to the canal as to successfully exclude the United States from any considerable participation in such local trade as might result from the opening of the canal, at the same time establishing advantageous positions from which to threaten our possible military operations in time of war. The Department trusts that

[245] SDDF, File 838.802/1, Meyer to Knox, 21 June 1910.
[246] SDDF, File 838.802/3, Furniss to Knox, 20 July 1910.

steps may be successfully taken to prevent the accomplishment of either purpose.[247]

There is no better indication of the similarity of naval and State Department concerns than the single notation, "This is very important," which the Latin American Division placed upon this naval document. Moreover, both the Department of State and Furniss did treat the issue as very important. Furniss intensified his efforts to convince President Simon that some devious motives must lurk behind the European desire to acquire so many sites for coaling stations. The distances between the Haitian ports, he argued, were so short that commercial vessels would rarely, if ever, need to refuel; hence the purpose must "be to establish numerous warship fuelling points which would place the United States, the friend and protector of Haiti, at a disadvantage."[248] The Department of State felt sufficient concern to deliver an *aide-mémoire* to the Haitian minister in Washington which asked his government, as a mark of its friendship for the United States, to make no arrangements which the United States regarded as inimicable to the best interests of the Republic of Haiti. This flowery protestation of concern for the Haitian welfare was soon followed by a specific request that President Simon postpone any final decision until he and his government had an opportunity to examine new proposals about to be made by an American syndicate which "the Government of the United States hopes to find so beneficial to Haiti as to merit its sanction."[249] These gambits were eventually successful, though Furniss had his moments of doubt, especially when he learned that several of the sons of the Haitian president were deeply involved in the proposed schemes. However, the Haitian legislature eventually modified the proposed contracts and, by removing those features to which the United States most objected, made them far less attractive to the European syndicates. Furniss shortly became convinced that the concessions would now be of so little value that Rankl and his associates, to cut their losses, would be willing to sell them to any interested American group.[250]

The perennial problem of the Mole St. Nicholas, Haiti's finest harbor, arose a year later. An American syndicate notified the Department of State that it expected to lease the Mole but wished an opinion from the Department before proceeding further. The initial reaction

247 SDDF, File 838.802/1, Meyer to Knox, 21 June 1910.

248 SDDF, File 838.802/3, Furniss to Knox, 20 July 1910.

249 SDDF, File 838.802/8b, *aide-mémoire* given Haitian minister on 20 August 1910.

250 SDDF, File 838.802/4, Furniss to Knox, 19 August 1910, and /8 and /9 of 14 and 17 October 1910.

of the diplomats was favorable. Since the proposed concession would be entirely American owned, the Latin American Division anticipated the Navy's approval.[251] But the General Board was again skeptical. It still feared the establishment of fueling stations on Haiti no matter who controlled them. Such stations, at which large supplies of coal would be maintained, would be unprotected in time of war, liable to seizure by America's enemies, and therefore a menace to the United States. The admirals endorsed in principle the idea that American citizens should enjoy the benefits of Caribbean trade expansion, but they wanted first to be certain that the number of bases in Haiti was severely limited, the quantity of coal maintained at them kept at the minimum, and the ownership clearly American.[252] The Navy, in short, still lacked confidence about its ability to control the Caribbean. It remained prone to fears of vague dangers, and, in this instance, worried that Haitian coal depots would serve as a temptation to potential enemies. Knox, it should be added, communicated all of the Navy's observations to the American syndicate in mid-1912; thereafter nothing was heard from the group while his administration remained in office.[253]

6. Insurrection in the Caribbean: Haiti, Santo Domingo, Cuba

Both Haiti and the Dominican Republic experienced political disorders during the years of the Taft administration. Indeed, beginning with the early months of 1911, insurrection was the almost constant state of affairs in Haiti. Constant also was the presence of American warships. At one time in 1911 no less than five American naval vessels were in Haitian waters, plus several European naval craft, while the Department of State never failed to ask the Navy to send a vessel to a trouble spot whenever one of its representatives requested naval assistance. By August 1911 Furniss had become so fearful of a general outbreak in Port-au-Prince that he asked the Department of State to give the naval command in Haiti virtually a free hand to act in any emergency. Standing orders, the minister claimed, should permit the Navy to prevent armed conflict within the Haitian capital and to take whatever action might be necessary to protect American life and prop-

[251] SDDF, File 838.345 consists of some 15 documents pertaining to the Mole that were collected between 1911 and 1913. They are all summarized in a covering memorandum prepared by the Latin American Affairs Division on 14 June 1913.

[252] SDDF, File 838.345/10, Meyer to Knox, 29 February 1912, /12, Andrews to Knox, 27 June, and /15, Winthrop to Knox, 1 August 1912; GB, Proceedings, 25 June and 30 July 1912.

[253] SDDF, File 838.345, summary memorandum of 14 June 1913.

erty.[254] Knox concurred. Back to the naval watch came the terse orders, "If hostilities between rival factions become imminent, define neutral zone and prevent fighting in the city. Land forces if necessary, safeguard American interests, and in general prevent any action detrimental to foreign interests."[255] The naval commander was, of course, asked to keep in touch with Furniss. Even so, it was a sweeping grant of discretionary authority to the Navy, an indication of the extent to which Knox and his associates were prepared to intervene in the Republic. But, on this occasion, the predicted emergency simply did not occur. The Navy then wished to reduce the number of vessels at Port-au-Prince to a single warship but was immediately confronted with Knox's personal veto. So widespread were American interests in Haiti and so great the chances of further disturbances, the Secretary of State advised, "that it will be necessary, for the present at least, to maintain a considerable naval force in Haitian waters in order to afford prompt and adequate protection."[256]

It was in the Dominican Republic that the strong hand of Philander Knox was most clearly demonstrated. Nothing was to be permitted to upset the operations of the customs receivership. "Because of the position which the United States occupies in the collection and administration of the customs of the Dominican Republic," the State Department informed the Navy in 1911, "this Department would regard any political upheaval . . . as most unfortunate."[257] Thus, when rumors began to circulate that ex-President Morales was plotting a return to power, the State Department immediately saw to it that the naval command was furnished with orders which, without specifying ways and means, directed it to prevent any landing by Morales or his followers on the Dominican coast.[258]

Early in 1912 the Navy suggested that its standing orders were insufficient and that the absence of definite, specific instructions was a handicap to its officers in Dominican waters. Huntington Wilson, William Doyle (the head of the Latin American Division), and, eventually, Knox himself collaborated in producing the desired guidelines. Their document was fully indicative of the spirit of their Caribbean policy. The United States, it argued, was deeply concerned with the preserva-

254 SDDF, File 838.00/625, Knox to Meyer, 5 August 1911, summarizing Furniss cables.

255 SDDF, File 838.00/632, Winthrop to Knox, 5 August, indicating orders sent by Navy Department.

256 SDDF, File 838.00/645-48, Latin American Affairs memorandum, 7 August 1911, Winthrop to Knox, 11 August 1911, and Knox to Meyer, 12 August 1911.

257 SDDF, File 839.00/326e, H. Wilson to Meyer, 16 February 1911.

258 SDDF, File 839.00/326f, and /333, H. Wilson to Meyer, 20 February 1911, and Latin American Affairs memorandum, Doyle to H. Wilson, 19 February 1911.

tion of law, peace, and constitutional order in the Dominican Republic as a consequence of the "rights and obligations granted to and imposed upon" that country by the treaty of 1907. Political stability in the Republic was absolutely essential and must be maintained so that the receiver general of the customs could perform his duties without interruption. It therefore followed that "civil disturbances of all kinds are therefore much to be deprecated and should be avoided as interfering with that maintenance of constitutional law and order which is absolutely necessary to the discharge of the above duties." But, the Navy was also told, the administration never wished it to operate independently of civilian guidance. Whenever action was contemplated, there must always be a full exchange of views between the naval officers on duty in Santo Domingo and the Legation at the capital.[259]

The lengths to which the State Department was willing to go to enforce that policy became obvious in the summer of 1912 when officials of the Latin American Division decided that the moment for decisive intervention had arrived. Dominican politics had, in their view, deteriorated rapidly since the preceding autumn when the assassination of President Ramon Caceras had brought the Victoria regime into power. In departmental eyes the Victoria government was a clear disaster; it was plagued by rising disorders, handled its finances as poorly as the pre-1907 regimes, and—a cardinal sin—interfered with the customs receivership; and it was also unable to cope with an unresolved border controversy with Haiti. Nor did the various revolutionary groups appeal to the Department of State, for they, it was alleged, did not represent "the best elements" in the Republic.[260] The American minister at Santo Domingo City, W. W. Russell, urged outright intervention and American control of the country as the only way to assure order and justice. "Without our effective control," Russell advised, "one administration here would be as good as another." His preferred remedy was to land American troops ostensibly to protect the customs houses but actually to use their presence "to dictate by persuasion or force a policy beneficial to the country."[261]

Assistant Secretary Huntington Wilson had already lost his patience with the Dominicans. He personally drafted and sent to Taft a long memorandum which argued that, if the Dominican situation were permitted to fester, the entire Caribbean policy of the United States would soon be discredited. His solution, which won Knox's approval, involved a dual approach. First, the United States would inform both

[259] SDDF, File 839.00/465, Memorandum, Doyle to H. Wilson, 10 January 1912, and Knox to Meyer, 15 January 1912.

[260] SDDF, File 839.00/659, H. Wilson to Taft, 19 September 1912.

[261] SDDF, File 839.00/657, Russell to Knox, 19 September 1912.

the Haitian and Dominican governments of its intention to run the disputed boundary line once and for all and then to enforce it by a border patrol operated by the customs receivership. Second, a few days thereafter, the Dominican government would be informed that the best interests of the Republic required the resignation and removal from the Victoria government of the Minister of War and Marine. The absolute prerequisite for success, Wilson insisted, was the assignment to Santo Domingo of a first-class warship, with an adequate landing force aboard—"the arrival of this ship to synchronize with the presentation of the note." Similarly, a war vessel must be sent to Port-au-Prince, "in the event that the Haitian attitude upon the boundary line shall prove such as to require this show of interest." Wilson, aware that the Navy had plans of its own to assign all available ships to duty at a forthcoming naval review, argued strenuously that "this is preeminently a case where naval vessels are necessary to the support of diplomatic representations, and one where there are at stake such grave matters of policy and national interest that the need is, in fact, paramount to all ordinary considerations." If the Dominicans resisted, the State Department was prepared to press its demands to the ultimate limits—short of outright hostilities—that could be justified under the treaty of 1907 and "the whole theory of our relations with that Republic." Contemplated actions included the forcible occupation of the customs houses and the rupture of diplomatic relations. Wilson also suggested that if President Taft agreed to press these demands, then the chief of the Latin American Division as well as a high-ranking military officer ought to be sent to the Dominican Republic in an effort to obtain compliance.[262]

This, in essence, was the course of action eventually followed. William Doyle and General McIntyre of the Bureau of Insular Affairs were appointed special commissioners by Taft. Their first assignment was actually to report back to Washington whether or not the suggested note of Huntington Wilson should be presented and, if so, to recommend methods to implement it. They were sent aboard the *Prairie*, which had a complement of 750 marines, and were authorized to use the marine force to re-establish control over the Dominican customs houses if that proved necessary.[263] Once arrived at the Dominican capital, they called for additional naval reinforcements. Knox approved their request, "since it is believed by the Department that the presence of these gunboats in Dominican waters would be of great moral value and thus result in strengthening the hands of the Commis-

262 SDDF, File 839.00/659d, H. Wilson to Taft, 19 September 1912. See also Rodman, *Quisqueya*, 118.

263 SDDF, File 839.00/664, H. Wilson to Doyle and McIntyre, 24 September 1912.

sioners and enable them to bring the purposes of this government . . . to a much earlier and more satisfactory conclusion."[264] Both War and Navy Departments, incidentally, were fully prepared for full-scale involvement. The General Board pulled its long-established Haiti-Santo Domingo plan from the files and lent it to Doyle's group, while the Army General Staff prepared a detailed report on its plans for an Army occupation to follow any naval landing.[265] Such action ultimately proved unnecessary. The presence of the superior force commanded by Doyle and McIntyre was more than sufficient. The Victoria government caved in, without even the necessity of landing the 750 marines. Before long a meeting on the *Prairie* had produced not only the resignation of some of Victoria's cabinet but the end of his regime and its replacement by one headed by Archbishop Nouel.[266]

Cuba was even closer and more immediate to the Navy. During the Taft administration, the Navy was involved in Cuban affairs almost to the extent that it had been in the palmy days of Roosevelt. Also, as in the preceding years, two issues—Guantanamo and revolution—concerned the Navy.

The original grant of land for Guantanamo, as noted in an earlier chapter, had left the Navy dissatisfied. "I have never visited Guantanamo Bay since that time," the commander of the Atlantic fleet once wrote Admiral Dewey, "without being impressed by the inadequacy of the cession and the certainty of its capture by any resolute enemy who chose to land on Cuban soil outside the limits of the station."[267] Diplomatic efforts to extend the base had begun, as we have also observed, before the second occupation of 1906 but came to an end when Root ruled that it would be inappropriate for the United States to press the issue while it was administering the government. The Navy reopened the question as soon as the occupation had ended and the Taft administration was in office. This time the Department of State was fully cooperative, and the American chargé d'affaires in Havana was instructed to find out if there was any willingness on the part of the Cubans to meet the Navy's wishes.[268] There was absolutely none. The Cubans, true to form, reverted to their familiar tactic of delay. The Cuban Foreign Minister simply turned aside the first inquiry by alleging "that he was exceptionally pre-occupied and couldn't give the matter proper attention." Soon the chargé accurately reported that the

264 SDDF, File 839.00/727, Knox to Taft, 29 October 1912.

265 GB, Proceedings, 17 December 1912; GS, Second Section, File 7428, Memorandum for the Chief of Staff, Crozier to Wood, 19 November 1912.

266 Munro, *Dollar Diplomacy*, 262-64.

267 GB, File 406, Pillsbury to Dewey, 27 December 1906.

268 SDNF, Case 4631/11-12, Adee to Morgan, 17 July 1909; GB, File 406, Meyer to Knox, 13 July 1909.

idea of enlarging Guantanamo was something "that the Cuban government would have preferred not to have to deal with." The political sensitivities of the Cubans, he forecast, were such that the Foreign Office would attempt to block any and all negotiations.[269]

A year later the Navy was back on the Cuban doorstep with a specific plan to trade its unused lease at Bahia Hondo for an extension of Guantanamo. Such a trade had first been suggested in 1906 but it was not until 1910 that it emerged as a full-blown, specific proposal, carrying the endorsement of all three service boards—General Board, General Staff, and Joint Board. The Joint Board's formal proposal, which was furnished to the Department of State, argued that Bahia Hondo was in a particularly rich and promising part of Cuba, an area which might in the future emerge as a major commercial and shipping center. But since the United States had leased land on both sides of the bay, America held a potential control over all seaborne traffic with Bahia Hondo. It therefore followed, the Joint Board suggested, that the cession of this valuable lease might be the appropriate carrot to dangle before the suspicious Cubans.[270]

Knox and his associates agreed. Minister John Jackson was instructed to reopen negotiations—and to make the usual argument that enlargement of Guantanamo was necessary "to enable the United States to maintain the independence of Cuba and to protect the people thereof as well as for its own defense."[271] After several false starts there then ensued several years of protracted negotiations which finally culminated in the signing of a treaty between the United States and Cuba for the cession of Bahia Hondo and the enlargement of Guantanamo.[272] But, alas for the Navy, it was a Pyrrhic victory. The Cuban Senate refused to ratify the treaty, thus denying to the Navy the land it so eagerly coveted.

The details of these lengthy negotiations are tedious in the extreme and need no elaborate examination. The State and Navy Departments cooperated throughout but had to contend with the Cuban predilection for postponement—the first of which was a plea to suspend negotiations until after forthcoming Cuban national elections.[273] The still unsettled issue of the Isle of Pines was again introduced and complicated the discussions.[274] But there were also complications on the

269 SDNF, Case 4631/13-14, Dearing to Knox, 16 September 1909. This material is also in GB, File 406.

270 JB, Minutes, 31 May 1910; GS, File 5288, Dickinson to Knox, 3 June 1910; SDDF, File 811.345/15, Dickinson to Knox, 3 June 1910, enclosing Joint Board report.

271 SDDF, 811.345/24, H. Wilson to John Jackson, 8 September 1910.

272 SDDF, File 811.345/112, Beaupré to Knox, 27 December 1912.

273 SDDF, File 811.345/24, Jackson to Knox, 10 September 1912.

274 SDDF, File 811.345/119, Beaupré to Knox, 23 January 1913.

American side. For some months the Secretary of the Navy, George V. Meyer, had his own doubts about the trade and had to be convinced by the General Board.[275] There were leaks to various newspapers which prompted land speculators to buy up properties adjacent to the existing boundaries of Guantanamo in the hope of making a future financial killing.[276] There were issues of substance as well: the Cubans worried about American financial claims for the period of the second occupation and the extent to which these might affect the Guantanamo settlement, while the Navy long refused to forego its jurisdiction over the waters leading into Guantanamo Bay.[277] But finally in the summer of 1911 the negotiators produced an agreement which satisfied both the General Board and the Department of State.

For some months afterwards there was optimism about securing Cuban approval of the agreement. Then rumors began to redouble about land speculation. It was reported that the Cuban President was unwilling to sign because his government would have to pay two million dollars to acquire land whose true value was scarcely one-quarter of that figure. Soon the Cubans began to argue that the United States should increase the rental fee paid for the Guantanamo lease—which then stood at the nominal sum of $2,000 per year.[278]

The Navy, growing worried, sought Presidential assistance and submitted a great bundle of documents to Taft. It argued that speed was essential since yet another session of the Cuban Senate was drawing to a close with no action imminent.[279] Taft and Meyer both asked Secretary Knox, who planned a visit to Cuba, to use his influence to expedite the affair.[280] Naval officers participated in a full-dress conference with top-ranking officials of the State Department in an attempt to get an intensified diplomatic effort.[281] It was all to no avail. For months the sticking point remained the annual rent. Taft had adopted the argument, with which the Navy concurred, that the cession of Bahia Hondo ought to be sufficient in itself and that the most the United States could consider was a token increase in the Guantanamo rental. Thus, the case dragged on into and through the summer of 1912—the Cubans insisting on $25,000 per year and the State Depart-

[275] SDDF, File 811.345/29, Jackson to Knox, 31 October 1910, reporting Meyer's hesitations.

[276] SDDF, File 811.345/79, Beaupré to Knox, 3 February 1912.

[277] SDDF, File 811.345/54, Jackson to Knox, 12 April 1911, and /51, Meyer to Knox, 28 February 1911.

[278] SDDF, File 811.345/74-76, Beaupré to Knox, 19 and 26 December 1911.

[279] SDDF, File 811.345/90, Taft to Knox, 17 February 1912.

[280] *Ibid.*, and /91, Meyer to Knox, 16 February 1912.

[281] SDDF, File 811.345/94, Memorandum of the Solicitor, 27 April 1912.

ment, following the advice of the Navy, offering one-tenth of that figure. Finally a compromise figure of $5,000 was reached, and the two
governments formally signed the agreement in December of 1912.[282]

It was now the turn of the Cuban senate. In raising objections it was
undoubtedly as skillful as the more famous Battalion of Death that
fought the Versailles Treaty in the United States senate in 1919. But
its problem was more simple: given Cuban sensitivities to Yankee imperialism, no Cuban senator, with national elections pending, wanted
to assume political responsibility for ceding national territory to the
United States Navy. The gambit was to raise obstructions, to delay—
and to leave the treaty for the *next* senate to handle after the election.
Which, of course, is precisely what happened. President Gomez gave
repeated promises of action, but late in the spring of 1913 the Senate
adjourned without having voted on the treaty. That was that: despite
the best efforts of the State and Navy Departments, of the Joint and
General Boards, and of William Howard Taft, the endeavor failed.[283]

Only a brief postscript is required. A year later the Department of
State received word from Cuba that the senate was at last ready to act
and that only a few details of the treaty would have to be renegotiated.
John Bassett Moore, the Solicitor in Bryan's Department of State,
urged the Navy to make its suggestions at once since the United States
would have to move rapidly to take advantage of the unanticipated
opportunity. Next morning the Aide for Operations, Commander
Sypher, appeared in the Office of the Latin American Division of the
Department of State. To the complete surprise of the diplomats
Sypher announced that the Navy was considering "a complete change
of plans . . . in connection with the expansion of Guantanamo." He
asked for a delay of three to four days so that the planners could complete their work.[284] The Navy missed the deadline. In fact it was not
until July 1915—two years later—that the State Department learned
what the Navy had in mind. At that time naval planners told the State
Department that, with the help of the United States Geological Survey,
it was investigating the possibility of obtaining water from artesian
wells drilled within the limits of the existing base. There was therefore
no need for diplomatic action on the extension of Guantanamo until
the geological study was complete.[285] That about finished the project.

[282] SDDF, File 811.345/97-112, various documents in this file for the period April
through December 1912.

[283] SDDF, File 811.345/117-122, Beaupré to Knox, 22 January, 27 February and
19 March 1913.

[284] SDDF, File 811.345/126, Latin American Affairs Division memorandum, Long
to Gibson, 20 January 1914.

[285] SDDF, File 811.345/129, Daniels to Lansing, 16 July 1915.

In the 1920s, for instance, a formal inquiry brought the statement that the Navy had now abandoned all interest in the enlargement of Guantanamo.[286] In 1930 the Council on Foreign Relations asked Dana Munro, the head of the Latin American Division, what had happened to Bahia Hondo. Munro replied promptly, if inaccurately, "An agreement of 27 December 1912 designed to restore Bahia Hondo to Cuba was ratified by this country on February 24, 1913, but it was not ratified by the Government of Cuba and therefore has not become effective."[287]

Although American troops departed from Cuba in 1909, the Taft administration continued to express concern about the possibility of further political disorder. Many in Washington continued to doubt the ability of the Cubans to conduct their affairs. Intervention within the framework of the Platt Amendment was in fact more than just a possibility on several occasions during Knox's tenure in the Department of State.

Late in December 1911 political tensions began to grow in Cuba over a decree by President José Gomez which forbade army officers to involve themselves in politics and, above all, to take an active role in the Veterans Association, an organization of former officers who had served in the insurrection against Spain. The American minister was afraid that the Cuban president might, under pressure, revoke his decree, thereby sanctioning military meddling in politics and opening the way for political disorders.[288] He envisioned a situation in which "we would have to intervene to restore order" and persuaded Knox to inform President Gomez that the United States expected him to uphold the laws in force and to preserve Cuba's republican institutions.[289] Soon, to the rejoicing of the Department of State, Gomez announced that he was prepared to keep the veterans associations under strict control. But in the interim there had been "veiled hints" that the United States might have to intervene if the situation deteriorated.[290]

Knox's diplomacy apparently created a furor in the War Department. On the day after the Secretary of State had sent his strong warning to the Cubans, Henry Stimson had a long discussion with his newly-appointed Chief of Staff, General Leonard Wood. Wood, of course, had already run one Cuban occupation and had his own decided opinions about what was best for Cuba. He thought that Knox's

[286] SDDF, File 811.345/135, Roosevelt to General Crowder, 29 July 1921.
[287] SDDF, File 811.345/177, Dana Munro to Martha Anderson, 11 January 1930.
[288] SDDF, File 837.00/541, Beaupré to Knox, 5 January 1912.
[289] SDDF, File 837.00/541, Knox to Beaupré, 5 January 1912.
[290] Munro, *Dollar Diplomacy*, 474-77.

message had been "alarming" since it had virtually threatened American intervention unless Gomez cracked down on the veterans. He observed that Secretary Stimson was apprehensive lest the United States be drawn into a situation that would once again require direct intervention. The Chief of Staff confided to his diary that

> It seems to me that we are going altogether too fast in this matter and are swinging the big stick over the little countries to too great an extent. The action taken in regard to Honduras, the bullyragging of Chile and other countries, is doing more to overthrow the good effects of Mr. Root's policies than all else combined. The Cuban situation, while presenting nothing alarming, is annoying; there is nothing serious as yet unless we irritate them into an attitude which will require another intervention.[291]

Wood, always cocksure of his own opinions, may have been a biased witness but his assessment of the effect of Knox's policies on Latin opinion was far from incorrect.

The spring of 1912 produced another Cuban crisis, an uprising of various groups of Negroes against President Gomez. As the movement gained in force, it also increased in complexity. Minister Arthur Beaupré first thought that it had been provoked by Cubans who wanted an American intervention, later decided that the Cuban President was implicated and hoped to use the revolt as a means of guaranteeing his own re-election.[292] The somewhat curious behavior of government troops when facing the Negro rebels added to American suspicions. Thus, there was a mood of some caution in the Department of State. By late May, however, both Beaupré and American naval officials in Havana advised a concentration of naval forces prepared either to protect American lives and property or to conduct a full-scale intervention if that became necessary.[293] A conference between officials of the State and Navy departments produced an order sending all ships then in the vicinity of Guantanamo to that base with instructions to await further orders to cope with a situation that "seemed seriously disordered." The Marine Corps was also ordered to get as many men as possible to Guantanamo. Within a few more days the Navy indicated that it had nine vessels in readiness—including the flagship of the Atlantic Fleet and a hospital ship, a force obviously ready for a major operation. But, as in 1906, the orders given the Navy were cautious. Naval commanders were instructed to intervene only to protect

---

291 Wood Papers, Diary, 16-17 January 1912.
292 SDDF, File 837.00/596, Beaupré to Knox, 22 May 1912, and /600 of 23 May.
293 SDDF, File 837.00/612, Beaupré to Knox, 25 May 1912.

American lives and property and were not authorized to intervene in Cuban politics.[294] Knox put the government of President Gomez on notice to "come to its sense of responsibilities" and suppress the rebellion lest the United States be compelled "to consider the need for giving protection itself to American interests."[295]

By June, as the situation worsened, Gomez was requesting emergency powers from his Congress, while Beaupré was emphasizing a potentially serious danger to foreign residents. The Navy informed the State Department that it was prepared for major landings; the Army provided Knox with a collection of maps, prepared in the two previous occupations, of every major foreign interest on the island.[296] Outbreaks within Havana were followed by the arrival of two American war vessels in that city's harbor, and some troops were posted on Cuban territory adjacent to the Guantanamo naval station. While Gomez protested the sending of the ships, he apparently indicated a willingness to accept American troops in his country on the grounds that their presence would provide protection for foreign interests and at the same time free his own soldiers for operations against the rebels.[297]

But the third occupation never occurred. As in 1906 the State Department remained reluctant to assume responsibility for a full-scale intervention. Knox always maintained that the vessels sent to Havana had been dispatched solely to provide a place of refuge for foreigners and for "such moral effect as they might have to calm the situation." Outwardly at least he seemed to hope that the Cubans, with American prodding, could themselves control the Negro uprisings.[298]

Washington relied, then, on the moral effect of warships strategically placed in Cuban waters and fully prepared to intervene if ordered. Beaupré came to accept this solution especially when, by late June, the Cuban government began to quell the uprising through its own efforts. But both he and Admiral Osterhaus, the senior naval officer present, strongly urged retention of the warships "for moral effect if not upon a far more serious duty." Both American officials were firmly convinced that it was the arrival of American warships in Cuban waters which had finally prodded the Cuban government into positive action against the rebels. Osterhaus, in his report, noted that the

[294] SDDF, File 837.00/619A, Knox to Meyer, 23 May 1912, and /638, Winthrop to Knox, 30 May 1912.

[295] SDDF, File 837.00/643, Knox to Beaupré, 30 May 1912.

[296] SDDF, File 837.00/655, /660, and /671, Beaupré to Knox, 1-3 June 1912; also, /689, Winthrop to Knox, 3 June 1912, and /690, Robert Shaw Oliver to Knox, 3 June 1912.

[297] SDDF, File 837.00/693, Beaupré to Knox, 5 June 1912.

[298] SDDF, File 837.00/737a, Knox to Beaupré, 10 June 1912.

Cubans were at last making serious efforts to end the disturbances and was positive that "these efforts are due to the presence of our own ships in Cuban waters and vicinity and ready to act promptly should the occasion arise."[299]

Once again, however, Knox's handling of the Cuban question struck a sour note with his critic, Leonard Wood. In early June, at a time when intervention had seemed a real probability, Knox formally requested the Army to prepare the 11th Cavalry, the 5th, 17th, and 29th Infantry Regiments, plus a battery of field artillery. To Wood this was an extreme and foolish measure, another indication of Knox's incapacity. At lunch the same day he chanced to notice Knox and Huntington Wilson seated at an adjacent table and engaged in a whispered conversation which, the Chief of Staff assumed, could only have concerned Cuba. That night he recalled the scene in his diary: "It would be hard to imagine two men who know less about it, and from the way the Cuban situation is being handled by the State Department, it can be depended upon to develop a formidable amount of trouble before we take any common sense action." Leonard Wood, naturally, had his own solution, a nostrum which he freely offered to many government officials but for which he found no takers. He wanted naval vessels sent up and down the eastern coast of Cuba, with their sailors given plenty of shore leave so their presence would be widely noticed. The Cuban government should also be asked to invite the Navy to conduct practice landing operations—in short, various devices whereby American military personnel would be highly visible throughout Cuba but without any official intervention. "This would be reported by every Negro coming in for tobacco and ammunition," Wood claimed, "and would soon reach the ill-organized and entirely purposeless groups of Negroes who are now causing so much anxiety."[300]

The general also, and on his own responsibility, chatted with the Cuban minister in Washington about the uprisings—and was told that his ideas were being forwarded to the Gomez regime in Havana. Wood tried to convey a warning that the United States government was seriously concerned by the revolt but also ventured the opinion that there probably would be no intervention. He went on to predict, however, that if intervention did occur, the Army would merely garrison Cuba at major strategic locations and expect the Cuban army to do its own fighting against the Negroes. He recorded in his diary that he remained silent when the Cuban minister asked if he would be in charge of the occupying forces and suggested that Cuban opinion

[299] SDDF, File 837.00/799, Beaupré to Knox, 18 June 1912, also forwarding views of Osterhaus.
[300] Wood Papers, Diary, 7 June 1912.

would be much less hostile if he were selected.[301] It is impossible to tell if Wood's marginal involvement on the fringes of Cuban diplomacy had any appreciable effect. But, since he had once governed Cuba, it is likely that his observations had some effect on its government. And Beaupré later complained that the Cuban government circulated rumors that Wood might be sent to investigate the Negro demands and would insist that the rebels be given a place in government. But whatever the effect, or however the Cuban government may have sought to employ Wood's name, it was an early precedent of actual military involvement in the processes of diplomacy.

7. MEXICO: "THERE IS A GOD IN ISRAEL AND HE IS ON DUTY"

Both William Howard Taft and Woodrow Wilson were to discover in Mexico and its revolution of 1911 an issue of the greatest complexity and difficulty. The historian of American foreign policy also finds, to his surprise, that an almost incalculable amount of American time and energy went into the "Mexican problem" that began midway in Taft's administration and was still unresolved on the eve of America's entry into World War I. Moreover, in the evolution of the Mexican policy of both administrations the military were to play a significant role, one which affected both the formulation and implementation of that policy.

In early 1911, when the first signs of revolt stirred in Mexico, Taft's sympathies were entirely with the conservative government of President Porfirio Diaz. In reply to an early request "to do something" about Mexico, Taft reacted sharply:

> I don't know what Ed Thatcher wants. Does he think we ought to intervene in Mexico and uplift the downtrodden citizens who attract his attention? Of all the people who are annoying, the uplifters without any sense are the most so. My own impression is that Diaz has done more for the people of Mexico than any other Latin American has done for any of his people; but the truth is they need a firm hand in Mexico and everybody realizes it.[302]

By no stretch of the imagination could Henry Lane Wilson, Taft's ambassador in Mexico City, have qualified as an uplifter. He grew increasingly perturbed by the facts of political disorder and especially by the many signs that this was not a typical Latin revolt but a genuine social revolution against the established order. Eventually Wilson would be personally involved, at the very least, in providing intellec-

---

[301] Wood Papers, Diary, 8 June 1912.
[302] Taft Papers, Letterpress, Taft to Horace Taft, 19 January 1911.

tual support for the Mexican conservatives who sought in vain to stem the tide. By early March 1911 he had become sufficiently alarmed to hasten to Washington to express his fears personally to the President. To judge by Taft's subsequent account of their discussion, his ambassador was close to panic. For the President was told that

> Mexico was boiling . . . General Diaz was on a volcano . . . and the small outbreaks were only symptomatic of the whole condition, in which 90% of the people were in sympathy with the insurrection; that a general explosion was probable at any time, in which case he feared that the 40,000 or more Americans would be assailed and American investments of more than a billion dollars would be injured or destroyed because of the anti-American spirit of the insurrection.[303]

Taft clearly was shaken. To his former mentor, Roosevelt, he wrote of the "volcano-like conditions" in Mexico, while to Knox, then vacationing in Florida, he underlined his fears for Americans in Mexico and the need to protect them "should the explosion come."[304]

In the absence of Knox, the President, for one of the few times in his presidential career, took the initiative in a matter of foreign policy. He summoned his service secretaries along with General Wood and Admiral Wainwright to the White House for an immediate conference. It was decided to mobilize a division of 20,000 men just north of the border in Texas, to stage a series of maneuvers with these troops, and to keep them in Texas for at least several months—in short, to be prepared in the event that the explosion feared by Henry Lane Wilson actually occurred. Taft's military advisers believed that such a mobilization would also be in the best interests of the Army. Both Secretary Dickinson and Leonard Wood affirmed that "as this was just the season for maneuvers in Texas, they thought it would be an excellent thing for the army and navy to have a mobilization at Galveston, San Antonio, and Los Angeles."[305]

Yet Taft, it must be emphasized, did not contemplate an actual intervention. His policy for Mexico resembled the tactics he and Knox had pursued in dealing with the smaller Latin states: to impress Mexico by the "moral force" of military power displayed on its border. The President promptly dispatched several letters to Leonard Wood in which he emphasized that the purpose of the mobilization was to "hold

---

[303] Taft Papers, Taft to Wood, 12 March 1911.

[304] Taft Papers, Taft to Roosevelt, 22 March 1911; Knox Papers, Taft to Knox, 11 March 1911.

[305] Taft Papers, Taft to Knox and Roosevelt, 11 and 22 March 1911.

up the hands of the existing government and [it] will have healthy moral effect to prevent attacks upon Americans and their property in any subsequent general internecine strife." Massed American forces on the border would spur the Mexican government to hold firm and at the same time give pause to those who might be contemplating violent action against American interests. It was also his duty as commander-in-chief, Taft believed, to have troops available for prompt action if the Congress should actually direct him to send forces into Mexico to protect Americans and their properties.[306] But this, again it must be emphasized, was an eventuality that the President did not anticipate. He wrote Admiral Wainwright that the very presence of American troops in Texas should prevent the need for intervention. But even if they did not, he would not make the decision himself, for "I seriously doubt whether I have such authority under any circumstances, and, if I had, I would not exercise it without express Congressional authority."[307]

Taft therefore sought to minimize the implications of the coming mobilization. He insisted that public announcements by the War Department must emphasize that the mobilization of troops was solely for maneuvers, merely a training exercise that fell well within routine military operations.[308] When certain sensationalist accounts began to appear in both the Mexican and American press, Taft carefully instructed the State Department to advise the Mexican government to pay no attention to them since the mobilization was not against Mexico and should be of no concern to its citizens.[309] Certain American editors were provided with confidential summaries of Taft's conferences and correspondence on Mexico and requested not to disclose their contents, even to their own newspaper staffs.[310]

But it was a sticky policy to maintain. As Philander Knox pointed out, there was an excellent chance of a "shindy" in Congress,

what with de la Barre [the Mexican ambassador] howling for strict enforcement of neutrality, with Wilson throwing fits about the imminence of Diaz going up in an explosion, with Americans with interests in Mexico demanding protection against real and fancied dangers, and Americans with no interests in Mexico but with large newspaper investments at home wanting to see the worst happen; with the Monroe Doctrine constantly requiring a measure of benevolent supervision over Latin American countries to meet its logical

[306] Taft Papers, Taft to Wood, 12 March 1911.
[307] Taft Papers, Taft to Admiral Wainwright, 12 March 1911.
[308] Taft Papers, Taft to Knox, 11 March 1911.
[309] Taft Papers, Taft to Adee, 12 March 1911.
[310] Taft Papers, Taft to Knox, 27 March 1911.

requirements; with the delicate entente with the Latin which has been nourished and maintained largely in the past upon champagne and other alcoholic preservatives.[311]

But were Taft's procedures sufficiently effective? The President remained certain that it was correct policy not to spell out the complexities of his approach; the moral effect of simply putting troops in Texas "would be quite as great whether we were to express our purpose or left it to be inferred."[312] Both Huntington Wilson and Leonard Wood thought that Taft was leaving too much to inference. The Assistant Secretary, who wanted to seize the shining moment to press certain demands on the Mexicans, wrote: "I believe that it would have been better to make no bones about it and to let it be understood as a matter of course that we wanted adequate troops within reach in case of some unlooked-for-eventuality involving violence to American and foreign life and property." He would explain the suddenness of the mobilization with the "cover story" that there had been much criticism of the efficiency of the Army and that Taft wished to give it an assignment that had to be accomplished in a hurry.[313] The Chief of Staff felt similarly. Both he and Secretary Dickinson had advised the President "to come out and say that the troops were going to strengthen the patrol and to be able to protect our interests if necessary, but he deemed it wiser to proceed as he did."[314]

As events proved, there was in fact plenty of room for misinterpretation. Military leaders, then concerned with plans for the anticipated Council of National Defense, found in the Mexican situation yet another valid argument in behalf of the need for better military and diplomatic coordination. "We are now engaged in preparing plans to meet possible contingencies in Mexico," one of their spokesmen wrote, "and are so seriously handicapped by not knowing what the State Department's policy would be should developments necessitate our intervention that the work cannot be intelligently prosecuted. All we can do is to prepare plans to meet what we *think might be the desires of the Administration*, and this, of course, multiplies our work greatly."[315]

There was immediate friction with the Navy. Within a few days after he had ordered the mobilization, Taft received an unexpected protest from the government of General Diaz. The Mexican president complained that orders given to units of the United States Navy to visit ports on both coasts of Mexico might very well produce a state of

311 Knox Papers, Knox to Taft, 15 March 1911.
312 Taft Papers, Taft to Knox, 11 March 1911.
313 Huntington Wilson Papers, Wilson to Knox, 10 March 1911.
314 Wood Papers, Diary, 29 March 1911.
315 GS, File 6320-8, Wotherspoon to Commander Hill, 13 April 1911.

general public alarm in his country. Diaz asked the President to make a public statement that would tranquilize Mexican opinion and indicate that the movement of American warships had nothing whatsoever to do with the coming Army maneuvers in Texas.[316] Taft was taken completely by surprise. As part of his overall program he had approved a long-anticipated naval plan to hold battleship maneuvers in the Gulf, but he had approved no orders to send smaller vessels into Mexican ports.[317] But Mexico was at once given the required assurances, while the Navy, no less rapidly, was told not to send any of its ships into Mexican harbors.[318]

The more Taft reflected upon the incident, the more angry he became. In his first phone call to the Navy Department he made the point that he "had not been informed of the orders which sent these vessels to Mexican ports."[319] He confided to Theodore Roosevelt his suspicion that the Navy had, on its own initiative, decided to patrol Mexican coasts. "The Navy," he added, "is anxious for a contest and has to be held in leash."[320] If so, it was released in no uncertain terms. Secretary Meyer shortly was the recipient of a strong letter from the President which re-emphasized his surprise at the Mexican protest and the fact that he had never been told about the sending of the ships during his conferences with his military advisers. But the burden of Taft's letter was his contention that while the maneuvers in Texas actually helped the Mexican government to maintain order,

> any movement of vessels to Mexican ports must give rise to misconception by the Mexican people and is likely to arouse their suspicion of our intentions. I hope you will see that these small fry do not appear any more in Mexican ports, and that you will keep all your maneuvers to the north of the border line.[321]

Taft, in short, drew a clear distinction between the role of the Army and the Navy. The mobilization reduced the danger of border incidents; it helped the border patrol to keep the insurrectionists from getting assistance on the American side of the line; and it could even, he thought, be interpreted as strengthening American neutrality. But naval visits to Mexican ports were in an entirely different category. For once the Taft administration recognized the potential drawbacks in trying to impress a Latin country with a display of naval power, al-

---

[316] Taft Papers, Taft to Adee, 12 March 1911; Knox Papers, Adee to Knox, 12 March 1911.

[317] Taft Papers, Taft to Meyer, 14 March 1911.

[318] SDDF, File 812.00/921, Taft to Adee, 12 March 1911.

[319] Taft Papers, Taft to Meyer, 14 March 1911.

[320] Taft Papers, Taft to Roosevelt, 22 March 1911.

[321] Taft Papers, Taft to Meyer, 14 March 1911.

beit a far larger and more important country than a Central American or Caribbean republic.

The furor over the "small fry" was subsequently explained away by the Navy. Beekman Winthrop, the Acting Secretary, calmed Taft with a letter which argued that, in point of fact, the incident "needs little explanation." The Navy, he said, had long planned to relieve certain vessels stationed in Panama on both sides of the Isthmus. The Mexican protests had been occasioned by nothing more than the fact that these ships, and the relieving vessels, had stopped at a few Mexican ports en route to and from Panama as part of this planned, routine movement.[322]

For some time afterward the Mexican pot boiled less violently. Those concerned with American policy seemed satisfied. To be sure, when American consuls in Latin America were asked to report public reactions to the Texas maneuvers, they indicated a general Latin suspicion that the United States had in mind other purposes than the training of soldiers.[323] But Leonard Wood seemed pleased, believed that the mobilization was going well, and convinced himself that Taft's action meant "we were not going to stand for any nonsense or any action that would render it necessary for foreign governments to intervene to protect the rights of their citizens."[324] Even Henry Lane Wilson was at least momentarily appeased. His government's policy, he told the State Department, "has steadied the hand of the Mexican government and brought it to a realizing sense of its responsibilities in the protection of the life and property of foreigners and the American population are profoundly gratified and feel a sense of security which is arresting the heavy tide of emigration of American women and children to the United States."[325]

By this stage of affairs, the Army was for once playing a larger role in American policy than the Navy. Ambassador Wilson now believed that the small ships should not have been permitted to stop at Mexican ports and his strongest request was only for the presence of a few naval vessels within easy access of Vera Cruz "to be available in case of extreme necessity. To that extent, and to that extent only should the Navy be utilized with reference to the Mexican troubles."[326] Consequently few reports from naval officers found their way into the files of the Department of State, while, by contrast, reports from the Army began to appear in quantity, especially since border troubles were

[322] SDDF, File 812.00/922, Adee to Taft, 13 March 1911.

[323] SDDF, File 812.00/956A, H. Wilson to American legations in various Latin American countries, 15 March 1911.

[324] Wood Papers, Diary, 29 March 1911.

[325] SDDF, File 812.00/1027, Henry Lane Wilson to Knox, 20 March 1911.

[326] SDDF, File 812.00/1275, Henry Lane Wilson to Knox, 27 March 1911.

continuous. Frequently these provided information on which the administration acted. When, for example, Army sources indicated that numbers of Americans were continuing to flee Mexico, the President at once asked Knox to make a special investigation.[327]

Taft continued to pursue a "correct" attitude, making it clear that "I am not going to be pushed into intervention in Mexico until conditions are such as to leave no doubt in the minds of the people that intervention ought to be undertaken. The burdensome consequences of such action no one appreciates more than I do."[328] With the continuation of border incidents, the Governor of Arizona recommended that the border guards be permitted to fire across the border in retaliation and even cross into Mexican territory. Taft vetoed the suggestion. Such actions, he felt, could readily be misconstrued by the Mexicans and might also serve to build up such pressure in the United States for a general intervention that the Administration would not be able to resist it.[329]

After Francisco Madero had succeeded Diaz, the revolution continued to intensify. There was a new alarm in February of 1912 which brought General Wood to the White House for a conference with Taft and Secretary Stimson. The President, disturbed by recent outbreaks in Mexico, directed Wood to institute additional precautionary measures: troops were to be prepared, the mobile forces made ready, and the border guard strengthened for any eventuality. The President for the first time officially authorized both military services to begin serious staff planning for a possible full-scale operation in Mexico. Next day Wood again saw Taft and Stimson and "impressed upon them that any operations must be directed to the quick and effectual seizure of the City of Mexico and the holding of the central plateau; to fool around with little expeditions and split up our forces would simply mean the massacre of our people and court disaster from a military sense."[330]

Army and Navy planners, now given a green light, began to coordinate their operational plans. Neither service, of course, had been idle before that time. The General Board, as part of its routine planning procedures, had been working on a Mexican war plan since 1909; this document, comparable to its various Caribbean plans, had actually been completed before the revolution began in 1911.[331] Moreover, Sec-

---

[327] SDDF, File 812.00/1045, Taft to Knox, 20 March 1911.
[328] Taft Papers, Taft to Oscar Straus, 6 May 1911.
[329] Taft Papers, Taft to Governor Sloan, 18 April 1911.
[330] Wood Papers, Diary, 4 and 5 February 1912.
[331] GB, File 425 (War Plans), Memorandum of 23 November 1909.

retary Meyer had felt, at the very beginning of the Mexican troubles, that the Navy might draw a heavier assignment than Taft initially anticipated. In March 1911 he had therefore instructed the fifth division of the Atlantic fleet to keep in contact with a force of 2,100 marines, who were themselves to be kept prepared for a quick embarkation. "There is some probability of general insurrection in Mexico," he had cabled, "and it will be necessary to protect American interests, to prevent the importation of arms, and possibly to seize Vera Cruz and hold it until our Army arrives."[332] Since that date the Navy had steadily been revising its standing Mexican plan.

Similarly, the Army War College had studied various aspects of a possible war situation with Mexico long before 1911. General Tasker Bliss, after examining existing plans in the spring of 1911, worried that they were out of date since Army planners had assumed as a working hypothesis that the entire Mexican nation would be united in resistance to the United States. The revolution, he thought, might well have invalidated this underlying assumption.[333] General Wood, as Chief of Staff, disagreed. He advised the War College that its planning staff should assume, revolution or not, that the Mexicans would be a united people in the face of an American intervention: "The character of President Diaz is such that he will go down fighting or not at all, and every interest on his part favors the creation of sufficient provocation to *force armed intervention* and thus save himself by directing the energies of the Mexican Insurrection against the United States."[334] Not every one, to be sure, shared Wood's estimate of Diaz, but Army plans did continue to proceed on the assumption that any American intervention would trigger massive Mexican resistance from all elements of the population.[335]

In early 1912, then, the two services tried to coordinate their individual plans into a single joint operation. The Navy's plans called for the seizure of Vera Cruz and its employment as a base for later Army operations against Mexico City, with other Mexican ports on the Pacific and the Gulf being seized or blockaded as necessary. The Army, arriving three days later, would have the major role: the conduct of a full-scale drive upon Mexico City. In the Army War College equally grandiose plans began to evolve, involving not only the four regular divisions of the U. S. Army but also a dozen "militia" divisions, the capture of Mexico City, and the possible occupation of all of northern

[332] Nav Rec Confid Ltrs, Meyer to Commanding Officer, 5th Division, Atlantic Fleet, 6 March 1911.
[333] GS, File 6474/9 (War Plans—Mexico), Memorandum of 22 April 1911.
[334] GS, File 6474/17, Memorandum of Chief of Staff, April, 1911.
[335] GS, File 6474/30, General Mills to Wood, 19 March 1912.

Mexico, presumably to guard against "atrocities" against foreign residents. Assuming that all internal opposition to Madero would cease, the Army planners believed that they would encounter organized resistance from a Mexican force of 40,000 to 50,000 men in their drive from Vera Cruz. To be on the safe side, they wanted to be able to put 130,000 American troops ashore at Vera Cruz. Since the regular Army remained minuscule, this force would require the services of upwards of a hundred thousand volunteers or militia.[336]

The Joint Board, examining these plans early in 1912, produced a document which combined the plans of the two services, defined the responsibilities of each, and submitted it to the White House for approval. After Taft's signature was obtained, the plan was returned to each service.[337] This, incidentally, was the second set of general war plans which Taft had recently seen and blessed; two months earlier he had similarly approved the Joint Board's plan for possible operations in Cuba.[338] The President did not, of course, participate in the planning processes of the services, but when joint plans were completed, he did examine them and indicate his approval in writing.

Taft may have initialed the Mexican Plan but he still neither intended nor expected to put it into operation. In the summer of 1912, at a time when border disturbances had again increased and there was much public discussion in the United States of the possibility of intervention, the State Department produced a long memorandum, the work of Solicitor J. Reuben Clark, which both summarized existing policies and indicated the framework within which the Administration intended to operate. According to Clark, there were only two principal options: direct intervention by the United States Army and Navy or reliance upon the government of Mexico to protect American lives and property. President Taft had ruled out the former course of action since (and Clark underlined the point) direct intervention would mean war against a united Mexico and reprisals against American citizens. "Intervention would not have been war," Clark maintained, "it would have been murder." After rejecting the possibility that the United States might recognize the belligerent status of one of the insurgent groups, Clark concluded that the only appropriate policy for the United States was to press American claims upon Mexico and avoid direct interference. In international law, he observed, intervention on

[336] GS, File 6474/21, War College memorandum, 16 February 1912, /27 and /30, Mills to Wood, 15 February and 19 March 1912, and /32, Wood to Mills, 7 March 1912.

[337] JB, Minutes, 15 April 1912; for the President's approval, see JB, File 325, Hilles (Taft's Secretary) to Meyer, 3 May 1912.

[338] JB, File 325, Hilles to Meyer, 2 March 1912.

behalf of claims could not be invoked until those persons involved "have exhausted the remedies afforded by the foreign country for the redress of such wrongs."[339]

Nevertheless, midway through 1912, Taft's attitude began to harden, and he authorized more pressure against Mexico:

> We are not going to intervene in Mexico until no other course is possible, but I must protect our people in Mexico as far as possible, and their property, by having the Government understand that there is a God in Israel and He is on duty. Otherwise they will utterly ignore our many great complaints and give no attention to needed protection which they can give.[340]

The Lord now donned the uniform of a United States naval officer, and His duty was no longer restricted, as in 1911, to American territorial waters. The Navy resumed its long standing role in Latin affairs. In the summer of 1912 Knox formally requested the Navy to send a warship "on a friendly and casual visit" to Mexico. But the purpose of this "casual visit," the Secretary specified, was to produce a "desirable moral effect upon the minds of the local population" and to cause "greater respect to be shown in the future both to this Government and to the citizens of the United States resident in Mexico." Friendly visits to Mexican ports would presumably promote good relations but they would also leave the impression "of the strength and power of our navy." Knox even suggested that the naval commander assigned this duty might be given the discretion to spend additional time at various ports if, in his judgment, such action would make the Mexicans more aware of his vessel.

The State Department also suggested to the Navy that comparable visits to the Gulf ports of Mexico might be even more valuable than stops at the smaller towns on the Pacific coast. Knox thought it best to send a battleship to such Mexican ports as Tampico, Vera Cruz, and Puerto Mexico, "since the presence of a really formidable vessel at these places would not only attract much attention locally but would indeed be noticed much more by the people in the interior of the country than a vessel visiting the west coast, which is a much more isolated section."[341] Needless to say, the appropriate orders were soon drafted in the Navy Department. In Mexico City, Ambassador Wilson was told to inform the Mexican government that the visits were entirely friend-

339 Knox Papers, Memorandum by J. Reuben Clark, "The Mexican Situation," 1 October 1912.
340 Taft Papers, Letterpress, Taft to A.B. Farquahar, 11 September 1912.
341 SDDF, File 812.00/4422a, Knox to Meyer, 13 July 1912.

ly in character and that such "casual visits" were the common practice of all nations.[342]

There was, however, an immediate operational difficulty. The Navy, though willing to comply, simply did not have sufficient ships available. Many of its vessels were at that time already committed to other political missions elsewhere in the Caribbean and Central America.[343] In the absence of any formal machinery for policy coordination, the most that the Department of State could do was request, cajole, and attempt to persuade the Navy to change assignments. The *Vicksburg*, for example, had scarcely been assigned to a mission on Mexico's west coast when she managed to knock a hole in her bottom and put herself out of action. The Navy claimed that no replacement was available. The Latin American Division of the State Department rather pointedly suggested that the Navy might recall a vessel from its Nicaraguan patrol or even withdraw a ship from the China station, but the admirals insisted that the need was more urgent in Nicaragua and in the Far East.[344]

In any event there was an increasing American restiveness about Mexico in the summer and fall of 1912. It was feared that the center of revolutionary disturbances was shifting to the western and more remote areas of Mexico. In these circumstances the Department of State was now willing to entrust naval commanders with considerable discretion to cope with disorders as they felt best. The commander of the ill-fated *Vicksburg*, for example, was told to watch developments in and about Guaymas and, if a sudden emergency threatened life and property, "to take such steps to afford them protection as may commend themselves to his discretion under the circumstances."[345] Meanwhile, in Mexico City, Henry Lane Wilson intensified his fulminations against the Madero regime; indeed, his admiration for the ousted Diaz was exceeded only by his detestation of Madero. Typical was a dispatch of August 1912:

Human life is not safe and property rights have no value whatsoever. Entire villages have been burned, their inhabitants, men, women, and children slaughtered and mutilated indiscriminately, plantations have been ravaged and burned, trains have been blown up and derailed and passengers slaughtered like cattle, women have been ravished and men mutilated with accomplishments of horror

[342] SDDF, File 812.00/4438, Winthrop to Knox, and Knox to Henry Lane Wilson, 17 July 1912.

[343] SDDF, File 812.00/4663a, Adee to Meyer, 17 August 1912.

[344] SDDF, File 812.00/4953, Memorandum of Latin American Affairs Division, 26 August 1912.

[345] SDDF, File 812.00/4681, H. Wilson to Meyer, 24 August 1912 and /4686a, Adee to Meyer, 20 August 1912.

and barbarity which find no place in the chronicles of Christian warfare. . . . In the midst of this appalling situation . . . the Federal government sits apathetic, ineffective, and either cynically indifferent or stupidly optimistic.

He was convinced that all legitimate American interests would be driven from Mexico "unless this Government is taught in due season that every American and every American interest in Mexico expects and must receive the same measure of justice that a Mexican or Mexican interest would receive in the United States." Nevertheless his invective, as usual, ran ahead of his suggestions for action; he was still reconciled to a policy of protests and did not demand intervention by force of arms.[346]

While Taft was adhering steadfastly to his non-intervention policy, he could tell the Assistant Secretary of State that "I had a talk with Wood yesterday, and they have perfected their plans down to date." When he received another unsatisfactory reply to a protest he had sent Madero, Taft informed his Secretary of State that "I am getting to a point where I think we ought to put a little dynamite in for the purpose of stirring up that dreamer who seems unfitted to meet the crisis in the country of which he is the President."[347] The "dynamite" consisted of tightening border procedures and increasing the naval watch. The Army, which had asked about its powers to arrest Mexican rebels known to be on American soil, was authorized by Taft to make the arrests, while the Department of State readily found precedents for such action.[348] In October the Department of State approved special visits by naval vessels to both Tampico and Vera Cruz, particularly since the latter city seemed to be in danger from an insurrectionary movement led by one Felix Diaz. Henry Lane Wilson was then authorized to inform the Mexican government, concurrently with the arrival of the warship, that the United States "hoped" there would be no fighting in and around Vera Cruz.[349] There was an immediate Mexican protest. Madero claimed that the level of excitement in Vera Cruz was already so high that the arrival of an American warship would surely be misconstrued and serve as a cause for further disorder. The Department of State turned down his protest, professing not to understand how the Mexican government could object when Vera Cruz was already in rebel hands and the United States therefore only "fulfilling a perfectly

346 SDDF, File 812.00/4899, Henry Lane Wilson to Knox, 28 August 1912.

347 SDDF, File 812.00/5392 and /5697, Taft to Knox, 5 September and 14 December 1912.

348 SDDF, File 812.00/5166, Memorandum for Adjutant General from General Wotherspoon, 28 September 1912, and /5168a, H. Wilson to Stimson, 2 October 1912.

349 SDDF, File 812.00/5253, Adee to H. Lane Wilson, 19 October 1912.

obvious and imperative duty on its part toward Americans and American interests at that port."[350] Again the naval officer in command was given wide latitude. While he was enjoined to observe strict neutrality between the contending factions, he was also given permission to afford protection to Americans and American interests "in such ways as commend themselves to the discretion of the Commanding Officer." He might, Knox added, "with the general interest of the [State] Department in mind, act in all instances and at all times in accordance with his own discretion." It was a broad and nebulous warrant and one for which the Secretary of State apologized; his department, he admitted to the Navy, had insufficient information about conditions in Vera Cruz to be able to issue more specific instructions.[351]

But the outcome in Vera Cruz at this time was unspectacular. The Diaz movement fizzled out after only minor pyrotechnics. Every one involved in the affair, however, was convinced that the arrival of the *Des Moines* at Vera Cruz had been beneficial in preserving order.[352] About the same time, Livingston Schuyler, chargé d'affaires in Mexico City during an absence of Henry Lane Wilson, began to recommend a far wider use of warships. With disorder rampant throughout the country and Madero barely hanging on to power, "we should have warships in every Mexican port, and they should be prepared to remain indefinitely. The United States must be ready for any eventuality as the Madero administration is absolutely impotent to bring about even a semblance of peace and order."[353] This, however, was too strong for Washington. Schuyler was informed that vessels could be sent only to protect American interests and could not "plausibly" be dispatched for any other reason.[354]

The dispatch of a warship to Tampico in the fall of 1912, as part of the general operation just described, had important implications for naval policy—indeed, long-range implications which did not become fully apparent until after Woodrow Wilson had become President. Until the autumn of 1912 the Navy had concentrated its war planning upon Vera Cruz, the port which guarded the approach to Mexico City. Tampico first came to the special attention of the General Board late in 1912 in connection with the presumed need to protect millions of dollars of American oil properties in that city. What happened at that time was that an agent of the Standard Oil Company sent a long letter

[350] SDDF, File 812.00/5276, Schuyler to Knox, 18 October 1912.

[351] SDDF, File 812.00/5347A, Latin American Affairs memorandum, Latchford to Dearing, 17 October 1912, to which is attached a copy of Knox's instructions to Meyer.

[352] SDDF, File 812.00/5315, Consul Canada to Knox, 23 October 1912.

[353] SDDF, File 812.00/5333, Schuyler to Knox, 23 October 1912.

[354] SDDF, File 812.00/5333, Huntington Wilson to Schuyler, 23 October 1912.

to General William Crozier, chief of the War College Division of the General Staff. The gist of this letter was that the oil properties at Tampico were of such vital importance to Mexico that the Army and Navy should seize that port at the very outset of any major operation in Mexico. The Mexican rail system, it was argued, could be paralyzed by such measures.[355] Crozier was impressed, forwarded the letter to General Wood. The Chief of Staff, in turn, sought the support of the civilian heads of the War Department in bringing the matter to the attention of the Navy.[356] But once Tampico and its oil had been called to the naval attention it took little effort to get the General Board to add Tampico to the Mexican War Plan. A revised version of this plan, dated December 1, 1912, included Tampico as one of the two ports (Vera Cruz, of course, was the other) to be seized by the Navy immediately upon the outbreak of hostilities between the United States and Mexico.[357] Thus the military services, spurred by the Standard Oil Company, were drawn to Tampico, the site of the famous naval incident in the spring of 1914 which provoked Wilson's direct military intervention in Mexico.

Towards the end of 1912, however, the Department of State again began to have second thoughts about the value of naval visits. It not only withdrew the *Des Moines* after Vera Cruz became quiet but also, in the somewhat surprising words of Huntington Wilson, began to suggest that "the continued presence of the vessels may militate against the more than usually friendly relations prevailing towards Americans in those ports at this time."[358] It now requested of the Navy only that ships be kept within a three-day cruising distance, much to the continued displeasure of Schuyler in Mexico City who wanted to continue the naval watch for its presumed effect on both rebels and government.[359] In any event, it was not until January 1913—after Woodrow Wilson's election but some six weeks before his actual inauguration—that the Mexican problem again erupted into full crisis. The murder of Madero followed by the successful coup of General Huerta provoked a last spasm of activity on the part of the outgoing administration.

[355] For changes in military planning, see GS, File 6774/112, General Carter to War College Division, 4 September 1912, an instruction to bring the Army's plans up to date. On the Standard Oil involvement in the Tampico planning, see /169, Crozier to Wood, 12 October 1912.

[356] GS, File 6774/169, Oliver to Meyer, October 1912.

[357] GS, File 6774/186, Mexican War Plan, as revised, 1 December 1912, and /174, Dewey to Meyer, 23 October 1912, indicating the great importance attached by the military to Tampico. See also GB, File 425 (Mexican War Plans), Dewey to Meyer, 2nd endorsement on communication of 22 October 1912.

[358] SDDF, File 812.00/5459A, Huntington Wilson to Meyer, 8 November 1912.

[359] SDDF, File 812.00/5314, Schuyler to Knox, 17 November 1912.

Many and varied crosscurrents affected this last effort of the Taft administration. Taft and Knox were "lame ducks," thoroughly repudiated in the November elections, and in an awkward position to make commitments. Moreover, by the time of the murder the State Department had finally come to question the quality of Henry Lane Wilson's reporting from Mexico City. The Ambassador, who had returned to his post at the opening of the new year, resumed his practice of sending vitriolic telegrams; indeed, he became virtually apopleptic, charging that Madero had "become a despot . . . and the dreamer of Coahuila, who essayed the role of Moses, is rapidly shriveling to the dimensions of a Castro."[360] But, as Fred Dearing of the Latin American Division pointed out, one of his angrier reports appeared to have been composed solely of excerpts from the front page of a single anti-Madero Mexican daily:

> It would seem that no efforts were made on the part of the embassy to verify the news transmitted to the department; that the newspaper information is uncertain and vague at best and apt to be played up in a more or less sensational way . . . almost all of the pessimistic reports from the Embassy during the recent past seem to have been made up in the same way—i.e., wholly from a cursory reading of this one newspaper printed in Mexico City.[361]

Knox began to make polite but pointed inquiries of Wilson about his pessimism and the sharp difference between his messages and those of Schuyler. As might be expected, these drew angry retorts from the Ambassador; Knox eventually withdrew from the verbal fray and merely cautioned Wilson to be prudent in his future comments.[362]

Immediately after Madero's murder, Ambassador Wilson began to demand an American military response. Noting that he had himself organized a foreign guard to protect foreign citizens in Mexico City, he insisted that Washington must now send a sufficient number of capital ships to make a real impression on the Mexicans and include a large enough marine complement to render whatever assistance might be required. In telegram after telegram he hammered on the theme that the 5,000 Americans resident in Mexico City were at the mercy of the ravaging hordes of revolutionaries who sought to avenge the murder of Madero. Henry Lane Wilson, whose own connections with the Huerta group were soon to be a source of great embarrassment to the United

---

[360] SDDF, File 812.00/5904 and /6068, Henry Lane Wilson to Knox, 20 January and 4 February 1913.

[361] SDDF, File 812.00/5904, Latin American Affairs memorandum by Dearing, 27 January 1913.

[362] SDDF, File 812.00/5912B, Knox to Henry Lane Wilson, 21 January 1913 and Wilson's reply of 2 February 1913.

States, believed that he himself could be the instrument for solving the Mexican crisis. If given general powers and instructions of "a firm and perhaps menacing character," the ambassador was confident that he could negotiate an end to the civil strife, at the very minimum bring about helpful talks between the contending parties.[363] Philander Knox was not impressed. He observed that if the talks collapsed or if Wilson's scheme was rejected by the Mexicans, there was real danger that the United States might be unwillingly drawn into direct intervention —which was, he emphasized, still the last resort of policy. He was unwilling therefore to authorize more than the cautionary measures already taken.[364]

The Secretary of State was closely following the recommendations of the Latin American Division of his department which advised the outgoing administration not to pursue Henry Lane Wilson's program unless it was fully prepared to make good on its threats. The Division said also that it would be necessary to request Congressional approval to use the Army and Navy, while it observed that if hostilities developed, the incoming Democratic administration would have to prosecute the war but would "have none of the responsibilities of the state of affairs found to exist when it came to power."[365]

The United States therefore limited its response to the Madero murder and the Huerta *coup*. It sent several capital ships to Tampico and Vera Cruz, with some smaller vessels to lesser ports. But though the naval force was sizable, the orders to the Navy emphasized that the visits were strictly for observation and reporting events; no new instructions for the protection of foreigners were issued; and the naval commanders were to show no bias in dealing with the conflicting parties. In sending the ships, Knox insisted, he was merely responding to "the fresh necessity of great caution due to the uncertainty of the new conditions caused by the uprising in the Mexican capital."[366] The attitude remained one of watchful waiting. The number of warships was gradually increased, and, in mid-February, after a conference between State and Navy Department officials, two more battleships were sent from Guantanamo to Vera Cruz.[367]

Henry Lane Wilson clearly itched to get his hands on the levers that controlled this naval force. He pointedly inquired about the degree of control that he could exercise over the newly-arrived warships and

[363] SDDF, File 812.00/6075 and /6092, Henry Lane Wilson to Knox, 10 and 11 February 1913.

[364] SDDF, File 812.00/6092, Knox to Henry Lane Wilson, 12 February 1913.

[365] SDDF, File 812.00/6092, Latin American Affairs memorandum from Doyle to Knox, 12 February 1913.

[366] SDDF, File 812.00/6082, Knox to Henry Lane Wilson, 10 February 1913.

[367] SDDF, File 812.00/6145, Winthrop to Knox, 13 February 1913.

asked for authority to act immediately in any new crisis without further instructions from Washington. He was sharply rebuffed by Washington. Knox bluntly informed his ambassador that the vessels had been sent solely to gather information and make reports. Moreover, since recent information from Mexico City seemed to indicate that there was growing stability, "there would seem to be even less reason for the Navy to change the orders which have been given to its ships at the request of the Department of State. . . . While the Department appreciates your anxiety, it feels requirements are such that it would be inadvisable to instruct you as you request."[368] Even Huntington Wilson was showing caution. When he casually learned that Taft had just transferred the Fifth Army Brigade from Omaha to Galveston, he sensed the danger of newspaper stories about the troop movement and their effect on Mexican opinion; he therefore sought the President's approval of a statement that the transfer was a routine military move and unconnected with the Mexican disorders.[369] Still, even though Taft and Knox refused to anoint Ambassador Wilson with additional powers or to approve measures which might upset the then delicate balance in Mexico City, they did increase their general military precautions. A cabinet meeting in mid-February, for example, produced a decision to station a naval transport at Guantanamo with 1,200 marines aboard and to prepare an additional force of 750 marines for any eventualities. Taft and Knox exchanged many notes with each other about the number and type of ships that should be made ready, discussed at length the question of whether or not the battleships should have marines aboard, and reached the firm conclusion that it made both diplomatic and military sense to station battleships, with marines aboard, at ports like Vera Cruz.[370]

Taft and Knox found no resolution to the Mexican dilemma before leaving office. When Woodrow Wilson and William Jennings Bryan took direction of American foreign policy in March, 1913, naval vessels were on station at various Mexican ports and their orders remained unchanged. Taft and Knox had certainly and clearly resisted Henry Lane Wilson's desire to employ those warships for his own purposes. Similarly they had continued to adhere to the long-established policy of non-intervention—often, it should be added, courageously and in the face of mounting domestic pressures to intervene. Early in 1913 it would have required a major provocation to tempt them to act,

[368] SDDF, File 812.00/6149, Henry Lane Wilson to Knox, and Knox to Wilson, 14-15 February 1913.
[369] SDDF, File 812.00/6370, H. Wilson to Forster, 22 February 1913.
[370] SDDF, File 812.00/6259, Taft to Knox, and Knox to Taft, 10 February 1913.

all the more so as a result of their repudiation in the elections of the preceding November. But the possibility that the United States would use force was always present, always under discussion. Above all, Philander Knox never wavered in his belief that the show of force was a valuable instrument of diplomacy. He firmly believed in impressing the Mexicans with the visible signs of American naval power and in leaving the inference that, if the Mexicans committed certain transgressions, that power might well be unleashed. Just before the administration left office, in late February of 1913, Admiral Southerland, an officer with long experience in Latin America, sent Knox a sheaf of telegrams on Mexico. The gist of these messages was that an entire division of the Navy should be sent to visit each of Mexico's major ports and that such a force would have a great and valuable impact upon Mexican opinion.[371] Knox agreed. His reply to Admiral Southerland expressed the very essence of his belief in the great value of the Navy in achieving the political ends of the United States:

> In the opinion of this Department, few things will work so successfully toward the re-establishment of peace and order in Mexico as an effective but unoffensive display of the great naval power of the United States. Not only will the local population be left with a wholesome regard for the might of the United States government but the central government in Mexico City will be kept in a state of watchful regard; watchful to prevent any incident which might provoke the use of this great power and, by pointing out the likelihood that it will be used in certain circumstances, be materially strengthened and braced in dealing with any recalcitrant elements in the country.[372]

This statement extolling the deterrent virtues of the Navy might well serve as the epitaph for an administration which, in all its Latin dealings, pursued but variants of this approach.

The last act of the Mexican drama was played against a general background of events in Latin America which made the outgoing administration fearful that all established Latin American policies would crumble when Woodrow Wilson came to power in March. Taft and Knox did not fear the incoming Democrats as much as they feared the Latin reaction to the inauguration. In early February of 1913 the Department of State began to pick up rumors that the inauguration of

---

[371] SDDF, File 812.00/6274, Knox to Meyer, 25 February 1913, in reply to Southerland's cables to the Navy Department, especially his cable of 18 February. See also /6292 for a copy of this dispatch.

[372] SDDF, File 812.00/6274, Knox to Meyer.

Wilson would be the signal for all the heretofore repressed revolutionaries to rise throughout Central America and seek to topple the existing regimes. According to the Latin American experts in the State Department, the danger was real since these revolutionaries misinterpreted the campaign statements and promises of Woodrow Wilson. They presumably believed that the President-elect was so committed to the repudiation of imperialism and "dollar diplomacy" that the incoming administration would sit back idly and permit revolution throughout Central America.[373] Assistant Secretary Huntington Wilson was particularly outraged. He was so alarmed that he went beyond normal channels to try to communicate his fears and apprehensions directly to the President-elect; he sent a long series of letters and memoranda through an intermediary, a personal friend of Woodrow Wilson, who was asked to bring them to Wilson's personal attention. The essence of these communications was the argument that all the riff-raff in Latin America, all the disorderly elements that had been held in check by the sane policies of Taft and Knox, were about to come to the surface in one grand saturnalia of disorder. Huntington Wilson wanted Woodrow Wilson to be on his guard and, above all, in his Inaugural Address, to warn the Latin dissidents that the new administration neither meant to reverse established Latin American policies nor intended to give free license to Central American disorders.[374] While this was a thinly disguised attempt by Huntington Wilson to commit Woodrow Wilson to those policies of Taft and Knox in which he so firmly believed, it was also a genuine expression of the Assistant Secretary's fears.

Taft and Knox were similarly exercised. In early February Knox sent a special message to the Navy in which he commented on these same rumors and asked that two war vessels be dispatched to both the Pacific and Caribbean coasts of Central America.[375] William Howard Taft personally endorsed the request and particularly commended it to his admirals.[376] The obvious result was that within three days the Navy informed the State Department that it was fully prepared to send vessels to Honduras, El Salvador, Nicaragua, Guatemala, and such other countries as might be necessary. The Navy's plans were impressive: five ships were to make many stops in many countries. Moreover, the commanders of these vessels were not to be given any information about the purpose of their visits; they were simply to be told

[373] SDDF, File 813.00/799, numerous dispatches covering the period 5-8 February 1913.

[374] Huntington Wilson Papers, H. Wilson to S. Bertron, 31 January 1913.

[375] SDDF, File 813.00/799, Knox to Meyer, 8 February 1913.

[376] SDDF, File 813.00/799, Hilles (Taft's Secretary) to Knox, 5 February 1913.

to confer with American consuls in the various ports and report their observations back to Washington.[377]

Taft gave his written approval to this plan. When advised of the fears of Philander Knox and Huntington Wilson, he had wired them that "The President . . . acknowledges the receipt of your confidential letter of February 4 relative to the rumor that the incoming administration will reverse the policy of this Administration toward Latin America, and to say that he has directed the Secretary of the Navy to send the vessels in accordance with your recommendations."[378] American consuls and ministers in Central America were told of the State Department's forebodings and to expect the warships in mid-February.[379] When it appeared that the growing Mexican crisis might interfere with the Central American operation, President Taft specifically charged the Navy to let nothing interfere with its accomplishment.[380]

Thus the Taft administration ended as it began. In March 1909 it had used the Navy to implement its political goal of keeping ex-President Castro from returning to power in Venezuela. In February 1913 it sent its warships on a political mission to Central America, still and always zealous to prevent any reversal of a cherished policy of preserving law and order near the Panama Canal. In this last endeavor, as in the many which had preceded it, Taft and Knox remained consistent in their belief that the dispatch of naval vessels would be "in the nature of a moral persuasion and a show of interest on the part of this country in the continued peace of Central America."[381]

[377] SDDF, File 813.00/799, Winthrop to Knox, 7 February 1913. See also Nav Rec Confid Ltrs, Meyer to Commanding Officer of the *Tacoma*, 11 February 1913.

[378] SDDF, File 813.00/799, Hilles to Knox, 5 February 1913.

[379] SDDF, File 813.00/799, Knox to American ministers in Central America, 8 February 1913.

[380] SDDF, File 812.00/6259, Taft to Knox, 10 February 1913.

[381] Nav Rec Confid Ltrs, Meyer to *Tacoma*, 11 February 1913.

CHAPTER FIVE

Wilson and Bryan: Moralism and Military Power

1. THE CLIMAX OF CIVIL SUPREMACY

JUST a few weeks after Woodrow Wilson had been inaugurated as President a short but sharp crisis erupted in Japanese-American relations. During the course of that crisis the military services, especially the Navy, recommended to the new administration that it adopt certain specific measures of military preparedness intended to prevent any Japanese surprise attack upon America's Pacific possessions. The Cabinet, after full discussion, rejected them. Soon, however, both Wilson and Josephus Daniels, his Secretary of the Navy, concluded that the Army and Navy were trying to force their hands and, worse still, were continuing to put pressure upon them after the responsible civilian authorities had determined the course of American policy. Daniels, as we have previously mentioned, joyously recorded his great pleasure at the President's anger at this military transgression and his stern determination that there would be no more war planning after the administration had decided against it. The Secretary of the Navy was equally pleased to carry out Wilson's instructions to telephone Admiral Bradley Fiske and inform him that there should be no further meetings of the Joint Board until there had been further discussions with him.[1]

The Wilsonian record contains not a few similar incidents. General Tasker Bliss recalled a day in the fall of 1915 when the Acting Secretary of War, Henry Breckinridge, showed him a tiny clipping from the *Baltimore Sun* which had made the President tremble and turn "white with passion." The clipping mentioned that the General Staff was supposed to be engaged in making plans for use in case of war with Germany. The President had not only demanded an investigation but also threatened to relieve every Staff officer on duty in Washington. Nothing, to be sure, came of this episode, for Bliss correctly pointed out that the General Staff had been created by statute in 1903 precisely for the purpose of making war plans and for years had been studying war plans for possible conflict with many different enemies, of which Germany

---

[1] Daniels Papers, Diary, 17 May 1913. (Now of course available in published form in Cronon, *Cabinet Diaries*.)

was but one. But War College work was thereafter camouflaged and, at least according to Bliss, handicapped by the President's attitude.[2]

Yet these two incidents do reveal much of the spirit with which Wilson, Daniels, and, it should be added, William Jennings Bryan, approached the civil-military relationship. They were even more determined than Taft and Knox to maintain the principle of civil supremacy, but, unlike their predecessors, they were also motivated by a desire to prevent militarism and military values from infecting civilian policy. Daniels, for example, was strongly opposed to the ideas of those in the Navy who continued to advocate a Council of National Defense and a stronger, more centralized naval establishment; to him it meant, simply, the Prussianization of the American military system and the loss of civilian values.[3]

Sometimes the administration's attitude bordered on pettiness and showed itself in matters of little consequence. Woodrow Wilson's own sense of the proprieties even extended to the off-duty entertainment of his officers. He was once outraged to read in the newspapers that members of the Military Order of the Carabao, a convivial assembly of officers and men who had once served in the Philippines, had sung at one of their reunions a number of ribald old Army songs which poked fun at the American government. It was not funny to Wilson. He fired off a stiff note to his two service secretaries in which he asked that the men responsible for the program be administered a "very serious reprimand" for their disrespect.[4] He was by no means mollified by the response that the program had been in jest and that the songs sung by the Carabao had been part of the entertainment at every reunion since 1899:

> What are we to think of the officers of the Army and Navy who think it "fun" to bring their official superiors into ridicule and the policies of the government which they are sworn to support with unquestioning loyalty into contempt? If this is their idea of fun, what is their idea of Duty? If they do not hold their loyalty above all silly effervescences of childish wit, what about their profession do they hold sacred?[5]

Also, as we have previously observed, both Wilson and Secretary of War Lindley Garrison were outraged when Colonel Gorgas made

[2] Frederick Palmer, *Bliss, Peacemaker* (New York, 1934), 106-07.

[3] Daniels Papers, Diary, 26 January 1915.

[4] Daniels Papers, Wilson to Daniels, 22 December 1913.

[5] Daniels Papers, report of Frank McIntyre, J. R. Alshire, and P. B. Howard to Secretary of War Garrison, 16 December 1913; the quotation is from a letter, Wilson to Daniels, 22 December 1913.

public statements about the Panama tolls controversy, for they regarded it as part of the "common law of the Army" that military men did not speak out on political matters.[6]

The administration's desire, to be sure, went deeper than the simple concern to chastize officers who appeared disrespectful or to prevent military discussion of controversial political questions. The overriding objective was to make certain that policy was made by civilians and not by military men. Wilson himself was quick to spot officers who appeared to disagree with his policies and to anticipate the problems that might ensue. In the summer of 1913, for example, Daniels showed him a letter from Admiral Frank Fletcher, then the senior naval officer stationed off Vera Cruz. Fletcher had written at some length of the inevitable necessity of an American intervention in Mexico to settle those problems which the Mexicans could themselves never resolve. He had concluded by informing Daniels that he had naval forces "ready upon your call, and I have again called attention to the advisability of having gunboats available to send to the small coast towns where bandits are increasing."[7] The implications of Fletcher's comments were not lost upon Wilson who immediately drafted his own reply to Daniels:

> I hope that you feel sure that Admiral Fletcher will do nothing on his own initiative and without orders. He is so decidedly of an opinion which does not correspond with our own that I have been wondering about that point a little since seeing in the papers yesterday that Lind [Wilson's personal representative in Mexico] spent a couple of hours with him.[8]

When the ill-fated intervention at Vera Cruz did occur, Wilson made it abundantly clear that there would be absolutely no military initiatives; policy was to be made solely in the White House. General Funston, whose Army troops had relieved the naval occupying force, was strictly forbidden to take any action which might increase tensions at the Mexican port. Indeed, he was told to do nothing without express authorization from Washington—"even should your own judgment indicate that something other than what is now being done you will, before acting, communicate fully with the Department and await instructions."[9] When one minor incident threatened to have widespread

---

[6] Papers of Lindley M. Garrison, Princeton University Library, Garrison to Wilson, 21 and 24 March 1913.

[7] Daniels Papers, copy of Fletcher to Daniels, 24 July 1913, and forwarded to the President on 11 August.

[8] Daniels Papers, Wilson to Daniels, 11 August 1913.

[9] Wilson Papers, File VI, War Department, Memorandum of Adjutant General, Wood to Wilson, 26 April 1914 (copies of orders prepared for General Funston). See also Garrison Papers, Box 13 of which contains a sheaf of orders and instruc-

political repercussions in Vera Cruz, Secretary Garrison advised Funston: "The duty of the Army is to carry out a policy, not to inaugurate one. The time for the Army to display its qualities is when it is ordered to perform a duty and shows excellence in doing so."[10]

2. CRISIS WITH JAPAN, MAY 1913

The Japanese crisis burst unexpectedly upon an administration which was committed to undoing the Far Eastern policies of Taft and Knox and which had just attempted to demonstrate its opposition to "dollar diplomacy" by withdrawing from the six-power consortium that had been formed to finance railway construction in China. It was triggered by the introduction into the California legislature of a series of so-called alien land laws whose purpose was to deny Chinese and Japanese the right to own land in that state. It was first discussed by the cabinet in late April at which time Wilson, hoping to prevent final enactment of the measure, sent William Jennings Bryan, his new Secretary of State, to California for urgent talks with the governor and legislators. But Bryan's mission was a failure, the legislation was finally approved, and the administration had to deal with the international consequences of a law which, every one realized, was "very offensive to the Japanese who are sensitive and regard it as a reflection on their race."[11] On May 13, 1913 Wilson read to his cabinet the protest that had just been received from the Japanese government. It was agreed by all present that the Japanese protest was much stronger than necessary, certainly stronger than the situation warranted. But the cabinet also agreed that Baron Chinda's note should not be interpreted as a threat and expressed nothing "except a very earnest desire to secure the same rights for the Japanese in California that are given to other aliens."[12]

In the General Board of the Navy the sentiments were far different. During the late winter and spring the Board had been at work on routine revisions in the Orange Plan, and in fact approved a new strategic section of the plan on the 29th of April.[13] The Orange Plan, it will be recalled, advanced a defensive strategy for the opening stages of any conflict with Japan, assumed a Japanese offensive at the onset of war,

---

tions sent to Funston. Typical is an order of May 2nd which reads, ". . . you will have to endure whatever blockade you are now suffering . . . and must make no aggressive move against any one who has not attacked you."

[10] Garrison Papers, Garrison to Funston, 9 May 1914.
[11] Daniels Papers, Diary, 22 April 1913.
[12] Daniels Papers, Diary, 13 May 1913.
[13] GB, Proceedings, 29 April 1913.

and anticipated major, and probably successful, Japanese attacks on America's possessions in the Pacific. The planners, in short, expected serious initial losses to the Japanese, losses which, in their judgment, would be all the more probable if the Japanese were able to launch a surprise attack or mount their offensive before the United States had an opportunity to prepare and concentrate its own limited, scattered defensive forces.

By 1913 the Navy's outlook, as well as its ambitions, were far more limited than they had been scarcely a decade earlier when the future had appeared so bright. The Orange Plan, to be sure, postulated an eventual victory that would come after the United States had launched a vast trans-Pacific offensive that would regain all lost territories and smash the Imperial navy. But its analysis of the situation at the beginning of a war was grim. For example, in February 1913 the General Board had agreed that no useful purpose was served by keeping advanced base materials in the Philippines or Hawaii; this equipment, the admirals recommended, should be transferred to Guam and used to bolster the temporary defenses of that island against a Japanese attack. The Board went on to observe that the entire advanced base concept had validity in the Far East only if the United States maintained comparatively strong naval units in the Pacific, units powerful enough to use the advanced base equipment in seizing and establishing bases for further offensive operations. But with American naval strength in the Pacific at the absolute minimum, the equipment possessed no usefulness. The Asiatic fleet then in being could undertake only the most limited of operations and could make use of the advanced base materials only if it was engaged in war with a Far Eastern enemy whose power was equally deficient. In war with a first-class power, such as Japan, the advanced base materials would possess no value unless the entire American fleet happened to be stationed in the Pacific at the beginning of hostilities—an eventuality which, of course, the strategists could scarcely even imagine. It followed, therefore, that the General Board wished now to abandon the whole advanced base concept in the Pacific and transfer the equipment to Guam, "whose defenseless position makes it imperative to do something to place it in a state of defense."[14]

The Japanese protests about the California land laws stirred the admirals and captains to a state of not inconsiderable excitement. On April 29th there was a meeting of the General Board attended by both Secretary Daniels and his principal assistant, the young and zealous Franklin D. Roosevelt. The admirals proposed a series of actions intended to get the Pacific defenses in a state of readiness to withstand

[14] GB, File 408, Dewey to Meyer, 26 February 1913.

any surprise Japanese attack. Daniels at once ruled out several of the recommendations: coaling the reserve Atlantic fleet and concentrating the Asiatic fleet in the waters of Manila Bay. For the moment, however, no objection was raised to the other suggestions of the General Board: the return of certain vessels to American ports, the speed-up of naval repairs, and the hastening of preparations to move the famous drydock at Subig Bay to the presumed safety of Manila harbor. Three days later Roosevelt, showing signs of the same enthusiasm that his cousin Theodore had exhibited on the eve of hostilities with Spain, cabled key personnel in certain naval yards that, on receipt of future instructions that specifically referred to this particular communication, they should proceed to put their stations on a war footing, establish additional guards, restrict all visitors, and replenish all stocks and supplies. Roosevelt also informed these men that, in advance of the later instructions, they might now assemble the heads of their various departments "in secret council" and begin discussing the plans they would implement at a later date—taking care of course to impress on all hands that these matters must be kept strictly confidential.[15] On the following day the General Board recommended to Daniels that the Army should officially be informed of the "steps that have already been taken looking to possible war and those in contemplation when the Government deems that the time has arrived to proceed openly in measures of preparation."[16]

By the 8th and 9th of May the General Board was calling for the implementation of some of the basic assumptions on which the strategy of the Orange Plan was founded. It wanted to get the Atlantic fleet prepared for eventualities; two armored cruisers in the Mediterranean should be called home; battleships and cruisers then in Mexican waters should be withdrawn and fitted out for actual military operations; and preparations should be gotten underway to assemble a fleet of at least seventeen battleships at Culebra or Guantanamo.[17] On the 9th the Board called for a reassignment of cruisers; those on station with the Asiatic fleet should be sent at once to Honolulu.[18] This request was also in keeping with the tenets of the Orange Plan, for it had long been assumed by the Navy that these cruisers would be lost in any initial engagement with the Japanese and that they should be withdrawn to Pearl Harbor well in advance of hostilities, where they would serve as the nucleus around which the great reinforced battle fleet would

15 GB, Proceedings, 29 April 1913, and File 425, Roosevelt to various navy yard commandants, 2 May 1913.

16 GB, File 425, Dewey to Daniels, 3 May 1913.

17 GB, File 425, Dewey to Daniels, 8 May 1913.

18 GB, File 425, Dewey to Daniels, 9 May 1913.

form. The General Board advanced two arguments in support of its proposals. First, such precautionary measures were urgent "in order to minimize the disadvantage to the United States in the event war should be declared in the Pacific." Second, their implementation would be a deterrent to Japanese action, thereby serving the cause of peace and the avoidance of war.[19] The admirals were true believers of the old military adage, *si vis pacem, para bellum*.

By this time both the Army as well as the Joint Board had become involved in discussions about the "crisis." Early in May of 1913 General Wood suggested the immediate advisability of joint Army-Navy talks about preparations the two services might make in common to meet what he termed "possible trouble in the Pacific area."[20] On the 8th of May the Joint Board met and heard an extended discussion of the Navy's plans to concentrate fleet units at Manila and Honolulu.

Much of this preliminary planning was definitely brought to the attention of President Wilson. The recommendations of the General Board which emerged from its meetings on the 8th and 9th of May were put into a letter that Assistant Secretary Roosevelt personally took to the White House. Wilson directed "no action" for the present, and the letter was duly filed in the desk of the Aide for Operations.[21] A second letter merely bears a note, written by Roosevelt, that Wilson had approved it in principle but that its contents would only be taken up in due time if and when the President gave his approval.[22] Wilson, in short, was cognizant of what his naval staff was considering and recommending but unwilling to endorse their requests.

Adding to the complexity of the planning procedures was the sharp difference of opinion which began to emerge between the two service secretaries, Lindley Garrison and Josephus Daniels. The former clearly shared the apprehensions of Wood and the General Staff; in mid-May, for example, Garrison told his Chief of Staff that Japanese-American relations were becoming critical and that the United States should take all the precautions that could be instituted without exciting too much public attention.[23] Thus, with Garrison's tacit approval, General Wood was able to direct that two companies of infantry be sent to Hawaii within the next thirty days to reinforce the meagre defenses of Oahu as well as to instruct General Bell, then commanding in the Philippines, to put sufficient forces on Corregidor, under the guise of conducting maneuvers, to guard against any surprise attack. Josephus

19 GB, File 425, Dewey to Daniels, 8 May 1913.
20 Wood Papers, Diary, entries of 5 and 8 May 1913.
21 GB, File 425, endorsement, signed N. L. Jones on the 8 May 1913 correspondence.
22 GB, File 425, endorsement, signed N. L. Jones, on the 9 May correspondence.
23 Wood Papers, Diary, 13 May 1913.

Daniels, however, resisted the recommendations that came from his naval advisers and was unwilling to implement their suggestions. Daniels, indeed, suspected that the two most militant of the admirals, Bradley A. Fiske and William F. Fullam, would have welcomed a chance to fight the Japanese. He was opposed to their suggestions on principle and confided to his diary:

> I have observed that if a man puts a gun on his shoulder and walks down the street, particularly down a street in which he knows there is a man with whom he has some misunderstanding, it is pretty likely to cause the other man to get a gun himself and that death or something else serious results, whereas if the man had not started out with the gun on his shoulder, the difficulty would have ended peaceably.[24]

It is small wonder, then, that on several occasions Admiral Fiske, the Aide for Operations, complained to Leonard Wood that he was having "a great deal of trouble" with Daniels.[25] In these circumstances, incidentally, it was Roosevelt, who shared the fears of the admirals and endorsed their plans, to whom the militants turned. It was he who was entrusted by Fiske and Fullam with the task of putting their recommendations before their recalcitrant Secretary. Young FDR, needless to say, was pleased to cooperate.[26]

The result of this military activity and planning was a full-scale cabinet discussion on the 13th of May at which the leading members of the the administration debated the extent to which they could accept the many recommendations coming from General Board, General Staff, and Joint Board. Baron Chinda's protest, as noted, was read to the group. In the extended discussion that followed Garrison generally sided with the views of the Army and Navy boards, while Daniels—with support from Wilson as well as Bryan—remained steadfastly opposed to any military measures of any sort. But Daniels, whatever his personal views on the subject, did read to the cabinet a long and carefully prepared statement which Admiral Fiske had submitted on behalf of the General Board. Fiske's statement, disarmingly enough, began with the argument that the Navy did not expect current tensions to lead to war. Nevertheless, he contended, precautionary measures should be instituted since many aspects of Japan's military and political situation had to be taken into account and, if war did develop, the United States would face many handicaps in fighting the Japanese.

[24] Daniels Papers, Diary, 13 May 1913.
[25] Wood Papers, Diary, 13 May 1913.
[26] Frank Freidel, *Franklin D. Roosevelt: The Apprenticeship* (Boston, 1952), 221-23.

What followed, then, was essentially a blend of the familiar logic of Mahan and the navalists with the basic assumptions of the Orange Plan. Fiske's memorandum, for example, emphasized the pressures of population upon the Japanese, the infertility of the Japanese soil, and the latent pressure for expansion—all of which, to a Social Darwinist and disciple of Mahan, made war at least a possibility. He also emphasized that, if war came, Japan could occupy both the Philippines and Hawaii, then withdraw her fleet to home waters and challenge the United States to wrest these conquests from her—all of which were standard assumptions of the Orange Plan.

Fiske pointed out that the United States could retaliate by sending her united fleet into the Pacific, blockading Japan's home islands, and bringing war home to the Japanese. But such an operation would take several years, while the Japanese, a frugal people, could certainly survive for an extended period of time. The real test, therefore, was not Japan's capacity to resist but America's will to sustain a long, drawn-out struggle waged at great distance and great cost. Fiske was certain that the Japanese had long since taken all of these possibilities into account and, knowing that many Americans hoped to dispose of the Philippines at some future date, might well have concluded that the United States "after an inglorious and expensive war of two years duration" would be willing to make peace on the basis of ceding the Philippines:

> It is conceivable that Japan may conclude—*may already have concluded*—that, if she should go to war with the United States, she could, by enduring a period of privation and distress lasting two years, acquire possession of both the Philippines and the Hawaiian Islands. Her war against China supplies a precedent for such a procedure.

Fiske, as spokesman for the General Board, had presented a foreboding picture, an example of the deep strain of naval pessimism that, in times of apparent crisis, rose to the surface. But his recommendations were limp: to forestall Japanese plans the United States must institute certain preparatory moves, the most important of which was to transfer to Manila the three cruisers currently in Chinese waters.

The General Board's analysis, in many ways a curiously accurate forecast of Japan's expectations in 1941, had no persuasive powers in May 1913. Wilson's advisers found it both too hypothetical and too dangerous. Daniels himself countered with the argument that any movement of naval vessels would simply encourage the "yellow press" to warlike speculations and that sensationalism in the press, in turn, might provoke the sensitive Japanese to adopt measures that otherwise could be avoided. Moreover, the cabinet, having debated the Chinda protest, simply did not regard the Japanese note as foreshadowing the ominous consequences predicted by the Navy.[27]

But both services continued to discuss the issue of naval and military preparations after the cabinet session on the 13th. On the following day the Joint Board formally recommended that the three cruisers in China be sent to Manila to bolster that city's defenses. In this request, the hand of the Army was clearly visible. The General Staff, as we have noted previously, had long worried about the state of Philippine defenses. It had always questioned the Navy's contention that, with luck, American forces could hold out in the fortress of Corregidor until eventual rescue. Hence it was the Army spokesmen who were most insistent about transferring the cruisers, since they wanted to add their naval firepower to Manila's defenses. But it was also apparent that the Joint Board was by now fully exercised. In a second letter, sent the same day, the Joint Board recommended the dispatch of eleven cruisers, five destroyers, and four submarines to Hawaii, with an additional two warships sent to the Canal Zone to strengthen its defenses.[28] Bradley Fiske also continued his own personal crusade to convince Josephus Daniels by providing his civilian chief with yet another, and even longer, memorandum which emphasized not just the possibility but the probability of conflict with Japan. It was another catalogue of Social Darwinist truths; Fiske maintained that Japan might choose the road to war because of unremitting population pressures for expansion, the peculiar ability of Japanese to thrive in warmer climates, and the "fact" that it was the United States which blocked Japan's access to the warmer regions of southeastern Asia.[29] The Army General Staff, meanwhile, was intensifying its revision of the Army version of the Orange Plan. A modified version was completed and approved by Wood and Garrison by late May. It was founded upon the same set of assumptions as the Navy's plan, since it anticipated the loss of the Philippines (save, possibly, for Corregidor) and postulated that for upwards of three months Japan would enjoy "practically undisputed control of the Pacific." It was a formidable document, prepared in great detail; there were, for example, copies of telegrams to be sent Army commanders in the Pacific, the text of conscription legislation to be submitted to the Congress, and drafts for many Executive orders

[27] The material in the preceding paragraphs is based on the May 13th entry in Daniels' diary, which includes a copy of Admiral Fiske's memorandum that Daniels read to the cabinet. The best general discussion of the debate in the Cabinet is to be found in Link, *New Freedom*, 289-304.

[28] JB, Minutes, 15 May 1913; Daniels Papers, Diary, 15 May 1913; Wood Papers, Diary, 15 May 1913.

[29] Daniels Papers, Diary, 16 and 17 May 1913.

necessary to put the plan into operation. Everything, in short, was ready for the President's signature.[30] (Parenthetically it might be noted that the prepared text of the telegram that would have been sent to the Army garrison in Hawaii was much more explicit and succinct than the fateful "war warning" dispatched by the War Department to General Dewey Short at Pearl Harbor some twenty-eight years later. The 1913 warning contained no ambiguities: "War with Japan is imminent. Be prepared to resist the enemy with all the forces under your command. . . . Put into effect the plans now on file in your Department for the land defense of the seacoast forts of Oahu." [31])

Woodrow Wilson was still being kept informed of the recommendations coming from his military services. On the 15th Secretary Garrison brought him several Staff recommendations about the number of civilian employees of the Philippine government who should be permitted to seek refuge on Corregidor as well as plans for Army maneuvers in Panama. Garrison also raised again the issue of moving units of the fleet to Hawaii and the Philippines. But Wilson was unmoved. General Wood later recalled the Secretary of War's discussion with the President as "an unsuccessful talk."[32]

A second cabinet meeting, held on Friday, May 16th, was also devoted to a thorough discussion of the Japanese crisis. Before his cabinet assembled, Wilson met privately with Garrison and Daniels, for he greatly desired a unanimous recommendation from his two service secretaries. But Daniels and Garrison were still poles apart. The Secretary of the Navy, expressing the opinion to which he had consistently adhered, claimed that any movement of American warships would simply inflame the Japanese and might actually create the circumstances that would lead to open conflict. Garrison, on the contrary, argued that the United States had the right to move its naval vessels where and when it pleased. The Secretary of War, clearly reflecting the views of the General Staff, contended that if the Navy could assemble its ships in the Philippines, then it might be possible to stage a successful defense of the islands. Garrison, as a civilian, was prepared to yield to the recommendations of the military experts. "It would be a mistake for us, who know so little about war," he told Wilson and Daniels, "to ignore the advice of the Joint Board." While Wilson clearly sided with Daniels, he concluded that the issue was of such great importance that a second, full cabinet discussion was mandatory and that no final decision would be reached before that debate.

[30] GS, War College Division, File 7280, Japanese War Plan, especially /2 and /7, 15 and 19 May 1913.

[31] GS, War College Division, File 7280/7, 19 May 1913.

[32] Wood Papers, Diary, 16 May 1913.

In the cabinet discussion of May 16th it appeared, at least for a time, as if a majority supported Garrison and the military planners. Garrison, needless to say, presented the recommendations of the Joint Board, while Daniels attempted to refute them. He was joined in his opposition by Bryan. Finally, Wilson made his ruling:

The Joint Board, of course, has presented the military aspect of the situation as it sees it, and it may be right, but we are considering this matter with another light, on the diplomatic side, and must determine the policy. I do not think any movement should be made at this time in the Pacific Ocean, and I will, therefore, take the responsibility of holding the ships where they are at the moment.

That same evening, at a White House garden party, Wilson and Daniels held a whispered conversation about the decision. As the Secretary of the Navy recalled their discussion, the President said, "At one time I think we had a majority of the Cabinet against us, but when I looked down the table and saw you upholding what you thought was the right course, it cheered my heart. We must not have war except in an honorable way, and I fear the Joint Board has made a mistake." Also on that same evening, after the cabinet's decision had been reported to him, a disgruntled General Leonard Wood recorded his sentiments in his diary: "Apparently Bryan and Daniels are against any degree of military preparedness whatever and do not realize in any way the possible gravity of the situation and the great disadvantage of failure to take reasonable precautions by getting things in shape." But for Wood there was at least one ironic consolation. He had been one of the vehement Army critics who had forced the Navy to abandon its plans to develop Subig Bay into a first-class installation, and he had continued to complain about the maintenance of any and all facilities at that location. Now he was witnessing naval fears for the safety of their unprotected ships, drydock, and other materials still at Olongapo. It was turning out, Wood gloated, just as he predicted. The Navy would have no worries if the admirals had only been willing to accept the Army recommendation that all naval facilities in the Philippines should be permanently situated in Manila Bay where their protection was at least feasible.[33]

The debates over military preparations in the Far East had so far proceeded in accordance with the accepted canons and procedures of policymaking. General Wood might complain, as he did, that as Chief of Staff he saw "nothing of the President" except at official functions and unfavorably contrast his relationship with Wilson to the associa-

[33] The preceding paragraphs are based on the Wood and Daniels diaries for the period 15-16 May 1913.

tion he had enjoyed with his friend, Theodore Roosevelt.[34] Nonetheless, the service boards and their chiefs had been afforded a full opportunity not only to present their proposals to their civilian superiors but also to get them debated in detail by the cabinet. However much Daniels abhorred the concepts of Admiral Fiske, he nonetheless did present them in full to his colleagues in the cabinet. President Wilson had been kept informed of the ideas emerging from both the General and the Joint Board; moreover, even while rejecting their advice, he had made it clear that he respected their right to present their suggestions. The decision had, in the last analysis, gone against them on the sound principle that political and diplomatic considerations were more fundamental than military logic.

The trouble between Wilson and his military advisers erupted on the following day, Saturday, May 17th. In the morning Fiske brought Daniels still another recommendation from the Joint Board. It was dated the 16th, that is, the day of the decisive cabinet meeting. The admiral insisted that its contents—another suggestion for further concentration of naval vessels in the Hawaiian Islands—must be transmitted to the President even though the cabinet had already made its decision. The Secretary, unable to convince Fiske that the issue was settled, finally agreed to show this recommendation to Wilson later in the day. But Daniels began to get irritated. First, Admiral Fiske called on him a second time with further suggestions for naval action; then, he was visited by a newspaper reporter who asked him pointblank if he approved the recommendation of the Joint Board that naval vessels should be moved. Convinced that the naval staff was trying to force his hand and was leaking information to the press, Daniels sent for Fiske and complained about the leak. At the end of the business day he went to the White House and related these events to the President. Wilson was angered by the newspaper leak but even more displeased by the apparent fact that the Joint Board had held another meeting and made further recommendations *after* the cabinet had reached its decision. It was this which provoked him into saying that the Army and Navy officers had no right to hold such a meeting after the responsible civilian leaders of the administration had reached their decision and communicated it to the services. "And I wish you to tell them," Wilson warned, "that if this should occur again, there will be no Joint or General Boards. They will be abolished." On the President's instruction, Daniels then called Admiral Fiske and informed him that there should be no further meetings of the boards until he had had an opportunity for further discussion with him.[35]

[34] Herman Hagedorn, *Leonard Wood* (New York, 1931), 138.
[35] Daniels Papers, Diary, 17 May 1913.

Civil supremacy had thus been upheld against improper military pressures. The services had been justly rebuked for trying to force a change in policies determined by their civilian superiors. So, at least, Josephus Daniels chose to interpret the event. His memoirs exult over the stand of the civilian against the military.[36] Certainly one major aspect of his analysis was correct. Those who had argued in behalf of the primacy of the political and diplomatic aspects of the Japanese crisis of 1913 were right in their assessment of the presumed danger as well as in their reading of the Japanese protest. Japan had meant no threat, there had been no prospect of war, and the "crisis" evaporated almost as rapidly as it had first blown up on the horizon.[37] The militants in the Army and Navy had again been the victims of their own inflated fears of Japanese intentions, above all victims of their world outlook which made them interpret international affairs almost exclusively in terms of strife and conflict, competition and war.

Nevertheless the entire episode cannot properly be interpreted as a textbook example of the triumph of civilian virtue over military vice. Josephus Daniels, for example, was not so much objecting to the military recommendations *per se* as he was protesting their timing. Even when he was arguing with Lindley Garrison, the Secretary of the Navy readily conceded that there had long been tension with Japan and that, in his judgment, the Taft administration should have kept the entire American fleet in the Pacific Ocean. At one point, in a moment of candor, he told Garrison that if he had known in March, when he first came into office, what he learned since then, he personally would have given such orders for the concentration of the fleet! And he followed this with admiring comments about the adroit way in which Theodore Roosevelt had checked the Japanese by his use of the American fleet. Though he chose to show the liberal-pacifist side of his nature in his memoirs, Daniels had no quarrel with the basic concept of using the fleet to impress a possible enemy, to show its power as a technique of peacekeeping. His primary objection was always that a sudden, unexpected movement of American warships, at a time of political tension, would not be a deterrent but an irritant. His diary, incidentally, shows that, like Garrison, he also had qualms about disagreeing with the professional judgment of the naval experts.[38]

Similarly even the flare-up between Wilson and the military leaders was something less than a heroic confrontation of civil and military. The famous letter of May 17th—the letter which so roused the Presi-

[36] Josephus Daniels, *The Wilson Era: Years of Peace, 1910-1917* (Chapel Hill, 1944), 161-68.

[37] Link, *New Freedom*, 303-04.

[38] Daniels Papers, Diary, 16 May 1913.

dent's ire—had in fact been prepared on the preceding day, *before* the cabinet had made its decision, and at a time when even Wilson conceded the right of the Army and Navy to make suggestions about a policy not yet finally determined. The Joint Board had hoped to get it to the White House in time for the cabinet meeting. But there had been one of those typical delays in the military channels, and the letter never got to Secretary Daniels until the following morning. Admiral Fiske, whose militancy was obvious, may have used bad judgment in pressing the issue at that time, but it was not the purpose of the Joint Board to exert additional pressure on Wilson to change his mind after the cabinet had met. General Leonard Wood, indeed, explained all of this to Wilson at a White House ceremony on the 19th and assured the President that it had never been the intention of the Joint Board "to annoy him by a succession of letters." Wilson responded that he was certainly glad to know this, since from his vantage point it had seemed clear that the military were trying to coerce him. The Joint Board did suspend its meetings for a time, but it was operating as usual in October of 1913. Moreover, since it did not normally meet in the summer months, the loss of meetings was scarcely noticeable. At the October session, incidentally, Wood told his fellow officers of his efforts to explain the entire misunderstanding about the message to President Wilson.[39] It might also be added that the entire incident—crisis with Japan as well as dispute with military leaders—vanished so rapidly that after May 20th there was no mention of the friction with the service boards in any of the notes that Daniels took at cabinet meetings. Thereafter his only note on the overall crisis with Japan was a reference to Bryan's statement that Japan would prefer to let time rather than armaments decide the differences.[40]

Two years later Daniels wrote the epitaph for the episode in a letter to Wilson:

> It is probable that newspapermen will ask you about Congressman Gardner's statement that you ordered the Joint Board of the Army and Navy to hold no further meetings. You may not recall the facts, and so I write to say that, after publication of their actions, during the delicate Japanese situation, which you disapproved, you directed me to say to the naval members not to attend another meeting until you gave such orders for a meeting. A few days thereafter you told me to say that meetings might be held but you wished no action decided upon in the Pacific pending the Japanese land discussion. . . . My own view is that . . . it is not necessary to give an answer

[39] JB, Minutes, 9 October 1913; Wood Papers, Diary, 13 October 1913.
[40] Daniels Papers, Diary, 20 May 1913.

to any statement he [Gardner] makes, but your judgment will be better than mine.[41]

3. The Caribbean and the Incident at Tampico

It is one of the paradoxes of the Wilson era that his administration, theoretically dedicated to the elimination of "dollar diplomacy" and the treatment of Latin states as equals, nonetheless created a record of intervention which, as Arthur Link has pointed out, was "unparalleled before or since in the history of the western hemisphere."[42] The many reasons for this record—diplomatic inexperience, the desire to promote the spread of democratic institutions, the unstated but no less real concern for the security of the route to the canal, and a host of other significant reasons—have been examined by many historians and need not once again be explored in detail.[43] But certainly the paradox was present, even if only implicitly, at the outset of the new administration. Wilson's press release of March 11th spoke of the desire to cultivate Latin friendship; it also—and here Wilson was in fact responding to Huntington Wilson's warning about the danger of forthcoming revolutions in Central America—contained a stern sentence that his administration would "have no sympathy with those who seek to seize the power of government to advance their own personal interests or ambition."[44]

The new administration's interest in naval bases furnished clear evidence that the regime of William Jennings Bryan and Woodrow Wilson was not going to reverse established trends in the Caribbean. Within only two months after he had become Secretary of State, Bryan had personally endorsed a scheme to purchase the Mole St. Nicholas in Haiti. It also seems clear that the proposal had matured in the Latin American Affairs Division, not in the Navy Department. Indeed, it was only after the plans were well underway that Bryan told the President that he intended to send copies of the proposal to the War and Navy Departments for their opinions.[45] Thus, while the military did give

---

41 Daniels Papers, Daniels to Wilson, 10 April 1915.

42 Link, *New Freedom*, 327.

43 See, for example, John Blum, *Woodrow Wilson and the Politics of Morality* (Boston, 1956); N. Gordon Levin, *Woodrow Wilson and World Politics* (New York, 1968); as well as Link's concise *Wilson the Diplomatist* (Baltimore, 1957). On Bryan see, R. D. Challener, "William Jennings Bryan," in Graebner, *Uncertain Tradition*, and Selig Adler, "Bryan and Wilsonian Caribbean Penetration," *Hispanic-American Historical Review*, xx, no. 2 (May 1940), 198-226. There is also some useful information in the most recent study of Bryan, Louis Koenig, *Bryan: A Political Biography* (New York, 1971), 502-51.

44 Link, *New Freedom*, 320.

45 Papers of William Jennings Bryan, Manuscripts Division, Library of Congress, Bryan to Wilson, 14 June 1913.

their sanction, their role was strictly secondary—and considerably different from the era of Roosevelt when their views had been sought before any such scheme was initiated.

The proposed purchase of the Mole did, of course, have certain "Bryanite" touches. Residents of the area to be ceded would have had the option of choosing either American or Haitian citizenship; if they chose to sell their lands, there would have been guarantees that they would receive full market value for their properties. But, in essence, it was still a lineal descendant of all the other proposals for naval bases that had emerged in the years since the Spanish-American War. The Haitians would be asked to cede a strip of land twenty miles in depth so that it could be defended from land attack and the American forces would not be restricted to harbor defenses.[46] Bryan appeared only half informed about certain aspects of the proposal. He told Wilson, for example, that, after examining charts of the harbor, he was impressed by the value of the Mole as a naval base—but then added that, even if the site was not intrinsically valuable, it was worth obtaining it simply to keep it out of the international market and European temptation.[47] This alone would indicate that Bryan and his new assistants were pursuing the same lines of thought and accepting the same logic that had long prevailed in the State Department of Knox and Huntington Wilson.

Once Wilson had approved the plan, Assistant Secretary of State Fred Osborne conducted the negotiations with the Haitians. He, too, advanced arguments which were something less than new, principally the contention that, to provide better protection for the Windward Passage, the United States needed a second fortified naval station on the other side of the passage from Guantanamo. Osborne, in turn, met counterarguments from President Oreste which paralleled those that American diplomats had long encountered on similar ventures. The Haitian President assured the Americans that he personally would rather see the United States in possession of the Mole St. Nicholas than any other country, but unfortunately the Haitian constitution forbade the sale of national territory. The United States, he added, might make an offer for future consideration, though it could not involve the outright cession of territory. In any event, Oreste concluded, the issue could not be discussed until some future date when his regime would be more firmly established and his political enemies less advantageously situated.[48]

Osborne applied no pressure and settled for what was probably his

[46] Bryan Papers, Bryan to Wilson, 20 June 1913.
[47] Bryan Papers, Bryan to Wilson, 14 June 1913.
[48] SDDF, File 811.34538/1, Furniss to Osborne, 9 July 1913, a summary of the discussions.

principal objective: the receipt of a pledge from Oreste that the Haitians would not entertain propositions for the Mole from other countries and would not sell it to any private concessionnaires, even those entirely American in composition. The Latin American division, as we have seen, had long been skeptical about private concessions, feeling that the original owners might at some future date be tempted to sell out to foreign interests. It was particularly dubious at that time about one group of New Yorkers who were interested in securing a lease on the Mole. Thus, when Osborne got the desired Haitian promises, he was satisfied. On his return to Washington he expressed entire satisfaction with his mission, suggesting that the Haitians might well have granted a concession to the New Yorkers if the government had not made clear its opposition to private concessions of this character.[49]

But the Department of State continued to keep a watchful eye. In 1914, when a new Haitian government sought diplomatic recognition, the American minister was instructed to inform the incoming regime in Port-au-Prince that the United States wished the question of the disposition of the Mole to remain unchanged.[50] The same State Department interest in bases also revealed itself in Nicaragua, where Bryan and his associates, revived the Nicaraguan treaty, first proposed by Knox, to secure a canal option and, among other details, a naval base on the Bay of Fonseca. When the proposal was submitted to Congress, it included a General Board recommendation that such a base would add to the safety of the Canal. But, again, it was a naval memorandum dated long after the Administration had begun its campaign on behalf of the treaty and showed once more how the Navy was being used to support civilian policy rather than initiating the requests for bases.[51]

But it was in Mexico that the full dimensions of Wilsonian policy and its many paradoxes were revealed. Here indeed was the moralist who wished to see the brutal, dictatorial Huerta replaced by a democratic leader; here also was the interventionist who, thwarted in his desire to help Mexicans reach American standards of virtue, seized upon the flimsiest of pretexts to launch a direct intervention into Mexican affairs. Wilson's handling of the Mexican revolution forms, without question, one of the most controversial, most frequently criticized, chapters in the history of his administration. It is a record which, however laudable the President's intentions may have been, was marred by multiple errors of omission and of commission.

The story of Mexican-American relations during the Wilson years has been told in detail in many excellent studies, and it would serve no

---

[49] SDDF, File 811.34538/2, Osborne to Bryan, 19 July 1913.

[50] SDDF, File 838.00/855, Bryan to Furniss, 26 February 1914.

[51] On the Nicaraguan treaty, Bryan papers, Bryan to Wilson, 31 July 1913, 15 January and 12 June 1914. See also Link, *New Freedom*, 335.

useful purpose to chronicle its lugubrious course in these pages.[52] From the viewpoint of the history of civil-military relations, however, it fully illustrates the central paradox of Wilson's relationship with all of Latin America. That is to say, it presents a case study of an administration which wished to repudiate the imperialist past and become a good neighbor but which ended up using military power to coerce an unwilling Latin neighbor in a fashion that outdid both Roosevelt and Taft.

The new administration had absolutely no desire in the spring of 1913 to intervene in Mexico. Wilson might fulminate about Huerta and refuse diplomatic recognition, but intervention was clearly ruled out. To be sure, at the very outset of his administration Wilson decided that the ships sent by Taft and Knox ought to remain in Mexican waters lest their immediate return to American ports be interpreted as a sign of American satisfaction with conditions under the Huerta regime. But both Daniels and Bryan wished for their early departure, and the naval watch was soon reduced drastically.[53] Cabinet discussions led to a clear consensus that, whatever one thought about Huerta, the United States should adopt no policies which suggested American interference. In these early discussions there was even the feeling, as Daniels once expressed it, that the entire Mexican problem was simply "a contest between English and American oil companies to see which would control."[54]

William Jennings Bryan had opinions far different from those of Philander Knox about the protection of American lives and property in Mexico. He believed that the United States might properly and officially request the Huerta regime to grant a safe conduct passage to American residents who sought to leave the country. But force could be used by the United States to protect or rescue its nationals only if Mexican authorities refused an official request for such safe conducts. It would, above all, be morally wrong to send American troops into Mexico to protect the property of American citizens who were unwilling to leave the country. Expressing a point of view which he was to expound at length when German submarines began to sink Allied shipping, Bryan contended that such an intervention would be tantamount to putting "property rights ahead of human rights—to put the dollar

[52] The best is Howard Cline, *The United States and Mexico* (New York, rev. edn., 1963).

[53] Daniels Papers, Diary, 11 April 1913. But see also a remarkable message from Bryan to all American legations in Latin America in which the Secretary of State wrote at length on the need to develop tolerance and a willingness to make mutual concessions in handling the Mexican problem. SDDF, File 812.00/6522, Bryan to American legations, 8 March 1913.

[54] Daniels Papers, Diary, 13 April 1913.

above the man—and war entered into for this purpose would put this country upon a level with those nations which have extended their territory by conquest."[55] Thus, when the new administration discussed its policy with regard to the destruction of American-owned railroad properties in Mexico, Bryan remained firm, along with Daniels, in his belief that the United States could do no more than try to arrange a safe convoy out of Mexico for those American rail employees who wished to leave. The United States certainly could not order its armed forces into Mexico "to help those who wanted to stay and protect their property."[56] About this time Admiral Southerland asked Daniels for instructions about possible naval operations. The Secretary of the Navy responded that, while the protection of American property was important, the Admiral should also remember that "nobody told Americans to go into Mexico and buy property, and if they do so they must not expect any more protection than others get."[57] It was in this frame of mind that both Wilson and Daniels scrutinized naval reports, as we have previously seen, to make certain that there were no naval initiatives by militantly inclined officers of the fleet.

Secretary Garrison, on the other hand, did not share the outlook of Bryan and Daniels. From the outset he argued, on pragmatic grounds, that the United States ought to recognize the Huerta government since there was no viable alternative to his regime.[58] As time passed Garrison began to feel that some sort of military intervention was inevitable. He was also not averse to using information obtained from his own officer corps to buttress his arguments. In the fall of 1913 the Secretary of War received a lengthy letter from Brigadier General James Parker, at that time commander of a cavalry brigade stationed at Fort Sam Houston in Texas. The nub of Parker's letter was a strong plea for intervention in Mexico as the only way to secure the necessary reforms in that country.[59] Garrison, without attributing his source, used the information supplied by Parker in his own correspondence with the President. He later wrote the general that, "while I do not feel that I am justified in saying it directly to the President, I am utilizing your facts as a basis for my communications to the President."[60] It was another example of the informal, roundabout way in which the views of military men could pierce the "civilian curtain" and be brought to bear on matters of civilian policy.

55 Bryan Papers, Memorandum, Bryan to Wilson, 19 July 1913.

56 Daniels Papers, Diary, 15 April 1913.

57 Daniels Papers, Daniels to Admiral Fletcher, 13 August 1913.

58 Garrison Papers, undated memorandum attached to Garrison to Wilson letter of 5 June 1913. Also Daniels Papers, Diary, 20 May 1913.

59 Garrison Papers, Brigadier General James Parker to Garrison, 20 October 1913.

60 Garrison Papers, Garrison to Parker, 12 November 1913.

Officers of the Army and Navy did not share the administration's views about the virtues of non-intervention. But they were not all militants or extremists. Some certainly realized that much of the growing public agitation to "do something" about Mexico was rooted in emotion, prejudice, and self-interest. General Leonard Wood clearly understood that many of the complaints which came from the border areas of the Southwest were to be discounted. As Chief of Staff he was sent in April 1913 to investigate conditions on the Rio Grande, an area from which were emerging loud complaints about Mexican depredations. Wood's report showed a notable lack of sympathy for the Texans:

> In general it may be said that the reports which have been sent to the War Department concerning alarm and disturbances on the American side of the border have been in almost all instances false. The attitude of the Governor of Texas has been one of politics, trying to build on public sentiment. Have been no disturbances on our side of the line, and people in Texas not alarmed. The appeals for troops from the Big Bend has been based entirely upon a desire to apparently sell supplies.[61]

The General Staff, of course, continued to perfect its Mexican war plan, basing its revisions in the spring of 1913 on the new assumption that, while Huerta might control his own forces, he would never be able to rally a united Mexico and its limited military resources against the United States.[62] Those naval officers familiar with the Mexican scene continued to believe that they were sailing near a powder keg that might explode at any moment. Admiral Southerland, for example, personally told Daniels in April 1913 that, in his judgment, war with Mexico was always possible on no more than a 24-hour notice, that naval vessels should be prepared to occupy all major west coast ports, and that the Navy, in general, should be ready to "over-awe" the Mexicans with superior force.[63] Admiral Fletcher, whose attitude toward intervention had so displeased Wilson, continued to be pessimistic about the Mexican future. By February 1914 he was writing directly to Daniels that the situation at Tampico, which had so far remained peaceful, was becoming ominous. He predicted that the Constitutionalist forces—that is, the revolutionary group headed by Carranza which Wilson clearly favored and was then trying to patronize—

[61] Wood Papers, Diary, 2 May 1913. Also Garrison Papers, Wood to Garrison, 26 April 1913.

[62] GS, War College Division, File 6474/270, Memorandum, Crozier to War Plans Committee, 24 June 1913 and /275, a revised version of the Mexican War Plan, 29 July 1913.

[63] Daniels Papers, Diary, 19 April 1913.

would soon occupy the city, with the usual looting and shooting to follow. Fletcher described the local situation as so tense and complex that the commander on the spot could be guided only by his own judgment.[64]

In any event, as the Constitutionalist opposition to Huerta spread and as Wilson became more and more embroiled in political and diplomatic efforts to unseat Huerta, the United States never did remove its naval watch. Whatever its hopes may have been in the spring of 1913, the administration continued the patrol initiated in the Taft period. Indeed, around Tampico, which in early 1914 became the focal point in the growing conflict between Huerta and Carranza, the number of American naval craft increased as the tensions rose. By the time of the famous incident of April 9, 1914, when a Mexican shore patrol arrested American sailors, there were at least six vessels in the immediate vicinity.[65] By early 1914, moreover, it was widely, and erroneously, believed that the Huerta regime would soon collapse and that, if this occurred, there was genuine danger of serious disorder in Mexico City. In these circumstances a reluctant Wilson now talked with both Daniels and Garrison about the possibility that the United States would have to mount a relief expedition to rescue its beleaguered citizens in the Mexican capital.[66]

Naval officers were still held under tight rein, even tighter than under Taft. When Fletcher was sent to Tampico in November 1913 to observe that troubled scene, he was specifically instructed that there could be no landing of his naval forces unless and until Washington approved—and then only if the admiral had previously advised his superiors that there was absolutely no other way to save the lives of Americans and other foreigners resident in Tampico.[67] Although controls were tight, information was meager. Wilson's Mexican policy was intensely personal, and to the Navy his purposes often seemed obscure. Admiral Fletcher soon complained that he, the senior officer, was ill-informed about national policy. Requesting the services of a certain Captain Huse, the admiral begged Daniels to provide Huse with special briefings in Washington before his departure for Tampico. "The slightest impressions I get from Washington," he informed the Secretary of the Navy, "as to the trend of sentiment in the administration, and your opinion, are of the greatest assistance to me in shap-

64 Naval Records, Area Files, 1911-1927 (Caribbean), Fletcher to Daniels, 24 July 1913, and Daniels Papers, Fletcher to Daniels, 4 February 1914.

65 Daniels Papers, an undated memorandum entitled "The Tampico Incident" prepared within the Navy Department as a summary of the events leading up to and following the incident.

66 See in the Daniels Papers a series of lengthy letters exchanged between Daniels and Fletcher between 5 and 7 January 1914.

67 Daniels Papers, copy of orders sent to Admiral Fletcher, 23 November 1913.

ing my conduct, for you must admit that my instructions are very meager."[68]

In April 1914 the long-anticipated showdown occurred at Tampico. That city, as we have seen, had recently emerged as the focal point of the Mexican revolution and had also become increasingly important in naval planning because of its oil facilities. The principal details of the incident at Tampico are familiar. On April 9th some sailors from the *Dolphin*, who had gone ashore in a launch to purchase gasoline, were arrested by Mexican authorities. They were marched for several blocks through the streets of Tampico but eventually marched back to their boat and released. The general commanding Huerta's forces in the area made an immediate verbal apology, but Rear Admiral Henry Mayo, the American officer in command at Tampico, was not satisfied. The arrest, as he later put it, had received so much publicity that he believed that he had to demand a formal Mexican disavowal, punishment of the arresting officer, and—what, of course, became the nub of the controversy—a formal salute to the American flag to be delivered within twenty-four hours.[69]

The arrest occurred at a moment when the American President, long incensed with Huerta, was deeply involved in efforts to obtain his removal from power and attempting to impose Wilsonian concepts of democratic virtue upon the Mexicans. The Tampico incident furnished a pretext—possibly, the charitable word should be justification—for action upon which Wilson immediately seized. The reaction in Washington to Mayo's report was instant. Significantly there was no immediate disposition to ask questions of the Navy or seek verification of the facts reported by Mayo. William Jennings Bryan, for example, simply and immediately forwarded the admiral's message to Wilson. It was a true copy, to which the Secretary of State added only the notation, "I do not see that Mayo could have done otherwise."[70]

From this unfortunate beginning the crisis grew with increasing rapidity, since the administration resolved to compel Huerta's government to bow to Mayo's demands. On the 11th of April the embassy in Mexico City was informed that the admiral's ultimatum had been communicated to Wilson and received the President's approval. Since the Mexican insult to the American flag had been "open and public," Bryan noted, there was no reason why "the salute should not be cheerfully given." (The administration did give the Mexicans a few extra days in which to comply. Since it was Holy Week, most Mexican offices

[68] Daniels Papers, Fletcher to Daniels, 4 February 1914.

[69] Wilson Papers, Series II, Bryan to Wilson, 9 April 1914; Nav Rec AF Caribbean, 1911-1927, Mexican File, Fletcher to Daniels, 9 April 1914. The best secondary account is Robert Quirk, *An Affair of Honor* (Lexington, Ky., 1962), 1-77.

[70] Wilson Papers, Bryan to Wilson, 9 April 1914.

were closed, and it was proving difficult to get in touch with the appropriate government officers.[71]) On the 14th it was decided to send units of the Atlantic Fleet to Tampico. Six days later, after a flurry of meetings, the administration decided to seize the city of Vera Cruz.

The decision to intervene was an administration decision—above all, Wilson's decision, for the role of Bryan was both indecisive and vacillating. It cannot be said that it was "made" by the United States Navy. A militant admiral anxious to punish the Mexicans may have initiated the episode, but the forthcoming decision was the President's. Moreover, as we shall shortly observe, not a few of the naval recommendations were overruled. Still, Army and Navy leaders did get an opportunity to express their opinions, were consulted on several crucial aspects of the evolving situation, and, in the last analysis, shaped and influenced at least the fringe of Wilsonian policy.

It was not until the 13th of April, four days after the arrest of Mayo's sailors, that the Department of State began to ask the Navy to supply answers to questions that might well have been asked earlier if the Wilsonian disposition had been different. After giving Admiral Mayo instructions on the procedures to employ if the Mexicans rendered the required salute, Bryan then asked him to indicate the specific language he had used in demanding the salute to the flag and why he had specified that the flag must be raised.[72] More significant, however, was the reaction in the administration when Huerta, as part of his sustained campaign to thwart Wilson's purposes, advanced the counterargument that Mayo's sailors had violated Mexican law by landing at a prohibited area in a city under martial law. This at least gave momentary pause to both Bryan and Robert Lansing, the shrewd legal counsellor of the State Department who was already beginning to make his mark. Bryan, who by then would have welcomed a way out of the impasse, told Wilson that, if Huerta was correct, then the United States could scarcely demand "as much as we could have demanded if we were clearly within our rights." Lansing, in turn, observed that the administration would have to take into account the fact that the Navy was violating the state of martial law then in force at Tampico.[73] At this juncture Bryan turned to the Navy and the General Board for a further opinion. He received back an extended memorandum which contended that the naval personnel had gone ashore on official duty and were therefore clearly acting within their rights under international law. The General Board's opinion, prepared by Admiral Fiske, further

[71] Wilson Papers, copy of Bryan to O'Shaughnessy, 11 April 1914, and O'Shaughnessy to Bryan, same date.

[72] Wilson Papers, copy of Daniels to Fletcher, 13 April 1914.

[73] Wilson Papers, Bryan to Wilson, 13 April 1914, two memoranda, one of which notes Lansing's opinions.

maintained: "It is a recognized principle of international law that public national vessels carry with them an element of extraterritoriality by which they are considered as part of the country to which they belong." Extraterritoriality extended to the small boats and launches of a larger public vessel. Thus the sailors in the whaleboat were included within the extraterritorial immunity of the *Dolphin*. They should, said the General Board, have been immune from "ordinary municipal interference"—indeed, were "absolutely immune in much the same way as an ambassador is immune within his embassy." The Mexicans and not the Americans had therefore violated international law. The General Board, in its righteous defense of international law, went further. Even if Mayo's sailors had committed some offense against Mexican law, the proper remedy for the Mexicans was not to arrest the Americans but simply to request that they return to their vessel and then to report what they had done to the Mexican military command in the Tampico area.

> Instead of doing this, however, the Mexicans committed the double wrong of taking the men, in uniform, out of a man-of-war's boat flying the flag of the United States, and also marching them and others, including a commissioned officer, through the streets of the city, under arrest.

What made the incident all the more reprehensible to the General Board was the fact that the Americans were unaware of having violated any Mexican laws and had had no intention of doing so. They did not know that they were landing in a prohibited area; they would never have gone ashore at that point if they had been properly informed; they carried no arms or ammunition and were simply trying to purchase gasoline.[74]

Fiske's memorandum was not merely sent to President Wilson. Special care was taken to inform him that it represented the unanimous opinion of the General Board, and Bryan advised him to read it carefully before sending further notes to Huerta.[75] In considerable contrast to its attitude during the Japanese frictions a year previously, the administration was pleased to accept a naval recommendation. In his own dispatches to Huerta, Bryan not only used some of the General Board's arguments but even adopted some of its phraseology. Bryan's note, which pressed for Mexican compliance with Mayo's demand for a salute, emphasized the absence of warnings about the prohibited areas at Tampico, stressed the innocence of the landing from the

---

[74] Wilson Papers, copy of Fiske's memorandum sent to Daniels, 13 April 1914. The memorandum was prepared by Fiske in consultation with the General Board.

[75] Wilson Papers, Daniels to Wilson, 13 April 1914.

whaleboat, and adopted the Navy's argument that the correct procedure would have been a request for the sailors to return to the *Dolphin* and not their arrest. The Secretary of State argued that under international law arrest could not be considered excusable.[76]

The Department of State also consulted naval authorities about the niceties of saluting procedure, especially the appropriate American response if and when the salute was rendered. The General Board informed Bryan that, under established procedures, a Mexican salute would imply a return salute to the Mexican nation by United States vessels present.[77] Given the nature of the quarrel and the national sensitivities involved, this was by no means a trivial concern. Much of the diplomatic debate between Mexico City and Washington revolved around Huerta's proposal—which Wilson rejected—that there be simultaneous salutes by both nations. Moreover, in any circumstances, the Mexicans insisted that there must be some American response. But Wilson, of course, had refused to grant diplomatic recognition to the Huerta government and was afraid that any American response to a Mexican salute, however it was rendered, would imply American recognition of a government he despised.[78] On this point in particular the Navy offered reassurance. A return salute, so ruled the Navy's experts on protocol, would simply be a salute to the Mexican nation as a whole and would carry none of the implications that the President feared. The Board cited several precedents from naval experience, especially one involving Honduras in 1894, in reaching its verdict.[79] These answers from the General Board, along with other and more technical matters, were soon incorporated in the various instructions sent to Mayo and Fletcher.[80]

The General Board provided advice which was included in the messages of the Department of State and, indeed, had some influence in the development of policy. But the officers on the spot in Mexico got no free hand at all, for Wilson and his advisers were taking no chances that local initiatives would force their hand. On the 14th it was decided, as we have noted, to order the Atlantic Fleet, under the command of Admiral Charles Badger, to Mexican waters. Before Badger sailed, Daniels sent Fiske to brief him and make certain that he fully understood the administration's policy. Fiske came armed with many

[76] Wilson Papers, Bryan to O'Shaughnessy, 14 April 1914, a note which bears a striking resemblance to the General Board recommendations.

[77] Wilson Papers, the Fiske memorandum of 13 April.

[78] Quirk, *Affair*, 59-63, for a summary of the argument. See also Wilson Papers, O'Shaughnessy to Bryan, 15 April 1914; Bryan to O'Shaughnessy, 16 April 1914; O'Shaughnessy to Bryan, 17 April 1914; and Wilson to Bryan, 19 April 1914.

[79] Wilson Papers, the Fiske memorandum of 13 April.

[80] Wilson Papers, Daniels to Wilson, 16 April 1914, a letter which outlines the orders sent by the Navy to its officers in Mexico.

documents, provided his own summary of events to date, and tried to be explicit about Wilson's objectives. He told Badger that the administration intended to enforce Mayo's demand for a salute but that, if Huerta refused, "force would probably be resorted to"—though, he added, Wilson earnestly wished to avoid war with Mexico. Badger made notes while Fiske was talking, after which he composed a letter to Josephus Daniels so that the Secretary of the Navy would have evidence in writing that he had been informed about the administration's stand. Daniels, in turn, was pleased with Admiral Badger's note. He passed it on to Wilson with the observation that he was satisfied from its tenor that "I impressed your views on him as strongly as I could."[81] Similarly, Admiral Fletcher kept one of his aides stationed in Mexico City at the American embassy so that his command could keep in touch with the evolution of diplomatic policy.[82]

But although the naval commanders were well informed about the firmness and general purpose of the administration, they remained uncertain about the specific measures that might be pursued. Those at Vera Cruz got few hints about the action that might be taken if Huerta stuck to his refusal. Even before he left for Mexico, Admiral Badger was well aware of the fact that he had no direct orders about how he was to proceed once he arrived off Tampico. He asked for further instructions specifying how naval actions commensurate "with the show of force should be taken." Badger himself was personally convinced that any landing of sailors or the seizure of even a single Mexican gunboat—indeed, any use of force—would be an act of war. It would, he argued, "involve the most serious consequences, and the United States government must be prepared for them."[83]

As early as the 15th of April Wilson had informed certain Congressional leaders that, in the event of a final refusal by the Mexicans, he might authorize seizure of Tampico and Vera Cruz and possibly a "peaceful blockade" of Mexico. Even before Badger's naval forces had been ordered to Mexico, Lansing had been searching the State Department's records for precedents which would justify the President in using force against the Mexicans.[84] The naval establishment, however, did receive one full-fledged opportunity to recommend a course of action to pursue. Over the weekend of April 18-20, Daniels put a series of direct questions before the Board: what should be done if Huerta rejected the American demands? How far could the President pro-

[81] Wilson Papers, Daniels to Wilson, 16 April 1914, including a copy of Badger's note written for Daniels on the 15th.

[82] Daniels Papers, Fletcher to Badger, a report of naval operations from 21 to 30 April 1914, dated 13 May 1914.

[83] Wilson Papers, Badger to Daniels, 15 April 1914.

[84] Quirk, *Affair*, 50.

ceed, without securing specific authorization from Congress, in instituting such measures as the seizure of Mexican ports, the establishment
of a pacific blockade, or even the establishment of a formal military
and naval blockade?[85]

The General Board not only returned detailed answers but went beyond the framework of the questions asked of it. It first rejected the
idea of acting without Congressional approval on the grounds that its
recommendations were such that Wilson should obtain legislative approval before instituting them. The admirals were strict constitutional-
ists who believed that Wilson's executive authority could not be exercised without Congressional sanction. Moreover, their stand on this
point was but the logical consequence of their formal recommendations. They wanted the United States to use both its land and its sea
forces to impose its demands on Huerta and, in addition, to establish
a belligerent and *not* a pacific blockade. Such a program, they reasoned, required Congressional approval and went far beyond the executive powers of the presidency.

The admirals rejected the idea of simply seizing a few customs
houses or even of seizing one or two Mexican ports. Such measures
would be acts of war, would inevitably cost American lives, but would
not be effective against an entire nation. Similarly, a pacific blockade
would be useless. The United States, the General Board observed, had
never previously attempted to establish a pacific blockade nor, in addition, had it ever recognized the right of other countries to enforce a
peaceful blockade against American shipping. A pacific blockade, the
Board argued, could never be made effective against the ships of other
countries and would only result in the diversion of the Mexican carrying trade from American or Mexican vessels to the shipping of other
countries. A pacific blockade, it added, would have no effect on the
shipment of arms and ammunition to Huerta. Thus, having eliminated
the seizure of one or two ports or the establishment of a pacific blockade as adequate responses, the General Board concluded that the only
viable course of action was to impose on Mexico a full-scale belligerent
blockade. It was a solution, Admiral Dewey argued piously, that arose
out of the General Board's sincere desire "to propose measures which
will be effective and least likely to cause international complications."[86]

These recommendations were not permitted, even within the naval
establishment, to go unchallenged. Admiral Victor Blue, serving at this
critical juncture as Acting Secretary of the Navy in the temporary absence of Daniels, did not think that the proposal for a belligerent
blockade went far enough. He reconvened the Executive Committee

[85] GB, File 425, Victor Blue to the Secretary of the General Board, 18 April 1914.
[86] GB, File 425, Dewey to Daniels, 18 April 1914.

of the General Board and made a fervent plea in behalf of implementation of the long-standing Mexican Plan—that is, the seizure of Tampico and Vera Cruz followed by a full-scale march on the Mexican capital to be conducted by the Army. Blue's recommendation was not well received; a majority of the Executive Committee was satisfied with the proposal for a blockade. Those opposed to Admiral Blue argued that any attempt to implement the Mexican Plan would lead to an unnecessary loss of American lives and would antagonize Latin American opinion far more decisively than a blockade. The Committee unanimously voted not to change its recommendation.

Admiral Fiske then asked for advice on an entirely different subject: what should the Navy advise in the unlikely event that Huerta actually agreed to render the salute? The members of the General Board were unwilling to give him formal satisfaction. They fell back to the familiar grounds of the traditional separation of civil and military authority. Since the administration had not asked for a formal statement on this point, they could not, or so they maintained for the record, make an official recommendation—not unless Secretary Daniels asked them to do so in writing. For the record they made a flowery statement which averred that any recommendation along the lines suggested by Admiral Fiske would involve a matter of policy "which does not come within the purview of the General Board."

But the naval policymakers did not believe in showing leniency toward the Mexicans. Their formal statement had been conditioned by their cautious respect for established traditions. But the members of the General Board were quite willing, if not eager, to compose a private, "informal" guide for Fiske's use. In this they said quite bluntly that, in the unlikely event of Mexican compliance with the American demands, such compliance would solve nothing. The fleet should remain assembled in Mexican waters until the disturbances in that country were at an end. It was also their "informal opinion" that the present moment appeared to be "the time to insist on reparations for past insults and injuries to Americans and foreign persons and property and to demand that these acts of hostility immediately cease." It suggested that the United States might properly demand Huerta's resignation and also insist that Carranza compensate Americans in Mexico for the damages that he and Pancho Villa had caused. Thus, while their formal advice paid the usual lip service to the separation of civil and military matters, their informal advice was militant, bellicose, *and* political.[87]

The debate within the General Board provoked the scorn of General

[87] GB, Proceedings, 19 April 1914. The minutes of this meeting of the Executive Committee of the General Board are as complete a set of minutes as any in the entire General Board file from 1900 to 1917.

Wood who, as usual, was reveling in the discomfiture of the naval establishment. Wood was also anxious to carry out the provisions of the Mexican Plan, especially the seizure of a port. He thought that the proposed blockade was simply absurd. He was convinced that the Navy had chosen that solution simply because the admirals were afraid of losing a million dollar vessel in an assault on Vera Cruz or Tampico. The Navy's foolish recommendation was, in Wood's eyes, simply the inevitable result of "having broken down old men handle the matter."[88]

In any event, and before these issues could be resolved, Huerta rejected the American ultimatum. Then, on the 20th, Washington suddenly learned that a German steamer, the *Ypiranga*, was about to arrive at Vera Cruz with a cargo of munitions for the Huerta forces. These events produced a mood of urgency, if not panic, in Washington and a day of frantic conferences about the nature and timing of the American response. The military leaders had one more opportunity to express their views to Wilson who, indeed, actively sought their counsel. On the 20th of April there was a cabinet meeting in the morning, a session of the Joint Board during the day, and—after Wilson had addressed Congress in the afternoon—a special White House conference in the evening that was attended by the two service secretaries, Admirals Fiske and Blue, General Wood, and Bryan.[89] The military came fully prepared. Wood, for example, brought to the White House a folder which contained all the variants of the Mexican Plan, various strategic studies of Vera Cruz and Tampico, and a dozen other items. But, if Wood's diary can be trusted, it was difficult for the conferees to agree on the appropriate retaliation—even though, earlier in the day, it had been decided to shift the locus of operations to Vera Cruz, a decision which, in turn, meant not only changing the destination of Badger's Atlantic Fleet from Tampico to Vera Cruz but also meant that Admiral Mayo's ships were pulled out of Tampico, the very spot at which the trouble had all started. The Navy was apparently still reluctant, in view of the General Board's recommendation, to endorse a landing at Vera Cruz, while it was the Army which argued most strongly for such action. It was probably only the predicted arrival of the German steamer at Vera Cruz that swung the balance. Finally, early in the morning of the 21st, the conferees agreed to carry out an immediate naval occupation of the customs house at Vera Cruz. At 3:00 A.M. the naval forces were alerted for such action, and at 8:00 A.M. the orders to go ashore were received at Vera Cruz. Civilian and military were ultimately in accord on the landing at Vera Cruz. "The

---

[88] Wood Papers, Diary, entries of 18 and 20 April 1914.

[89] Various aspects of this particularly chaotic day are well described in Quirk, *Affair*, 78 ff., and Link, *New Freedom*, 399-400.

President asked each of us," Wood later recalled, "if this should be done, and we all agreed." But the conferees had remained undecided about the course of action to take at Tampico, from which port Mayo's ships had been removed when news of the *Ypiranga*'s imminent arrival reached Washington. It was decided to wait for another report from Admiral Fletcher before deciding what action to take at the port where the salute should have been rendered.[90]

There had been a confident expectation—shared by Wilson and by Admiral Fletcher—that the Mexicans would yield the customs houses without opposition. The naval forces, however, soon found themselves involved in a sharp, day-long fight for possession of the city.[91] Once ashore the naval commanders were perplexed by the nebulous and extremely untidy situation. Admiral Badger observed, "The entire situation is serious. We have seized Vera Cruz but have no belligerent rights other than those we ourselves assume and which may cause international complications." He soon received a copy of the Congressional authorization, approved on the 21st, to use armed force against the Mexicans. But Badger found this authorization of little solace. "After carefully reading it," he reported, "the commander-in-chief is uncertain of his powers in the circumstances. He is exercising and must exercise powers which can, with strict legality, only be employed in time of war—for war at this place actually exists."[92] Admiral Mayo was equally perplexed:

> The situation appears to be decidedly strange, and the Mexican side regards war as existing. So far as I am able to learn or infer, the government of the United States does not yet consider that a state of war exists, and therefore no war measures can be taken by any naval commander. It is not believed that such a state of affairs can continue indefinitely.[93]

The Army soon relieved the naval occupying force at Vera Cruz, and the Army command, like that of the Navy, also began to complain about the state of war that was not war and the restrictions placed

[90] GS, War College Division, File 6474/310, "Papers used by General Wood in Conference with President Wilson on 20 April 1914," and Wood Papers, Diary, 20 April 1914. See also the cryptic report of the Joint Board meeting in JB, Minutes, 20 April 1914. The Wilson Papers contain a vast collection of communications to and from military officers on this date.

[91] Daniels Papers, Fletcher to Badger, 13 May 1914, the report of naval activities in Mexico from 21 to 30 April. There are also many individual reports from naval commanders in the Daniels Papers that bear on the customs house seizure.

[92] Naval Records, Area Files, 1911-1927 (Caribbean), Badger to Daniels, 23 April 1914.

[93] Daniels Papers, report from Mayo to Badger titled "Activities at Tampico from 17 April to 30 April 1914."

upon it.[94] Ultimately General Tasker Bliss was moved to send a long, angry letter to the War College which charged that the inflexible war plans of the College and the General Staff had placed the Army in a situation at Vera Cruz which in no way corresponded to existing realities or to the assumptions of the planners. A successful war plan, Bliss maintained, "must fit the conditions which exist when the execution of the plan has to begin, or at least must be capable of being made to fit." This, the general charged, had not been the case, for the Army's plan for Mexican operations had been based "upon a relatively clear-cut proposition instead of the horrible confusion that now confronts us." All of the Army's plans had assumed that there would be an organized government in Mexico City and that the Army's immediate assignment would be to launch an offensive against the capital. But Woodrow Wilson had refused to permit any such move, with the inevitable result that the Army, committed to its rigid planning assumptions, found itself handicapped by great organizational and operational difficulties. This state of affairs, according to Bliss, had arisen because the War College and the General Staff, in drawing up their Mexican plans, had never dreamed that Vera Cruz could be occupied without a declaration of a state of war or that the Army would be forced to halt with the mere occupation of that Mexican port: "A year ago I warned that State would hold on to the last moment, that State would give no warning to the War Department to quietly get ready in anticipation of possible failure of diplomatic negotiations." Thus, as far as Bliss was concerned, the entire Mexican War plan had been proved worthless, and even if an order should actually come through to proceed to Mexico City: "The State Department, which had nothing to do with the preparation of your plan, will have interfered with its execution to the extent of allowing the largest possible force of combined rebels and federals to concentrate at the City of Mexico and the maximum time for destruction of roads and of defenses."[95]

In all countries military men, once committed to action, chafe against limited, restricted war and the demands of politics. Their sense of order is disturbed by operations conducted without a declaration of war and the consequent untidiness of their powers and authority. It is therefore not surprising that both Army and Navy complained about their situation after the landing at Vera Cruz. But the reason for their discomfiture is not hard to find. Woodrow Wilson, who had never anticipated Mexican resistance, was appalled by the loss of American

[94] In the Garrison Papers there is a thick file of orders sent by the War Department to Funston, and these clearly reveal the close restrictions placed upon the Army.

[95] GS, War College Division, File 6474/347, Bliss to Wotherspoon, 9 June 1914.

lives in the fighting and, above all, determined not to become embroiled in general war with Mexico. He rejected all pleas, strongly made by Garrison, to institute a blockade or to implement any portion of the Mexican War Plan by a move in the direction of Mexico City. He therefore laid down the strictest of orders that the retaliation against Huerta would be limited to the occupation of Vera Cruz. To the military the initial landings at that port were, in accordance with all their previous planning, to have been but the prelude to further and more extended operations; to Woodrow Wilson they were a military finale.[96]

In any event, Wilson immediately determined that there would be no local initiatives, no local incidents in Vera Cruz. Moreover, Josephus Daniels, in the face of all the previous planning, was reluctant to have the command at Vera Cruz pass from the Navy to the Army, specifically from the hands of Admiral Fletcher to those of General Funston. Daniels did not so much want to protect the interests of his own service as he wished to make certain that a man of "proven judgment" remained in control of affairs. The Mexican situation was so perilous that Fletcher, a man who understood its delicacy, was to be preferred to Funston who, though equally able and resourceful, was "a Rooseveltian in method, I fear that he may do something that may precipitate war."[97] Daniels lost his argument, but he need not have worried, for when Funston did take over the command at Vera Cruz, he too was placed under the most stringent of orders. Garrison, who went to considerable pains to emphasize that his instructions came at the express direction of the President, made it clear that Funston was to do absolutely nothing that might create further tensions or to extend the area of military occupation. He did relent to the extent of informing Funston that the War Department would, however, welcome his reports and recommendations for action.[98] Funston's eventual reward for obedience was a commendation from the Secretary of War for his caution and prudence throughout his period of command.[99]

The United States ultimately escaped from the Vera Cruz intervention without further conflict—at least in part because the Army and Navy commanders, initially armed with plans of heroic proportions, were reduced to executive agents of the firm Presidential will. But the entire Mexican episode had, if nothing else, its ironic dimensions. On the 20th, when Badger's Atlantic Fleet was diverted to Vera Cruz and Mayo also ordered to that city, the Navy lost control of Tampico. Ad-

[96] Wilson Paper, Memorandum from Wood to the Adjutant General, 26 April 1914.

[97] Wilson Papers, Daniels to Wilson, 25 April 1914.

[98] Garrison Papers, Garrison to Funston, 9 and 10 May 1914.

[99] Garrison Papers, Garrison to Funston, 24 November 1914.

miral Fletcher, on his own authority, tried to reverse Mayo's orders, but it was too late. Admiral Mayo had already sailed from Tampico. Thereafter, and after the fighting at Vera Cruz, no one wished to run the risk of attempting a return to the harbor of Tampico lest there be further bloodshed. The Navy was never again in a position to enforce the Admiral's now almost forgotten ultimatum that Mexican authorities at Tampico must salute the Stars and Stripes.[100]

4. THE EVE OF THE EUROPEAN WAR

While Funston was still in occupation at Vera Cruz, an Austrian archduke was assassinated in the faraway European city of Sarajevo. Within weeks the European nations, bound to one another by interlocking military alliances, had plunged into the holocaust that was to be World War I. Wilson issued a sweeping neutrality proclamation and contended that the preservation of neutrality would be a sign of America's self-possession. The immediate outbreak of war in Europe had no major impact either on the conduct of American diplomacy or upon the military services. In August and the first few weeks of September 1914, to be sure, there was a truly monumental exchange of correspondence between the State and War Departments. But these messages dealt with emergency measures to charter commercial vessels to rescue Americans stranded in Europe and to remove them from the battle zones. The initial and principal impact of the European war on American foreign policy involved the effort to find ways and means to bring United States citizens back to the safety of the Western Hemisphere.[101]

Gradually the situation changed. The war, which Europeans had expected to last no more than a few months, turned into stalemate. As the conflict dragged on, as the British blockade began to affect neutral shipping, and as the Germans resorted to submarine warfare, American foreign policy—Wilson's neutrality program—was deeply affected. With the passage of time, too, the civil-military relationship was to change. The basic framework, the institutions and organizations, remained very much the same, but the setting became far different. All the old, established assumptions about America's role in the world began to crumble as the Great War became the first modern total war.

It is for this reason that this study terminates with the outbreak of the war in Europe in the summer of 1914. Whatever happened in the relationship between, on the one hand, the White House and the State

100 Daniels Papers, two reports from Fletcher to Badger, 13 May 1914; Badger to Daniels, 9 May and 3 June 1914.

101 Garrison Papers, Memorandum of conference of heads of departments in respect to emergency conditions in Europe, 5 August 1914.

Department and, on the other, the War and Navy Departments, must be studied against the backdrop of the European conflict and America's reluctant but growing involvement in it.

The three episodes that have so far been considered—the Japanese-American crisis, the attempt to purchase the Mole St. Nicholas, and the intervention at Vera Cruz—were representative of civil-military relations prior to the outbreak of the European conflict. They indicated, too, the paradoxes of the Wilsonian approach: the suspicion of militarism but the willingness to use force, even on flimsy pretexts; the rigid control over the military but also the fact that Army and Navy leaders were not entirely closed off from the policymaking process. One might, to be sure, have examined other interventions, especially in the Caribbean, for Wilson was thoroughly embroiled in both Haiti and Santo Domingo well before World War I had become the first concern of policy. By September 1913, for example, Bryan, acting to support the Bordas regime in Santo Domingo, was asking the Navy to send warships to certain Dominican ports to help the government maintain its blockade of a rebel group; by the summer of 1914 the Secretary of State was bluntly informing the Dominicans that "the United States will . . . employ such force as is necessary to maintain constitutional government and put down insurrections"; and, when the Bordas regime, with which the Administration was now at odds, seemed recalcitrant, Wilson was prepared to yield nothing, indeed, in his words, was ready to "insist upon full and literal compliance. . . ."[102] In Haiti, where revolution had broken out against President Oreste Zamor, the United States was prepared for direct intervention in the summer of 1914 and by October, after sending a battleship and a transport loaded with marines to the Haitian capital, was informing the naval commander that his job was "to take charge of Port-au-Prince and . . . restore Charles Zamor to his Cabinet functions."[103] But detailed examination of these events is unnecessary. The spirit and purpose behind these interventions was not significantly different from what had animated the President's Mexican policy, while the Navy was likewise used in a familiar fashion to enforce American demands. These interventions were more direct and blunt than those of Taft and Knox, but they differed only in degree and not in kind.

More important, however, is the fact that the ultimate American action—the actual military occupation of these two island republics—did not take place until after the European war had become the overriding concern of American foreign policy. The landings in Haiti occurred in the summer of 1915, while the proclamation of a military government

---

[102] Link, *Struggle for Neutrality*, 502, 514.
[103] *Ibid.*, 516-28. Charles Zamor was Oreste Zamor's brother.

in the Dominican Republic was, by accident more than design, delayed until the spring of 1916.[104] But by that time the setting for American diplomacy had in fact been revolutionized by the war. Indeed, at a later date, Secretary Robert Lansing, justified the entire Haitian operation in terms of a German threat to take over the Haitian customs and secure the Mole St. Nicholas.[105]

Such an interpretation, of course, raises great difficulty for the historian. Those who have tried to demonstrate that considerations of the "balance of power" affected Wilson's policies towards Germany have not been able to sustain their case.[106] Similarly, those who have examined the voluminous Caribbean materials in the files of the State Department have been unable to find hard evidence of any European threat to Haiti or the Dominican Republic.[107] Indeed, once the European nations had become locked in total war, it is straining credulity to imagine how any one of them—least of all blockaded Germany—would have had either the inclination or the opportunity to intervene in the Caribbean. Moreover, pre-war tensions in Europe were so great that it is difficult to take seriously Bryan's fears, expressed in May of 1914, that there was danger of a joint Franco-German venture in Haiti; they seem, at best, an example of the Secretary's continuing naïveté.[108]

But considerations related to the European war did affect the Wilson administration's Caribbean policies after August of 1914. The familiar if irrational fear of German intentions was still present, indeed was revived. Though the historian can readily discount Lansing's evidence, it is nonetheless true that the Secretary of State did think in 1915 that the Germans might try to establish submarine bases in the Caribbean.[109] In the fall of 1916, when the Navy once again made a specific request for Samana Bay, both Daniels and the General Board raised not only the German spectre but also the presumed need of the Navy to possess this base as a means of assuring absolute American control of the Caribbean in the event of involvement in the European war.[110] The negotiations for and the purchase of the Danish West Indies were speeded at least in part out of the fear that Germany might be tempted to conquer Denmark and thereby acquire a foothold in the

104 Montague, *Haiti*, 207 ff., and Munro, *Dollar Diplomacy*, 352 ff., are the best secondary accounts.

105 Robert Lansing, *War Memoirs* (Indianapolis, 1935), 310.

106 See, for example, Edward Buehrig, *Woodrow Wilson and the Balance of Power* (Indianapolis, 1955).

107 Link, *Struggle for Neutrality*, 535 devotes a long footnote to this issue and refutes Lansing's "evidence."

108 Link, *Struggle for Neutrality*, 521.

109 Lansing, *Memoirs*, 19-29 (copy of his memorandum to Wilson on 11 July 1915), and 310.

110 SDDF, File 811.34539/1 and /2, Daniels to Lansing, 29 August and 22 December 1916.

Hemisphere.[111] And by early 1917, after professing that he was personally free of suspicions of Germany, even Wilson could justify sending naval units to support a Cuban government on the grounds that "so many things are happening, we cannot afford to let Cuba be involved by German plots."[112] These fears of Germany may then, as in the past, have been irrational or even used as a smokescreen for other motives, but they were assuredly present. In any event, to set them in proper perspective as well as to analyze the total content of civil-military relations after 1914 requires a separate study which would focus on the many ways in which the war in Europe began to affect both foreign and military policy. It is best, then, to terminate this study of admirals, generals, and American foreign policy with the firing of the guns of August—before the familiar assumptions of American policy were breached by the first of the global wars of the twentieth century.

[111] Department of State, *The Lansing Papers, 1914-1920* (Washington, 1940), II, 503-04, a copy of Lansing's 4 December 1915 memorandum to Wilson.
[112] Daniels Papers, Diary, 27 February 1917.

CHAPTER SIX

Conclusions

A FEW modest conclusions are clearly in order. In many respects this book has been limited to a static analysis of certain aspects of civil-military relations in the general area of American foreign policy. The limitation was in large part imposed by the materials available, above all, by the episodic nature of the military's involvement in the formulation of American foreign policy. But it must again be emphasized that the institutions necessary for a sustained and evolving civil-military relationship never developed in the United States between 1898 and 1914. While the concept of a Council of National Defense had its proponents, it failed to attract widespread support, and even some of those who advocated the proposed Council saw it more as a device to secure larger appropriations from Congress than as an institution that would develop a coherent national security policy. Existing institutions, moreover, simply did not evolve. By 1914 Root's General Staff, which had been designed to create bold, new policies, was just as bogged down in parochial military detail as it had been in its early years; the General Board remained a purely advisory body and did not emerge as the policymaking organ of the Navy; and the Joint Board, often little more than a primitive device to lessen interservice rivalries, lost rather than gained influence over the years.

The preceding pages have suggested some of the principal reasons why these institutions failed to develop. Many, of course, lay outside the military establishment and were beyond its ability to influence. The vast majority of Americans remained convinced that two vast oceans provided absolute security, were isolationist in their world outlook, and believed that the United States could readily avoid involvement in any European conflict. Viable institutions, therefore, would emerge only when Americans began to fear that their national security was genuinely threatened—and that moment was not to arrive until the very eve of World War II. But institutional development was also inhibited by the weight of inherited traditions and established attitudes about the proper role of military men in a democratic society. While this book has indicated that Army and Navy officers did have some voice in certain foreign policy decisions, there was always resistance, always a desire to keep the military in the subordinate place assigned to them in Anglo-American society since the time of Cromwell. Such attitudes were always present whether the specific situation involved a Wilson and a Daniels who were worried about a presumed attempt by the Joint Board to force their diplomatic hand or a Taft and a Knox who were always prepared to use the armed forces as an instrument of policy but determined that they would function only as the ever-obedient servants of civilian will. Yet the reverse side of the civil-military relations coin is no less important. Men like Dewey had grown up with and learned to accept the "givens" of their status. They did not believe that it was the proper function of military men to exercise a "political" role; rather they felt that it was the responsibility of the civilian leadership to determine national policy and then tell the military what it was and how it was to be executed. Indeed, many of their complaints suggest that they wanted not so much to share in the actual policymaking process as to be furnished with firm guidelines and directives. In any event, military men were reluctant to assert themselves, often producing only cryptic recommendations or generalized statements that obscure all but the purely military aspects of their thinking. The historian who tries to assess their role is often forced to work backwards; from a purely operational document he must try to infer the assumptions and ideas on which it was based.

Given such a framework of institutions and attitudes, the determinant in the civil-military equation was, and could only be, the factor of personalities and the network of personal relationships within a particular administration. In recent years no President or Secretary of State has been able to escape the recommendations of the Joint Chiefs —recommendations, it should be added, which now come from officers who themselves command the services of a vast array of specialists and sophisticates in every field of military endeavor from advanced game theory to electronic espionage. And that vast hierarchy known in today's shorthand as "The Pentagon" has countless ways of influencing public policy along the entire length of Pennsylvania Avenue. But, prior to World War I, a President was free to listen or not to listen to his military advisers except in rare moments of national emergency. The case of Theodore Roosevelt proves the point. Roosevelt did involve the United States in world affairs and possessed at least a rudimentary appreciation of the impact of the European balance of power upon the United States, but he failed to transmit much of this to the public or to his own successors. His accomplishments in foreign affairs were largely personal and, indeed, seemed idiosyncratic to the public; when he left office only a handful of Americans believed that their country had any stake in the maintenance of the European balance. What was true in foreign relations was also true in civil-military relations. Roosevelt was a President whose avocation, if not passion, was things military, who wrote endless pages about the proper caliber of naval guns and the correct thickness of armor plate, and who corresponded almost daily with Leonard Wood about the prospect of putting 5,000 troops ashore at Canton. He certainly listened to his military advisers, but he listened to them primarily as individuals; the relationships were, again, personal and idiosyncratic. During the Subig Bay controversy he expressed a petulant willingness to read the views of the Joint Board about the disposition of the fleet, but he also strongly indicated that he would make no promises about heeding their opinions. Thus, in military as in foreign policy, Roosevelt laid no foundations for institutional development, for the transmission of methods and procedures beyond the time of his own presidency, or for moving beyond a civil-military system that rested on a network of personal relationships. The historian interpreting the Taft or Wilson periods must still continue to focus on the factor of personalities rather than institutions. Indeed, though the military were used more often and had more to do, in the years after Roosevelt many of them wished to return to the days when there was a president in the White House who understood them and communicated with them.

Yet, as it was argued earlier, it remains all too easy to emphasize the static if not the negative dimensions of civil-military relations in American foreign policy. In the Federal archives as well as in private papers in the Library of Congress there is an abundance of material which attests to the military dimension in American foreign policy after the Spanish-American war. Only a small number of historians have made use of these materials. Professional historians have, on the whole, long been alienated from the soldier and the sailor. Not a few have regarded military history as a subject inappropriate for humanistic scholarship, while others have been repelled by the old fashioned "drum and trumpet" school of military history which seemed to exist solely to chronicle the accomplishments of Great Captains. Nor has the Department of State played entirely fair with its own published records. Its official publications for the years from 1898 to 1914 simply do not reflect the considerable volume of reports and correspondence of military officers that are preserved in the Department's own archives. The *Foreign Relations* series prints selected documents which originate in the civilian sphere and only rarely publishes those that came to the State Department from the War and Navy Departments. For example, any historian who based his study of American policy towards the Chinese revolution on the *Foreign Relations* volumes for 1911 and 1912 would find a representative selection of the messages from Minister Calhoun. But he would find nothing from Admiral Murdock, and, if he relied on these volumes, he simply would not know that the naval officer was reporting in equally great detail and that, from his vantage point on the Chinese coast, was interpreting the revolution quite differently from the civilian minister located in the Manchu capital of Peking. The 1909 and 1910 volumes present the same difficulty with respect to Nicaragua. There is simply no trace in them of the acerbic reports and recommendations of Admiral Kimball who advocated a line of policy in Nicaragua completely at odds with the State Department in Washington and the American diplomatic personnel in Nicaragua.

Similarly historians have often identified themselves with the civilian policymaking process and have ignored the military except when, as in the instances of actual armed intervention, their exclusion was impossible. Dana Munro's *Intervention and Dollar Diplomacy in the Caribbean, 1900-1921* is one of the most exhaustive and detailed examinations of the Latin American policy of the United States that any scholar has yet written. Yet in the many pages devoted to Nicaragua, there is, again, not a single reference to Kimball.

All of which suggests that by omission the official publications of the Department of State, as well as a considerable amount of the scholarly literature, have made a particular policy or specific episode appear more "civilian" than in fact it was and have made the military appear even more peripheral than they actually were.

This conclusion is being written at a time when scholars are severely, and properly, criticizing the militarization of American foreign policy in the recent past. The continuing horror of Vietnam has led an ever widening number of Americans to re-examine national priorities and, especially, to question the influence of the military and of military values upon American society. In the 1970s antimilitarism and pacifism are far more prevalent than they were even at their previous peak in the decade of the 1930s. It would be tempting, as well as fashionable, to conclude this study with an attack upon the admirals and generals for their Social Darwinist myopia, their excessive faith in the instruments of coercion, or their belief in the preservation of order and stability through military power. It would also be tempting, given the present concern with racial issues, to cite the many examples, from the Caribbean to China, in which the racial biases and feelings of racial superiority affected their judgments as well as their recommendations. Indeed, given the current mood of nostalgia, it might even be an appropriate conclusion for this book to argue that the United States was a healthier society in the years before 1914 when the military services knew their place and when, if they were tempted to stray, were put back by virtuous civilian traditions and practices.

But the literature of American history is already reasonably well stocked with critiques of the military mind, and another lengthy broadside hardly seems necessary. It should be sufficient to point out that the officers of the army and the navy were insufficiently educated in political affairs, were isolated from the mainstream of civilian thought as well as policymaking, and were often compelled to rely upon their own insufficient sources of information. In consequence they did produce many a document which bordered on fantasy. It is difficult to think of a more charitable word to describe the Black Plan which, it will be recalled, rested on the dubious assumption that William II would launch his fleet across the Atlantic and engage the United States Navy in a great battle in the Caribbean for mastery of the hemisphere. Even if comparable though less virulent strains of Germanophobia can be discovered within the State Department of those years, such ideas reflected no rational analysis but only a doctrinaire acceptance of Social Darwinisn in its crudest form and a literal adherence to the tenets of Alfred Mahan. Worse still, the Black Plan reflected no awareness of the current actualities of the European alliance system or of the policies then being pursued by the European states. It was, at best, a "worst possible contingency" approach which failed to consider the options that were really available to Germany. Similarly, the General Staff was certainly correct in advising against any large-scale participation in the Chinese revolution on the sensible grounds that the United States did not have enough available troops to conduct an effective intervention. But the Army planners were right for the wrong reasons. They envisioned a European commitment of upwards of 100,000 troops in China, a force in which any American contribution would indeed have been invisible if not actually lost. But the idea that the European powers were themselves in any position to dispatch 100,000 troops to China—or, indeed, could work together in sufficient harmony to produce such a force—reveals only that the General Staff was light years removed from a genuine or sophisticated understanding of international affairs. The early strategic plans of the General Board also indicate that the admirals had at best a mechanistic understanding of how the international system functioned. They assumed, for example, that since France and Russia were allies in Europe, they would also work together in the Far East. Nowhere in the naval literature was there an appreciation of the fact that France was an uncertain ally in the Far East precisely because the French feared that their entente with Russia might draw them into unwanted conflict with Britian arising out of Anglo-Russian rivalries in Asia. Similarly, amidst all the fears expressed about European intervention in Santo Domingo in 1904 and 1905, there was no informed political analysis of the actual situation in Europe at that time—a situation which, in view of the Russo-Japanese war and the concurrent Moroccan crisis, made it highly unlikely that any European nation would have believed it politic to become involved in a Caribbean dispute with the United States.

Yet, as has also been previously noted, sweeping generalizations about the "military mind" must be regarded with skepticism. This is not merely because, as this study has indicated, the services turned out occasional atypical officers like Murdock and Kimball but rather because the so-called "military mind," as it is conventionally defined, existed almost as frequently in civilian as in military circles. The preceding pages have pointed to the numerous occasions when consuls and ministers were, if anything, more prepared to solve a problem of local unrest by calling in a gunboat or who were eager to suggest a base site that the navy could acquire. The "deterrence theory" advanced by Taft and Knox to deal with the Mexican revolution rested squarely upon what they regarded as a wholesome display of American military power on the Texas border as well as in Mexican coastal waters, while a Huntington Wilson believed with real conviction that the best way to obtain his diplomatic goals in Haiti and Santo Domingo was to synchronize the presentation of demands with the arrival of warships. If it is agreed that one of the basic attributes of the "military mind" is a tendency—even a preference—for reliance upon the direct or indirect use of the instruments of coercion to resolve political questions, then such an outlook is to be found almost as frequently among civilians as among military officers of the period. Indeed, it is at least an arguable proposition that the greatest threat to humane and prudent policy is often not the army or navy officer but the "militarized civilian"—the political leader or government official—who believes in the effectiveness of force but who may actually not be as aware as the military officer of the difficulties in applying force or even of the limits of military power. The recent publication of the *Pentagon Papers* suggests that this problem has by no means been confined to the first two decades of twentieth-century American foreign policy.

There is, however, one particular facet of American foreign policy and military thought about that foreign policy which deserves special notice. With the Spanish-American war the United States not only became involved in the Caribbean and in the Far East but also, however the term is defined, began to emerge as a "world power." But the world of 1900 was an imperialist world, and the values of imperialism prevailed everywhere in it. The imperial powers dealt in the currency of naval bases, spheres of influence, colonies, naval demonstrations, gunboat diplomacy, and interventions in the internal affairs of presumably "backward" countries. As A. E. Campbell commented on the attitude of the European states towards the Boxer Rebellion, "To none of the powers of the time was China anything more than an object of policy, an enormous expanse of territory and a huge population to be exploited commercially, and if possible politically."[1] Similarly, William L. Langer noted, "Hardly anywhere in the diplomatic correspondence does one find any appreciation for the feelings of the Oriental or of any sympathy for the crude efforts made at reform. The dominant note was always that force is the father of peace and that the only method of treating successfully with China is the method of the mailed fist."[2] One of the fascinations for the historian who examines this period in the history of American foreign policy is to try to follow the halting, groping manner in which the relatively small, elite group of Americans who cared about international affairs sought to come to grips with that imperialist world and to define a viable set of policies to cope with the new problems that now confronted American diplomacy. A very few, of whom Roosevelt was the leader, were intellectually prepared to plunge completely into world politics and even play the balance of power game; others, like Elihu Root, might be concerned with maintaining order and stability but still sought to attain their goals through legal or juridical solutions; while those who followed William Jennings Bryan clung to their vision of America as the city set upon the hill that should only attempt to redeem a corrupt world through its own shining, democratic example. Also, as has been noted, though American leaders actually adopted varying policies and pursued changing tactics, their public pronouncements still described goals and objectives in terms of inherited traditions and were couched in the language of idealism, morality, and legalism. Even when American leaders embarked upon new policies—such as Theodore Roosevelt's frankly interventionist approach to the Caribbean—they frequently chose to justify their ventures in terms of the traditions and shibboleths of America's isolationist past. Thus, to make his policy palatable to the public, Roosevelt chose, and chose deliberately, to anchor it in the sacred tradition of Monroe.

But the admirals and generals, as we have seen, approached this imperialist world on its own terms and accepted its values without pausing to ask questions. They did think in terms of military power and of the need to possess bases from which that power could be exerted; they trusted in intervention as the best way to preserve order; and they believed in the inevitability of international conflict as a concomitant of imperialist rivalry. In handling Caribbean questions, the

[1] Campbell, *Britain and the United States,* 158.
[2] William L. Langer, *The Diplomacy of Imperialism* (2 vols., New York, 1935), II, 704.

civilian leaders both shared and implemented many of their ideas and values. A John Hay was fully prepared to try to secure almost the full range of the bases that the navy wanted, while the various interventions of Roosevelt, Taft, and Wilson clearly showed that political leaders were willing to use the instruments of force to preserve order and guarantee American interests in a region which they, like the military, considered an area of vital strategic importance. But in the Far East neither the course of events nor the results were the same. The United States had become involved in an area where it confronted great powers and not small, underdeveloped Latin countries. In the Caribbean the United States enjoyed a virtual monopoly of power and could indeed impose its will by barely raising its military voice. But in Asia, where the interests of Japan and the European powers clashed and conflicted, the United States was not only a newcomer but militarily weak. The military planners were contending—indeed, it was the very heart of their argument—that if the United States wished to compete in that world of Asian power politics, then it must be prepared to use the instruments of coercion and play according to the then accepted rules of the imperialist game. Roosevelt at least understood that proposition; indeed, he ultimately tailored his diplomatic policies to conform to military and political realities when he sought accommodation with Japan. Moreover, notwithstanding the obvious deficiencies and distortions in the case that the military tried to make, the admirals and generals were pointing to something that civilian leaders often forgot or ignored in formulating their Far Eastern policies throughout the decades after 1900: namely, that neither legal, juridical solutions nor pronouncements of principle are always or even necessarily effective and that in an imperfect world the successful statesman, regrettable as it may be, does on occasion have to come to terms with the naked issues of power and force. The officers of the army and navy were therefore pointing ahead to one of the great and unresolved dilemmas of American foreign policy in Asia in the years before Pearl Harbor, a dilemma which arose specifically from the fact that, while the United States did acquire a host of political and moral obligations in the Pacific after 1898, it did not possess the power to sustain them or its position in times of ultimate crisis. One is by no means simply an apologist for the military if he observes, as did the admirals and generals, that from the time of the Open Door notes to the attack on Pearl Harbor, American foreign policy in the Far East suffered from the discrepancy between, on the one hand, its political commitments and obligations, and, on the other, its military ability to support them in the face of an ultimate challenge.

The opening pages of this book also posed the question whether a study of civil-military relations in the general area of foreign policy would produce any useful generalizations about two polarized yet widely held interpretations of twentieth-century American foreign policy—the "realist" critique of historians like George Kennan and the essentially economic interpretation of the New Left. It scarcely seems necessary to comment further about the limitations of the former view which suggests that the American diplomatic record is best understood in terms of its legalistic and moralistic components. Viewed from the perspective of civil-military relations, that critique scarcely applies to the Caribbean where, even in the days of Elihu Root, the gunboat lurked not far over the horizon of his treaties and courts of Central American Justice, while the very persistence of a military dimension to the Open Door suggests, at the very minimum, that the realist interpretation is something less than complete. Moreover, as these pages have suggested, American leaders often merely employed the language of tradition and morality to win popular acceptance for new policies that in reality involved participation in a world of imperialist values.

But the materials in this book sustain as well as amplify the case that can be made for interpreting 1898 and its aftermath as a deliberate search for an "informal" or "insular" empire. In both the Caribbean and the Far East the admirals, with occasional assists from the generals, were quite consciously trying to build a network of operating bases and fixed positions from which American military power could be radiated. While the effort of the General Board did suffer from inconsistencies and weaknesses in argumentation, the naval planners put forth a number of quite systematic proposals and statements about their presumed needs. Moreover, it should be emphasized that their most persistent efforts came not in 1898 or as part of the euphoria of wartime expansionism but in 1900 and immediately following. To be sure, there were reasons for that delay; in 1898 the Navy was disorganized, compelled to rely on the *ad hoc* recommendations of Mahan's hastily assembled strategy board, and did not produce even a semblance of systematic strategic thought until the General Board was created in 1900. Nonetheless, the principal effort came in 1900 and afterwards, especially in the Far East after the logistical and operational difficulties of the Navy in the Boxer Rebellion had made naval officers acutely aware of the actual limits of their power.

What the navalists wanted would still have been an "insular" empire though it would scarcely have been "informal." It would clearly have remained insular for there were no calls for territorial acquisition on the grand scale. But the American empire would have been greatly extended—extended, indeed, well beyond either the geographical or political limits of "informality"—if the military had managed to secure all of the sites that they either systematically or sporadically coveted. In Latin America, it will be recalled, the proposals included points as far removed from the Isthmus of Panama as Peru and the Galapagos Islands, while in Asia the program called for an American military presence on or directly adjacent to the Chinese mainland. The latter would have involved not only a geographical outreach of several thousand miles but also a more direct American commitment to and involvement in Chinese affairs—in a part of the world where the interests of all the great imperialist powers were then contending and clashing. It scarcely seems that "informal" is an appropriate term for such an empire which at its periphery would have been committed and involved in the very center of the great power antagonisms of the turn of the century. But in any event it can certainly be argued that the Navy's quest for bases, along with the modest support it received from certain Army officers, represented a challenge to the limits established in 1898. It was in essence an attempt to expand the range of "informality" and "insularity" well beyond the gains of the Spanish-American war which no longer seemed sufficient to the military strategists.

The New Left interpretation, however, focuses upon the economic motivation. Bases are regarded simply as the means whereby the demands of the marketplace can be served. Naval literature, as we have seen, certainly did place considerable emphasis upon the ways in which an American navy could meet the needs of an expanding American commerce. And in the Taft era when, for example, it was thought that Haiti was about to cede coaling stations to Europeans—naval writers emphasized that the opening of the Panama Canal would increase the economic importance of the Caribbean. Yet it remains questionable whether any deep-seated economic motivation really underlay the Navy's expansionist program. The economic thought of the General Board was in actuality little more than a derivation from Mahan's interpretation of history through seapower. It was simply an elaboration of Mahan's thesis that nations, with Great Britain serving as the model, achieved greatness by expanding their overseas commerce and that the essential purpose of a navy was to protect that commerce and fight the wars that commercial expansion produced. The emphasis in naval thought was always upon creating a rationale that would justify not only the existence but the further strengthening of the Navy itself. It is, indeed, by no means an untenable hypothesis that many of the economic arguments put forth by the Navy were deliberately phrased in such manner because naval spokesmen thought that this was what their civilian superiors wanted to hear and also that it was the best way to make their case before Congress and the public. In the industrialized America of 1900, in which business interests predominated and were worried about the economic future, what could be more logical than to try to advance the Navy's credibility by arguing that the job that the Navy could do best was the advancement of American overseas commerce? Moreover, it might be added, not a few naval officers were themselves jealous of those who had achieved economic success and often scornful of businessmen who put economic interests ahead of all others. More than a few traces of this naval disdain for the business ethic appear, for example, in the reports of Admiral Kimball complaining about the attitude of Americans in Nicaragua as well as in the correspondence of junior officers in Santo Domingo who felt that the Clyde steamship line lacked any concern for the national interest and cared only about the profits to be gained by the subsidization of Dominican insurrections.

Finally, the introduction posed the question about the extent to which America had reconciled force with diplomacy in the years from McKinley to Wilson. In the Far East, as the preceding paragraphs have just argued, there was clearly no effective reconciliation. At the most it can be argued that the admirals were pointing to the discrepancies between American commitments and American power, or that a Theodore Roosevelt, coming to appreciate the limitations on American power, adjusted his Asian policies accordingly. If China was "saved" from partition, it was not because of American political or military policy but more simply because of the workings of the European alliance system and the mutually deterring fears of imperialist rivalries. In the Caribbean there was short-run reconciliation and success —if by "success" it is meant that the policies pursued seemed to achieve their stated objectives. Revolutions most assuredly were deterred, deflected, and suppressed throughout the Caribbean, and a considerable degree of American-style law and order was imposed. And Europe stayed out. But even this degree of "success" must be qualified. By the turn of the century Great Britain, facing the rise of German naval power in Europe, was quite prepared to relinquish her onetime role in the Caribbean, while, for various reasons, the other powers were almost equally willing to let America put on the badge of the policeman of the hemisphere. Which meant, quite simply, that the United States was "successful" in the Caribbean because—and unlike the situation in Asia—there were no outside challengers among the great powers. In the Caribbean the United States enjoyed carte blanche to take full advantage of the great discrepancy between the power available to her and that available to any small Latin country in whose affairs she determined to intervene.

Nor, indeed, was American policy always successful even according to its own objectives and standards. While intervention in Nicaragua may have quelled one insurrection, it helped to keep an unpopular regime in office and thereby spawned another revolt—and another appearance of the Navy and the Marine Corps. Success, in short, helped to start an insurrectionary cycle. Moreover, by 1911, with the outbreak of revolution in Mexico, the United States was coming to face a situation which could not be controlled by gunboat diplomacy, for the Mexican revolution was a social revolution fueled by the forces of nationalism. Wilson at Vera Cruz was the first to have to confront the implications of this new kind of revolution—and the first also to realize that the traditional show of force or landing of sailors was not going to deflect the revolution or achieve American purposes.

In the long run, therefore, there was no reconciliation between force and diplomacy. American leaders, civilian as well as military, accepted an interventionist ethic; they subscribed to Taft's conviction that they "were living in an age when the intervention of a stronger nation in the affairs of a people unable to maintain a government of law and order . . . becomes a national duty and works for the progress of the world." In Latin America intervention produced bitter resentments, and "successes" were counterproductive, for they stirred the fires of Latin nationalism, and by the end of World War I the dominant mood in all Latin countries was becoming a strong anti-Americanism. Moreover, in Latin America both military and civilian policymakers had equated order and stability with sound finances and conservative governments. No thought had been given to the political and social consequences of American policy: how, for example, an intervention might work for the benefit of an entrenched clique or elite, might stir popular resentment, and might stimulate the very forces of instability that American policy had sought to prevent. Similarly, in Asia, American interventionism built long-term resentments. Americans, civil as well as military, thought of themselves as the benefactors of China and deluded themselves with the belief that their interventions were somehow different from those of the European imperialists. Years later, in the aftermath of World War II, they were to be stunned when the force of Chinese nationalism turned against them and branded them equally imperialist.

Bibliography

UNPUBLISHED MANUSCRIPT SOURCES

I. *Private Papers*

Manuscripts Division, Library of Congress

General Tasker H. Bliss
Charles J. Bonaparte
William Jennings Bryan
General Henry C. Corbin
Josephus Daniels
Admiral George Dewey
John Hay
Philander C. Knox
Admiral Alfred Thayer Mahan
William M. Moody
Admiral George Remey
Elihu Root
Admiral Charles Sperry
William Howard Taft
Admiral Henry Clay Taylor
Woodrow Wilson
General Leonard Wood

Firestone Library, Princeton University

Lindley M. Garrison

Ursinus College Library, Collegeville, Pa.

F. W. Huntington Wilson

II. *Official Records*

A. DEPARTMENT OF STATE—General Records of the Department of State, National Archives, Record Group 59

Between 1898 and 1914 the State Department employed no less than three different, and frequently confusing, filing systems. The now familiar "decimal file" did not come into operation until 1910.

From 1898 to 1906 all correspondence between the State Department and the two military departments is to be found in the Miscellaneous Letters file, under the general heading of Domestic Correspondence.

These are bound volumes, arranged in a strictly chronological order—that is, all the "domestic correspondence" of a given day is filed together regardless of the subject matter. Moreover, to add to the difficulty, the incoming correspondence is bound separately from the outgoing correspondence; there is one set of volumes for letters addressed to the Secretary of State, and another for his replies.

From 1906 to 1910 the Department used the so-called "numerical file." All of the correspondence, including dispatches, whether of domestic or foreign origin, that related to a particular topic was given a "case number" and filed together—thus "Case 8258," for example, deals with the world cruise of the White Fleet and contains all the documents which relate to that topic. In 1910 the "decimal file" was instituted, and, with its official index, the records of the State Department at last became truly accessible to the researcher.

For the earlier period, the following special files were used to supplement the Miscellaneous Letters materials:

Consular Despatches: From Santo Domingo City (1898-1900), from Chefoo (1898-1902), from Newchwang (1901-1902), from Shanghai (1900-1902).

Ministerial Despatches: from the U.S. Minister to China (1898-1902), from the U.S. Minister to Korea (1901-1903).

Instructions from the Department of State to the Peace Commission at Paris (1898).

Correspondence of the Director of the Bureau of the American Republics with the Secretary of State.

Correspondence of the Japanese Legation in the United States.

B. DEPARTMENT OF THE NAVY

1. Papers of the General Board of the United States Navy, formerly Naval Records Center, Arlington, Virginia, now in National Archives.

General Board papers are in three categories:

a. Proceedings and Minutes. Bound volumes of the minutes of all meetings of the General Board from 1900.

b. Letters. Seven bound volumes for the period 1900-1914, comprising letters and reports between the Board and, primarily, the Secretary of the Navy.

c. General Files. The following were most useful:

404 and 404-1 Oversea bases
405 Subig Bay
406 Cuban naval stations, Guantanamo

408 Advanced bases (including China and Korea)

409 Overseas bases (scattered documents relating to many proposed sites)

414-1 Coaling stations, general (includes final report of 1898 Strategy Board)

420 Naval building policies, distribution of the fleet

422 Guam

425 War plans

438 International law

446 Naval policy

2. Office of Naval Records and Library, National Archives, Record Group 45

Record Group 45 is, on the whole, the best source for naval materials prior to 1914. There is, to be sure, some material of value in Record Group 80, General Records of the Department of the Navy, especially in its General File, 1897-1926. But this file is exceptionally frustrating to use and, more important, the file has long since "been considerably depleted by the Office of Naval Records and Library" (see James Masterson, "Preliminary Checklist of the General Records of the Department of the Navy, 1804-1944," National Archives PC 31 [46-20], December 1945).

Within RG 45, the so-called "Subject" and "Area" files are the most important:

a. Subject File (ca. 1775-1910). Most notably those items under the index headings: Governmental Relations—Domestic and Foreign, Naval Policy, Protection of Individuals, International Law.

b. Subject File (1911-1927). Especially Haiti, Nicaragua, Margarita, Venezuela, Ecuador, and Galapagos, Mexico.

c. Area files (1900-1909). Caribbean (Area 8) and Far East (Area 10).

d. Area files (1911-1927). Central Pacific, South East Pacific, Caribbean.

Also of great value were certain collections titled "Confidential Correspondence," notably:

e. Translations of messages received in cipher (1888-1910), 5 volumes.

f. Confidential letters sent (1898-1914), 7 volumes.

g. Confidential communications, Asiatic station (1904-1905).

Finally, copies of various naval war plans (Japan, Germany,

Mexico, Nicaragua, Haiti-Santo Domingo) are to be found in the collection, under the reference National Archives Folders 136 through 142, Op. 29.

C. WAR DEPARTMENT

1. General Records of the War Department General Staff, National Archives (Old Army Section), Record Group 165

Various documents and reports originating within the War College Division, the Second Section of the General Staff, and the Chief of Staff, from 1903 on.

2. Records of Joint Army and Navy Boards and Committees, National Archives, Record Group 225

a. Joint Board. Minutes and Communications—contains both the minutes of Joint Board meetings from 1903 on and correspondence with the two service secretaries.

b. Joint Board General Files, especially files numbered from 301 to 351.

PUBLISHED SOURCES

United States Congress, Senate, *Diplomatic History of the Panama Canal*, 63rd Congress, 2nd Session, Document 474, Washington, 1914

United States Navy Department, *Annual Reports of the Secretary of the Navy, 1899-1914*

United States Department of State, *Right to Protect Citizens in Foreign Countries by Landing Forces*, Memorandum of the Solicitor for the Department of State, October 5, 1912, Washington, 2nd revised edition, 1929

United States Department of State, *The Lansing Papers, 1914-1920*, 2 vols., Washington, 1940

Books

Albertini, Luigi, *The Origins of the War of 1914*, 3 vols. (London: Oxford, 1952-57)

Allen, G. W., ed., *The Papers of John Davis Long, 1897-1904* (Boston: Massachusetts Historical Society, 1939)

Bailey, Thomas A., *Roosevelt and the Japanese-American Crises* (Stanford: Stanford University Press, 1934)

Beale, Howard K., *Theodore Roosevelt and America's Rise to World Power* (Baltimore: Johns Hopkins University Press, 1956)

Bernstein, Barton, *Towards a New Past: Dissenting Essays in American History* (New York: Random House, 1968)

Bishop, Joseph, *Charles Bonaparte, His Life and Public Services* (New York: Scribners, 1922)

Bixler, Raymond W., *The Foreign Policy of the United States in Liberia* (New York, Pageant Press, 1967)

Blum, John M., *The Republican Roosevelt* (Cambridge: Harvard University Press, 1954)

———, *Woodrow Wilson and the Politics of Morality* (Boston: Little, Brown, 1956)

Braisted, William, *The United States Navy in the Pacific, 1897-1909* (Austin: University of Texas Press, 1958)

Brassey's Naval Annual, 1903 (Portsmouth: J. Griffin, 1903)

Brodie, Bernard, *Sea Power in the Machine Age* (Princeton: Princeton University Press, 1941)

Buehrig, Edward, *Woodrow Wilson and the Balance of Power* (Indianapolis: Indiana University Press, 1955)

Calcott, W. H., *The Caribbean Policy of the United States* (Baltimore: Johns Hopkins University Press, 1942)

Campbell, A. E., *Great Britain and the United States, 1895-1903* (London: Longmans, 1960)

Campbell, Charles, Jr., *Anglo-American Understanding, 1898-1903* (Baltimore: Johns Hopkins University Press, 1957)

Challener, Richard D., *The French Theory of the Nation in Arms, 1866-1939* (New York: Columbia University Press, 1955)

Cline, Howard, *The United States and Mexico* (Cambridge: Harvard University Press, 1953)

Coles, Harry L., ed., *Total War and Cold War* (Columbus: Ohio State University Press, 1961)

Craig, Gordon A., *The Politics of the Prussian Army* (New York: Oxford, 1956)

Crane, Katherine, *Mr. Carr of State* (New York: St. Martin's, 1960)

Cronon, E. David, *The Cabinet Diaries of Josephus Daniels, 1913-1921* (Lincoln: University of Nebraska Press, 1963)

Cuff, Robert E., *The War Industries Board in World War I* (unpublished dissertation, Princeton University, 1966)

Cummings, Captain Damon, *Admiral Wainwright and the U.S. Fleet* (Washington: Government Printing Office, 1962)

Daniels, Josephus, *The Wilson Era, Years of Peace, 1910-1917* (Chapel Hill: University of North Carolina Press, 1944)

Davis, Calvin P., *The United States and the First Hague Peace Conference* (Ithaca: Cornell University Press, 1962)

Dennett, Tyler, *John Hay: From Poetry to Politics* (New York: Dodd, Mead, 1934)

Dennis, A.L.P., *Adventures in American Diplomacy, 1896-1906* (New York: Dutton, 1928)

Deutrich, Mabel, *Struggle for Supremacy*: *The Career of General Fred Ainsworth* (Washington: Public Affairs Press, 1962)

Earle, E. M., ed., *Makers of Modern Strategy* (Princeton: Princeton University Press, 1943)

Esthus, Raymond, *Theodore Roosevelt and Japan* (Seattle: University of Washington Press, 1967)

Fiske, Bradley A., *From Midshipman to Rear Admiral* (New York: The Century Co., 1919)

Fitzgibbon, R. H., *Cuba and the United States, 1900-1935* (Menasha, Wisconsin: Collegiate Press, 1935)

Freidel, Frank, *Franklin D. Roosevelt: The Apprenticeship* (Boston: Little, Brown, 1952)

Graber, Doris, *Crisis Diplomacy*: *A History of U.S. Intervention Policy and Practice* (Washington: Public Affairs Press, 1959)

Graebner, Norman A., ed., *An Uncertain Tradition*: *American Secretaries of State in the Twentieth Century* (New York: McGraw-Hill, 1961)

Griswold, A. Whitney, *The Far Eastern Policy of the United States* (New York: Harcourt, 1938)

Hagedorn, Herman, *Leonard Wood*: *A Biography* (New York: Harper, 1931)

Halle, Louis, *Dream and Reality* (New York: Harper, 1958)

Hammond, Paul Y., *Organizing the Common Defense* (Princeton: Princeton University Press, 1961)

Harbaugh, William, *Power and Responsibility*: *The Life and Times of Theodore Roosevelt* (New York: Farrar, Straus and Cudahy, 1961)

Harrington, Fred, *God, Mammon and the Japanese* (Madison: University of Wisconsin Press, 1944)

Healy, David F., *The United States in Cuba, 1898-1902* (Madison: University of Wisconsin Press, 1963)

Howe, M. A. DeWolfe, *George von Lengerke Meyer*: *His Life and Public Services* (New York: Dodd, Mead, 1919)

Huntington, Samuel, *The Soldier and the State* (Cambridge: Belknap Press, 1957)

Iriye, Akira, *Across the Pacific*: *An Inner History of American-East Asian Relations* (Cambridge: Harvard University Press, 1967)

Jessup, Philip, *Elihu Root*, 2 vols. (New York: Dodd, Mead, 1938)

Kennan, George, *American Diplomacy, 1900-1950* (Chicago: University of Chicago Press, 1951)

Koenig, Louis, *Bryan*: *A Political Biography* (New York: Putnam, 1971)

Langer, William L., *The Diplomacy of Imperialism*, 2 vols. (New York: Knopf, 1935)

Lansing, Robert, *War Memoirs* (Indianapolis: Bobbs-Merrill, 1935)

Lederer, Ivo, ed., *Russian Foreign Policy*: *Essays in Historical Perspective* (New Haven: Yale University Press, 1962)

Leopold, Richard, *Elihu Root and the Conservative Tradition* (Boston: Little, Brown, 1954)

Levin, N. Gordon, *Woodrow Wilson and World Politics* (New York: Oxford, 1968)

Link, Arthur L., *Wilson*: *The Struggle for Neutrality* (Princeton: Princeton University Press, 1960)

————, *Wilson*: *The New Freedom* (Princeton: Princeton University Press, 1956)

————, *Wilson the Diplomatist* (Baltimore: Johns Hopkins University Press, 1957)

Livesey, William E., *Mahan on Sea Power* (Norman: University of Oklahoma Press, 1947)

McCain, W. D., *The United States and the Republic of Panama* (Durham: Duke University Press, 1937)

McCormick, Thomas J., *The China Market*: *America's Quest for Informal Empire, 1893-1901* (Chicago: Quadrangle Books, 1967)

Marder, Arthur, J., *The Anatomy of British Sea Power* (New York: Knopf, 1940)

————, *From the Dreadnought to Scapa Flow* (London: Oxford, 1961)

Mayo, Lawrence S., ed., *America of Yesterday*: *The Journal of John D. Long* (Boston: Atlantic Monthly Press, 1923)

Millis, Walter, *The Martial Spirit* (New York: Literary Guild of America, 1931)

Miner, Dwight, *The Fight for the Panama Route* (New York: Columbia University Press, 1940)

Montague, L. L., *Haiti and the United States, 1714-1938* (Durham: Duke University Press, 1940)

Morgan, H. Wayne, *Making Peace with Spain*: *The Diary of Whitelaw Reid, September-December, 1898* (Austin: University of Texas Press, 1965)

Morison, Elting E., *Admiral Sims and the Modern American Navy* (Boston: Houghton, 1942)

————, ed., *Letters of Theodore Roosevelt*, 8 vols. (Cambridge: Harvard University Press, 1951-54)

Mowry, George, *The Era of Theodore Roosevelt, 1900-1912* (New York: Harper, 1958)

Munro, Dana G., *Intervention and Dollar Diplomacy in the Caribbean, 1900-1921* (Princeton: Princeton University Press, 1964)

Nelson, Otto L., Jr., *National Security and the General Staff* (Washington: Infantry Journal Press, 1946)

Neu, Charles E., *An Uncertain Friendship*: *Theodore Roosevelt and Japan, 1906-1909* (Cambridge: Harvard University Press, 1967)

Nevins, Allan, *Henry White* (New York: Harper, 1930)

———, *Hamilton Fish* (New York: Dodd, Mead, 1936)

Palmer, Frederick, *Bliss, Peacemaker* (New York: Dodd, Mead, 1934)

Perkins, Dexter, *Hands Off*: *A History of the Monroe Doctrine* (Boston: Little, Brown, 1941)

Pomeroy, Earl S., *Pacific Outpost*: *American Strategy in Guam and Micronesia* (Stanford: Stanford University Press, 1951)

Pratt, Julius W., *America's Colonial Experiment* (New York: Prentice-Hall, 1950)

Pringle, Henry F., *The Life and Times of William Howard Taft*, 2 vols. (New York: Farrar and Rinehart, 1939)

———, *Theodore Roosevelt* (New York: Harcourt, 1931)

Puleston, W. D., *The Life and Works of Alfred Thayer Mahan* (New Haven: Yale University Press, 1939)

Purcell, Victor, *The Boxer Uprising*: *A Background Study* (Cambridge: Cambridge University Press, 1963)

Quirk, Robert, *An Affair of Honor* (Lexington: University of Kentucky Press, 1962)

Reid, J. C., *The Manchu Abdication and the Powers, 1908-1912* (Berkeley: University of California Press, 1935)

Rodman, Seldon, *Quisqueya*: *A History of the Dominican Republic* (Seattle: University of Washington Press, 1964)

Roskill, Captain W. W., *The Strategy of Sea Power* (London: Collins, 1962)

Schilling, Warner, *Admirals and Foreign Policy, 1915-1919* (unpublished dissertation, Yale University, 1953)

Sprout, Harold and Margaret, *The Rise of American Naval Power, 1776-1918* (Princeton: Princeton University Press, 1939)

Stimson, Henry L., and McGeorge Bundy, *On Active Service* (New York: Harper, 1947)

Stirling, Yates, *Sea Duty* (New York: Putnam, 1939)

Tansill, Charles, *The Purchase of the Danish West Indies* (Baltimore: Johns Hopkins University Press, 1932)

du Val, Miles P., *Cadiz to Cathay* (Palo Alto: Stanford University Press, 1940)

Varg, Paul, *Open Door Diplomat* (Urbana: University of Illinois Press, 1952)

———, *Missionaries, Chinese, and Diplomats* (Princeton: Princeton University Press, 1958)

Weigley, Russell, *Towards an American Army* (New York: Columbia University Press, 1962)

Welles, Sumner, *Naboth's Vineyard*, 2 vols. (New York: Payson and Clarke, 1928)

White, Leonard D., *The Republican Era: 1869-1901: A Study in Administrative History* (New York: Macmillan, 1958)

Williams, William A., *American-Russian Relations, 1781-1947* (New York: Rinehart, 1952)

Willock, Roger, *Bulwark of Empire* (Princeton, privately published, 1962)

Wilson, F. W. Huntington, *Memoirs of an Ex-Diplomat* (Boston: Bruce-Humphries, 1945)

Zabriskie, E. H., *Russian-American Rivalry in the Far East* (Philadelphia: University of Pennsylvania Press, 1946)

Periodicals

Adler, Selig, "Bryan and Wilsonian Caribbean Penetration," *Hispanic-American Historical Review*, xx, no. 2 (May 1940), 198-226.

Alger, Philip, "Professional Notes," *United States Naval Institute Proceedings*, xxix, no. 2 (June 1903), 493-95.

Braisted, William R., "The United States Navy's Dilemma in the Pacific, 1906-1909," *Pacific Historical Review*, xxvi, no. 3 (August 1957), 235-44.

————, "The Philippine Naval Base Problem, 1898-1909," *Mississippi Valley Historical Review*, xli, no. 1 (June 1954), 21-40.

Coletta, Paolo, "McKinley, the Peace Negotiations, and the Acquisition of the Philippines," *Pacific Historical Review*, xxx, no. 4 (November 1961), 341-50.

Esthus, Raymond, "The Taft-Katsura Agreement: Reality or Myth," *Journal of Modern History*, xxxi, no. 1 (March 1959), 46-51.

Fiske, Bradley A., "American Naval Policy," *United States Naval Institute Proceedings*, xxxi, no. 1 (March 1905), 1-80.

Greene, Fred M., "The Military View of American National Policy, 1904-1940," *American Historical Review*, lxvi, no. 2 (January 1961), 354-77.

Grenville, J.A.S., "Great Britain and the Isthmian Canal, 1898-1901," *American Historical Review*, li, no. 1 (October 1955), 48-69.

Hains, P. C., "An Isthmian Canal from a Military Point of View," *Annals of the American Academy of Political and Social Science*, xvii, no. 2 (May 1901), 397-408.

Hood, John, "The Pacific Submarine Cable," *United States Naval Institute Proceedings*, xxvii, no. 3 (September 1900), 477-80.

Langer, William L., "Farewell to Empire," *Foreign Affairs*, XLI, no. 1 (October 1962), 115-30.

Livermore, Seward, "American Naval Base Policy in the Pacific," *Pacific Historical Review*, XIII, no. 2 (June 1944), 113-35.

———, "American Strategic Diplomacy in the South Pacific," *Pacific Historical Review*, XII, no. 1 (March 1943), 42-49.

———, "Theodore Roosevelt, the American Navy, and the Venezuelan Crisis of 1902-1903," *American Historical Review*, LII, no. 3 (April 1946), 452-71.

———, "Battleship Diplomacy in South America," *Journal of Modern History*, XLI, no. 1 (March 1944), 31-48.

May, Ernest, "The Development of Political-Military Consultation in the United States," *Political Science Quarterly*, LXX, no. 2 (June 1955), 161-80.

Minger, R. H., "William H. Taft and the United States Intervention in Cuba in 1906," *Hispanic-American Historical Review*, XLI, no. 1 (February 1961), 75-89.

———, "Taft's Mission to Japan: A Study in Personal Diplomacy," *Pacific Historical Review*, XXX, no. 30 (August 1961), 279-94.

Morton, Louis, "War Plan Orange: A Study in Military Strategy," *World Politics*, XI, no. 2 (January 1959), 221-50.

Rippy, J. Fred, and E. Parks, "The Galapagos Islands: A Neglected Phase of American Strategic Diplomacy," *Journal of Hispanic History*, IX, no. 2 (March 1940), 37-45.

Rippy, J. Fred, "The Institution of the Customs Receivership in the Dominican Republic," *Hispanic-American Historical Review*, XVII, no. 4 (November 1937), 419-57.

Stockton, Charles, "The American Inter-Oceanic Canal: A Study of the Commercial, Naval, and Political Conditions," *United States Naval Institute Proceedings*, XXVI, no. 4 (December 1899), 752-97.

Taylor, H. C., "The Fleet," *United States Naval Institute Proceedings*, XXIX, no. 4 (December 1903), 799-807.

———, "Memorandum for a General Staff for the U.S. Navy," *United States Naval Institute Proceedings*, XXVI, no. 3 (September 1900), 441-48.

Walker, Asa, "Notes on Cuban Ports," *United States Naval Institute Proceedings*, XXVI, no. 2 (June 1900), 333-40.